HISTORY OF THE

HISTORY OF THE SHAN STATE

FROM ITS ORIGINS TO 1962

SAI AUNG TUN

SILKWORM BOOKS

The publication of this book was partially funded by the Toyota Foundation.

ISBN: 978-974-9511-43-5

Published in 2009 by
Silkworm Books
6 Sukkasem Road, T. Suthep
Chiang Mai 50200 Thailand
info@silkwormbooks.com
http://www.silkwormbooks.com

The maps in this volume were redrawn by Ms. Carole Duval, Mrs. Eliane Leterrier, and Guy Lubeigt of the UMR 8586 of the Sorbonne University, the National Scientific Research Centre of France (CNRS).

Typeset in Janson Text 10 pt. by Silk Type
Printed and bound in Thailand by O.S. Printing House, Bangkok

5 4 3 2 1

Contents

Maps

Illustrations

About the Author

Sai Aung Tun is above all an academic and a scholar of history, although he was involved in the political life of his country during the socialist regime and later became a member of the National Convention (1993) to shape the future constitution of Myanmar. A fervent nationalist like all the Myanmar citizenry, he is also a devoted Shan Buddhist. Through his postings in Myanmar he made acquaintance with many monks and religious persons, participated ceaselessly in the construction of numerous pagodas, and therefore has become a well-known pagoda-builder.

Sai Aung Tun was born in 1932. He matriculated in Hsipaw (northern Shan State) and was appointed as tutor in the History Department of the University of Rangoon in 1957. Sent to the University of Denver (Colorado), he obtained an MA in International Relations. He then began a career as a government servant and, in 1961, he was promoted to head the History Department of Taunggyi College in the capital of Shan State. From 1964 to 1968 he was posted to the Department of History, Arts and Science of the University of Mandalay (Mandalay Division), and later transferred to head the History Department of Magwe College (Magwe Division). From 1970 to 1980 he assumed the post of principal of Myitkyina College (Kachin State) and then switched to a political career during the socialist regime. He was elected as a member of parliament for the constituency of Mogaung (Kachin State), where a large Shan community is located. From 1980 to 1985 he was recalled to the capital and appointed principal of the Institute of Foreign Language of the University of Yangon. In 1985 he was elected a State Council member in Hsipaw, his native town, and remained in this position until 1988.

In 1992 Sai Aung Tun was appointed vice chairman of the Myanmar Historical Commission, where he joined the remaining members of the Myanmar academic community (Dr. Than Tun, U Tun Aung Chain, U Hla Thein, U Thet Tun [former ambassador to France], Daw Ohn Kyi, U Than Htut, U Thaw Kaung [former chief librarian, Universities Central Library], Dr Ohn Khine, Dr Khin Maung Nyunt, and Daw Ni Ni Myint). Presently professor emeritus of international relations, he conducts

PhD and MA classes at the University of Mandalay-Yangon and continues to receive and help many visiting foreign scholars.

In the years preceding the Golden Jubilee of the Historical Commission (1955–2005), Professor Sai Aung Tun was instrumental in preparing and realizing the publication of more than forty volumes detailing the mostly unknown works of his colleagues on the commission. This achievement, coupled with the yearly organization of international conferences held in Yangon, effectively put an end to several decades' isolation of Myanmar scholars and opened up a new era for developing a relationship with the outside world.

Guy Lubeigt
Docteur d'Etat
Senior Research Officer (Centre National de la Recherche Scientifique)
Permanent Representative in Myanmar and Thailand

Acknowledgments

It had long been my intention to write a history of Shan State from the earliest times to the 1960s. But my aim went unrealized because financial limitations did not allow me to carry out the research necessary for the project. I looked around for sources of support that might enable me to conduct my research. On my way to Bangkok, I met Dr. Chatthip Nartsupha from the Chulalongkorn University and Professor Renoo Wichasin from Chiang Mai University, both of whom had a keen interest in Shan studies. Dr. Chatthip Nartsupha invited me to his house, where we discussed my research project in his library. He had a big collection of materials on the Shan and he allowed me to make use of it for my research project. They both suggested that I apply for a research grant from the Toyota Foundation. One of my very close friends, Dr. Thaw Kaung, who is a member of the Myanmar Historical Commission, also advised me to apply for a research grant from the foundation. I would like to thank these three scholars for their encouragement and the valuable suggestions they gave me.

With a letter of recommendation from U Tun Aung Chain, secretary of the Myanmar Historical Commission, I sent my application to Mr. Norio Kanie, the managing director of the Toyota Foundation.

The research grant was promptly given, and for this I would like to express my deepest thanks to Mr. Norio Kanie and also to the two program officers, Mr. Alan Feinstein and Mrs. Yumiko Himemoto-Hiraishi, who came to Yangon and explained to me in detail how I should make use of the research grant and the rules and procedures that I should observe.

Having obtained the research grant, I wasted no time and immediately began my research. I went through the collections of the Universities Central Library, the Yangon University Library, the Library of the Universities Historical Research Center and the National Archives Department, gathering the information and materials that were relevant to my project. All the librarians and the staff members were very cooperative and I would like to thank them for all their help.

I also made a research trip to Shan State, visiting Taunggyi, Lashio, Muse, Nam Hkam, Mong Mit, Keng Tung, and other places of historical importance, interviewing local scholars, collecting local chronicles, copying historically important manuscripts, and taking photographs of antique items, old monasteries, old *haw* (residences of Shan chiefs), and the products of cottage industries. For the information and materials I acquired I owe a debt of gratitude to all the local scholars and friends, especially to Dr. Sai Mawk Hkam (Lashio), Sao Sukhamin (Tang Yan), Long Karn Hkam (Lashio), Sai Pan Seng (Mandalay), Sai Myat Aung (Mandalay), Sai Hkun Noom (Muse), Sai Kyaw Naing (Muse), Nang Sandar (Muse), Sai Hsar Aye (Nam Hkam), Sai Yee Pu (Nam Hkam), Sai Than Nyan (Nam Hkam), Sai Yee (Keng Tung), Long Tang Kae (Taunggyi), Sao Noi Mao Hkun (Putao), Long Hong Hkam (Keng Tung), Long Tip (Keng Tung), Sai Sam Tip (Keng Tung), Sai Aik Pao (Yangon), Long Heng Shwe Aye (Yangon), Dr. Sai Sang Aik (Yangon), Hkun Wun Tip (Yangon), Sai Thet Win (Yangon), Nang Vo Seng (Yangon) and all the executive members of the Shan Cultural and Literary Committees of Yangon, Mandalay, Taunggyi, Lashio, Muse, Nam Hkam, Mong Mit, and Keng Tung, who rendered me every possible help in my research.

I also visited Taunggyi Museum and obtained many valuable manuscripts and received photographs of historically important museum pieces. For the help I received, my thanks go to the museum curator, Nang Lao Ngun, and the members of her staff.

The grant also allowed me to go abroad for the collection of material relevant to my research. There are a lot of documents, reports, manuscripts, and personal letters about the British Administration in the Shan States at the India Office Records in the British Library in London and in the Scott Collection of the Cambridge University Library. While in London, my research would not have been possible without the help of Reverend Sao Dhammasami and Reverend Sao Jotika, who personally took me to the British Library, and Sai Pang, Anita Jain, Saye Khaeo Pang, Tzai Seng Pang, Sai Mong, Sai Onn Mong, Dr. Kyaw Thinn and Sao Phong Kaeo (Owei), Dr. Richard Tun Nyunt, Dr. Ye Lin Hock and Shwe Phyu Thaw, U Maung Maung and Daw Than Than Myint and Sao Noon Oo, who provided me with accommodation and transport to the libraries and museums around London. I would like to thank all of them for their very kind help. I would also like to thank Daw San San May and other staff members of both the British Library and the Library of Cambridge University for helping me to get all essential materials for my research.

I also owe a great debt of gratitude to Sao Hso Hom, my old classmate, who lives in Australia, who was kind enough to help me organize my research. He also read through my research paper, especially the last four chapters which dealt with the proposal for revising the constitution in whose discussion he participated more than forty years ago.

I would like also to thank Dr. and Mrs. David Rachael Hall of Cambridge, who read through parts of my research work and gave me good advice about the format of my research, and also to Dr. Justin Meiland of Mahidol University, Bangkok, for his valuable advice.

Another scholar who helped me organize my research project was Dr. J. N. Phukan from Guwahati (Assam). I also thank him for his very kind help.

I should not forget to mention U Tun Aung Chain, secretary of the Myanmar Historical Commission, who not only wrote a letter of recommendation when I applied for a research grant but also patiently and thoroughly went through my project paper from beginning to end, correcting the errors I had committed in writing the paper. I thank him from the bottom of my heart.

Last, but not least, I would like to express my sincere thanks to my research assistants U San Win, Daw Mie Mie Lwin, Daw Hmwe (Nang Hom), Daw Lya Lya Win, my computer programmer Dr. Sai Sang Pe (Mong Yai), and Dr. Guy Lubeigt and his staff for preparing all the necessary maps. They gave me every possible help in accomplishing my research project. Remaining mistakes and shortcomings are my sole responsibility.

Finally, I would like to thank Ms. Susan Offner for her editorial work and Ms. Trasvin Jittidecharak for her help in publishing this book.

November 2004

Preface

A history of the Shan state from the earliest times to the 1960s is here presented to inform the general reader about the migration of the Shan ethnic people from their old settlements around the Hwangho-Yangtze region to Southeast Asia until they reached Myanmar. It is also believed that the Shan people entered Myanmar beginning in the first century AD. They generally occupied most of the areas in the northwest, north, northeast, and east of Myanmar proper. But the area of their greatest concentration was in the eastern part, called the Shan State. From their base in the Shan Plateau, the Shan tried to invade the plain region of Myanmar several times and to control the heartland of the country. They were able to do so only after the fall of Bagan. They dominated the political stage of Myanmar for a few centuries and founded three historically important capitals in the heartland of Myanmar at Pinya, Sagaing, and Inwa (Ava). After the decay of the Shan dynasties Myanmar was unified under a most able king, Bayinnaung. From there Shan history merges with that of Myanmar.

I should have written a complete history of the Shan State in all its cultural, economic, social, and political aspects. But owing to financial constraints and a lack of time to do wider and deeper research, I could write only a short history under a grant from the Toyota Foundation with a time limit set at one year.

The migration of the Shan people to Southeast Asia and finally to Myanmar was a lengthy and strenuous process. In their long march to Myanmar the Shan stopped many times on the way to establish a number of dynastic kingdoms whenever and wherever they could find good valleys. The size of their kingdoms depended mostly on the size of the valley. Most of their kingdoms were small with the exception of Nan-chao and Mong Mao Long, which developed into empires with many notable political, social, and economic achievements. The Shan brought with them their culture of wet-rice cultivation wherever they migrated and settled for food security, which was considered an important element of national power in the old days.

It took three thousand years at least for the Shan to march down to Myanmar from their original home in China. They were always on the move due to the restlessness of their character. When they did not quarrel and fight among themselves, they would move gently and quietly along the rivers until they found a new valley with fertile land, tender grass, and fresh water to establish their traditional *baan* and *mong* or kingdoms. When they fought among themselves, or encountered new forceful immigrants, or neighbors, their migration became more forced and violent, as in when the floodgate opened during the invasion of the Mongol military forces led by Kublai Khan in AD 1287.

Bamar and Shan became united whenever they encountered foreign invasions or wars. In the long course of its history, Myanmar intermittently had wars with its neighbors, China, Thailand, Assam, and Manipur, and also with Great Britain. There were glorious periods in its history when Myanmar fought foreign wars during the reigns of King Anawrahta, Bayinnaung, and Alaung Paya. The Shan contingents gallantly fought together with Bamar to win against the foreign foes.

In the three wars with the British, the Shan sacrified thousands of lives in guarding Myanmar sovereignty. Myanmar fell into the hands of the British in 1885, and both Shan and Bamar became colonial subjects of the British for nearly a hundred years. During the British rule in Myanmar, the Shan states were separated from Myanmar proper in accordance with the British policy of "divide and rule."

At first, the British had no idea how the Shan states should be ruled. Finally they readopted the method of the Myanmar kings to rule the Shan states through their own chiefs. They held out the olive branch to all Shan chiefs, persuading them to submit and vow allegiance to British power. Many Shan chiefs did, and *sanad*, or appointment orders, were issued to the Shan chiefs who were required to rule their states in accordance with the terms stated in the *sanad*. By those terms, many traditional and hereditary privileges and rights were curbed and the positions of the Shan chiefs were no better off than in the time of the Myanmar kings. This created dissatisfaction among the Shan chiefs. They were under the tight control of the British commissioner and governor. In 1922 the British introduced reform, and all the Shan states were placed under the institution of the Federated Shan States. A council was created, having the British commissioner as its chairman and the British resident as its secretary. The Shan chiefs were members of the Federal Council but their roles were merely advisory. They had no legislative and executive powers at all. The Shan chiefs presented memorandum after memorandum stating their grievances and dissatisfactions and appealed for reform and an increase of most of their privileges and rights in administering their states. The British turned a deaf ear to their appeals and were slow to introduce reasonable reforms. Political agitation took place in 1930 when a roundtable conference was held in London to discuss the question of the separation of Myanmar from India. The Shan chiefs sent another memorandum and requested permission to participate in the roundtable conference and ascertain the position of the Shan States after the separation of Myanmar from India. But they received no favorable response from the British government. The Shan States were not only separated from Myanmar proper but placed under the Frontier Area Administration created by the British authority.

The Second World War broke out and the Japanese invaded Myanmar. The Shan States came under the Japanese military administration and were also separated from Myanmar proper. Moreover, two prominent Shan states, Keng Tung and Mong Pan, were given to the Thai government by the Japanese military authority as royal gifts without the knowledge or agreement of the Shan people.

In 1945 the world war came to an end. The Japanese withdrew from Myanmar and the British reoccupied it. The Shan States were again placed under British rule. But a political awakening took place in Myanmar proper as well as in the Shan States. The people from Myanmar proper began their political campaign for independence. What happened then in the Shan States? In 1946 the First Political Conference was held in Pang Long, organized by the Shan chiefs. Representatives of the hill peoples and representatives of Myanmar proper including the governor and Frontier Service personnel were invited. The question was raised: "Politically, where do we go from here?" The representatives from the hills and from Myanmar proper came to realize that the time had come for them to forge political unity and demand independence. Leaders from Myanmar proper and the hills discussed their common political causes and objectives and all came to agree on a demand for independence. A preliminary agreement was obtained and all agreed to hold a larger and more dynamic political conference at the same place in 1947. According to schedule, the Second Pang Long Conference took place in February 1947. The Myanmar delegation, led by Bogyoke Aung San, and all the representatives of hill peoples arrived. Political discussions were held continuously until a consensus was reached to demand independence from the British government. Under the signed historic Pang Long agreement all pledged to unite and to demand complete independence.

Independence was given on January 4, 1948. A tragic incident took place on July 19, 1947. Bogyoke Aung San and his comrades including the Shan leader Sao Sam Tun were assassinated.

A parliamentary government was adopted after independence together with a quasi-federal state. After a decade of trial, it became apparent that the clauses and articles provided in the constitution did not meet the needs of the nationalities. They began to see the omissions and the loopholes and the need for amendment and reform. It was the Shan leaders and the people of Shan state who were the first to point out the weakness of the constitution. They were joined by other nationalities and all agreed to reform the constitution. The Shan produced a document called "A Proposal for the Amendment of the Constitution." A national seminar was held in Yangon in a broadcasting station. Before the discussions were finished a coup d'état took place and the country was left without a constitution. That is a short history of the Shan state from the earliest times to 1962. The pages that follow flesh out the background, circumstances, decisions, and events presented in this brief overview.

Abbreviations

AFPFL	Anti-Fascist People's Freedom League
KMT	Kuomintang
KNDO	Karen National Defense Organization
NUF	National United Front
Pa-Ah-Ma-Sa	Pa-O National Association
Pa-Ah-Ma-Pha	Pa-O National Organization
PVO	People's Volunteer Organization
SCOUHP	Supreme Council of United Hill Peoples
SEATO	Southeast Asia Treaty Organization
SSHPO	Shan State Hill People's Organization
SSPFL	Shan State People's Freedom League
SSPO	Shan State People's Organization
USSPO	Union of the Shan State People's Organization
Ya-Pa-La-Pha	Shan State People's Liberation Party

1

The Shan in Myanmar

One unique feature about the Union of Myanmar is that, according to the 1931 census, more than one hundred national races had been living together as members of the same family since time immemorial, sharing all sorts of joy and woe in the long course of their history. In the early parts of their history of ups and downs, there were times when they fought each other like foes and there were also times when they could establish cordial and harmonious relations to become kinfolk and friends. Sometimes they were subject to each other, but most of the time they became good partners working and helping each other for the common goals of achieving sociopolitical and economic development, defending national territorial integrity, organizing national consolidation, maintaining national sovereignty, and striving for the assurance to have equal standing with other members of the world community. Each of these national ethnic groups has greatly and substantially contributed something to the development of this country according to the best of its ability, and each has also hoped to enjoy the fruit of its contribution according to its need.

Now, of the many national ethnic groups living in this multinational Union of Myanmar, the Shan are the largest, occupying different parts of the country, especially the eastern plateau called Shan State. More than that, the Shan people have a history and cultural tradition of their own and a developed literature and religion, Buddhism.

In fact, the Shan have played many prominent roles in the task of organizing Myanmar to become a sovereign nation like today. The Shan helped found the Upper Myanmar capitals like Pinya, Sagaing, and Inwa (Ava) and many *baan*, *mong*, and *keng* in the northwestern, northern, northeastern, eastern, and southeastern parts of the country, taking responsibility for defending the Myanmar border areas from being encroached and infringed on by alien powers. At that time, there were no national or standing armed forces like today. The task of defending these areas lay totally in the hands of the Shan levies.

When the Myanmar kings established their Bagan Empire and began their territorial expansion, it was the Shan who provided contingents of fighting soldiers. In the internal work of construction the participation of the Shan as good donors was recorded in the stone inscriptions of Bagan, especially in the promotion of religion and its activities.

In the long course of history, there are many historical evidences of the Shan closely and actively cooperating with the Myanmar kings in their wars with neighboring countries and the victories achieved over foreign foes. There is historical proof of the roles that the Shan contingents and their chiefs played in the Myanmar conquest of Chiang Mai, Ayutthaya, Assam, and sometimes in war with China.

In critical situations the Shan never hesitated to help, especially when there were foreign wars. In the First, Second, and Third Anglo-Myanmar Wars, the Shan provided the best fighting soldiers, including Shan women, under the command of their feudal chiefs. Many Shan sacrificed their lives in these three wars and many others in the past. The Shan never betrayed the sovereign in the times of monarchy. The Shan patriots even hatched a plan to rescue King Thibaw on his way from the palace to the Gaw Wein jetty in Mandalay.

U Aung Myat, the *saohpa* of Waing Hso (Wuntho), became much enraged on hearing of King Thibaw's capture by the British. He gathered forces around him and, with the Shan patriotic forces, rose against the British despite a warning from Kinwunmingyi not to do so. As a lone fighter, he continued to fight on until he was defeated owing to the superior quality of British arms. But he never surrendered to the British. He took refuge in Mongna-Sanda, a Tai Nue Shan state of the border area on the Chinese side. He came back to Myanmar at the invitation of the government only after independence was achieved.

Again, the role of the Shan people came to the fore during the Myanmar struggle for independence. Bogyoke Aung San led the Myanmar delegation to London without Shan representatives to negotiate for independence with the British prime minister, Clement Attlee. There, the question arose regarding the participation of the frontier people of the hill regions in the political struggle for independence. Independence without the hill regions and their people would not be complete or meaningful. At this juncture, the Shan leaders and representatives of other nationalities organized a political conference at the strategic town of Pang Long in the Central Shan States in February 1947. There, heated, thorough, and serious political discussions took place and finally a political breakthrough was achieved. All representatives attending the conference unanimously voted to join hands with the Myanmar leaders in their struggle for independence. That historic agreement signed between the leaders of the plain region and the leaders of the hill region greatly affected the negotiations in London, and independence was granted to Myanmar on January 4, 1948. More than that, the Pang Long Agreement was a historic landmark in many ways. First, it was the first national unity achieved between the leaders of Myanmar proper and the frontier hill region. Second, it was the historic creation of the First Modern Union of Myanmar on February 12, 1947. Third, it freed Myanmar as a whole from the colonial bondage that had been imposed upon the people for nearly a century. Fourth, it led to the restoration of national sovereignty to the new nation, the Union of Myanmar. Finally, it helped Myanmar to become a sovereign nation on equal footing with other members of the United Nations Organization.

Even from the cultural and religious points of view, the Shan and Myanmar are closely akin to each other. The major link in the cultural and religious kinship of these races is Buddhism of the Theravada School. The two peoples, in fact, share not only a common religious faith but a large body of customs, ceremonies, folk beliefs, and values related to Buddhism. For centuries the Shan and the Bamar were socially, economically, and religiously mixed, and they mingled and intermarried. The Shan speak the Myanmar language much more fluently than the Myanmar speak Shan. All national tasks or responsibilities laid down by the Union Government were equally shared and faithfully carried out by all the national ethnic peoples of the country including the Shan.

WHO ARE THE SHAN?

The Shan belong to the Mongoloid stock of the Tai ethnic group who are spread over southwestern China, Hainan, Vietnam, Laos, Thailand, Cambodia (Kampuchea), Myanmar, and northeastern India in Assam. They are also known by a variety of names depending upon the color of their costumes, teeth, and tattoo. Sometimes they are called to accord with the names of the streams, the rivers, the lakes, the forests, the plains, the hills, the mountains, and the valleys where they live. On the basis of the color of the dress, there are names like Tai Lam (Dam, black), Tai Kau (white), Tai Leng (Deng, red), Tai Lai (striped waistband). Those who live by the Red River are called Tai Leng (Deng) and by the Black River Tai Lam (Dam), etc. J. G. Scott in his book *Gazetteer of Upper Burma and the Shan States* gives a list of Tai names[1] as does Professor Nomal Chandra Gogoi in his article "Tai, Htai and Dai: Origin, Evolution and Dissemination of Tai Culture in China and Southeast Asia with Special Reference to the Ahoms of Assam."[2]

Regarding the original home of the Tai people, historians and ethnologists have been making intensive investigations, but the result is still far from being satisfactory. However, the scholar Max Muller ventures to say:

> the original seat of the Tai or Siamese branch of the Indo-Chinese peoples, called Shan by the Burmese, was in Central Asia and it was from that area that these people were the first to migrate towards the south and settle along the rivers Mekong, Menam, Irrawaddy and Brahmaputra.[3]

Dr. B. Laufer, Curator of Anthropology, Field Columbian Museum, Chicago, remarks:

> the early home of the peoples of eastern Asia was in the upper reaches of the Hoang-ho or Yellow River of China, . . . from this centre the Tibetans migrated westward; the early tribes of Indo-China, southward; and the Chinese southeastward.[4]

On the course of the Tai migration to the south, Professor P. Gogoi in his article, "The Tai and the Tai Kingdom," written in 1969, has this to say:

> The history of their migration is a history of long centuries of struggle which they had to carry on both against the Chinese imperial pressure from the north and against the powerful neighbors in the south, resulting in the succession of glorious periods of their supremacy in China, Burma, Laos, Assam down to the modern times.[5]

Later, through intensive field researches carried out by Chinese and foreign scholars, the general consensus is that the real home of the Tai people or the region where they developed as a well-known or distinctive race had been in southwestern China and that, in the course of time, due to the pressure of the new immigrants from the north, they continued to move along the big rivers and their tributaries that flowed from or through China to Assam, Myanmar, Laos, Thailand, Vietnam, and Cambodia, like Brahmaputra, Chindwin, Ayeyarwady (Irrawaddy), Shweli (Nam Mao), Than Lwin (Salween, Nam Kone), Menam, Mekong, Black River (Nam-me-lam/dam), and Red River (Nam-me-leng/deng).

WHERE WAS THEIR EARLY HOME?

Generally, the Tai ethnic people were believed to have their early settlements around the fertile basins of the Huanghe or Yellow River and the Yangtze River. But the actual location of their original homeland is very difficult to ascertain. For that, further research and investigations will have to be undertaken. Regarding the story of the spread of the Tai into southwestern China, information could be available from the study of the Chinese historical annals, the dynastic records, and the chronicles of the periods concerned.

The Tai ethnic people are believed to have migrated into China even before the Chinese themselves. That was why they were called the elder brothers of the Chinese. The history of the pre-Chinese period revealed the existence of the Tai state of Ngu or Wu. It was believed that Ngu or Wu State was located around the mouth of the Yangtze River. The area controlled by this state consisted of the modern province of Kiangsu and its adjacent region. The Tai ethnic people living in China in the early days were called white barbarians and black barbarians, and sometimes they were known as people with golden teeth as described by Fan Ch'o, a Chinese official of the Tang dynasty. In his book *Man-shu*, he stated:

> The "black-teeth" barbarians, the "gold-teeth" barbarians, "silver-teeth" barbarians, "tattooed-leg" barbarians. . . . The "black-teeth" barbarians use lacquer to lacquer their teeth. . . . The "gold-teeth" barbarians use gold carved plates to cover their teeth, and the "silver-teeth" barbarians use silver to cover their teeth. When they have business to go out to interview people, they use these as an adornment. . . . The "tattooed-leg" barbarians engrave the skin above the ankle and below the shin, all round with lines and patterns. . . .

From the beginning of their history, the Tai people were good agriculturists. They were well known for wet-rice cultivation, which they took with them to every place they moved to and settled in. As a means of communication, the Tai language was widely used and spoken. Many Tai words were incorporated into the Chinese language in later days. According to the Statistical Account of the Province of Kwanghsi (Guangxi), out of nineteen words, twelve are Tai. In AD 1172 a Chinese resident of Kwanghsi gave a short list of nine words of their language and almost all were found to be Tai.[6] Obviously the Tai spoken language was once quite influential and spoken by ethnic groups around the fertile region of the Yellow River.

In their long march to the south, southwest, and west, the Tai never failed to establish their kingdoms and empires whenever the situation favored it. The Chinese historical annals revealed the emergence of the Tai Confederated States, known as Ts'u. Where was Ts'u then? Ascending the Yangtze River to the present province of Hupeh, that would be the seat of the Ts'u state. According to the sinologist Mr. Parker, Ts'u was the largest of the Tai Confederated States of ancient times, covering the vast area of land northward between the Yangtze and Yellow rivers, including the old Tai state of Ngu or Wu and all the regions southward to the sea.[7]

Regarding the widely spread Tai ethnic race, the scholar S. Hallett remarked that the Tai not only stretched far away eastward, perhaps to the Chinese Sea, but also formed one of the chief ingredients of the Chinese race.[8]

Another pre-Chinese period of the Tai state was called Pang or Pan-hu and it was predominant in central China, south of the Yellow River. The Pang people occupied the area of the northeast of Sichuan and the west of the Honan. The generic name of the people of Pang was Ngao or Yao or Great. They should be considered the oldest stock of the Tai ethnic people. Their language and words spoken at that time were recorded in the annals of the eastern Han. It is also found that out of eight words on the list, five are Tai. Pang State had been in existence since the twentieth century BC. The Pang people were not subdued by the Chinese until the end of the eleventh century AD and they did not acknowledge the supremacy of the Chinese emperor. The chief of Pang State was once recognized as king of Siang-yang (Hupeh) and governor of King-chou. His realm contained eighty thousand villages.[9] Pang State was contemporary with and rival of the Chinese Han dynasty. The two states established friendly relations and gave mutual help to each other. The political existence of the Great Pang State was, however, destroyed by Shang Wu-ting in 1231 BC. After a lapse of 767 years, the old Pang state was revived with the help of the Tchou people. The second seat of Pang State lay between the Yuen and the Wu rivers, west and southwest of Tung-ting Lake, a mountainous region.[10]

Another group of the Tai ethnic people settled at the headwater of the Yangtze River and occupied the region at the intersection of Honan, Hupeh, and Nang-hwui provinces. From there they extended their territory westward in the Kiu Lung (green wilderness of thick wooded area) range of the mountains, forming the boundary between Shansi and Sichuan provinces.[11] Professor M. Terrien de Lacouperie assumed the area to be the original cradle of the Tai race.

Moving to western Sichuan in about 2000 BC, another Tai ethnic group set up a new kingdom known in history as Ta Mung or Great Mung. This group was recognized as the progenitors of the Tai ethnic group of Tongking of Vietnam.

The Tai ethnic people were always on the move and they never tired of finding a new place and establishing new *baan*, *mong*, and *keng*. They were required to do that to maintain their identity, their cultural heritage and wet-rice cultivation culture, and their values and right to exist as a civilized people like other nationalities.

A twin city-state established by another branch of the Tai ethnic group was called Pa and Lung. These two states played an important part in the subsequent history of the Tai race. The seats of both Pa and Lung states were in western Sichuan. The Pa had relations even with Ts'u as early as 600 BC. There is evidence of Pa princesses married to Ts'u kings. The Chinese annals also mention how the ruler of Hia Ki sent his minister, Mang Tu, to Pa State to establish friendship between the two kingdoms in 1971 BC. The Chinese annals also state that near the Pa was the Lung. The Chinese called the Lung people Lung-jen and the Pa people Pá-yi. The Pa people lived under a government of their own.[12] The dynastic histories of the Hou-han-shu (the later Han dynasty, AD 25–250) and the Tsin Shu (the history of the Tsin dynasty, AD 265–420) give a long description of the Pa kingdom and the prominent role it played during the dynastic periods of the time. Wu-hsiang was described as a hero king who helped to found the State of Pa in eastern Sichuan.

The Pa people spread to Hupeh (Hubei) and Hunan and then moved down to the Yangtze River and then to the Chia-ling and Ch'u rivers. A branch of the Pa people was known as Tsung. They also established a kingdom called Tsung.[13] They settled in the Hunan-Guizhou border region. During the Han dynasty, the native people who lived along the Yu River of the Lang-chung were Tsung people.[14] The *Hua-yang-kuo-chih* also explains that T'ang Chu was an old Tsung kingdom. In Sichuan there was a place called Ch'u where settlements of Tsung people could be found. Another stock of Tai ethnic people who inhabited the regions in western Hunan, southern Kuei-chow (Guizhou), and eastern Yunnan were called Chung or Chung-chia and those in western Kwanghsi (Guangxi) were called Chuang. They all spoke the Tai language with variant dialects. During the Chou dynasty (1122 BC to 255 BC) Pa State was on equal footing with other feudal states of China, like Ch'in to the north, and Ch'u and Teng to the east.[15] These states sometimes fought each other and sometimes established cordial relationships.

Shuh was another Tai state in western Sichuan. The limits of the Shuh kingdom, according to Ch'ang Chu, the author of the *Hua-yang-kuo-chih*, were from the Pao-hsieh route on the north to Nanchung on the south. The Pao-hsieh route was a valley in Shensi province. In the modern period, this route linked up with Shensi and Sichuan provinces. Nanchung was a vast province, including southern Sichuan, western Guizhou, and most parts of Yunnan. The king of Shuh at that time was called "Wang Ti."[16]

The *Hua-yang-kuo-chih* also said that the states of Shuh and Pa were contemporary and rivalrous. Sometimes they were at war with each other.[17] The Shuh king appointed his brother to assist in his administration and that post was called "Chia-meng."[18] The translation of Chia-meng could be Kyem-mong used in the later period by Tai chiefs.[19] In 316 BC, Shuh and Pa were conquered and annexed by Ch'in.[20]

The Tai in Sichuan during the Han dynasty (206 BC–AD 220) were known as Pan-hsun. The Pan-hsun people set up their numerous settlements along the Yu River during the third century BC. They were good cultivators as well as courageous fighters. The Han kings, whenever they had trouble with the neighboring states and were unable to defeat them, enlisted the help of the Pan-hsun people to fight for them. The Han king called them "Marvelous Troops" and conferred titles on them and very often exempted them from taxation as a reward for their victories over the enemies.[21] They remained loyal subjects of the Han emperor.

For many centuries the Tai ethnic people were the dominant race over a wide strip of land on the left side of the Yangtze from Sichuan to the sea. But they were always followed by the long stretching arm of the Chinese race. From southwestern China, the Tai ethnic group known to the Chinese as Pai-i made another move to enter the remote province of the western frontier, Yunnan. These Pai-i people referred to themselves as Ai Lao or Ngai Lao.

THE EMERGENCE OF NAN-CHAO

The Tai ethnic groups, in the long march to southern and southwestern China, were able to revive and reestablish their kingdoms and dynasties intermittently in various localities. Some of these were shortlived; others lasted for centuries. The history of this period showed that the Tai people were unable to unite their petty feudal kingdoms into a large and powerful state until the emergence of Nan-chao in the seventh century.

In AD 650 the Ai Lao rulers united and organized six Chao states into one powerful confederated state named Nan-chao. The six Chao states that were thus united were:

1. Mung–Hi–Chao
2. Che–Chai–Chao
3. Chien–Lang–Chao
4. Shi–Lang–Chao
5. Teng–Shan–Chao
6. Mung–She–Chao[22]

Nan-chao State was the creation of the Ai Lao (Ngai Lao) branch of Tai people. They were a tough and vigorous Tai group, having great ability and organizational skills, through which they managed to organize mobile armed forces composed of the ethnic nationalities living within Nan-chao, and to create an effective administrative machinery to control Nan-chao. That the Ai Lao created Nan-chao can be gleaned from the Chinese history *Chin T'ang Shu*, which states:

> The Nan-chao barbarians were originally a sort of Wu Man (Black barbarian) tribe. Their surname is Meng. These barbarians call their kings Chao. They claim to be descendants of the Ngai Lao (Ai Lao). For generations they dwelt in Meng-She-Chou and were chieftains there. It is east of old Yang-Ch'ang of the Han dynasty and west of Yao-Chou. Formerly their chiefs were six: hence their names Lu-Chao. . . .[23]

As regards the location and extent of Nan-chao State, the Chinese history *Hsin T'ang Shu* described it thus:

> Nan-chao is called Hao-to, Lung-wai (Dragon's Tail), Chu-mieh, and Yang-Chien Mang-She Chao is to the south of the others, hence the name Nan-chao. It lies between Yung-Ch'ang and Yao-Chu, south of the Iron Bridge. On the east it adjoins the Ts'uan; on the southeast it is connected with Chao-Chih (Tonkin); on the west with Mo-ch'ieh-t'o (Magadha); on the northwest it joins T'u-fan (Tibet): on the south it joins Nu-wang (probably Sip-Song-Pan-Na); on the northeast it connects with Ch'ien-wu. The king's capital is Yang-Chu-Mieh city (Ta-li-fu). Another capital is Shan Shan-fu (Yunnan-sen).[24]

If the accounts in the *Chin T'ang Shu* and *Hsin T'ang Shu* are considered authentic, then we are provided with a very good estimate of the size and power of Nan-chao. To administer such an extensive empire effectively, the Nan-chao rulers introduced an elaborate governmental organization which included:

- entrusting ministers with the power to decide matters of state
- appointing governors, army officers, officers to preside over finances and public works. There were even officers in charge of horses, cows and the collection of taxes; officers for the management of secret businesses; officers in charge of the palaces . . .
- parceling out lands to the officials according to their ranks, to village communities, and to the farmers
- conscripting all able-bodied men into military service. The army was divided into four departments, each having its own flag. The soldiers were supplied with helmets and with shields of copper and rhinoceros hide, with coats and trousers of leather. A leader was appointed over each one hundred men, an officer over each one thousand, and a commander in chief over four armies.
- appointing six viceroys for outside regions and dividing the kingdom itself into

ten *kien* (Perhaps *kien* could be the same word as today's "Keng" in Shan State, "Chiang" in Thailand, and "Xiang" in Laos).

- encouraging the people from K'uh-Tsing Chou to Tien Ch'i to cultivate wet fields, feed silkworms with oak leaves, weave and embroider fine silk fabrics, sift gold from the sand, and raise horses.[25]

The Ai Lao chieftains, who had been engaged in wars with the Chinese for many years, came to realize the need for a strong and united Tai State to contain the steadily growing encroachment of the Chinese. They were also aware of the weakness of the feudal administration. Thus they carried out reforms to bring the six Chao states into the united confederated state of Nan-chao and to set up a powerful military force.

Who were responsible for the greatness of Nan-chao and the restoration of Tai political power? Sao Saimong Mangrai provides the following names of some of the Nan-chao rulers:

1. She-lung
2. Ka-tuh-mang
3. Tuh-lo (alias Sinulo)
4. Lo-sheng-yen
5. Yen-koh
6. Sheng-lo-p'i brothers
7. Koh-lo-feng, adopted by no. 5
8. P'i-lo-koh, son of no. 6 and nephew of no. 5[26]

Likhit Hoontrakul also gives the following names and dates of the Nan-chao rulers:

1. Mung-Si-Nu-Lo	650–674
2. Lo-Sing-Yen	675–711
3. Sing-Lo Pi	712–727
4. Pi-Lo-Ko	728 –747
5. Ko-Lo-Fung	748–779
6. Yi-Men-Sin	780–795
7. Sin-Ko-Kian	796–812
8. Kian-Lung-Sing	813–818
9. Kian-Li-Sing	819–823
10. Hung-Jew	824–858
11. Tien-Lung	859–877
12. Lung-Shun	878–902
13. Chang-Mai-Szu	903–927
14. Chao-Shan-Chen	928
15. Yang-Kan-Chen	929–937
16. Tuan-Szu-Ping	938–1094
17. Kao-Sheng-Tai	1095–1096
18. Tuan-Chang-Shun	1097–1253[27]

The Nan-chao monarchs, having firmly established their power, tried to establish friendly relations with China. King Sinulo (AD 650–677), soon after coming to the throne, sent an embassy to the Court of China to conclude a treaty of friendship with the Tang emperor Kaotsong. That treaty remained in force for many years. Nan-chao–China friendship was maintained and peace between the two countries was restored. Pi-Lo-Ko (AD 728–747) was also successful in his attempt to renew the treaty of friendship with China and even signed a treaty of military alliance in order to wage war against the Tibetans. Ko-Lo-Fung (AD 748–779), who succeeded Pi-Lo-Ko, also went on a friendly visit to China as soon as he became king. But on his way to the Chinese court, he was insulted by the governor of Hunan. The incident led to his invasion of China and the capture of some cities after his return from the Chinese court. A few years later the Chinese emperor sent an expedition to punish Ko-Lo-Fung, but it failed. Aware of the Chinese anger and anticipating another war with China, Ko-Lo-Fung concluded an alliance with Tibet. The expected Chinese invasion of Nan-chao came in AD 754. There were heavy casualties but once again the Chinese suffered a defeat. When Imohsun (Yi-Men-Sin) (AD 780–795) succeeded Ko-Lo-Fung, he signalized his accession to the throne by invading China. However, he was defeated and had to sue for peace. A treaty of friendship was signed with the Chinese emperor recognizing him as king of Nan-chao and conferring on him a gold seal.[28] On his part, Imohsun promised to abandon his treaty of friendship with Tibet. The Chinese emperor, satisfied with the behavior of Imohsun, sent an envoy to Nan-chao to mark the occasion of friendship. The envoy was received with great pomp. “Soldiers lined the roads and the horses’ harness was ablaze with gold and cowries. Imohsun wore a coat of gold mail and tiger-skin and had twelve elephants drawn in front of him.”

Having secured peace and established friendship with the Chinese in the east, Imohsun turned his attention to other neighboring states for territorial expansion. He first invaded Tibet, captured sixteen towns, and took much booty.

In AD 829 one of Imohsun’s successors invaded China. He captured Sui-Chu, Yong-Chu, and Kong-Chu and brought back captives and skilled artisans who soon raised Nan-chao to the level of China in the fields of art, literature, weaving, and cottage industries. In AD 858 Tokin was brought under Nan-chao. Tsui Lung (Tien-Lung) (AD 859–877), who came to the throne of Nan-chao in AD 859, assumed the title of emperor. This angered the Chinese emperor Suentsong of the Tang dynasty and war broke out between China and Nan-chao. The forces of Nan-chao besieged the Chinese city of Chang Tu on several occasions. Peace was restored between China and Nan-chao when “Fa” or Lung-Shun (AD 878–902) came to the Nan-chao throne. The Chinese emperor sent his envoy to the Nan-chao court and a marriage was arranged between the daughter of the Chinese emperor and the son of the Nan-chao ruler to strengthen the relation of friendship.

Nan-chao remained an independent state on an equal footing with China for centuries. It was finally destroyed on January 7, 1253, by the Mongol forces of Kublai Khan.[29]

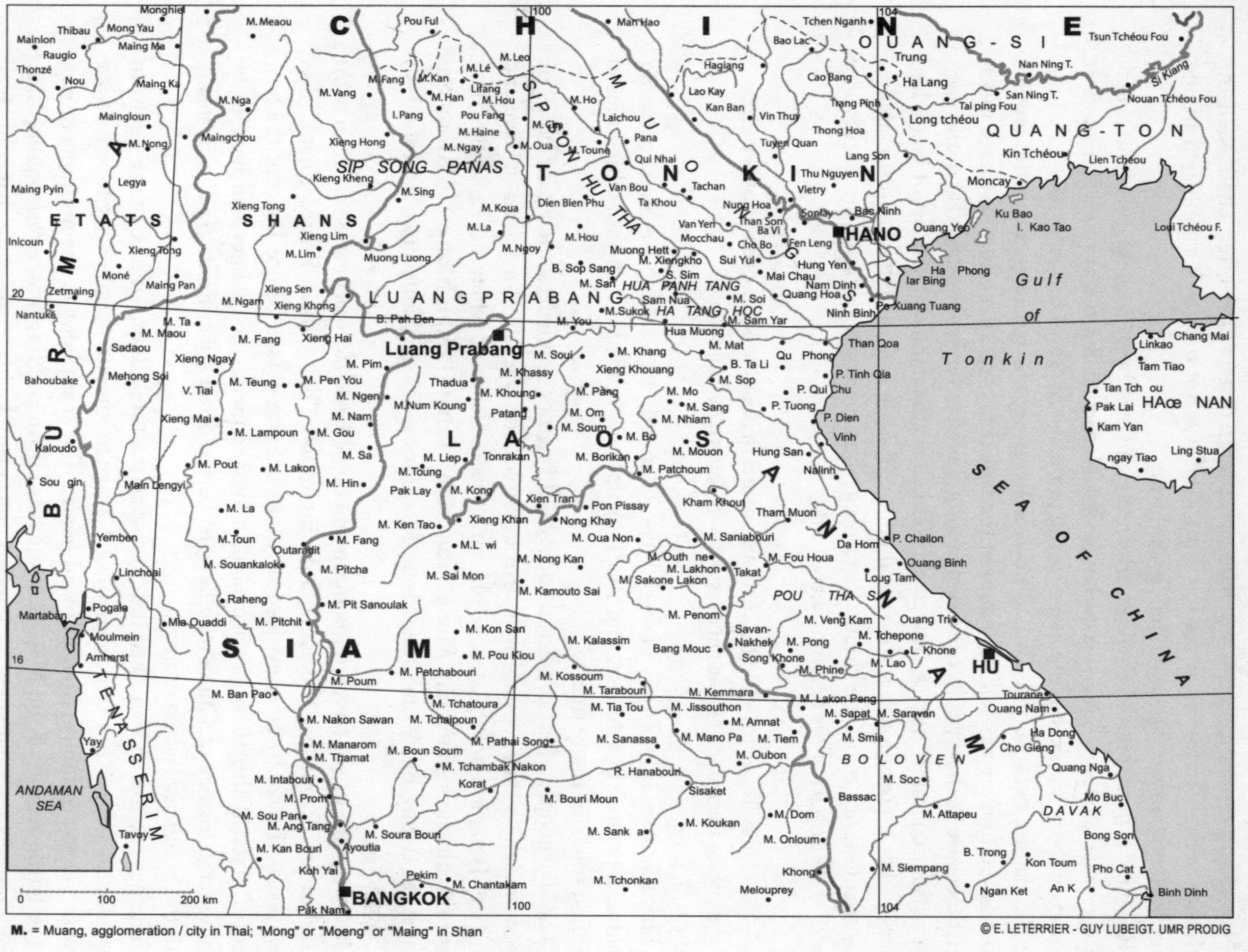

MAP 9. Indochina and the Tai-Lao dependencies

Nan-chao's reputation as a powerful confederated state that often challenged the authority of the Chinese emperor in China itself was not only well established among neighboring countries but extended far and wide.

Recently a new theory has been advanced and has been a cause for controversy among some scholars. This theory holds that Nan-chao State was not a Tai state. It does so on the grounds that the names given in the list of Nan-chao rulers do not sound like Tai names, because the Tai had no rule for using the last element of the father's name as the first element of the name of the son. This argument does not have much merit, because such a system prevailed among Tai Mao or the Dehong Tai in the past. They also used family names. Moreover, a check on the names on the list of Nan-chao rulers makes it apparent that the rule linking the names of the father and son applies only to a few, not to all the rulers. Regarding Shan names N. Elias in his *Introductory Sketch of the History of the Shans* pointed out:

> Shan kings frequently changed their own names in honour of some remarkable event, assumed the name of some ancestor, or were known by a surname.[30]

The Chinese called this powerful confederated Tai state Nan-chao, meaning "southern prince" in Chinese, and the Tai sometimes called it Lan-sao, which means "million rulers or many rulers."

The Tai people often preferred to have old names applied to their new cities or kingdoms which they reestablished. For example, Lan was used for Lanna in Thailand and Lan-Tsang in Laos. The same old names were also used when the Tai in the Shan State rebuilt their states like Mong Hsu, Mong Lung (Long), Mong Yai, Mong Yu, Mong Pai, Mong Pa, Mong Nai, Mong Paw, Mong Tsing, Waing Hso or Mong Hso or Tso, etc.

It is yet too early to pass judgment on whether Nan-chao was or was not a Tai or Ai Lao creation. Regarding this issue, a distinguished Thai scholar, Prince Thani,[31] has this to say: "I have to be convinced by more definite details before I accept the new theory." Even if this theory is accepted, a long sequence of changes will have to be made or the history of China may have to be rewritten covering its past relationship with the Southeast Asian countries.

The destruction of Nan-chao did not signal the total disappearance of the Tai from the political stage. After the downfall of Nan-chao, the Tai people went looking for a new center to reestablish their political power. The main body of the migrants moved to the fertile region of the Mao near the Shweli River. Here was a vast region, large enough to accommodate new settlements and covered with fertile lands that could feed a large population. The Tai emigrants from Nan-chao chose this area to establish their new empire known as Mong Mao Long.

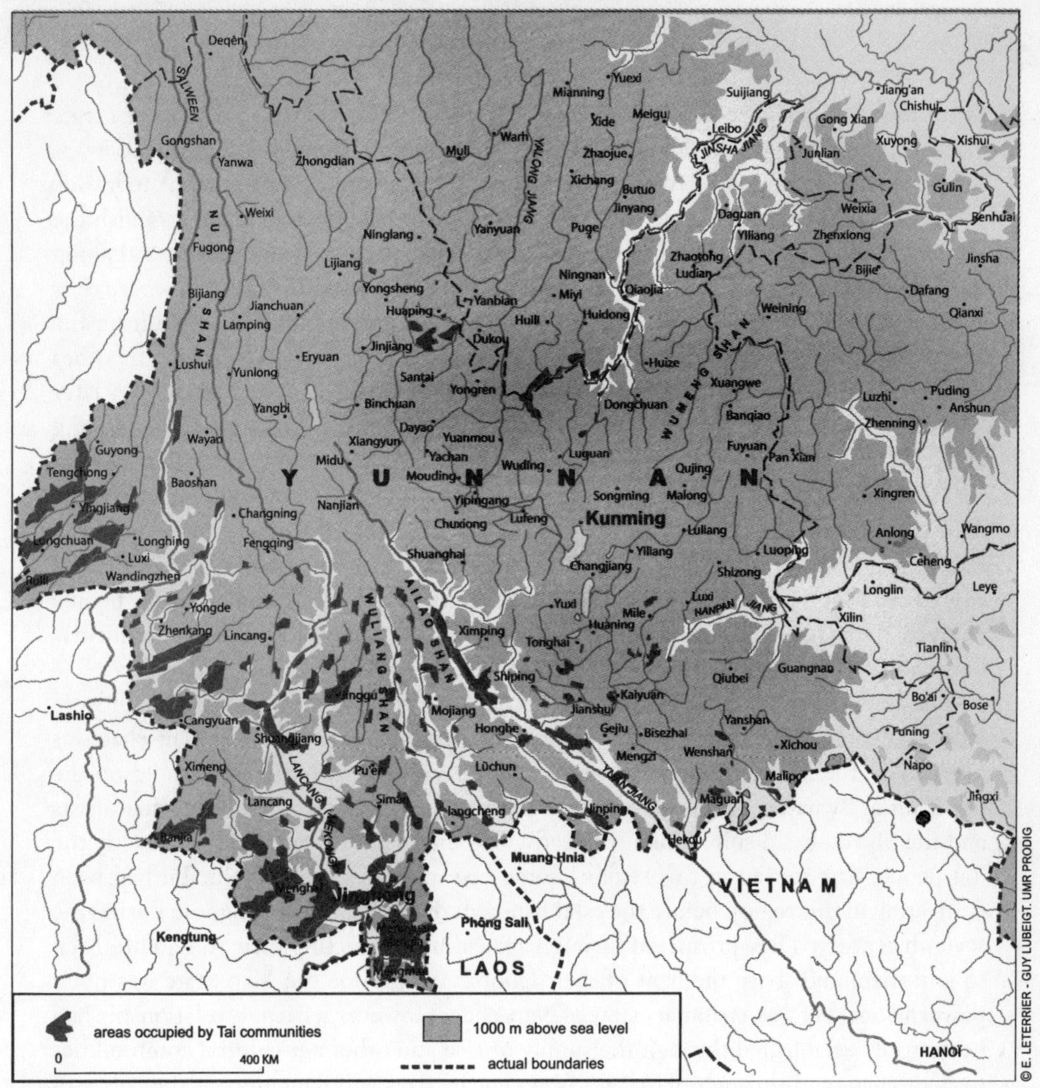

MAP 10. Areas occupied by Tai peoples in Yunnan

THE RISE OF THE MAO KINGDOM OF THE TAI

From the geopolitical point of view, the Mao region was located in a most strategic place. From this region the Tai people could enter Upper Myanmar very easily. So it was simple for them to cross the Ayeyarwady (Irrawaddy) and the Chindwin rivers to invade north Rakhine. From the same base they were able to occupy Assam and establish the satellite kingdom of the Ahom Shan. They were also able to ascend northward along the Ayeyarwady or the Nam Kieo River to occupy the Hkamti Long area, where they established small principalities, each ruled by its own ruler. The Tai people from the Mong Mao area also moved south along the Ayeyarwady River, to be joined by other groups coming down from the Shan state to settle in Upper Myanmar, where they later founded kingdoms and dynasties in Pinya (Panya), Inwa (Ava), Sagaing, Kale, Hsaung Hsop, Waing or Mong Hso, Mohnyin, Mong Kwang, Mong Mit, and Bhamo (Wan (Baan) Maw). The Shan state itself was filled with these Tai immigrants who created their petty feudal states like Hsen Wi (Theinni), Hsi Paw (Thipaw), Mong Nai, Mong Pai, Yawng Hwe (Nyaungshwe), and Keng Tung, each with its own feudal ruler. To the east of the Mao region lay the imperial kingdom of China, with which the Tai people enjoyed trade relations in times of peace. However, wars also occurred frequently between China and the kingdom of Mao.

The lands along the Shweli River (Nam Mao) were fertile and productive, but were still very sparsely populated when the Tai people came in to settle. After Nan-chao was overrun by the Mongols, new Tai immigrants from that area arrived to build up the population. By nature and profession the majority of the Tai people were agriculturists and the Shweli basin suited them perfectly. It is difficult to ascertain when exactly the Tai people first settled in this region. Some historians believe that the Tai had been cultivating in this region before the establishment of the Nan-chao kingdom during the seventh century. They prospered through agriculture, attracting their Ai Lao brethren to join them and share the fruit of their labors. At the time the Mao State was not a powerful one, but was a tributary state of Nan-chao. However, a friendly relationship had been firmly established through the supply of rice and other agricultural commodities to Nan-chao, and through marriages between the sons and daughters of the rulers of the two kingdoms. When the Tai from Nan-chao joined their brethren in this region, the basis was established for the future greatness of Mong Mao Long. The Ai Lao brought with them their knowledge of administration as well as their military skills to help build Mong Mao Long into a powerful sovereign state. The Ai Lao also brought with them their cultural heritage in art, literature, architecture, weaving, and other craft industries, which later flourished among the Tai Mao. Defeated but not dispirited the Ai Lao forged a unity with the Tai Mao and worked together with their brethren to reestablish an independent and powerful Tai state.

Many Tai sayings and proverbs were revised and used to support a state policy that emphasized unity among the Tai, which encouraged working hard together for the common good, and which urged young and old, men and women, boys and girls to join hands to revive the former glory and achievements of Nan-chao in the kingdom of Mong Mao Long.

To mention a few of these sayings or proverbs, there was one saying that went "Bend yourself to the ground and you will one day prosper." The saying encouraged the Tai Mao of the time to work harder to transform the entire fertile valley of the Shweli into green fields of rice. The Tai were a very security-conscious people who always considered food an essential and effective element of national power, and they have always bent their energies toward the earth and worked hard as good agriculturists.

A second saying was "One tiger dies and another tiger rises up. One dragon dies and another dragon replaces it." This saying was supposed to assure the Tai people that whatever had happened in the past, whether they had tasted victory or defeat, was not a cause for worry, because such things happened whether one liked it or not. What was more important was to continue to work hard and to put more effort into regaining what had been lost. In other words, one should keep on working hard until one achieved one's objective. This saying helped the Tai Mao to create a new leadership for the task of building their new kingdom.

A third saying was: "The food is more delicious when it is eaten together; the burden is much lighter when it is shouldered together." This saying encouraged the Tai Mao people to unite, work hard, and share responsibilities for the good of the new kingdom. The Tai Mao believed that each individual should contribute according to his or her ability and that each would receive according to his or her needs.

A fourth saying went: "Girls must lift the lighter part of the timber pillar, boys the heavier end." Fairness and cooperation had to go together as girls and boys of the time joined hands in contributing labor in the construction of the new Mao kingdom, which took some time to become great.

At least forty-five kings of Mong Mao Long may be identified, although some of them may have been legendary rulers. The list of kings includes:

1. Hkun Lai	568
2. Ai-Dyep-That-Hpa	638
3. Hkam Pong-Hpa	678
4. Hkam Sap-Hpa	?
5. Hkam Sip-Hpa	703
6. Ni-Fa-Mong	763
7. Sao Hkam-Hpa	783
8. Sao Hkai-Hpa	834
9. Sao Han-Hpa	868
10. Sao Tao-Hpa	901
11. Sao Powt-Hpa	933
12. Sao Won (*Wan*) Hpa	960
13. Sao Hon-Hpa	983
14. Sao Hau-Hpa	996
15. Sao Lip-Hpa	1014

16. Hkun Kwot-Hpa	1035
17. Sao Tai-Hpa	1050
18. Sao Lu Lu	1062
19. Sao Sang Mwun	1081
20. Sao SangYaw	1096
21. Sao Tai-Hpa	1103
22. Sao Hseng-Nga	1112
23. Sao Lu-Chu (*Chio*)	1123
24. Sao Nga-Cho (*Chio*)	1137
25. Sao Hkun-Ming (Mong)	1145
26. Sao Hkun Kum (*Gum*)	1163
27. Sao Tai Pum	1171
28. Sao Tai Laing (*Long*)	1188
29. Pam-Yau-Pung	1203
30. Sao Ai-Mo (*Mong*). Kang Nang	1210
31. Sao Kwan Hpa (Hso-Hkan-Hpa)	1220
32. Sao Pin-Hpa	1250
33. Tai Peng *or* Sao Hkam-Hpa	1282
34. Sao Wak-Hpa	1285
Interregnum	1315
35. Ai-Puk	1324
Interregnum	1330
36. Sao Ki-Hpa *or* Tai Pong	1339
37. Tai Lung	1346
38. Sao Lwei *or* Sao Tit-Hpa	1396
39. Sao Ngan-Hpa	1415
40. Sao Lam-Kon-Hkam-Hpa	1448
41. Sao Hum (*Hom*) Hpa	1461
42. Sao Ha-Hpa	1490
43. Sao Pim-Hpa	1496
44. Sao Hum (*Hom*) Hpa	1516
45. Sao Poreing	1604[32]

(See also appendix 1.)

The kingdom of Mong Mao came to be known as Mong Mao Long ("Long" meaning great) only when Sao or Hso Hkan Hpa came to the throne in 1220.

The history of the Mao kingdom begins with a legend. There was once a Mao prince in the Shweli valley who got married to a dragon princess. She bore him a son named Hkun-Tung-Hkam, who had mythical powers, and his mother came to help him whenever he was in need. When he came of age, Hkun-Tung-Hkam sought the hand of a princess, the daughter of another Shan (Tai) ruler in Yunnan. But gaining the hand of the princess was difficult, because the beautiful Shan princess was kept in a palace on an island in the middle of a big lake. Her father had proclaimed that whoever could reach the island and strike the palace gong there without using a bridge or a boat would be given his daughter in marriage. Hkun-Tung-Hkam accomplished the task very easily with the help of his magical powers and of his dragon mother, who came and stretched herself across the lake to the island on which the palace was situated. The prince walked over the waters of the lake upon the back of his mother, struck the palace gong and gained the hand of the beautiful princess, as promised by her father. Hkun-Tung-Hkam returned to the Mao kingdom with a big retinue of attendants and escorts. He built a palace and lived happily there with his wife, as king and queen of the Mao kingdom. According to the chronicle his ascension took place in 763, fifteen years after the kingdom of Nan-chao. Hkun-Tung-Hkam ruled over the Mao kingdom without internal or external disturbances for seventy-two years. After his death Hkun-Tung-Hkam was succeeded by his son Hkun-Lu. The kingdom of Mao enjoyed peace under his rule for eighty years and he was succeeded by his son Hkun-Lai. Hkun-Lai's rule lasted thirty-six years up to 951. The accounts of the reigns of Hkun-Lu and Hkun-Lai and of the rulers who followed them are legendary, and since they are lengthy as well as imaginative, I shall not repeat them here. During this legendary period, the Mao kingdom was not very powerful or very extensive. Its domain covered a few states around the Mao valley and the China-Myanmar border. However, the Mao kingdom developed noticeably with the decline of Nan-chao.

In 1220 the greatest Tai ruler of Mong Mao, Hso-Hkan-Hpa, came to the throne. His main objective as king of Mong Mao was to recover all the Tai territories lost during the Nan-chao period. In order to realize his plan for expansion, he organized a powerful army. Then he marched up to Mong Se-Long or Yunnan-fu (Kunming). The Chinese governor, caught unawares by this sudden attack, could not resist Hso-Hkan-Hpa. He therefore proposed a peace agreement to which the Mao king agreed. The agreement ceded to Hso-Hkan-Hpa, Mong-Ti-Mong Men (Teng-Yueh), Yong-Chang, and several principalities down the Cambodian River that previously belonged to the Nan-chao king, including the Shan states. The *Hsen Wi Chronicle* mentions that a large part of the Mon kingdom of Lower Myanmar, including Bago (Pegu), Yangon (Rangoon), and Mawlamyaing (Moulmein), all principalities of importance of Laos, and Hsen Wi itself, were also brought under Mao control.[33]

Encouraged by his success in the south, Hso-Hkan-Hpa prepared his armed forces to invade northern Myanmar and to annex Assam. He organized his army into three divisions. One was led by his brother Sam-Long-Hpa, who was the most outstanding military commander of his time, and the other two divisions were led by able ministers. Hso-Hkan-Hpa mounted three military expeditions: one against northern Rakhine, the second against Manipur and Kachar, and the third against Assam. As a result of these expeditions all of northern Myanmar, northern Rakhine, and Assam were brought under the rule of the Mao kingdom. The Assamese ruler agreed to pay tribute to the Mao king, a tribute which included twenty-five ponies, seven elephants, twenty-four viss (86 lbs.) of gold and two hundred viss (720 lbs.) of silver, to be paid every three years. When Sam-Long-Hpa, who had led the expedition to Assam, returned home with his victorious army, the two other generals who were jealous of his military and diplomatic achievements, falsely reported to Hso-Hkan-Hpa, the king, that Sam-Long-Hpa, his brother, was conspiring against him. On the orders of the king, Sam-Long-Hpa was poisoned to death and, becoming the guardian spirit of Mong Kwang, is worshiped by the people of that region up to the present day.[34] Hso-Hkan-Hpa's killing of his brother was a great mistake because Sam-Long-Hpa was a military as well as a diplomatic genius and had played a very considerable part in building up Mong Mao into the extensive kingdom of Mong Mao Long.

The two brothers, Hso-Hkan-Hpa and Sam-Long-Hpa, were both military commanders who took active command of their forces. Hso-Hkan-Hpa took direct command of the southern front and led the campaign to recover all the territories lost during the rule of Nan-chao. His brother, Sam-Long-Hpa, took command of the western front, which included Myanmar and Assam. Through the efforts of the two brothers, the following states and principalities were brought under Mong Mao rule:

1. Mong Mit, comprising six *mong*: Bhamo (Baan Maw), Molai (Mong Leng), Ungbaung Hsi Paw, Hsumhsai, Singu, and Taguang.
2. Mong Kwang, comprising ninety-nine *mong*, among which the following were the most important: Mong Long (Assam), Kassei (Manipur), part of Rakhine, Yaw country, Kalay, Hsang-hsop, Maing Kaing, Mong Yaung, Mong Kwon, San-Kring Hkamti, Mong Li (Hkamti proper), Mohnyin (Mong Yang), Mautsobo, Kunnung-Kunmum (Mishnu country), Kang-Sei (Naga country).
3. Hsen Wi, comprising thirty-nine *mong*
4. Mong Nai
5. Kung Ma
6. Chiang Sen
7. Lan-San (Lin Zin)
8. Bagan
9. Yun (Chiang Mai)
10. King-lung (said to be Kieng Hung, Kiang-Yung-gyi of Cheili)
11. Kiang-laung (said to be a district north of Ayutthaya)
12. Mong Lem
13. Tai Lai (Tali-fu)
14. Wanchang (Yung Chang-fu)
15. Palaung country (Tawng Peng)
16. Sang-Pho (Songpho country)
17. Karen (Kayin) country
18. Lawaik
19. Lapyit
20. Lamu
21. La-Khaing (Arakan, meaning probably that portion not under Mong Kwang)[35]
22. Ayutthaya (Siam)

23. Tawi (Tavoy)
24. Yunsaleng

Hso-Hkan-Hpa died in 1273 after ruling for thirty-five years. He is recognized as the greatest of the kings of Mong Mao Long because of his achievements, and among Tai rulers, second only to Koh-Lo-Feng of Nan-chao.

There was one exceptional occasion, when an alliance was made between the Mao and the Chinese rulers for a joint invasion of Myanmar to capture the city of Bagan (Pagan) in 1284.

In the south a Shan named Magedu, having secured the support of the king of Sukhothai, established himself as king of Martaban. Later he assumed the title of Wareru in 1287 and founded a dynasty among the Mon which lasted 255 years.

Chiang Mai was annexed to the Mao empire in 1295 and Cambodia became a tributary state of the Mao.

Wars between the Mao and China did not cease but were continued by both sides, whenever a favorable situation presented itself. In 1343 the Chinese undertook a military campaign against the Mao, which failed. Fifty years later they launched another offensive against Mong Mao Long. A bitter battle occurred and the Chinese suffered defeat with great losses.

In 1413 the Mao king, Hso-Ngan-Hpa, went on the offensive and invaded Yunnan with the intention of taking the capital Tali-fu. He was, however, driven back by the Chinese forces from right under the walls of the capital. He withdrew but was further pressed by the Chinese. Unable to withstand the Chinese assault, he fled to Inwa (Ava), where they put on a show of force to pressure the Myanmar king to give up Hso-Ngan-Hpa. Hso-Ngan-Hpa, seeing that the situation was unfavorable, chose to kill himself by taking poison rather than surrender. The Chinese dried his corpse and took it back to China to be presented to the Chinese emperor.

The Chinese looked upon Mong Mao Long as a thorn in their side and continuously tried to eliminate it. From 1448 to 1515 the Chinese launched a series of military offensives against Mong Mao Long. The rulers of Mong Mao Long who succeeded Hso-Hkan-Hpa were weak and lacked the ability to organize an effective army or to consolidate the peoples and the territories which had been acquired into a compact state. The Mao empire was extensive but very loose and too decentralized for effective mobilization of its citizens into an army. Moreover, the prolonged wars against the Chinese had exhausted its resources and dragged the morale of its people to a low ebb. In contrast, the Chinese military kept growing in strength and made fresh encroachments on Mong Mao Long. Worse still for Mong Mao Long, Myanmar toward the west had become unified under an able king, Bayinnaung, who had not only been consolidating his kingdom but was expanding into neighboring states. The Mao rulers were confronted with a war on two fronts, one in the east against the Chinese, and the other in the west against the Myanmar. Mong Mao Long was being squeezed between China and Myanmar.

In 1562 Bayinnaung of Bago (Pegu) sent an army of two hundred thousand men under the command of his son and his brothers to invade Mong Mao Long by way of Bhamo (Baan Maw). The Mao king was compelled to acknowledge himself a vassal of the king of Bago. The city was spared but the Mao kingdom as a sovereign state ceased to exist.

WHEN DID THE TAI ENTER MYANMAR?

As to when exactly the Tai entered Myanmar, scholars differ in their opinion. Some believe that the Tai migrated into Myanmar before the Christian era, and others said it was after that. The migration was sometimes gradual as it was the unique character of the Tai to be restless and to always feel the itch to move to new places where there were tender leaves and clean water. But sometimes their migration could be violent due to wars among themselves or with foreign powers, which pressed them to move to a new place in a torrential fashion as when Nan-chao was destroyed by the Mongol force in AD 1253. The migration at such times was like a flooded river in the rainy season, very forceful.

Dr. Cushing, after long research on the Tai, remarked:

> the migration of the Tai into Burma probably began about two thousand years ago, although Shan and Burman tradition place the irruption several centuries earlier. What we can gather from Chinese history would seem to point to the same date.[36]

History reveals that the Shan were already present in Myanmar in the pre-Bagan period. A legendary hero who bore a Shan name appears in Bagan prehistory. Pyu-Sao-Hti, who helped to beat off a ferocious animal threatening the peace of Bagan, is believed to be descended from the Shan ethnic race. After peace was restored he organized the multi-ethnic nationalities around the area to form united village communities, which later became Bagan, the capital of the first Myanmar empire.

The story of the founding of Ta-kwong (Tagaung in Myanmar) City State in Upper Myanmar on the left side of the Ayeyarwady (Irrawaddy) River and the coming down of its ruling chiefs Maha Thanbawa and Sula Thanbawa to establish a new kingdom in Lower Myanmar was closely linked with the Shan chronicles of the old days. The northern Shan chronicles also tell, as myth or folk history, how the Shan came down from the mountains of southern Yunnan into the Mao valley of the Shweli River to form a beachhead to migrate into Myanmar. (See map 5)

When they entered Myanmar, the Tai immigrants were given new ethnic names by ethnic nationalities in Myanmar. The Tai were then known to Bamar as Shan, to the Kachin, the A-chiang, the Azi and the La-shih as San, to the Ma-ru as Sen, to the Ta Arng of Palaung as Tsen, to the Was as Shem, to the Mon as Sem, and to the Yunnanist as Pai-yi. But the Shan referred to themselves as Tai.

Professor Luce published a long research paper on the Shan entitled "The Early Syãm in Burma's History" in the *Journal of the Siam Society (JSS)* in which he stated:

> I have got on to cards about 150 dated entries in Yuan Shih relating to the history of Dai (Tai) peoples, and perhaps 200 under the early Ming.[37]

He also mentioned that the word *Syãm* was discovered more than twenty times in the stone inscriptions of Bagan, the earliest one in AD. 1120. He also found that one *Syãm* became a *Syambyan* in one stone inscription. *Syambyan* was an old Mon title conferred on a high government official. The word *Khanti* was also often found in the Bagan inscriptions to prove that the Khanti Shan had been living in Myanmar since the old days. Mention was also made in the Bagan inscriptions about the existence of Khanti Shan settlements in the six Kharuin of the Minbu District on the west bank of the Ayeyarwady River about eighty miles from Bagan.[38]

According to Professor Coedès, the word *Syãm* was found in a Cham inscription of the eleventh century and also on the bas-reliefs of Angkor Wat in the twelfth century.[39]

Now, in order to make an easy study of the Shan people in Myanmar, they are classified into five sections:

1. The Shan who occupy the northwestern part of Myanmar
2. The Shan who occupy the northeastern part of Myanmar
3. The Shan who occupy the eastern part of Myanmar
4. The Shan who occupy the southeastern part of Myanmar
5. The Shan who occupy the central and lower parts of Myanmar

1. Shan of the northwestern group include all those who are scattered over northern Myanmar proper from Manipur, Assam (Ahom) to Bhamo (Baan Maw). Over this stretch of land, the Shan established their *baan* and *mong*, especially where they could find fertile land and good flow of water for their traditional wet-rice cultivation, which they brought with them from China. There sprang up many *mong* such as Mogaung (Mong Kwang), Mohnyin (Mong Yang), Mong Waing Hso (Wuntho), Mong Kale (Kale), Mong Hsaung Hsop (Samjok or Thaung Thut), Mong Singkaling Hkamti (Singkaling Hkamti), which are situated about sixty miles above the junction of the Uyu and Chindwin rivers. Moreover, there were many Shan settlements from Yaw country to Motsobo or Shwebo in the old days. The Hukaung-Tanai Valley was also occupied by the Shan, and Mong Kung or Main Kaing was once the old capital of the areas. The Hkamti Shan moved up along the Nam Kieo or Ayeyarwady River to set up a large settlement by the river, Malika, and named the place Hkamti Long or Great Hkamti or Bor (father) Hkamti. The Hkamti Shan made this place their native home for a long time and in the course of time they established eight *mong*, each with its chief called *saohpa*.

1. Mong Lokhun
2. Mong Masi

3. Mong Lon Kyein
4. Mong Manse Khun
5. Mong Man Neu
6. Mong Langda
7. Mong Lang Neu
8. Mong Yak

Of all the *mong* in the northwest only two, Mohnyin (Mong Yang) and Mogaung (Mong Kwang), had historical significance. They were independent states of Upper Myanmar and exerted their influence over the other states in the northwestern part of the country. Myanmar history gives a vivid account of how the Mohnyin chief actively participated in the political struggle to control Inwa.[40] He even established himself as king of Inwa and was succeeded by *saohpa* of Ohnbaung of modern Hsi Paw.

In the chronicle of Mogaung, Sao Hsam Long Hpa was known to be the first *saohpa* and general commanding the Mao troops. He was the brother of the Mao king, Sao Hso Hkan Hpa. Under his rule there were ninety-nine *saohpa*, who acknowledged him as their overlord. He organized an army and crossed over the Ayeyarwady River and the Chindwin River to invade north Rakhine, Manipur and up to Assam where he helped to establish the Ahom Shan dynasty. According to the Assamese Buranji, the first king of Ahom Shan was Sao Hso Ka Hpa, a royal relative of Sao Hsam Long Hpa. (See Sam Lung-pha in appendix 2.)

Ney Elias in his book, *Introductory Sketch of the History of the Shans*, describes how Sao Hsam Long Hpa came from Mong Mao to establish Mogaung and how he pursued the territorial expansion to the west and exerted his authority over the newly conquered states.[41] The Manipuri chronicle also mentions the influence which Mogaung exerted over Manipur. Mogaung shifted its capital two or three times according to the chronicle and traces of the old sites and other historical remains like pagodas, temples, and clumps of fruit trees and other big trees can still be found. It was considerably larger than Bhamo (Baan Maw) and bore every trace of being the capital of the old days. Mogaung also had a fertile area of cultivated plain, extending southward to Mohnyin, north to Kamaing and west to Indawgyi. The internationally known jade mine Hpa Kang is located in Mogaung.

In the old days the north of Kat Hsa or Katha was inhabited by Tai Leng or Myanmarized Shan. The Kadu, Pwon (or Hpon), and other ethnic nationalities were probably mestizos, but more Shan than the others.

After the British annexation, the Shan in the northwest were separated from the main bulk of their kinfolk from the Shan States, having a different administration. The Shan in the northwest belong to the Tai ethnic groups of Tai Leng and Tai Hkamti and have a similar culture and belief in Buddhism. But they have different written scripts. The Tai Leng are gradually losing their written language and only old people and learned monks are able to read and write. Even the spoken language is losing its grip. Only the Tai Leng of remote parts and Indawgyi areas are able to communicate with each other through their own Tai Leng language. The Hkamti Shan seem to be able to maintain both their written and spoken language. The Hkamti Shan introduced a reform in their written script, and textbooks and readers were published by the Hkamti Shan Literary and Cultural Committee. In some of the Hkamti Shan communities, there are literacy campaigns sponsored by the Literacy and Cultural Committee. Owing to the lack of funds and support, their activities cannot cover the whole area of the Khamti Shan communities. Both Tai Leng and Tai Tai Hkamti are very fond of telling stories. There are a lot of folktales and stories of all kinds told by the old folks to the young people, mostly about how the Shan came through the mountain passes and along the rivers to establish their *baan* and *mong* in these parts of the country. The legendary story of the founding of Mohnyin, Mogaung, Waing Hso, and Mong Mit and the migration to Assam through difficult paths is widely told and known to all Shan living in northwestern Myanmar.

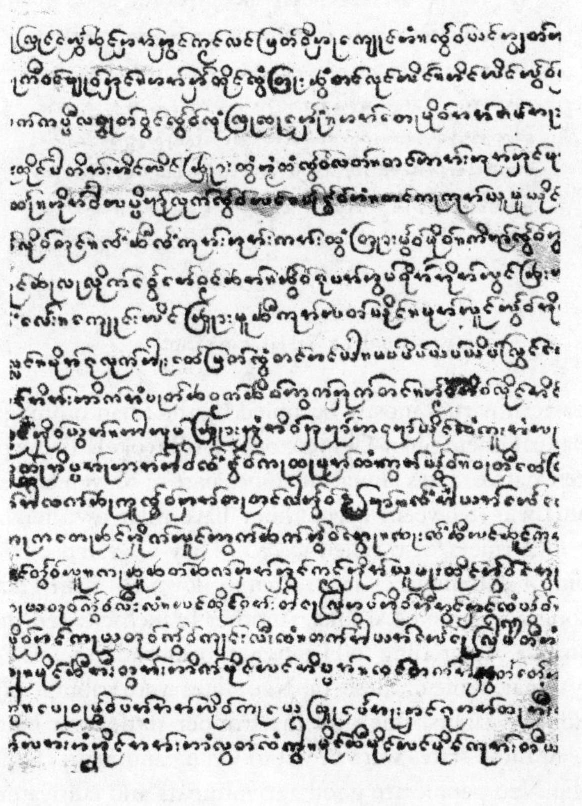

FIGURE 1.1. Tai Leng script.

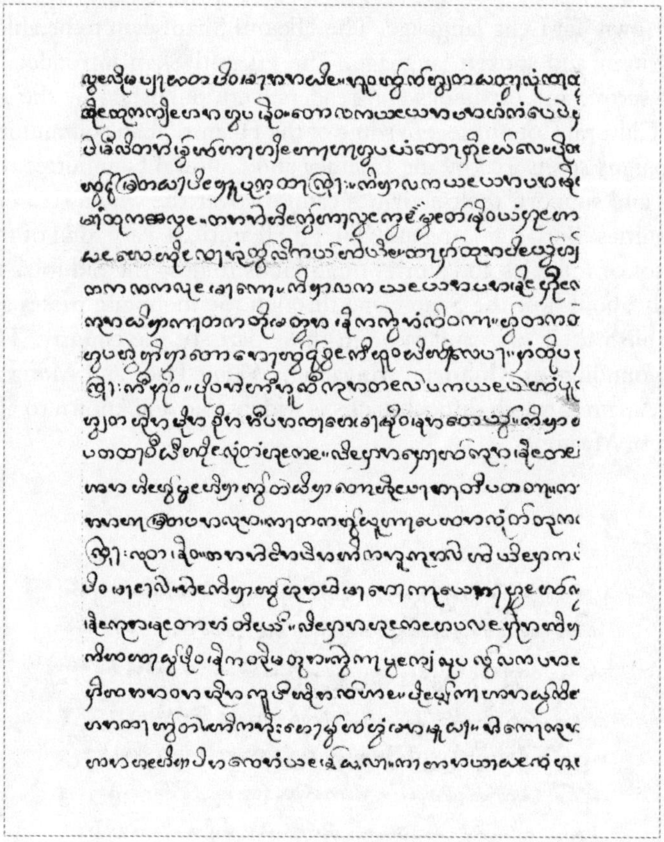

FIGURE 1.2. Tai Hkamti script.

2. The northeastern part is mostly occupied by the Shan ethnic people called Tai Neu (the Myanmar call them Shan-Chinese or Shan-Tayoke). These people, called Tai Dehong, have their native states along the upper part of Shweli and along the eastern bank of the Than Lwin (Salween) River. They have their own feudal administrative system and their own rulers, also called *saohpa*. They migrated into the Bhamo area and set up a chain of communities from Bhamo down to Nam Hkam, Muse, Hsen Wi, Hsi Paw, Mong Kung, and Lai Hka. Another branch crossed the Than Lwin to Mong Liem, Mong La, Keng Tung to Hsiphsaungbana and to Laos. Before the British annexation of Myanmar, some of these Tai Neu states were tributaries to the Myanmar kings with autonomous rights. But after the frontier settlement between the British and the Chinese, all these states were ceded to China and many Tai Neu migrated to Myanmar. The Tai Neu people are good agriculturists and cultivators and engage in wet-rice and sugar-cane plantation and other garden crops. The Tai Neu women wear dark-blue turbans and black skirts and broad silver and jade bracelets in various shapes and designs. The Tai Neu chiefs all speak Chinese, but the mass of the population

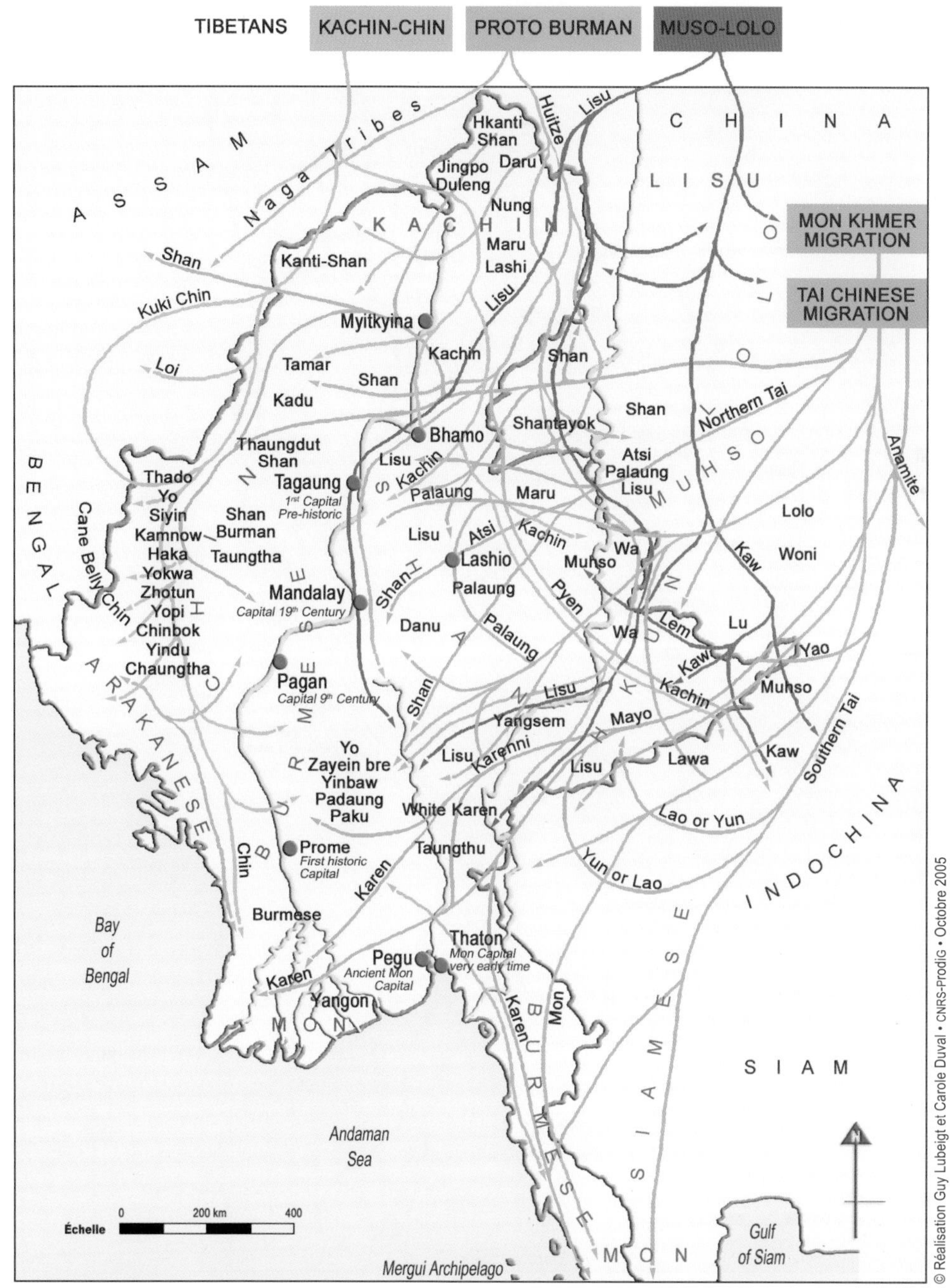

(Adapted from chart of probable migration waves into Burma, compiled by J-H. Green, in Enriquez 1933, ch. 4)
NB: Map represents the historical, ethnological, and linguistic knowledge of the 1920s.

MAP 1. Races of Myanmar and waves of migration

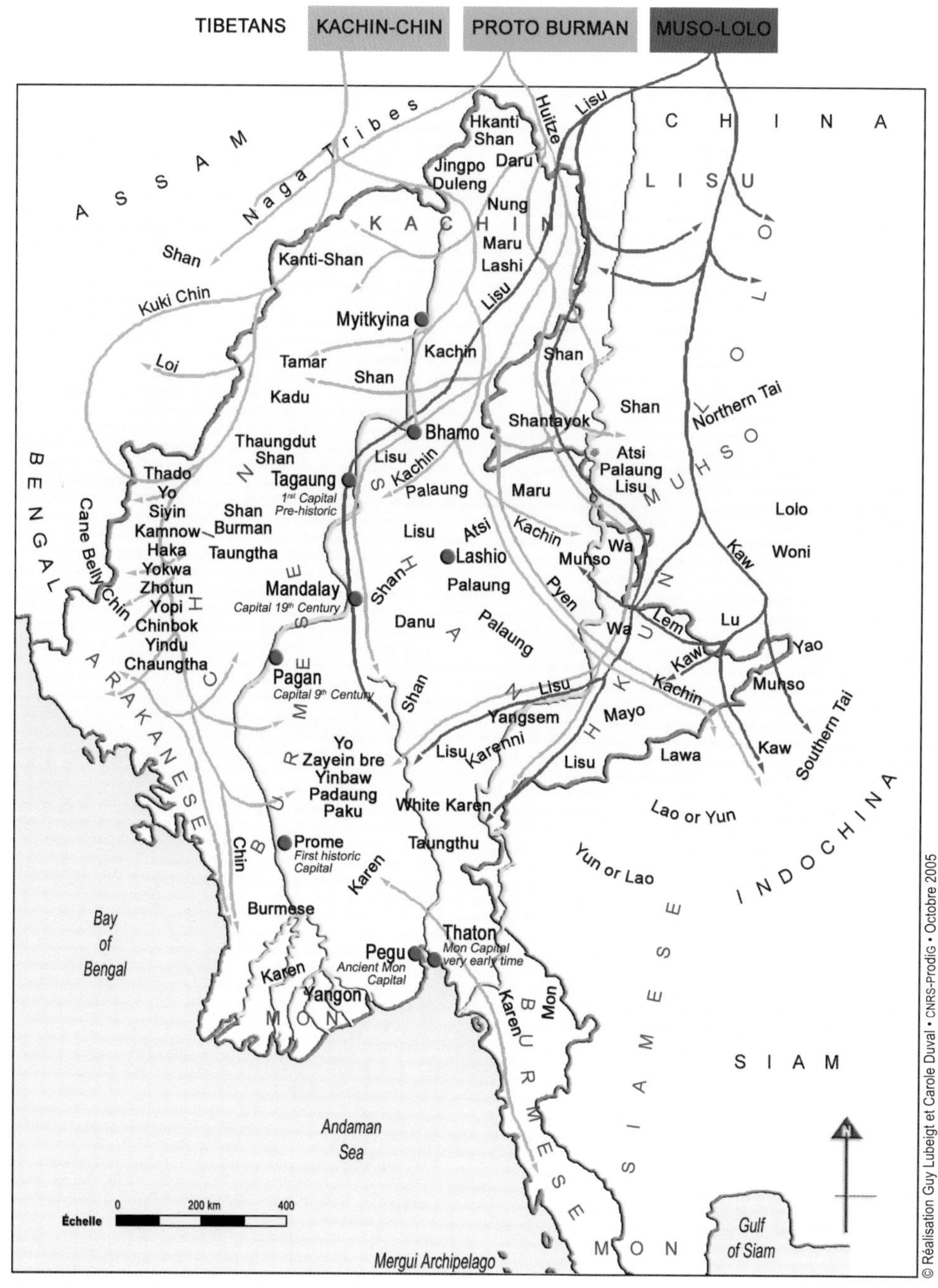

(Adapted from chart of probable migration waves into Burma, compiled by J-H. Green, in Enriquez 1933, ch. 4)
NB: Map represents the historical, ethnological, and linguistic knowledge of the 1920s.

MAP 2. Tibeto-Burman migrations

MAP 3. Probable origin of the Tai people

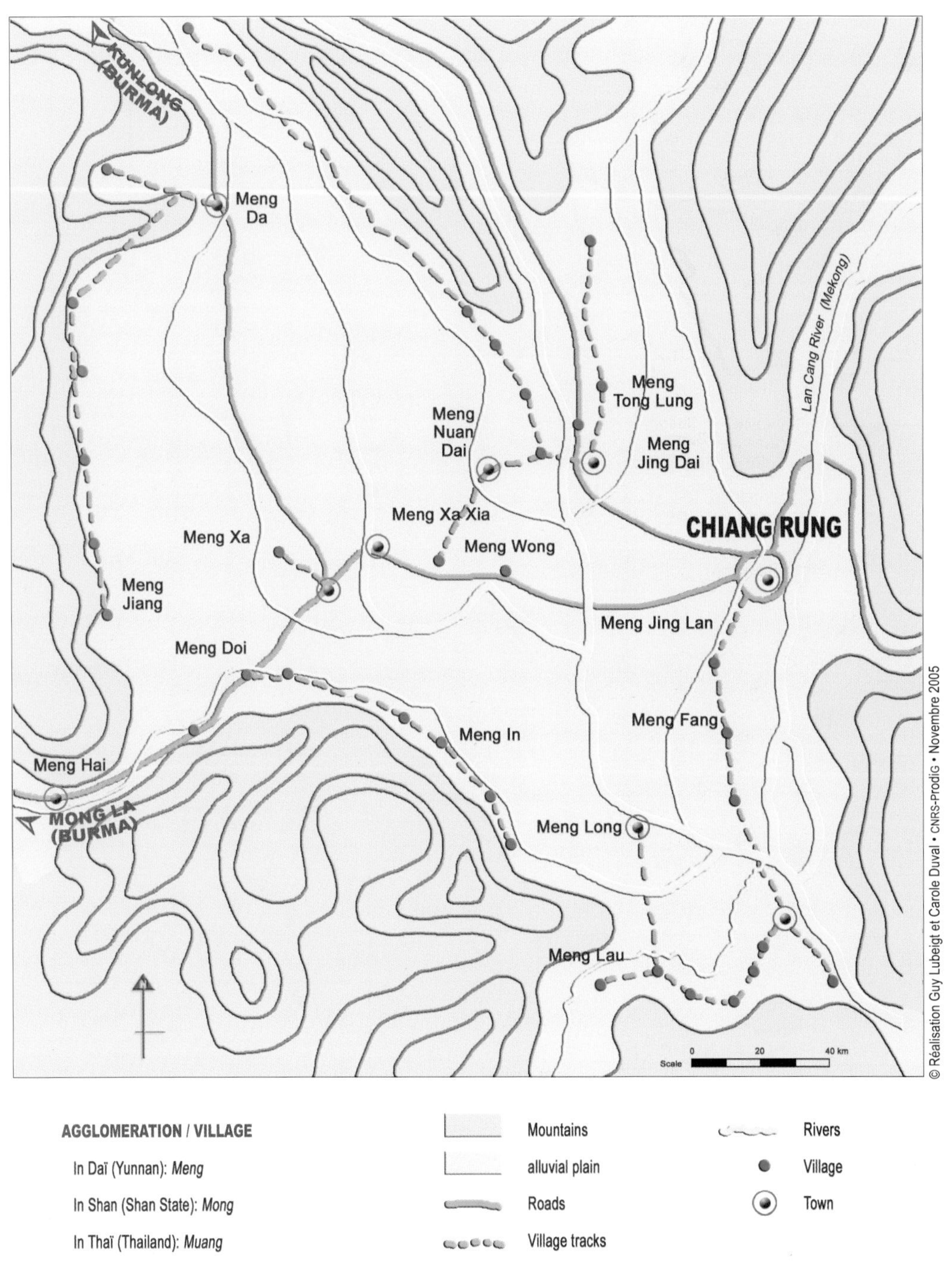

MAP 4. Location of Tai villages in the Chiang Rung (Jinghong) plain

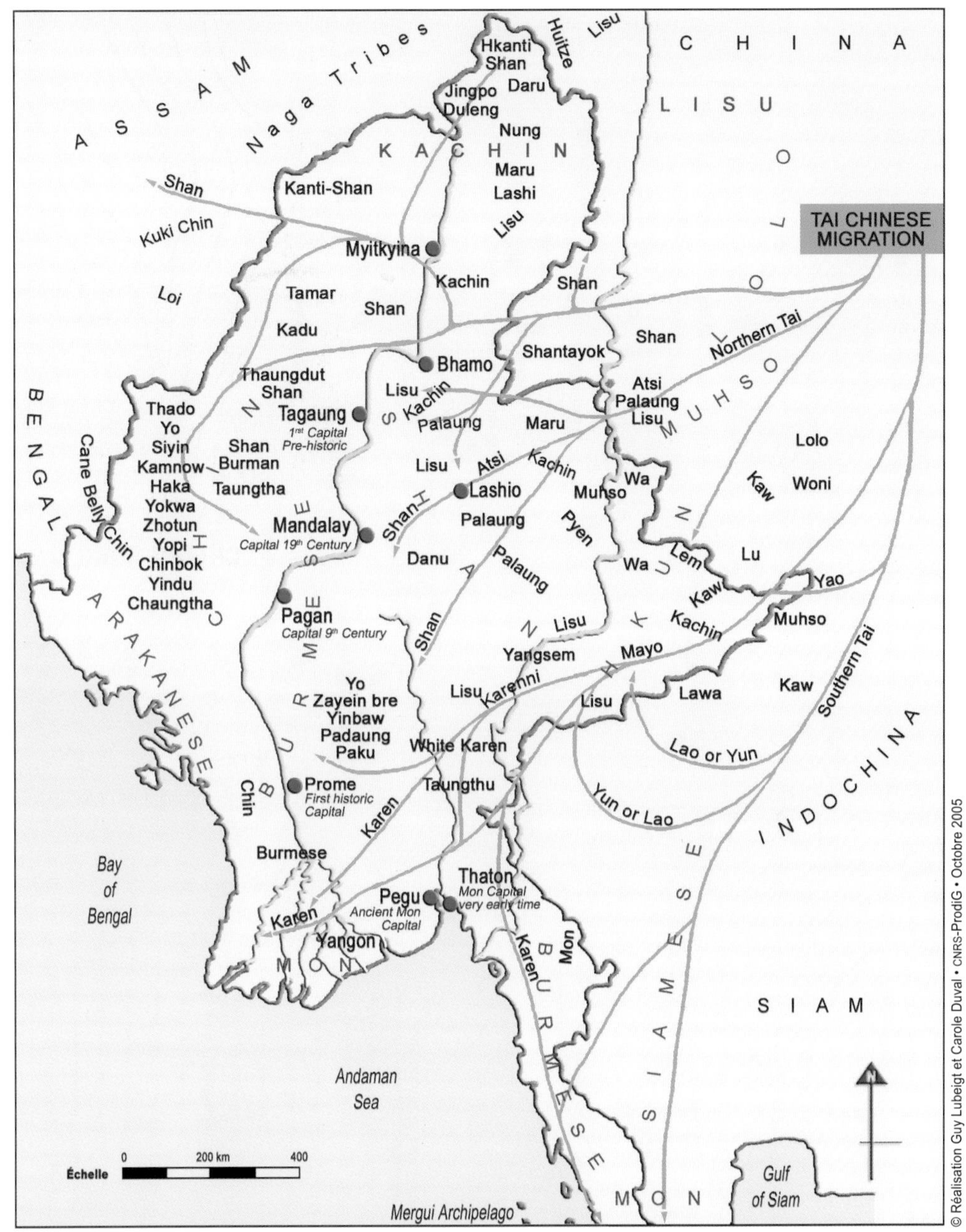

(Adapted from chart of probable migration waves into Burma, compiled by J-H. Green, in Enriquez 1933, ch. 4)
NB: Map represents the historical, ethnological, and linguistic knowledge of the 1920s.

MAP 5. Tai-Chinese migrations

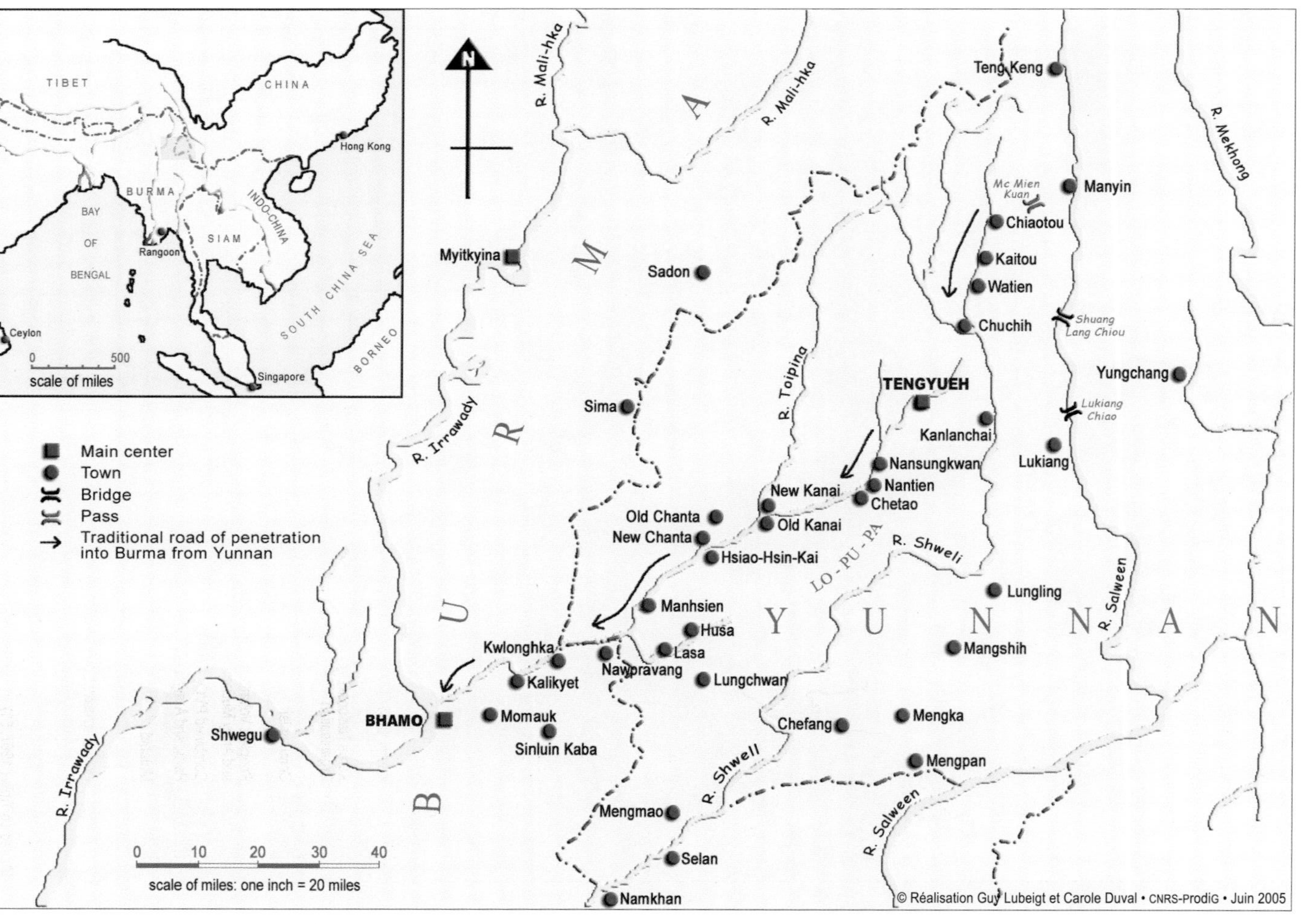

MAP 6. The Myanmar-China borderland

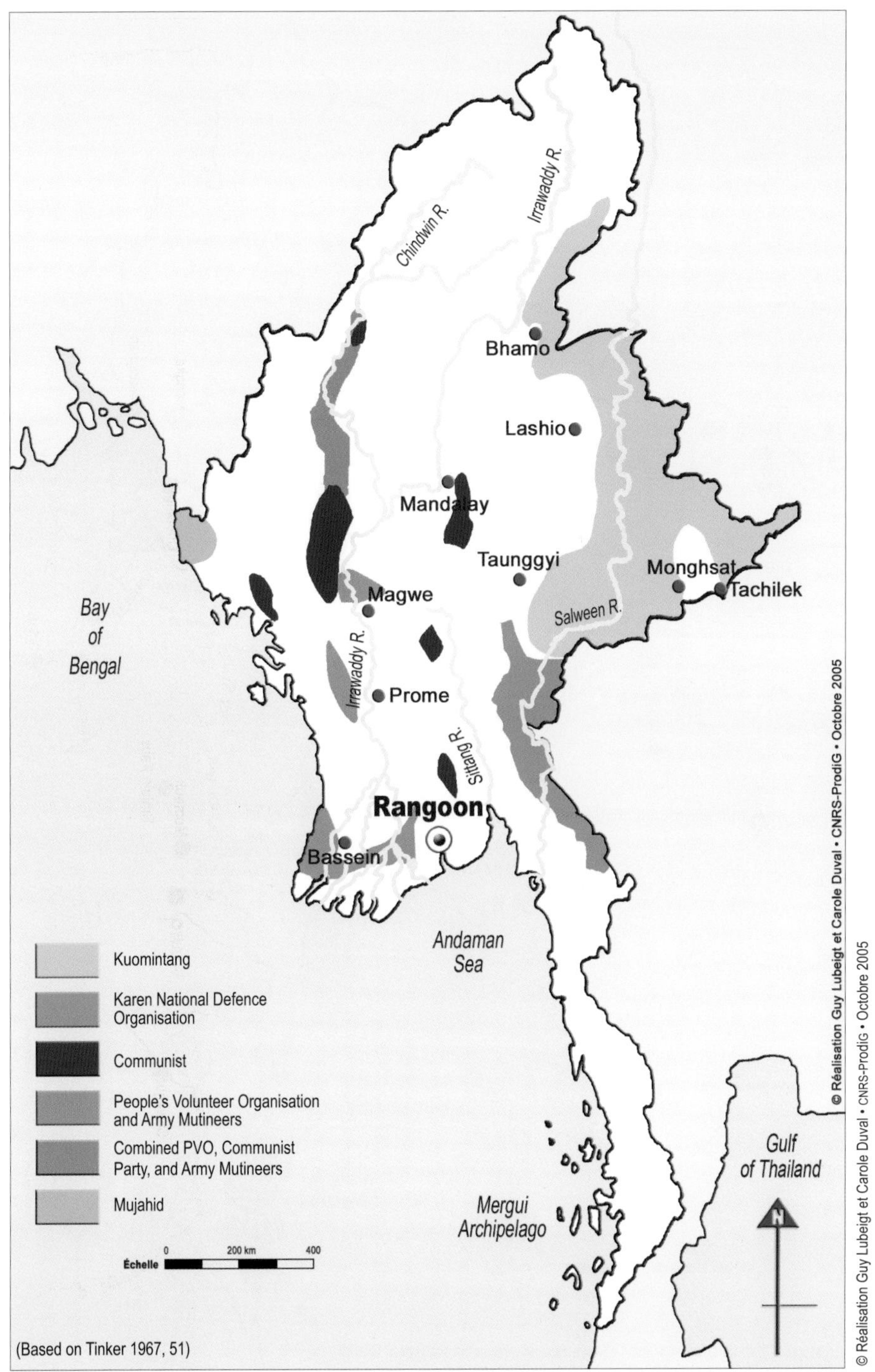

© Réalisation Guy Lubeigt et Carole Duval • CNRS-ProdiG • Octobre 2005

MAP 7. Territory held by the KMT, 1953

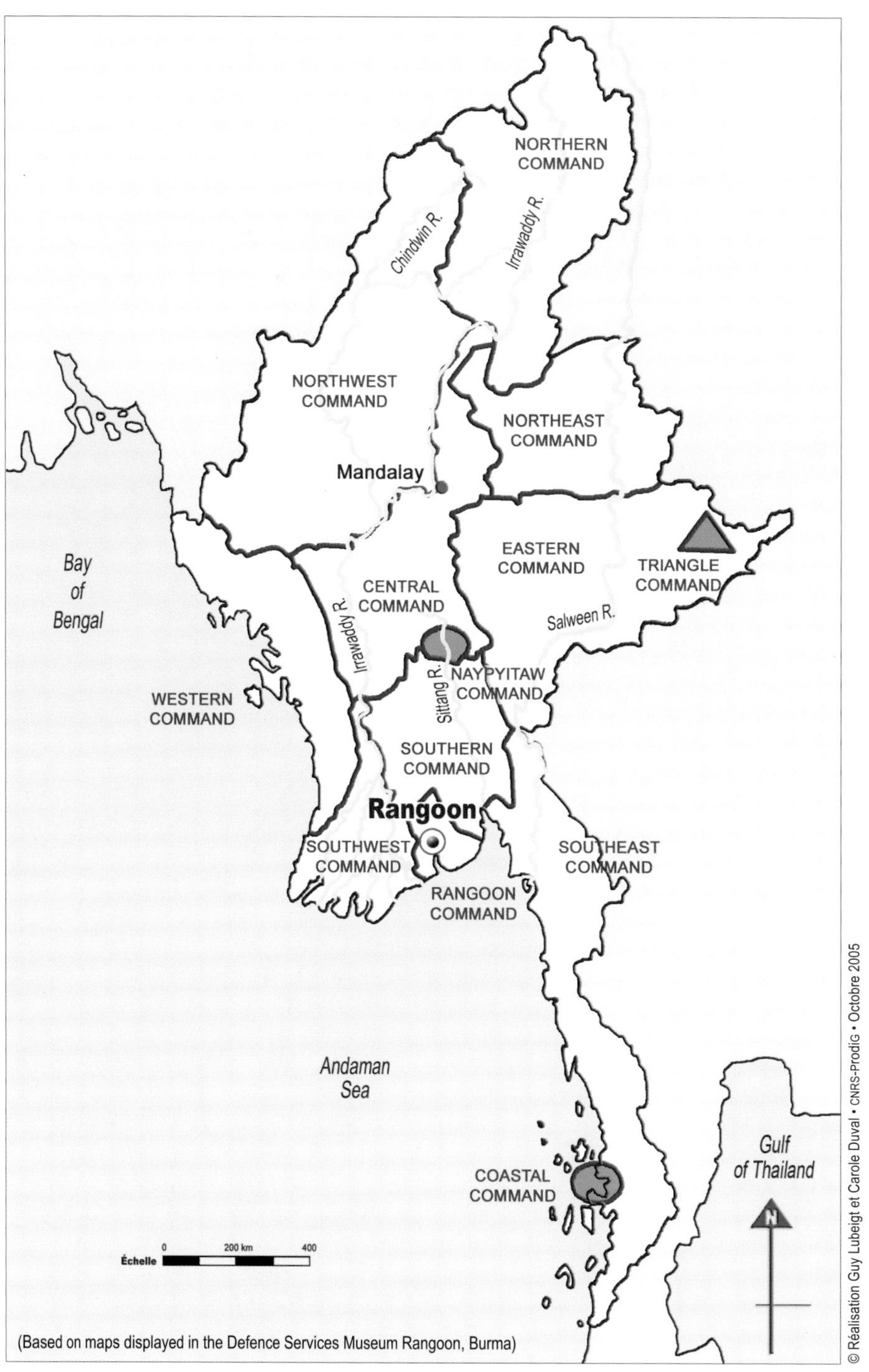

MAP 8. Tatmadaw regional commands, 2001

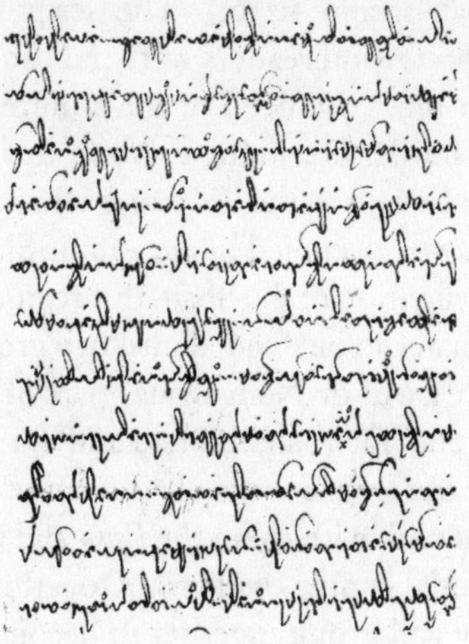

FIGURE 1.3. Tai Neu script.

FIGURE 1.4. Tai Hkun script.

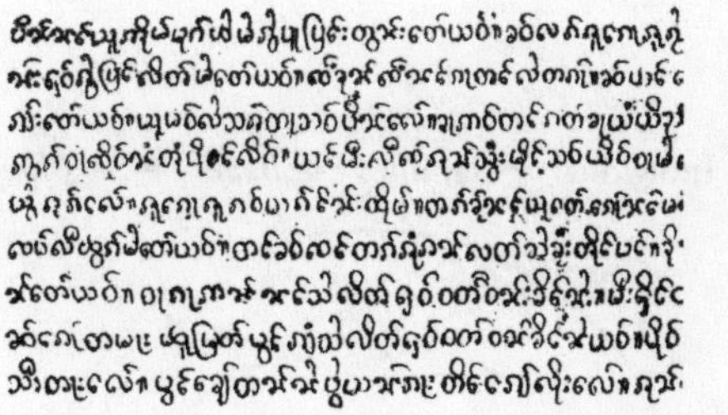

FIGURE 1.5. (*Above, upper r, and r*) Tai Long script.

remain distinctively Tai. They have their written script, which looks like bean sprouts and which the Shan call *Lik Hto Ngouk* (bean-sprout script). The script has been reformed to keep up with modern times. Textbooks and readers were published by the Tai Neu Literacy and Cultural Committee to meet the need of the children. Those Tai Neu who live on the Chinese side of the border are quite active in their literacy campaigns. Ethnologically the Tai Neu people belong to the Tai Long ethnic group.

3. The eastern part of Myanmar proper is mostly occupied by the ethnic Shan group of Tai Long or Shangyi. Because of the mass occupation of the Shan, this region is called the Shan Plateau or Shan State. The eastern Shan can be divided into two groups. The group that occupies the Trans-Salween (Than Lwin or Nam Kone) part of the river included Tai Hkun, Tai Lu, Tai Lem, Tai Neu and Tai Yuan, Tai Lao and Tai Htai. But the Shan who occupy the Cis-Salween part of the river are mostly Tai Yai or Shangyi. Wherever the Tai people migrated they always took with them the *baan* and *mong* system. *Baan* is a village and *mong* is a state. Individual families will group together to form a *baan*. Many *baan* over a wide area of territory will group together to become a *mong*. Over the Shan Plateau there are many *baan*, *mong*, and *keng* forming the Shan States or Shan State. The social structure and cultural system of the Tai are represented in the diagrams by Oliver Raendchen (see fig. 1.6 and appendix 3.)[42]

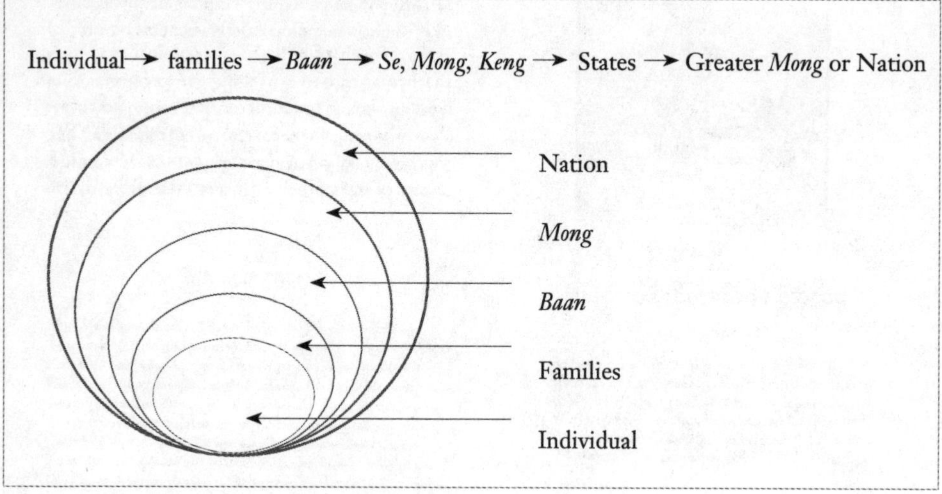

FIGURE 1.6. The Tai social system. (Raendchen, *Tai Culture* 7:2)

Keng Tung is the largest state of the Trans-Salween region. The Hkun and the Lu people may be considered the majority of the population. The Hkun language is akin to Lu of Hsiphsaungbana, northern Thailand, and Lao. Like other Tai dialects, it has at least five tones. The Hkun script has been reformed and modified and is now used and understood even by the Laotian people. Before the sixteenth century, the letters of the Hkun script were rectangular, but now they are round and easier to write and read. The Hkun Literary and Cultural Committee has published some textbooks and readers for their children. Piles and piles of palm manuscripts can be found in all the Hkun and Lu monasteries but they are mostly religious. Keng Tung people, Hkun, Lu, Yuan, Tai Lem, Tai Neu, Tai Lao, and Tai Htai, have very close communication with neighboring countries Thailand and Lao as there is no language barrier between them.

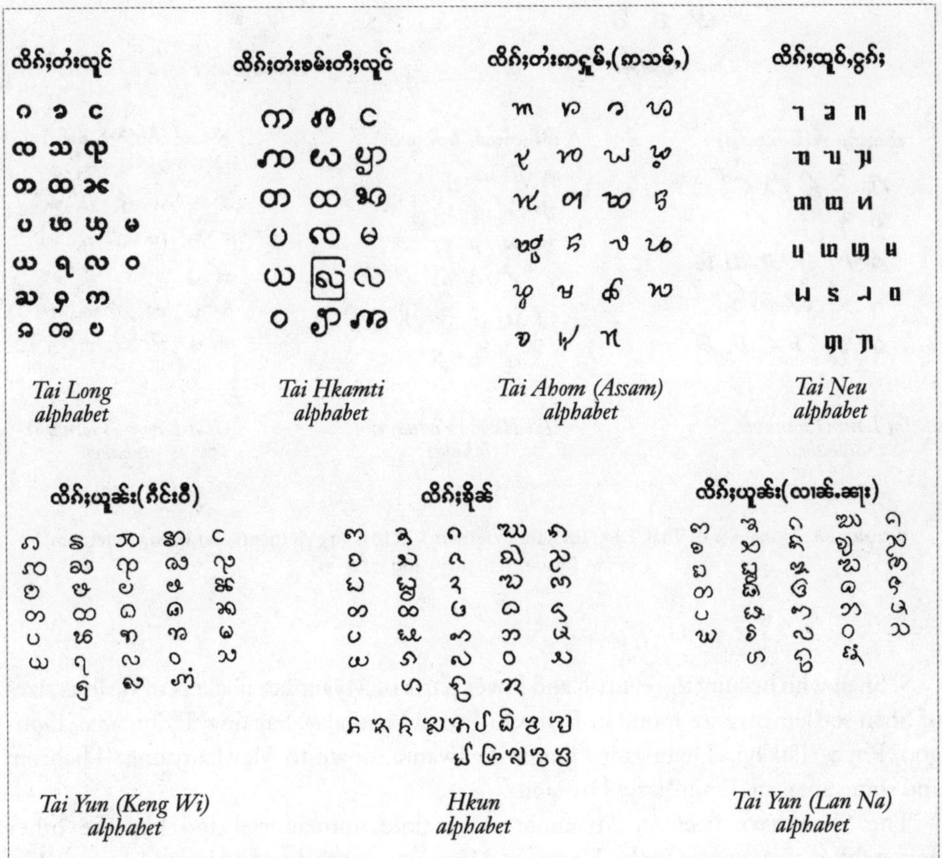

Tai Long alphabet | *Tai Hkamti alphabet* | *Tai Ahom (Assam) alphabet* | *Tai Neu alphabet*

Tai Yun (Keng Wi) alphabet | *Hkun alphabet* | *Tai Yun (Lan Na) alphabet*

FIGURE 1.7. Alphabets of Tai Long, Tai Hkamti, Tai Ahom (Assam), Tai Neu, Tai Yun (Keng Wi), Hkun, Tai Yun (Lan Na).

4. The Shan of the southeast have settlements in Kayah State. Shan communities are found all over the place especially in Hpa Saung. Through this beachhead some Shan extend their settlements right into Thailand in Mae Hong Son and regions along the Kayah Tai–Thai border. The Shan inhabiting this area are mostly Tai Yai or Shangyi and use the Tai Yai script for their written language.

FIGURE 1.8. Alphabets of Thai, Lao, Tai Lam (Vietnam), Tai Hkao (Vietnam), Tai Laeng (Vietnam). (Shan Reader (History) 2004, 50–51)

5. Shan who occupy the central and lower parts of Myanmar, pockets of various sizes of Shan settlements are found in Pyin Oo Lwin, Mandalay, Sagaing, Pyinmana, Taungoo, Phyu, Taikkyi, Tharawady, Thonese, Twante, down to Mawlamyaing, Thahton, and some areas in Tanintharyi Division.

The Shan have been in Myanmar since time immemorial and like the other nationalities they consider the Union of Myanmar as their native home because they have helped to construct it. They live in harmony with other national ethnic minorities and are always ready to help maintain this country as a sovereign nation now and in the future.

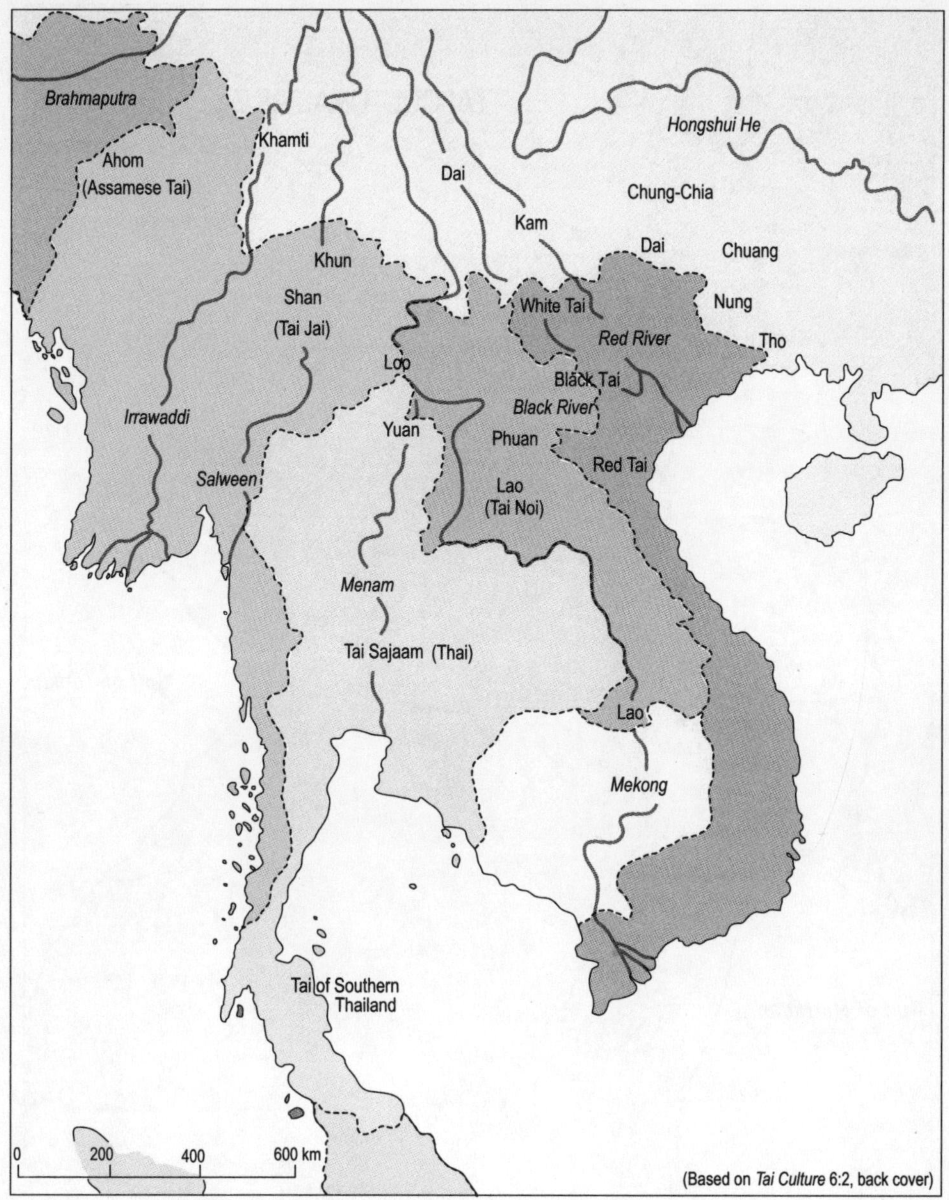

MAP 11. Tai-speaking ethnic groups in Southeast Asia

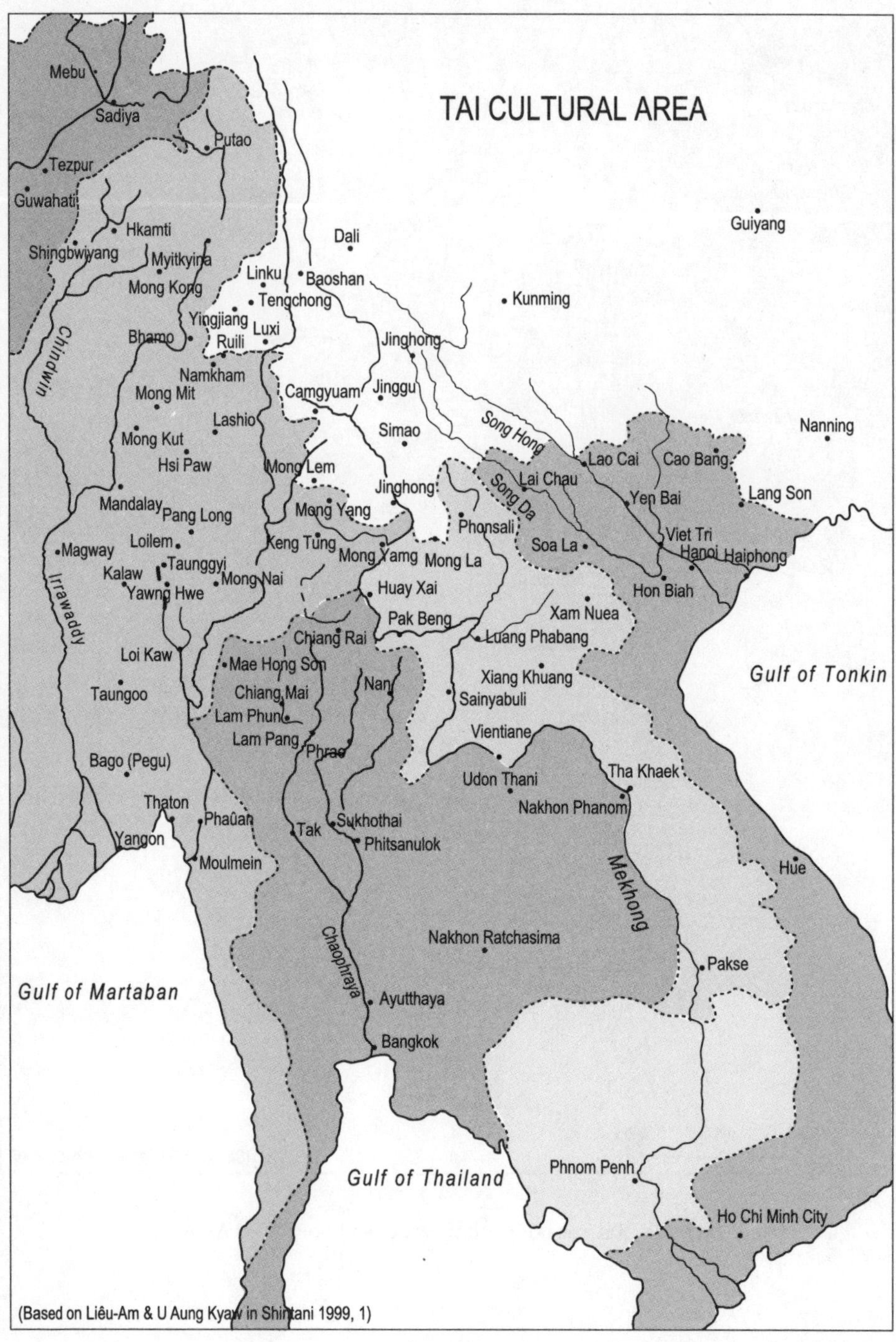

MAP 12. Tai cultural area

2

Shan State

LOCATION, BOUNDARIES, CONFIGURATION, AREA, AND POPULATION

Shan State forms the eastern portion of the present Union of Myanmar between latitudes 19° 17′ and 24° 13′ north, and longitudes 96° 10′ and 101° 11′ east, having an area of about 60,155.277 square miles (155,801.4 sq. km) and a population of 3,716,841. It consists of 52 townships, 1,936 wards, and village tracts.[1] The shape of the country is roughly that of an obtuse-angled triangle, with the obtuse angle pointing north, with its base near the plain of Myanmar, and its apex on the Mekong River. Shan State is bounded by Kachin State on the north, the People's Republic of China on the northeast, the People's Democratic Republic of Laos on the east, Thailand on the southeast, Kayah State on the south, Mandalay Division on the west, and the Ruby Mine area on the northeast.

THE THAN LWIN (SALWEEN) RIVER

The most outstanding feature of Shan State is its longest, wildest, and most picturesque river, called Nam Khone in Shan, Than Lwin (Salween) in Myanmar, and Lu Kiang (or Nu Kiang, Lu-Tzu Kiang) in Chinese and having its source in the Tibetan Highlands. This river begins in China, but for most of its length it cuts through the larger portion of Shan State from north to south, until it empties itself into the Gulf of Martaban. The Than Lwin not only separates the country into two parts but also constitutes a formidable barrier that prevents the Shan people of Cis-Salween and Trans-Salween (Than Lwin) from having easy communication with each other.

The Than Lwin does not flow gently. There are rapids and falls along its course, because of the reefs of rock which run across its bed. Sudden falls from one to several feet produce a very rough and violent flow of water. Sometimes pointed rocks of various formations jut out of the water and they can be very dangerous for any type of navigation. Huge rocks are strewn along the course, and great rugged mountains can be seen towering on both sides of the river. In the rainy season the water is quite full and the surface of the water even, but the velocity of the current is so tremendous that it is impossible for any type of boat or craft to be propelled up the river. The average difference between high and low water level of the Than Lwin throughout Shan State is between sixty and seventy feet and in some places as much as ninety feet.[2] During the summer season, when the water is low, sandbanks and cliffs emerge, adding to the scenic beauty. Geologists believe that the entire course of the Than Lwin is through paleozoic or Archaean rocks and that the deep rocky troughlike character of its valley[3] continues to within a few dozen miles of the sea at Mawlamyaing (Moulmein).

The Than Lwin has many tributaries flowing into it from the right. Some are long, some are short, some are large and some are small. Among the largest are the Nam Nim and the Nam Kyat. The tributaries entering from the left are the Nam Ting (or Teng), the Nam Nang, and the Nam Hka. The Nam Ting takes its source from the neighborhood of Shunning-fu in China and flows from the east to enter the Than Lwin. The Nam Nang begins its course from the Mothai country and the Nam Hka flows through the Wa States to join the Than Lwin from the left bank.

Another important tributary of the Than Lwin in this area is the Nam Pang. This river has its headwaters in the hills between Loi Leng and Loi Maw in southern Hsen Wi State and flows parallel to the Than Lwin from north to south, separated from it by the intervening hills of Loi Maw, Loi Se, and Loi Lan. The Nam Pang finally comes to join the Than Lwin from the right bank, just a few miles below the village of Keng Hkam, in Southern Shan State.[4] The Nam Pan has a few tributaries of its own flowing down from Loi Leing and Loi Maw, and farther south it is joined by small streams which water the region near Tang Yan and Mong Yai. A bridge was built across the Nam Pang at Man Kat on the Lashio-Tangyan road.

The Nam Ting is another important tributary of the Than Lwin, and it rises in the hills of the north in Mong Kung and flows southward to Mong Nai, then Lang Hkay, where it actually comes to within fifteen miles of the Than Lwin. It then turns southwest and enters the Than Lwin just fifteen miles above the boundary of Kayah State. West of Nam Ting is another tributary called Nam Pawn which has its source in the hills of Lai Hka State and flows southward into Kayah State to finally join the Than Lwin. Another stream, named the Nam Tam Hpak, has its source in the Ho Pong area. It drains the eastern half of the central region and runs parallel to the Nam Pawn. West of the Nam Tam Hpak lies the Nam Pilu, which waters much of the Myelat area, enters Ang Le (Inle) Lake, and then leaves it in a southerly direction to form the Lawpita Falls, where a big hydroelectric plant supplies electricity to many industrialized zones in Myanmar. After that the Nam Pilu disappears underground, flowing through an unknown channel to join the Nam Pawn and then the Than Lwin. In the final stage, the Than Lwin enters the sea at the Gulf of Martaban by two river mouths, one to the north and one to the south of Bilugyun Island. The southern mouth of the river is used by ocean-going craft to enter the port of Mawlamyaing.

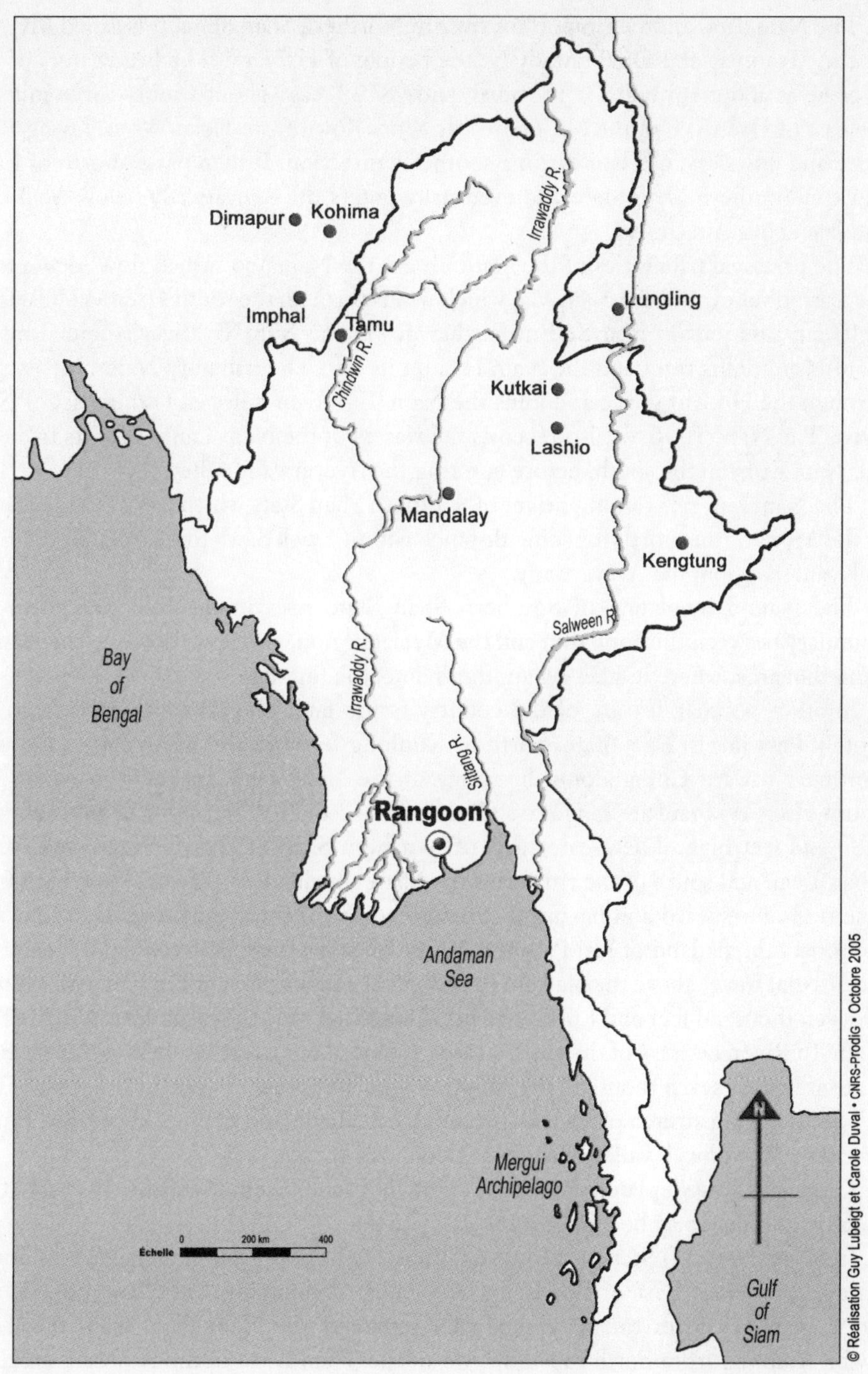

MAP 13. The rivers of Myanmar

The Nam Tu is another important river in Northern Shan State. It is called Myitnge by the Myanmar and Dokhtawady by the people of Hsi Paw. The headwaters of this river lie at about latitude 23° 18′ north and 98° 28′ east, about twenty-three miles to the east of Hsen Wi, in the Na Ti area. It winds down from Hsen Wi to Tawng Peng State and flows east of Hsi Paw, in a southerly direction. It then passes north of Lawk Sawk in Southern Shan State and eventually enters the Ayeyarwady below Mandalay and just above Ava (Inwa).[5]

The principal tributaries of the Nam Tu are the Nam Yao, which flows down from the Lashio valley, and the Nam Ma, which winds through the south Hsen Wi hills from Loi Leng and joins it near Se En. Farther down, the Nam Tu River is joined by the Nam Hsim on its right and the Nam Hka on its left. The tributary Nam Hpe Se runs through the Ho Kut gorge and joins the Nam Tu fifteen miles east-southeast of Nam Maw. The Nam Tu River also receives the waters of the Nam Lang, with its tributary the Nam Et from the south, before entering the Ayeyarwady valley.

The Nam Zawgyi is another river of Southern Shan State which has its fountainhead in the Myelat, runs north for some distance within Lawk Sawk State, then flows down to Kyaukse to join the Ayeyarwady.

The Nam Paunglaung of Southern Shan State rises in the hills that form the boundary between the Yamethin and the Myelat region, and flows down to the plain of Yamethin area, where it takes on another name, the Sittaung.

Another peculiar feature of the country is the fault or rift, which runs from the Goteik Pass in Hsi Paw State, north to Kunlong ferry on the Than Lwin, and then continues toward China along the valley of the Nam Ting. In between North and South Hsen Wi State are ranges of hills known as Loi Hpa Tan and Loi Sak, about six thousand feet high. The greater part of Northern Shan State, which lies west of the Than Lwin and south of the rift forms the Shan tableland, or plateau, stretching from Hsum Hsai eastward and having an average height of three thousand feet. This area comprises the flatland of Hsi Paw and Mong Yai states and is intersected by many hill masses that tower above the plateau. In eastern Hsi Paw there are Loi Pan with a height of seven thousand feet and Loi Leng with a height of nine thousand feet. North of the Nam Tu River, because of the fault, a mass of mountains stretches up into Tawng Peng State as high as seven thousand five hundred feet. The northern portion of North Hsen Wi State is a big stretch of upland affected by the fault, and a series of paralled ranges extends to the Shweli valley in the northwest.

Large and grassy upland plains about nine thousand feet high exist in this part of the country and they may be looked upon as a plateau.

In South Hsen Wi State or Mong Yai, there is a huge outstanding mass of mountain called Loi Leing. East of Loi Leing is a range comprising Loi Maw, Loi Se, and Loi Lan. They form the watershed that separates the Nam Pang from the Than Lwin. Running from north to south, east of the Than Lwin in the Ko Kang area, are mountain tracts and peaks as high as seven thousand feet. South of Ko Kang in Sonmu State are ranges of hills and valleys throughout the rest of the Trans-Salween portion of Northern Shan State, and they form the watershed between the Than Lwin and the Mekong.

In Southern Shan State the principal hill ranges run generally from north to south. Near Kalaw, Loi Sindaung (or Loi Tsang) and Loi Myinmati are prominent, with an average height of five thousand feet. A bold block of hills 7,678 feet high lies east of the Loi Menetaung in Pang Tara. East of that, the Loi Tsang range divides the valleys of Yawng Hwe and of the Nam Tam Hpak. Farther east, separating the valley of the Nam Tam Hpak and the Nam Pawn, are Loi Mai and Loi Maw with peaks over seven thousand feet. East of this there are no well-defined continuous hill ranges, the country up to the Than Lwin consisting of a high plateau cut up by valleys. Near the frontier, the country for the most part consists of rugged and lofty masses of hills.

The Myelat area is characterized by open rolling downs, large tracts of which are treeless and rather dry. East of Myelat the scenery changes from tropical to alpine, and the physical nature is different. Then comes the Yawng Hwe valley. The lowland around this area is well watered. Yawng Hwe valley displays alternate expanses of park-like savannah, forests and well-tilled land, with the great Ang Le Lake in the center.

NONG ANG LE (INLE LAKE)

Nong Ang Le or Ang Le Lake, which is known worldwide as a tourist destination, lies on the plateau of the southern Shan state of Yawng Hwe. It attracts thousands of tourists from Myanmar proper, and from the rest of the world, because of its scenic beauty, floating gardens, floating market, and leg-rowing fishermen. A well-known festival is held on the lake every year in October, to honor the images of the Buddha called Phaungdaw-U Hpa Sao. A regatta is also held in conjunction with the festival. Young men and women in traditional dress, sing and dance and participate in this Regatta Festival, the men rhythmically rowing their boats in a standing position, using the muscle power of their legs. It is an awesome scene to watch.

Nong Ang Le lies within the state of Yawng Hwe, at a height of three thousand feet and at latitude 22° 35′ north and longitude 96° 57′ east. The lake occupies the central part of a trough between two ranges of hills which run from north to south. An alluvial plain has been formed on the western side, and is gradually extending itself into the water. Several streams run through the plain and form a swampy area between land and water. One of the streams flows down from the dried lake-basin of Heho eight hundred feet higher than Nong Ang Le. On the western side a rather large stream enters the lake by several mouths and some streams also flow down to the lake from the northeast. On the eastern side a few streamlets enter into the lake; they are all very short and many of them dry up in the summer. From the southern end of the lake a larger river flows out and makes its way southward.

The lake is about fourteen miles long and five or six miles wide. Its depth varies with the seasons. In the rainy season the depth at the deepest part is about twenty feet, but in the dry season in March, it is twelve feet deep. The average depth of the lake is about seven feet. The bottom of the lake is overgrown with long and tangled weeds, which sometimes rise almost to the surface. The water is very clear in summer and one can see the aquatic animals and a variety of fish at the bottom, as if they were in an aquarium. All the silt brought down by the streams is deposited before it reaches the middle of the lake. The floating islands, which are massed together at the edge of the lake, are one of its most characteristic features.[6] Crops and vegetables of all kinds can be grown on these floating islands all the year round.

GEOLOGICAL ASPECTS OF THE SHAN PLATEAU

The Shan Plateau massif which occupies the whole eastern portion of the country and extends southward into Tanintharyi (Tennasserim) can be classified as a part of the Indo-Malayan mountain system, which has existed as a geomorphological unit since the close of the Mesozoic age.

The Shan Plateau massif which constitutes the portion of the western edge is quite well defined and well marked, both physically and geologically. It rises abruptly from the valley and for four hundred or five hundred miles the edge is formed by a long strip of granite or gneiss. The predominant rocks in the Shan Plateau are gneiss, which yield rubies and other gemstones, and massive limestone of the Devonian-Carboniferous periods. Rocks of all ages, from Precambrian to Jurassic, occur in the massif, and deposits of the later Tertiary period and Pleistocene epoch occupy old lake basins. In the Precambrian rocks-dominated area around Mogok or Mong Kut are the principal "ruby mines." The rocks around Bawdwin Nam Tu in Northern Shan State, according to the geologists, are associated with the ancient volcanic rocks of argentiferous galameo type, and extensive deposits of silver and lead ore are quite common.[7]

Another feature of the plateau is that its surface, for the most part, is undulatory. In several places there are lakes, but their sizes are shrinking, including Ang Le Lake. The general elevation of the plateau is about three thousand to four thousand feet above sea level. Some portions of Shan State are composed of limestone into which the rivers cut deep gorges like the Gokteik Gorge. Although Shan State is considered a plateau-dominated country, it has also various systems of ranges of hills and mountains varying in height in different places. The highest is Loi Ling at about 8,771 feet.

Shales or rocks of fossile submetamorphic type and limestones of the Paleozoic era occur in different places in the Shan Plateau. To the east of Hsi Paw, thick beds of red sandstone are folded in among the limestone and a calcareous band in these has yielded brachiopods and other fossils which are classified as Jurassic or Lower Cretaceous.

Formations of redstones, sandstones, clay and coal seams, and alluvial deposits can also be found in different parts of Shan State, especially around Lashio, in the valley of the Nam Yao River and also in the valley of the Nam Ma. Farther south are deposits of Tertiary clay and sandstones containing seams of coal.[8]

The oldest rocks consist of gneiss with veins of synite and granite east of Taunggyi. Fossiliferous beds of the Permian period are also found around the region east of Taunggyi in Southern Shan State.[9]

CLIMATE, TEMPERATURE, AND RAINFALL

Shan State has a monsoon climate with three seasons, the summer, the rainy and the cold season. As a whole, the climate is temperate and salubrious. In the area around the Hsi Paw and the Than Lwin valleys, the climate can be very hot in summer and very humid in the rainy season, with a maximum temperature of about 96° F and a minimum of 65° F in the cold season during January and February, a dense wet mist and fog hangs over the deep valley areas, especially the Hsi Paw, Than Lwin, and Mawk Mai valleys, for some hours after sunrise. In December and January, frost is quite common in upland regions north of Hsen Wi, Mong Yai, Loi Mwe in Keng Tung and sometimes even in the treeless plains of Myelat in Southern Shan State.

In the summer season, the heat during the day in some places of the lowland region is quite considerable, but the temperature always drops at night. Comparatively speaking, Shan State has a pleasant climate in summer because of the cooling breeze that sweeps over it. This accounts for the hill stations like Kalaw (4,000 feet), Taunggyi (4,700 feet), Loi Lem (4,500 feet), Nam Hsan (5,300 feet), Kut Kai (4,000 feet), and Loi Mwe (5,700 feet) of Eastern Shan State. Many holiday-goers drive up to these places to take refuge from the summer heat in the pine forests and breathe the cooling breeze that rustles through the trees.

The Shan Plateau has quite a good rainfall for its forests and for the cultivation of crops and vegetables. The average annual rainfall, except on the highest ranges, is sixty to eighty inches, which is good enough for the growth of teakwood. On the highest mountain ranges the rainfall is much heavier, especially around Tawng Peng in Northern Shan State.

ADMINISTRATIVE DIVISIONS

A considerable number of native states and principalities of the Shan had been scattered all over the Shan Plateau since time immemorial. As to when exactly these petty states were founded, nobody can ascertain. According to legend and local chronicles, the state of Mong Nai was founded in 519 BC, Hsen Wi in 441 BC, and Hsi Paw in 423 BC. Whether these dates should be taken as authentic or not, the fact remains that these states existed long in the past. When Nan-chao and Mong Mao Long were in their heyday, these states were their tributaries. Sometimes when the Chinese emperors in the east or the Myanmar kings in the west were strong and powerful, these states pledged their loyalty to them and sent tribute. However, their autonomy and the right to run their own affairs were never questioned.

Shan State may be divided into three parts.

The first part, Northern Shan State, comprises the following:

1. Lashio State
2. Hsi Paw State
3. North Hsen Wi State
4. Mong Yai State (South Hsen Wi State)
5. Tawng Peng State
6. Mong Mit State
7. Wa State (Mong Lun)

The second part, Southern Shan State, comprises the following:

1. Yawng Hwe State
2. Mong Pai State
3. Lawk Sawk State
4. Samka State
5. Nawng Wawn State
6. Hsa Htung State
7. Wan Yin State
8. Ho Pong State
9. Nam Hkok State
10. Mong Nai State
11. Lai Hka State
12. Mawk Mai State
13. Mong Pan State
14. Mong Pawn State
15. Mong Nawng State
16. Mong Kung State
17. Mong Sit State
18. Kehsi-Mansam State
19. Keng Hkam State
20. Mong Hsu State
21. Mong Sang State
22. Keng Lom State
23. Hsa Mong Hkam State
24. Kyauk–Ku State
25. Loi Ai State
26. Loi Maw State
27. Maw State

28. Maw Nang State
29. Maw Son State
30. Nam Hkai State
31. Nam-Lok State
32. Pang Mi State
33. Pang Tara Stste
34. Poi La or Pwe La State
35. Ye-ngan or Ywa-ngan State
36. Loi Long State
37. Myelat State
38. Taunggyi State

The third part, Eastern Shan State or Trans-Salween State, comprises:

1. Keng Tung State

FORMATION OF FEUDAL ADMINISTRATION

The prevalent form of administration of these states in the past was feudal. The *saohpa* was head of state, or *mong*. *Sao* is the Shan word for ruler, lord, king, master, or prince; *hpa* means sky. Thus *saohpa* means Lord of the Sky. The idea of the *saohpa* as "Lord of the Sky" is akin to the Western idea of the divine right of kings. The belief was that, like the sky, the *saohpa* descended from above and had the right to rule their subjects as they pleased. By virtue of this concept, the *saohpa* became the ruling class of Shan society with their special god-given right to rule their subjects. This concept was deeply rooted in the minds of the Shan people, whose conservatism ensured the survival of the feudal system for many centuries on the basis of the divine right of the *saohpa*. The *saohpa* held all powers, and as sole rulers over their subjects and *mong*, their actions were never questioned. The *saohpa* often used their powers firmly and effectively. The feudal administration pivoted around the *saohpa* and for good or bad, they bore the responsibility for their people.

Now, how was the feudal administration organized? It was organized upon the *baan-mong* system, similar to the one that had been practiced among the Tai Dam of northern Vietnam in the past and assisted by the cooperation of an administrative staff that included Kyem Mong, Naw Mong, Ngam Mong, Kao Mong, Htao Mong, Pu Heng, Pu Kang, Pu Mong, and Pu Kye. Regarding the *baan-mong* organization of the Tai Dam of northern Vietnam, a distinguished scholar, Oliver Raendchen, in his research paper "Social Aspects of the Ban-Mong System of the Tai Dam in Northern Vietnam," presented at the Sixth International Conference on Thai studies held in Chiang Mai from October 14 to 17, 1976, says:

> The Tai Dam village, called *ban* (*baan*), comprises as average 40–100 families, living in houses on stilts. The *ban* has well-defined boundaries and often it is surrounded by a bamboo Hedge. A *ban* owns a distinctive area of land, separated into rice-fields, plantations, pastures, and forests. Rice-fields and plantations are owned by families; pastures and forests are commonly owned.
>
> Several ban, usually all the villages in one valley form a *mong*, which traditionally came under the authority of a *phia* (noble), a *chao* (lord), or a *mot chao* (group of lords). The *chao* or *mot chao* ensured administration and determined the obligation of members of the commune (Dang/Cha/Lu U 1993. p. 117). The *mong* existed independently of each other.[10]

In the case of Shan State, each *baan* or *wan* could consist of fifty to two hundred households and was administered by the *pu kye*, who was head of the village. Several *baan* would form an *aing* and several *aing* would form a *mong* whose head was the *saohpa*. In Shan State any *aing* that had one thousand families would have an administrator called the *pu hein*. He was the key man of the provincial administration and was assisted by the *pu kang* and the *pu hmong* but mostly by the *pu kye*, the other key figure in administration at the local level, who worked in coordination with the *pu hein* in provincial matters. The working together of the *pu kye* and *pu hein* in a well-coordinated and efficient manner ensured stability in the province, and the *soahpa* depended upon them for the peace and prosperity of his *mong*.[11] The *saohpa* relied on the *pu kye* and the *pu*

FIGURE 2.1. H.R.H Prince of Wales's visit to Mandalay, 1922. Duke of Windsor, Edward VIII and *saopha*. *Standing l–r:* Loi Kaw, Mong Mit, Lawk Sawk, Mong Kung. *Sitting l–r:* Mong Yai, Hsi Paw, Yawng Hwe, H.R.H Prince of Wales, Governor Sir Reginald Craddock, Keng Tung, Mong Nai, Tawng Peng. (Photo courtesy of Sao Hkam Yap Hpa)

FIGURE 2.2. Village houses. (Milne 1910, 112)

FIGURE 2.3. *Saohpa's haw,* or palace, at Keng Tung. (British Library Collection no. 92/2 (B), 1890s)

hein for the collection of taxes and revenue and for the conscription of soldiers, in time of war, and supplied food and necessities to the family of the *saohpa*, owed allegiance directly to the *saohpa*, and could not be easily dismissed for improper behavior. The posts of *pu kye*, *pu kang*, *pu hmong*, and *pu hein* were hereditary, sons succeeding their fathers with the approval of the *saohpa*.

The central organ of government was located in the *haw*, or residence, of the *saohpa* and called the *rom* (office) *saohpa*. Here the *saohpa* was assisted by a number of officials and by the *kyem mong*, or heir-apparent, who was usually the eldest son of the *saohpa*, and normally succeeded him upon his death. The post of *naw mong*, usually occupied by the second son, was more or less titular, without much power or many duties attached to it, the *kyem mong* being the person of the central government.[12] The *ngarm mong*, *kao mong*, and *htao mong* were appointed from among the senior citizens and the relatives of the *saohpa*. They were experienced men with a deep knowledge of administration and statecraft. They were also men of great integrity and morality. They enjoyed the confidence and respect of the people, and it was through them that the people presented their grievances to the *saohpa* for redress. The *saohpa* sought their advice on problems of administration and they freely gave their advice and suggestions. But they acted only in an advisory capacity, the *saohpa* accepting or rejecting their advice as he wished. However, during the absence of the *saohpa* or during a vacancy in his leadership, these elderly officials took care of the affairs of the *mong*.[13]

The *saohpa* in Shan State remained embedded in their feudalism and were not able to organize their *mong* into solid kingdoms like Mong Mao Long or Nan-chao. Perhaps they were not allowed to do so by their powerful neighbors, China and Myanmar, which promptly cut down their power whenever it showed any signs of growth. The *saohpa* remained divided in the course of their history, wasting time and resources in internal intrigues, squabbles, and internecine strife. They were also kept busy supplying contingents of military levies to their powerful neighbors, to whom they owed allegiance. The topography of Shan State also constituted a physical barrier which prevented the forging of unity and the creation of a greater state surpassing their *mong* in size and power.

ECONOMIC SITUATION IN THE FEUDAL SHAN STATE

The economic system practiced by the Shan in the past was feudal, based upon a rural-agricultural system of self-sufficiency, which was also sustainable. There were no major industries and no large-scale production of consumer goods, in terms of either quantity or quality. Only a few cottage industries existed, producing household goods for everyday use; their production was localized and there was no import or export on any substantial scale. There was little or no use of money as a medium of exchange, for transfer of goods was accomplished through a barter system. Within the limits of this feudal economic system, the people were fairly well-off and happy in their own way.

This feudal economic system, which persisted for centuries, became so deeply rooted in Tai society that the Tai people could not imagine that there could be any alternative to this feudal system. This was a greal drawback for the Tai people, and a cause of the ultimate destruction of the feudal administrative system. The Tai failed to keep up with the new politico-economic system that was evolving around them in the changing environment. To this day, Tai societies in some parts of Southeast Asia remain feudalistic and appear to be reluctant to adopt a developed economic system that would affect their old lifestyle. Ways and means must be found to help these conservative Tai to merge into the modern technological agri-economic system that is developing rather rapidly in the world today.

AGRICULTURE

Agriculture has been the most important and principal occupation of the Tai people, not only of the present day, but also of the past, ever since the time they lived around the region which lay between the Hwang-ho and Yangtze Kiang rivers in China. The Tai people may even be considered one of the earliest pioneers in the profession of wet rice cultivation. They worked the land with heart and soul, using their traditional method of cultivation, spending much time and labor to master the art of rice growing to ensure their survival as a race. In the past all the members of the Tai family involved themselves in the growing of rice, each extending his or her helping hand, husband and wife, son and daughter, and even domestic animals like buffaloes, bullocks, and elephants (see figs. 2.8, 2.12) cooperated in the agricultural work of growing rice, all making an investment of time, labor, and materials for the production of rice.[14] Rice was in fact a staple food crop of the Tai people and also a major economic crop of Tai society. For the Tai, food meant security, and the Shan rulers considered food to be an element of national power. They believed that whoever commanded the paddy field, or *na*, would command the

FIGURE 2.4. Plowing rice fields.
(Milne 1910, 150)

FIGURE 2.5. Tai Hkamti elephant plowing.
(From International Conference on Comparative Studies of the Dai Culture, 2003, back cover)

FIGURE 2.6. Water wheels, or *kon nam*, used in Lang Hko, Southern Shan State.
(Photo by Sai Seng Kham, 2003)

destiny of their kingdoms. Their first priority after the annexation of new lands was to make their subjects, the Tai farmers, create new acres of *na* to be added to existing ones for the growing of more rice. From the Hwang-ho and the Yangtze Kiang region to Assam, and then eastward to Thailand, Laos, Vietnam, and back to Sichuan, Kuei-chow (Guizhou), and Kwangtung, across the Asian land, millions and millions of acres of endless *na* were created by Tai ethnic groups migrating in different directions. Their empires, kingdoms, and dynasties may have disappeared from the map of Asia, but the precious legacy of their creation, the *na*, have been left, marking the site of their old settlements. Many of these Tai ethnic groups stayed on in their kingdoms as good farmers and good agriculturists who kept producing rice as food for the nations to which they owed allegiance. Moreover, the Tai people were responsible for the extensive spread of the *na* culture to other ethnic nationalities living in China, Vietnam, Assam, and Myanmar. Together with the knowledge of rice cultivation they transmitted Tai words for paddy fields and rice-growing implements such as *na*. Thus *na* culture was adopted and practiced by many rice growers of Asia and Southeast Asia.

The Tai people became greatly experienced in rice planting and were especially well known for their system of wet-rice cultivation. Rice planting culture became an integral part of their lives, as they involved themselves deeply in the cultivation of rice and accumulated the rich knowledge of it.

In their long march which led them into Southeast Asia the Tai never failed to find areas or regions where soil was fertile and water plentiful. With their primitive technology they built dams, weirs, and water wheels, *kon nam* in Shan, to divert water from creeks, streams, and rivulets leading to the valleys for the cultivation of rice and other kinds of vegetables. The economy of wet-rice cultivation in the valleys became the basis of Shan life and culture in Shan State, and the Shan cultural foundation was deeply rooted in this agriculture.

In Shan State the majority of the Shan people choose to live in rural areas where they can easily and freely engage in rice cultivation, either in the fields or in the valleys or on the slopes of the hills and mountains. Shan State is fully dominated by agriculture and it can be termed a rural-agricultural-peasant dominant world. All cultivable lands in Shan State were under the control of the Shan State chiefs, the *saohpa*, who were the sole owners of the land. The farmers who worked the land, strictly speaking, did not own the land as their private property. The land was given to them to cultivate: it was not hereditary property, nor was it transferable. The *saohpa* took much care to see that all cultivable land remained firmly in the hands of the Shan farmers and peasants.

Agricultural work undertaken by the Tai peasants during the feudal period in Shan State involved a great deal of hard labor. The work included:

(a) Selecting the region where paddy fields, or *na*, could be systematically created.
(b) Mapping the irrigation system in order to have a sufficient amount of water for the *na*.
(c) Choosing suitable places where dams, or *hpai*, could be properly built.
(d) Marking the site where weirs could be built to divert the water.
(e) Looking for appropriate places where waterwheels could be placed to carry the water to higher areas.
(f) Carefully preparing for the seedling, or *wan ka*.
(g) Plowing the other fields, or *na*, for transplanting, or *som na*.
(h) Fixing the date for harvesting, or *pat khao*.
(i) Collecting the sheaves for stacking, or *pum khao*.
(j) Arranging for the threshing, or *paw khao*.
(k) Transporting the paddy from the fields to the granaries at home, or *yong khao*.
(l) Sending the paddy to the nearest mills or to the pounding mill, or *tam khao*.
(m) Holding the ceremony of offering the new harvest of rice to Lord Buddha and to the chief monks of the village monasteries, or *pwe lu khao mai*.
(n) Finally giving a great feast to the community, celebrating with music, dancing, singing, and exhibiting their agricultural success in the form of a crop-fruit-flower vegetable show and prize for outstanding crop products of the year.

The Tai people were happy after the harvest season; all the granaries were full with rice and paddy. They would take a few baskets or bags of surplus rice to the nearby market for sale and to exchange for other commodities.[15]

RICE-GROWING SYSTEM IN SHAN STATE

Rice is grown extensively on all arable land in Shan State. The preparation for rice cultivation is made as soon as the first showers of the monsoon have softened the ground sufficiently to enable the plow to penetrate the soil, and the actual plowing usually begins at the end of May or the beginning of June.

Preparing the Seedlings

The rice plants are first grown in nurseries, where the ground is carefully and thoroughly plowed and harrowed back and forth several times until the seedbed is fine with soft mud. Before sowing in the nursery, the water is drained off the field. The seeds that are to be sown are placed in bags or woven baskets and soaked in water until they show signs of sprouting. The main advantages of using sprouted seeds are that time can be saved and germination can be improved. Sprouted seeds also get a root-hold in the soil more readily than unsprouted ones and are less liable to be washed away by a downpour. The sprouting seeds are taken out of the bags and baskets and drained by being spread on mats, but care has to be taken to ensure that the seeds do not become too dry. When well drained the seeds are carried in the baskets to the nursery where they are sown, broadcast by hand, very thickly over the prepared field. At the beginning it is necessary to keep the water level low in the nursery field. After ten days the young rice plants will be an inch or two in height. Then they will need plenty of water for a quick growth.

Preparing to Transplant

While the young plants are growing in the nursery, the other larger fields are prepared for the transplantation. Plowing is done by going round and round in the field in a counterclockwise direction, and sometimes backward and forward, the farmer guiding the buffalo as it drags the plow through the soft mud. The Shan farmer prefers buffaloes to bullocks because they are not only stronger but easier to maintain. But only one buffalo is yoked during the plowing and harrowing. The coulters used by the Shan farmer are mostly made of wood; some are made of iron. But all the implements used by the Shan farmers, such as plows, plow-beams, plowshares, yokes, clod-breakers, weeding knives, long-handled mallets, hoes, spades, harrows, rakes, etc, are mostly made by Maingtha blacksmiths and local craftsmen. The implements are primitive and crude, but are widely used by the cultivators of Shan State. The plowing begins as soon as the ground is fully soaked with irrigation water or rainwater. The farmers take their buffaloes to the fields before daybreak and plow the whole morning until noon, when there is a one- or two-hour break for lunch, and a few minutes' nap in a little field hut, or *htain na*. Then they continue plowing their fields until the sun sets. For protection from rain, wind, and sun, they use locally made raincapes made from the leaves of the screw pine (which the Shan call *tway*) and a large bamboo hat called *kup*, made from the leaf sheaths of the bamboo. One farmer and his buffalo can plow at least one-third of an acre in a day of six working hours.

Transplanting

When the rice plants in the nurseries are thirty days old, they are ready for transplantation to the larger fields that have been well prepared by plowing and harrowing. The Shan farmers have a lovely tradition during this time of the year. Transplanting is the work of the community for the Shan people and the cultivators extend a helping hand to one another. The first farm owner informs the community that his fields stand ready for transplanting, and on the assigned day the villagers all come to the fields and help in the transplanting. It is customary for the farm owners to offer a delicious meal for all the helpers and it becomes a great feast for the day. In this way they go around and help one another in transplanting until all the fields are green with rice plants. It is an enchanting scene to watch the whole community joining together in this work of transplanting. This kind of community cooperation among the Shan is called *aou wun kan*, which means "helping each other in reciprocity."

When transplanting, the seedlings are plucked (it is called *htway ka* in Shan) in the nursery, tied into bundles, carried to the field, and given to the helpers, men and women, boys and girls, who are waiting ankle-deep in the mud. They work the whole morning and break for lunch at noon, then continue to transplant field after field until the whole area is fully planted.

The seedlings are set one foot apart from each other and their roots are pressed down into the soft mud as quickly as possible with a rhythmic movement. During the transplanting, the men and women choose to wear old jackets and old trousers rolled up to the knees, or old shirts and leggings. All wear large hats with strings tied tightly under their chins to protect them from the sun or driving rain. Bending down the whole day to sow the plants is hard and back-breaking work, and standing in the muddy water, sometimes swarming with leeches and insects, is also unpleasant. But the Shan peasants are inured to such hardship, and they laugh, sing, and tease one another while working, keeping the traditional community spirit alive for the occasion. If someone among them works slowly and if he is a boy they will unmercifully tease him. Telling him not to work slowly like a water snail, they secretly place a bundle of seedlings in his little basket (called *pem* in Shan) which he wears slung at the back of his waist, and sing: "Oh, look! Oh, see! Someone is moving so slowly, so very slowly, the little plants of paddy are growing on his basket."

The fields are left flooded after the transplanting in July, until a month before the harvest. The whole village community again works together when the harvest season arrives. As at the transplanting the farm owner provides food for the day and the whole village turns out to reap field after field until all the harvest is gathered. Reaping is always done by hand using a small sickle with a finely serrated edge. At the time of reaping, the

FIGURE 2.7. Paddy planting. (Milne 1910, 152)

rice is tied into bundles and left on the ground to dry for at least seven days.

The reaping begins in September and goes on to October and even as late as November, depending on the variety of rice, because some varieties ripen later than others.

The rice bundles are tied together to make sheaves, and the sheaves are heaped into stacks and carried to the threshing floors. In Shan State the threshing floor is usually located in the paddy fields, being just a plot scraped smooth and plastered over with buffalo dung and clay to give it a hard, smooth surface. The method of threshing is still primitive and done by a number of buffaloes being driven round and round over the sheaves of rice until the grains lie in heaps on the threshing floor. Another way of separating the grain from the straw is by beating the sheaves against the hard floor by hand. The stalks are held firmly and the ears are repeatedly struck, sometimes on a flat stone, until the grains fall off.

Winnowing

Winnowing is done when there is a breeze. The grain is handed up, basket after basket by a man on a tripod bamboo platform six to eight feet high, from which it is allowed to trickle to the ground. With a sufficiently strong breeze, the wind blows away the lighter grains' short pieces of straw, chaff, and dust, leaving a fairly clean heap of grain on the ground. Threshing and winnowing are carried out from the beginning of January till about the end of February, a lot of time and energy being spent on them. With the grain winnowed, the farmer puts aside the portion of rice required by his family for the following year, pays his rent, the wages of his laborers, and the fee for the hire of buffaloes, all payments being made in rice. With the consent of his family, he sells the surplus rice to traders from the town. The rice reserved for family use is put into bags or baskets and carted home, there to be stored in the *yong khao*, a woven bamboo granary about seven or eight feet tall and plastered with clay.

During the planting period, at least three offerings symbolizing the religio-socio-ritual belief of the Shan cultivators are performed. The first offering is made to *hpi sao mong*, the guardian spirit of the state; and *sao hso hpaik*, the spirit of the White Tiger, as part of the preparation for the sowing of seeds in the nursery. It is called *pwe wan ka* in Shan. The offering includes steamed rice, fruits, flowers, water, candles, and incense sticks. Prayers for a good yield and good rainfall are made by members of the cultivators' family.

The second offering is performed after the reaping and just before the threshing. This time the offering includes either steamed glutinous rice or cooked rice, pumpkins,

FIGURE 2.8. *Wat* Ho Kung in Keng Tung, Southern Shan States. (British Library Collection no. 92/3 (35), Neg. no. B. 14597, 1890s)

sweet potatoes, fruits, popcorn, flowers, water, candles, and incense sticks. They pray and thank *hpi sao mong*, the guardian spirit of the state, *sao hai*, the guardian spirit of shifting cultivation, and *sao na*, the guardian spirit of crop fields, for providing them with good yields of crops for the year. The ceremony is called *pwe pat khao* in Shan. When the work of threshing and storing the grain in the granaries is finished, the celebration begins. The Shan cultivators believe that all the guardian spirits are responsible for the good yield of their crops and for the good rainfall. Before the Shan became Buddhists, they sacrificed animals and offered them to the spirits, but now they offer only rice, fruits, flowers, water, candles, and incense sticks.

After the harvest, the Shan farmers steam or cook the first yield of rice and offer it to the Buddha, at home, at the pagoda, or at the monastery. A bagful or basketful of new rice is sent to the presiding monk of each nearby monastery. Then all the farmers celebrate a big ceremony for the new harvest either at the nearby *wat* or at a public building. With the whole village community participating in the ceremony, the presiding monk of every monastery is invited to deliver a sermon, to have lunch, and to accept bags and baskets of rice and other offertories. Guests from other communities are offered a hearty and delicious lunch to symbolize the successful harvest. Participants bring along their music competition and an exhibition of various crops, vegetables, fruits, and flowers. The winners are given prizes of money and certificates, and honored for their high achievements.[16]

The Shan cultivators do not forget the contribution of the bullocks and the buffaloes that have helped them in the plowing, threshing, and transporting and give these animals special feed of rice mixed with boiled rice or chopped hay mixed with bran, or *ham*, sesame cake, or *chi nga* or groundnut cake, for their helpful assistance in the fields. After the harvest and a good feed, the buffaloes are released to take care of themselves in the nearby jungle, until another plowing season arrives.[17] Oblong wooden bells, with two or three strikers hanging like tongues inside the mouth, are attached to the neck of the buffaloes before they are released. The ringing of the wooden bells can be heard from quite a distance and serves to indicate the location of the buffaloes.

Broadcasting

In certain regions of Shan State broadcast sowing of rice is also practiced. But it is not a very popular method, because of the difficulty of regulating the water properly and satisfactorily. Owing to this difficulty, the growth of rice, when using this method, is very uneven; gaps occur and rice plants have to be transplanted repeatedly from other fields. Broadcast sowing is usually practiced where enough water is lacking and where the laborers for transplanting are scarce. The Shan farmers are traditionally more used to transplanting than to broadcasting, so broadcast sowing has not been widely adopted.

Manuring

In the past, the Shan cultivators had no knowledge of chemical fertilizers and even today many do not use them. Mostly they refrain from using any fertilizer at all. But in certain regions some farmers use cow dung or buffalo dung as natural fertilizers. The problem is that dung is not available in large quantities. In some places paddy husk is also applied as fertilizer. Shan farmers also know that bat guano serves as a good fertilizer, but again this is not much used, because it is not available in quantity. The Shan farmers do not seem to be too bothered about fertilizers, preferring to rely on the natural fertility of the soil. But they are gradually being briefed to apply chemical fertilizers to increase the yield of the rice crops.

Pests and Disease

Damage caused by insects, pests, and fungal disease is exceptional and hardly exists. However, in certain regions, considerable local damage is sometimes done by insects, rats, crabs, and, occasionally, wild elephants, small deer, and wild pigs to fields near the forest area. Grain in storage is also spoiled by insects, pests, and rats.

Insects and pests harmful to the rice plants are:

1. Rice hispa (*Hispa cenecens*)
2. Stem borer (*Schoenobius bipanetifer*)
3. Leaf-cutting caterpillar (*Spodopera mauritia*)
4. Rice case worm (*Nymphda depunetalis*)
5. Ear-cutting caterpillar

The hispa, the leaf-cutting caterpillar, and the case worm are most common, and they usually appear in the early part of the season and attack nurseries and the newly transplanted fields. They attack when the plants are still young and weak. But when the plants have grown stronger, there is almost no danger of being attacked by these pests. The stem borer and the ear-cutting caterpillar usually come at the time when the crop is ripening, but the damage they do is not as great as the damage done by the crabs, or *pu.*[18]

Pu *(Crabs)*

Land crabs are quite common everywhere in Shan State, especially in the irrigated areas. They can harm the nursery grounds and also the newly transplanted areas by making holes. Such holes can do direct damage to plants, and can also damage indirectly by obstructing the flow of water into the fields. To reduce the danger, crabs are caught and put into wide-mouthed earthenware pots and dumped elsewhere or sold in the market. Crabs also serve as food for Shan farmers.

Rats

Rice fields located near forests where rats have their breeding grounds are liable to be attacked. When food in the jungle like the flowering bamboo, roots, fruits, and nuts become scarce, rice fields are invaded en masse by the ground rats, which cut the plants and eat up most of the grain. The cultivators can bring the rats under control by destroying their holes, trapping them, hunting them down with dogs and sometimes by using poison.

Birds

Birds, especially the ubiquitous sparrow and also flocks of parrots, cause considerable damage to the crops almost every year. Their danger is diverted by keeping them away through the use of scarecrows or by netting them and selling them in the market and sometimes eating them as a delicacy.

Other Animals

Rice fields situated at a distance from the village or near foothills and thick forests are liable to be damaged by wild elephants, wild pigs, and small deer. They can spoil a considerable area of the rice fields, but such damage rarely happens. These animals can be scared away by shooting, beating dry bamboo, iron buckets, or any hard material, to make a rhythmic frightening noise, or by firing off firearms if the villagers have any.

Diseases

Diseases usually found in the rice fields are bunt (*Tilletia horria*) and false smut (*Ustilaginoidea virens*). But the incidence of these diseases is quite negligible.

Another widespread disease discovered in the rice field is sclerotial disease (*Sclerotium oryxoe*). This disease mostly attacks the stems of the plants. The most reliable method of beating it off is to breed resistant varieties of rice.

Another disease that troubles the farmers is eelworm disease, which is caused by minute parasitic eelworms. It can be easily checked by burning the stubbles in the fields.

Stored Grain Pests

The two common stored grain pests are the rice weevil (*Calandra oryzoe*) and the caterpillar of the moth Sitotroga Cerealella (*Oliv*). The first type of pest usually occurs in grain stored throughout the rainy season. To avoid these pests, one should carefully and properly clean the grain before storing it. The caterpillars of the Sitotraga Cerealella can cause some damage, but are not as dangerous as the rice weevils and can be combatted by removing them before they multiply.

SHIFTING CULTIVATION

In Shan State the majority of the Shan farmers engage in wet-rice cultivation. To grow rice by this method farmers must transform a vast area of wasteland into fields, or *na*. The creation of *na* is possible only in lowland or flatland regions. In Shan State every possible area has been converted into *na* for wet-rice cultivation. Millions of acres of *na* located in various parts of Shan State and Myanmar are mostly created by Shan farmers. In creating these millions of acres of *na*, the farmers use only spades and locally made tools and implements. The *na* has become an important means of production for the Shan cultivators. Their survival depends on their possessions of the *na*, and the *na* has become their source not only of income but of political power as well. The Shan farmers believe that their future prosperity depends on how much harder they can work in wet-rice cultivation. They are very greatly devoted to this occupation, about which the Shan have a proverb, "*Kom na taw lin mong, tay herng yu one nung,*" which means "Bend yourself to the ground and you will one day be prosperous."[19] It is not impossible for everyone to hold *na* in Shan State. Those who are poor, or are late immigrants to this land, or who live in remote parts up in the hills are not able to own *na*. They have no alternative but to choose other areas for rice cultivation. Since only the hilly regions are left for them to grow rice, they have to choose the hills to grow rice and they practice shifting cultivation, or *hai* in Shan. The meaning of *hai* in Shan is "crying." The *hai* cultivation is so very laborious and difficult, and the *hai* farmers have to undertake so much hard work that tears sometimes come streaming down their eyes; hence, the name.[20]

People who have almost no opportunity to possess the *na* practice in fact shifting cultivation. The *hai* has become a subsistence economy for them. The people who engage in *hai* cultivation usually live far from towns and from centers of advanced culture. The *hai* farmers are culturally backward and are naive and isolated from culturally advanced people. They are landless and unable to find other means of economic resources within an undeveloped region. They start off with shifting cultivation, but once they gain control of the lands they are working on, their agriculture can take on various forms of permanence, provided they are not subjected to pressure, which makes them landless again. In a way, shifting cultivation is at the start of the process of transforming wild, forested landscapes into developed culture landscapes.

Simply described, "shifting cultivation" is a tilling process which shifts from place to place, usually every year. The tillers roughly clear a patch of jungle, ordinarily by setting fire to the trees and undergrowth on a hillside during the dry weather. Then when the rains come and soften the soil, the *hai* farmer sows his seeds among the roots and stumps of trees. Three or four months later the *hai* farmers gather whatever the *hai* yields, which is usually very little and just enough for their survival.[21]

Shifting cultivation is practiced by *hai* farmers in various forms, depending on the topography of the hills and mountains, the space available, and the condition of the soil in that area.

To understand the characteristics, features, and quantitative elements of the shifting or *hai* cultivation, the following points must be noted:

1. It is practiced chiefly by simpler cultures of small population, and sometimes is used by almost everyone faced with cropping system expediencies.
2. It involves human labor, using mostly hand tools and almost no power tools.
3. The principal and primary tasks involve the felling and cutting of trees and slashing and burning to dispose of the vegetation debris after drying.
4. Different systems of crop planting are used in given fields with multiple and specialized cropping systems.
5. The frequent shifting or *hai* cultivation is sometimes without the knowledge of the authorities.
6. Crops obtained from *hai* cultivation are primarily used for subsistence.
7. The use of permanent dooryards, near-homestead gardens with multicropping system and cultural power.[22]

The practice of shifting cultivation is greatly criticized for the damage done to the environment, and for the destruction of virgin forests. Soil erosion, the unnecessary cutting down of valuable trees, the loss of flora and fauna, and the damage done to vegetation are attributed to shifting cultivation. New laws and regulations have been issued to prevent the practice and expansion of *hai* areas, and action has been taken against *hai* cultivators for breaking the law. Sometimes the burning of the *hai* has started forest fires. Thousands of acres of virgin forest have been lost to forest fires starting from the *hai*. As a consequence of *hai* cultivation many varieties of orchids, wildflowers, raspberries, medicinal herbs, and many vegetables used as food have been destroyed, and the natural habitat of wild animals and game has also become very limited.

New adjustments and compromises between men and nature are badly needed. Problems that the poor *hai* cultivators face should not be ignored. Strict enforcement of laws and severe punishment for violations should not be imposed arbitarily on the *hai* cultivators. Their problems should be sympathetically considered and new lands or areas for them to cultivate should be demarcated or *na* be given to them in exchange for their *hai*. They should be helped financially to develop wastelands into new *na* and thereby transform them into *na* cultivators, or they should be helped to enter new professions or occupations so that they can abandon the practice of *hai* cultivation. If *hai* cultivation is properly regulated and managed, the damage to Shan State can be avoided. No doubt, in order to reduce environmental damage to forest and degradation, which is a problem at present, the further expansion of *hai* cultivation should be discouraged, and alternative occupations found for *hai* cultivators.

Moreover, a better work plan for the extraction of timber should be drawn up and carried out to curtail the illicit overcutting of trees. New forest reserves should be established to limit exploitation and to enlarge areas for game sanctuary and species of precious fauna, some of which are found in no other forests of the world.

Another factor that should be considered is the search for feasible substitutes for firewood and charcoal, which are domestic fuel. In Shan State and in Myanmar firewood and charcoal are widely used, but no figures exist on the tonnage annually used as domestic fuel. The fuel problem has become a national concern, and if we do not stop the exploitation of our forests for fuel, for cultivation, for construction, and for export, we risk becoming victims of environmental depletion in the future.

PLANTATION AND GARDEN CROPS

Rice, being the principal staple food grain of the Shan people, is grown in every cultivable place in Shan State. But the Shan farmers are also aware of the need to grow other crops too. The majority of the Shan are not wheat consumers and wheat is grown chiefly for the foreigners living in Shan State. Potatoes, capsicums, onions, garlic, beans, peas, chilies, soya beans, sweet potatoes, and groundnuts are produced in large quantities, both for domestic use and for export. Potato has become one of the major cash crops of Shan State. It is extensively grown in Heho, Aung Ban, and the Myelat area in Southern Shan State. It is distributed to other parts of Myanmar as a cash crop of the Shan farmers. Onion and garlic are mostly grown in the rice fields after the rice is harvested.[23]

The fields are thoroughly plowed again after the harvest and grow large quantities of onions, garlic, chilies, water chestnuts, groundnuts, and sweet potatoes. Shan garlic is well known throughout the country.[24] A special kind of small onion is grown only in the Muse-Nam Hkam areas. It is used for making pickled onions, a favorite food of the northern Shan people.[25] Soya bean is another special crop of the Shan farmers, especially of the North. Soya bean, or *hto nau* in Shan, is a crop which is heavily consumed by the

Shan people who, for that reason, have come to be known as *tai hto nau*, or the soya bean-eating people. *Hto nau* is very nutritious. A great variety of delicacies are made from the soya bean, like *hto hpu*, *hto hpu hpaik*, bean curd, *hto hpu yen*, *hto nau yen*, and *hto nau nam hpit* being the special food of the Shan people made from the soya bean.[26] Soya beans are now extensively grown in all parts of Shan State for domestic use and for foreign export.

Other important crops like maize, millet, corn, sugarcane, and indigo are also produced by Shan cultivators. Sugarcane plantations have become widespread because of the present high demand. There are three varieties of sugarcane in Shan State—black, red, and white. The cane is crushed in a locally made press turned by a buffalo and the juice is boiled in a long process and made into molasses, called *nam oi* in Shan, which is then sent to the sugar mill to be refined into sugar. Yawng Hwe has long been famous for its sugarcane plantations and there is a sugar mill nearby in Mong Sauk.[27]

Cotton, or *Kwi*

Cotton, or *kwi* in Shan, is cultivated over a large area in Shan State, mostly for domestic use. There are two varieties of cotton, brown and white, named according to the color of the cotton balls. The Shan people spin their own yarn and weave their own cloth at home from the cotton they get from their fields.

Taung (Leaves for Rolling Cheroots)

Another economic crop which cannot be ignored is *taung len ya* in Shan, leaves for rolling cheroots. These *taung* trees are grown only in Shan State and nowhere else. They produce leaves which are used locally as cheroot wrappers after being picked, dried, and pressed. In olden days there were as yet no cigarettes. The Shan people and all other indigenous nationalities in Shan State smoked local cheroots, wrapped with the leaves of the *taung*. Since such leaves are produced only in Shan State, dealers in this business find it quite profitable. Demand for the leaves is increasing, and plantations for this kind of crop can be found in Loilem, Hsi Hseng, and Kyauk Than in Southern Shan State and in the Mong Kay area in Northern Shan State.[28]

Ya Mai, or Tobacco

Tobacco, or *ya mai*, is also grown in Shan State as a cash crop. The American tobacco seed introduced into the Lang Hko circle of Mawk Mai State by the *saohpa* has proved fairly successful so far.[29] The consumption of tobacco is quite high in Shan State and in Myanmar. The first tobacco produced by Shan State was from Lang Hko, where the soil and climate are good for the crop. The tobacco produced from this area is sent to cigar and cigarette factories in Shan State and in Myanmar. The tobacco grown in Shan State is of the Virginia type and of high quality. A factory producing high-quality tobacco for pipe smokers was established in Lang Hko and its products have been distributed all over Myanmar.[30]

To get edible sesame oil, or *nam man nga*, and groundnut oil, or *nam man hto*, sesame and groundnut are widely grown in Northern and Southern Shan States. The Shan farmers also have plantations of pineapple, damson, and coffee, producing more crops than needed for domestic use. In fact more canneries should be introduced to solve the problem of surplus fruits. Jackfruits are also produced in abundance, and hundreds of them rot away and are wasted each year because there are more jackfruits than can be consumed in the area. There is also a need to introduce food technology to preserve these overproduced fruits.

Tangerine (*Citrus nobilis*, sour)

Tangerine or orange is widely grown in all parts of Shan State. It is a small slender evergreen tree fifteen to twenty-five feet high and mostly armed with small auxiliary straight thorns. The leaves are small, oblong to oval and two to four inches long, acute, and blunt. The flowers are small, white, and solitary. The fruit is generally two to four inches in diameter, globose to oblong with a sweet-acid or bitter vesicular pulp. The skin is fairly smooth and thin with yellow or orange color.

The fruit known locally as "orange" is cultivated mainly in the Shan Plateau especially in Hsi Paw of Northern Shan State and in Lawk Sawk of Southern Shan State. It is also grown in the deep, narrow, tropical valleys of the Than Lwin or Nam Khone tributaries. Those grown in Kantu Long in Mawk Mai State are said to be unequaled anywhere for their size and flavor. In other states there are small-scale plantations of oranges but due to their long distance from the railway stations or transportation center and markets, they are less known and not so carefully attended.

Careful pruning is very essential. The nonfruiting branches and water sprouts, as well as those branches which tend to crowd the plant, should be cut or done in the early stages in order to build up a healthy body of the plant.

There are several fungal diseases and insect pests of citrus, and among the most serious insect pests are the caterpillars of the lemon butterfly *Papillio demonleus, Linn*, which appear during the rainy season and if not checked in time multiply and strip the leaves of the plant.

Among fungal diseases, citrus scab and citrus canker are the most dangerous. If not checked in time, they could cause considerable damage.

Cutting off all diseased branches and burning them and spraying the plants with Bordeaux mixture will help to keep the disease in check.[31]

The fruits are divisible into two types, those with loose skins and those with tight skins. The season for oranges in Shan State is from December to March.

Nowadays the people from urban areas consume more fruits, and the demand for oranges is increasing. Trade in them has become quite important and the growers have begun to invest more for the extension of their plantations. Owing to the gradual improvement of transportation to the urban markets, fruit growing is becoming important in the economy of valleys of Shan State.

Coconut

Coconut is grown in Shan State, but not on a big scale. It needs a hotter climate than is found in many parts of Shan State, and only the areas around Lang Hko (of Lang Hkay) in Southern Shan State are favorable for coconut plantations.

Banana

Bananas of different varieties are also grown all over the Shan State. *Kwei som*, a variety which is not sweet but which helps digestion, is very much liked by the Shan people. Children are usually offered *kwei som* in preference to other varieties of banana, and it has become a traditional monk's offering among the Shan people. The offering made to monks always includes a bunch of bananas and a coconut. In the backyard of every Shan house, a banana grove will always be found. The banana leaves are useful in many ways, especially for wrapping the local Shan cakes called *khao mon haw*.

Tea

The tea plantation is quite well established in Northern Shan State especially around Loi Long/Tawng Peng State where the soil and climate are good for tea plants. It has become the special crop of the Palaung and Shan people. Tea is also grown in other parts of Shan State, but the quality of the tea of Nam Hsan, Tawng Peng area, is the best. Loi Long and Tawng Peng have a mass of hills, ranging about six thousand feet above sea level where the temperature is favorable for growing tea. The soil in this region is dark, brown clay loam, which is good for the tea crop. The tea plant belongs to a species of indigenous wild tea shrubs. Pieces of land covered with dense forest are usually chosen for developing a tea plantation. The seed is collected in November and sown in nurseries in February. The plants are kept for one or two years until they are two or three feet high, and then transplanted on the slope of the hills in August and September. No manure is used but the plants are regularly watered in the dry season. Weeding is done occasionally. The plants are allowed to grow freely and no pruning is done. Vacant places are filled up every year. The leaves are picked when the plant is four years old and it will continue bearing new leaves for up to ten or twelve years. Tea leaves are picked three times a year, from March to October. The first picking, made between May and July, is supposed to yield leaves that have the best taste and flavor, and which are called *moe lut shwe hpee*. The second picking is called *ka-kang*. The taste and flavor change because the leaves have been affected by the touch of rainwater. The third picking is called *ka-hawt*. The leaves picked at this time are rough and have lost most of their taste and flavor and are sold at the lowest price of the three.[32]

During the British period, the processing of tea was increased by a factory at Nam Hsan, in Tawng Peng Substate, operated by the Bombay-Burma Corporation.

Ginger

Ginger, or *ching*, is another important crop of the Shan farmers. Ginger produced in Shan State is sent to other parts of Myanmar where it is pickled and eaten with fried peas, garlic, sesame, and chili.

Mustard

Mustard, or *hpak kaat*, is the most popular vegetable of the Shan people and of the other national minorities. In every household mustard is grown, either on a small or large scale. There are many varieties of mustard. Mustard oil is produced from the mustard seeds by using the local presses, which are turned by buffalo or by bullocks. The oil is used for cooking and for medicine. There are a great number of recipes for preparing the mustard for the table, and the Shan know them best. Mustard leaves are very often pickled and mixed with chili powder, onion, garlic, and other flavorsome ingredients. Pickled mustard leaves are eaten in a variety of ways. They are mostly cooked or fried with meat of any kind and have become the most common food of the Shan people, who for that reason are called *tai hpak kaat*, or mustard-eating people. In their daily meal the Shan people always include *hpak kaat* and *hto nau* of soya bean.[33]

Coffee

Coffee plantation has been introduced into Shan State and is now in great demand. But coffee plantation is possible only where there is a mild climate, neither too hot nor too cold. Coffee also needs fertile soil and plenty of shade. Coffee has become a popular drink in Myanmar and it is extensively grown in Chin, Kachin, and Shan states. Nawng Hkio, Kyaukme, Hsum Hsai, Hsi Paw, and Pyin Oo Lwin in Northern Shan State are quite suitable for coffee to meet the demand for both domestic use and export.

Betel

Betel-vine gardens are also numerous, especially around the Yawng Hwe region.

Indigo Gram

Indigo is also grown in a considerably large area, but the demand for it is not so great.

Other Garden Crops and Fruits

Other garden crops like guavas, sweet potatoes, watermelons, cucumbers, tomatoes, cauliflowers, cabbages, radish, custard apples, strawberries, eggplants, okra, turmeric, lime, yams, cotton, indigo, cinnamon, pumpkin, gourd, and corn are also grown mostly for domestic use.

Fruits like papayas, peaches, apples, plums, apricots, mangoes, pomegranates, pineapples, jackfruits, and damsons are also widely grown all over Shan State for home consumption and for export.

IRRIGATED CULTIVATION

In certain regions of Shan State, including cultivable highland areas, Shan farmers have practiced irrigation for rice growing. This has not been done on a very extensive scale, because large irrigation works involve heavy investment, modern technology, know-how, and long-term management. During the feudal period in Shan State there was no well-organized and properly managed system of irrigation. The irrigation system in existence at that time was very primitive and run by local cultivators. The feudal authority did not appear to have taken much interest or responsibility in this work. A large portion of the irrigation work was left to the farmers to undertake, and local cultivators were made responsible for the irrigation works in their cultivated areas.

Farmers living in cultivated areas had a common interest in getting sufficient water for their rice fields during the planting season. It was quite important that the water be equally shared and properly regulated for the benefit of all farmers. Problems sometimes arose among the farmers about an equitable flow of water to their fields. For example, farmers with fields lower down the canal or stream might not get sufficient water for their fields, because farmers with fields in the upper part used up all the water for their own fields.

Despite such problems, Shan farmers have shown a spirit of cooperation in the construction of dams, timber weirs, sand weirs, and water wheels (see fig. 2.6), and in the digging of new channels, canals, and waterways leading to their fields. Dams and weirs in Shan State were mostly built near the sources of water, near big falls and springs, drainage basins and across streams to divert water into lakes or reservoirs or directly into their fields and farms through water channels, canals, and waterways. In some places water wheels were used to raise the water from streams or rivers to high ground, and then let the water flow along the waterways to cultivated areas. But the method used to build these dams, weirs, and water wheels was outdated, and the materials used were mostly wooden posts, crude timber, bamboo, rock, stones, and earth. The dams and weirs could not withstand the force of the water during heavy rains and were good only for one year. Renovating, repairing, mending, and replacing materials had to be carried out every year before the rainy season began. Sometimes the dams were built with branches of trees and plaited bamboo-work and plastered over with mud, sand, and stone, and very often they were carried away by the force of the stream. The farm community would rebuild the dam, each farmer who had irrigable land subscribing his quota of labor. That was an admirable aspect of the agricultural community. But farmers have endured much hardship because of the traditional methods of their irrigation. It is now time for modern techniques to be applied, in order to obtain a better system of irrigation which would help increase the production of our staple food and export commodity, rice. To keep up with the present increase in population and the high demand for rice, both for domestic consumption and for export, the Shan farmers should adapt to the new techno-agro-economic environment and use a modern irrigation system for future development.

Already by the 1980s, the state authority took a very keen interest in providing Shan farmers with a modern irrigation system, and the following well-organized and well-managed dams and canals have been built:

1. Heho Valley Irrigation Canal
2. Banyin Irrigation Canal
3. Nam Kut Dam
4. Nam Kat Dam
5. Mong Pa Liao Dam
6. Nam Yan Diversion Canal
7. Mong Hsat Valley Dam
8. Mong Lwi Weir
9. Mong Lin Dam

More dams are being built in other parts of Shan State. These systems now supply water to over twenty thousand acres.[34]

In the future, Shan cultivators hope to increase the production of rice and other agricultural crops, both for domestic consumption and for export to neighboring countries, by making use of a more up-to-date irrigation system. Shan State has more than enough of water resources in its natural brooks, streams, rivers, springs, natural reservoirs, lakes, falls, drainage basins, and valleys. The question to resolve is, how to properly and systematically divert or channel the water to distant rice fields and farms. For the optimum use of its water resources, a modern irrigation system needs to be carefully charted out and introduced.

More dams, weirs, diversion canals, waterways, and embankments must be built, using strong and durable materials such as iron, steel, and concrete instead of crude timber, wooden posts, bamboo, sand, and earth, which require annual repair and waste a lot of farmer's time, labor, and energy.

Mechanized farming should also be introduced and up-to-date farm machinery used in plowing, reaping, threshing, winnowing, and storing. To double the crop production, chemical fertilizers should be applied. Mixed farming should also be introduced to increase the income of the farmers. The Shan cultivators should switch from the feudal socioeconomic type of agriculture to a modern techno-socioeconomic type if they are to improve their lot in the future world. Modern farming with a better system of irrigation is quite costly, and a huge investment will have to be made and financial assistance given to the agriculturist. Perhaps loan banks charging low rates of interest will have to be established to help those farmers who are in need of financial assistance. Moreover, workshop training or demonstration centers should be opened to help farmers learn modern techniques of agriculture. It is now time to start doing something about it.

NATURAL FORESTS: FLORA AND FAUNA

A good growth of forest vegetation anywhere in the world depends on three main factors: optimal temperature, good rainfall, and fertile soil. The presence of these three elements, especially a good amount of rainfall, helps to create useful forest areas with a variety of timber, bamboo, medicinal herbs, orchids, wildflowers, and all sorts of flora and fauna in Shan State. Natural products or forest products obtained from these forests help to sustain the economy of the Shan people.

Teak (Tectona grandis)

Teak is the most important forest product of Shan State. It is grown in regions where the annual rainfall is about sixty to eighty inches and where the altitude does not exceed three thousand feet above sea level. In Northern Shan State teak forests are found around Hsi Paw, Tawng Peng, North Hsen Wi, Kain Gyi, and Nam Ma. There are also considerable teak trees along the deciduous belt, mostly parallel to the streams in Shan State. Good reserves of forest rich in teak exist in the drainage basin of the Than Lwin, Nam Tu, Mekong, Nam Pawn, and Paung Laung or Sittaung.

Mong Nawng also had a good area of teak forest, but unfortunately it was destroyed by reckless cutting and illicit extraction. That danger is gradually threatening other areas. Small patches of teak natural regeneration areas are common in Mong Mit. They also occur along the tributaries of the Than Lwin, Nam Pang, and Nam Teng. Regions around Keng Hkam, Mong Nai, Mawk Mai, Mong Pu, Mong Hsat in Southern Shan State are known for good teak-bearing reserved forests. But some of these have been exhausted owing to reckless and uncontrolled exploitation. Teak forests found in the drainage basins of the Than Lwin, Nam Tu, Mekong, Nam Pawn, and Paung Laung or Sittaung are considered to be of high quality. A great number of teak logs are extracted from these areas and floated down the Than Lwin to the Kado forest depot just north of Mawlamyaing. The teak forests in the Nam Tu drainage areas are located near Lawk Sawk, and the extracted logs are floated down the Nam Lang and then to Nam Tu to be collected in the rafting station at Inwa. The teak trees around Keng Tung are extracted and sent to neighboring countries by various means of transportation. The Nam Pawn teak forests include the valleys of Nam Pilu and Nam Tam Hpak. These forests have also been overexploited and only a few hundred teak trees are left. The teak trees of the Paung Laung drainage basin include the Loi Long region, but it has been overexploited and is almost exhausted.

Extraction, Girdling of Teak

Girdling is the process of cutting away a ring of sapwood about three inches wide around the base of the tree until a continuous surface of the darker heartwood is exposed. The tree dies gradually, having been deprived of its sustenance that normally rises through the vessels in the sapwood. Three years after girdling, the trees gradually lose moisture and their barks and become sufficiently dried and light enough to be able to float.

Felling and Logging

Felling of teak trees is done by both axe and saw. The general principle in logging teak is to crosscut to the largest dimension that can be extracted under local hauling and floating conditions. Timber other than teak is also crosscut into logs in lengths of eighteen feet, unless logged for a special purpose. A drag-hole is made at the end of every log so that it can be dragged by chain.

Dragging

After felling and logging, the logs are dragged to the nearest streams or rivers, which they will be floated down during the rainy season. Dragging is mostly done by buffaloes in easier terrain and by elephants in more difficult and undulating terrain. Before floating, any obstruction in the streams that can disturb the floating like fallen trees and other snags has to be removed. Sometimes rocks obstruct the waterway and have to be blasted away to ensure smooth floating. Throughout the floating season extensive use has to be made of the elephants to keep the logs on the move and maintain constant floating. The logs then make their way downstream to the rafting station, where they are lashed together into rafts. Teak rafts are made in sections of about twenty logs lashed together with canes, each raft consisting of at least ten sections. The building of rafts and their safe handling through the hazards of obstructions, rapids, sandbanks, and traffic on the main rivers require a high degree of skill and technique by those who undertake the work.

Description of the Teak Tree

The teak *mai hsak* trees have rounded crowns with tall cylindrical boles, which are often buttressed at the base and sometimes fluted. The leaves are unusually large, about one or two feet long. The upper surface of the leaf is quite rough but the underside is quite smooth. The bark of the teak tree is gray or light brown. The tallest teak found in Shan State was as high as one hundred fifty feet, weighed about ten tons, and was discovered in the Shweli forest of the old Mao region.

When the green teak is girdled, the sapwood is light yellow and the heartwood is chocolate. When dry it turns a golden brown and sometimes shows dark streaks. With age and exposure to the air, the wood then turns dark brown. When teak is freshly cut it is rough and oily to the touch and has the smell of old leather. The virtue of teak lies in its strength, durability, and unshrinkability. It resists attacks of fungi and white ants. It lasts a long time, even in constant contact with water.

During the British occupation of Shan State, teak was used as railway ties on a trial basis, and was found that they could last for at least twenty to twenty-five years. Teak has a high density and is long lasting without artificial preservation. That is the real beauty of the teak in Shan State.[35]

Teak in Shan State occurs in the mixed forests and contributes about 10 percent of these forests. Shan State production before World War II was about 7 percent of the total production of Myanmar.

Use of Teak

The British, when they first annexed Myanmar, paid great attention to the teak forests, finding ways to systematically preserve them and extract them for the benefit of their teak traders. Moreover, they had come to discover that teak had many uses. For example, the pre-eminence of teak as shipbuilding timber has been recognized for centuries because of its strength and durability. During the British administration in Myanmar, teak retained its popularity in shipbuilding and was used in the construction of warships, liners, cargo vessels, motor or sailing yachts, ferry steamers, and launches.

Teak is also much used for house-building and for household furniture of all sorts because of its durability and freedom from movement due to expansion and shrinkage. It is also immune from the attacks of white ants and termites. Paneling, flooring, stairways, fireplaces, window seats, doors, and window frames are also made of teakwood.

Mai Pek, or Pine (genus Pinus)

Pine forests cover the hill-slope at altitudes higher than eight thousand feet in areas around Kalaw, Kut Kai, North Hsen Wi, Mong Yai, Loi Mwe, a large part of North Keng Tung, Ko Kang, and Wa states. There is another indigenous pine species called *Pinu merkysu*, which grows at a low altitude of five hundred feet. In fact, pine forests are quite common in Shan State, covering many square miles. Sometimes the pine occurs together with oak and chestnut trees. In areas higher than six thousand feet, indigenous pine forests gradually get thinner and are replaced by dark-foliaged evergreen hill forests which contain magnolia, lauriniae, and rhododendrons.

Mai Pao, or *Ingyin* (*Pentaeme suavis*)

Ingyin, called *mai pau* in Shan, is grown in regions of Northern Shan State, especially in Mong Yai and Mong Long. Ingyin is next to teak in importance because of its usefulness and durability. It reaches about eighty feet in height and five to six feet in girth. It is a tree that should be felled green rather than killing it by girdling first. The timber is widely used in Northern Shan State as building timber, and the Myanmar Railways Department during the British administration used it as railway ties. It was also used in the mine shafts in the Nam Tu mine, and in the oil wells in central Myanmar, and also as structures or buildings because of its immunity to the attack of white ants.[36]

Mai Hak, or *Thitsi* (*Melanarrhuca usitata*)

Thitsi, called *mai hak* in Shan, is a tree with a clear bole, common in the hill forests of Shan State up to thirty-five hundred feet. The average height of *thitsi* is fifty to sixty feet. It is a medium tree with a rounded crown.[37] The wood is dark red, heavy, dense, hard, and very durable. It is used in making house posts, which give very long service, in building bridges, and in making tool handles, anchor stocks, and plows. It is a black varnish tree. *Mai hak* is mostly found around Hsi Paw, on the northern slopes of Loi Leng, and in the Manhsaung area of Mong Yai. The gum or oleoresin extracted from it fetches a good price and is mostly used in making lacquerware. It has many other uses in furniture work.

Mai Yoam, or *Thitkado* (*Cedrela toona*)

Thitkado, or *mai yoam*, is another useful tree that grows in both Northern and Southern Shan States. The tree is usually eighty to one hundred feet in height and six to eight feet in girth. The wood is reddish, scented, and easily worked. It is resistant to the attack of white ants, and shrinks and swells in response to changes of atmospheric humidity. It is mostly used by Shan farmers to make sheaths for knives and swords.

Paper Mulberry (*Broussontia papyrifera*)

The paper mulberry, which the Shan call *mai has*, grows naturally in various parts of Shan State, especially around the areas of Hsi Paw, Mong Kung, and Keng Lom. The bark of the tree serves as raw material for the making of Shan paper, which is distributed widely throughout Myanmar.

Silk-cotton Tree (*Ceiba pentandra*)

The silk-cotton tree, or *mai niu* in Shan, is found everywhere in Shan State, the fruit being used for stuffing pillows, and in the old days for stuffing pads inserted under the pack saddle of bullocks, mules, and monkeys. It is a large tree reaching a height of one hundred thirty feet and having a girth of twelve feet. The wood is whitish, soft, and open-textured. It is not normally durable, but lasts well underwater. It is also subject to discoloration and is not immune to the attack of borers during open-air seasoning. Its timber is used for making canoes, troughs, cheap furniture, toys, small boxes, casks, coffins, matchboxes, and packing cases. It is also turned into wood pulp.

Bamboo (the genus *Bambusa, dendrocalamus*)

Bamboo grows everywhere, in a great variety, along the slopes of hills, in the valleys, and in the vicinity of villages, and is used extensively in the making of household articles and in construction. The Shan lifestyle being impossible without the bamboo, it has more uses than any other plant in Shan State. It is a source of food, weapons, baskets, clothes, implements, furniture, shelter, domestic utensils, bridges, water conduits, water wheels, dams, road surfacing, rafting material, paper, and weir, etc. Bamboo has also become a promising source of pulp on a commercial scale. It also furnishes materials for houses, which use it for walls, rafts, floors, roofs, and even as posts and beams. It is also used for fencing, mats, handles for tools, knives, and countless other purposes. Bamboo also has industrial uses, notably to buoy up nonfloating timbers for transport by water and to serve as dunnage, i.e. loose packing material that protects a ship's cargo from damage. Bamboo also serves as raw material for making paper pulp.

***Mai Sa-lam*, or *Pyinkado* (*Xylia dolabriformis*)**

Pyinkado, or *mai sa-lam*, is a hard, heavy, strong, and durable timber that is also resistant to the attacks of white ants. It is used for heavy construction work and also for railway ties. Under favorable conditions *pyinkado* can reach to a height of about 120 feet and a girth of 12 feet. The wood is reddish brown.

The felling of the *pyinkado* tree is done while it is still green. After seasoning it, it becomes very hard and destructive of tools. It is considered the world's best timber and is used for construction work and freshwater locks, piling, rubbing fenders, gangways, chutes, and other works subject to hard wear and rough usage or for purposes where great durability under exposed conditions is required. It is a favored wood for house posts and stands well underwater. It is also used for carts, yokes, agricultural implements, and so on.

***Mai Chi-tawk*, or *Padauk* (*Pterocarpus macrocarpus*)**

Padauk, or *mai chi-tawk*, is a moderate tree having a height of about sixty to eighty feet and a girth of eight feet. The wood is hard, stronger than teak or oak, very durable and steady, and the best all-round utility timber in Shan State as well as in Myanmar proper. The *mai chi-tawk* timber is red, with beautiful curled and mottled figures showing through the color. It is used for cart wheels, frames of boats, carriages, wheels, parquetry, flooring, general cabinetwork, and general furniture. It takes wax or French polish very well. The range of shrinkage and movement is quite small, and the wood may be recognized as definitely steady.

***Mai Hsa Hpong*, or *Pyinma* (*Lagerstraemia flos reginae*)**

Mai hsa hpong, or *pyinma* in Myanmar, is found throughout the forests in Shan State, especially along the stream banks and flat alluvial plains. The average height of the tree is seventy feet and, in favorable soil, the height can go up to one hundred feet. The wood is light-brown, hard, elastic, and strong. It is much used for building construction and for boats. It will float, if allowed to stand for two years after girdling. It has a certain immunity against white ants and durability underwater.

***Mai Htaeng*, or *In* (*Dipterocarpus tuberculatus*)**

Mai htaeng, or *in* in Myanmar, is a tree reaching a height of seventy to one hundred feet and a girth of five to six feet. It occurs all over Shan State in regions where the *ingyin* grows. The timber is reddish brown, hard, and easily worked. It is not immune to white ants but is durable under cover. It is available in large quantities and is useful for building cheap houses, carts, boats, and for many other purposes.

***Mai Nyu* (*Shorea obtusa*)**

Mai nyu, or *thitya* in Myanmar, is a large tree which grows in low-hill regions. It reaches one hundred feet in height and seven to eight feet in girth. The wood is very closely related to *ingyin* or *Pentaeme suavis*. It is hard and very durable and is mostly used for railway ties, bridges, general construction, buildings, carts, and rough furniture. It is immune to white ants.

Other Plants

From 2,500 feet to 4,000 feet, the hills and mountains of Shan State are covered with vegetation of a different character, and also large trees of different species like Dipterocarpus, Turpinia, Dalbergia, Caesalpinia, Bauhinia, Terminalia, Lagerstraenia, Strychnos, and Quercus. There are other species of shrubs and herbaceous plants too. Different varieties of ferns, mosses, and lichens are found in every forest in Shan State. Species of Ranunculus Clematis, Viola, Polygala, Hypericum, Primula and Swertia are plentiful in Shan State forests. Moreover, tropical genera like Lespedeza, Codonopsis, Ipomoea, and many other types of labiate grow all over the Shan hills.[38] There are also many wild plants such as crab-apple, wild pear, wild cherry, pink cassia, gul mohur or flamboyant, yellow laburnum, jacaranda, blossoming shrubs, creepers, and wildflowers of all sorts. Varieties of beautiful and lovely orchids are also seen hanging in big trees of deep forests in Shan State and these add to the beauty of Shan land.

Fauna

The forests of Shan State have been the habitat of many species of fauna for centuries. In the thick forests and deep valleys, in the bamboo groves of various varieties, in the streams and rivers with rapids and falls, in the swamps and ponds, lakes and reservoirs, tributaries and basins, grassy lands and rolling hills, caves and holes, cliffs and boulder rocks, mountain peaks and slopes of hills, birds and fowls, fish, insects, creatures, animals, and fauna of different species enjoy an environment of abundant fruits, food, fresh water, and air.

Brown-antlered deer, barking deer, panolia gede, pigs and hares are found in the localities where there is both water and vegetation, fruit, and food appropriate to them, especially near jungles of scrubby thorn, low tufts of grass, and bushes. During the rainy season, the deer cast off their horns and when the new ones come up as tender growth, they usually avoid associating with the does to escape from being bitten by them. They also avoid living in the dense forests so that their horns will not be caught by creepers. Being the fleetest of animals, they prefer living in the open country to be able to run better and faster when they encounter enemies.

The hare is a lovely creature and a very speedy one. It is not so easy to catch. At first it makes a casual or leisurely hop as if about to stop. But when it turns a corner, it surprisingly doubles its speed, leaving pursuers far behind. When the hare is captured, the hunter usually pulls off its tail for good luck. The hare usually lives under a low tuft or bush, making a smooth bed by beating the ground with its rump.

In the deep valleys and in the dense jungles with a certain degree of humidity, bison, wild bull, and antelope are found, sometimes accompanied by elephants, leopards, wild pig, and barking deer. These animals are considered very unfriendly to human beings, but they also avoid making the first attack on human beings unless they are forced to, or in unavoidable circumstances. When chased by the bison, a man should lie flat on the ground, because the beast, having a short and thick neck, cannot reach down to attack him. When a deer is chased by a wild dog, it will run across a stream with the idea of throwing the wild dog off the scent. But it will also turn and fight when pressed or forced into a corner.

The wild pig will be found rearing its children in nests built of grass. The tops of the nest are sloped like thatched roofs in order to keep out the rainwater.

Leopards, or *hso hpai* in Shan, when encountering men in the jungles, will not approach to harm them, but will play havoc for a while and then disappear. The leopard has the habit of scratching the ground to sharpen its claws when it feels it is about to meet its prey. It will crawl up trees at night to catch sleeping fowls. The bite of the leopard on its animal prey is always at the neck or throat. It has a very strong jaw and its grip is very firm, and there is no way that the victim can struggle, resist, or escape. The victim is always dragged to a secluded place where it is killed and devoured.[39]

Various species of reptiles also exist in Shan forests. There are many kinds of snakes, which Shan call *ngu*, like rat snake, viper, cobra, and hamadryad of several kinds. The rat snake is quite common, and occasionally eaten by the people. Its flesh tastes very much like that of fish. Vipers are very poisonous and dangerous to humans, but they are rarely found in Shan forests. These snakes are mostly found in dry and hot regions. The Russel's Viper is viviparous and people believe that when the young ones are mature, they eat their way out of their mother's body and cause her death. Hamadryads are also very dangerous to people and vengeful. If any one of them is killed, its mate will sooner or later come to exact revenge upon the aggressor. There are also other kinds of nonvenomous and fangless snakes in the Shan forests.

The boa constrictor is a handsome snake and grows to a large size. It feeds on animals up to the size of the barking deer, and does not attack human beings unless it is forced to. People believe that this snake hypnotizes its victim by displaying its navel. Sometimes, when the jungle is burned, the boa constrictor will take to the swamp pool and lie submerged to catch its prey when it comes to drink.

Lizards of different varieties are also found in the forests of Shan State. Some are poisonous and some are not. The local people have certain superstitions about some lizards. The *phut mwe*, called *len* by the Shan, is believed to bring bad luck and poverty to any house it may enter. But it is edible and its eggs are considered a delicacy.[40]

Different species of tortoise (*tao*) are also found in the valleys and streams, near the foothills and in the rice fields, in Shan State during the rainy season. Both tortoise and turtle are eaten, and their shells made into combs and other ornaments. Their eggs are obtained by following their tracks, and sometimes dogs are brought in to track them down by their scent.[41]

Among the game birds are the jungle fowl, partridge, two or three varieties of geese, snipe, golden plover, duck and teal, which usually arrive in summer from neighboring countries and leave in the rainy season. The hawk is quite a common jungle bird which can be found in various regions of Shan State. It also has the habit of migration. The pea-fowl, pheasant, kalig, imperial pigeon and green pigeon, and other jungle fowls abound in the Shan forests.

Predatory birds like the eagles are also found in woody areas. They usually come out only when darkness falls, to search for their food. Owls commonly found in Shan forests are mostly the forest owl, horned owl, and the screech owl. Birds like the nightjar, jay, pheasant, crow, crane, and many others as indicated in the second list below are also found in Shan State.

Animals

1. Bison
2. Elephant
3. Rhinoceros
4. Tiger
5. Leopard
6. Bear

7. Gaur
8. *Tsine* or *saing* or *Bos sondacious*
9. Sambar
10. Hog deer
11. Barking deer
12. Swamp deer
13. Goat
14. Hare
15. Monkey of several varieties
16. Gibbon white-browed, or *Hylobatis hoolock*
17. Hog
18. Porcupine
19. Jungle cat
20. Civet cat
21. Fox
22. Squirrel
23. Wild dog
24. Jackal
25. Scrow
26. Snake of several varieties
27. Teal
28. Viper
29. Hamadryad (King Cobra)
30. Cobra
31. Python
32. Harrier (hound)
33. Elk

Birds

1. Babblers
2. Bamboo bird
3. Barbets
4. Bee-eater
5. Bittern
6. Bulbuls
7. Copper-smith
8. Crane
9. Crow
10. Cuckoo
11. Dove
12. Egret
13. Hawk
14. Himalayan eagle
15. Honey sucker
16. Hornbill
17. Kestrel
18. Lark
19. King crow
20. Kingfisher
21. Lapwing
22. Laughing thrush
23. Magpie robin
24. Minivet
25. Munias
26. Nightjar
27. Osprey
28. Owl
29. Ox bird
30. Pheasant
31. Pied harrier
32. Peafowl
33. Roller
34. Sandpiper
35. Shama
36. Shrike
37. Sun bird
38. Thrush
39. Vulture
40. Wagtail
41. Warbler
42. Weaver bird
43. Woodcock
44. Woodpecker
45. Wood snipe
46. Cormorant
47. Duck
48. Gamecock
49. Geese
50. Grebe
51. Jungle fowl
52. Kite
53. Tern
54. Water fowl

Other fauna found in Shan State are wild bees, wasps, hornets, and several varieties of butterflies.

The Elephant

Elephants, *tsang* in Shan, are considered the most sagacious of all the jungle creatures. They are very cooperative and united in time of danger. When the sense of danger approaches, they will take a favorable position to protect themselves or their young ones. That is what we call protection by sentinel kin. Elephants are also found to enjoy comradeship in times of trouble. When an elephant is wounded and unable to keep up with the herd, its companions will help it.

The elephant is considered a member of the forest fauna of Shan State. It is the most useful animal for such heavy work as timber extraction. In the past the elephant played quite an important role in feudal warfare as a war machine. Nowadays they play an important role in the economy. In Shan State the economic exploitation of the forest would not have been possible without the elephants. This also applies to Myanmar.

The elephant found in Shan forests is different from the Indian elephant. The Shan elephant is powerfully built, but it is much smaller and much more compact than the Indian elephant. It also has much smaller ears than the Indian and the African elephant. Another difference is that only the male elephants bear tusks.

Of all the animals, the elephant is the only creature that has the power to handle heavy timber, especially on slopes, in difficult terrain, in rocky areas full of boulders, and in muddy sand and water.[42]

The pulling, pushing, and dragging of hundreds of thousands of logs in Shan forests are done by elephants. The elephant does the job where the machine stops. The machine needs petrol, diesel, or electricity, and a mechanic; the elephant needs only fodder and a mahout, and its power never fails.

Wild elephants are captured by two methods—the *mela shikar* and the Kasen stockade. The first method is used by the Hkamti Shan who capture elephants in the Myitkyina area, the Hukaung valley, and the Hkamti Long forests in the extreme north of Myanmar. In this method, the elephanteer needs much more courage and skill. He must mount a tame elephant and ride up alongside a selected animal in the wild herd. Then he must, by all means, try to slip heavy rope nooses around the leg and neck of the wild elephant and secure it to a tree.

The other and more common method, the Kasen stockade, is used throughout the country. In this, a large funnel-shaped stockade is built with heavy timber and disguised with foliage. Then the wild herd is gradually driven into a narrow passage, about the width of an elephant, and the gate at the end of the passage is dropped and the animal is trapped and becomes a prisoner. Then the elephant is tied up with heavy ropes and removed to a separate stall through openings made in the walls. It is tied up and left to starve for some time, and then watered and fed by hand until complete acquaintance is secured between the elephant and the attendants. Within a few weeks the captive becomes quite amenable, but the shock of the capture remains, and it takes at least two years of humane and gentle treatment before it can be fully fitted for heavy work.

Tame female elephants are allowed to consort with wild tuskers and they can breed freely. The period of gestation is about twenty months. It is the usual case for one baby calf to be born at a time. The young newborn calf is about two to three feet high at the shoulder and is covered with long coarse hair. It looks very attractive and as it grows, it becomes very playful and mischievous. One peculiar fact about the elephant is that the mother of a young calf is almost invariably assisted in her maternal duties by self-appointed "aunties" or nurses from the herds.[43] The she-elephant takes her duties very seriously and, in the event of danger and outside interference, she will stand to defend the calf, just as the mother does. The young elephant will follow its mother for eight or ten years, and gradually it is accustomed to being handled and ridden. It is also trained to carry a miniature elephant basket, until it comes up to the age of eight or nine, when it will be given a certain weight of baggage to carry.

The lifespan of the elephant is approximately the same as that of man. The elephant is mature at age twenty, but its best working age is from twenty-five to forty-five, and it can work up to the age of seventy or more. Some elephants have lived up to one hundred years.

Elephants are usually good-tempered beasts. But sometimes, they can be temperamental and dangerous to human beings. Therefore they need to be carefully and firmly

FIGURE 2.9. Plowing with elephant. (Photo by Sao Nwe Pe Taung of Putao, 1998)

handled. Another peculiar characteristic of the male elephant is that, on reaching maturity, it becomes subject to periodical paroxysms of excitement. Its temporal gland becomes enlarged, and from the ducts which lie on each side of the head below the temples an oily discharge oozes out. This stage of the condition is known as mush and occurs quite frequently. During this period some elephants become very unruly, violent, and destructive. Their sexual desire increases enormously. If they are not securely fettered and kept under close supervision, they will wander about and attack and crush everything in sight.

Regarding the height of the elephant, a full-grown male elephant's height is about ten feet at the shoulder, and for the female it is about eight feet. The longest elephant tusk ever recorded is about eight feet, nine inches long and its girth is about one foot six and three quarters of an inch.

The feeding of elephants does not pose too much of a problem. In their wild state, elephants spend most of their time feeding on bamboo leaves, wild grass, climbers, leaves of trees, fruits, and even barks of trees. Elephants eat only green fodder. They generally spend the day in dense forests and will sometimes come out of the jungles to raid crops in the fields. They sleep very little at night but will doze during the day and sometimes lie down to sleep. If they are well fed and well treated, they will flap their ears and make low rumbling noises. But when they are angry, they will scream and trumpet loudly.

Although elephants have a heavy body, they can climb mountains quite easily, and they are also good swimmers. Crossing a stream in deep water poses no problem for the elephant. They may not have good eyesight but they have an acute sense of smell and hearing. Their skin may be tough and thick, but they are extremely sensitive, and that is why they keep on splashing water over their bodies to wash off insect pests and dust. They like to have a good supply of water for themselves and sometimes they are found digging down in stream beds to get it. Being a heavy animal, the elephant cannot trot or gallop or run or jump like a horse, but it can move very fast if it wants to. That is the wonder of the elephant.

The elephants in the Shan State are mostly and widely used to extract timber in the forests. After heavy work the elephants are let loose into the jungles to forage for food. But their forefeet are shackled with iron fetters to which is tied a long tethering chain so that they cannot wander too far away. They will also have, hanging around their necks, a wooden clapper, or *hok* in Shan, so that the mahout can know their location while they go grazing in the jungle. Male elephants are given much heavier work than female elephants. Under some conditions a male elephant will move two hundred tons of teak logs from stump to floating stream or river, for a season.

On the whole, the elephant is a good companion, loyal servant, faithful friend, intelligent, cooperative, helpful, and never tires of serving human beings. It is in fact a treasure. Let us try our best to preserve our environment, so that our elephants may survive with us in Shan forests.

Forest Protection

Nowadays, if we observe the forests of Shan State closely, we will discover that they are faced with acute threats of depletion, degradation, deforestation, and destruction. The Shan forests are exposed to natural dangers of one kind or another such as forest fires, storms, floods, erosion, volcanic eruptions, earthquakes, and changes in the weather, which sometimes damage the forests. But the greatest damage that has been inflicted on the forest in the Shan State has come from man himself. Man has become the greatest enemy of the Shan forests. Man sometimes does not comprehend the simple fact that if an agricultural crop is destroyed, it will be a loss for only one year, but if a forest is destroyed it can mean a loss of a hundred years. Man also fails to realize another simple fact: that it will take nearly a hundred years for a young or new forest to develop into maturity. If he were aware of these facts he would not have committed himself to the business of reckless exploitation, uncontrolled extraction, and excessive and illicit cutting of his valuable and precious trees. If he were more conscious of the environment, he would not so carelessly throw away his lighted cigarette butt into the bush, to cause wild forest fires that damage not only the forest but human beings as well.

Of course, there are laws aimed at preventing man from doing damage to the forests. But they do not seem to be very effective thus far. We see everywhere ongoing illicit activities that cause deforestation. Greater efforts have been made to put a stop to the destruction, but the results remain far from satisfactory.

For the future survival of the forests and their flora and fauna, which help to sustain the economy of Shan State, a much more effective set of laws and a program of forest production must be introduced and applied, as suggested below:

1. A close check and supervision should be maintained over the extraction carried out in the forests by private agencies.
2. Stern action should be taken against those who commit forest theft and fraud.
3. Laws on the extension of grazing grounds and farmlands should be imposed.
4. Measures should be taken to prevent the spread of forest fires.
5. Programs for preventing erosion should be adopted and soil conservation measures introduced.
6. Preventive measures should be taken to protect trees from attacks by pests, diseases, and fungi.
7. Plans to remove deadly creepers that might damage valuable trees should be drawn up and carried out.
8. Public education on the interdependence between human beings and the environment should be introduced in the school syllabus.
9. Multireforestation programs should be introduced, from village to national levels.

LIVESTOCK FARMING

Livestock farming is carried on quite extensively in Shan State. Cattle are bred everywhere not for their beef or milk, but for domestic use and for pack-work. Bullocks are sold to the traders to be used as pack animals to transport goods and commodities to parts of Shan State and even down to Mandalay in Myanmar. In the feudal days pack animals were used as the most common means of transportation. The Shan people are quite religious and abstain from slaughtering cattle for beef. They do not milk cows and they allow calves to suckle at will. Bulls roam freely with the herds. In Myanmar, cattle are used to plow the fields, but the Shan farmers rarely use them for plowing. Instead, they use buffaloes very widely. The buffalo is bred everywhere in Shan State and is used in plowing and other agricultural work. The buffalo is also used for pressing sugar cane, groundnut, and sesame, to extract edible oil. It is sometimes used also as a transport animal in place of the bullock. Since Shan became Buddhists, they have given up killing buffaloes as a sacrifice. But the Wa and Kachin peoples still use buffaloes as sacrificial animals at their spirit-worship ceremonies.

Ponies are also bred in Shan State for domestic use as pack animals. The ass, the donkey, and the mule are also bred in Shan State, but on a very small scale. Mong Kung, Kehsi Mansam, Mong Nawng, and Yawng Hwe in Southern Shan State and Kokang, Ta Mong Nge, Muse, Nam Hkam, and Hsen Wi are known for breeding these animals. Sheep and goats are also bred for meat but not very extensively.

Shan State has very wide and good grazing grounds, providing favorable opportunities for large-scale cattle farming. We hope that such an enterprise will come into being one day, for the benefit of the Shan farmers.

MINERAL RESOURCES

Shan State is very rich in mineral resources. A lot of them are lying idle underground and so far no attempt has been made to tap them for the benefit of the people living in Shan State. Coal deposits have been found along the valley of the Nam Yao in Lashio, bordering the Hsen Wi area. Low-quality coal has been found widely scattered around the areas of Mong Yaw and the valleys of Nam Ma, Nam Pawng in Mong Yai and Hsi Paw states. Lignitic coal has also been discovered near Nam Pat in Mong Yai. A large quantity of tourmaline deposit is also located near the Nam Pai River in Mong Long of Hsi Paw State. Southern Shan State is also known for its deposits of coal, which have not yet been developed. These lie in the areas of Lai Hka and Myelat, though their qualities appear to be inferior.

Gold has been found in many places in Shan State, but not in quality and quantities as good or great as other metals. Most of the gold is found in the form of dust and nuggets. Larger gold pieces have also been discovered, but not in great quantities. Gold is mostly washed from the sand of streams neighboring the deposits, and washing for gold is widely and regularly carried on at the many points along the Than Lwin and the Shweli rivers, and many streams in Mong Wa. The valley of the Nam Ma, a small tributary of the Than Lwin River, is well known for its heavy gold deposits. Once there was a project to obtain gold by dredging and hydraulic methods, but it did not materialize. Gold washing has become very popular as a local business for people who cannot get employment anywhere. After harvest, villagers and farmers go to the forests and valleys to look for deposits of gold dust. Gold collectors and purchasers follow the caravan of gold washers with a bagful of money to buy the gold dust that has been obtained, before it is smelted into gold bars at their homes or at some secret location. Another known deposit is located near Hopai in Lantau Circle in Mong Yai State. A few veins of gold are also believed to exist along the valleys of the Nam Yang Long and the Nam Hka near the area of Wan Pet Ken.

Wolfram is mined on the Mong Pai-Pyinmana border area, lead and silver in the Nam Tu. The Bawdwin mines in Tawng Peng State produce various metals. In 1936 the Bawdwin lead mines produced seventy-three thousand long tons of lead and forty-five thousand long tons of zinc as well as substantial quantities of antimony, silver, copper, and gold. The Bawdwin mine was probably the world's leading lead and silver mine owing to the high silver content of the ore.[44]

Silver and lead are found in Tawng Peng State and Mong Yai State near the areas called Kong Hka and Loi Leng. Mong Wa is also known for its deposits of silver, especially around the area of Mong Hka. Lead is another metal mostly found in Wa State. Large deposits of lead are located in the areas east of Mong Long, Loi Long, and San Tong. In Southern Shan State silver, lead, and plumbago are mined on a small scale in Myelat.

Iron occurs in some quantity in Lai Hka and in Sam Ka. Copper has also been discovered in the Myelat area, but not in large quantities. In Northern Shan State iron is extracted at Hsop Tung in Hsi Paw State near the Mong Tung area. Silver mining, on a large scale, has been in progress for years at the Bawdwingyi mine, situated in the valley, ten miles southeast of the village of Kat Lwi and about six miles north of Pang Yang in Tawng Peng State. Other metals like lead and copper are also extracted from small mines located in this area, but only in small quantities. The hills around this area were honeycombed by the Chinese miners in the old days. They were the first to mine manually without modern equipment. Many of them died of malaria and other diseases while mining in this area. Human skeletons in chains have been discovered together with shafts and other local mine equipment, as well as long rows of beehive-shaped smelting ovens and stone bridges built across the streams in the valleys.

Salt was discovered in Mawko near Baw Gyo, six miles west of Hsi Paw. It has been mined there since 1506, according to local records of the area. But salt mining carried on in this area is very old-fashioned. Villagers use only locally made ovens to boil salt water and dry the salt the local way, using bamboo mats of all kinds. The salt is then packed in leaves of the teak trees, in packets tied with thin bamboo strips. The salt produced here has a somewhat bitter taste, so the demand for it is not so good. It is sold to local people when, as sometimes happens, salt from Mandalay is unavailable. Modern technology should be introduced to further develop the salt mine and scientific analysis made to reduce the bitter taste.

Another mineral enterprise undertaken by the Shan people is the extraction of saltpeter from bat guano. Bat guano is collected from the limestone caverns located throughout Shan State. The Wa people are mostly engaged in extracting saltpeter from the guano, and during the cold season they bring their saltpeter down to the Tang Yan bazaar to sell or exchange it for other commodities. In Southern Shan State, saltpeter is collected in Mong Pan and in the Nam Tok and Nam Teng areas.

A few spinels of inferior quality have been discovered in Mawk Mai State and elsewhere.

Pottery clay is another mineral product of Shan State, produced mostly in Mong Kung, Yawng Hwe, and Sam Ka states.

Laterite occurs everywhere, and limestone has been widely used in constructing houses and government buildings. Lime-burning is an occupation that is widespread in Shan State.

Other minerals like rubies, sapphires, and spinels are found in the gravel beds in Mong Kut, which formerly belonged to Shan State, Mong Mit, and the Mong Long part of Hsi Paw State. During the British regime, the Myanmar Ruby Mines Company Limited operated on a large scale at Mong Kut and elsewhere under license, using modern machinery. Nowadays the government is the sole owner of all the ruby mines, and private enterprises can do business only for a specified period of time, and only under special permission. New discoveries of ruby-bearing minerals have been made in Mong Hsu in Central Shan State. Jade and amber are found mostly in Hpa Kang and Mong Kwang. These areas were once under the suzerainty of Shan *saohpa*.

Highly technical knowledge and heavy capital investment are essential to develop the mining industry in all its aspects in the Shan State.

ARTS AND INDUSTRIES

Cotton

Cotton is a product of Shan State. It is grown everywhere and can easily be obtained from the Shan bazaars. Coarse, strong cotton cloth, called *man* or *wan* by the Shan, is produced in great quantity, especially around Nam Lan in Hsi Paw State. There are two kinds of *man*, the white and the brown. The brown *man* is the better quality and known for its durability because it is made from red-flowered cotton.

Home-spun cotton cloth is produced throughout Shan State. Almost every Shan house has a loom, and everyday clothes of the Shan people are produced mostly at home. The implements used for weaving cotton into cloth, such as the loom, the spinning wheel, and other tools, as well as the methods of cleaning, dressing, spinning, and weaving, are identical with those of Myanmar. First a cotton cloth is woven in pieces about a yard in width, and cut up, to make clothing like shirts, trousers, skirts, coats, and so on. Jackets or tops for women are woven separately, and other pieces of cloth are added to the main body of the garment either at the bottom or at the top. To enhance the beauty of the jackets, the cloth is sometimes woven of mixed cotton and silk yarn. Cotton blankets, bags, towels, turbans, shoulder wraps, and many other articles designed gracefully and artistically are produced, but are rather expensive.

In North Hsen Wi and Mong Yai curious sleeping webs of cloth with zigzag diamond patterns in black, red, green, and yellow are beautifully woven. To make the piece more attractive, weavers sometimes use silk as the weft. Robes for the monks are also specially woven at home. Farmers and the common people in Shan State love to wear homespun clothes and dresses. They live a simple life and dress in a simple way. Glittering and expensive dresses are used only on auspicious occasions and at religious festivals held at the pagodas and monasteries. The Shan dye their own clothes, using different barks of trees, stick-lac, and indigo to get different colors. For a yellow dye, they use the bark of the jackfruit tree and turmeric roots, and for a red dye, sapan wood and stick-lac.

Silk

The rearing of silkworms is done only on a small scale in Shan State, the silk needed for home industries being imported from Laos, China, and Myanmar. Skirts, trousers, turbans, coats, jackets, shoulder wraps, and any other items made of pure silk are very expensive. They are meant for the elite class, chiefs of states, and rich men. Occasionally gold and silver threads are sewn into the silk, the cloth acquiring more glitter according to the amount used. Nong Ang Le in Yawng Hwe has become a well-known center for the silk cottage industry. Sarongs, or *hpatong* and *hsin* in Shan, are produced and sold to the people of Myanmar. Silk yarn is dyed different colors before being woven into cloth.

Bamboo Baskets

Bamboo is widely used in Shan State. The furniture used in Shan homes is mostly made of bamboo. Bamboo is also used for commercial purposes. Transportation is very poor in the Shan State and the Shan mostly use bullocks as a means of transportation. Long caravans of bullocks, carrying goods and commodities to different parts of the Shan State, can be seen during the dry season. Mules, donkeys, and elephants are also used as pack animals. Each pack animal carries two bamboo baskets, one hanging on either side of its back. All sorts of goods are put in the two baskets, especially rice and tea. These pack animals transported tea to Mandalay, the capital city of Myanmar in those days, and on their return journey they carried other commodities needed by the Shan people. These baskets are manufactured where bamboo can be obtained, and Hsi Paw is known for producing the best quality of baskets for pack animals.

Another bamboo product of the Shan State is the *pem*, or small basket used by Shan farmers. The *pem* has a string attached, tied around the farmer's waist so that he has the basket behind his back to hold things when he goes to work on the farm or in the field. His lunchbox, betel box, pipe, tobacco, cheroot, knife, and sickle will be put in this small basket for use at the work site. These *pem* are either made at home or bought from the bazaar.[45]

Other baskets of different designs and sizes and shapes are produced in Shan State depending on the availability of good bamboo.

Bamboo Hats, or *Kup*

To protect themselves from the rain or the heat of the sun, Shan wear bamboo hats. Different parts of Shan State produce different kinds of bamboo hats. Farmers wear large bamboo hats when they go to the fields; the children, small bamboo hats when they go to school. Nam Hkam is known for the large-sized bamboo hats for the farmers, but Mong Nawng produces the finest bamboo hats for women. Once, it was the fashion for Shan damsels to wear beautiful bamboo hats from Mong Nawng, or *kup Mong Nawng*. The best bamboo for making such hats grows in the Mong Nawng area.

FIGURE 2.10. Various Shan hats, or *kup*. (Photo by Sai Aung Tun, 2002)

FIGURE 2.11. A Shan couple wearing *kup*. (Photo by Sai Aung Tun, 2002)

In many places in the Shan State a variety of hats are made of the leaf sheaths of the giant bamboo, which the Shan call *kup mai pok*. The leaf sheaths fall off from the giant bamboo when they are fully grown. They are collected and flattened out under heavy stones. Then these leaf sheaths are cut into the lengths and sizes required and sewn together by hand to become a hat. Sometimes gold and silver threads are inserted in the sewing to make the hat more beautiful and decorative. When old Shan men wear their hats they do not remove their turbans, and to keep the hats from being blown away by the wind, they attach a string to each side of the hat and tie the string under the chin. Young men who want to look smart use silver chains to fasten their hats.[46]

Tway, or Rain capes

In the old days, Shan farmers used the *tway* to protect themselves from the rain and the wind. During the rainy season when the farmers go to the fields, they have to bend the whole day transplanting the paddy. Sometimes the wind is very strong and the rain is heavy so that they are soaked to the skin. They do not have raincoats to protect themselves, the only material they have hung on their backs is a rain cape. The *tway* is locally made with the leaves of the screw pines, of which one can find plenty in the Shan forests. These leaves are gathered and spread out to dry in the sun. There are little points, like horns, on either side of the leaf, which have to be removed. The leaves are then cut according to the lengths required. Then they are sewn together to become a *tway*, or waterproof coat or cover. The *tway* has many uses. Mostly it is hung on a man's back to protect him from the rain. *Tway* are also used by traders to cover baskets to protect their goods from dust and rain. Sometimes the *tway* is also used as a mattress by the farmers when they take a nap in their little field huts. The *kup* and *tway* are the twins that the Shan farmers use to protect themselves from the dust, rain, sun, and wind.

Bamboo Mats, or *Hsat*

Bamboo mats of different sizes and shapes are produced everywhere in Shan State. They have a variety of uses. The rough bamboo mats are bigger and used for drying paddy in the field and for drying tea leaves. The smooth ones are used at home as a floor covering. The finest bamboo mats are woven in Keng Tung and used as mattresses during the summer and when one goes to observe the Sabbath at the monastery during Lent. They are usually kept at home for special occasions and used when elderly or religious people come for a visit.

Grass mats are also woven, mostly in Tang Yan and Nam Hkam. Mats are called *hsat* in Shan. The ordinary mats are called *hsatpyu* and woven with the skin or outer part of the bamboo. Another kind is called *hsatnu* or *hsatchaw* and is made from the inner part of the bamboo. A variety of *hsat* and baskets of various designs are brought to the bazaar for sale on market days.

Bamboo Lunchbox, or *Ep Khao*

The lunchbox, or *ep khao* in Shan, is widely used in the Shan State, especially by the farmers. When a farmer goes to his farm, to the fields, or into the forest, he always carries his lunchbox, which is made of bamboo. Glutinous rice is always put in the box, with soya bean cake or *hto nao* for lunch. The lunchbox is either made at home or bought from the bazaar. Lunchboxes are largely produced in Mong Nawng, Mong Hsu, Lai Hka, Kehsi Mansam, and Mong Kung, in Central Shan State. These bamboo boxes are also used in many other ways. They are made in a variety of designs, but only from the finest bamboo.

Chopsticks

Chopsticks are used by the Chinese as an eating utensil. While the Europeans use the knife and fork, the Chinese use chopsticks and the Indians and many Southeast Asians use their fingers. Nowadays the use of chopsticks has become popular in Shan State, and the people of Muse-Nam Hkam use chopsticks widely. Even children are quite skillful in the use of chopsticks. The best way to eat noodles is by using chopsticks. In many restaurants in Southeast Asia today, chopsticks are placed together with forks and spoons on the table, and many European tourists have learned to use chopsticks. These chopsticks made from bamboo are produced in Shan State. There are also chopsticks made of plastic nowadays, but bamboo chopsticks are still in great demand, and they are much better for picking up food. Bamboo chopsticks are not slippery, so one can pick up pieces of food or meat firmly and easily.

Shoe-making, or *Sok Tin*

Shan shoes are mostly made of buffalo or cow hide. Occasionally deer skin and tiger skin are used to make shoes, but they are very expensive and not easily available. When making shoes, iron hobnails are driven into the soles to ensure their durability. In the Muse–Nam Hkam area, the Tai Nua people use cotton cloth to make their shoes. Cotton shoes are convenient and light, but they can be easily soaked when worn during the rainy season, and their durability then becomes limited. A variety of sandals are also produced in the Muse–Nam Hkam area and some of them are made from hay stalks and dried grass. In many places wooden clogs are also produced and are widely used by Shan women during the rainy season.

Pottery

All sorts of pottery are produced in Shan State in the form of pots, bowls, jars, flower vases, water bottles, teapots, ornaments for the pagoda, and even toys for the children. These are mostly glazed a greenish shade, or a red ocher or a dull black. Burned paddy husk is mixed with clay to get the black pottery. Mong Kung produces the best pottery in Shan State. Other towns also produce pottery of their own designs for the needs of the local people. Clay water-bottles and *chatties*, or earthenware pots, are also manufactured in Tapong and Nambon; and other villages in Mong Yai, Mong Pan, and Mong Tung in Hsi Paw; and in Nam Hkam and Kokang.

FIGURE 2.12. Pottery in Nam Hkam, Northern Shan State. (Photo by Sai Aung Tun, 2002)

Ironwork

Iron is produced in Shan State and the method used is very primitive. Only local tools are used to dig out the metal. A well-known place for iron extraction in the old days was located in Loi Namtin Hills, west of the Pang Long and Man Pong circles in Lai Hka State. There are a few shafts on the side of the hill where iron ore is extracted. A furnace is established on a nearby site and smelting is done, using charcoal made from pinewood. The furnace is made of earth with two openings in the heat. The extracted ore is pounded until it becomes a fine gravel and this is put into the furnace, a handful at a time through the upper opening. The process produces crude metal, which is taken to the bazaar for sale. Smiths buy the metal from other towns, and make it into plowshares. Hpaung Hseng circle in Mong Nai is famous for manufacturing plows for the farmers. Ironwork of all sorts produced by smiths of nearby circles or villages is carried to Pang Long, where there is a big market and demand for such material.

The smelting as well as the making of iron implements involves much hard work and requires at least five or six people to do the job. Iron implements produced are mattocks, axes, tripods, spades, swords, knives, scissors, plowshares, choppers, and other agricultural implements. In the Northern Shan State, Nam Hkam is well known for its production of such local hardware. Mong Hsa smiths are also famous for producing a variety of agricultural hardware. They set up their forges everywhere in town to produce such implements.

There are also skilled ironsmiths in the Nong Ang Le area of Yawng Hwe, who turn out many iron implements needed by the Shan of the south. Around the Phaung Daw Oo pagoda, shops sell these implements produced by the smiths of Ang Le–Yawng Hwe.

Lacquerwork

Shan State is known for its fine lacquerware. The chief center for this industry is Lai Hka. It was believed that the craft of making lacquerware was brought to Lai Hka by immigrants from the Yuan country of Lanna and Laos. In those days there seemed to have been a trade relationship between the Lai Hka people and the Yuan people. The craft was also spread to other parts of Shan State. Small lacquer industries are located in Yawng Hwe at Ywa-ma and Tha-lei at the heart of Ang Le Lake, not far from the famous Hpaung Daw Oo pagoda. During the British occupation the industry also developed in Mong Nai, Mong Mit, and other areas. But owing to isolation and difficulties in communication and transportation and lack of support, lacquer industries in these areas no longer exist. One good thing is that because of the relative remoteness of Shan State from chief commercial centers, many traditional Shan lacquerware shapes and designs can still be found today. The popular lacquer products of the Shan State are mostly betel box *kun-it*, the *hsun-ok*, the *kalat*, and the *daung-lan*. Another well-known product was *pwe-daw-ok*, a huge royal food container made especially for the Shan chiefs. The Shan also practice *yun* work. The Shan *yun* works are much better than those of Bagan, because floral and geomantic motives prevail in Shan *yun* work, usually in red and yellow on a black background, or yellow and black on a red background. In many cases the designs and shapes are executed in a carefree and abstract manner.

The popular product of the Ywa-ma and Tha-lei area is a small eight-inch-high *kalat* made from woven bamboo. Mostly the *kalat* are left undecorated to serve as stands for objects offered to the pagoda. Ywa-ma and Tha-lei also produce *hsun-ok* for the annual Hpaung Daw Oo festival held each year in late September or early October at Ang Le Lake.

Keng Tung is also noted for producing an unusual type of partially gilded lacquer basket, called *kok-kau tak* in the Shan language. It resembles a bowl on four short legs and is used as a container for rice flour or paddy popcorn at religious festivals, and for meritorious services. The industry at Keng Tung died out for a number of years but has recently been revived. At present, a well-known craftsman for this profession is U Mu Lainda and his family. All his sons and daughters are trained in this craft and one of his sons has got a scholarship to attend the government-sponsored institute at Bagan. U Mu Lainda was once invited to Japan to a seminar on the lacquerware industry. He should be further encouraged and supported to maintain this traditional craft in Keng Tung for future generations.

Well-known Shan lacquerware can be found in:

1. Denison University: *pyi-daung* (1933).
2. Victoria and Albert Museum: betel boxes and small bowls, *bi-it* (1894).
3. Museum of Mankind (London): Shan *bi-it*.
4. University Museum of Archaeology and Anthropology, Cambridge: a wooden lathe, betel box.

FIGURE 2.13. *Bi-it* cosmetic box, formerly in the possession of the *saohpa* and his consort, the Mahadevi of Laihka. H: 12", late nineteenth century, Taunggyi Museum.

FIGURE 2.14. Close-up of a prevalent floral motif on Shan *hsun-ok*.

FIGURE 2.15. A decorative gold-leaf panel which was possibly part of a manuscript chest from Ang Le in the Shan States. Late eighteenth to early nineteenth century. 20" x 17". (Figs. 2.13, 2.14, 2.15 from Sylvia Fraser-Lu, *Burmese Lacquerware* (Bangkok: Orchid Press, 2000) 162, 164, 82. Reproduced by permission of Orchid Press.

FIGURE 2.16. A gilded *hsun-ok* with relief-molded decoration. H: 24", early twentieth century, Taunggyi Museum.

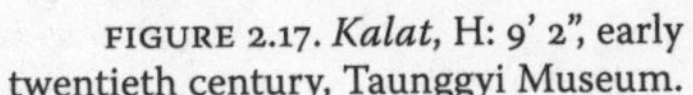

FIGURE 2.17. *Kalat*, H: 9' 2", early twentieth century, Taunggyi Museum.

FIGURE 2.18. Detail of a *bi-it* that once belonged to the wife of the former *saohpa* of Lai Hka, Taunggyi Museum

FIGURE 2.19. *Ko-kau-te* (rice container) from Keng Tung illustrating excellent gilded *thayo* work. H: 4", early twentieth century. *Left:* Seal indicating it was made in Keng Tung. (Collection Leslie/Kuloy, Photo by John Everingham)

FIGURE 2.20. Shan lacquerware in Shan State Museum, Taunggyi. (Photo by Sai Aung Tun, 2004)

5. Pitt River Museum, Oxford: Shan bowl. (1888)
6. Taunggyi Museum, Shan State, Myanmar: excellent examples of many types of Shan lacquerware—a trio of *kalat*, fine *hsun-ok kalat* with a twelve-inch-high *bi-it*, other *yun* works.[47]

A variety of lacquerware like betel boxes, *bi-it*, cups, trays, cigarette and cigar or cheroot boxes, flowerpots, water bottles, and bowls are produced and sold to different parts of Shan State, especially during the pagoda festival, and also to other parts of Myanmar.

Silverwork

Silverwork is produced mostly in Pang Long, which is well known for its good workmanship. Silversmiths melt the old silver rupee coins, bars of silver, and other metals to produce a variety of silverware which includes betel boxes, cigar boxes, cheroot boxes, water cups, hairpins, rings, jewelry, goblets, bowls, trays, daggers, and swords of many designs. The daggers and swords sometimes have hilts as well as sheaths of silver and even gold. In the old days the bowls of tobacco pipes were made of silver and sometimes the mouthpieces. Bracelets for the women in the old days were made of copper and decorated with knobs and balls of silver, but nowadays the knowledge of silverwork is dying out. Some of the raw materials for the silversmiths were obtained from local mines in Nam Tu–Pang Hai in Northern Shan State and Baw (Maw) Saing area in Southern Shan State.

Brasswork

Brasswork is also produced in certain parts of Shan State. Large monastery bells, bullock bells, elephant bells, Buddha images, tattooing implements, brass buckles for belts, and betel-nut pounders are manufactured or cast by the local smiths for local use.

Shan Paper, or *Se-Hsa*

Shan paper is generally popular for its durability and its variety of uses. It is used for pagoda decoration, for making umbrellas, for wrapping articles, goods, and other commodities, for writing purposes, for making *parabeik*, or Shan folded books, to write Buddhist scripts, for copying stone inscriptions and many other uses. The paper is produced in considerable quantities throughout the Shan State, especially in the area where the raw materials, the *hsa* trees, are available. But high-quality Shan paper is produced largely in Mong Kung, Lai Hka, Keng Tawng, and Keng Rom in Central and Southern Shan State. The paper is manufactured from the bark of the *hsa* tree, which grows wild everywhere in the Shan forests. However, nowadays the manufacturers of Shan paper face the problem of an acute shortage of *hsa* bark due to the reckless overcutting of the *hsa* trees. It is high time for preventive measures to be taken seriously to conserve these trees for the future, and for steps to be taken to systematically culture the *hsa* species for further propagation and cultivation. In fact a systematic replanting of *hsa* trees with the help of agri-technology should be started right now to enable the local paper-making industry to survive in the future and to benefit local paper producers.

FIGURE 2.21. *Parabeik*, or Shan folded books. (Photo by Sai Aung Tun, 2003)

Pickled Tea and Dried Tea Industry

The pickling of tea leaves is an important industry of the Palaung and Shan people, mostly in Tawng Peng, Hsi Paw, Mong Hko, Ko Kang, and Pang Long (Southern Shan State). Tea leaves plucked from the plantation are brought home in the evening and steamed over a cauldron of boiling water. The steamed leaves are then spread on a mat and rolled by hand for some time, and then they are thrown into pits and compressed by means of heavy weights. After a few days the leaves ferment and become pickled tea. To make dried tea, the steamed leaves are rolled by hand and then spread on mats to dry in the sun. After a few days, water is sprinkled on the leaves, which are dried again for some time. Then the dry leaves are sifted through a big bamboo sieve. Only such leaves that pass through the sieve are selected as dried tea. The pickled tea is put into bamboo baskets and the dried tea leaves are put into gunny sacks and transported down to Mandalay, or to other parts of the Shan State by caravans of bullocks, mules, and donkeys for sale. Both pickled tea and dried tea leaves are used extensively in the whole of Myanmar. Eating pickled tea with garlic, green chilies, fried peas, beans, dried prawns, and a dash of lime and oil has become very popular among the Myanmar people. Drinking of plain tea made with the dried tea leaves is also very popular, and a cup of plain tea is offered to guests and everyone who drops in for a visit. Every house, either in Shan State or in Myanmar, keeps a good tea set, complete with pot and cups and a lacquer plate or bowl for pickled tea and the other delicacies to go with plain tea, in accordance with Shan custom.

Boat Making

Boat making is another local industry practiced by Shan, who live along the banks of the rivers Nam Khone (Than Lwin), Nam Tu, Nam Ma, Nam Yao, Nam Pawn, Nam Zawgyi, Nam Paung Laung, Nam Teng, Nam Tam Hpak, and so on. These rivers flow through uneven terrain of hills, mountains, deep valleys, and gorges, full of rapids and falls in their long course toward the sea, or into the large rivers like the Ayeyarwady (Irrawaddy) and the Mekong. The Ayeyarwady and the Mekong are bigger and wider than those in Shan State. The flow of water in these big rivers is more gentle and stable and no obstacles are encountered in their course down to the sea. Motorboats and steamers can travel far and wide on those rivers and they have become quite useful for commercial and other purposes. The Shan rivers are not navigable, because of the natural characteristics which pose threats to travel by motorboats and steamers. The local people living along the rivers have not much choice but to use little narrow boats or canoes as their means of communication and transportation. Small boats and canoes are widely manufactured for use on these rivers. The local people use local tools and local methods to make their own boats or canoes. First they have to go into the forests to pick an appropriate tree for use in making their boat or canoe. After careful selection, they fell the selected tree and drag it down to the riverside, where it is hollowed out till only an outer skin of about one or two inches is left. Then the belly of the boat is coated with tar or black varnish extracted from *mai hak* (*Melanorrhoea usitata*). The boat is kept upside down to dry in the sun for a few days. After that it is placed in the water to test its buoyancy. If everything goes well the boat is used as a means of transportation. Generally such a boat or canoe is manned by two men, one at the bow and one at the stern. Both men use long paddles to push the boat up against the current.

Boats used in Ang Le Lake are much bigger and wider, and they have outboard motors attached and can travel much faster and carry more passengers and more goods, and other commodities. With such boats, the people of Ang Le travel much more easily from village to village around the lake, and can transport their farm and water products much more quickly to Yawng Hwe and thence overland to Taunggyi and to various parts of Shan State and Myanmar.

Drum or *Kong* Making

A drum is called *kong* in Shan. The Shan *kong* is made of a cylindrical hollow wood covered at one end with a tightly stretched membrane or fine skin or parchment. The *kong* is considered the main and most important traditional musical instrument of the Shan people.

Generally there are two types of the Shan *kong*. The first is a short type called *kong kon pot* in Shan, and the other one is a long and heavy type called *kong kon yao* in Shan. Other instruments which go with the *kong* are a pair of cymbals and a set of gongs of different sizes, tones, and sounds. When beaten with hands, these *kong*, especially the long and heavy ones, give out a booming sound that can be heard from far away.

Kong making is a cottage industry and can be found in various parts of Shan State. But this industry is very small-scale and is established not on commercial and profit motives, but only to keep the cultural heritage and traditional values alive.

FIGURE 2.22. A band with drum, gongs, and cymbals. (Milne 1910, 66)

In making a *kong*, a special tree or wood will have to be chosen, especially light and durable wood. The easiest and most common tree to use is a jackfruit tree. To make the *kong*, the craftsman uses only local tools. The *kong* is usually painted black on the upper part, red in the middle part, and again black in the lower part. Before it is sold, the *kong* is thoroughly tested for its smooth sound by craftsmen or experts in this profession. They will carefully and attentively listen to the beat of the *kong* and its sound from nearby and far away. Synchronization of the beating of the *kong* and its accompanying instruments is very important. They must be harmonious to be able to arouse the happy mood of both the participants and the dancers. Playing *kong* requires teamwork and the musicians must understand each other. Coordination among them is very important, so they must be very careful not to lose the rhythm of the *kong*. The freehand dance, stick dance, and sword dance can be performed with the *kong* and its accompanying instruments. On auspicious occasions, *kainaya* (sacred bird), peacock dance, and *tonia* dance (mythic animal) are performed. Such performances of dance are staged at the pagoda festivals and at other *pwes*, social or religious gatherings.

The *kong* and its instruments are considered traditional cultural heritage materials and are not to be misused or misplaced. The Shan follow a custom regarding the *kong* and its instruments that no one is supposed to jump, cross, or sit over these instruments.

If anyone breaks this custom, he is censured, and the *kong* and its instruments will have to be sprinkled with soap-nut water to drive away the bad influence that might befall the *kong* and its instruments. The *kong* has its magic power. Its beating and booming sound can change the mood of the people. As soon as the Shan people hear the vibrating and booming sound of the *kong*, they become very lively.

The *kong* and its accompanying instruments are mostly owned by the community for its use. Well-to-do people also keep the *kong* for family use when they perform religious ceremonies. Those who are in need of the instrument can come and request its free use. The *kong* and its instruments are very well kept in the corner of the upper part of the house. The *kong* is always kept in a standing position.

The *kong* owned by the community is kept in the house of the headman called *pu kye* or *pu hein*. Sometimes it is kept in the monastery with the consent of the chief monk.

FIGURE 2.23. Drum making in Nam Hkam. (Photo by Sai Aung Tun, 2003)

FIGURE 2.24. Various kinds of *kong*. (Photo by Sai Aung Tun, 2003)

3

The Shan Hegemony in Upper Myanmar from 1287 to 1555

In Myanmar history, the years from 1287 to 1531 are recognized as the period of Shan kings in Upper Myanmar. This period witnessed the successful establishment of the three historically famous cities of Pinya, Sagaing, and Inwa (Ava) by the Shan kings. Inwa became a well-known capital recognized as the center of Myanmar political power by Westerners for whom Inwa meant Myanmar and who very often referred to the Myanmar Court as the Court of Inwa.

According to Myanmar historical records, Myinsaing and Pinya were founded by the Shan kings, eight of whom ruled Myinsaing and Pinya from 1298 to 1364. They were:

1. Athinhkaya	1298
2. Yazathinkyan	1298
3. Thihathu	1312
4. Usana	1324
5. Ngasishin	1343
6. Kyawswa-nge	1350
7. Narathu	1359
8. Uzana Byaung	1364

(See appendix 4.)

Sagaing was founded by the Shan kings, and seven ruled it from 1315 to 1352:

1. Sawyun	1315
2. Tarabyagyi	1323
3. Shwetaungtet	1336
4. Kyaswa	1340
5. Nawrahtaminye	1350
6. Tarabyange	1350
7. Minbyauk Thihapate	1352

(See appendix 5.)

Inwa was founded by the Shan kings. Nineteen ruled it from 1364 to 1552 as given below:

1. Thadominpya	1364
2. Nga Nu	1368
3. Minkyiswasawke	1368
4. Tarabya	1401
5. Nga Nauk Hsan	1401
6. Minhkaung	1401
7. Thihathu	1422
8. Minhla-nge	1426
9. Kalekytaungnyo	1426
10. Mohnyinthado	1427
11. Minrekyawswa	1440
12. Narapati	1443
13. Thihathura	1469
14. Minhkaung	1481
15. Shwenankyawshin	1502
16. Thohanbwa	1527
17. Hkonmaing	1543
18. Mobye Narapati	1546
19. Sithukyawhtin	1552

(See appendix 6.)

In Lower Myanmar as well the Shan influence was predominant with the accession of Wareru as king of Martaban in 1287. His dynasty ruled from 1287 to 1526. The rulers of the Wareru dynasty were as follows:

1. Wareru	1287
2. Hkun Law	1296
3. Saw O	1310
4. Saw Zein	1324
5. Zein Pun	1331
6. Saw E Gan Gaung	1331
7. Binnya E Law	1331
8. Binnya U	1353
9. Razadarit	1385
10. Binnyadammayaza	1423
11. Binnyaran	1426
12. Binnyawaru	1446
13. Binnyakyan	1450
14. Mawdaw	1453
15. Lady Shinzawbu	1453
16. Dammazedi	1472

17. Binnyaran	1492
18. Takayutpi	1526

(See appendix 7.)

THE FALL OF BAGAN (PAGAN) AND THE RISE OF THE SHAN

The Mongol invasion of Bagan in 1287 and the flight of King Narathihapate (or Tarokpyemin, meaning "the king who fled from the Chinese") to Bassein (Pathein) in the south brought an end to the period of Bagan's glory started by King Anawrahta in 1044. Later successors were so weak that they were unable to retain the power of Bagan. A political vacuum was thus created, shifting the center of political gravity to the Myinsaing area where Shan were predominant.

The Shan penetration into Myanmar goes back to a date since before the first century AD. The Shan movement was sometimes slow and peaceful, but at other times it was forceful, depending on the pressure from the north. In the process, Shan settlements, known by such terms as *mong*, *se*, and *keng*, were founded in the river valleys in the north, northwest, east, and northeast of Myanmar. The size of these settlements depended on the extensiveness of the valley. From the northwest region down to the east of Myanmar such polities were founded as Mong Hsaung Hsop, Mong Khaing, Mong Yang, Mong Kwang, Mong Waing Hso, Mong Mit, Mong Mao, Se-lan, Mong Hsen Wi, Mong Hsi Paw, Mong Kung, Mong Lai Hhka, Mong Nai, Mong Pan, Mong Mawk Mai, Mong Pai, Mong Yawng Hwe, Mong Lawk Sawk, Keng Hung, Keng Tung, Keng Sen, Keng Tawng, Keng Hkam, Keng Lom, Keng Lap, and Keng Mai, encircling the Upper Myanmar plain which later became the center and scene of power struggles among the various feudal chiefs.

Even during the pre-Bagan period, the Shan had been in Bagan. But they did not involve themselves in local politics. They were peaceful settlers of the region rendering services in building pagodas and in agricultural work, and joining the royal contingents in fighting foreign wars and the wars of territorial expansion of the Bagan kings. Many stone inscriptions in Bagan mention the donation and donors of the meritorious works of the Shan in Bagan. In the pre-Bagan days, a Shan prince named Pyu-Sao-Hti was well known for wiping out the ferocious animals that troubled the people of Bagan and for uniting the Pyu, Myanmar, and Shan living in the area.

The legendary Shan princess named Sao Mon Hla, a daughter of a Shan king of Se-lan, who became the queen of Anawrahta, established an important Shan-Myanmar link. Anawrahta, on his way back from China, stopped in Se-lan to establish friendly relations with the Shan king who was as powerful as himself in the Mao area. They exchanged greetings and royal presents. The Shan king, to cement the relationship more firmly, married his only daughter, Sao Mon Hla, to Anawrahta. She was taken to Bagan and installed as a royal consort. Sao Mon Hla was very beautiful, very religious, and a devoted Buddhist. She had not wanted to get married and would have preferred to

FIGURE 3.1. Shwezaryan pagoda built by Sao Mon Hla, Shan princess.

remain single throughout her life. But she was asked by her father to marry Anawrahta. As it was not customary to go against the wishes of the royal father she was married to Anawrahta. On arriving in Bagan, she was extremely happy to have the opportunity of meeting the most highly esteemed Buddhist abbot, Shin Arahan. Very much absorbed in his teaching, she became a staunch devotee of Theravada Buddhism and strictly observed the five precepts in her daily life. She practiced meditation as taught to her by the chief abbot. She kept herself engaged in the meritorious activities of the court and her popularity went far beyond, arousing the attention of rival queens in the palace. Jealousies prevailed and plots to bring about her downfall were hatched without her knowledge.

She was so pure in thought, word, and deed that the sacred relics of Buddha came to dwell in her earrings and one night these relics emitted bright lights of different colors, to the amazement of many people in the palace. The rival queens and those who were jealous of her position and wished to accomplish her downfall accused her of being a witch who had the power of emitting unholy rays of bright lights. The matter was reported to the king. On hearing the word "witch," Anawrahta's mind darkened. He lost his sense of balance, and his love for Sao Mon Hla turned into hatred. She was driven out of the palace right away. She and her entourage set out from the palace on foot without ill feelings toward either the king or anyone else in the palace. It was the beginning of her misfortune. She had never had the experience of walking barefoot from Bagan to the Shan land. She made many stops on the way. Just before climbing the Shan hills, she made a final stop at Shwezaryan, east of Mandalay. The water of Shwezaryan stream that flowed down from the Shan hills was so clean, clear, and fresh that she could not resist the temptation to take a bath. She stopped by the river to bathe. But when she took off her precious earrings and was about to place them on her skirt, the relics from the earrings suddenly flew up into the sky, emitting colorful rays of bright light. She then came to realize that the sacred relics had been dwelling in her earrings. She prayed for the relics to come back and she made a solemn vow to enshrine them in a pagoda for the benefit of the Brahmas, spirits, and human beings and to worship them in order to gain merit. While a small pagoda was being built a troop of guards arrived from Bagan with orders to kill her and her entourage if the entrance gate of the pagoda was found not turned toward Bagan. Fortunately the main entrance of the pagoda faced the correct direction and Sao Mon Hla's life was spared.

She made a last effort to push herself up the hills of the Shan plateau. When she reached Baw Gyo, her father and brother came down to receive her with a big army. The Shan forces were about to march on Bagan to avenge the insult. But legend says that the march on Bagan was stopped by the intercession of the chief monks from Bagan, who explained to the Shan commanders the consequences of war, the loss of lives on both sides, and the endless animosity that would continue after the war between the two peoples. Anawrahta also sent a message of regret that satisfied the Shan king. The Shan forces withdrew and war was avoided for the good of the two sides. In order to ensure the security of the border Anawrahta built a number of fortified towns along the foothills of the Shan plateau. But this measure was not effective during the rule of weak kings of Bagan. Shan immigrants slipped through the mountain passes to occupy the upper plain of Myanmar especially in the area of Kyaukse.

A massive Shan migration took place after the destruction of Mong Mao Long by the Mongol army. It was, indeed, like the opening of the floodgates and nothing could prevent this new migration into the Upper Myanmar plain.

By the thirteenth century the Shan had gained a foothold in the Kyaukse area ready for the further expansion of their settlements. Kyaukse was a region located in a strategic position commanding the trade route to the Shan hills. Interregional trade flourished at the time. Shan traders with their pack animals brought down Shan products to Upper Myanmar and took back Kyaukse products to the Shan hills. This lucrative trade between the two regions encouraged more Shan traders to venture down to Myanmar plains. More and more Shan farmers joined this stream of migration into Kyaukse. With their advanced technique the Shan migrants reclaimed marshy wasteland around Kyaukse and turned it into a fertile and productive land of wet-rice cultivation. Kyaukse was also a convenient place from which they could easily get back to the Shan hills when there was trouble. Among the new immigrants to Kyaukse was a Shan prince named Thinghkabo, who had lost his chance to become the chief in his native state. Thinghkabo also led the other Shan to renovate the abandoned old weirs, dams, and canals. A new irrigation system was introduced and multicrop cultivation was also encouraged to make the place the granary of Upper Myanmar.

Almost at the same time crop production declined in Bagan. Owing to excessive deforestation around Bagan, rainfall greatly decreased. Consequently its land became dry and unproductive, and the annual crop yield was now insufficient to feed the people of Bagan. The Bagan people had to depend on the Kyaukse Shan farmers for supplies of rice and other foodstuffs. Kyaukse also served as a human resource center, and soldiers needed for royal service were conscripted mostly from the area. Thinghkabo and his sons soon had the opportunity to render service at the royal court of Bagan. His sons became members of the royal guards of Bagan. They served well and faithfully. Because of their loyalty and good service to King Narathihapate they were awarded the governorship of the Kyaukse region. The eldest son of Thinghkabo was conferred the title of Athinhkaya and made the governor of Myinsaing; the second son was appointed chief of Mekkaya with the title of Yazathinkyan. The youngest son was given Pinle and was known as Thihathu.

Their stay at the Bagan court was most fruitful. They had the opportunity to come into association with many princes and princesses including the queen mother, Queen Saw. One of their sisters was married to the son of Narathihapate and they became part of the royal court. They also learned the statecraft of the Bagan kings and the management of the daily affairs of the palace.

After the death of Narathihapate, the three Shan chiefs began to feel that they could set up an independent rule of their own in Myinsaing. The Kyaukse people looked up to them because of their wealth and political power. The Kyaukse people enjoyed economic prosperity and political stability under their rule. The people of the region stood united under their leadership.

Kyawswa, the new king who came to the throne of Bagan, was so weak that he was unable to control territories beyond the capital, whereas the three Shan chiefs were strong enough to exercise their authority not only within their own territory but also over the adjoining regions. Another weak point of Kyawswa was that Queen Saw felt ignored because he failed to pay attention to her. She was very much annoyed with the new king and she felt that her influence in the court was diminishing. She hatched a plot to oust young Kyawswa from the throne. She secretly sent her plan to the three Shan brothers and asked them to help her. Well acquainted with the queen mother whose help had made them chiefs, the three Shan brothers invited Kyawswa to the consecration of a monastery in Kyaukse they had built. When Kyawswa came, he was seized and forced to become a monk to live in the monastery. The queen mother went back to Bagan, where she became supreme again. Young Saohnit, the son of Kyawswa, was enthroned but the real power was in the hands of Queen Saw.

Kyawswa and his son Saohnit, feeling the effects of the Shan power, appealed to the Chinese emperor for help to reinstate the rightful king to the Bagan throne. The Chinese came down with an army of twelve thousand soldiers. The three Shan brothers fortified their cities and laid out a defense strategy to resist the Chinese.

The Chinese besieged the three walled cities of Myinsaing. On the walls, the Shan soldiers mounted ballista and in one assault the Chinese lost five hundred soldiers from the arrows, blocks of stone, and beams hurled down on them.[1] The two sides fought fiercely and the Chinese suffered heavy casualties. The Shan princes and their followers were mostly war veterans, having fought in many wars of the past. With their new techniques of warfare, they easily beat off the Chinese who, having to march from a very far distance, were exhausted by the time they reached Myinsaing. Moreover, the weather demoralized them and the shortage of rations for the soldiers contributed to their defeat. Finally, the Shan showed the chopped head of Kyawswa to the Chinese, signalling that there could be no hope of a restoration of the late dynasty to the Bagan throne. For peace, the Chinese generals were offered 700 ticals of gold and 2,200 ticals of silver and many other items of precious gifts. The generals were so pleased with the presents that they asked their soldiers to help build the irrigation works of Kyaukse, i.e. the Thindwe canal. The Shan were happy that at the feast the youngest brother Thihathu composed a triumphant war song and sang it:

The Chinks came down the passes,
Roaring, boys, roaring;
The rain of their arrows
Pouring, boys, pouring.

The withdrawal of the Chinese troops was in fact a victory for the Myinsaing Shan. They were recorded as being outstanding in their military strategy and their diplomatic initiative, making the Chinese withdraw from the Myanmar soil. It also marked the end of the Chinese involvement in Myanmar's domestic affairs. To further cement the cordial relationship between the two countries, the Shan kings sent envoys to China in 1308.[3]

The victory over the Chinese was followed by the death of the two elder brothers, Yazathinkyan and Athinhkaya, leaving the youngest brother, Thihathu, to rule the country. Thihathu soon felt the need of a new capital commanding access to the Ayeyarwady. Accordingly a site was chosen where, as tradition goes, a golden flower was discovered at the digging of the foundation for a pagoda. The construction of a new palace was started at the site and after its completion, Queen Saw with her royal entourage from Bagan came on invitation to attend the opening ceremony. At the ceremony Thihathu was honored with a golden belt and a golden tray, the symbols of royalty since the time of Anawrahta (1044–77). Queen Saw was recognized as a queen mother and a good friend and royal adviser to the Shan kings. Thihathu followed the style of the old Bagan kings. He married the daughter of Narathihapate who had been married to her half brother, Kyawswa, and had a son named Uzana. (See appendix 8.) Thihathu also had another son by his marriage to a Shan wife. His name was Athinhkaya Sao Yun. He crossed over the river Ayeyarwady and established a new city called Sagaing, extending his rule up to the Manipur frontier. He set up a new line of Shan kings that lasted for forty-nine years.

After the death of Thihathu (1312–24), his son Uzana succeeded him. This king ruled for twenty years and abdicated in favor of his brother Kyawswa, and became a hermit. Kyawswa later assumed the title Ngasishin (1343–50), "Owner of Five White Elephants." He reigned eight years and was succeeded by his son, who also was named Kyawswa. After a reign of nine years Kyawswa was succeeded by his brother Narathu. When Narathu came to the throne, he tried to exert his influence on Sagaing, but unable to do so, he invited the Mao Shan to attack Sagaing. On hearing the news of the coming of the enemies, the people fled and abandoned Sagaing. Finding nothing to fight, the Mao Shan turned on Narathu, who failed to give them help. Pinya was bitterly attacked and King Narathu was carried away to Mong Mao.

Another prince named Uzana Byaung came to the throne, but he was so weak that he could not exercise authority over the country. After three months another prince, Thadominpya, took his place in 1364, thus ending the Myinsaing dynasty that lasted for sixty-six years.

Thadominpya (1364–8) was believed to be a descendant of the ancient kings of Tagaung on his father's side, but on his mother's side he was the grandson of the Shan king of Sagaing, Athinhkaya Sao Yun. He was a dynamic, courageous, but ruthless person. He removed all his rivals in Sagaing as well as in Pinya. He was the founder of Inwa city. After consulting his royal astrologers he selected the site of the new capital at the convergence of the Myitnge and the Ayeyarwady. Since the site was low-lying, swamps were drained off. The city walls were carefully and systematically charted out and in the center the golden palace was built on February 25, 1365, with much pomp and splendor befitting the auspicious ceremony. The city's classical name is Ratanapura, the City of Gems.[4] Professor Hall makes the following remark:

> As the capital of upper Burma, and, after 1634, of the whole of Burma, its name became so closely associated with the country itself that Europeans came to refer to upper Burma as the 'Land of Ava' and to the government as the 'Court of Ava', even when the capital was at Amarapura or Mandalay.[5]

Thadominpya then set out to suppress those who revolted against him. The first campaign was against Theinkathu of Sagu. There he contracted smallpox. While he lay dying, Thadominpya ordered one of his trusted men, Nga Nu, to rush back to Inwa and kill his beautiful queen, Sao Ummer, so that she might not fall into the hands of his successor. Nga Nu did go back to Inwa. But instead of killing her, he married her and crossed over to Sagaing to be the king there.

An interesting aspect of Thadominpya was that once he captured a notorious thief-dacoit-robber, called Nga Tet Pya. This thief was so clever that no one from the king's security force could capture him. One night, Thadominpya set out from the palace alone to capture the man. He succeeded and Nga Tet Pya, who had become his prisoner, was asked, "Now, you have become my prisoner, name any weapon by which you would like to be killed—sword, hackle, axe, spear, or iron spit." The notorious thief calmly answered, "Since I am now in your hands, you can execute me with whatever weapon you prefer. I am ready to die. But the last wish I would like to make is this. I would like to marry your beautiful queen Sao Ummer." Thadominpya was not angry or insulted by this. He thought that such a courageous man should not be killed and appointed the notorious thief his security guard and Nga Tet Pya served him well and faithfully. Thadominpya died in 1368 after a reign of three years.

Minkyiswasawke (1368–1401) came to the throne in 1368. He was also a Shan king, related to Narathihapate and the three Shan brothers. Earlier he was taken captive to Arakan (Rakhine) with his brother and father in 1333 and was brought up in Arakan. After his release he became governor of Amyin in Sagaing. When he became king the first measure he took was to build a weir at Zidaw and to improve the irrigation system of the area. Next he set out to Meikhtila to repair the embankment of the lake. While in Meikhtila he met a local scholar named Wunzin, whose local knowledge surprised the king. Wunzin was taken to the royal court and appointed adviser to the royal crown. He served very well and on many occasions his suggestions met the interest of the king. He also helped to solve many internal and external problems encountered by the king. He was conferred the royal title of Wunzinminyaza and continued to render his services to successive kings of Inwa up to 1422.

Most of Minkyiswasawke's time was engaged in fighting the Mon-Shan. The wars between Shan-Myanmar in the north and the Shan-Mon in the south went on for a long time without any decisive victory for either side. It was a drawn-out war and went on for many years, causing heavy casualties on both sides and loss of lives and property and much damage to villages and cultivation. Royal princes and princesses of both sides were captured and some died in the fighting. Many able military commanders gave their lives in battle. The feudal character of the wars was fully displayed as in other wars of the feudal age.

From 1287 to 1539 Chiang Mai Shan migrated into Lower Myanmar. At first they came to trade but later they settled down as cultivators around Thahton, Martaban, and Bago and became involved in local politics. Outstanding among them was a person named Magadu. He was born in Doonwun, Thahton. When he grew up he went to Sukhothai to become an elephant stable boy at the Thai Royal Court. For his good services he was promoted captain of the royal guard. He went with the king on every expedition so that he became acquainted with the king's daughter. One day, during the absence of the king, he eloped with the princess and took her to Doonwun. In 1281 he raised a rebellion against Aleimma, the governor of Martaban. Killing the governor, Magadu declared himself the king of Martaban. He took a new title and came to be known as Wareru. He then made an alliance with the Mon chief Tarabya and they launched an attack against Bago. By 1287 they both occupied all territories south of Prome (Pyi) and Taungoo. A quarrel broke out between the two leaders over the division of the conquered lands and they challenged each other to a single combat on elephant. Tarabya was defeated and captured. On the intercession of the chief monk, Tarabya's life was spared. Later Tarabya planned another secret plot against Wareru, who was warned by his daughter who was the wife of Tarabya. Tarabya was caught and killed, and Wareru became supreme in Lower Myanmar. He made Martaban and Doonwun his capital alternately up to 1269, then moved to Bago and set up his dynasty in 1287. The dynasty lasted to 1526 with its last king Takayutpi. (See appendix 7.)

Wareru obtained recognition from his father-in-law, the lord of Sukhothai, who gave him a white elephant as a royal gift. Wareru is well known in history for his achievement in the compilation of the traditional laws called Dhammathat. It consisted of laws ascribed to the ancient Indian sage, Manu, and was brought to Lower Myanmar by the Hindu colonists.[6] This law book is known as the *Wareru Dhammathat*. It was a digest of the Laws of Manu, compiled at his behest by monks from the writings of earlier scholars preserved in the monasteries. It was the earliest law book in Myanmar and is still extant.[7] It is a Shan contribution to the development of ancient Mon-Myanmar laws.

Myinkyiswasawke at first tried to establish friendly relations with the southern states, especially with Bago (Pegu). In 1371 he met Binnya U, the king of Bago, and exchanged gifts such as betel boxes, spittoons, and items of pomp and grandeur. They agreed to draw a boundary line between the two states. But the situation changed when Razadarit came to the throne in 1385. His uncle, who was against him, wrote to Minkyiswasawke to help him oust Razadarit as follows:

> I, Laukbya, lord of Myaungmya, bow at thy feet, O King of the Golden Palace at Ava, and pray that thou march against Razadarit before he is firm upon his throne. I will

> bring men by water; when we have conquered him, do thou keep the heartwood and leave the bark (from *Razadarit Ayedawpon*).[8]

With this message of request Minkyiswasawke marched down south with his troops, and fighting took place mostly in the delta up to 1422. He could not dethrone Razadarit and the war dragged on for a long time.

The Shan from Kale, Mong Yang, Mong Kwang, Mong Mit, Hsi Paw, and Yawng Hwe swarmed down partly to help the Inwa kings in their war against the Mon-Shan in the south and partly to settle down for good in the plains of Lower Myanmar. Some historians say that it was a war of migration of Shan from the north to Inwa and to the delta. The Inwa troops used two routes to invade the delta: one through the Sittaung valley and the other through the Ayeyarwady and then the Hlaing River to attack Hmawbi, Dagon, Dala, and Myaungmya. The war fought between the Bago king and the Inwa king at that time was not like the wars we know today. The fighting was very irregular and without regular armies. The soldiers went home during the rainy season for cultivation and resumed the fighting as soon as the dry season began.

In 1371 the two Shan chiefs of Kale and Mong Yang fought each other. They both asked for help from Minkyiswasawke. He consulted the wise minister Wunzinminyaza, who said, "Temporize and let them fight it out till they are exhausted and you get both."[9] In 1393 the chief of Mong Yang came down to attack Sagaing. But Thilawa of Yamethin who drove off the Shan to Shangon, twenty miles north of Sagaing, repulsed the Mong Yang Shan.

In 1374 the Arakanese (Rakhine) people requested Minkyaswasawke to send someone to fill the vacant throne of their country. He sent his uncle Sawmunkyi to rule Arakan. But his rule was very short because he died in 1384. Minkyaswasawke then sent one of his sons to succeed Sawmunkyi, but he proved oppressive and was recalled to Inwa.

Taungoo was another southern state that gave trouble to Minkyiswasawke. Its chief, Pyanchi, was very friendly with the Bago chief. Minkyaswasawke asked his brother who was the chief of Prome to get rid of Pyanchi. A plot was laid and Pyanchi fell into it and was captured and killed.

Minkyiswasawke died in 1401 at age seventy, leaving the war with the Mon unfinished, to be continued by his successors.

Minhkaung (1401–22) succeeded his father Minkyiswasawke in 1401. He was married to a Maw Shan princess, and a son named Minrekyawswa, believed to be a reincarnation of Bawlawkyandaw, the son of Razadarit, was born to them. This young Shan-Myanmar prince was known as a great warrior. At age thirteen he led an expedition against the Arakanese who encroached on the Myanmar territories of Yaw and Laungshe in Pakokku. The expedition was successful and the Arakanese king Narameikhla was driven out of his country and took refuge in Bengal. A Myanmar prince, Anawrahtaminsaw, was appointed king with Sawpyechantha as his queen at age thirteen. She was the sister of Minrekyawswa.

The *saopha* of Onbaung (Hsi Paw) and Yawng Hwe tried to make trouble with Minhkaung, but fighting was avoided on the timely advice of Wunzinminyaza. Minhkaung married off one of his nieces to the *saopha* of Hsi Paw. The non-Burmanized Shan chief of Kale and Mong Yang also made trouble, but were beaten off. To appease China, Minhkaung sent a goodwill mission to Yunnan. At the instigation of Razadarit the Hsen Wi chief came down to attack Inwa, but was repulsed by Minrekyawswa. In the single combat on elephants, the Hsen Wi chief fell and peace was restored. Two Shan chiefs from Mawke and Mawden also encroached on Myedu territory north of Shwebo, but the young prince Minrekyawswa also drove them off.

While Minhkaung was occupied with the Shan affairs in the north, Razadarit took the opportunity to raid Myanmar territories. He even went up the Ayeyarwady to attack Inwa, but he made a mistake. On his way up the river, he did not take Prome, Myedu, and Bagan but left them in the hands of his enemies. He camped at Sagaing, beating his war drum and threatening to capture Inwa. Minhkaung could not do much except close himself up in the fortified city of Inwa. Finally a monk bearing many gifts interceded with Razadarit on behalf of Minhkaung. Hearing the preaching of the monk, Razadarit agreed to withdraw. He built a *zayat* (rest house) at Sagaing and left. While he was on the way the Myanmar burned his *zayat* and also intercepted his forces. In Prome the Myanmar garrison fought the Mon force and even captured Razadarit's daughter. Minhkaung also swooped down with a bigger force. All the Mon forces on the east bank of the Ayeyarwady were wiped out. It happened because Razadarit did not listen to the advice on strategy of his two commanders, Byat Za and Deinmaniyut. The Mon garrison at Thayetmyo fell and a Mon commander who was the father of the two queens of Razadarit was captured and taken prisoner by Minhkaung.

The two minor queens, fearing for the death of their father, appealed to Razadarit to make peace with Minhkaung and to get back their father. Byat Za, who was consulted by Razadarit, said that he was not concerned with the women's tears but only with the victory of the king. But he was bribed with gold and other presents and finally gave his consent to the king making peace with the Myanmar.

Peace was made and the two kings exchanged gifts and honors. They had dinner together and prayed together at the Shwesandaw pagoda in Prome to establish eternal love, peace, and friendship. In addition a marriage ceremony was arranged at Bago between Minhkaung's sister and Razadarit. Peace was good for both the Myanmar and the Mon. Thousands of lives were spared because of peace. Farmers were happy because they could till their lands peacefully. But the peace was short-lived. Trouble arose over the succession to the Arakanese throne and the appointment of the crown prince in Inwa. When Minhkaung's son Minrekyawswa was appointed crown prince, Minhkaung's younger brother Theiddat became furious. He rebelled and took refuge in Bago, seeking the help of Razadarit. Minhkaung also sent a message to the Chiang Mai chief to attack Bago. The message was intercepted and sent to Razadarit. Razadarit broke the pledge of peace, and sent Mon troops to support the rival claim. The Arakanese troops with the help of Mon soldiers were able to dethrone

Anawrahtaminsaw and execute him. Razadarit took his young queen Sawpyechantha into his harem.

On hearing the news of his daughter's capture and falling into the hands of Razadarit, Minhkaung could not control his anger. Despite good advice from Wunzinminyaza, he chose an all-out war against Razadarit even at the rainy season. He marched down the country, ravaging village after village until he reached Pankyaw, where he was checked.[10]

One night while in camp, he was nearly killed by the Mon commander Lagunein, who slipped into his camp and stole his betel box and ruby sword. Minhkaung was shocked at this, knowing that his security was at stake. He broke through the siege line and escaped. His soldiers defended him well during his escape, but many of them fell in the fight, like a bundle of bamboos being broken and scattered.[11] He also lost his queen Shinminauk, the Maw Shan mother of Minrekyawswa, and the southern queen Shin Bo-me, who fell from her elephant and got lost in the jungle.

On hearing of the capture of his sister and his mother, Minrekyawswa became a fiend. He enlisted Shan and Myanmar in his force and made the decision to invade the Mon country by sea and by land. He was so furious that he said, "As a crocodile eats his victims, so will I rend the flesh of the Mon."[12] Most of the fighting took place in the delta region. Both sides suffered heavy casualties, and great damage was done to the villages and cultivation. Razadarit had to retreat and was confined to Bago and Martaban. The rest of the country fell into the hands of the Myanmar. But Razadarit was a veteran king and warrior and could not be underestimated in his knowledge of strategy and tactics. The tide of war turned in his favor at the last battle near Twante, in which Minrekyawswa was ambushed by Razadarit and also his chosen commandos. After getting about a hundred gashes, Minrekyawswa's elephant became maddened, shook him off, and crushed his thigh. Crippled, he crawled away to take refuge under an *Okhne* (*streblus asper tour*) tree. A search was mounted and he was found and taken prisoner to Razadarit's camp. He refused all the treatment offered to him and died during the night. His body was exhumed at Dala and his ashes and bones were put in a golden pot and dropped into the water at Mahtiwa at the mouth of the river near Twante. No major fighting took place after that.

His son Thihathu, born of a Maw Shan queen, succeeded in 1422. He took over his father's queen, Shin Bo-me. He marched down to the Delta to help settle a quarrel among Razadarit's sons. He came back to Inwa with a Mon princess Shin Saw Pu and crowned her queen consort to the dislike of Queen Shin Bo-me. Shin Bo-me secretly invited the Onbaung *saopha* to get rid of Thihathu and he was shot to death with an arrow in 1426 near Aungbinle in Mandalay.

Inwa was temporarily ruled by the *saopha* Kalekye Taungnyo (1426–27), who married Shin Bo-me. Mohnyinthado attacked Inwa, and drove out Kalekye Taungnyo and Shin Bo-me, who fled to Arakan. Kalekye Taungnyo died on the way near Shwesettaw. Shin Bo-me was brought back to the palace again. She became queen for the fifth time and finally died childless. Shin Saw Pu also became queen consort of Mohnyinthado, but

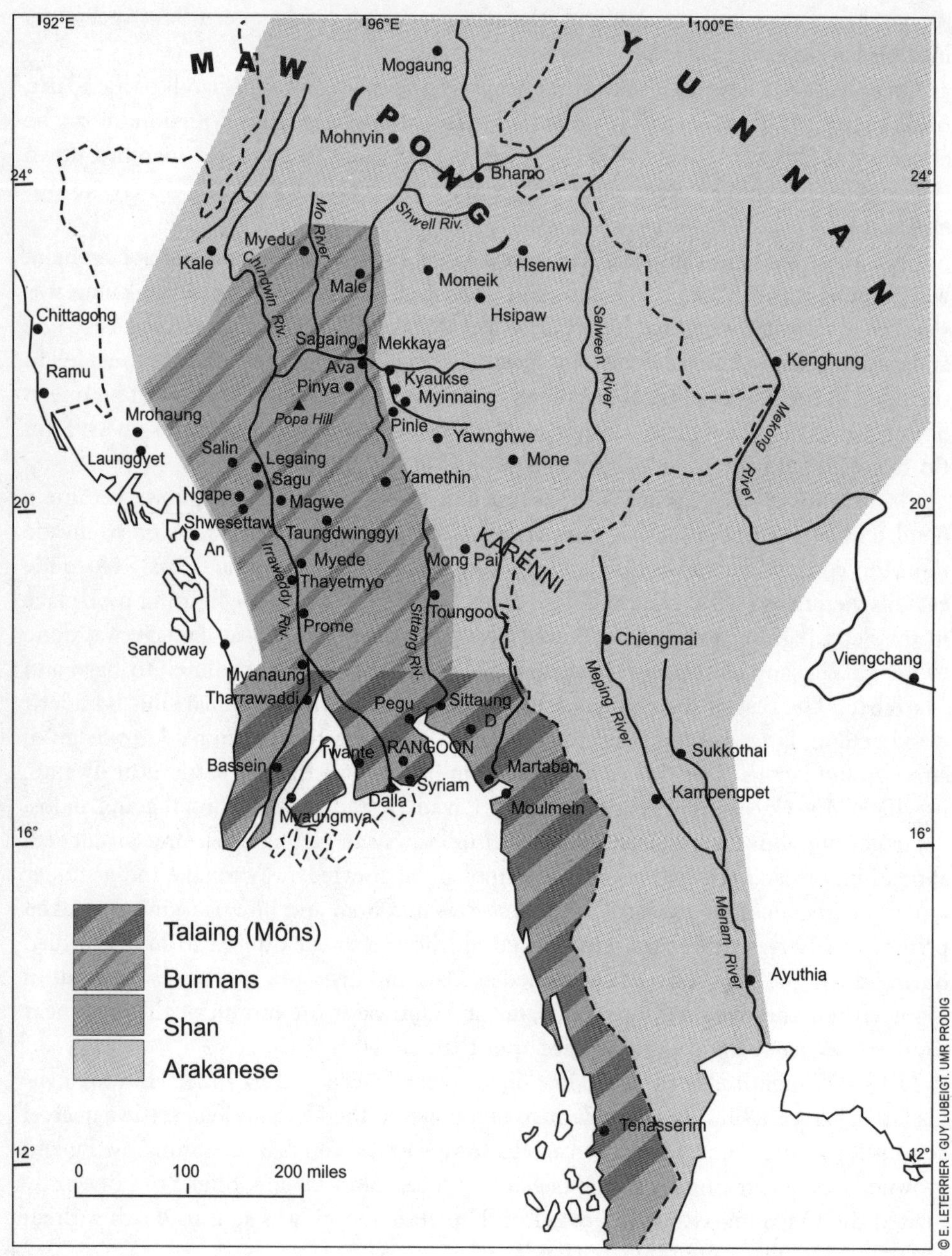

MAP 14. Shan dominion, 1287–1531

she felt tired of living in Inwa and she fled to the Delta in 1430 with the help of two Mon monks.

Mohnyinthado's reign was attended by troubles in all parts of the country. Taungdwingyi, Yamethin, Pinle, Shan, and Mon States rose against him. During his time a European named Nicolo di Conti, a merchant from Venice, came to Myanmar. He wrote a very interesting account of Myanmar of that time.

The outstanding religious achievements of Mohnyinthado's reign included building a huge monastery called Kyaungdawgyi, two miles west of Sagaing. He also built Yadana Zedi or Payabyu pagoda and enshrined sacred relics. Mohnyinthado was also known for a minor alteration he made in the calendar. He died in 1440 and was succeeded by his two sons Minrekyawswa (1440–3) and Narapati (1443–69). Minrekyawswa's rule was very short and he died in 1443. His brother, who was formerly a governor of Prome, succeeded him in 1443 and was very soon confronted with rebellions from the chiefs of Kale and Mong Yang. But they were easily subdued. Narapati marched up to attack Mong Mao Long, ruled by the Shan chief, Hso Ngan Pha. Hso Ngan Pha was captured and brought down to Inwa. The Ming emperor, who was interested in the trade route to Upper Myanmar, also found Mong Mao Long an obstacle and he accused the Mong Mao chief Hso Ngan Pha of attempting to revive the Nanchao empire. So he decided that Mong Mao Long should be wiped out and its king captured and brought to the capital. A long struggle took place between the Shan and the Chinese that lasted from 1438 to 1461. The Mao Shan were sandwiched between the Chinese in the east and the Shan-Myanmar in the west. Finally Mong Mao Long was destroyed, and the Chinese marched down to Inwa and demanded the surrender of Hso Ngan Pha to them. Narapati refused but in the meanwhile Hso Ngan Pha committed suicide and his body was dried and taken to China. Narapati also acknowledged the overlordship of the Chinese and was given a gold seal and appointed "Comforter of Ava."[13] The Chinese force also helped Narapati to restore peace and order in Yamethin before they went home. Narapati died in 1469 and was succeeded by his son Thihathura, 1469–81.

Thihathura was a weak king and the neighboring states were free from his control. In the north Mong Yang became powerful and aggressive. In 1472 Thihathura asked China to suppress Mong Yang. But his request was not effective, because Mong Yang and China were on good terms. The states on the Shan plateau were at war with one another and Thihathura could do nothing about it. Disorder prevailed everywhere. In this chaotic situation Thihathura died in 1481.

Minhkaung and Shwenankyawshin, who came to power after the death of Thihathura, could do nothing to improve the chaotic situation of the country. But Myanmar literature flourished during this period. Many outstanding scholars emerged whose high standard of writing contributed to the development of Myanmar literature. Taking the opportunity, the Mong Yang (Mohnyin) force invaded Inwa and in 1527 it fell to the Mong Yang chief Sao Long, who made his son, Hso Han Hpa (Thohanbwa), king of Inwa and went home.

Hso Han Hpa (1527–43) is mentioned in Myanmar history as a full-blooded savage. He destroyed pagodas and killed monks whom he thought would rebel against him at Taungbalu south of Inwa in 1540. His right-hand man, Minkyiyannaung, finally killed him. Minkyiyannaung was offered the throne but he refused, saying that he was too old and not of royal blood. The throne then was offered to the chief of Hsi Paw named Sao Hkun Mong (Hkonmaing) in 1543. He was brought down to Inwa with great pomp and splendor. Sao Hkun Mong planned to unite Shan and Myanmar into a united country. But his plan failed because his reign was very short. He died in 1546, after ruling for three years. Before he came to Inwa, he called a conference at Hsi Paw, assigning all his brothers, sons, and nephews to different parts of the Shan states as chiefs. They were all to follow strictly the precedent of paying annual homage to Inwa. That set a precedent which was unfailingly observed in later generations of kings. Sao Hkun Mong's son Mobye Narapati, the *saohpa* of Mong Pai, succeeded him in 1546. He also failed to unite either Shan or Myanmar to support his rule. Taungoo was building its power under Tabinshwehti. In the north Mong Yang was still aggressive and planning to ally with another Shan chief who was against the Inwa king, Sithukyawhtin of Sagaing. Inwa was attacked. Narapati fled to Taungoo and asked Bayinnaung for help. He was kept there but when Bayinnaung captured Inwa in 1555, he did not restore Narapati to his throne. This marked the end of the Shan rule in Inwa, which lasted from 1287 to 1555.

SUMMARY OF THE SHAN DYNASTIC PERIOD (1287–1555)

- Large-scale migration of Shan began in 1287 with the destruction of Mong Mao Long by the Mongols, leaving the Shan with no choice but to make a forceful penetration into the valleys of northern Myanmar. The Shan intrusion coincided with the political vacuum caused by the weakness of the Bagan kings in the later Bagan period.
- The Shan kings were noted for their achievement in the founding of the three historic capitals of Pinya, Sagaing, and Inwa, which up to the present day are recognized as centers of Myanmar arts, crafts, and culture.
- A long struggle ensued for domination of the plains of Upper Myanmar, for, according to the geopolitical theory of the time, whoever controlled Inwa commanded the heartland and also controlled Myanmar. The control of Inwa was thus the central political object for the feudal kings of the day.
- In the long struggle the Shan were split into two. One group who came down to the plain of Myanmar first, gradually adopted Myanmar culture and Buddhism and, mixing and mingling with the native people, finally became assimilated to become what we call Burmanized or Myanmarized Shan. The other group was the non-Myanmarized Shan, who came down later from the valleys of the north and northeast. The struggle to dominate Inwa turned into a struggle between Myanmarized and non-Myanmarized Shan and into cultural clashes between the two ethnic groups.

• The same pattern was repeated in Lower Myanmar with the coming of Magadu (Wareru) and his followers, the Chiang Mai Shan, and the establishment of his dynasty, which lasted from 1287 to 1526. They were also assimilated into Mon culture and Buddhism, and mingled with the natives to become the Shan-Mon ethnic people. They gradually lost their Shan characteristics. The war between Lower Myanmar and Upper Myanmar at that time could be termed a war between the Shan-Mon kings of Lower Myanmar and the Shan-Myanmar kings of Upper Myanmar.

• During the Shan dynastic period both Shan-Mon and Shan-Myanmar kings were listed as possessors of the sacred white elephant regarded as a symbol of royal power, prestige, and glory. Wareru had a white elephant, given him by his father-in-law, the king of Sukhothai, as a gift of glory. Thihathu, the Pinya Shan king, recovered a white elephant from Sa Hmon stream and conferred on himself the title Ta-Si-Shin Thihathu, "Owner of One White Royal Elephant." Kyawswa, another Shan king, obtained five white elephants, and the title of Ngasishin Kyawswa was conferred on him as owner of five white elephants.

Kyawswa himself participated in the hunt for white elephants. The first white elephant he captured was near Indwelun. It was named Pale Ta Mu. The second white elephant was found near Hmon Taw Myaung Kyat and named Maha Kaythaya. The third one was caught in the foothill of Pyet Taung and was conferred the title Than Myan Swa. The fourth one was trapped near Sa Hmon Hpya and was honored with the title of U Paw Thahta. The last one was seized north of Tha Ban Kaing village and its royal name was Chit Swa Ma Re.

The capture of five white elephants by Kyawswa created a psycho-political impact on his brother Uzana, who was the king. On hearing the news of the five white elephants, Uzana felt inferior to his brother Kyawswa in power, prestige, and glory. So he abdicated in favor of Kyawswa, who became the prestigious king as Ngasishin Kyawswa, "Owner of the Five White Elephants." In the later period, rivalry and competition for the possession of white elephants became a serious issue in feudal politics and a cause for wars, damaging property and claiming many innocent lives.

• Regarding religious beliefs, there can be no doubt that the Myinsaing Shan were good Buddhists even before they arrived in Kyaukse. When Thihathu became king, he first built the Shwe Gu pagoda, but because of floods it did not last long. When the capital Pinya was established, Thihathu followed the procedures of the Bagan kings. He consulted his royal ministers, astrologers, and chief monks and built Nan, Myo, Atwin Shwe Kyaung, and excavated the Htaukshay and Kan Hla Lakes that were an essential feature of the new capital.

He also paid regular attention to the worship of the Triple Gems and gave daily offerings of food (*soon*) to monks inside the palace.

Religious teaching and learning were also promoted. Laymen and monks who devoted themselves to the propagation of Buddha's teaching were encouraged and honored. Thihathu also took a great interest in attending to their material needs. He installed Yahantha Shin Htwe, Shin Theikpasatku as his great teacher in matters of religion.

• A ceremony enshrining the Therira sacred relics which were obtained from Anawrahta was held at Shwezihkon, and the remaining two relics were given to the minister Ponnya to be enshrined in the Sagaing Ponnya Shin pagoda.[14]

• Uzana (1325–69) was another Shan king who was also known for his religious activities. He is well remembered for building the seven monasteries, called Saga-ku-na Kyaung, at Pinya.

The first monastery was named Zabuka and donated to Thudhammathami. The second, named Wailuwun, was given to Shin Nya-na Teza, who was well versed in Buddhist literature and Abidhamma. The third monastery was named Ain-naing and administered by Shin Warapatta, who devoted himself to the study of San, Alinka, grammar (Thadhar), Nyar, Kalap, Widet, Thamti, Bhahi, and astrology. The fourth monastery, named Zaytawun, was cared for by Shin Gu-na-birama, who belonged to the Bagan Shin Ananda sect. The fifth was popular as Kala Kyaung monastery and managed by Shin Ardhaik-sa-ranthi, who also belonged to the Bagan Shin Ananda sect. The sixth was known as Myauk Zun monastery and managed by Shin Thu-da-mana Linkara. The last one, named Taung Zun monastery, was looked after by Shin Thiriponnya. An auspicious ceremony of planting a bodhi (banyan) tree was performed at the northeast corner of Taung Zun monastery. Arrangements were made to offer cultivated lands with sufficient number of slaves to support these monasteries.

Shin Thiriponnya also assigned the minister Anandapyitsi to complete the building of the Shwezihkon pagoda left unfinished by his father. After that a grand pagoda festival was celebrated for the benefit of all beings and for sharing the merit.

• Cavalry forces, as part of the war machine, played an important role during the Shan hegemony in Upper Myanmar. The Shan relied much on cavalry forces for quick attacks on enemies. Moreover, horses were widely used in those days as means of communication, transportation, and warfare. Shield-bearing troops were also attached to the mounted force. These cavalry forces were well organized and well distributed at suitable places. They were called *myin su* (horse troops) and *kar su* (shield-bearing troops).

• Elephantry was also organized and elephants were trained for warfare. Each good war elephant was given a name. A special selection of elephants was made for the king and courageous commanders. Prominent fighting elephants were well remembered in history. Some leading elephants won many battles and were honored with special titles. The Shan were mostly good horse and elephant riders. They used these animals as parts of their war machine since the time they were in China. The Shan princes very often chose single combat on either elephant or horse as a symbol of bravery and manly fight, and these combats were a special feature of the feudal wars.

• As a feature of his religious activity, Ngasishin Kyawswa built a pagoda named Lay Myet Na Paya southwest of Pinya.

• Athinhkaya Sao Yun (1315–23), the founder of Sagaing, built up all cavalry forces. He classed all fighting horses into various groups and posted each in a separate region of the country. The cavalry forces were well looked after and given free land to maintain them. The shield-bearing troops were also organized in the same way.

• As for meritorious work, Sao Yun built the Setkya monastery west of Sagaing. Lands and slaves were also offered to support the monastery. In the same way his brother, King Tarabya (1323), built a big monastery called Thathana Kyaung east of Sagaing with his mother. Another brother, Shwetaungtet (1336), went and offered a fine piece of cloth and prayed to become king at the Thamantasa pagoda in Amyin.

King Kyawswa (1340) also built a monastery called Abayagiri Kyaung. Lands and slaves were also offered to maintain the monastery. King Nawrahtaminre (1350) built a monastery called Minre Kyaung, also with offering of cultivated lands and slaves. Tarabyange (1350), soon after coming to the throne, built a Saga monastery with cultivated lands and slaves. Minbyauk (1352), as his work of merit, built a pagoda called Zihkon on the tenth waxing of the moon in the month of Tabaung.

Most of the Sagaing kings had great interest in building monasteries rather than pagodas to accommodate the increasing number of monks of the time. Their religious activities were quite limited compared with those of the Myinsaing and Inwa kings. But some important stone pillars with inscriptions recording their religious works were raised like the Shin Saw Kyi pillar, Sao Ummar Pyathat monastery inscription, Saw Taw U Kyaung inscription, Pinya Kyaung inscription, and others.

Thadominpya one of the Inwa kings, retored the ruined embankment of Nga Kyin In (Lake), Kyaukmaw In, In Bu In, and Ohne In. He offered cultivated land and slaves to support the Bagan Shwezikhon pagoda. Minkyiswasawke built the pagoda called Zihkon in 745 on the advice of the Arakanese abbot who had been his religious teacher since he was young, and who conferred the highest title of Maha Theinkaraza on him. He also paid great attention to the advice of the Myanmar abbots and built another Zihkon and a monastery in Ywathitkyi.

• Mohnyinmintaragyi (1427–40), noted for his devotion to the worship of the Triple Gems, carried out the following meritorious works:

Pagoda	Monastery	Location
1. Yatana Zedi	A golden monastery	Sagaing
2. Yan-aung-myin	A golden monastery	Sagaing
3. Zihkon Zedi	A golden monastery	Nyaungyan
4. Zihkon Zedi	A golden monastery	Amyin
5. Zihkon Zedi	A golden monastery	Anya-pan-pyin
6. Zihkon Zedi	A golden monastery	Shein-Ma Ga
7. Zihkon Zedi	A golden monastery	Myohla (north)
8. Min-hkaung-gyi Paya	A golden monastery	Pinya
9. Zihkon Zedi	A golden monastery	Mye-ne
10. Zihkon Zedi	A golden monastery	Yazagyo
11. Zihkon Zedi	A golden monastery	Pa-hkan-gyi
12. Zihkon Zedi	A golden monastery	Thit-sint
13. Zihkon Zedi	A golden monastery	Taunggyi
14. Zihkon Zedi	A golden monastery	Wa-yin-toke

15. Zihkon Zedi	A golden monastery	Pyi
16. Zihkon Zedi	A golden monastery	Bagan-Nyaung-nwe
17. Zihkon Zedi	A golden monastery	Hkan-taw
18. Zihkon Zedi	A golden monastery	Inwa-myit-nge
19. Zihkon Zedi	A golden monastery	Myin-mi
20. Zihkon Zedi	A golden monastery	Nga-lein-hkwe
21. Zihkon Zedi	A golden monastery	Taung-pa-lu
22. Zihkon Zedi	A golden monastery	Kwan-zi-kye
23. Zihkon Zedi	A golden monastery	Pinya
24.	A golden monastery	East Pinya
25.	A golden monastery	Myin-hkontaing-taing
26.	A golden monastery	Pyin-zi-myo
27.	A golden monastery	Htan-taw
28. Chantha-gyi pagoda	A golden monastery	Minbu
29.	A golden monastery	Sagaing

- During the reign of Mohnyinmintaragyi (Mohnyinthado), five Buddha relics were brought from Ceylon (Sri Lanka) by the two Buddhist abbots, Sri Thuddhamma Linkara and Thihahla Maha-tha-mi, in 1430. A big ceremony was held to welcome the sacred relics by the king and courtiers and people at Prome. The five relics were enshrined in the Yatana Zedi on the west of Sagaing on Saturday, the Full Moon of Tabaung, in the year 797, Myanmar Era. A grand golden monastery of brick nogging with 78 doors was also built and donated to the two abbots who brought the sacred relics. A stone pillar, called Yatana Beikhman Kyaung, was set up with an inscription about the building of Htu-pa-yon monastery (east) by his daughter and nephew Uzana.
- The first intercourse with the Westerners was made during the reign of Mohnyinthado by the visit of a merchant of Venice, named Nicolo di Conti. He wrote a short account of what he had seen in Myanmar.
- Mohnyinthado was assisted by three brave brothers named Bayagamani, Yazathinkyan, and Yan-lo-kywe. The first brother, Bayagamani, was an excellent tactician and won many battles against the enemies. The second brother, Yazathinkyan, held posts of defense as well as administration and was a reliable adviser to the king on administrative affairs. The third brother was a military commander of the king's army and a cool-headed commando. For their excellent military services, the king awarded them titles and gold and other presents. With the gold they received from the king, they built two pagodas, Pyi-neik-pan and Mahi-ringana.[15]
- Mohnyinthado was not only a Buddhist but a traditionalist. He observed the local tradition of sacrificing animals to the Mahagiri spirit in 787, soon after coming to the throne.
- Mohnyinthado made a small alteration of the calendar after being advised by the abbots of Sagyo and Min Kyaung that such alterations would bring peace and prosperity to the people and the country. But the minister Yazathinkyan warned him that such an

alteration would affect the life of the king. But Mohnyinthado said, "I must not hesitate to do it, if it is for the benefit of all beings. Knowing the ill effects that might befall the people, I will not refrain from doing so. History will remember me as a king of no courage and if I must die, let me die. I will not be put into a song as the king who was afraid to do his duty."[16]

A big ceremony of great pomp and splendor to alter the calendar was held north of Taungpalu, and south of Inwa, in Ngwe-zin-zay-yat, attended by all the ministers, princes, princesses, and courtiers. Donations of gold, silver, elephants, horses, cattle, all sorts of rice and crops, lands, and slaves were made. The alteration of the calendar was the elimination of 798 years from the current year of 800 and a new calendar was begun with the remaining 2. The king died shortly after making the alteration.

• Mohnyinthado proved himself a good king. He strictly observed the ten precepts of a good king. He was very considerate to his people and had a balanced view of their complaints and their troubles. He always looked to past administrative experience as a guide for the present and future development of the country. He was very generous and did not hesitate to give away what he had and was always ready to improve the lot of his people. The principle of loyalty had to be strictly observed for those who served him. Industry and vigilance were his key abilities in managing state affairs. He always looked for new ideas and new plans to improve his internal administration. He was also a courageous man with a high quality of statecraft.

He also took measures to renovate ruined or deteriorating pagodas and temples in his capital from either his own funds or funds collected from his ministers and the people.

Those who were forced into prostitution in Inwa, Bagan, and Nyaung U were given aid and funds were collected from his ministers and other donors to resettle them. Some of his concubines and other ladies-in-waiting who were guilty of sexual misconduct were forgiven and made to marry and live a proper family life. Fifteen minor queens and a minister's wife who committed petty theft were forgiven and helped to resettle without punishment. Such arrangements for unfortunate people were made one hundred fifty times during his reign. For thirteen years King Mohnyinthado devoted himself to such humanitarian works. Finally to have a permanent mark of his good work, he donated cultivated lands and other valuable materials for the maintenance of pagodas, temples, and monasteries.

4

Relations between the Myanmar Kings and the Shan Chiefs before the British Occupation

It is right for a government to pursue policies that secure internal stability and national unity and lead to external cordiality with neighbors or foreign powers. Any government that pursues a wrong or rigid policy that is incompatible with the internal situation, the people, and the country suffers a political setback. The same consequence also occurs when the external policy of the government does not conform with the external situation.

Relations between the Myanmar kings and the Shan chiefs before the British occupation were based on the policy laid down by the central court of Inwa (Ava) and implemented by the ministers, *bohmu mintha*, *sitke*, *nakhan*, and *saray* (secretary), who were sent to capitals of the *saohpa*. Other components of the central policy consisted of loyalty, allegiance, voluntary services, regular tributes, and taxes needed by the central government headed by the king.

Often the change of suzerains in the central court of Inwa affected the operation of the internal as well as the external policy. But sovereignty remained permanent unless disturbed by external war or foreign powers. In such times, officials who held the reins of administration had to be flexible to maintain the trend of social, economic, and political progress that had been achieved as vital interests of the state. In case a need arose for a change of policy because of a change of sovereign, the new policy should be better and sounder than the previous one.

The policy pursued by the Inwa court in its internal affairs was very feudalistic and rigid, but its implementation was very simple, in the modern sense. The main criterion of the central policy was to secure the loyalty of the subordinate chiefs, accompanied by annual tributes and voluntary services, supply of contingents in times of war and rebellion, and payment of taxes needed by the king for his domestic uses. In return, the subordinate chiefs got a *sanad*, or letter of appointment, from the king confirming their legitimacy as rulers of their states, along with regalia, titles, and finally the right to manage their internal affairs without interference from the central government.

However, such a pledge of allegiance was not considered enough. The chiefs had to send their sons and daughters to the court of Inwa as assurance of their good behavior at home. If the fathers' behavior at home was good and peaceful the children were trained to become acquainted with and acquire the Myanmar administrative system. That was also a way to establish an intimate bond between the families of the Shan chiefs and those of their suzerains. The Shan chiefs apparently appreciated such arrangements, because they found no sharp differences between the Myanmar royal administration and the Shan feudal administration. Some of the Shan chiefs took the king's palace as a model to build their own *haw* (residence), and adapted and practiced the court ceremonies of the royal court at Inwa to gain prestige in the feudal world of the Shan chiefs. In fact, the royal administration of the Inwa court became the prototype of the feudal administration of the Shan States. Whenever a Shan princess permanently attached to the royal palace was chosen to become a queen or royal consort it was considered a political triumph of the Shan feudal lord. Some of the Shan princes who got married to Myanmar princesses became royal servants at the central court. Royal titles were conferred on some who became provincial administrators in Myanmar proper. But in time of crisis and the insubordination of their fathers, those princes and princesses did not go unpunished. They were virtually hostages at the royal court and could be imprisoned, tortured, and even executed. Revolt by a subordinate chief against the central government was a serious offense and was ruthlessly suppressed. His property was confiscated, his state was devastated, and he was expelled or outlawed.

Not surprisingly, the royal government occasionally practiced a divide-and-rule policy as a political expediency. Feuds were fostered among different groups of feudal chiefs. Sometimes rival aspirants and claimants to the throne were left to settle their problems by force of arms, and the winner was confirmed as *saohpa* by royal patent only after paying a heavy tribute. Usually the Shan States were administered by the royal government through *saohpa*, *myosa*, and *ngwehkunmu* under the surveillance of Myanmar officials stationed at their capitals. But those officials stationed in the Northern Shan States were accountable directly to the royal court in Mandalay, and those who were in the Southern Shan States had their office in Mong Nai. Garrisons were also established at strategic points in the Shan States. The number of soldiers, guns, and ammunition was classified and fixed. Relations between Myanmar officials and the *saohpa* depended much on the personality of the resident officials as well as that of the chiefs. The royal court sometimes issued codes of conduct and regulations to be observed by the Myanmar officers. Dr. Richardson, who visited Mong Nai in the Southern Shan States in 1837, gave the following account of the *bohmu mintha* and *sitke daughee* stationed there.

> The Myanmar resident in Mong Nai in 1838 was Bo-hmu Mintha Meng Myat Boo (General Prince Meng Myat Boo, a half brother of the king's son of a Shan princess), the General who commanded at Melaun during the late war with us, and has been, since peace, governor of all the Shan countries from Mobie . . . His deputy . . . is the

> Setkay Daughee [*sitke dawgyi*], who has several officers under him; and there are at the court of each of the other Tsoboas [*saohpa*] two Tsetkays [*sitke*], also appointed from Ava. These Tsetkays, particularly the chief one, lord it over the Tsoboas; to him the chief authority belongs and all the external relations of the country [are] committed; and the royal orders are sent to Monay [Mong Nai], from whence they are forwarded by the Tsetkays; but the Monay Tsoboa has no authority to call any of the others. The lesser Tsoboas have no Tsetkays and are looked upon as merely Myosas.[1]

Regarding the manners and pretension of the *sitke*, Dr. Richardson writes:

> I sent the Shan interpreter and some of the most respectable of the traders to notify our arrival to the Tsoboa or Tsetkay Daughee and claim protection from the mob. They were stopped by the latter Chief . . . He questioned them in the most arrogant manner as to who they were, where from, and what they wanted . . . he replied that I should not see the Tsoboa until he was fully informed of our errand, that we had no right to enter the Kingdom by this road, . . . In the evening a Seray, or secretary, came out to my tent; he mentioned to the people outside, though not to me, that he had been sent by the Tsetkay. He was dressed in a handsome and heavy fur jacket with the hairy side in, though the thermometer in the tent was about 680 . . . He questioned me as to what I wanted here, and wished to know why I had not brought letters to the Tsetkay . . . I explained again the reason of my coming unprovided with letters to the Tsetkay &c., by the fact of the Commissioner of Moulmein not being aware of the existence of such an officer, &c. My visitor had served in the late war; he had been a sort of Aide-de-camp to the old General of the Shans, Maha Nay Myo, &c.; had taken part in the affair at Wattigam, and bore a part in Zimbike, when the old General was killed, with several of the Shan Tsoboas and two of the three wives of the Laygea (Lai Hka) Tsoboa who, dressed in male attire . . . to have done good service against our troops at the seven stockades near Rangoon.[2]

Dr. Richardson later met the *sitke*, who insisted that he must first go to *yuem-dau* (the *yum*, or a courthouse) to report his arrival. It was a place where all lesser chiefs assembled to get instruction from Meng Nay Myo Yadza Norata (the secretary). The *sitke* would take Dr. Richardson to the *saohpa*. But Dr. Richardson had to take off his shoes at the *yuem-dau*, which he refused. He was taken to the *lum* or *yuem* to see the *saohpa*. He was asked to sit at the *coontsen*, the flank about a foot high which surrounds the central pillars of the *yuem*. Inside the flank was the *sitke dawgyi*, Meng Myat Boo's representative and former governor in his absence of all the Shan States; the royal *sitke*. . . two *nakhan* and two *boo-dawgyi*, and also Meng Nay Myo, the secretary. Then the *sitke* began to lecture and accused Dr. Richardson of trespassing on the territory without an order from Meng Myat Boo and the king from the capital. His language became so arrogant that Dr. Richardson protested. The *saohpa* was not allowed to come inside the *coontsen*. He was to sit outside. When the interview with Dr. Richardson was over, then the *saohpa* was allowed to come in. The *saohpa* entered the *coontsen* with four gold *chattah* and about fifty or sixty men armed with muskets, *dha*, and spears, and a member carrying *thanleat*.[3]

The *saohpa* was about sixty-eight years of age. His manners were mild and gentlemanly. His *haw*, or palace, had a gilded roof of five stories; the *pyathat*, or royal spire, surmounted by a *hti* (*chathah*), or gilded iron ornament, so called; the hall where guests were received was about forty feet square excluding a large verandah which surrounded it; the center portion, a square of thirty feet, was raised about eighteen inches, with four rows of pillars, which supported the high roof, three in each row and ten feet apart; the innermost four of the two center rows were gilded, and the *yaza bolen* (throne), which was very handsome, was lower and better proportioned than those of the Siamese (Thai) Shan *saohpa*. The gold appeared burnished at the distance at which Dr. Richardson sat, though the art of burnishing was not known to the Burmans. At each side of the throne stood a large white muslin umbrella, furled with two rows of gold plate attached to fringes near the outer edge; on it were a small gold crown, a scepter, a chowree, an *ottar daun*, and the royal red velvet slippers, forming the five insignia of royalty (*meng hmeauk yaza ngaba*). The only other furniture in the room was a gilded chair and a common clumsy Burman bedstead. There might be about one hundred muskets ranged in different parts of the hall.

Just before the British occupation of the Shan States about ten thousand Myanmar soldiers were kept in the Shan States. There were about twelve *saohpa* at that time, four of them beyond the Than Lwin and the contingents they were required to furnish to the Myanmar government numbered to over ninety thousand men. While Dr. Richardson was in Mong Nai, an order came from the royal court of Inwa to supply about a thousand men to help suppress Prince Tharawady's rebellion. About three hundred fifty Myanmar families were in Mong Nai at that time. But they lived entirely on the support of the native people and *saohpa*. The Shan very often complained about the expenses they had to meet and of other oppressive acts committed by the Myanmar *sitke*.[4]

The *saohpa* also had absolute power over their subjects. Sometimes the feudal chief was also oppressive and imposed heavy taxes on the people especially when the royal court of Inwa demanded more money. Unable to bear the oppressive taxation, the people moved to the neighboring states. There were also times when the *saohpa* could not meet the demands of the royal court and resorted to armed rebellion against the royal government.

Mostly *ngwehkunmu* governed the Myelat area. They were responsible to the Myelat *wun*, who was directly appointed by the king. The people of Myelat, mostly Danus, were always treated by the Myanmar kings as tributaries and not as part of Myanmar proper.

It was often seen that the Myanmar kings married Shan princesses and made them queens or maids of honor. During the time of King Mindon, the Mong Nai queen was one of his majesty's favorite wives and for that the Mong Nai *saohpa* was given special privilege, and special insignia were offered to him. Cordial relationship between the Myanmar kings and the Shan chiefs depended much on their personal characters. King Mindon could establish a cordial relationship with many Shan chiefs because he carefully observed their autonomous rights and imposed reasonable taxes on them. Mindon Min also realized that he could rely much on the support of the Shan chiefs in internal and foreign wars. Most of the Shan chiefs were loyal to him. The Hsi Paw *saohpa* came down with his own contingents to help him when Mindon was faced with a palace rebellion against him (*Hsi Paw Chronicle*). He also understood the reliability of the Shan forces that had fought against the British during the Anglo-Myanmar wars of 1824 and 1852.

During this period, a durbar was very often held in Mong Nai between the *saohpa* and his ministers and provincial administrators to discuss state matters and also the question of succession when the ruler of a state died. Special durbars were held by order of the royal court on the death of a ruler and when orders from the royal court were to be explained to the Shan chiefs. These assemblages were held mostly in the *yum*. In this there was a long raised platform running from east to west in the center of the audience hall. At the western extremity of this, the *bohmu min* sat on a platform facing the east. In front of him sat the *wundauk*, who accompanied the *bohmu* when the latter paid his visit. Behind the *wundauk* sat the *sitke-gyi*, then the *nakhan* and other subordinate officials, and at the eastern side were ranged bodyguards. To the left of the *bohmu min* but below the platform was a square enclosure fenced with red cords. In this the *saohpa* arranged themselves at their pleasure or according to mutual agreement, the Mong Nai *saohpa* occupying the post of honor, that nearest to the *bohmu*. The *saohpa* was nearly in a line with the *wundauk*, a little to the left front of the *bohmu*. Beyond them and facing the *nahkan* were the *myosa*, also in a red-fenced enclosure, like that of the *saohpa*. Behind these enclosures were others, in which were gathered the *ahmat* and *myosa*—the officials of the *saohpa* behind the *saohpa* and those of the *myosa* behind their masters. The *ngwehkunmu*, if any were present, took rank with the *amatgyi* of a *saohpa*.

At the palace in Mandalay, the Shan chiefs sat straight in front of the throne behind the princes of the blood and the ministers of state, who took station right and left of the throne.[5]

The Myanmar kings of the Konbaung period seemed to have realized the importance of cooperation between the royal court and the chiefs of the Shan States, especially King Mindon, who was considered the most enlightened of the Myanmar kings. The two Anglo-Myanmar wars had made him realize the importance of national unity and the indispensable role of the Shan chiefs who voluntarily contributed contingent after contingent in time of foreign wars and internal rebellions. One way to bring cordiality between the king and the Shan chiefs was to confer titles on them for their loyalty, for their cooperation in time of peace, for their contribution of fighting forces in time of war, for their regular payment of tax money, and finally for their annual tributes to the royal treasury. In those days royal titles were conferred on both Myanmar and Shan chiefs as follows:

Titles bestowed on Myanmar kings

King Mindon	*Thiri pawara wizara nanda yathapandita Maha dhamma raza dhiraza.*
King Thibaw	*Thiri pawara wizara nanda yathatilawka dhipati pandita maha dhamma raza dhiraza.*

Titles bestowed on Shan *saohpa*

1. Shan State of Keng Hung, or Kyaingyungyi
   Zawti Nagara Maha Wuntha Thiri Thudhamma Yaza.
2. Shan State of Keng Tung, Keng Chang, or Kyaington, Kyaingchaing
   Pyinsala Ra-hta Maha Wuntha Dhamma Yaza.
3. Shan State of Mong Nai, or Mone,
   Kambawza Ra-hta Maha Wunthiri Pawara Thudhamma Yaza.
4. Shan State of Hsen Wi, or Theinni,
   Thiri Ra-hta Maha Wuntha Pawara Theta Thudhamma Yaza.
5. Shan State of Yawng Hwe, or Nyaung Shwe
   Kambawza Ra-hta Thiri Pawara Maha Wuntha Thudhamma Yaza.
6. Shan State of Mong Pai, or Mobye
   Kambawza Maha Wuntha Thiridhamma Yaza.
7. Shan State of Mong Pan, or Maing Pan
   Kambawza Thiri Maha Wuntha Dhamma Yaza.
8. Shan State of Lai Hka, or Legya
   Kambawza Ra-hta Maha Wuntha Thiri Thudhamma Yaza.
9. Shan State of Mong Pu, or Maing Pu
   Kambawza Ra-hta Wuntha Thiha Dhamma Yaza.
10. Shan State of Mawk Mai, or Mawkme
    Kambawza Rahta Maha Wuntha Thiri Yaza.
11. Shan State of Loi Long, or Taungbaing
    Maha Thiri Pappada Thura Yaza.
12. Shan State of Mong Mit, or Momeik
    Gantala Ra-hta Maha Thiri Wuntha Yaza.
13. Shan State of Hsawng Hsup, or Thaung Thut
    Mawriya Maha Wuntha Thiri Yaza.
14. Shan State of Waing Hso, or Wuntho
    Maha Wuntha Thiri Zeya Thohonbwa.
15. Shan State of Kale, or Theinnyin
    Mawriya Thiri Maha Wuntha Dhamma Yaza.
16. Shan State of Kanti, or Hkamti
    Maha Wuntha Durein Yaza.

Titles for *myosa*

17. Hsum Hsai, or Thonze
    Thiri Ra-hta Maha Wuntha Thudhamma Yaza.
18. Mong Pawn, or Maing Pun
    Thiri Maha Tho-nganbwa.
19. Sam Ka, or Saga
    Maha Yaza Tho-nganbwa.
20. Hai Long, or Helon
    Maha Zeya Tho-nganbwa.
21. Kantarawady, or Karenni
    Pappada Kyawgaung.
22. Hsi Paw, or Thibaw
    Kambawza Maha Wuntha.

Myook

23. Mong Long, or Maing Lon
    Nemyo-minhla Raza.

Ngwehkunmu

24. Maw Hson, or Bawsaing
    Nemyo-thiri Raza.
25. Poi La, or Pwehla
    Nemyo-thiri Raza.
26. Pang Tara, or Pindaya
    Nemyo-raza Nawrahta.

Da-kunhmu

27. Pong Ma, or Pon-mu, or Kun-mu
    Thiri Maha Raza Tho-nganbwa.[6]

When relations between the local chiefs and the central king were cordial and on good terms the people were happy because they could till their fields and produce food without disturbance. When the chiefs of near and far had good relations, they kept themselves busy complimenting each other and conferring titles, regalias, emblems of royalty, rich clothing or finery, and royal costumes according to their status and rank to open a new chapter of universal brotherhood among the chiefs of the feudal age.

The above is a summary picture of the relationship that existed between the royal government headed by the kings and the local government controlled by the Shan chiefs. Now, it would be necessary here to see the relationship between the local public or the Shan peoples and the king and also their own chiefs. The relationship between the central government and the local public did not seem to exist at all, because the king gave full authority to the Shan chiefs and his *bohmu mintha*, *sitke*, *nahkan*, and *saray-dawgyi* to rule on his behalf. The Shan chiefs wanted full autonomous rights to manage their own internal affairs. They did not seem to like interference from the king or any one from the central government. They wanted to have absolute power to rule over their subjects without any restraints or constraints from above or from outside. Their action against or for the public was not subject to any laws of justice or injustice. There might be customary laws or individual moral consideration, but a despotic ruler could set aside such laws. All this depended on the personality of the individual ruler. But the rulers were mostly despotic in their character, thinking, behavior, and outlook. Under the circumstances, the Shan people as a whole had to work hard, firstly to have enough food for themselves, secondly to fulfill their social and political obligations to regularly and punctually pay all kinds of taxes to their own chiefs, and finally to pay extra taxes to meet the demands from the royal government made through the Shan chiefs. Taxes were imposed more heavily when a coronation took place, when queens were promoted in their status, when princes and princesses had ear-boring ceremonies and rites of novitiation, when important state functions were performed, and finally when there was state emergency.

In addition to taxation, another burden called voluntary services was borne by the Shan people. They were called to give free services for whatever the chief of the state wanted to do. The worst side of voluntary services was the requirement to go to war either for the local chiefs or for the royal crown. Most of the Shan chiefs loved to fight each other. Fighting among them was like playing a card game. The same thing was true of the royal kings. There were always intrigues or plots in the struggle for power, rank, title, and prestige. In all these the people suffered, mostly the farmers who formed the backbone of feudal society and the most productive force of the country. What they hated most was war, whether it was among themselves or with foreign powers. When these domestic or foreign wars broke out, they had to abandon their farms and render military service without any payment. The service they contributed was not only free of charge; they had to provide their own rations and their own weapons because the weapons and rations given by the state or chiefs were not sufficient. Most of the farmers were not trained for warfare. Many were killed although it was not worth the sacrifice in domestic wars against their own people, their own relatives, their own kith and kin, in the interest of the members of the royal family and the family of the ruling class, the privileged class, the class of permanent exploiters.

The people, especially the farmers, were exploited generation after generation and they remained a permanently exploited class, throughout their lives during the centuries of feudal domination. No statistics of fallen soldiers, no pension, no compensation, no reward, no honor and no state funeral ceremonies, no meritorious *soon* (meal) ceremony was made to mark their noble sacrifices. In the long period of the feudal age there were no public schools, no welfare centers and no law courts where the people could complain about their hardship or injustice and redress their grievances. They were totally isolated, their ears closed, their eyes blind, and their lives miserable. Their knowledge of domestic affairs did not go far beyond the boundary of their rice field, and their knowledge of international affairs did not go far beyond the news of their chiefs making a state visit to the royal court in Mandalay. That was the lot of the Shan people at that time. They were drowned in the sea of despotism or shut up in the complete darkness of the feudal age. They suffered long under feudal rule, their senses numb, and their nerves inactive. They did not know what to do even when feudalism was removed and the dawn of democracy and modernization set in. They were still bewildered.

This gives the general picture of the network of relationships between the rulers and the ruled during the feudal period, which lasted for centuries. It provides us with bitter historical lessons about a past which should not be repeated and which should be avoided at all cost. We should not be blind to these historical facts, which weakened our national unity, national progress, and national sovereignty. We must have the courage to remedy our past mistakes.

FIGURE 4.1. Royal regalia offered to the Shan chiefs (*saohpa*) by the Myanmar king (*Hsi Paw Chronicle*)

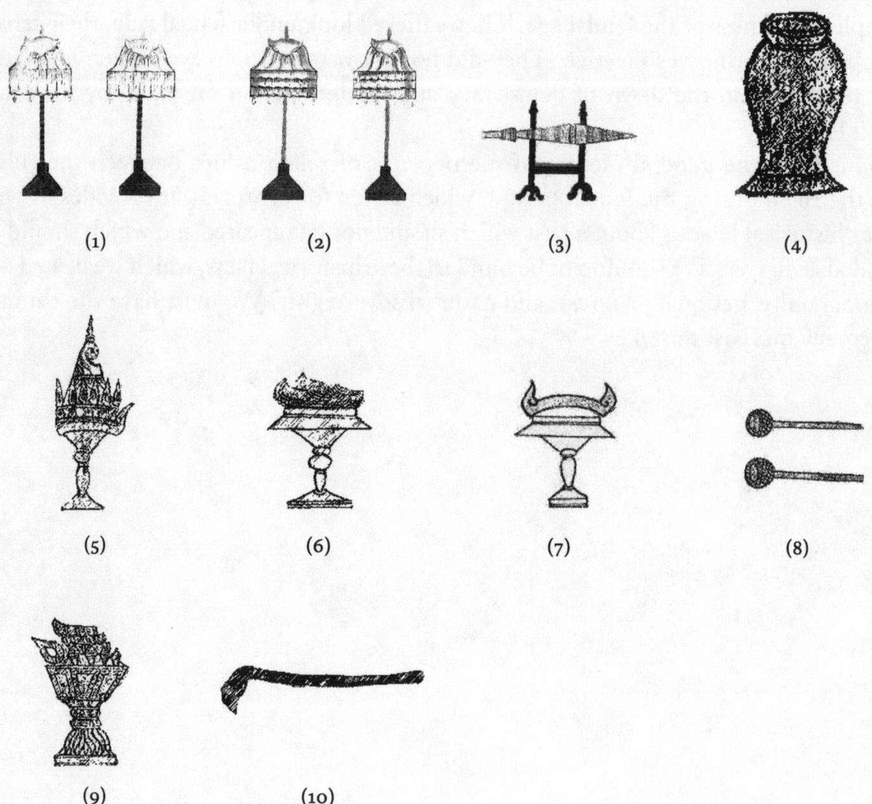

(1) Two royal umbrellas in red, with golden flowers decorating a tier of four banyan leaves, adorned in gold at the canopy and the pinnacle
(2) Royal white umbrella with thirty-six golden banyan leaves of three tiers adorned in gold at the canopy and pinnacle. The gilded shaft is five cubits (2.5 yards) long.
(3) Sheath of a royal dagger in white, adorned with rubies on the seven metal rings. Each of the two ends of its golden handle is also adorned with a ring of precious stones.
(4) Golden spittoon
(5) Distinctive headgear worn by Shan royalty adorned in fifteen gold pedals and fifteen neen tree leaves
(6) The gold foot-weary slippers
(7) Decorated golden frontlet
(8) Gold earplugs
(9) Betel cup depicting the twelve signs of the zodiac and decorated with rubies in three stripes, associated with teapot decorated with rubies in three stripes and three segments of betel rolls adorned with rubies in the fringes. It is a complete set of betel casket.
(10) Royal sword made of alloy of gold and copper put into a scabbard colored white and decorated with golden thread and inserted in a red bag of wooden cloth

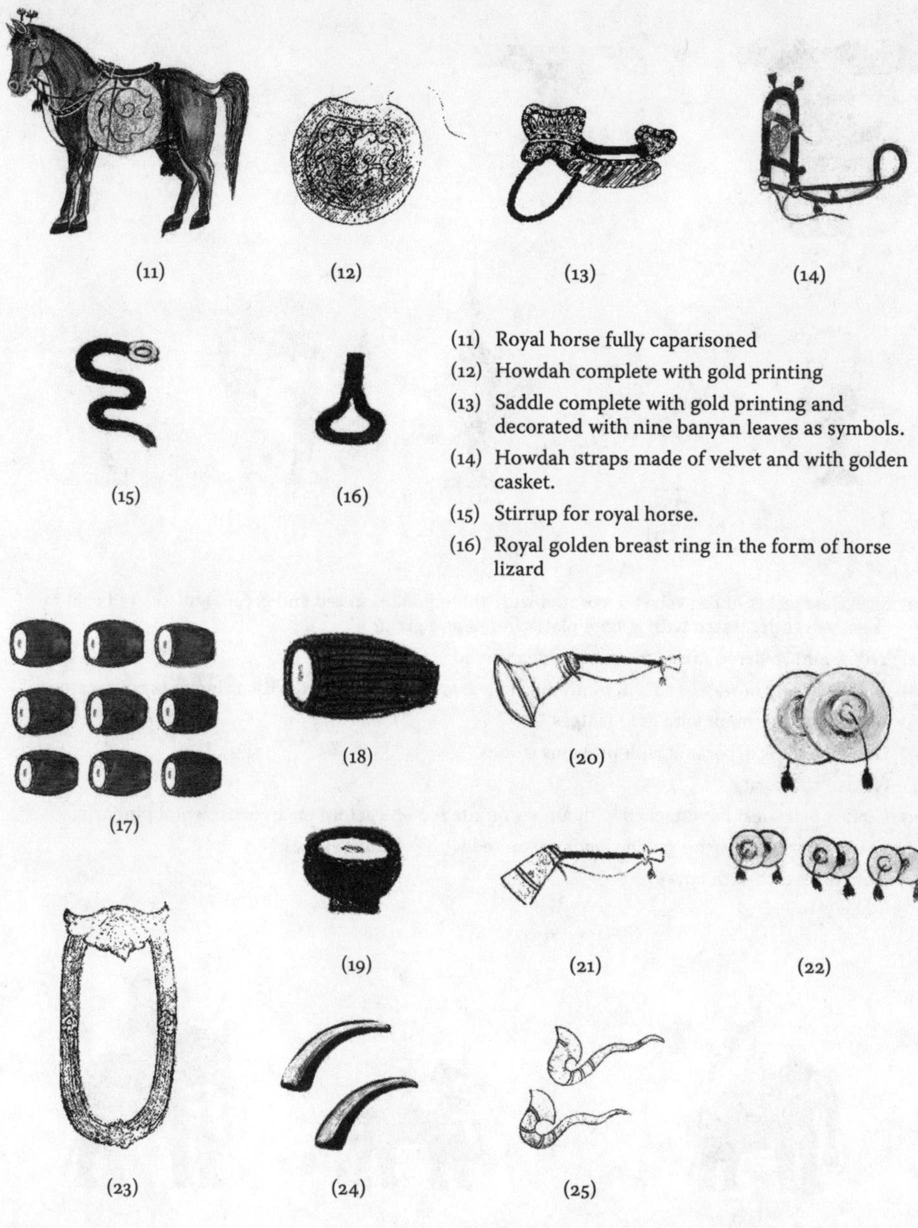

(11) Royal horse fully caparisoned
(12) Howdah complete with gold printing
(13) Saddle complete with gold printing and decorated with nine banyan leaves as symbols.
(14) Howdah straps made of velvet and with golden casket.
(15) Stirrup for royal horse.
(16) Royal golden breast ring in the form of horse lizard

(17) Nine red drums
(18) Small drum
(19) Short drum
(20) Large silver oboe
(21) Small silver oboe
(22) One large pair of bronze cymbals, and three small pairs
(23) Royal sash with fifteen rings and a necklace decorated with rubies in the middle and precious stones in the fringe
(24) Two horns
(25) Two bugles/whistles

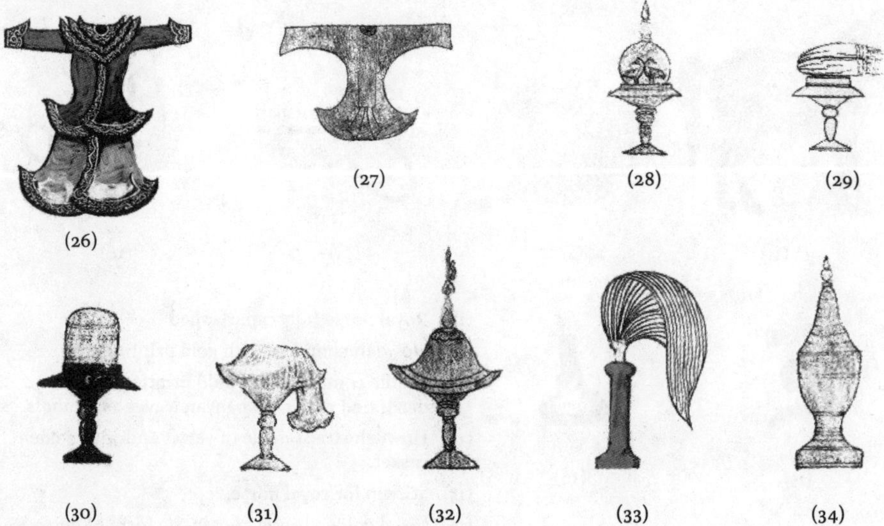

(26) (27) (28) (29) (30) (31) (32) (33) (34)

(26) Sleeveless jacket in red velvet decorated with golden plates in red and green. Full-skirted coat in green velvet decorated with golden plates in red and green
(27) Yellow embroidered dress, made of golden thread
(28) Golden casket in wax in a form of mythical bird which is decorated with a ring of precious stones.
(29) White royal garment with gold fringes
(30) Gold betel box decorated with precious stones
(31) Golden royal hat
(32) Golden palm-leaf hat attached with amber on the top and set up on an ornamental pinnacle.
(33) Yak tail fly-whisk with a golden shaft decorated with precious stones
(34) Gold betel dish with cover

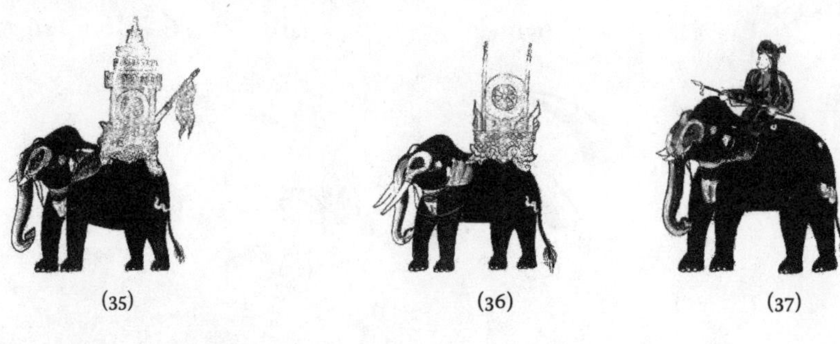

(35) (36) (37)

(38)

(35) Elephant howdah decorated in gold and diamonds at top; flag stand
(36) *Kadaung* – elephant saddle
(37) Royal female elephant
(38) Royal young male elephants

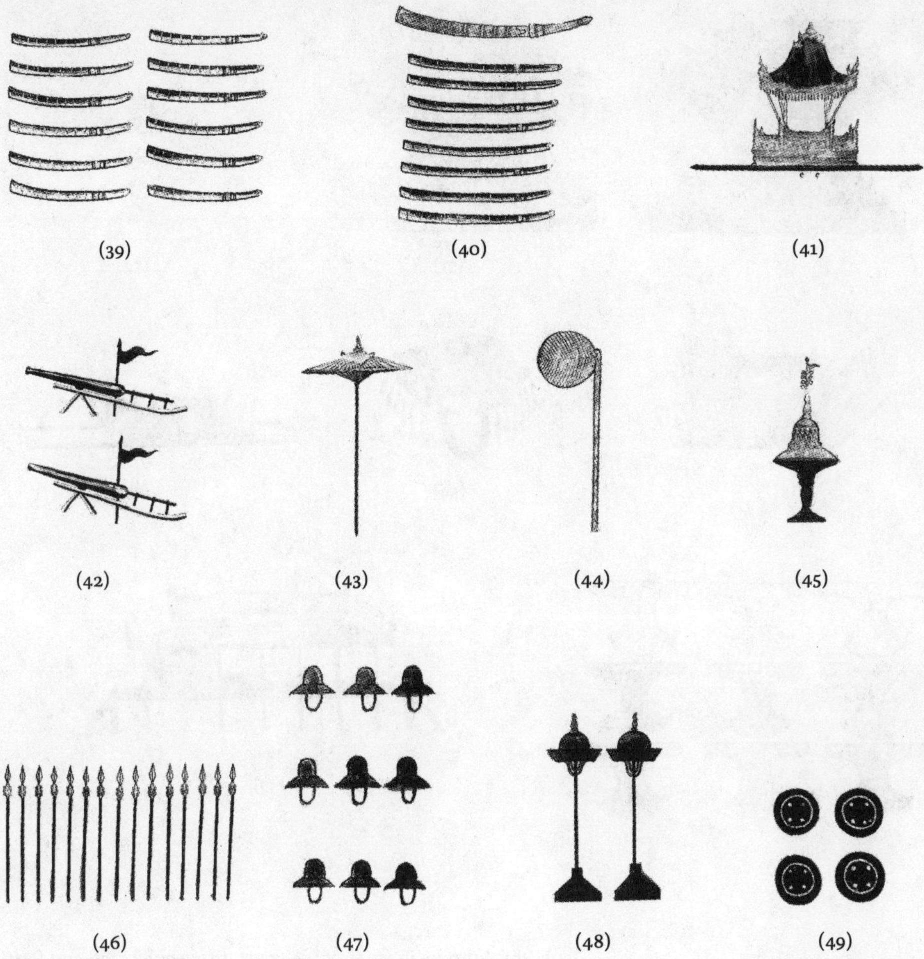

(39) Twelve royal swords in golden frames
(40) White scabbard with a flat handle
(41) Litter
(42) Two guns
(43) Royal golden umbrella
(44) Royal golden fan
(45) Golden bonnet/cap with fifteen gold decorative upright leaves adorned with two lines of precious stones
(46) Sixteen spear-men from Mong Nai Troop
(47) Nine helmets
(48) Two royal Kyaing staffs with golden top
(49) Four golden shields

(50) 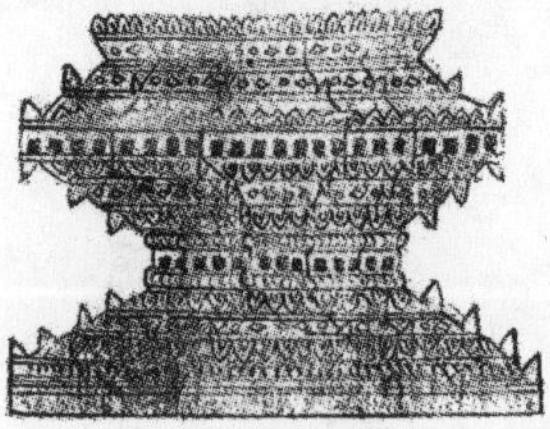 (51)  (52)

(53)  (54)  (55)

(56)  (57)

(58)

(50) Royal throne in front of the court, three cubits tall and four cubits wide, painted in reddish color

(51) Royal throne in front of the *haw* is three cubits tall and four cubits wide, adorned with gold

(52) Royal seal

(53) Couch with head-rest decorated in golden color

(54) Golden palanquin with velvet whish

(55) Golden palanquin

(56) Nine velvet gowns/robes decorated like the skin of pangolin

(57) Court with two-tiered successive roofs, with terracotta tiles, painted in reddish color inside

(58) Walls of a *haw* in brick, 150 tas (1050 cubits), with four gates

5

Political Situation in the Shan States before the British Occupation

The political situation in the Shan States after the death of King Mindon and before the British occupation was very chaotic. His son and successor, King Thibaw, was very weak and unable to unite the chief ministers who were so divided in their views about almost every issue of state either domestic or foreign. Moreover, the palace was infected with all sorts of intrigues hatched by the ambitious queens, princes, princesses, and ministers. The key player in these plots was Queen Supayalat. She was very ambitious, and to secure her husband's ascension to the throne she masterminded plot after plot to eliminate her opponents. King Thibaw was completely under her thumb, and she became the chief director of state affairs. Thibaw's role as king gradually diminished and the central government lost the dynamism to exert its power throughout the country. The cordial relationship between the king and the Shan chiefs that had existed since the time of King Mindon was terminated, and none of the ministers at the royal court or the king took interest in mending the situation. The relations went from bad to worse. The only interest cherished by the royal court in that critical period was exaction of more and more money, taxes, and tribute from the Shan chiefs. The mismanagement of state affairs was another cause for the deterioration of the economic and political situation in Myanmar. Revolts against the central authority took place in the Shan States.

The Mong Nai chief was the first to rise against King Thibaw. Mong Nai was the largest, wealthiest, and the most powerful state of southern Shanland. Its capital had been the residence of the king's military representatives. King Mindon took much care not to displease the chief of Mong Nai, preserving a cordial relationship between the two rulers. King Mindon married the daughter of the Mong Nai chief and she became one of his favorite queens. Through her, the political position of the Mong Nai chief at the royal court became prominent. But the situation took a sharp turn when King Thibaw took over. The relationship between the king and the chief deteriorated with the imprisonment of the Mong Nai queen by King Thibaw. More taxes were demanded from the Shan chief, and Mong Nai State was dismembered by giving Mong Hsat to

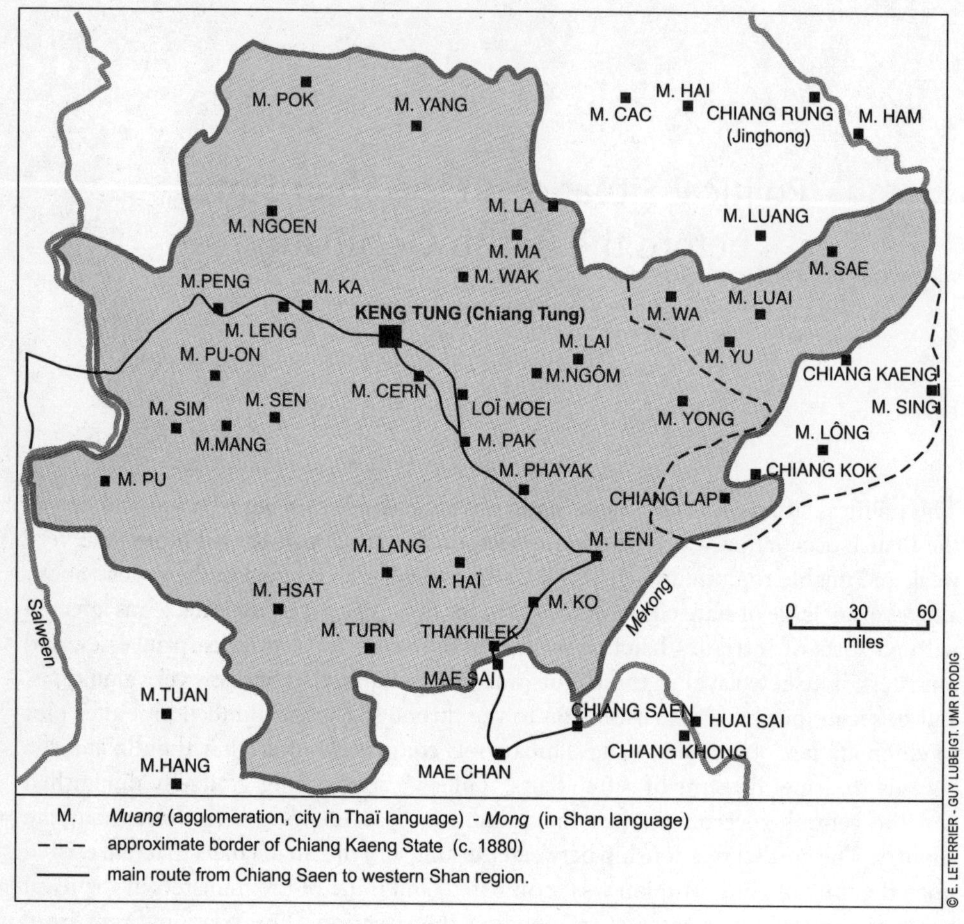

MAP 15. Keng Tung State, c. 1880

the chief of Mong Pan. Again the district of Mong Hsat that belonged to Mong Nai reverted to the chief of Mawk Mai. Up to this time the *saohpa* of Mong Nai, Sao Hkun Kyi, did not lose his patience, still acknowledging the suzerainty of King Thibaw.[1] The relationship between the two rulers was further strained over the appointment of the *myosa* of Keng Tawng, a substate of Mong Nai, against the wishes of the Mong Nai chief. The displeasure of the Mong Nai chief was aggravated by the appointment of Twet Nga Lu, who was antagonistic to the Mong Nai chief, as regent to the young *myosa* of Keng Tawng.

Twet Nga Lu was a man of low birth and a son of a fisherman who lived in Ta Kaw by the side of the Than Lwin River. He became a monk and then went to Mandalay. While in Mandalay he committed a flagrant sin with a woman of the Mong Nai family, for which he was unfrocked. To settle all these controversies, the Hluttaw (parliament) ordered the Mong Nai chief in November 1883 to present himself at the royal court in Mandalay. Knowing what would happen to him, he delayed his departure. Fearing his flight from his state, the Myanmar *sitke* and his soldiers tried to capture the Shan chief by force. But Hkun Kyi struck first by surrounding and attacking the Myanmar garrison. Three volleys were fired, followed by fierce fighting. Four hundred Myanmar soldiers were killed, including *sitke* Alon Myowun, and only about one hundred escaped to Yawng Hwe.[2]

A punitive force was sent to Mong Nai. Other Shan *saohpa* from the north and from the south were ordered to march with the Myanmar force with their own levies and contingents.[3]

The neighboring chieftains who were related to him and who shared a common hatred against King Thibaw for his aggressive measures against them joined the Mong Nai *saohpa*. They were *saohpa* and *myosa* from Lawk Sawk, Mong Nawng, Mong Hsat, and Mong Pyein. The contest was unequal and the combined royal force was too powerful for them. The Mong Nai *saohpa* and his comrades fled to the Trans-Salween state of Keng Tung, where they were well accepted and well treated by the Keng Tung chief, Sao Hkam Hpa.[4]

The capital with its multitude of beautiful religious monuments, monasteries, and temples was razed by the royal army. For siding with Mong Nai, Lawk Sawk was taken and given to Yawng Hwe. Mong Nawng and other states were ravaged as punishment for helping Mong Nai.[5]

The Keng Tung chief had severed his allegiance to King Thibaw, before the arrival of the fugitive chiefs, over the question of appointing the Keng Hung chief by the royal court against the nominee of the Keng Tung chief. Upon this the *saopha* of Keng Tung, Sao Hkun Hti, executed the Myanmar political officer in 1882, including his guards numbering about thirty. The Keng Tung *saohpa* and his forces marched on Keng Hung to depose the Myanmar nominee and establish his candidate as ruler of Keng Hung.[6]

The political situation west of the Than Lwin River was anarchic. Usurpers and de facto rulers ran most of the states west of the Than Lwin. Myanmar forces were withdrawn and disappeared after the British occupation of Mandalay, leaving the warlike chiefs of the hills to shape their own destiny. Fighting between and within the states went on, accompanied by the depredations of a number of gangs of robbers, looters, dacoits, and warring groups. Communications were cut off and trade stopped. Both the winning and the losing side conscripted farmers. Plantations were left unattended, rice fields were abandoned, and farmers did not know who would reap the crops. Villages and towns were deserted. People moved to safer areas and many went to settle in Laos, Thailand, and the British territories in Lower Myanmar.

In the meanwhile, the fugitive chiefs led by the Keng Tung and Mong Nai *saohpa* formed a confederacy with a politico-military objective to dethrone King Thibaw and enthrone a more benevolent prince in his place. They established a Confederacy military force with each chief contributing levies and contingents. The political and military situation was quite favorable at that time for the Shan *saohpa* to set up an independent Shan state with one of them as king, but it was far from their thinking and they did not seem to entertain this idea at all.[7] They preferred having a sovereign lordship over them, having been accustomed to it, and they did not want the sovereignty to be disturbed or the monarchical system discontinued. All they wanted was a much more benevolent king than a tyrant. They preferred having their traditional right to manage their internal affairs without interference either from the royal court or from their military representatives stationed at their capitals.

The leaders of the Confederacy seemed to have lost track of political developments in Upper Myanmar. They should have paid attention to the news of the dethronement of Thibaw and his exile to India and should have known that they would have to deal with the British politically and militarily, and not King Thibaw. They should have reanalyzed their military and political strategy to cope with the new situation. But they did not; instead they went ahead to look for a new Myanmar prince able to lead the Confederacy armed force.

Finally, the secret agent of the Keng Tung chief found a Myanmar prince of royal blood, the Limbin prince, who was living in Mawlamyaing. He was invited to Keng Tung to lead the Confederacy and he left Mawlamyaing in October 1885. Who was the Limbin prince? He was an illegitimate son of Einshehmin, who was killed in the palace rebellion of 1866. His mother was a dancing girl.[8] The young prince was taken into the king's household and survived the massacre. He shaved his head, wore the yellow robe, disguised as a noble monk, and escaped to Yangon. The British government protected and educated him in St. John's College. He was appointed magistrate of a small town in Tenasserim. But he was later relieved of his post for incompetence. He was also found inciting rebellion in Upper Myanmar. He was finally given a pension and permitted to live in Mawlamyaing.

The Limbin prince got news of the British occupation of Mandalay and King Thibaw's dethronement and exile to India, but he kept it to himself. He might have thought that should the British reestablish the monarchy and install a king it could possibly be him. But it did not come out as he calculated. He arrived at Keng Tung on December 10, 1885. A general meeting with the fugitive chiefs from the Trans-

Salween States was held. At that time the active members of the Confederacy were Mong Nai, Lawk Sawk, Mawk Mai, Mong Pawn, Mong Nawng, Mong Sit, Keng Hkam, Mong Ping, Hsa Htung, Ho Pong, and the Myaelat principalities. They laid down the following objectives:

1. To establish the Limbin prince as an independent sovereign.
2. To uphold the pledge of allegiance to the Limbin prince.
3. To restore the states and territories from the hands of the de facto rulers to their de jure rulers.
4. To take every measure to withdraw the Myanmar force from the Shan States.
5. To persuade the remaining Shan chiefs to join the Confederacy of their own free will and, if necessary, by force of arms.
6. To restore peace, trade, and religion to the Shan States.
7. To achieve unity under the new suzerain authority and to quell anarchy in the Shan States.
8. To strengthen the armed forces of the Confederacy. Member states were required to contribute levies or contingents.
9. To set up a temporary palace for the Limbin prince in the fertile valley of the Tampak at Manyin, east of the Yawng Hwe Lake.[9]

The Limbin prince also made a solemn promise that if he became king he would not exact taxes unduly from the Shan chiefs, would respect the autonomous rights of the Shan chiefs, and would agree to the new rule of the chiefs paying obeisance to the king only once in three years.

At the same time that the Limbin prince became the head of the Confederacy, the British occupied Mandalay, and King Thibaw was dethroned and exiled to India. Hence the challenge that was originally planned against Thibaw had to be diverted against the British. In that case what would be the stand of the Shan chiefs? The Limbin prince knew well the fighting ability of the British forces and their training and equipment. He was for a while caught in the horns of a dilemma and he seemed to have lost direction, so that he could only make an ambiguous appeal to his forces to resist the British. The Shan chiefs, on the other hand, assumed that it would take the British a long time to pacify Upper Myanmar and would have no time to invade the Shan States as some hardliner chiefs like Lawk Sawk and Mong Nai thought. The *saohpa* believed that the British, whoever they were, were also usurpers of the Myanmar throne and were to be driven out of the country.

The Limbin Confederacy war machine started to roll across the Than Lwin in 1886 with the aim of taking back states and lands from the usurpers as soon as possible. It first invaded Mong Nai, the Mong Nai and Lawk Sawk *saohpa* taking the lead. Mong Nai was easily recaptured and the usurper Twet Nga Lu driven out. Twet Nga Lu fled to his old native land Keng Tawng and started forming an anti-Confederacy group. Lawk Sawk was also quickly and easily taken back from the protégé of the Yawng Hwe chief. The Yawng Hwe chief became the archenemy of Sao Waing, the chief of Lawk Sawk,

FIGURE 5.1. The Limbin prince. (Ni Ni Myint 1983, 116)

for taking his state in his absence. Lai Hka, Mong Kung, and Kehsi Mansam joined the Twet Nga Lu group by the order of the royal court of Mandalay. Some de facto rulers also grouped around Twet Nga Lu and remained neutral, waiting for the British to come to their rescue. The Confederacy forces, led by the chiefs of Mong Nai and Lawk Sawk, reached Mong Nai on March 21, 1886, and the Limbin prince and his force arrived on April 8, 1886. The prince sent letters calling on other Shan chiefs to join the Confederacy. The remaining Myelat *ngwe-hkunmu* joined and the Confederacy became more powerful and its position was much strengthened.[10] It attacked Keng Tawng where Twet Nga Lu had his resistance base. Keng Tawng was easily overrun and Twet Nga Lu fled to Lai Hka to regroup his soldiers, assisted by the chiefs of Lai Hka, Mong Kung, and Kehsi Mansam. The Confederacy forces then directed their attacks on Lai Hka, Mong Kung, and Kehsi Mansam. These three states were destroyed, razed from end to end, as punishment for siding with the Myanmar court.[11] The Confederacy forces scored one victory after another, the credit for these successes going to Sao Hkun Hti of Mong Pawn. Sao Hkun Hti had a military brain and was a good fighter and marksman. In addition, he also had organizing ability and diplomatic skills. Mong Pawn was a small state situated between Lai Hka and Taunggyi, and Sao Hkun Hti was ambitious to expand his state like the other chiefs.

Mawk Mai, taking advantage of the victory scored by the Confederacy forces, encroached on Mong Pan. The Mong Pan chief, unable to defend himself, fled across the Than Lwin. His capital was pillaged and many villages were destroyed and deserted.

Yawng Hwe was the only state left outside the Confederacy. The Yawng Hwe chief was asked many times to join the victorious group, but he refused. Yawng Hwe had an internal problem. In the old days, it was very pro-Myanmar and its chief, Sao Maung, was brought up at the royal court during King Mindon's reign. After the British occupation of Mandalay, Sao Maung and his followers came back to the Shan States, but he was ambushed on the way by the Lawk Sawk troops and wounded. He retired back to Myanmar and authorized his brother Sao On to administer Yawng Hwe on his behalf. Another half brother, Sao Chit Su, also made a claim to the Yawng Hwe throne, but Sao On easily defeated him. With the help of the neighboring chiefs of Sam Ka, Maw Nang, Hsa Mong Hkam, and Pang Mi, Sao On was able to withstand the attack of the Limbin Confederacy forces.[12]

Having heard the news of the British occupation of Mandalay and Upper Myanmar, Sao On chose to ally himself with the British rather than with the Confederacy. He believed that it would be difficult for the Confederacy forces to beat off the British. While withstanding the threats of the Confederacy, he sent a request for help to the deputy commissioner stationed in Kyaukse in May 1886:

> Let the hereditary Shan chiefs be maintained. Let us come under your protection. Attempts have been made and are being made by ambitious chiefs to set up Burmese princes in their name to dominate the rest of the states . . . Assure us of protection . . . and tell us what you want to do.[13]

This was the state of affairs in the Southern Shan States up to May 1886. Now let us turn our attention to the Northern Shan States and see what was happening politically. The four prominent states in the north were Hsi Paw, Hsen Wi, Mong Mit, and Tawng Peng. As in the south, there were intrigues and power struggles. The main players on the political chessboard of the north were Sao Hkun Hseng, chief of Hsi Paw State, and Hkun Sang Ton Hong, chief of Hsen Wi State. Tawng Peng and Mong Mit were little disturbed, except for a small factional strike for the control of a minor chief.

Following the fall of Mandalay, the Myinsaing prince and the Hsen Wi chief Naw Mong were released from prison. They quickly went up to the Shan hills to organize a resistance movement against the British. The Myinsaing prince sent orders to various chiefs in the Northern Shan States to contribute levies and contingents and to rise against the British.

The prince, knowing that the Hsi Paw chief, Hkun Hseng, was an influential leader, wrote to him requesting arms, ammunition, and soldiers:

> In former times a Ceylonese monarch, Duttagamani, crushed the Tamil invaders to prevent the downfall of the religion.
>
> I shall wage a ruthless war against the heretic English Kalas, so that I may be able to save my religion, preserve the Royal Dynasty, and secure the happiness of the people. Therefore the Sawbwagyi (Saohpa Long or Great Saohpa) is directed to bring men and arms.[14]

Most of the prominent chiefs of the Northern Shan States did not show much interest in the resistance movement against the British or in the reestablishment of either Limbin or Myinzaing as their national sovereign. Their interest was the internal reconsolidation of their own states.

Let us look at the role played by Hkun Hseng in the politics of the Northern Shan State. Hkun Hseng was the de jure ruler of Hsi Paw State. But he was absent from his state during the rule of King Thibaw. The imposition of heavy taxation on him by King Thibaw and his refusal to send his contingents to march against Hkun Kyi of Mong Nai earned him a bad reputation and he was blacklisted by the royal court. To avoid direct confrontation with King Thibaw, which he thought unavoidable, he fled to Lower Myanmar to take refuge under the British, but he did not submit himself to their authority. He lived in Yangon as a good citizen but maintained himself as a prince in exile and, as legitimate chief of Hsi Paw, claimed the traditional prerogative rights and the power of life and death over his subjects. He also kept a body of hereditary retainers. While living in Yangon, he was haunted psychologically by the conspiracy of King Thibaw. One day, he shot two of his retainers to death and for that he was arrested and tried before the Recorder in Yangon and sentenced to death. Later the sentence was commuted and he was released on condition that he left British territory. He left and made his way to the Karenni State, where his very close friend, Sawlapaw, chief of state, supplied him with funds, arms, and men. With his small contingent he returned to Hsi Paw. When he arrived in March 1886, he found his hometown in ruins, his ministers in hiding, and his enemies encamped. Naw Mong, the Hsen Wi chief who had been imprisoned in Mandalay, was released when the British occupied Mandalay. He joined the Myinzaing resistance camp. By order of the Myinzaing prince, Naw Mong became chief of Hsi Paw just before Hkun Hseng arrived back. Hkun Hseng viewed him as a usurper and, recruiting more soldiers and his own men who were still loyal to him, established himself as the *saohpa* of Hsi Paw in July.

After firmly consolidating his old state, Hkun Hseng turned his attention to absorbing the neighboring states of Hsum Hsai and Mong Long in the west and Mong Tung in the south. Taking advantage of the chaotic situation, and before the British could send their force, he invaded the three states, which all fell before him. Then he appealed to the British for recognition as chief of Hsi Paw, Hsum Hsai, Mong Long, and Mong Tung.[15]

Hkun Hseng did not join the Limbin group or the Myinzaing group. He did not believe that these two camps could beat the British, whose army was powerful and unbeatable. He adopted a policy of nonconfrontation with the British. He and the chief of Yawng Hwe, Sao On, would be considered pro-British Shan chiefs. Moreover, Hkun Hseng felt he owed great gratitude to the British for commuting his death sentence and for releasing him to leave British territory and return to Hsi Paw. He wrote the following letter to the chief commissioner on November 16, 1886:

> Thanks to the Chief Commissioner and the Government of the Queen Empress, I was enabled to return to Hsi Paw . . . I remember this act of kindness by night as well as by day. I have been trying to persuade the other Shan chiefs to abstain from warfare among themselves and to accept the rule of the British Government.[16]

Sir J. George Scott, in an article published in *The Asiatic Quarterly Review*, July 1869, gave the following remark:

> The Saohpa was ambitious but shrewd; he was absolutely unscrupulous, but his misfortune had taught him craft. He held back just long enough to avoid being

> premature in a declaration of business to British authority, and yet sent in letters early enough to claim the credit of spontaneity, when it was determined that the peace of Burma, not less than that of the Shan States, bound the British Government to take over the suzerainty of the country. The Saohpa himself paid a visit to Mandalay, was present at the New Year's parade. There and obtained from the enthusiasm of the moment and glamour of his eventful career, terms which were perhaps more liberal than justice demanded.[17]

After hearing the news of the occupation of Mandalay by the British, Hkun Hseng went to Mandalay to make direct contact with the British and was exempted from tribute for ten years. He came back to Hsi Paw and brought G. E. Bridges with him as his adviser. He also agreed to accept a British adviser to manage his domestic affairs. He visited England in 1893 to have his eyes treated. During his stay there he was given the honor of being presented to Her Majesty, the queen. He was given the CIE title and became a member of council of the government of Myanmar.

Next to Hsi Paw on the east was Hsen Wi State, one of the biggest northen Shan states. For nearly a quarter of a century, this state had its own political turmoil. Fighting erupted between the chief of Hsen Wi and his subordinate, Hkun Sang Hai, a militia leader who returned from Keng Tung. He led a military contingent to Keng Tung to help defend it against an attack by the Siamese. Sang Hai was a good fighter. He won the battle over the Siamese and came back to Hsen Wi. Misunderstanding and suspicion arose between Naw Hpa, the chief of Hsen Wi, and Sang Hai, the chief of militia, over the murder of Ahmat Seng Ting Kam and his seven sons. Ahmat Seng Ting Kam was the grandfather of Sang Hai.[18]

They fought each other for a long period of time. Finally Naw Hpa was defeated and the throne of Hsen Wi fell into the hands of Sang Hai, who became the chief. For his defeat, Naw Hpa was summoned to Mandalay and jailed. The royal court sent its *sitke* one after another, with Myanmar forces but they were unable to get into Hsen Wi. They made their headquarters at Lashio and could control only a few villages around it. The Mandalay king had no choice but to issue orders to other Shan chiefs to combine their forces and march on Hsen Wi to dethrone Sang Hai. Instead of challenging the combined forces, Sang Hai withdrew into the wild hills of the Wa States. Naw Hpa was reinstated as chief of Hsen Wi and remained so some years. But Hsen Wi was badly ruined and divided into several substates.

Sang Hai adopted the title of *hkun* (lord) and became Hkun Sang Hai. He reappeared and took control of the northern portion of Hsen Wi. The southern part of Hsen Wi came under the rule of another leader named Sang Awe, later known as Pookchok, leader of administration. Naw Hpa, the legitimate ruler of Hsen Wi, took refuge in Mongsi. For his defeat by his enemies he was again summoned to Mandalay for another explanation. Knowing what would happen to him, he did not go down to Mandalay. Instead, he sent his son, Naw Mong, who was imprisoned on behalf of his father.

Hkun Sang Hai began to consolidate his position in northern Hsen Wi. He also recruited another rebel leader named Hkun Sang Ton Hong, whose fighting ability excelled any rebel in that area. Hkun Sang Hai married off his daughter to Hkun Sang Ton Hong to confirm his loyalty to him. Hkun Sang Ton Hong's former name was Sang Yon Ko. He was born in the village called Ton Hong near the Than Lwin River. Like Hkun Sang Hai, he was a born fighter and a good strategist. Because of his excellent fighting ability, Hkun Sang Hai made him his lieutenant. When Hkun Sang Hai died, Hkun Sang Ton Hong took his place and became the most influential politico-military leader of Hsen Wi. Hkun Sang Ton Hong could easily take over the throne of Hsen Wi. By the time Mandalay fell, he had firmly established himself on the Hsen Wi throne and proclaimed himself chief of the state.

Naw Mong, whom Thibaw put into prison, was released after the fall of Mandalay. He made his way back to Hsen Wi to obtain his throne back from Hkun Sang Ton Hong. Although Naw Mong could organize some fighting men from Lashio and Mong Yai, he could not drive Hkun Sang Ton Hong out of Hsen Wi. Instead Hkun Sang Ton Hong dealt his opponent Naw Mong a final blow. Pookchok's forces were also driven down to the southern part of Hsen Wi, and Hkun Sang Ton Hong nearly reached the point of complete victory over his enemies before the British intervened. A truce was secured. Negotiations between the two opponent chiefs and other elderly Shan took place under British mediation. Finally all agreed to split Hsen Wi State into two. The northern part of the territories was placed under the rule of the chief of Hsen Wi with its capital Hsen Wi. The southern territories were put under the chief of Mong Yai with its capital Mong Yai. Hkun Sang Ton Hong was recognized as *saohpa* of Hsen Wi and Naw Mong was confirmed as *saohpa* of Mong Yai. The political chaos that had developed since Mindon's time finally came to a temporary end with the intervention of the British.

6

A Military Expedition to the Shan States

The chief commissioner followed closely the news of political developments in the Northern and Southern Shan States and became convinced that a military expedition was necessary to quell the chaotic situation. So a plan for a military expedition was drawn up and all military and political officers accompanying the expedition were thoroughly instructed what to do and what not to do. Being the nearest crisis, the problem in Hsi Paw was tackled first. Since the fall of King Thibaw the trade route to the Northern Shan States had been blocked because of the infestation of robbers and dacoits plus the anti-British activities organized by some princes, especially the Myinsaing prince and his followers. The prince had been organizing some of the local chiefs to rise up against the British. Moreover, the chief of Hsi Paw had been consolidating his position with the plan to absorb the neighboring small states of Hsum Hsai in the west, Mong Long in the northwest, and Mong Tung in the southeast.

In the Southern Shan States news of the Limbin Confederacy crossing the Than Lwin to capture Mong Nai and lay siege to Yawng Hwe, and a frantic request from Sao On, the Yawng Hwe chief, reached the chief commissioner, who was convinced that a military expedition was necessary to rescue Sao On and to solve the Limbin problem.

After making a political assessment of the situation, the chief commissioner, Sir Charles Bernard, expressed his view:

> Until we act, the interstate fighting and the inroads of the Limbin prince will not abate . . . we shall very soon cause defeat and deposal of gathering render the Limbin prince . . . the longer we delay, the more chance there will be of the parties hostile to the British . . . and of the Shan powers being turned actively against us . . .[1]

A column of troops under Colonel E. Stedman with Civil Officer H. Thirkell was immediately sent to Hsum Hsai in November 1886. Gangs of robbers and bands of dacoits that had been dominating the routes to Hsi Paw were quickly cleared and anti-British activities were suppressed. Hkun Hseng, the chief of Hsi Paw, also sent his levies to help clear the trade route to Mandalay. After a few weeks, caravans of pack mules and pack bullocks carrying goods were streaming down to Mandalay to reestablish business between the Ayeyarwady (Irrawaddy) Plain and the Northern Shan States. The chief of Hsi Paw, Hkun Hseng, went down to Mandalay in January 1887, and was received with pomp and grandeur. He acknowledged the British suzerainty, and for that was rewarded a remission of tribute for ten years and also promised a supply of arms and ammunition when in need to deal with his opponents and the anti-British elements. The absorption of Hsum Hsai, Mong Long, and Mong Tung into Hsi Paw State was also approved. Naw Mong, the usurper of Hsi Paw, and his ally, the Myinsaing prince, and his followers were driven out and peace was restored.

After that the chief commissioner turned his attention to the southern problem. He took the war theater in the Southern Shan States more seriously and more carefully. The policy of the olive branch, carrot and stick was to be applied with great care. But he was convinced that the method was simpler than the pacification of Upper Myanmar. In Upper Myanmar the British had to deal with a disintegrated mass and it was much more difficult. But in the Shan States the British had to deal with the Shan chiefs. If the Shan chiefs could be persuaded to acknowledge the British supremacy the whole problem could be solved without a fight and a saving of men, lives, and money.

To implement this program, efficient and farsighted political officers with military and administrative experiences were required. The first choice went to Arthur Heddings Hildebrand, deputy commissioner of Tharawady district in Lower Myanmar. He had experience in dealing with the native people of Karenni State when he was a member of the mission to demarcate the boundary between Karenni and the Shan State of Mong Pai.

As for the assistant political officer, James George Scott was chosen. He was about thirty-five years old with average height and a commanding manner. Being a teacher at St. John's College, he had experience dealing with people of various walks of life. He had a keen interest in the study of people, their nature, culture, and beliefs. He had already written a book on Myanmar life and custom. He was impetuous, courageous, and aggressive, but he was considerate. He was also sharp and quick in making decisions as well as executing them. He was also an administrator scholar. He was highly known for his voluminous writing, the *Gazetteer of Upper Burma and the Shan States*.

The date for the expedition was set on January 16, 1887. The route to the Southern Shan States was very difficult due to the rugged terrain and thick forests. But Colonel Stedman decided to take the shortest route which passed through Kyatsakan, Gegauk, Pyindeik, to the Singu valley. When the troops reached Gegauk valley on January 15, a clash took place and three Shan were killed. At Pyindeik another attack broke out, killing two Shan. In the Singu valley a sniper fired a few shots at the British troops without any casualty and two flags of the Limbin force were found. There were signs of resistance at Nam Hkom. The Limbin Confederacy prepared for attack but the British used their mountain gun. One shell was fired at the Limbin force, killing eight enemies. The expedition troops reached Pwela, the principal town of the Myelat area. There, nine *ngwehkunmu* tendered their submission in person. On January 30 a letter was sent to the chief of Lawk Sawk, Sao Waing, asking him to cease his attack on Yawng Hwe and to negotiate, under British mediation, whatever causes of dissatisfaction he had with the Yawng Hwe chief. But Sao Waing refused, accusing Sao On of committing dacoity by taking over his state in his absence. There could be no possibility for negotiation, since the British had come to aid Sao On, his arch-enemy. The political officer Hildebrand sent another note demanding Sao Waing to meet him at Heho and to disband his troops. Hildebrand assured him of his position as chief of his own state and of noninterference in his domestic affairs. The main intention of the British was to put an end to the distressing situation. Again Sao Waing refused to meet the British demand. The British troops marched past Heho to Bawrithat pagoda about three miles from Yawng Hwe. Here Colonel Stedman gave orders to encamp for a while. Sao On, the chief of Yawng Hwe, was relieved by the arrival of the British troops. But Sao Waing showed no sign of withdrawal. Instead, he reinforced his defense at Kugyo with eighteen hundred fighting men, commanded by his father, Hkun Beke. Sao Waing himself took command of another fort at Bangwe three miles farther north. Hildebrand tried his last correspondence and gave the chief of Lawk Sawk another chance. Again there was no response.

On February 9, 1887, at midnight, the British troops moved to attack the Kugyo headquarters located about seven miles from their encampment. From one thousand yards away the British troops fired two shells at the Kugyo fort, followed by mounted and infantry attacks, and fighting took place at close range. The whole position fell into the hands of the British with twenty-four Shan killed and three British soldiers wounded. The Lawk Sawk *saohpa* finally abandoned further resistance and retreated to his own state. That was the first breakdown of the Limbin Confederacy.

After the fall of Kugyo, the following day the expedition entered Yawng Hwe. British officers rode on elephants provided by Sao On. Along the road were people joining the procession to welcome the British troops. British officers were well treated and entertained in bamboo sheds with all sorts of Shan delicacies. After that the site for a fort was chosen six miles to the south of Yawng Hwe, where the ground was slightly higher and healthful. The fort was named after Stedman, as suggested by the political officer Hildebrand. The submission of the *myosa* of Sam Ka was secured and a letter from the *saohpa* of Mong Pai was received stating his happiness at the arrival of the British troops. Friendly letters were sent to all chiefs of the Confederacy including the Limbin prince assuring them that there would not be any change in the system of government of the old days, or the customs and religion of the Shan people. Sao Waing, the chief of Lawk Sawk, was informed again of the promise to pardon his obstructive conduct and activities, but to no avail. Messengers from Lai Hka, Mong Kung, and Kehsi Mansam also arrived with letters from their chiefs acknowledging British supremacy. The *myosa* of Sam Ka, Loi Long, and almost all *ngwehkunmu* from the Myelat area recognized the British overlordship. Chiefs of Yawng Hwe and Mong Pai did the same thing. But the chiefs of the Limbin group, including the prince himself, showed no sign of submission. Oaths of allegiance among them were renewed to stand and fall together in any event that might transpire. At the same time the chiefs of Mong Nai and Mong Pawn wrote to the chief commissioner justifying their actions against the Yawng Hwe chief. They accused Sao On of committing criminal acts by harassing and plundering neighboring states, especially Lawk Sawk. For that he would have to be punished and disposed of by force of arms. They also stated in their letter their willingness to talk with the British about peace in the Shan States.

More letters were sent to Sao Waing, the chief of Lawk Sawk, and to the Limbin prince. But there was no progress. Meanwhile Mong Pai was having trouble with the Karenni, and J. G. Scott went down the Balu Chaung with a few soldiers to settle the situation. At the same time the superintendent wrote another letter to Hkun Hti, the chief of Mong Pawn, to invite the members of the Confederacy to meet him, including the chiefs of Lai Hka, Mong Kung, and Kehsi Mansam, hoping to settle the question of submission once and for all. But that was turned down by Hkun Hti, who said it was impossible to get the confederates at this time and that the chief of Mong Nai, Hkun Kyi, was not available, because he had gone to Kantarawady for a meeting with Sawlapaw. Sawlapaw, chief of the Karenni, was organizing the local chiefs to move against the British. Sawlapaw and Hkun Kyi also formed an alliance to wage a defensive and offensive war against the British. The British were now left with no choice but to resume their military campaign. Their first target was the Lawk Sawk chief, Sao Waing. The final letter was sent to him to submit or face military action and be eliminated forever.

No favorable response came. The British troops moved toward Lawk Sawk. Sao Waing offered neither submission nor fighting but fled and the British entered Lawk Sawk on April 11, 1887. With the consent of the people Bo Saing was asked to take temporary charge of the state. The British troops continued their march on Ho Pong from Lawk Sawk. Hkun Hti, the chief of Mong Pawn, said he could not come to see the superintendent, because he was besieged by the Lai Hka, Mong Kung, and Kehsi Mansam forces. The Lai Hka chief and his allies also wrote to the superintendent informing him that they would send a troop of a thousand men to help him in his march to suppress Mong Nai. Meanwhile, two letters arrived, one from Twet Nga Lu and the other from the chief of Mong Pan, who appealed to the superintendent for help because they had been driven out of their states, Keng Tawng and Mong Pan, by the forces of Mong Nai and Mawk Mai. It was a crucial time for the superintendent to decide what to do in this situation.

At that point representatives from Nawng Wawn and Nam Hkok arrived with the message that they agreed to acknowledge British supremacy. These two states were insignificant in the size of their territories, but they were active members of the Confederacy. The superintendent was encouraged morally because he saw a split in the Confederacy. The British troops moved up to Mong Pawn to rescue Hkun Hti from being attacked by Lai Hka and its allies, to woo him to the British, and to reconcile Lai Hka and its allies with Mong Pawn.

When the British troops arrived at Mong Pawn, the forces of the two sides were in their stockades ready to fire at each other. The superintendent met Hkun Hti and asked him to stop firing at his opponents. Hkun Hti agreed to stop on condition that the other side did the same. Here, J. G. Scott with his Shan interpreter went to the other stockade and negotiated with the Lai Hka and its allies. Firing not only stopped; the Lai Hka, Mong Kung, Kehsi Mansam alliance also agreed to withdraw their troops to their own states.

Hkun Hti, the chief of Mong Pawn, entered into a political negotiation for the exemption of tribute for the first year, for the tribute to be reduced or revised, and for British garrisons to be stationed at Pekon, Mong Nai, and Hsen Wi as in the old days but not at Fort Stedman. Hkun Hti also demanded that Keng Tawng be ceded to Mong Nai. Hkun Hti and Hildebrand discussed many other things concerning his politics and his attitude toward the British and his submission to British authority. Hildebrand found Hkun Hti very interesting and recognized him as a military strategist, a good shooter, and an able diplomat—resourceful, intelligent, jovial, and good-natured. He acted as a spokesman for the Confederacy on political and military affairs. Hildebrand realized that Hkun Hti was the key man of Confederacy politics. If he could be persuaded to side with the British, then the back of the Limbin Confederacy would be broken. Hkun Hti also came to realize the military strength of the British. He suggested that the superintendent and his troops should go to Mong Nai for further negotiations with the Mong Nai chief as well as the Limbin prince. He also promised to help. On May 5, 1887, the British troops with Hildebrand and his assistant J. G. Scott reached Mong Nai. Hkun Kyi, the Mong Nai *saohpa*, and Scott entered into serious negotiations, each paying a visit to the other and finally the Mong Nai chief agreed to the British proposal. Regarding Hkun Kyi's negotiation with the British, Scott gave the following remarks:

> Thus Hkun Kyi was assured the dignity of a partner with his conqueror. . . . the calm dignity and self-confidence of a *sawbwa [saohpa]*, who despite humiliation, would calmly issue orders to his neighbours, his neighbours, greatly impressed . . . they saw in it, not arrogance and braggadocio, but nobility and a mark of the esteem in which the *sawbwa* was held by those about him.[2]

Hkun Kyi also asked permission to fly a Union Jack at his *haw*. The request was given, the troops presented arms, and the bugle sounded with the Mong Nai people watching the new flag unfurling at the top of a bamboo pole. Hkun Kyi then wrote to the neighboring chiefs to acknowledge British authority as he did. The Mawk Mai chief also invited the British officers and Scott, and a lieutenant with a few soldiers to make a quick visit to Mawk Mai. They were cordially received and negotiation was immediately carried out. Without any difficulty the allegiance of the *saohpa* of Mawk Mai was obtained.

The Limbin prince and Scott then entered a new round of negotiations. These two knew each other very well. When Scott was a teacher at St. John's College, the Limbin prince was a student. But the negotiation did not go too smoothly. The Limbin prince was now in a critical situation, thinking about his future status, where and what political and financial guarantee he might have, or what he could secure from the British. It took him a few days to seriously consider the terms offered to him. Finally the Limbin prince wrote a letter to Scott asking him for assurance on three points:

1. that he should be free from all criminal process
2. that he should be allowed to take with him his elephant, ponies, and other movable property, and that he should be given Ks 250/ as a monthly pension
3. that certain lands in Mandalay which belonged to his father be given back to him.

Most of this was agreed to by Scott and both signed the agreements.

The Limbin prince and his followers were escorted to Fort Stedman on May 13, 1887. The trip took eight days from Mong Nai to Yawng Hwe. On the way, throngs of people came out to see the prince, thinking that he was being taken to Mandalay to be enthroned as king. Finally the royal captive arrived at Fort Stedman and the whole fort was full of joy. The British troops held jubilee sports of all sorts. Those who rendered special services or help to the superintendent and his party were given a variety of presents including special invitations to the victory celebration. Letters of congratulations were also received from the chief commissioner and from the viceroy of India.[3]

After a few days' rest at Fort Stedman, the Limbin prince was brought down to Yangon for retirement. But he was denied the right to live there. Of his own choice he was sent to India. He was permitted to come back to Yangon in 1912 to 1915. When the First World War broke out, he was again sent back to India. At his request, he was allowed to come back in 1921 to Myanmar, where he lived until his death in 1933.[4]

Thus for a time the chaotic situation improved and both conquered and conqueror enjoyed the fruits of their achievement. But further efforts would have to be made by the officers concerned. The Shan States were far from pacified. And the final phase of pacification would have to be undertaken for the whole Cis-Salween areas.

7

Pacification of the Cis-Salween States

The first phase of the pacification in the Southern Shan States was achieved by the surrender of the Limbin prince, followed by the disintegration of the Confederacy forces. In the Northern Shan States, Hkun Hseng was restored to his own state, Hsi Paw. The feud between Hkun Sang Ton Hong and Naw Mong was solved by creating two divisions of the Hsen Wi State, the north and the south. The northern division was called Hsen Wi and given to Hkun Sang Ton Hong; the southern division was called Mong Yai and given to Naw Mong. All these settlements helped to bring temporary peace to the whole of the Shan States.

A great celebration was held at Fort Stedman to mark the victory over the Shan States and the cooperation between the Shan chiefs and the British officers. Special guests, foreign and native, were invited and entertained with a variety of Shan food and delicacies. Sports and fun fairs were also organized for both the soldiers and the public. People enjoyed meeting each other for the first time after a long period of factional war led by the Shan chiefs. Gifts and greetings were cordially exchanged between the Shan chiefs and the British officers of various ranks trying to acquaint themselves with each other. It was really a great moment for the Shan chiefs and for the Shan people to mark a change of sovereign from the Myanmar king to the British queen-empress. The British policy of olive branch and carrot and stick seemed to work very well in the first phase of occupation and pacification. The celebration at Fort Stedman ended smoothly. Soldiers shared the joy and satisfaction over the accomplishment of their first mission to the Shan States. Guests went home with remembrance of new friendships and new souvenirs from the Shan people. The Shan chiefs went back to their states uncertain about their future role as leaders of their own states, with new overlordship from a foreign land with which they were not well acquainted. On the other hand, the British political and military officers, like Superintendent Hildebrand, J. George Scott, Colonel Stedman, and the soldiers were quite satisfied and happy at having carried out their objective of occupation and pacification with very few casualties.

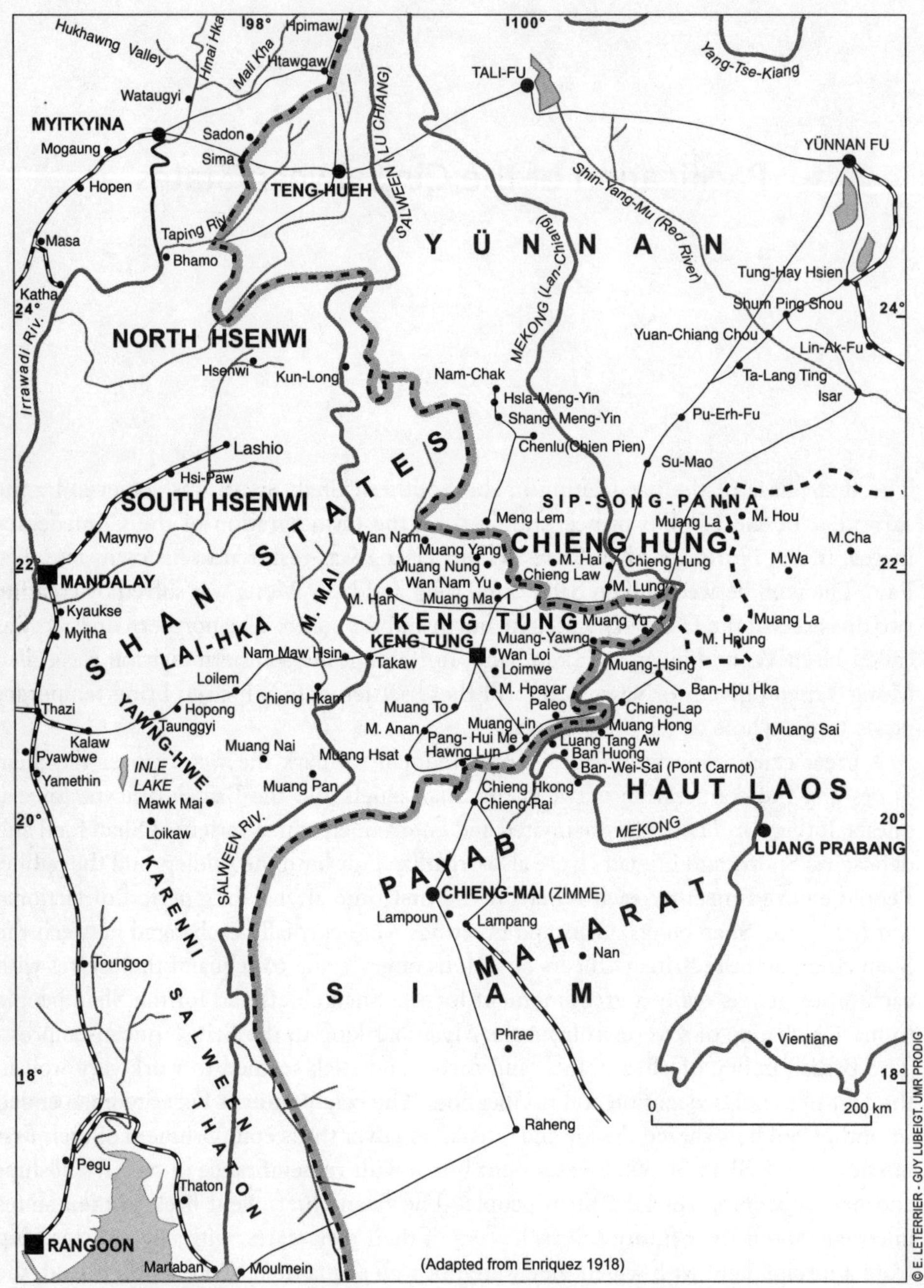

MAP 16. Eastern Myanmar border with Yunnan, Siam, and French Indochina

After that, Superintendent Hildebrand made a grand tour of the Northern Shan States with the British troops, leaving a few soldiers to guard Fort Stedman. The old rebellious chiefs in the south took the opportunity of Hildebrand's absence to renew their fighting against each other. When Hildebrand reached Mong Yai, he got the news of Twet Nga Lu invading Mong Pan and the taking over of Mawk Mai by the Karenni leader Sawlapaw. Old disputes over the illegal extraction of teak and timber along their borders occurred and Sawlapaw with his bands of aggressive followers attacked Mawk Mai and burned down everything including the monasteries. Marauding bands from the neighbors also shared in the spoils. Unable to resist, the Mawk Mai chief fled and a protégé of Sawlapaw was established as the new ruler. Twet Nga Lu also took the opportunity to occupy Mong Pan. Unable to defend himself, the Mong Pan chief, Hkam Leng, also fled. Twet Nga Lu's next step was to take over Mong Nai.

Hildebrand hurried down to Yangon to confer with the chief commissioner while his assistant, George Scott, was dispatched back to Fort Stedman immediately. In Mong Pai new feuds with another Karenni leader, Bobya, over the territorial problem recurred and fighting broke out. The chiefs of Loi Long and Thigyit made new territorial claims. Indein near Yawng Hwe also created political instability, and even the small principality of Ye Ngan had its own trouble over the question of succession. The chief of Yawng Hwe, Sao On, who lived under the protection of the British troops of Fort Stedman, also made territorial claims on the border tract of Kun Sat that belonged to the neighboring state Hsa Htung. The situation was also aggravated by the rumor spread by Sao On that the Chinese and the French were in alliance to declare war on Great Britain, that the French had taken over Calcutta, that the number of the British soldiers at Fort Stedman would be reduced, and so on.[1] Such rumors helped to encourage the rebellious leaders to expand their territorial activities.

Mawk Mai, as already mentioned, was invaded by Sawlapaw, who was very proud of himself for having remained aloof from the suzerainty of the Myanmar king in the old days. He was also anti-British in his attitude and believed that they had no right to occupy the Shan States and to interfere in his domestic affairs. They should be driven out. In his letter to the chief of Mong Pawn, he said:

> As for the coming of the Kulas [the British], let them come. We have no quarrel with them. If they mistreat us, we will cut them down. If they defeat us, we will bow down to them but not unless . . .[2]

Scott wrote to the rebellious chiefs to stop fighting each other. To those who refused, British troops would be sent to quell them. Hildebrand also sent an order to the Mong Nai chief to drive out Twet Nga Lu from Mong Pan. The Mong Nai chief took immediate action by sending a contingent to suppress Twet Nga Lu, but the Mong Nai contingent was ambushed and routed. Twet Nga Lu pressed on quickly to occupy Mong Nai. Mong Nai fell into his hands and the *haw* (residence) of the chief was occupied on May 3, 1888. On hearing this news, Scott with Colonel Sartorius, Lieutenant Fowler, and some sepoys immediately marched from Fort Stedman to Mong Nai to recapture the capital as well as Twet Nga Lu. On May 9, 1888, they approached Mong Nai and camped at a place eight miles away from the capital. A plan for a lightning strike against Twet Nga Lu was drawn up and carried out the next morning. Scott chose Lieutenant Fowler and six sepoys and led the charge. They galloped into the compound of the palace unnoticed. At that time most of the soldiers of Twet Nga Lu were out foraging. The action was quick and bold. Twet Nga Lu was unaware of their presence and was captured before he could grasp his gun, which lay close to him.

The *St. James's Gazette* reported on the recapture of Mong Nai and Twet Nga Lu:

> The recapture of Mone [Mong Nai] from the rebel leader Twet Nga Lu in the beginning of May is a good example of what rapid and determined action will do with a semi-civilized enemy. The relieving party under Colonel Sartorius, of the 1st Beloochees, started at daybreak . . . in the hills to the west of Mone . . . Mr. Scott, the Assistant Superintendent of the Shan States, with Lieutenant Fowler . . . and six men of the Rifle Brigade mounted on officers' ponies . . . they galloped straight on the palace, . . . the clatter of the hoofs brought Twet Nga Lu to a window. Mr. Scott knew him by sight, and with the assistance of a soldier, had the rebel tied to his own bed-post within two minutes . . . Twet Nga Lu had a repeating rifle loaded with sixteen cartridges lying by his bedside, but not the time to seize it . . . Twet Nga Lu bound and his chief leaders under guard . . . The capture of Twet Nga Lu is likely to have the most satisfying results. The disturbances that broke out in the Southern Shan States during April were mainly due to his advance and his intrigues, and now that he and his leaders have been captured the complete establishment of peace may be anticipated.[3]

Twet Nga Lu and his followers were taken to Fort Stedman as prisoners. Scott was honored for his success in capturing Twet Nga Lu and restoring peace to Mong Nai. The viceroy, the commander-in-chief, and the chief commissioner sent special letters of congratulations and telegrams to him. The telegram from the chief commissioner stated:

> Chief Commissioner congratulates you and Lieutenant Fowler on your extremely well executed dash on Mone and capture of Twet Nga Lu and thanks both of you and the men of the Rifle Brigade . . . after you have examined Twet Nga Lu's correspondence report result by wire . . . the prisoners including Twet Nga Lu . . . make over . . .to Mone Sawbwa for trial and punishment according to Shan custom . . . take care that Twet Nga Lu does not effect his escape . . . if the Mone [Mong Nai] Sawbwa sentence any prisoners to death for an offence other than murder suspend execution until you get orders on this point . . . Government of India has consented.[4]

At that time Superintendent Hildebrand had not yet been given judicial power to try prisoners or criminals. So Twet Nga Lu and his men were sent back to Mong Nai

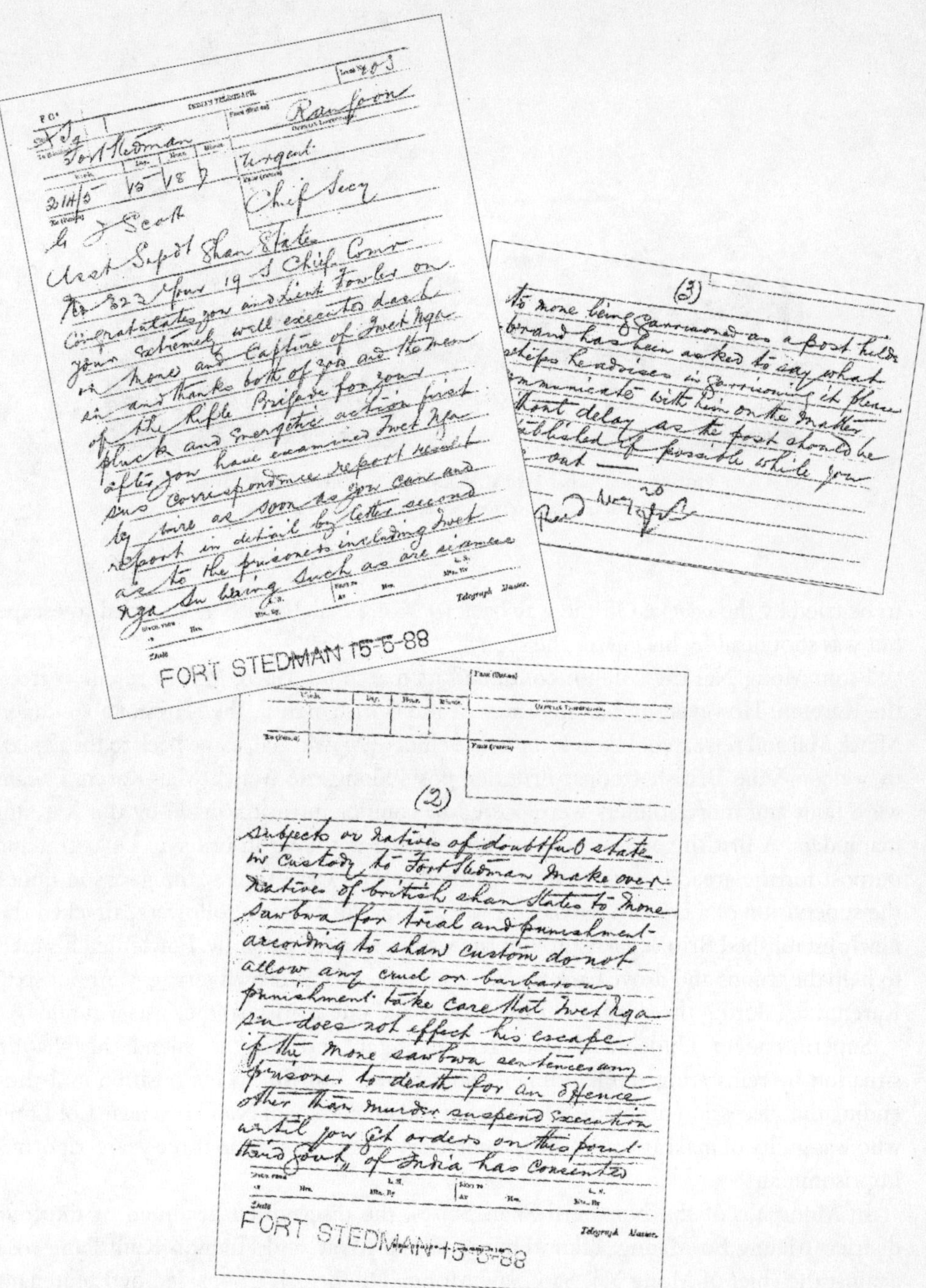

INDIAN TELEGRAPH
Rangoon
Urgent
Chief Secy
Fort Stedman
2114/5 15 18 7
G J Scott
Asst Supdt Shan States
No 322 Your 19-5 Chief Commr
Congratulates you and Lieut Fowler on
your extremely well executed dash
on Mone and capture of Twet Nga
Sin and thanks both of you and the men
of the Rifle Brigade for your
pluck and energetic action first
after you have examined Twet Nga
Sins correspondence report result
by wire as soon as you can and
report in detail by letter second
as to the prisoners including Twet
Nga Sin being such as are Siamese

Telegraph Master.

FORT STEDMAN 15-5-88

(2)

subjects or natives of doubtful state
in custody to Fort Stedman make over
natives of British Shan States to Mone
Sawbwa for trial and punishment
according to Shan custom do not
allow any cruel or barbarous
punishment take care that Twet Nga
Sin does not effect his escape
if the Mone Sawbwa sentences any
prisoner to death for an offence
other than murder suspend execution
until you get orders on this point
third Govt of India has consented

Telegraph Master.

FORT STEDMAN 15-5-88

(3)

to Mone being garrisoned as a post held
...brand has been asked to say what
...ships he advises in garrisoning it please
communicate with him on the matter
without delay as the post should be
established if possible while you
... out —

Recd [illegible] 20

FIGURE 7.1. Telegram from the chief commissioner, Yangon, to J. George Scott, received at Fort Stedman on May 15, 1888.

FIGURE 7.2. Durbar held at Mong Nai, Southern Shan States, after J. G. Scott ousted Twet Nga Lu, dated 1889.

to be tried by the *saohpa*. On the way back to Mong Nai, Twet Nga Lu tried to escape but was shot dead by his guard, the sepoy.[5]

From Mong Nai the column continued its march on Mawk Mai to rescue it from the Karenni. However, on hearing news of the British arrival, the Karenni abandoned Mawk Mai and retreated. Hkun Hmon, the chief of Mawk Mai, came back to the capital to welcome the British troops. Frontier posts along the Mawk Mai–Karenni State were built and more soldiers were posted to counter intrusion made by the Karenni marauders. A British garrison was established at Kantulong in order to be a strategic outpost for the area. Twenty-five fully armed sepoys were kept at the garrison under the supervision of a *subedar*. Sawlapaw, with a superior force of followers, attacked the newly established British garrison. But the sepoys resisted gallantly. Fowler led his men to help the troops and drove back the Karenni forces to their own territory. About sixty Karenni fell during the skirmish at the border and one British soldier was wounded.[6]

Superintendent Hildebrand inspected Ye Ngan and tried to mend the chaotic situation by reinstating the legitimate ruler Maung On Bin to his position and thus ending the succession problem. The chief of the small state of Nan Hkai near Loi Long who was guilty of making war in British territory was sentenced to three years' rigorous imprisonment.

In Mong Yai of the Northern Shan States, the disgruntled headmen of the four districts Maung Po Maung, Hkun Hpong, Hkun Myat, and Htamon Kum Pang rose against the chief of Mong Yai, Sao Naw Mong. The British troops, led by Lieutenant Daly, went to settle the problem. The four leaders were found guilty of committing rebellion, arrested, and put into the British jail in Mandalay. Some of their followers fled to Mong Lun to take refuge in the hills. In Hsi Paw it was found that Hkun Hseng could not restore peace and security in Hsum Hsai and Mong Long and he was warned that he would be forfeited to rule over those regions unless he could bring peace and security. Hkun Hseng took very stiff measures and peace was restored in the two regions.

After a year of experience in dealing with the Shan chiefs and the situation in the Shan States, the British administrative officers came to see the necessity of introducing modifications in the autonomous rights of the Shan chiefs. They also realized that close British supervision of the proper management of the state's affairs with fairness and justice had become quite necessary. As a first step in that direction, the Shan States were divided into two administrative divisions, the Northern Shan States and the Southern Shan States, in August 1888. The Northern Shan States were to be composed of Hsi Paw, Tawng Peng, North Hsen Wi, and Mong Yai under the supervision of Superintendent Daly and the Southern Shan States and the Myelat areas were placed under the management of Superintendent Hildebrand. Both officers were to be directly responsible to the government of Myanmar.

Daly and Hildebrand dealt separately with Mong Mit, another Northern Shan State, which had its own problem. Its ruler in 1874, Sao Hkun Ho, ruled Mong Mit till his death in 1885. He was succeeded by his son, Sao Khin Maung. As the son was young, a regency was formed and appointed to rule Mong Mit. Another rival claimant to the throne was Hkun Hkam Leng, a distant relative of Sao Khin Maung. He was the ruler of the neighboring state of Mohlaing. When the British annexed Upper Myanmar Hkun Hkam Leng was in Mandalay. He sought recognition as chief of Mohlaing and Mong Mit from the British in December 1885. The British government was not sure of the legality of his claim. He was granted a provisional *sanad*. When Hkun Hkam Leng went back home, the forces of the regency opposed him. Unable to beat them off, he appealed for British help. In August he was called to see the deputy commissioner at Katha and told to limit his claim to Mohlaing, but he refused. He organized the Kachin tribes to take Mong Mit by force. In April 1887 the chief commissioner visited Mong Mit and met the regency of Sao Khin Maung at Mogok. He recognized Sao Khin Maung as de jure *saohpa* of Mong Mit. Hkun Hkam Leng then allied himself with the Saw Yang Naing group who were fighting the British. But the British force defeated them all. Mohlaing State was partitioned and half was given to Bhamo and the other half to Mong Mit.

In April 1889 the infant ruler of Mong Mit was replaced by Sao Maung, the former *saohpa* of Yawng Hwe. He was quite mature and had experience in administration. He set up a new administration with the approval of the British and peace was restored to Mong Mit.

Now the British turned their attention toward the Trans-Salween States. But they moved toward these states with caution because their frontiers touched the foreign countries of China, French Indochina, and Siam. Letters were sent very often to the *saohpa* of Keng Tung to secure his allegiance. When Scott visited Mong Nai to confirm the allegiance of its chief Hkun Kyi, he wrote to the chiefs of Keng Tung, Keng Cheng, Keng Hung, and Mong Lin asking them to submit themselves to the new suzerainty of the queen-empress as they did to the Myanmar kings in the past. But because of unstable circumstances in Mong Nai, the representatives of Keng Tung did not arrive. For a year, negotiations between the Keng Tung chief and the British officers were not successful. The British became quite concerned that China and Siam would interfere in the frontier matters with Keng Tung. W. J. Archer, the British vice-consul in Chiang Mai, was asked to visit Keng Tung in May 1888 to get the opinion of the Keng Tung chief about the Cis-Salween States.[7] Moreover, the chief was not to enter into any treaty with any foreign power and was also asked to pay regular tribute as he did to the Myanmar kings. The British promised not to interfere with the domestic administration of the old days. The British government would also use its influence and protection to get suitable boundary lines drawn with Siam. The Keng Tung chief was also told to withdraw his force in Mong Pu which belonged to Mong Nai.[8] The *saohpa* accepted the general terms mentioned in the letter.

J. G. Scott and Captain F. J. Pink with a force of forty sepoys crossed the Than Lwin at Takaw and proceeded to Keng Tung. Scott had almost three years of experience with the Shan chiefs and could guess the result of a personal encounter. He planned to apply the policy of pomp and show in dealing with the Keng Tung chief. Approaching Keng Tung, Scott sent another letter asking about the arrangement the chief and his ministers had made for their accommodation and meeting when they reached Keng Tung. The chief minister and minor officers came to meet Scott and his party a few miles outside the capital. They were escorted to the site where the Myanmar had their garrison before. The following day, Scott and his party were officially received and a meeting was held with the *saohpa* and all his ministers and officers. A presentation of *sanad* to the *saohpa* was made. Scott gave a speech at the ceremony advising the chief to be loyal to the queen-empress, to keep peace in the state, and to open trade. All the ministers and officers were happy with the speech. They promised to cooperate with the British officers. But the *sanad* offered to the Keng Tung chief was different from those given to the other Shan chiefs. The recital in the preamble of the former subordination of the Shan chief to the Myanmar king was omitted. The tribute to be paid to the British was not to be money but, as in the old days, gold and silver flowers and miscellaneous articles of nominal value. The right of the government to revise the tribute was not mentioned, as well as the rights in forests and in minerals. The role of the superintendent in the administration was not included in the *sanad*. But the *saohpa* must accept the advice of the chief commissioner. Moreover, the Keng Tung *saohpa* was forbidden to communicate with any foreign power. The British had no plan to station troops in Keng Tung, and treated it as a state in subordinate alliance rather than a typical British subject state.

In April 1889, Scott and his party called on the other Trans-Salween States of Mong Pu, Mong Hsat, and territories that belonged to Mong Pan.[9] Mong Lun was another state listed as a vassal of King Thibaw. It was situated in the Northern Shan States bordering the Wa States. The Wa States could be divided into two parts: the interior belonged to the wild Wa and the outer part to the tame Wa that included Mong Lun as well. The tame Wa were mostly Buddhists and adopted the Shan culture. They used the Shan script and most of their religious literature was in Shan language. Most of their monks read, wrote, and preached in Shan. They dressed like Shan and their administrative system was like the Shan. Their chief was also called *saohpa*. Mong Lun State had its territories on both sides of the Than Lwin River. The British invited the Mong Lun chief but he never turned up. As the Wa States bordered China, the British were quite cautious in dealing with Mong Lun. The British were not well informed about the Wa, but like other Shan states, Mong Lun had to be brought to accept the suzerainty of the British. Mong Lun was also known as a refuge for rebels, dacoits, and defeated parties. They just disappeared in the hills of the wild Wa and returned when the situation became favorable to disturb the western side of the Than Lwin. Their activities became a concern to the British. Scott took the view that Mong Lun should be brought and kept under British protection and its chief must acknowledge the overlordship of the British as did the other Shan chiefs.

In 1889–90 a correspondence was opened with the chief of west Mong Lun, but he declined to accept British supremacy. In January 1891 British troops led by Daly marched on Keng Hung through the Wa States. The Mong Lun chief, Sao Maha, refused to meet Daly and fled into the interior part of the wild Wa. But his rival, Ton Hsang, received Daly cordially. Armed with a recommendation from Daly, Ton Hsang was recognized as *saohpa* of Mong Lun. The government of India was cautious in increasing its commitments east of the Than Lwin, fearing Chinese opposition. Scott was also instructed not to commit any act that might create problems and complications with China. He was instructed not to cross the Than Lwin and involve himself in the territorial problems of Mong Lun east of the Than Lwin. Scott took a different view and opposed the policy of not crossing the Than Lwin.

After a thorough investigation, he reported that China had never at any time had any authority over or dealing with Mong Lun and its chief. The noninterference policy of the government would definitely result in the Mong Lun State falling into the hands of China.[10] On October 21, 1892, the chief commissioner replied to Scott, accepting his proposal and allowing him to cross the Than Lwin whenever he considered it necessary.[11] Scott was happy with the reply and planned to cross the Than Lwin, capture Sao Maha, who disturbed the peace and whose attitude was anti-British, and to settle the territories of Mong Lun east of the river. Scott visited many places like Yang U, Nget Hting, Loi Long, Mawk Hpa, Mot Hsamo, Mong Hka, and Mong Hsaw, and tried to brief their chiefs and have them acknowledge British suzerainty, to ensure peace in their own states, to stop fighting each other and supporting Sao Maha who was anti-British, and to recognize the legitimate rule of Ton Hsang over both east and west Mong Lun. Sao Maha never came out to challenge Scott, but fled into the interior part of the wild Wa. Scott succeeded in bringing the Mong Lun chief and other minor chiefs of the Wa area to accept British allegiance over them.

8

The British Occupation and the Settlement of Frontier Problems

After Upper Myanmar was annexed in 1885, the Shan States became an appendix of the British possession of Myanmar. The British had no grasp of the boundary of the Shan States with Siam—where and on which side of a mountain, valley, or river it was—because there was no recognized fixed border during the rule of the Myanmar kings. The Shan chief knew where the frontiers of his state began and where it ended. But interstate warfare often changed the state frontiers. Additions and subtractions of territories were made after every feudal war and a new frontier was drawn up. After the occupation and pacification of the Cis-Salween Shan States, the British were reluctant to cross over the Than Lwin and occupy the territories of the Trans-Salween States for fear of having frontier problems with Siam, French Indochina, or China. At first the British wanted a natural boundary like the Than Lwin River or the Mekong as their eastern frontier. France and Siam had territorial interests, and established military outposts and garrisons in some areas. But no claims had yet been made to create military provocations against each other. The region was too remote and the means of communication was very poor. To send troops to such an area would be costly. The British had to undertake the task of occupation and pacification they had inherited from King Thibaw of Myanmar of which the Shan States were a part, but they lacked a preconceived policy or plan for this new land.

The Shan chiefs of this region had lost not only their sovereign rights but the autonomous rights they had enjoyed during the time of the Myanmar kings. Now it was the British responsibility to manage the affairs of the Shan States and to shape the destiny of the Shan chiefs. Some frontier chiefs regained their lost territories but some had to forgo their legitimate rights, had their lands transferred to foreign powers, and finally even lost the right to choose their own suzerainty. They were willing to serve, but in some cases they did not have such rights, and had to comply with the treaties they had made with foreign powers. They lost their hereditary rights over their own subjects. That was the heaviest price of foreign domination that the frontier chiefs and peoples had to suffer and sacrifice for reasons they did not understand. They had established their *baan* (village) and their *mong* (state) through countless efforts made over countless years, through deprivation, pain, and sufferings of many generations, and by the sacrifice of countless people. They had to make extreme sacrifices to preserve their dear lands of lebensraum and their survival in the midst of jungles, intractable mountains, hills, and forests. Alas, at the point of a gun and physical pressure and in disregard of morality and international law, they were sold to foreign powers like chicks and piglets at the open supermarket created by the superpowers of the time. Within two or three years of the British occupation the Shan people lost an enormous portion of their native land.

The first British interest after the occupation of the Trans-Salween areas was to delimit the frontier with Siam. The first dispute the British had with the Siamese (Thai) was over a small tract east of the Than Lwin. The area was quite mountainous, and about twenty to thirty miles wide. It extended from Keng Tung on the north to the southern extremity of Kantarawady, about one hundred fifty miles. The interest over this area was not for the land but for its valuable teak trees. The chiefs of Kantarawady, Mong Pan, Mawk Mai, and the Siamese claimed this area. Its northern portion comprised five small states—Mong Hsat, Mong Tung, Mong Hang, Mong Kyawt, and Mong Hta. The chief of Mong Pan claimed them. The two governments agreed to form a commission. A conference to examine the rival claims was held at Mong Pan in January 1888. The inhabitants of these states were mostly Shan who were from Mong Pan. They acknowledged the rule of the Mong Pan chief up to 1887, and after that the Siamese called the headmen of these states to drink the water of loyalty to the Siamese government. Four complied with the request, except the headman of Mong Hsat. Instead, he asked for help from the chief of Mong Pan and the chief of Keng Tung for his protection, which they granted.[1]

Following an inquiry, the British took control of the five states and gave back four to the Mong Pan chief. Only one state, Mong Hsat, was given to the chief of Keng Tung. The Siamese strongly protested but no action followed. Scott was dispatched to the area to support the claim of the Mong Pan chief. In December 1888 the problem of timber extraction came up. The *pawmong* (local chief) who was friendly to the Siamese permitted Kya Nyun, a contractor from Mawlamyaing, to extract timber in the area. Another contractor, Maung Ba Thaw, who held a lease from the Mong Pan chief, was already working in the area. The logs of Maung Ba Thaw were being stolen and, to protect them, the British sent two men to stamp the logs, but Ai Nan Pon, the *pawmong*, seized them. Scott, with a few sepoys, went to settle the matter. But the *pawmong* fled, taking his two prisoners along. Scott pursued the *pawmong* to recover the prisoners but to no avail. He then appointed a new *pawmong* and came back. The Siamese chief, with whom the *pawmong* and his prisoners took refuge, sent orders to the four headmen to renew their allegiance to the Siamese and tried to take Mong Kyawt. The Mong Pan chief sent his force to get it back.

Another dispute occurred between the British and the Siamese over the question of the Karenni rebellion. When the Karenni leader Sawlapaw waged war against the British, the British asked the Siamese to help, which they did. After the matter was settled the Siamese expected to get rewards from the British for their help. But the British just thanked them without any reward or compensation. The Siamese then occupied the Karenni territory east of the Than Lwin and clearly made it known to the British. The British asked the Siamese to withdraw. But they proceeded to work in the forests, stole logs, as well as one hundred elephants, and showed no signs of withdrawing from the area.[2]

During the political chaos in the Southern Shan States when Mawk Mai, Mong Pan, and Kantarawady were fighting each other, the Siamese took the opportunity to set up their garrisons in early 1889 at Meksakun and Mong Mau, which belonged to the state of Mawk Mai.[3]

In 1889 the Anglo-Siamese Commission decided to visit the disputed area. The British party, led by Ney Elias, marched from Fort Stedman with three objectives: (1) to make the Siamese withdraw from the Trans-Salween States of Karenni and Mawk Mai, (2) to settle the disputes over the violation of British territory, and (3) to demarcate the boundary line between British and Siamese territory.[4]

The Siamese party failed to appear and the British conducted an ex-parte inquiry and survey. They found a garrison with more than one hundred Siamese soldiers in Karenni territory. A minor incident took place when a Siamese army officer tried to block the way with his men. The British troops removed them at gunpoint and seized the Siamese officer. After discussion with the Siamese commander, the officer was released and his army restored.[5]

Ney Elias and his party then went to Mong Mau and Meksakun where the Siamese had their garrisons. Inquiring about the two little states, they found that they legitimately belonged to the Mawk Mai chief. The chief was allowed to reoccupy both Mong Mau and Meksakum. The Siamese withdrew their garrison and the problem was solved.[6]

Then the party moved to check the substates of Mong Pan, Mong Hta, Mong Hang, and Mong Kyawt. They were very sparsely populated and were almost deserted. But when the British reached the fourth substate of Mong Tung they found a force of one hundred fifty Siamese. The *pawmong* of that state was pro-Siamese and refused to communicate with the British except through the Siamese officer. This chief was found to have pledged his allegiance twice to the chief of Mong Pan and twice to the Siamese authority. His house was surrounded and he was arrested and put into prison. The Siamese officers were told that the four substates were the possession of the British and that the Siamese had no right to stay. The Siamese complied and another frontier problem was settled.

The party returned to Fort Stedman with all three objectives accomplished. Ney Elias prepared the boundary proposal, which was sent to the Siamese government. The British minister in Siam was instructed to press for the prompt withdrawal of the Siamese garrisons from Karenni State. Finally, the Siamese government agreed to withdraw all its troops from the land of the Karenni. Moreover, the Siamese Commission cooperated very well with the British, and a joint examination was made of the remainder of the frontier from Mong Tung to the Mekong River.

A proposal was also prepared to ask for compensation from the Siamese government for the damage done to the Karenni territories and for the loss of teak and elephants. But the government of India did not press the claim against Siam: instead it applied other means to compensate Sawlawi, the chief of Karenni State.

A boundary line between the British and the Siamese was drawn in 1893. A joint commission held its meeting at Mong Hang, a substate of Mong Pan east of the Than Lwin. Superintendent Hildebrand, assisted by H. G. A. Leveson, led the British commission, and Long Hkam Chat and Long Sarasit represented the Siamese commission. The joint commission was split into two parties: one assigned to work toward the Than Lwin, the other to work toward the Mekong. Markers were set up along the agreed places. Minor adjustments were made in some places and no major disagreements occurred.[7]

Hildebrand was instructed to use his own judgment where to establish the boundary pillars in two places in the upper division. One was in the district of Mong Ngam near Mekok, another in the Keng Sen plain near the Mae Sai River. The fixing of the most suitable boundary here required giving Keng Tung territory to Siam. The people there were unhappy about the transfer of their territory to a foreign power in April 1894. They were asked to move to Keng Tung State if they so wanted. They did not, because to abandon their native state and transfer their immovable property was difficult for them.[8]

In dealing with the Chinese over the boundary question, the British were more cautious in their moves. First, they were not sure where Chinese interests were in the Shan States and which states sent tribute to China and when. The British also did not know the relationship between China and Myanmar regarding the Shan States and the kind of relationship that existed between the Chinese chiefs and the Shan chiefs. There were a lot of questions the British had to ask and answer. The British officers were busy working to get more information—from Myanmar court records, state chronicles, histories, memoirs, journals, reports, and interviews, etc. Many British officers were assigned to gather information about China and Myanmar-Shan relationships in the past and present. The British would have to deal with another big power next to India. Moreover, there never had been a clear boundary between Myanmar, the Shan States, and China. The Sino-Myanmar influence over the Shan States was like a seesaw. Sometimes the Chinese were powerful enough to exert their influence on the Shan States and secure tribute from them. The same happened when the Myanmar were powerful. The Shan States had never been united to form or become a sovereign state and deal with either China or Myanmar on an equal footing. They had been pressured by both China and Myanmar in the course of their history to secure their allegiance. Sometimes there were occasions when the Shan States had to send tribute as vassals to both. Sometimes they were punished for not sending regular tribute to their suzerain authority. Such was the difficulty of the border states at the time. They were at the mercy of the two powers, China and Myanmar.

After Archer's visit to Keng Tung the British learned that there was no direct attempt from either China or Siam to control Keng Tung and the Trans-Salween States. Scott crossed the Wa States from west to east to Keng Hung. All these explorations and investigations were made to ascertain the places where China had its interests in these areas. Meanwhile the French were also penetrating the Upper Mekong from the east and the south. They had firmly established themselves in Cochin China in 1862. By 1885 their influence had reached the Chinese coastal area as far north as China proper. They penetrated farther into the Lao country and established their vice consul at Luang Prabang.[9]

The French also learned about the advancing British influence that had touched the bank of the Mekong River. In the same way, the British were also watching closely the French penetration along the Upper Mekong region into the kingdom of Laos. By now the main British interest was to secure the Mekong River as a natural boundary between the French and themselves. The British were worried about the frontier complications they would have to face. The Shan looked at these big powers with amazement. They did not know why in 1892, for no good reason and with no respect or regard for the opinion of the Shan and the Lu people, Keng Hung was given to China and Keng Cheng was ceded to Siam. The Shan lost a great portion of their territories for reasons they did not understand.

The Shan melon was then cut according to the need of the big powers. These Shan *mong*, or states, were established through a long evolutionary process involving endless efforts, hardships, struggles, and wars undertaken by the Shan peoples. But now, without their knowledge, their homeland was treated as a royal gift to be distributed among the big powers. Here, a little patience is needed to see how the territorial problem became a football game played by the big powers. The time had come now to demarcate the boundary of Keng Cheng with Keng Tung and Keng Hung. The task of demarcation was assigned to Superintendent Hildebrand, who was a member of the Anglo-Siamese Boundary Commission, to work jointly with the Siamese. But when the British reached the Mekong the Siamese commission refused to participate, saying it was not ordered by its government to do the job of demarcation. The work of demarcation was then excluded. After the surveyor had finished drawing the line of the boundary, Hildebrand proclaimed Siamese sovereignty over Keng Cheng and the fate of the little state was sealed.[10]

After this, another question arose whether Keng Lap, a tiny district, should be ceded to Siam or not. Keng Lap occupied a strategic location, controlling the principal ferry across the Mekong for traders of the neighboring states and Yunnan. Hildebrand thought it important to retain the portion of Keng Lap west of the Mekong under British control. It was obvious that Keng Lap belonged to Keng Tung, and the Keng Tung *saohpa* always appointed its headman. Moreover, the people of Keng Lap agreed to be subjects of the Keng Tung chief. Guided by the report of Hildebrand, the chief commissioner recommended to the government of India to keep the Cis-Mekong territories for the Keng Tung chief and to cede the Trans-Mekong territories to Keng Cheng, which now belonged to Siam.[11] But the whole question was again reviewed as a result of French intervention in the matter.

The French adopted a stiff attitude toward the affair. They demanded the cession of all Siamese territories east of the Mekong in 1893 and, to back the demand, sent gunboats to the Menam, alarming the British. The British also took similar measures. The situation thus became tense. A tripartite struggle over the region became imminent. The statesmen of the three powers were now to decide whether to solve the problem by peaceful means or by force. The remark of the British foreign minister, Lord Roseberry, on this situation was that:

> the British cannot afford to be the Knight Errant of the world, careering about to redress grievances and help the weak . . . to keep a buffer state between French frontiers and that of India in order that a vast expenditure and damage may not be incurred by the immediate proximity of a great military power on our northeastern flank.[12]

The Siamese government mulled over the French ultimatum given on July 20, 1893. In the meantime the French and the British demonstrated their naval strength in the Menam. If the two powers fought over Keng Cheng, Siam would be involved, the area of battle would be enlarged, and both French and British would have to consider the cost of war, its duration, the task of pacification, the work of administration, compensation, war indemnity, and other consequences of war. On the part of Siam many questions arose. Was Siam well prepared for the war? Would it have a chance to win? Or could it afford to lose? Would it be able to preserve its sovereignty? What territorial gain or profit did it expect to get? Its position was very precarious. The British interest in this situation was to create a neutral zone between the British and French spheres of interest. First, Great Britain advised Siam to accede to the French demands to retain its independence. A treaty was signed on October 3, 1893, by which Siamese territories (in fact these were Shan territories) on the east bank of the Mekong were ceded to France.

Being a weak power, Siam ceded all territories east of the Mekong to France. It was a wise decision. In fact Siam lost nothing. It was the Shan who lost their lands. The tension in the Menam now seemed to ebb a bit. The attention now turned to the demarcation at Keng Cheng between the British and the French.

Meanwhile the British were arranging to demarcate the boundary between Keng Tung and Keng Cheng. Under the treaty with Siam the French began to claim Keng Cheng as their possession. But here, to the surprise of everyone, G. C. B. Stirling, the British officer who was undertaking the work of demarcation, was ordered suddenly to proceed at once to Mong Hsing, the capital of Keng Cheng. The chief of Keng Cheng, the *myosa*, was informed of the cancellation of the British transfer of Keng Cheng to Siam. The sudden change in the situation was perhaps due to the fear of the British, growing out of the negotiation of Lord Dufferin in Paris, that the French might take over the disputed territory. To his great shock and amazement, the *myosa* was asked to send tribute to the British. Stirling was also ordered to provide all information possible about the situation east of Keng Cheng. On March 29, 1893, Stirling and his party arrived in Mong Hsing and informed the *myosa* of his mission. But the *myosa* refused to submit to the British without the consent of the Siamese government. The *myosa* explained how his state was formerly under the suzerainty of the Myanmar and Keng Tung chiefs, was transferred to the British and then to the Thais and then back to the British. He was puzzled over the jigsaw game of big-power diplomacy.

At the end of 1894, arrangements were made for the two commissions to meet at Mong Hsing for the demarcation of a buffer zone. The British arrived in Mong Hsing on Christmas Eve. The French failed to arrive, but their tricolor flag was flying at the top of the post near the *haw*, or residence, of the chief. The *myosa* also declined to meet the British commission led by J. G. Scott and his adviser, W. W. Warry. Scott asked one of his men to lower the flag and bring it to him. On New Year's Day the French commission, led by M. Pavie, arrived. The two chiefs of the commission discussed and agreed on the plan of operation as proposed by Scott, and M. Pavie virtually admitted that Keng Cheng was a British possession or position. But events took a sharp turn on the arrival of the French commander M. Lefevre, who boldly declared that Keng Cheng belonged to France and that the British were only visitors in the territory. Here came a crisis. The *myosa* was in trouble again. He could not decide to whom he owed his allegiance and from whom he should take orders. Who was his actual suzerain? The French leader, M. Pavie, who was a little sympathetic to him, proposed not to put too much pressure on him and let him be free and independent beforean agreement was reached between the two governments. The British agreed to this proposal. Then the flag question arose and only after a long and heated discussion did Scott agree to give back the flag to the *myosa* and not M. Pavie. The *myosa* then handed back the flag to the French leader. M. Pavie again asked the *myosa* to keep the French flag with him.

The joint commission held another meeting on March 20, 1893. But it could not reach agreement, owing to the French claim on all territories lying to the east of the Mekong plus a considerable tract west of the river, including Keng Lap. The British intention of setting up a buffer zone was also dropped. The settlement plan for Keng Cheng seemed to get nowhere but to deadlock, because the French showed no signs of compromise over the territories east of the Mekong. The French even made efforts to establish a fort near Keng Hkong to protect their interests east of the Mekong. Scott then urged the government of India to take steps to keep a permanent station of British troops to protect British interests in the area. But the chief commissioner was not in favor of keeping troops in Keng Tung. He even urged the government of India to recall the troops.[13] But the British home government took a different view about the question of keeping troops in Keng Tung. On receiving a telegram from the chief commissioner regarding the French moves to occupy Keng Cheng by all means, the British foreign secretary ordered the British political officers accompanied by British troops to proceed to Keng Cheng and remain there permanently and enforce British supremacy over the state.[14]

G. C. B. Stirling, who was a member of Scott's commission, was immediately told to proceed to Mong Hsing with his troops. A hundred men as a reserve force were to be kept in Keng Tung for an emergency.[15] A road from Mong Nai to Keng Tung was built with a telegraph line to improve communication in case of an emergency. Pavie, the French representative, showed no sign of retreat in his demand over all territories of Keng Cheng east of the Mekong. Scott, not to be outdone, laid claim to all Keng Cheng and its population. Pavie threatened to arrest any officer sent from Keng Tung who came to enforce law and order in territories east of the Mekong. Scott again declared that those officers would be protected with the use of force if necessary.

Stirling marched, as ordered, with 112 men under Captain Caulfield to Mong Hsing on April 22 and arrived on May 4. He was instructed to protest against the French occupation of the British territories and to ask them to leave and to hold firm over his position.[16] On arriving at Mong Hsing, Stirling invited the *myosa* to see him but he never turned up, though some of his ministers appeared. Stirling took the reins of administration into his hands. Ministers were asked to cooperate in the daily affairs of administration. A site for a garrison was chosen and quarters for the soldiers were built. The French representative from Keng Hkong, E. Dupy, wrote to Stirling protesting that the British had no right to occupy eastern Keng Cheng and insisting on the right to exert their authority over the territories mentioned in the clause in the Franco-Siamese Treaty of October 3, 1893.[17]

The position of Stirling in Mong Hsing was difficult. The *myosa* himself was not happy with the uneasy situation of his state. He remained in hiding to avoid being pressured from either side. The Keng Cheng ministers, too, without the presence of their chief, were unwilling to cooperate with Stirling. They were passively hostile to him as were the people of Keng Cheng who had no wish to be the subjects of the British or the French. They felt that they were part of Keng Tung State and they owed their allegiance to the Keng Tung and Keng Cheng chiefs and to nobody else. So their attitude toward Stirling was quite sullen. But they did not create any trouble against him. The revenue question arose, and Stirling had a hard time dealing with the state officials. The state ministers and officers were ordered to collect annual revenue for the British to demonstrate British authority over the people of Keng Cheng. The ministers refused to collect the revenue, saying that they needed the *myosa's* approval to do so.[18] Then Stirling took stern measures against them. He arrested some of them and put them into quarterguard with the warning that one of them would be deported each week to Myanmar until all of them had been deported. On hearing the news the *myosa* fled into French territory and asked for protection. The remaining ministers then collected the annual revenue of three thousand rupees and only then were the arrested officials freed.

The new French foreign minister, M. Barthelot, issued a statement insisting Mong Hsing be given to France as agreed in the Franco-Siamese Treaty. He also proposed a joint guarantee of Siam as a neutral state. The British foreign secretary, Lord Salisbury, was ready to negotiate.

Agreement between the two powers was reached on January 15. Under that convention neither party could send its armed forces into the region without the consent of the other. The region consisted of the basins of the Phetchaburi, Mekong, Menam, Bang Pa Kong rivers, and their tributaries.

There were some small territories around Mong Bang Tapan, Mong Pase, north of the basins of the Menam, Mekong, and Me Eng in which both parties enjoyed equal rights. But by the Franco-Siamese Treaty of October 3, 1893, France retained the rights in the twenty-five-mile zone on the right bank of the Mekong and the right to navigate in that portion. The two powers also agreed to maintain the independence of Siam, the Mekong serving as the boundary of both powers, France and Great Britain. In 1894 and 1895 separate agreements were signed with China and both powers enjoyed commercial rights in Yunnan and Sichuan provinces.[19]

Under the agreement, the territories of Keng Cheng that lay on the east bank of the Mekong were transferred to France. But a larger part of Keng Cheng was given to the British and was incorporated into Keng Tung State.

On May 9, 1896, the representative of France, M. Vacle, came to Mong Hsing to take charge of Keng Cheng. He asked Stirling, the British representative, to sign a statement admitting that the British occupation of Keng Cheng was a mistake and to transfer the revenue he had collected to the French. But Stirling refused to sign and to hand over the money. He agreed, however, to transfer the control of Mong Hsing. The transfer of authority was made on May 10, 1896, and the British marched back to Keng Tung.[20]

The Keng Cheng problem was solved. The Anglo-French rivalry over the land came to an end and secured Siam as a buffer state with its sovereignty intact. The war boats in Menam were withdrawn to their bases. But the Keng Cheng case had consumed a lot of time and effort of both parties. The cost of sending troops, and the war boats to cruise along the Menam River, was never announced and left unknown to the public. The big powers were unconcerned about the sufferings and woes of the chief and the people of Keng Cheng. Neither side took an interest in calculating the loss incurred by Keng Cheng in the power struggle. Keng Cheng felt relieved when it was released from being a pawn on the chessboard of the Anglo-French power politics on May 10, 1896. There was territorial gain for the British and the French but territorial loss for the people of Keng Cheng as well as the loss of autonomous rights which turned into a historical process to be remembered. The chief of Keng Tung was not happy about the Keng Cheng settlement. Keng Cheng had been part of Keng Tung State since time immemorial, and the acquisition of Keng Cheng was neither through war nor through force. Keng Cheng grew into a state by itself through the historical *baan-mong* process of the Shan. The amalgamation of Keng Cheng into Keng Tung State was through an evolutionary historical process of Shan being with Shan without force or war.

The British foreign secretary, Salisbury, was considered to have exercised rather sound judgment in withdrawing from Keng Cheng in the interest of Anglo-French peaceful relations. Because the disputed area was of little value it was not worth going to war over it. Geopolitically, Keng Cheng's location was too remote and inaccessible for the British. The agreement over Keng Cheng solved the Anglo-French-Siamese frontier problem.

As part of the plan to pacify the Shan States, the British had another major task to undertake: to settle the boundary between China and British Myanmar. The British did not know the exact extent of King Thibaw's domain, but they claimed that every tributary state of Thibaw should be their possession. The British political officers were asked to comb for information from the Myanmar archives, Chinese records, and local Shan chronicles, and interviews were conducted with frontier and local chiefs.

China exercised a certain degree of influence on the Shan States along the border with British Myanmar, mostly on the Chinese side of the border. But China occasionally exerted a political influence on the Shan States and Wa States on the British Myanmar side of the border. Before the overthrow of Thibaw neither Myanmar nor China had exercised authority over the Wa States. Mong Lun paid tribute to Hsen Wi only. But the Chinese became active after the annexation of Upper Myanmar by the British. When Daly led his troops through the Wa States to Keng Hung, China protested. Later China sent its agent to meet Ton Hsang in Mong Lun. During the Scott expedition it was known that Chinese influence had been established in the eastern Wa States but not inside. Such was the situation in 1893. But it had become necessary to establish a boundary line between China and British Myanmar to avoid border problems in the future.

FIGURE 8.1. Myanmar-China Boundary Commission. (Photo by J. G. Scott, British Library Collection no. 92/1 (54). Neg. no. B 12696 (pol), 1898)

Scott was very farsighted in this matter. He had a good idea as to how the demarcation line should be drawn and when and where. His previous visit to Mong Lun and the Wa States enriched his knowledge of the topographical situation of the area. He also learned how much the political influence the Chinese had in the Wa States and the dangers the British would encounter. With this historical and geographic knowledge as background, the British could easily make a diplomatic maneuver when the time came for practical negotiation to settle the border with China.

On March 1, 1894, negotiations between the two powers began and Scott made a proposal for the boundary between Wa States and China. The Chinese government accepted the proposal and an Anglo-Chinese Treaty was signed. Under the treaty the British renounced all claims to Mong Lem and Keng Hung. But the Chinese had to agree not to transfer these two states to any foreign power without the knowledge of the British government. The Chinese government failed to observe the provision and part of Keng Hung was ceded to France in June 1895. The British objected and asked for compensation, and the Chinese agreed to cede Kokang and an additional territory adjoining Hsen Wi on the western bank of the Than Lwin. Again, the Mong Lem and Keng Hung chiefs and people could not understand why their states were transferred to a new sovereign. What wrong had they done for such punishment? They were being sold or transferred to new powers for reasons they did not know. To whom should they complain about their territorial grievances?

Another convention was agreed on in Beijing on February 4, 1897, and another boundary line was demarcated between the Shan States and China, which has since remained. But the rugged part of the Wa States from the Nam Ting River to the Nam Ma River was incapable of demarcation and remained an area in which disturbances broke out in 1935–36 and 1936–37. An Anglo-Chinese commission was formed to investigate the rival claims of the area made by China and British Myanmar.

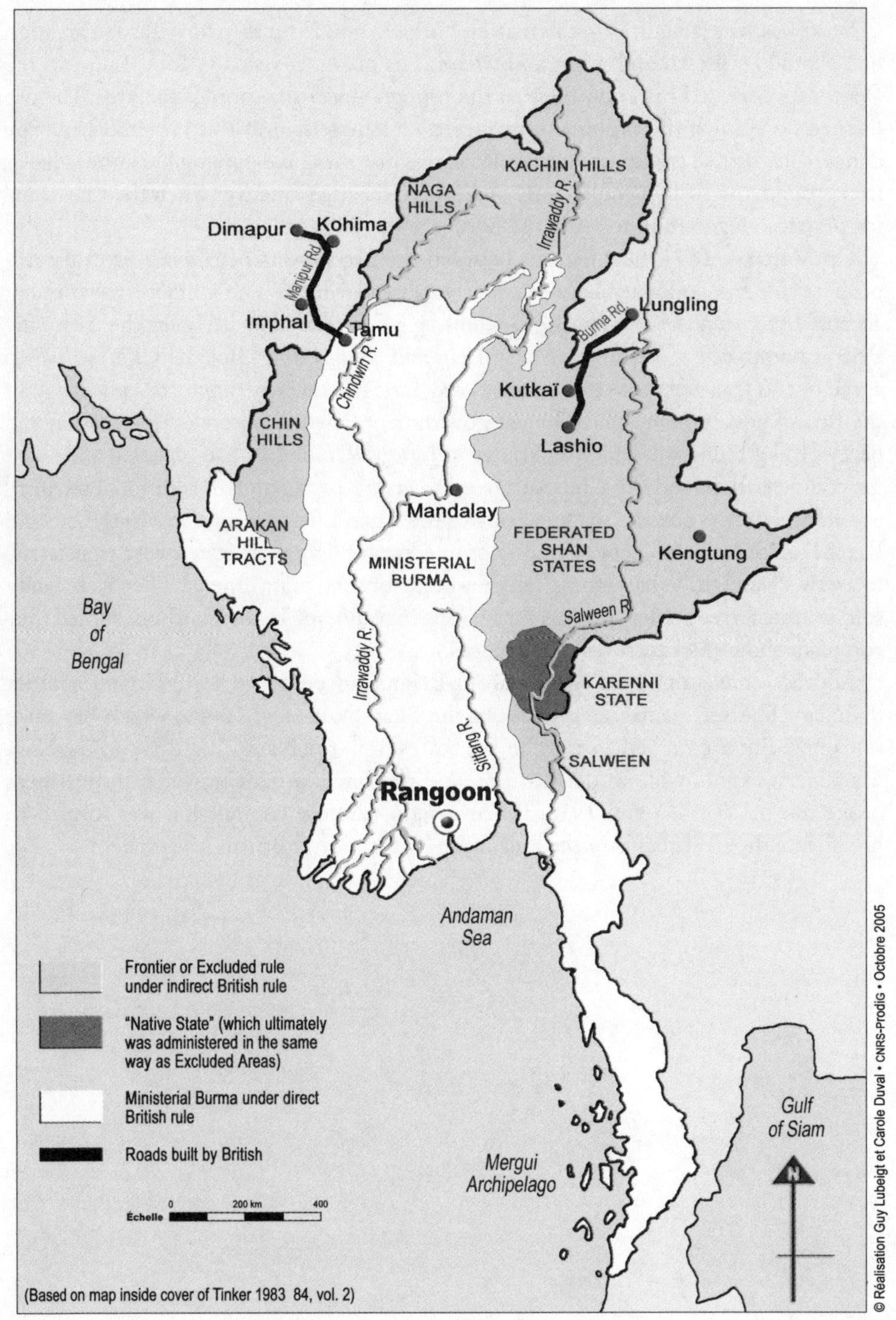

MAP 17. British colonial rule in Myanmar

9

The British Administration in the Shan States

When the British annexed Upper Myanmar in 1885, the Shan States, which were an appendage of King Thibaw's kingdom, were left unoccupied for a year or two, because the British had no definite plan how the Shan States should be annexed, occupied, and administered. Moreover, the British knowledge of the Shan, their culture, customs, traditions, and beliefs was rather limited. The topography of Shanland, its size and extent, and finally its long boundary that touched on China, French Indochina, and Siam (Thailand) were also ignored. The British were also not very well informed about the local political situation that had been developing in the Shan States in the first year of their occupation of Upper Myanmar.

J. G. Scott in his book, *Gazetteer of Upper Burma and the Shan States*, admitted as follows:

> Until comparatively recently our knowledge of the Shans was derived entirely from the Burmese history or from the information condensed from the journal of Dr. Richardson and Captain Macleod, by Colonel Yule in the thirteenth chapter of the Narrative of the Mission to the Court of Ava in 1855. The Burmese history was confused, fragmentary, and biased; the details of the explorers are very valuable in giving us details of intermediate history, but hardly help us to determine when the dispersion and segregation of the Shan race began and what their position was before these events took place.[1]

Pieces of information were gathered from the writings of Ney Elias, who wrote the *Introductory Sketch of the History of the Shan* (published in Calcutta in 1876), and from Mr. Parker, who translated the Chinese annals and discovered that the Shan kingdom of Tali-fu at one time came very near to overthrowing the Chinese Tang dynasty. From Reverend Dr. J. N. Cushing, who wrote a brief Shan history and ethnography in 1890, the British also got some information on the Shan, who once lived together with the Chinese as brothers and whose original homeland was in China before they came to Southeast Asia.[2]

Monsieur Terrien also supplied the British with information about the existence of a Shan empire called Nan-chao and about the Ai Lao people who very often raided the Chinese in the old days. Later, interest in Shan history began to rise and British political officers and scholars began to comb through Myanmar records and manuscripts and Shan local chronicles for more information. Interviews with local scholars, local administrators, *saohpa*, and frontier chiefs were intensively conducted to get information about the Shan and their history.

Meanwhile, the situation in the Shan States became chaotic and news of the fighting among the Shan chiefs, the formation of rival groups, the Limbin Confederacy, the rebellion organized by Twet Nga Lu, the revolt of the Karenni chief against the British, the anti-British campaign of Prince Saw Yang Naing and his followers, the political instability in Hsi Paw and North Hsen Wi kept coming in every day and struck an alarm bell for the British administrators. They realized that delay in taking action could threaten the stability of their newly acquired British territories of Myanmar.

The first step in maintaining stability was to confirm that the Shan States, which formerly belonged to King Thibaw, had now become the possession of the British government. Lord Dufferin issued the following statement on New Year's Day in 1886:

> By command of the Queen Empress it is hereby notified that the territories formerly governed by King Thibaw will no longer be under his rule, but have become part of Her Majesty's dominions and will . . . be administered by such Officers as Viceroy and Governor-General of India. . . .[3]

Even then Lord Dufferin was not so sure how the Shan States should be brought under British suzerainty. In his speech at Government House in Yangon (Rangoon) that he delivered to the Shan community on February 24, 1886, he said:

> I am much interested in the Shan nationality. Her Majesty's Government is most anxious to make you, and . . . all the inhabitants of the Shan States, feel how desirous we are to gain their confidence, to cultivate good will, and to do everything in our power to promote their trade and advance their general interests. You will be doing the Government a real service if you take any opportunity . . . of making their rules and the inhabitants of those States understand that the British Government is fully determined to respect their independence, to abstain from all interference, with their internal affairs. . . .[4]

The British chief commissioner, who had much authority in handling the affairs of the Shan States, was very careful in dealing with the Shan chiefs. He believed that the most important thing was to get their trust and confidence and if that could be achieved, he would have no difficulty in getting the submission of the Shan chiefs. To achieve that, he must first apply the olive branch policy, and if that failed, then he should adopt the carrot-and-stick policy.

The commissioner chose the policy of the olive branch when he telegrammed the government of India on November 25, 1886:

> I asked General Prendergast not to send his notice among the Shan and told him that we had no idea of governing them or converting them into British districts. . . . I gave him a first rate Shan interpreter who has travelled in the Shan States and suggested that if he had opportunity of communicating with Shan chiefs, he should tell them that the British would not interfere in internal autonomy of the large states, so long as they governed well, promoted trade and paid a moderate tribute.[5]

For over a year the British tried to convince the Shan chiefs of their good intention of noninterference and respect for autonomous rights of the chiefs, but the response was not satisfactory. Most of the Shan chiefs kept ignoring their appeals and requests. Only two chiefs, one from the Northern and the other from the Southern Shan States, were interested in making an alliance with the British. Hkun Hseng of Hsi Paw and Sao On of Yawng Hwe chose British help and protection. The remaining chiefs were divided on the issue of submission to British overlordship. The Limbin Confederacy opposed British supremacy over them; for them the question of confronting the British did not arise, since their objective was only to replace King Thibaw with the Limbin prince and not to fight the British. The other Shan chiefs were interested only in recovering their lost territories from usurpers and to punish them for robbing them of their legitimate rights. Twet Nga Lu was not interested in fighting against the British. He fought only to get the Mong Nai throne from Hkun Kyi. Sao Waing of Lawk Sawk tried to get back his lost territories from the Yawng Hwe chief and made war against the British only because the British protected the Yawng Hwe chief. The Keng Tung chief did not have a good reason to oppose the

FIGURE 9.1. Government House, Taunggyi, 1909. (British Library Collection no. 163/1 (151), Neg. no. B. 15699 pol, 1909)

FIGURE 9.2. Durbar Hall, Southern Shan State, 1909. (British Library Collection no. 163/1 (148), Neg. no. B. 15106 pol, 1909)

British. He was anti–King Thibaw over the questions of tax exaction and appointment of his candidate in Keng Hung.

This was the actual state of affairs in the Shan States. It did not prove to be as simple as the British believed. They became quite complicated and until this web of political complications was immediately tackled it could affect the security and stability of the eastern part of the British Empire. Finally the British political and administrative officers became convinced that both diplomatic and military means must be applied to solve the affairs of the Shan States. Within two years of intensive efforts using both the olive branch and carrot-and-stick policies, the whole of the Shan States was annexed, occupied, and pacified including the settlement of the frontier problem with China, French indochina, and Siam.

On February 4, 1890, the Foreign Department issued a notification about the form of *sanad* that was adopted with the approval of the government of India for issue to *saohpa* of the Shan States. The *sanad* were offered to the *saohpa* who ruled over big states, and also to *myosa* who ruled over substates of the *saohpa*, and also to *ngwehkunmu* who were chiefs of the Myelat principalities. The terms of the *sanad* to be observed by the *saohpa*, *myosa*, and *ngwehkunmu* were not the same. They differed from one another depending upon the location of the state, the situation prevailing at that time, and the general opinion of the chief commissioner, who decided on the appropriate terms to be included in the *sanad*.

Generally, the terms concluded in the *sanad* were:

1. Permission to administer the territory of the state with power to manage matters of law and order, revenue, and nomination of successor.
2. Rules, regulations, and conditions were prescribed by the chief commissioner and any chief who failed to observe them would forfeit the rights to rule over his state.
3. *Saohpa* were required to pay a fixed amount of tribute in cash for five years. The amount and duration would be revised by the chief commissioner as he thought fit.
4. The government reserved to itself the proprietary right of all forests, mines, and minerals. If the *saohpa* would like to work or lease any forests they could do so provided they paid royalty to the government.
5. Shan chiefs were required to administer their states according to the customary law but subject to the guidance of the superintendent of the Shan States not to oppress the people.
6. The Shan rulers were also required to maintain peace and order in their territories and to keep open trade routes. They were to pay compensation if traders or caravans were attacked within their territories.
7. The *saohpa* were also required to keep an agent who would live at the headquarters to keep the superintendent informed of what was happening in their states.

8. The Shan chiefs were required to accept the decision made by the superintendent if disputes arose within or without their states.
9. The Shan rulers must also provide land free of cost if the government decided to build a railway line through their states. They must help the government in every possible way.
10. The Shan *saohpa* were also forbidden to export opium, spirits, or fermented liquor into Lower Myanmar or other parts of Myanmar unless they paid duties and observed rules of customs.
11. The Shan rulers were required to deliver any criminals who took refuge in their territories at the request of the government officers.
12. The *saohpa* were not permitted to exercise any criminal jurisdiction over European and British subjects and such cases should be presented to the superintendent of the Shan States.
13. The *saohpa* were required to obtain permission for communication with states outside British India. (For details, see appendixes 9–15.)

REDEFINITION OF THE SHAN STATES

On May 4, 1886, the British Foreign Department issued Notification 791E which said, "... the whole of Upper Myanmar, including the Shan States, ... was declared to be part of British India."

Then under Section 8 of the Upper Myanmar Laws Act, issued in 1887, the Shan States were defined as follows:

1. The Northern Shan States (under the supervision of the superintendent, Northern Shan States)
2. The Southern Shan States (under the supervision of the superintendent and political officer, Southern Shan States)
3. The Myelat (under the supervision of the superintendent and political officer, Southern Shan States)
4. States under the supervision of the deputy commissioner, Myitkyina District
5. States under the supervision of the deputy commissioner, Upper Chindwin District

When the British took over the Shan States, they readjusted interstate boundary lines and amalgamated the small states into the big states to meet the needs of the British administration. Sometimes territories were taken from their original states and given back to their original owners to be in line with British administrative convenience. For example, Maw or Baw, which was placed under the control of the commissioner of Meikhtila Division, was afterward restored to its original position as one of the Myelat States.

In 1900 the small state of Nam Hkom was incorporated in the state of Kyaukku and ceased to exist. In 1902 the state of Mong Sang, or Mong Sin, was amalgamated with Mong Hsu State.

In 1917 the small state of Nam Hkai was incorporated in Loi Long.

In 1920 the substate of Keng Hkam was amalgamated with the state of Mong Nai.

In 1920 Mong Mit State was included in the Northern Shan States and separated from the Ruby Mine District of which it originally formed a part. But this district was placed under the Mong Mit chief, Sao Khin Maung, KSM.

In 1922 Maw Son (Baw Zaing) State was amalgamated with Yawng Hwe.

In 1926 Keng Lun was amalgamated with Kehsi Mansam.

In 1928 the small state of Loi Maw was amalgamated with Yawng Hwe State.

In 1930 Loi Ai (Lwe E) was amalgamated with Hsa Mong Hkam (Thamakan) and Nam Tok with Loi Long.

The unfortunate Trans-Salween States of Keng Hung and Mong Lem were ceded to China. Another Trans-Salween State, Keng Cheng, had part of its territories ceded to France and another part of its territories absorbed into Keng Tung.

The last unfortunate Trans-Salween state of Cheng Sen was ceded to Siam and all these states were excluded from the Shan States.

By virtue of the Myanmar Act of 1898, subsection 3, the lieutenant governor announced the following territories to constitute the Shan States:

1. The Northern Shan States comprising the following states were to be placed under the supervision of the superintendent, Northern Shan States.

Name of State	Dependencies
(1) Tawn Peng, or Taungbaing (2) North Hsen Wi, or Theinni (3) South Hsen Wi, or Mong Yai	
(4) Hsi Paw, or Thipaw	- Mong Long, or Maing Lon - Hsum Hsai, or Tonze - Mong Tung, or Maing Ton
(5) [a]Mong Mit, or Momeik	- Mong Lang, or Mohlaing
(6) East and West Mong Lun, or Mainglun	- Mawhpa - Hoklap - Mot Hai - Ngekting - Monghseng - Mong Pat

[a] The state of Mong Mit (Momeik) with its dependency was excluded from the Ruby Mines District and included in the Northern Shan States—vide Political Department Notification No. 32, dated November 4, 1920. (IA)

(7) All territories east of the Salween River not mentioned elsewhere in this notification, which on November 27, 1885, owed allegiance to the king of Myanmar and which still form part of Upper Myanmar	

2. The Southern Shan States comprising the following states were to be placed under the supervision of the superintendent and political officer, Southern Shan States.

Name of State	Dependencies
(1) [b]Keng Tung, or Kyaington	- Mong Pu, or Maing Pu - Mong Hsat, or Maing That - Hsin Mawng, or Thinbaung - Hsin Ywat, or Theinyut
(2) [c]Mong Nai, or Monè	- Keng Tawng, to Kyaingtaung
(3) [d]Yawng Hwe, or Nyaung Shwe	- Lai Hsat, or Lethet - Angley, or Inleywa - Kyawkhtap or Kyawktat - Hsikip, or Thigyit
(4) Mong Pai, or Mobye (5) Lawk Sawk, or Yatsauk (6) Lai Hka, or Legya	
(7) Mawk Mai, or Mawkme	- Mehsakun, or Mesakun - Mong Mau, or Maing maw
(8) Mong Pan, or Maingpan	- Mong Hta, or Mainhta - Mong Hang, or Mainghan - Mong Kyawt, or Maingsut - Mong Tun
(9) Mong Pawn, or Maingpun	
(10) Sam Ka, or Saga	- Pangmi
(11) Nawng Wawn, or Naungmun (12) Mong Nawng, or Maingnaung (13) Mong Kung, or Maingkaing (14) Mong Sit, or Maingzeik (15) [e]Kehsi Mansam, or Kyethi Bansan	

[b] See Political Department Notification No. 12, May 21, 1896.

[c] Kenghkam (Kyangkan) ceased to be a state and was amalgamated with the State of Mong Nai (Monè)—*vide* Political Department Notification No. 26, October 9, 1920.

[d] Includes Mawson (Bawsaing) which ceased to be a state and was amalgamated with the State of Yawng Hwe (Nyaungshwe)—*vide* Political Department Notification No. 44, September 20, 1922; also Loimaw, which was included in the State of Yawng Hwe by Political Department Notification No. 9, February 9, 1928.

[e] Kenglun (Kainglun) ceased to be a state and was amalgamated with the State of Kehsi Mansam (Kyethi)—*vide* Political Department Notification No. 28 (?), May 20, 1926.

(16) [d]Loi Long, or Lwelon (17) Hsahtung, or Thaton	- Tam Hpak, or Tabet - Mang Lon, or Letmaing
(18) Wanyin, or Bunyin	
(19) Hopong, or Hopon	- He Long, or Helon
(20) Nam Hkok or Nankok (21) Sakoi, or Sagwe (22) [e]Mong Hsu, or Mainghsu	

3. The Myelat area was placed under the supervision of the superintendent and political officer, Southern Shan States.

Name of State	Dependencies
(1) Maw Nang, or Bawnin	
(2) [g]Hsa Mong Hkam, or Thamakan	- Ma Kwe, or Magwe - Loi Ai, or Lwean - Tawngla, or Taungla
(3) [h]Pwela, or Pwehla (4) Maw, or Baw (5) Ye Ngan, or Ywangan (6) Pangtara, or Pindaya (7) Pangmi, or Pinhmi (8) [i]Loi Ai (9) [j] Nam Hkom	
(10) [k]Loi Maw (11) Kyong, or Kyon (12) [l]Nam Tok	

[f] Nam Hkai (Nanke) in the Myelat ceased to be a state and was amalgamated with the State of Loi Long (Lwelon)—*vide* Political Department Notification No. 6, March 2, 1917.

[g] Mong Sang (Maingsin) ceased to be a state and was amalgamated with the State of Mong Hsu (Mainghsu)—*vide* Political Department Notification No. 4, April 17, 1902.

[h] Loi Ai (Lwe E) ceased to be a state and was amalgamated with the State of Hsa Mong Hkam by Political Department Notification No. 21, April 22, 1930.

[i] Kyawkkuceased to be a state and was amalgamated with the State of Pwelaby Political Department Notification No. 10, February 9, 1928.

[j] Loi Ai (Lwe E) ceased to be a state and was amalgamated with the State of Hsa Mong Hkam by Political Department Notification No. 21, April 22, 1930.

Nam Hkom (Nankom) ceased to be a state and was amalgamated with the State of Kyawkku by Political Department Notification No. 10, dated February 9, 1930.

[k] Loi Maw (Lwemaw) ceased to be a state and was included in Yawng Hwe by Political Department Notification No. 9, February 9, 1928. These territories ceased to be part of the Myelat and are subject to the Shan States Customary Law in force in Yawng Hwe (Nyaungshwe) State—*vide* Political Department Notification No. 24, dated April 30, 1928.

[l] Namtok (Nantok) ceased to be a state and was amalgamated with Loi Long (Lwelon) by Political Department Notification No. 21, dated April 22, 1930.

4. State under the supervision of the deputy commissioner, Myitkyina[m]District.

Name of State	Dependencies
(1) Hkamti Long, or Kantigyi	

5. States under the supervision of the deputy commissioner, Upper Chindwin District.

Name of State	Dependencies
(1) Hsawnghsup, or Thaung Thut	
(2) Singkalaing Hkamti, or Zingalein Kanti	

[m] "Myitkyina" substituted for "Putao" by Political Department Notification No. 12, dated March 31, 1925.

During the early days of the British occupation, the authority and powers of the Shan chiefs and their officials were exercised without any legal sanction. The Shan States Act of 1888, which came into effect in February 1889, made a little modification to the feudal powers. By section 11 of that Act the civil, criminal, and revenue administration of every Shan State was vested in the chief of state but subject to the restriction specified in the *sanad*, or order of appointment, granted to the chief. Under the same section, customary laws were allowed to be practiced in the administration of each state, but they must be in accordance with justice, equity, and good conscience without opposing the spirit of the law of British India. With two years of experience with the Shan chiefs and their administrative system, the British came to realize that the feudal administrative system lacked the essence of British justice in many civil and criminal cases and in programs of public welfare. Limitations of the autonomous rights of the Shan chiefs were then imposed in the appointment *sanad* of the Shan chiefs. With that emerged the British Administration in the Shan States. Moreover, the power to appoint officers of the states and to regulate their powers and proceedings was vested in the governor.

After pacifying the Shan States, the British took measures to introduce their administration in Shanland. Shanland is a vast area, with many hills of various heights and deep valleys; thick forests with difficult means of communication and transportation. The size of the states and principalities depended on the size of each valley, and a feudal type of administration was the common system everywhere. Each state or principality was under its chief, the *saohpa*. They were so divided and never united, but they enjoyed their autonomous rights from the beginning of their history. They insisted on having that right throughout even after they had accepted the Myanmar kings as their traditional or legal sovereigns. The Myanmar kings thus reigned over the Shan people by remote control. They rarely visited Shanland but retained it through their chiefs. The

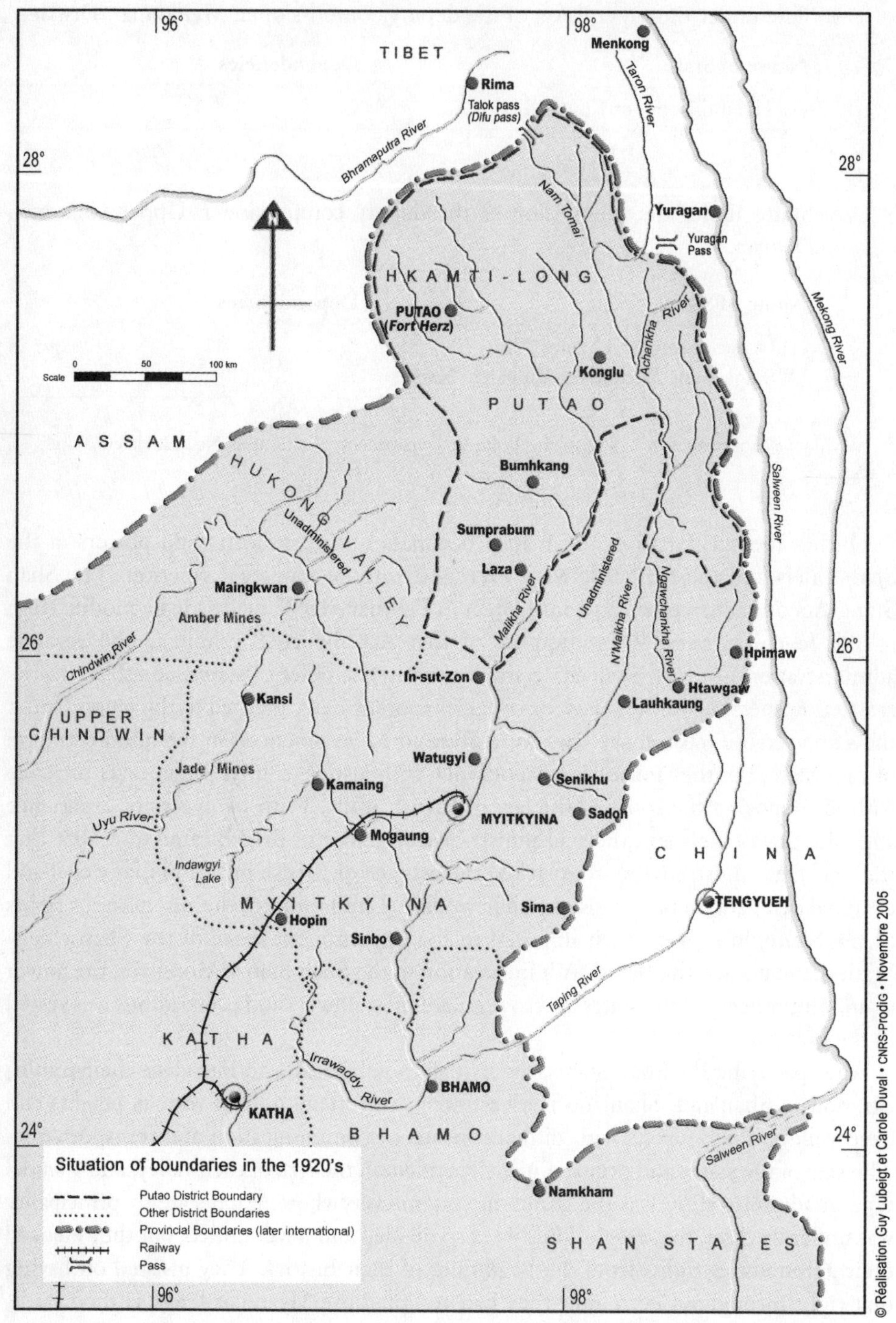

MAP 18. Putao region (northern Myanmar)

Shan people did not seem to mind much or care much about having the Myanmar kings as their sovereign. They had learned that there were times when Shan chiefs were kings of Myanmar and they gave the same allegiance, with no difference or peculiarity, as to whether the king was Myanmar or Shan. Now, the British came and the country called Myanmar lost its sovereignty and independence. The Shan chiefs, the Shan people, and the Shanland shared the woes suffered by the Myanmar. Now who were to be blamed for the loss of sovereignty and independence, the Myanmar or the Shan? Let us study the history of the Shan States and analyze the series of events, right and wrong, good and bad, and review the historical facts so as not to repeat the bad parts of our history.

The British in their new administration and for convenience divided the Shan States into North and South.

By 1922 the British administrators felt the need to reform the Shan States' administration. Before 1922 the Shan States administration was so decentralized and diverse that it was sometimes difficult to apply a uniform system of regulations, hindering the effectiveness and progress of the administration. The administrative officers felt that it would be much better and more efficient in executing the work plans of the administration and development of communication and other works if a system of coordination and pooling of resources could be introduced. A sense of collective contribution by all the chiefs to the all-round development of their states should be the criteria of the new system. A federated system was then introduced in the Shan States by Notification of No. 31, on September 17, 1922, which said:

FIGURE 9.3. At the Delhi Durbar, 1903. Four of the Southern Shan States chiefs in magnificent gold coats: Mong Pawn, Keng Tung, Mong Nai, Yawng Hwe. *Back:* Gantarawadi (Sawlawi), *center,* flanked by Bawlakay and Kye-bogyi. (Grabowsky et al. 2003, 230)

With the sanction of the Governor-General in Council and the consent of the Chief of the Shan States concerned, the Lieutenant Governor is pleased to declare that, with effect from 1st October 1922, the under mentioned Shan States and Notified Areas shall be known as the Federated Shan States:

Northern Shan States

Hsi Paw
Tawng Peng
North Hsen Wi
South Hsen Wi (Mong Yai)
Mong Mit
Mong Lun
Lashio (notified area)

Southern Shan States

Keng Tung
Mong Nai
Yawng Hwe
Mong Pai
Lawk Sawk
Lai Hka
Mawk Mai
Mong Pan
Mong Pawn
Sam Ka
Nawng Wawn
Mong Nawng
Mong Kung
Mong Sit
Kehsi Mansam
Maw Nang
Loi Long
Hsa Htung
Wan Yin
Hopong
Nam Hkok
Sa Koi
Mong Hsu
Hsa Mong Hkam
Pwe La
Maw
Ye Ngan
Pang Mi
Kyong
Taunggyi (notified area)
Loi Lem (notified area)
Kalaw (notified area)
Keng Lum[6]

THE FEDERAL COUNCIL OF SHAN CHIEFS

The Federal Council was the highest organ of the Federated Shan States. According to Notification No.18, issued on May 5, 1923, by the governor of Myanmar, the commissioner of the Federated Shan States would become the president of the council. The superintendent of the Northern Shan States would be the vice president and would preside in the absence of the president. While presiding over the council, the vice president would have the same powers as the president.

The assistant superintendent of the Shan States would be appointed secretary of the council. The duty of the secretary was to send invitations including the agenda to the members of the council for the meeting.

Under this scheme of federation, the Shan chiefs retained their autonomous rights in cases like collecting taxes, ensuring law and order, maintaining courts for the disposal

FIGURE 9.4. Saohpa of Hsi Paw, Sir Sao Hke. (Sai Aung Tun collection)

FIGURE 9.5. Saohpa of Yawng Hwe, Sir Sao Maung.
Yawng Hwe Museum, Southern Shan State

of criminal and civil cases, appointing their own officials, and controlling their own subjects but under the advice of the superintendents.

The Departments of Public Works, Medical Administration, Forests, Education, Agriculture, and to a small extent Police were centralized and placed under the control of the federation. States were required to contribute to the Federation Fund. Some portions of the fund were received from forests, minerals, and a fixed contribution by provincial funds. The federation was also required to pay a fixed proportion of its revenue to the government of Myanmar in place of tribute formerly paid by the states. The Federated Shan States then became a subentity of Myanmar with its own administration and revenue.

The chiefs could express their views on federal and general matters, including the budget, through the Council of Chiefs, including all chiefs of the rank of *saohpa* and four elected representatives of those of lesser rank. The commissioners of the Federated Shan States, the superintendent, political officers for the Southern Shan States, and the superintendent for the Northern Shan States were ex-officio members of the council. The agent of the governor in respect of the administration was the commissioner of the Federated Shan States, who was president of the council. The power of the High Court was vested in the commissioner. As superintendent and political officer, he could also try other cases. The governor was the High Court himself and could try other cases also. Departmental officers in the Shan States were also technical advisers of the superintendent and the commissioner in their subjects.

In 1922, under the original arrangement, the Federated Shan States formed part of the Northeast Frontier Division. But on July 1, 1925, there was a separate commissioner for the Federated Shan States, who could also perform his duties as superintendent or political officer of the Southern Shan States. The administration of the federation was different from that of the rest of Myanmar.

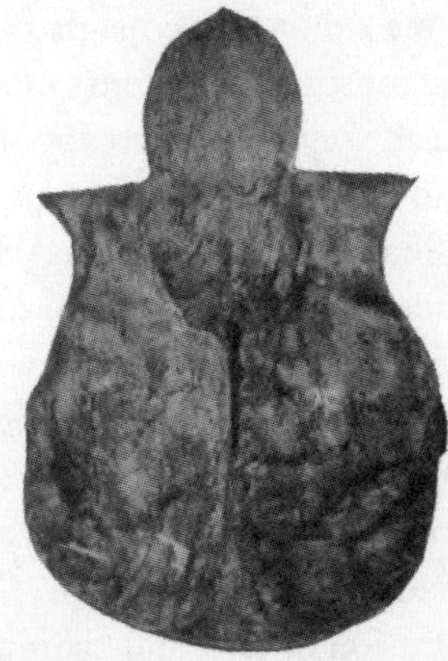

FIGURE 9.6. Helmet of Tai Hkamti soldier and leather jacket of Tai Hkamti soldier, Myitkyina Museum, Kachin State

In the Northern Shan States, at first, the criminal, civil, and revenue administration was vested in the chiefs, but there were limitations laid down in their *sanad* and restrictions imposed through the Shan States Act, or the Myanmar Laws Act.

Notification No. 11 of November 1890 also modified the customary law applied in cases of criminal and civil matters. The superintendent was empowered to revise punishment for criminal cases and had control over the administration of criminal justice. Revisionary power over criminal or civil cases was vested in the superintendent. The chiefs could not try any criminal or civil cases committed by a European or American or a government servant. Only the superintendent and assistant superintendent could try such cases.

According to the Federated Shan States Laws and Criminal Justice Order of 1926, the superintendent could exercise the power of the district magistrate and session judge and the assistant superintendent could act as a district magistrate by the Code of Criminal Procedure, sections 31 and 34 of 1898.

If the superintendents and assistant superintendents were Europeans or British subjects, they were also to act as ex-officio justices of the peace in the Shan States. The following *saohpa* were gazetted as additional session judges for the areas within their jurisdictions:

1. Keng Tung
2. Hsi Paw
3. Mong Nai
4. Tawng Peng
5. North Hsen Wi
6. Mong Mit
7. Yawng Hwe

The superintendent was empowered to withdraw from subordinate magistrates such cases as he thought fit. He could also take cognizance of any criminal case and try or refer it to a subordinate magistrate for trial. In certain Shan States the superintendent and assistant superintendent could act as registrars for births, deaths, and marriages. In some areas they could also appoint headmen. The above-mentioned acts also applied equally to the Myelat

The Shan States of Hsaung Hsop and Singkaling Hkamti in the Chindwin valleys were placed under the control of the deputy commissioners of Myitkyina and Upper Chindwin Districts. Separate laws and criminal justice orders were issued for these areas on June 21, 1926. But the power of the High Court was vested in the commissioner of Sagaing Division. The Shan States of Hkamti Long were put under the control of the deputy commissioner of Myitkyina District. For that area an administration order was issued on June 21, 1926. The regulation of the laws of that area included the administration of civil and criminal justice and the collection of revenue.

The procedures to be observed by the members for the conduct of business of the Federated Council were stated as follows:

The Governor of Myanmar is pleased to approve of the following rules for the conduct of business and the procedures to be followed in the Council of the Federated Shan chiefs:

1. The Commissioner, Federated Shan States, shall be the President of the Council. The Superintendent, Northern Shan States, shall be the Vice-President and shall preside in the absence of the President. The Vice-President when presiding over the Council shall have the same power as the President when so presiding.
2. The Council shall appoint a Secretary, who shall ordinarily be an Assistant Superintendent of the Shan States.
3. The Council shall assemble at least once in every year at a date and place to be appointed by the President to suit the convenience of members of the Council.
4. The Secretary shall send to each member a summons to attend each meeting, stating the business to be transacted thereat.
5. A member who wishes to move any resolution or ask any question at a meeting of the Council shall send a copy of such resolution or question to the Secretary not less than six days before the commencement of the meeting and a copy of such notice or question shall be circulated by the Secretary to the members of Council.
6. The President shall determine the business for each day of the period of the meeting and except with the leave of the President no business not included in the business of the day shall be transacted at any meeting.
7. Not less than twelve members shall be the quorum for the transaction of business.
8. The business of the Council shall be conducted in Shan or Myanmar, and shall, if the President so directs, be recorded in English or in Myanmar.
9. The President may adjourn a meeting of the Council either on his own motion or on a vote by the Council in that behalf.
10. The President shall preserve order and decide all points of order. A member may at any time submit a point of order for the decision of the President. No discussion of any point of order shall be permitted unless the President desires to take the opinion of the Council thereon.
11. A member desiring to make any observation on any matter before the Council shall speak from his place, shall rise when he speaks and shall address the President. If the President rises at any time the member then speaking shall resume his seat.
12. When, for the purpose of explanation during the discussion or for any sufficient reason, a member has occasion to ask a question of another member on any matter then under the consideration of the Council he shall ask the question through the President.
13. (1) The matter of every speech must be relevant to the matter before the Council.

(2) A member while speaking must not:

(a) refer to any matter of fact on which a judicial decision is pending;

(b) make a personal charge against a member;

(c) use offensive expressions regarding the conduct of any legislature within the British empire;

(d) reflect upon the conduct of His Majesty the King or the Governor-General or any Governor or any Court of Justice;

(e) utter treasonable, seditious, or defamatory words; or

(f) use his right of speech for the purpose of obstructing the business of the Council.

14. The decision of the Council on any matter requiring decision shall be taken by means of a question put by the President on a motion proposed by a member or otherwise.

15. Votes may be taken by a show of hands or in such other manner as the President may direct.

16. The decision of the Council shall be in accordance with the one on which the Council has given its decision in the same session.

17. A motion must not raise a question substantially identical with one raised in another motion.

18. After the member who moves has spoken, other members may speak to the motion in such order as the President may determine.

19. No member other than the mover shall speak more than once upon a question, but the mover shall be allowed to close the debate with his reply.

20. The President may address the Council at any stage before putting a question to move.

21. (1) An amendment must be relevant to the subject matter of the motion to which it is proposed.

(2) An amendment may not be moved which if carried would have merely the effect of a negative vote.

(3) After a decision has been given on an amendment to any part of a motion an earlier part shall not be amended.

(4) No amendment may be proposed which is inconsistent with a previous decision on the same subject matter given in the same period of meeting.

(5) The President may refuse to put an amendment which in his opinion is frivolous.

22. (1) When an amendment is moved, or when two or more amendments are moved, the President shall, before taking the sense of the Council thereon, state to read to the Council the terms of the original motion or and of the amendment or amendments proposed.

(2) It shall be in the discretion of the President to put first to the vote either the original motion or any of the amendments which may have been brought forward.

23. With the consent of the Council the President may require the attendance at any meeting of any officer in the service of the Federated Shan States. Such officer may be permitted to speak at the request of the President but shall have no vote.
24. With the consent of the Council any matter may be referred to a Committee appointed by the members with instruction to the Council on such matter by a given date.
25. The Council may resolve itself into a Committee for the discussion of any matter. In such case, the Council shall elect a Chairman in place of the President and the formal rules of debate shall be suspended. No resolution of such Committee shall have effect unless and until a motion for its adoption has been passed by the Council.[7]
26. The minutes of the proceedings of the Council shall be recorded by the Secretary and copies of the minutes relating to one meeting shall be circulated in English and Myanmar to all members at or before the end of the following meeting. The minutes as a whole shall be put to the Council for formal confirmation at the close of the last meeting of the session. After confirmation, they shall be signed by the President and, when so signed, shall be the record of the proceedings of the Council and shall be open to the inspection of each member of the Council.[8]
27. Notifications

(A) Boundary between the Possessions of Great Britain and France Foreign Department Notification No. 958E., dated the 22nd May 1895.

Whereas by a declaration in regard to Siam and the Upper Mekong signed and made on the fifteenth day of January 1896, it was agreed between Her Majesty the Queen-Empress of India and the President of the French Republic that the *thalweg* of the Mekong River should be the boundary between the possessions or influence of Great Britain and France respectively.

Know all men, and it is hereby proclaimed, that the *thalweg* of the Mekong River from the mouth of the Nam Huok northwards as far as the Chinese frontier is the limit of the possessions or spheres of influence of Great Britain and France respectively.

Also know all men, and it is further proclaimed, that the Governor-General in Council is hereby pleased to order that all lands and territories whatsoever situated within Her Majesty's possessions between the *thalweg* of the Shan State of Keng Tung shall henceforward form part of the said Shan State of Kengtung.

(B) The Eastern Boundary of the Keng Tung State Political Department Notification No. 12, dated the 1st May 1896

In exercise of the power conferred by section 8, subsection (3), of the Upper Myanmar Laws Act xx of 1886, and with the previous sanction of the Governor-General in Council the Chief Commissioner is pleased, in continuation of Notification No. 10, dated the 11th July 1895, and in supersession of so much thereof as refers to Keng Cheng (Kyaingchaing), to declare that the *thalweg* of the Mekong River from the mouth of the Nam Huok northwards as far as the Chinese State of Keng Hung for the purpose of the said Act and that all lands and territories situated within Her Majesty's possessions between the *thalweg* of the Mekong River as abovementioned and the existing frontier of the said Shan State of Keng Tung shall henceforward form part of that State.

(C) Foreign Department Notification No. 2, I. A., dated the 1st January 1903. Table of salutes to Shan sawbwa.

States	**No. of guns**
1. Keng Tung	9
2. Hsi Paw	9
3. Mong Nai	9

(D) Foreign Department Notification No. 1, I.C., dated the 1st January 1906.

State	**No. of guns**
1. Yawng Hwe	9

(E) Foreign & Political Department Notification No. 1, I. C., dated the 1st January 1918.

State	**No. of guns**
1. Kun Sang Awn	9

(F) Political Department Notification No. 17, dated the 10th May 1923. His Excellency the Governor is pleased to direct that the Council of the Shan States Federation shall be known in English as "The Federal Council of Shan Chiefs" and in Myanmar as "Kambawza Padethayaza Athin."

During the British administration in the Shan States, the classical names of states were officially retained (as can be seen in appendix 16).

Since its inauguration on October 1, 1922, the federation had never been popular among the feudal chiefs, *saohpa*, because they felt that they were not thoroughly consulted and the scheme was an imposition on them by the British. Its advantages and disadvantages were not thoroughly discussed, and the general feeling among the local chiefs was that by framework of this federation their executive powers had not only been reduced but had been deprived of most of their hereditary rights and status as the ruling chiefs of their states. They also felt that they had been compelled to give up too much of their traditional powers to the federation, which affected much of their hereditary status if looked at from the eyes of their Shan subjects. The general feeling of uneasiness and dissatisfaction was stirred up among the big chiefs of the big states, especially the four hereditary saluted Shan chiefs of Hsi Paw, Keng Tung, Mong Nai, and Yawng Hwe, including the *saohpa* of Mong Mit and South Hsen Wi. They prepared a memorial of grievances and the official claim to be classified and recognized as the same level of the princes of India equipped with full hereditary privileges and rights. They put that memorial to the governor in 1923.

The issue of *saohpa's* rights and status was then discussed between the governor and the deputation of the *saohpa* at Taunggyi in December 1924. But the governor rejected the proposal of the *saohpa* on the ground that the history and traditions of the Shan States were quite different from those of the Indian princes who ruled their native states in India. The Shan chiefs did not lose hope after their proposal was rejected. They kept on sending one memorandum after another from 1930 to 1939 demanding that their hereditary or traditional rights and status be restored to them.[9]

The meeting of the Federal Council of Shan Chiefs was held at Taunggyi on September 7, 1930, and there, a resolution was passed to send two *saohpa*—one from Mong Mit and the other from Yawng Hwe—as their representatives to attend and present their cases at the Roundtable Conference held in London between the Myanmar delegation and the British government on the issue of separation of Myanmar from British India. The two representatives were to present the interests of the feudal chiefs of the Shan States. They also hoped to lay before the British government the aim and the desire of the Shan chiefs. The summary of the 1930 memorandum was submitted to the British government at the Roundtable Conference in London (see appendix 17). The summary read as follows:

> On the occasion of the Burma Roundtable Conference held in 1930 to consider the constitutional future of Myanmar, the Federated Shan States sent two representatives, Sao Khin Maung, *saohpa* of Mong Mit and Sao Shwe Thaike, *saohpa* of Yawng Hwe to London to present their views and a Memorandum was submitted to the British Government in December 1930.
>
> The Memorandum first traced the history of the Shan States, relating that at the time of the British annexation of Upper Burma, despite some measure of Burmese ascendancy over the Shan States, the right of Shan Chiefs to rule their own states independent of Burmese control was not questioned; that, after the annexation, the Shan Chiefs were treated as sovereigns in their own right and the Shan States were incorporated into British India with the Chiefs becoming subjects of the Crown.
>
> The Memorandum stated that the Constitution of the Federation was framed without formal consultation with the Chiefs, who were made to consent to the Constitution at a single meeting, and that a sympathetic interpretation of the Constitution was impossible with British officers who were unacquainted with the customs of the Shan States and came with preconceived ideas.
>
> The Memorandum declared that in pre-Federation days, tribute was paid directly to the Government of India and not to the Government of Myanmar, and that administration of the two countries was not only distinct but completely different; that, nevertheless, the Shan States would not object to a future federal form of government with Myanmar on the following terms:

(a) that there would be no interference with the affairs of individual States;
(b) that their ancient rights, customs, religions, and privileges would remain unaltered unless modified by mutual consent;
(c) that the relationship would be on the same lines as that between the India States and British India; and
(d) that the hereditary rights of the Chiefs would be acknowledged and safeguarded by the British Government.

Asserting that under the existing system of administration the Chiefs had only nominal legislative and executive powers, the Memorandum called for the full freedom for the Chiefs in civil and criminal administration and in matters of revenue and the right to govern their States independently, and for the Council of the Chiefs, which was currently a purely consultative and advisory body, to be given the power to deal with all matters affecting the welfare and prosperity of the Shan States as a whole.

The Memorandum pointed out that the Indian Statutory Commission, which had not visited the Shan States and had no personal knowledge of their progressive state, had reported that the principal Chiefs of the Shan States "appeared to be very well contented with their present system of administration," but had made no mention of the reform in administration which the Chiefs desired and which had been presented in a Memorandum to the Commission.

The Memorandum declared that the ultimate ideal of the Federated Shan States was to acquire its independence under the British Crown, and that the restoration of wider powers to the Chiefs would, on the one hand, benefit the States in the development of the sources of natural wealth, and, on the other, fit them to acquire the same measure of independence as the Indian States.

Recalling that Sir Reginald Craddock, Lieutenant Governor of Myanmar, had, in a Durbar on 22nd March 1920, told the Shan Chefs, "the special powers, rights, and privileges which you have enjoyed in the past must be conserved for you in the future," the Memorandum declared that the Chiefs desired a reversion of their status, and that the original designation of the Chiefs as "Maharajah Sawbwagyi" should be revived.

The Memorandum proposed that if Myanmar were separated from India under a new constitution and the Shan States be treated independently of Myanmar, the political relations of the Shan States with the Paramount Power be through the Governor of Myanmar or the Viceroy of India.

The Memorandum also proposed that in external economic relations the Shan States should have the same powers as any independent Indian State, that the rights of the Chiefs to impose tariffs and customs be reversed, and that the Chiefs be given such share of the Central Revenue as receipts from customs, income, etc. as would be allotted to Myanmar in the future.

The Memorandum expressed the desire of the Chiefs to be given the same privileges and status as the Rulers of the Indian States.

The Memorandum suggested the following reforms with regard to internal affairs:

(a) That unless a special High Commissioner was appointed, the Governor of Myanmar should act as such, and that he be Chairman of the Council of Chieftains, and the senior Chief be Vice-Chairman and act as Chairman if the Commissioner was unable to attend.

(b) That matters of finance and assessment be administered solely by the Chiefs without the dictation of British officers.

(c) That, as against the current contribution of 50 percent of State revenues to the Federation for public works, education, health, and agriculture, 12½ percent be paid to correspond to the tribute paid by the Chiefs before the Federation.

(d) That, with regard to forests, mines, and minerals, 50 percent of the revenue be paid to the State concerned and 50 percent to the Federation.

(e) That communications (e.g. roads and bridges) be the responsibility of the Federation, while administrative buildings, markets, courthouses, etc. be the responsibility of the States.

(f) That education be administered by the individual States under the supervision of the Central Education Department.

(g) That public health be within the control of the individual States under the supervision of the Central Medical Department.

(h) That agriculture be left to the Chiefs under technical supervision.

(i) That the procedure in criminal jurisdiction should be carefully considered, with the rights of the Chiefs also recognized.

(j) That no alteration be made in civil administration.

(k) That the modification of the customary laws currently in force should continue, but absolute discretion was to be given to the Chiefs regarding local regulations and by-laws.

(l) That the above should also apply to the Myelat States which currently did not enjoy the privileges of administering the customary laws.

(m) That the State Budget be prepared by the Chiefs and be considered final.

(n) That the *sanad* presently in force should be revised to conform with the changes in tribute and status suggested in the Memorandum.

(o) That, in the event of the separation of Myanmar from India, there should be a definition of the rights of the Chiefs with regard to succession which should not be derogatory to their status.

AN ANALYSIS OF THE ADMINISTRATION OF THE FEDERATED SHAN STATES

The Federated Shan States was, in a way, created from the British point of view to help build up a uniform administrative system to the greatest possible extent for the whole of the Shan States. It was also created to pool the financial resources of the Shan chiefs for establishing and running major departments like Public Works, Medical Administration, Forests, Education, Agriculture, and Police for the benefit of the Shan people. On all these matters, the Shan chiefs could give advice but, according to the terms set down for the Federated Shan States, they had no power to initiate projects. Most of the administrative and public works were to be supervised and controlled by the commissioner, who was the president of the Advisory Council of Chiefs. He was to be assisted by the superintendents, who were also British. The power of the High Court for the Shan States was also vested in the commissioner, except in the trial of cases against Europeans or British subjects. Departmental officers of government formally under the Shan States were transferred from ordinary departmental control to become technical advisers to the commissioner in their respective fields of work.

In a way, the traditional hereditary rights of the Shan chiefs to rule their states were reduced. This later became a cause of dissatisfaction and friction in the relationship between the Shan chiefs and the British officers.

Ever since the Shan States became part of British India the Shan chiefs had lost the administrative authority over their states and their subjects. They had to acknowledge the suzerainty of the British and to observe the terms imposed on them in the *sanad*, or appointment order, issued by the British governor as had been done by the Myanmar kings in the old days. The *saohpa*, or local chiefs, were never treated by the British authority on an equal footing. After the federation, some *saohpa* were given power in some matters of civil and criminal judicial administration and revenue, but were subject to the control of the commissioner and the supervision of the superintendents of the Northern and Southern Shan States. They could not directly appoint their successors but had to obtain the approval of the commissioner. They could not make any direct communication with the governor or government of Myanmar without the knowledge of British officers concerned with administration of the Shan States.

In the case of the *saohpa* of the Northern Shan States, the means of communication with the governor was through the assistant superintendent, the superintendent of the Northern Shan States, and finally the commissioner, who was the agent of the governor. For the Shan States, the commissioner was the most powerful British officer. He was empowered to exercise the duties of the commissioner of the federation, the superintendent, and also the political officer.

The *saohpa* of the Southern Shan States had to go through two British officers in their communication with the governor, the assistant superintendent, and the commissioner.

The arrangement affected the prestige of the *saohpa* and the local chiefs. They felt they had been deprived of much of their authority and that they were just puppets or titular heads of their states, contrary to their hereditary status.

By the Civil and Criminal Justice Orders which were issued from time to time under the Myanmar Laws Act of 1898, the commissioner, the superintendent, and assistant superintendent were authorized to exercise general control over the administration of civil and criminal justice in the Northern and Southern Shan States within their jurisdiction and to exercise all the powers conferred on them by these orders.[10]

In accordance with the framework of the federation, the status, administrative power, and role of the *saohpa* were defined as follows:

1. The status of local chief was generally the same as that before the constitution of the Federation.
2. They had the right to nominate their heir or successor, subject to the approval of the governor and the commissioner of the Federation.
3. They had the right to exercise administrative powers in matters of civil and criminal justice and revenue, but with the guidance of the superintendent and under the control of the commissioner.
4. Appointments of local officers could be made by the local chiefs with the approval and control of the assistant superintendent, the superintendent, and the commissioner. (The Myanmar Laws Act 1898, section 12, subsection 1).
5. The *saohpa* and local chiefs were recognized as consultants giving their opinion without any legislated power.
6. The administrative role of the *saohpa* or local chiefs was very much restricted and confined to the internal administration of the states as subordinate staff.
7. All administrative officials and subordinates of general administrations of the States were appointed and controlled by the governor.

The *saohpa* felt that they had been deprived of their hereditary rights and made complaints.

Once, the *saohpa* of North Hsen Wi asked the president of the Council of Chiefs whether the *saohpa* had full power in the internal administration of their state. The president replied that the chiefs could exercise full power in the administration of the internal affairs of their state, but that it would have to be in accordance with the *sanad* granted to them, which stated that they were in all matters subject to the guidance of the superintendent and that they must further conform to any order issued by the governor.[11]

From its inauguration in October 1922, the federation was not popular among the Shan chiefs. The *saohpa* felt that they had consented to give up too much power in the federation, and a strong sense of dissatisfaction prevailed among them. Some *saohpa* of the large states who were anxious about their hereditary rights and status waited for an opportunity to submit a memorandum for the redress of their grievances and the restrictions imposed on them by the terms of the Federated Shan States.

A golden opportunity came in 1930 when discussions were held at the Roundtable Conference in London on the question of the separation of Myanmar from British India. A meeting of the Shan chiefs was held in the Council Hall in Taunggyi in

September 1930, where a resolution was passed to send the *saohpa* of Yawng Hwe and Mong Mit states as their representatives to participate in the Roundtable Conference and submit a memorandum making known the interests of the Shan States in general and the changes they wanted in their administrative status in particular.

The interests of the Shan States and the grievance of the *saohpa* were thus represented in the memorandum submitted to the British government in December 1930.

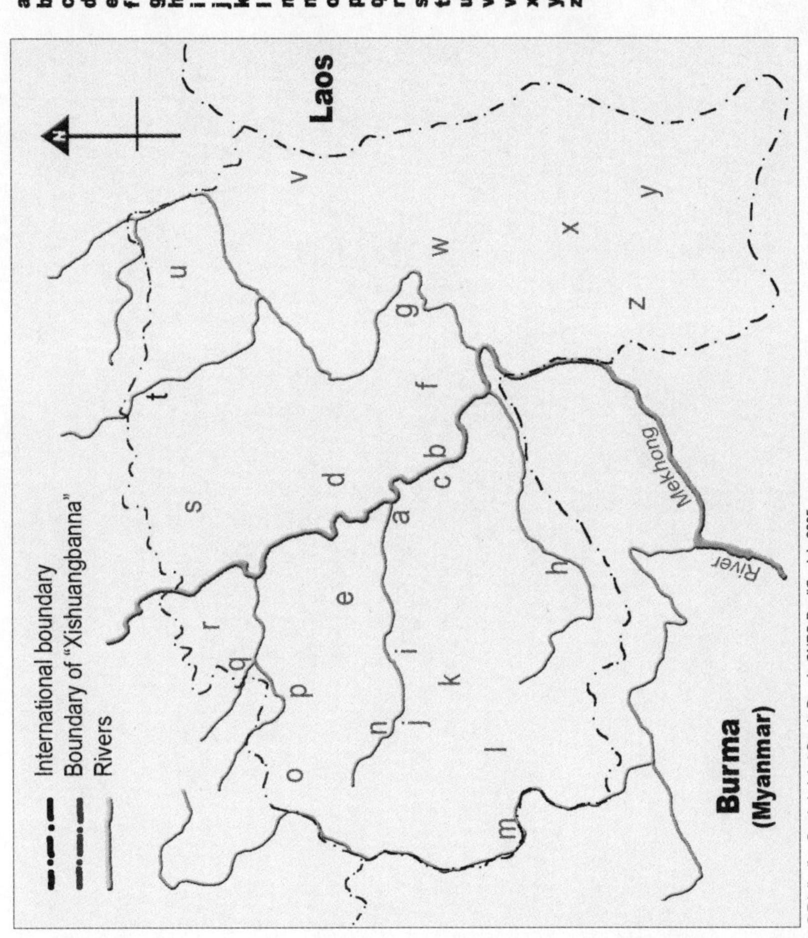

MAP 19. Locations of Moengs in Hsiphsaungbana

10

The Japanese Conquest of Myanmar and the Occupation and Partition of the Shan States

After two intensive air raids and heavy bombings that caused great damage and destruction, the Japanese army finally invaded Yangon on March 8, 1942. It occupied the city on March 9, unfurled the flag of the Rising Sun, and declared the country "occupied."[1] The quick Japanese success in Southeast Asia and in Myanmar was due to two factors. One was effective military operation, the other effective political propaganda. The Japanese army was well organized and mechanized according to its own standard. The soldiers were trained for fighting in rough terrain and thick forests and were well equipped. Many of them fought in the wars with Russia and China. The Western powers, which had previously dominated Southeast Asia and Myanmar, now shifted their attention to the home front in Europe, and these regions were neglected so that they easily fell prey to the Japanese army. The remaining defense forces of these powers were not well equipped or well organized. The fighting spirit of the soldiers was weaker than the Japanese. The sinking of the British battleships, *Prince of Wales* and *Repulse*, off the eastern coast of Malaya was a setback for the British navy and demoralized the British soldiers during this time.

Slogans like "Japan the leader of Asia," "Japan the protector of Asia," "Japan the liberator of Asia," "Japan the light of Asia," "Asia for the Asians," and propaganda like "Greater East Asia Coprosperity Sphere" were very attractive and effective in luring the support and the help of the Southeast Asian peoples including Myanmar, which had been exploited by Western colonialists for a long time.[2]

During a joint operation to invade Myanmar, the Myanmar patriotic group of the Thirty Comrades and the Myanmar Independence Army rendered effective cooperation, providing guides and topographical intelligence. For this help Myanmar was promised "independence," but whether the independence to be granted was genuine or nominal, real or false would have to be tested through cooperation, coalition, reconciliation, and patience. Gradually, the Japanese military authority began to notice the strong sense of Myanmar nationalism and a vigorous desire for a real independence and nothing less. Joint operations between the Myanmar Independence Army and the

Japanese Imperial Army did not go as smoothly as was thought. Occasionally misunderstandings and suspicions occurred, especially when a new town was liberated. For example, when Mawlamyaing was taken the Myanmar Independence Army would have liked to set up a provisional government, but the Japanese went ahead to establish a military administration, not caring what the Myanmar forces wanted to do.

Three months after the occupation of Yangon, an initial administrative system called the Central Administrative Committee, also known as the Free Myanmar Administrative Committee, was introduced with Dr. Ba Maw, who had been recently released from the Mogok (Mong Kut) jail, as its chairman. This newly established administrative system was soon replaced by a more reliable and suitable type of administration called the Myanmar Executive Administration on August 1, 1942, headed by Dr. Ba Maw. But important matters, like budget, defense, reconstruction, and military affairs, were controlled by Japanese advisers and officials. Moreover, higher Myanmar officials were required to take an oath of allegiance to the Japanese authority.[3] Despite that, Dr. Ba Maw and Myanmar officials still stuck to their slogan of "one blood, one voice, one command" even together with Nippon or trust Nippon.[4]

A piece of good news came to Myanmar on January 28, 1943, when General Tojo, the prime minister of the Japanese imperial government, announced on the radio, "At present Japan approves the construction of a Myanmar state. The aspiration of independence long cherished by the Myanmar will soon be realized."[5] The Preparatory Committee for Independence, consisting of twenty-two members, was formed on May 8, 1943. For further discussion of the matter a delegation composed of Dr. Ba Maw, Thakin Mya, Dr. Thein Maung, and Major General Thakin Aung San was invited to Tokyo. Everything went well and the granting of independence was confirmed. The Order of the Rising Sun, First Class with Grand Cordon, was conferred on Dr. Ba Maw, the Order of the Sacred Treasure, Second Class, on Thakin Mya and Dr. Thein Maung, and the Order of the Rising Sun, Third Class, with Middle Cords, on Major General Aung San. On May 8, 1943, the Myanmar Independence Preparatory Committee was set up with twenty-two members.

Another round of discussions took place between Dr. Ba Maw and General Tojo in July at Singapore.

With great pomp and grandeur an auspicious impressive ceremony was held in the main hall of Government House at Yangon on August 1, 1943, to mark the proclamation of independence for Myanmar granted by the Japanese government. Dr. Ba Maw became head of state called *naing-ngan-daw adipadi*. The Japanese military administration was dissolved. Dr. Ba Maw appointed the following people to be the members of his government:

1. Dr. Ba Maw — Prime minister
2. Thakin Mya — Deputy prime minister
3. U Ba Win — Home minister
4. Thakin Nu — Foreign minister
5. Dr. Thein Maung — Finance minister

6. Thakin Aung San	Defense minister
7. U Aye	Taxation minister
8. U Thein Maung	Justice minister
9. U Hla Min	Education and health minister
10. Thakin Than Tun	Agriculture minister
11. U Mya Yamethin	Commerce and industry minister
12. Thakin Lay Maung	Communications and irrigation minister
13. U Hla Pe	Forests minister
14. Bandoola U Sein	Welfare and publicity minister
15. U Tun Aung	Cooperation minister
16. Thakin Lun Baw	Public works recovery minister

A Privy Council composed of twenty members was also formed.

After that Dr. Ba Maw declared war against the United States and Great Britain. Myanmar and Japan signed a Treaty of Alliance which contained four articles:

1. The Japanese and Myanmar governments, for the purpose of prosecuting the Greater East Asia War, agree to cooperate in military, political, and economic matters.
2. The Japanese and Myanmar governments agree to cooperate in the construction, advance, and common prosperity of the Greater East Asia Coprosperity Sphere.
3. Matters of detail regarding the execution of the treaty will be negotiated when necessary.
4. The treaty will come into force on the date of signature.

Formal recognition was officially accorded to the new State of Myanmar on August 1, 1943. Mr. Renzo Sawada became the first Japanese ambassador to Myanmar. The Myanmar nation was recognized by Japan, Germany, Bulgaria, Slovakia, Croatia, Nanking, Manchukuo, and Thailand. Myanmar sent its ambassadorsDr. Thein Maung to Japan, U Ba Lwin to Thailand, Thakin Ba Sein to Manchukuo, and Thakin Tun Ok to China.

A Myanmar national flag of three colors, yellow, green, and red horizontal bands with a peacock-in-pride in green, blue, and red in a circular inset in the center was adopted together with the Myanmar National Anthem, which said:

> We are Myanmar forever,
> This is our country, our land, (Repeated)
> It is the duty of everyone to remember,
> This is our land, our country.

The territory of the new Myanmar up to September 25, 1943, was confined to areas around the valley of Sittang and Ayeyarwady rivers and Tenasserim (Tanintharyi). The

Shan States were not included in the new Myanmar up to that period. The question was where were the Shan States? Where did they go? Under whom were they placed or administered? No mention of Shan States was made when the Myanmar Executive Administration was formed on August 1, 1942. The Shan States did not come into the picture of the administration and their role in Myanmar's history was kept silent, making it very difficult to assess how much interest the Myanmar leaders took in the affairs of the Shan States. When Dr. Ba Maw and his ministers were invited to Tokyo to discuss the independence question, no Shan representative was included. In the same way, when Thakin Aung San and his ministers went to London to discuss the same question with British prime minister Clement Attlee in 1947, no Shan representative was involved.

Although the Shan States were part of Myanmar geographically or physically during the British occupation, they were not part of Myanmar, politically and administratively. They were separated from Myanmar; Myanmar proper was administered as part of British India with the Legislative Council, whereas the Shan States and other "excluded areas" were administered directly by the governor with his assistants. The practice of two administrative systems in one country fitted in very well with the policy of divide and rule of the British government of the time. Now, when Myanmar was conquered by the Japanese and given independence, the Shan States were not included and the Japanese kept these states to themselves. During the military operation in the Shan States, the Japanese forbade the Myanmar Independence Army to enter the Shan region.

The policy of the Japanese imperial government at that time was to use the Shan States as pawns on its Southeast Asian military chessboard. The Shan States were to be used as bait to entice Thailand and Myanmar to participate more actively and forcefully in the Japanese military campaign in Southeast Asia. In other words, the Shan States were to be used as gifts to both Thailand and Myanmar for their active participation in the Japanese scheme of conquest in Southeast Asia.

Geopolitically the location of the Shan States was very important at that time because they shared borders with China, French Indochina, Thailand, and Myanmar with the British military supply line of Myanmar Road passing through the Shan region. The Japanese army quickly invaded the Shan States after the fall of Taungoo. It swept up to Karenni and to the Southern Shan States, occupying the key road from Taunggyi to Lashio to block the Myanmar Road to China. There were three other main roads giving access to the Shan States, which the Japanese army made use of for its quick occupation of the Shan States. The first road connected Mandalay, the heart of Myanmar, with Lashio, the northern capital of the Shan States, and then to the border of China. Through this road the British sent arms and other war matériel to China. The second road was the one from Thazi to the Southern Shan States to the capital of Taunggyi and then to Keng Tung and to the Thai border. The British expected the Japanese to use this road to invade the Shan States. The third road linked the two from Lashio, Hsi Paw to Loi Lem and then to Taunggyi, and from there the road turned south to Karenni and beyond that to Taungoo in Myanmar. All these roads were well built by the British during their occupation of the Shan States and they all served well for the quick conquest of the Shan States by the Japanese. Moreover, in invading the Shan States, the Japanese used not only land forces but air power. Almost every big city and town in the Shan States was heavily bombed, killing many and destroying markets, schools, and public buildings. People were terrorized and fled to the jungle and remote parts of the country, leaving towns and cities deserted. Communication and transportation were cut off and government machinery was paralyzed. People suffered from starvation, diseases, and all kinds of miseries followed by stealing, looting, and dacoities. War is really terrible no matter who wins or loses.

The British evacuated Myanmar and the Shan States. During the evacuation, the British sought the help of China, and the Nationalist government of President Chiang Kai-shek agreed to send his troops. The 93rd Division of the Chinese army moved into Keng Tung State to guard the borders of French Indochina and Thailand. The 249th and the 55th Divisions moved in by the Myanmar Road to take up positions in Karenni and northward to protect the Thai border from Keng Tung to Myanmar.[6]

The Chinese soldiers were generally not well trained or well equipped like the Japanese. The Chinese were badly defeated by superior numbers and mechanized equipment, including airplanes, against which they had no defense.

Regarding the role and the position of the Shan chiefs and the Shan people before the Japanese invasion of the Shan States, Professor Clarence Hendershot, in his article "Role of the Shan States in the Japanese Conquest of Burma," in *The Far Eastern Quarterly* (May 2, 1943) made the following remark:

> Witnesses observed no active fifth columnists among the Shans, but there is reason to believe that at least some individuals in responsible positions were not happy to have the British go. Even since the latter began to impose their authority in 1887, certain of the chiefs have been restive. Some of them felt they had been duped. Before their forebears had submitted, they had been told that they would be granted as favorable conditions as they formerly had received from the king of Burma. But soon they discovered that their rights of taxation were restricted, their judicial power curtailed, and even their family matters regulated and that assembling of judicial procedure should precede execution, but the chiefs resented the instruction. Control of forests and minerals became a source of discontent. In the first agreements the British made no claim to these, but on discovering that the Burmese kings had collected revenue from forests and minerals, the British asserted similar rights. Concessions ultimately were made by the British but the problem was never settled to the satisfaction of the chiefs. Control of opium also became a source of friction in the states bordering China.
>
> The chiefs have been concerned, too, about the policy of the British in the matter of succession. Although there was nothing in the first settlements to that effect, the British constructed their agreements as purely personal and therefore automatically

> terminated on the decease of a chief. Normally an approved heir was permitted to succeed, but approval was not assured. Ten or more states disappeared by amalgamation, the number of units being thereby reduced to thirty-five.

Keng Tung, the largest state (about 12,000 sq. miles), and Hsi Paw, the richest, were, it so happened, under direct British control inasmuch as their chiefs were minors. On the approach of the Japanese, the chief of the strategically important state of North Hsen Wi, who had been uncooperative for years, retired to a house he had built in the hills. At least one other chief said he proposed to act similarly. One chief is reported to have said that if the Japanese came, he would not resist but for self-preservation would try to fit into their scheme of things. One chief is reported as probably having fled to India.

While witnesses agree that, unlike the situation prevailing in Myanmar, there were probably no fifth columnists, they disagree as to the actual attitude of the people and the chiefs. One witness believes the latter sincerely wanted the British to win but reconciled themselves to Japanese rule as a matter of expediency. Another is convinced that the Shan were ready to welcome the Japanese. A third observer is of the opinion that a minority, not more than 25 percent, was pro-Japanese, but that for the most part the people were simply pro-Shan. Perhaps the same can be said for the chiefs.[7]

THE SHAN STATES UNDER THE JAPANESE

After the conquest of the Shan States, the question was: how would these states be administered? Would the administrative model of the Myanmar Executive Administration be applied here? But a check of document No. 52 and the Japanese Military Administration Order No. 3 will show that there was no hope of the Shan States having a civilian administration. The military administration, on November 14, 1942, stated:

1. The Shan States Administration Office shall be established on November 25, 1942.
2. The organization and jurisdiction of the Shan States Administration Office are as described in a separate document "Organization and Regulations for the Shan States Administration Office."
3. The High Commissioner shall execute military administration in accordance with the "Governing Principle for the Occupied Areas Under the Hayashi Army Group" and the following summary. He shall also take over the military administration from the corps commander—Kiku, Tatsu, and Tate Corps—in their respective jurisdictional territories. (See appendix 18.)

The following are some of the important clauses extracted from *Burma: Japanese Military Administration, Selected Documents, 1941–1945* by Frank N. Trager:

- In executing military administration in the Shan States, simple and plain measures shall be taken and the existing traditional method shall be adopted. Especially in administering the territories under the control of the Shan chiefs, the existing system for the time being shall be utilized. Efforts must be made to avoid interfering in minor matters concerning local administration and to win popular support in order to facilitate the military administration.
- The Shan States Administration Office shall be established at Taunggyi.
- The army group commander and the superintendent of the military administration shall have direct control over the following eight subjects.
- There will be a high commissioner in the Shan States Administration Office. The high commissioner shall be under the superintendent of the military administration, carry out military administration within his jurisdiction. (See appendix 19.)
- Under the Shan States Administration Office, the High Commissioner's office, and the following departments with their respective chiefs and necessary personnel, shall be established.
- A court of justice, with a chief justice and necessary personnel, shall be established under the Shan States Administration Office.
- The Shan States Administration Office shall have jurisdiction over the old Feudal Shan States.
- Military administration of the Shan States shall be executed in accordance with the "Governing Principles of the Occupied Areas under the Hayashi Army Group."
- The Shan States Administration Office shall consist of Japanese officials and shall carry out a sound military administration. At lower level organizations in local areas Japanese officials shall be posted to positions of leadership.
- The army group commanders and the superintendent of the military administration shall have direct control over the eight subjects. (See appendix 20.)
- When employing natives for military administration organization, first preference shall be given to Myanmar.
- Regarding education, a plan must be made to spread the Japanese language.
- There shall be a Shan Chiefs' Council under the Shan States Administration Office.
- On the question of the reversion of the Shan States.
- A treaty between Japan and Thailand concerning the territories of the Shan regions.

After the establishment of the Shan States Administration Office in Taunggyi on November 23, 1942, the following Japanese officers were appointed office staff:

SHAN STATE OFFICE

Official Position	Rank	Name
High Commissioner	Chief, Civil Administration	Nishimura Takuma
Chief of General Affairs Department	Colonel	Nakada Saichiro
Chief of General Affairs Bureau	Lieutenant	Fujino Massao
Chief of Accounting Bureau	Civil Administrator	Sato Heishichi
Chief of Investigation Bureau	Civil Administrator	Suemune Yoshikaku
Chief Secretary in the High Commissioner's Office	Civil Administrator	Iwanage Umpei
Chief of Domestic Affairs Department	Civil Administrator	Kato Hitoshi
Chief of Sanitation Bureau	Army Engineer	Chiba Tomoyuki
Chief of Education Bureau	Civil Administrator	Iida Chu
Chief of Peace Bureau	Civil Administrator	Ohmi Ken
Chief of Police Bureau	Civil Administrator	Kubo Gemma
Chief of Economic Department	Civil Administrator	Omata Akiyoshi
Chief of Forestry Bureau	Army Engineer	Kawanaka Kizo
Chief of Commerce & Industry Bureau	Civil Administrator	Kinoshita Futatsu
Chief of Mining Bureau	Civil Administrator	Hiroi Tatsumi
Chief of Transportation Department	Civil Administrator	Sakamoto Ryunosuke
Chief of Public Works Bureau	Army Engineer	Moritani Masuo
Chief of Postal Service Bureau	vacant	
Chief of Judicial Department	Civil Administrator	Hayashi Yoshisuke
Chief Superintendent of Northern Shan States	Civil Administrator	Kuroe Shigeharu
Chief Superintendent of Southern Shan States	Civil Administrator	Takahashi Kunihira
Chief Superintendent of Karenni States	Civil Administrator	Kaneda Nobuo
Mayor of Taunggyi	Civil Administrator	Ogawa Issui
Mayor of Lashio	Civil Administrator	Togawa Takao
Mayor of Kalaw	Civil Administrator	Shinohara Yoshio
Mayor of Loilem	Civil Administrator	Yorinushi Shogo

(See appendix 20.)

FIGURE 10.1. Civilian trading company, Toyomenka, based at Shwe Nyaung, Southern Shan State. (From Sao Kiao Mong, Taunggyi)

Departmental Regulation for the Shan States provided for the establishment of the General Affairs Department. Under it were bureaus such as General Affairs, Investigation, Accounting, Financial, Education, Sanitation, Police Affairs, Public Peace, Mining, Commerce and Industries, Forestry, Agriculture, Land Transportation, Postal Service, and Public Works. (Also see appendix 21.)

To supervise the work of the bureaus, the Superintendent Department was established and the detailed duty regulations for the superintendents were also prescribed. (See appendix 22.)

A Judicial Ordinance of the Shan States was also introduced by the Japanese military commander of the Mori Army Group on July 7, 1943. The documents no. 60 contained fifteen articles concerning the judicial affairs of the Shan States. (See appendix 23.)

Though the period from 1941 to 1945 may seem to be short, for the people of the Shan States it was a long period of suffering. Their beautiful and peaceful land had turned into a war zone of British-Chinese and Japanese forces. The British Command sought the help of the Chinese Nationalist government and planned to defend the Shan States and Myanmar. The Chinese army was given the task to defend the Shan States while the British army and civilians evacuated to India. The Chinese army moved into the Shan States, taking positions in Keng Tung and Karenni and other strategic places along the Thai-Myanmar border, expecting the Japanese to attack from these areas.

The Japanese army made a quick move into the Shan States to block the Myanmar-China Road, the main artery of military supply to China.

What did the people of the Shan States do in that situation? Things were beyond their control. They kept watching the British evacuating to India. The path to India was not easy at all, because it passed through a series of thick jungles and forests and a number of rugged mountains full of ferocious animals. Soldiers, administrative officials and their families, businessmen, merchants, traders, doctors, and other British citizens including thousands of Indians and Chinese civilians moved across the Shan States. One column of people went to China and another to Bhamo, Myitkyina, and then to India. Time was short for them because the Japanese army was too quick for them. In the photographs taken during those days the evacuees looked very upset and miserable and some were bewildered, confused, and dazed. Their faces looked very uncertain, doubtful, with a loss of faith in themselves, because they were not sure whether they would make it to India or China. The fear of being captured, tortured, trapped, arrested, and executed pushed them on toward India or China—some on foot, some by rented car, some by bullock cart, some by elephant, and some lucky ones by plane in shifts from Myitkyina. In their long march to India and China, many unlucky ones died on the way, some from wounds, some from being attacked by dacoits or robbers or ferocious animals and others from being infected with incurable diseases, especially malaria, dysentery, and a mysterious virus unknown in the impenetrable jungles and forests. No one could help anyone much, everyone was struggling for his own safety. Life was precious and one could not afford to die especially at the hands of enemies. Crippled evacuees, wounded soldiers, weak old people, and people with contagious diseases sat appealing to the stronger ones for help from the roadsides. There was no other means of transportation by which they could hope to be rescued. The scene was very unpleasant.

They were chased and bombed by the enemies. Corpse after corpse lay scattered in towns, especially Lashio, Hsen Wi, and along the Myanmar Road, which came to be known as the Road of Death. Nobody cared to clear the corpses away and the air in the town became polluted and the stench caused another epidemic that killed hundreds of lives. The ones who suffered most were the Chinese soldiers and civilians. The Shan were drafted as porters by the British, Chinese, and Japanese armed forces. Many of them did not return home and nobody knew where they had been taken to. Even after the war was over, they did not return and were presumed dead. The loss of innocent lives, the casualties suffered by nonmilitary men were many. But there were no statistics, no compensation, no sympathy, no rewards, no honors, no recognition for their services, no witnesses, no rescuers, nor any kind of help. They just disappeared like the summer clouds not in the sky but in fields of battle and in fighting in which they played no part and for which they were not responsible. The same things happened when the Japanese retreated from Myanmar.

FIGURE 10.2. Leaders of the Greater East Asia Coprosperity Sphere nations at a conference in Tokyo, November 1943: General Hideki Tojo, the Japanese premier, in the center, with Dr. Ba Maw and Subhas Chandra Bose on the extreme left and right. (Maung Maung 1959, photo no. 6)

THE PARTITION OF THE SHAN STATES

The conquest of Myanmar and the invasion and partition of the Shan States by the Japanese and the occupation of Keng Tung and Mong Pan states by the Thai army were different episodes but parts of the same story of "The Greater East Asia Coprosperity Sphere," written by the Japanese imperial government. It was a big surprise that when Premier Hideki Tojo originally offered Myanmar independence he omitted mention of the Shan States. Then and there the fate of the Shan States was sealed.

On July 29, 1943, a deliberative mittee on the conclusion of a Treaty of Alliance between Japan and Myanmar held a meeting at the Imperial Palace. In attendance were the committee chairman, Mr. Suzuki, and committee members Tojo, prime minister and army minister; Shimada, navy minister; Ando, home minister; Aoki, Greater East Asia minister; Shigemitsu, foreign minister; and others. When the question was raised concerning the reversion of the Shan States, Tojo replied that he was considering the cession of some parts of the Shan States to Thailand and the remaining Shan States to Myanmar in the future in order to encourage Thailand and Myanmar to cooperate with Japan in prosecuting the war.

On the reversion of the Shan States to Thailand, Minami Jiro, a member of the committee, raised the issue whether the territory in question was the one east of the Than Lwin River. In reply, Tojo said that since many chiefs' domains were located on both sides of the Than Lwin River and he did not wish to divide them, he was considering assigning Keng Tung and Mong Pan states to Thailand and the remaining Shan States to Myanmar at the appropriate time. (See appendix 24.)

On August 18, 1943, the deliberative committee held another meeting, attended by Hara, president of the Privy Council; Suzuki, vice president of the Privy Council and the committee chairman; Tojo; Aoki; Shigemitsu; and others. At the meeting, Shimizu, a member of the committee, asked whether Myanmar was dissatisfied with the annexation of the two Shan States by Thailand. In reply, Premier Tojo related the circumstances when he had made the proposal during his interview with Dr. Ba Maw in Singapore and with Phibun in Bangkok on his trip south. He said that although Dr. Ba Maw had shown no sign of dissatisfaction with Thailand's annexation of the two Shan States, uneasiness might be entertained by the natives, and that therefore both matters should be left for consideration in Japan's future policies. In fact Dr. Ba Maw should have protested but he did not, thus sealing the fate of the two states, Keng Tung and Mong Pan. (See appendix 25.)

Regarding the transfer of the territories in the Malay States and the Shan regions to Thailand, a treaty between Japan and Thailand was signed at the meeting on August 18, 1943.

The articles included in the treaty (see appendix 26) were:

1. The Japanese government agrees to recognize the annexation by the Thai government of the Kelantan, Trengganu, Kedah, Perlis States, and their attached islands.
2. The Japanese government agrees to the annexation by the Thai government of the states of Keng Tung and Mong Pan of the Shan region.
3. The Japanese government agrees to terminate its administration, now being executed over the above areas within sixty days after this treaty takes effect.
4. The boundaries of the areas stated above in Articles 1 and 2 shall be based on the boundaries that exist as of the date of this treaty.
5. Detailed matters essential for the enforcement of this treaty shall be negotiated and decided upon by respective authorities of the two governments.
6. This treaty shall take effect on the date of signature.[8]

A meeting to conclude a treaty between Japan and Myanmar concerning the transfer of the Shan territories to Myanmar was held at the Imperial Palace on September 22, 1943. Hara, Suzuki, Tojo, Aoki, Shigemitsu, and the others attended the meeting.

In his report Suzuki stated the reason for transferring the Shan territories to Myanmar. It said: In order to induce Myanmar to increase its war effort and cooperation with Japan, Japan decided to recognize Myanmar's annexation of the Shan States. In an interview with Ba Maw during his trip south, Tojo had declared that Japan was considering action on the matter. Furthermore, the Japanese ambassador to Myanmar had recently reported that the Myanmar government desired the earliest possible annexation of the Shan region to Myanmar and that Japan's approval and recognition should coincide with the Myanmar celebration of its independence on August 25. This would be a most effective way to lift the morale of the Myanmar people in their support of the war effort. Consequently, the Japanese government decided on the annexation and negotiated with the Myanmar government. Both governments finally agreed on the following treaty provisions (see appendix 27).

> The Japanese and Myanmar governments, resolving to prosecute successfully, in close cooperation, the common war against the United States and Great Britain, and establish a Greater East Asia based on high moral principles, have agreed as follows:
>
> 1. The Japanese government agrees to recognize the annexation by the Myanmar government of the Karenni States, Wa States, and the whole of the Shan States with the exception of Keng Tung and Mong Pan states.
> 2. The Japanese government agrees to terminate its administration now being executed over the above areas within ninety days after the treaty takes effect.
> 3. Detailed matters essential for the enforcement of the treaty shall be negotiated by respective authorities of the two governments.
> 4. The treaty shall take effect on the date of signature.[9]

On hearing about the cession of Keng Tung and Mong Pan states to Thailand, the chiefs of the states and the Shan people were unhappy and felt that they were at the mercy of the Japanese imperial government. In the transfer of these territories to Thailand and to Myanmar, the Shan chiefs and the Shan people should have been consulted or at least their views should have been considered. The Shan chiefs and their people would have liked to express their feelings over the transfer of their lives, states, and properties to foreign powers. But there was no way through which they could send their appeal and petition. At that time, there were no agreements such as the Atlantic Charter, no nongovernment organization, no Red Cross agency, no human rights association, no trusteeship council and no United Nations organization where the Shan could have submitted their grievance on the transfer of their native lands to foreign powers without their consent.

The Shan people suffered the loss of their territories whenever there was war. For example, after the defeat of Myanmar in the Anglo-Myanmar War in 1824–26, the Ahom Shan dynasty together with Assam had to be given to British India. Again after the defeat of Myanmar in the Third Anglo-Myanmar War in 1885, the whole of the Shan States became colonies of the British, and the Shan territories of Keng Hung, Hsiphsaungbana, and Mong Lem were ceded to China, the State of Keng Cheng to France, and Chiang Saen to Thailand. Moreover, the Tai Neu territories in the areas of Dehong or upper Than Lwin like Nantien, Kang Ai, Chanta (Santa), Lungchuan or Mong Wan, Mong Mao, Chefang, Mangshih, Luchaing, Mengpein, Lasa, Husa, Kungyu, Mongtine, and Wanting were absorbed into China.[10]

Now with the defeat of the British during the Second World War, the whole of the Shan States fell into the hands of Japan. Under the treaties concluded between Japan and Myanmar, the Shan territories of Keng Tung and Mong Pan had to be given away to Thailand as gifts, and the Wa States, the Karenni States, and the remaining Shan

States had to be transferred to Myanmar. The Shan people did not seem to mind much at becoming part of Myanmar, because they had been together since time immemorial and they still remembered that they had helped found the cities of Pinya, Sagaing, and Inwa, making Myanmar their own country.

THAI DIPLOMACY AND THE ACQUISITION OF KENG TUNG AND MONG PAN STATES

When the Second World War broke out, Japan, under the banner of the Greater East Asia Co-prosperity Sphere, launched a military campaign into Southeast Asia to liberate the territories that had been under the domination of the Western imperialists. On December 8, 1941, Thailand was attacked by the Japanese at nine key points: by infantry forces at Battambang in Cambodia, by the air force at Don Mueang airfield, and by seven amphibious landings from the sea between Hua Hin and Pattani on the gulf coast. Thailand had never been colonized by any foreign powers in its past history; the British and French, having a common interest in keeping Thailand as a neutral and buffer state, had left it as an independent sovereign state. In the past, it had concluded commercial and territorial treaties with the British and acquired some rights and lands from them at the expense of the Malay States.

Although the fighting between the Japanese and the Thais at these points was fierce, it lasted only a few hours because Field Marshal Phibul Songkhram, the Thai head of government and leader at that time, felt that to fight against the Japanese who had superior fighting power would be suicidal, and ordered a cease-fire. The sinking of the British battleships, *Prince of Wales* and *Repulse*, convinced him that to side with Japan in the war would be advantageous to Thailand, and he decided to seek an alliance with Japan. On December 14 he signed a secret agreement with Japan promising to send Thai troops in the invasion of Myanmar. On December 21, 1941, Thailand and Japan signed a formal treaty of alliance in front of the Emerald Buddha at Wat Phra Kaeo.[11]

Believing that the Allies would be defeated once and for all, Phibul then declared war on Great Britain and the United States, for which the Japanese rewarded him with some territories from British Malaya and the British Shan States without there being historical justification for the reversion of these territories to Thailand.

Many Thais did not comply with Phibul's diplomatic action. The Thai ambassador to Washington, Seni Pramoj, did not deliver the declaration of war to the US secretary of state. But Phibul was determined to be on the winning side and to share the spoils of victory. That was the vital interest of his government at that time. In his plan to send the Thai army to Myanmar, he conceived the idea of creating a new "Northern Army" that would invade Myanmar and control the territories east of the Than Lwin River. He also wanted to take over the Karen territories, but the Japanese urged him to confine his ambition to the Shan territories only. Although the Japanese knew about the creation of the "Northern Army" they did not object to it in principle. But they had to consider Myanmar's reaction to it, even if not that of the Shan. When Dr. Ba

Maw was informed about the transfer of Keng Tung and Mong Pan states to Thailand, he was less than happy and commented, "Neither the Myanmar nor the Shan will be completely happy about the dismemberment of the Shan territory and its people," but he made no strong protest.

Phibul picked Luang Seri Raengrit to lead the "Northern Army." This man was well known in Bangkok for his patronage of the Royal Turf Club. The Thai soldiers were transported to Chiang Mai by train and from there carried their own supplies and trekked up the mountains to reach the Myanmar border. The Thai soldiers were not well equipped and inadequately armed and were poorly briefed on their mission in the Shan States. Meanwhile the Chinese military units of the Ninety-third Division moved down the Than Lwin valley to take up position in Keng Tung.

On May 3, 1942, twenty-seven Thai Air Force planes flew to Keng Tung and bombed the market where the Chinese troops were stationed. Many Chinese soldiers were killed, and they retreated. A few weeks later the Thai troops, led by Field Marshal Pin Choonhavan and General Chatichai Choonhavan, entered Keng Tung and the Thai flag was raised. Sao Mom Boon Wat, a member of the ruling family of Keng Tung, was asked to issue an order stating that the Thai government was in charge of the state,[12] and the Thais set up a local administration. The Thai troops were not popular but the Keng Tung public did not react too harshly against them. The Thai soldiers were seriously deficient in food and medical supplies. They suffered from malaria and dengue fever and Phibul had to order ten tons of quinine and foodstuff to be sent to his soldiers in Keng Tung. Phibul paid much attention to the Thai troops in Keng Tung but not to Mong Pan, where he sent only about a hundred military police and where they did not get along well with the public and clashes occurred very often.

By January 1943 the theaters of war in Europe as well as in Myanmar took a different turn. News of German defeats at Stalingrad and in North Africa, and the British move to the offensive on the Myanmar front reached Thailand, and the Thai authorities showed signs of worry. To these was added the news of Tojo's fall from power, forcing Phibul Songkhram to resign.

He was succeeded by Khuang Aphaiwong, whose government made it clear to the British that they renounced all claims to the Shan States and northern Malaya and that they would return these territories to Britain immediately when hostilities ceased. But the British did not seem able to forget being stabbed in the back by Japan's use of Thai territory to invade Myanmar and Malaya. The British prime minister, Winston Churchill, planned a punitive strike against Thailand, but American pressure prevented him from doing it.

The dropping of atomic bombs on Hiroshima and Nagasaki in August 1945, followed by the surrender of Japan, hastened the return of the Thai force in Keng Tung and Mong Pan to Thailand. Some Thai soldiers got married to Shan girls and settled down in Keng Tung to become citizens of the Shan States.

The remaining territories of the Shan States, the Wa States, and the Karenni territories were, under the Myanmar-Japan Treaty of Alliance, transferred to Myanmar in September 1943. There was general jubilation over their transfer and the head of state, Dr. Ba Maw, sent formal letters of good will to the Shan chiefs, *saohpa*, *myosa*, officers, and staff and invited them to Yangon and entertained them. Dr. Ba Maw then appointed the central government's home minister, U Ba Win, to be concurrently the high commissioner for the Shan States, the Karenni States and the Wa States, but it was really the deputy high commissioner, U Khin Maung Pyu, a native of the Shan States, who handled the administrative affairs of the Shan States.

For the actual ceremony of transfer from the Japanese high commissioner of the military administration to the high commissioner of the states, U Ba Win, Home Secretary U Paing, the deputy high commissioner, and Thakin Nu flew to Taunggyi. At the ceremony a Statement of Unification between Myanmar and the Shan States was issued. The actual letter of transfer was signed by the Japanese emperor and it was presented to the *adipadi*, or head of state, in Yangon.[13]

This is the story of how the Shan States were finally united to Myanmar after their separation in 1885.

11

The First Multinational Political Conference at Pang Long in 1946

The Myanmar lost the Third Anglo-Myanmar War in 1885 and the Upper Myanmar territories were annexed by the British. The Shan States, being part of the Myanmar empire, shared the same fate and had to acknowledge the overlordship of the British. In 1939 the Second World War broke out and the British evacuated from Myanmar, leaving the Shan States as prey for their enemies. The Japanese Imperial Army took control of the Shan States and gave Keng Tung and Mong Pan states to Thailand as royal gifts for being a good friend and for giving passage to the Japanese in the invasion of Myanmar. A military administration was imposed and the Shan States came under fascist rule for three years. The Second World War came to an end with the defeat of the Japanese and the British came back and resumed their administration over the Shan States for the second time.

For more than half a century the Shan States had been under continuous periods of foreign domination, and the Shan people also lived under fascist rule. During those years they suffered much spiritually and materially.

Now they began to feel that the time had come for them to make a political move to free themselves from the British. Politically speaking, the frontier peoples, including the Shan, were still underdeveloped. But the Shan, in comparison, were a bit ahead in their political outlook. The Shan leaders, the *saohpa*, made an effort to organize a political meeting at Pang Long, a little town of Lai Hka State in the Central Shan States. This first multinational political conference took place on March 26, 1946. Looking around for political allies, the Shan leaders found the Myanmar people from the plain region, who were politically, administratively, and economically more advanced and who had begun a political campaign to get freedom and independence from the British. It was immediately felt that political unity between the hill peoples (Shan and other ethnic nationalities) and the plain people (chiefly Myanmar) had become a necessity. "Freedom" had become a common objective for both peoples of hills and plain. In fact, these peoples had been living together in the same land and drinking the same water, sharing the same sovereignty, religion, culture, and traditions. They had undergone political, social, and economic hardships together during the darkest days of their history. They enjoyed economic prosperity, political freedom, social equality, and freedom of worship during the golden period of their history. Joy and woe were woven fine for these people during the long period of ups and downs of their history. They were found helping each other establish the Myanmar Naing Ngan (Union of Myanmar) of today.

Now the question was: who would take the initiative in arranging for these peoples to meet each other and where and how? Who would provide the venue, the facilities, and expenses for the meeting? It was finally decided that the Shan should take full responsibility for the successful implementation of the conference. The Shan leaders then took the risk to hold a conference at Pang Long on March 26, 1946. At that time the Federated Shan States were still under the British.

The conference was attended by representatives from other races including the Shan, Karen, Kachin, and Chin. A strong delegation of Myanmar leaders also took part. U Tin Tut, the governor, was invited but could not make it. The ex-premier, U Saw, and his men attended. U Nu and his team also came at the invitation of the Youth League.

The Pang Long Conference was, in fact, an event such as had never before taken place in the history of the hill peoples of Myanmar. Now all the scattered brothers of the hills were brought together at Pang Long for three objectives: to forge friendships, to secure mutual understanding with each other, and to lay a foundation for future cooperation. All the guests were greatly impressed by the generous hospitality and the high social and outstanding economic and agricultural standards of the people.

The first conference at Pang Long opened on March 26, 1946, and was presided over by the *saohpa* of Tawng Peng. At the start of the conference he announced that the object was not to make snap decisions but to hear what the representatives would like to say and to make decisions at leisure.

The governor was to be present and make a speech at this historic conference, but due to illness, he could not attend. His speech, delivered by Mr. Stevenson, director of the Frontier Areas Administration, was greeted with frequent and prolonged applause. (See appendix 28.)

The governor dealt with two subjects: the constitutional position and administrative reform in the Shan States, and the effort at economic development.

On the first subject: the administration of the hill areas would be under the direct control of the governor as in the past, to continue until the hill peoples themselves chose to join Myanmar proper. The British government hoped that the Shan States would soon join Myanmar proper in a form acceptable to both sides. The people of Myanmar proper were most anxious to include the Shan States in a fully self-governing Myanmar, and the people of the Shan States should give earnest and dispassionate consideration to the matter.

On internal administration, state advisory councils had been formed in every state which, it was hoped, would later develop into fully representative institutions in which the will of the people would be made known and brought to bear on the administration.

The administration of the Frontier Areas had been reorganized; its head was now in direct contact with the governor on the one hand and with the residents on the other. The former superintendents were now residents, and the assistant superintendents, assistant residents, reflecting the change in their role from the former superintendence of Shan States affairs to that of aid and advice.

The governor also proposed to establish advisory councils to the district officers in all subdivisions and districts of the Frontier Areas. The aim and duty of the district officers would be to train the advisory councils to accept responsibility so that they would later take over, item by item, all the spheres of local government and become a powerful force for development.

On the effort at economic development: the governor planned to initiate geological and agricultural surveys in the Frontier Areas to find ways of increasing the national income and the capacity to pay taxes in order to provide for schools, hospitals, traveling dispensaries, agricultural experimental stations, and other public services. The surveys would expand and collate information and enable the coordination of plans in all economic spheres. For example, irrigated cultivation would be increased in some areas, and the land for *taungya* cultivation would be used for more useful purposes, such as orchards and fuel and timber reserves; those nearest would be developed for industrial projects absorbing their products.

As communications in Myanmar were restored, improved methods of packing and refrigeration would be applied to increase and improve the trade with Myanmar proper in fruits, vegetables, and other farm products. Agricultural and marketing cooperatives would be formed and developed for this.

The Erosion Committee was revived; its anti-erosion work was one of the most important projects undertaken by the Federation, which hoped that it would receive pressing attention and support because wise use of the land was the foundation of all other economic activities.

In health, proposals were made for increased teaching facilities for nurses at Dr. Seagrave's hospital in Nam Hkam and an improved mobile service of surgical and medical teams. Besides the treatment and cure of disease, coordinated activities of many kinds were also needed to prevent disease; it meant improving the diet, building better and more hygienic houses, maintaining cleaner villages, and destroying the carriers of disease. As soon as adequate civilian supplies became available, the new weapons against disease—penicillin, DDT, and the new cures and preventives of malaria—would be brought into use in the Shan States. But local effort was also necessary—villages must be kept clean and sanitary, eatables must be grown to improve the diet, and better houses must be built for the children to grow up strong and healthy.

Local effort was necessary so that the available public money could be used for things that could not be done by oneself; for instance, in setting up a dispensary in the village, accommodation could be built by local effort, and public money used for equipment and medicines.

The same principles applied to the increase in educational facilities. If village tracts and circles took up the burden of providing buildings for schools, the number of schools, especially primary schools, would increase. On its part, the Frontier Areas Administration was considering a detailed plan for educational improvement in the Shan States, including providing for technical as well as academic training. As a special aspect of adult education, the training of craftsmen for cottage handicrafts needed attention, as increased production of minor village industries and improved marketing would increase income.

The state and regional councils should not be limited to political and administrative functions but should be made centers for disseminating information on cottage industries and technical improvement as well as help obtain patent rights.

There was need to develop and use to the full the natural self-reliance and inventive ingenuity which was the heritage of all hill peoples. The aim should be to ask nothing from the administration that could be done with one's own skill, brain, and energy, so that the assistance given would be of tenfold value. In self-reliance lay the real key to national resurgence and national progress.

The delegates to the conference made speeches stressing the need for cooperation among the hill peoples and the people from Myanmar proper. According to the secret British report, three were noteworthy. One was a Kachin, whose competence astonished even U Saw. But Thakin Nu's speech stirred up a storm. He lashed out at the British, accusing them of separating the hill peoples and the Myanmar people and only making them hate each other. His speech took the form of a diatribe directed against the British couched in immoderate terms. The *saohpa* were incensed at having one section of their guests publicly insulted by another at a meeting of this nature. The British officials and observers at the conference were not happy about U Nu's speech. They denied emphatically and asked "What have the Myanmar public done toward the hill peoples to win their love and faith?" It was through the influence of a section of the Myanmar who, while saying that we all belonged to the same race, blood, and home, called in our enemies, the Japanese, and caused the hill peoples to suffer miserably during the dark days that followed. But the result of U Nu's speech was also to the good, as it put other Myanmar leaders, including U Saw, on the defensive. U Nu's speech also had a deep effect on the Chin and Kachin delegations, who expressed their displeasure both at the immoderateness and at its lack of good taste in the circumstances in which it was delivered. Others also believed that the speech was ill advised and improper.

Mr. H. N. C. Stevenson, director of the Frontier Areas Administration, made the following remarks after hearing U Nu's speech:

> We are inclined to think that people who try to make unreal things real or to bluff the public are the ones who are responsible for the misunderstanding, suspicion and discord found to be existing between the Hill peoples and the Burmese. Now this is just one instance in a hundred. We would quote a thousand others. It is therefore an obvious fact that unless the Burmese leaders and people alike change their opinion

> about the Hill peoples and the treatment to be accorded to them there can be no hope of forming a real Federated Burma.
>
> On the other hand, if the Burmese will realize the situation and try to amend their past faults, we see no reason why there cannot be a real united Federated State of Burma. What we ask the Burmese to do is to be realistic and examine the facts. The British are our friends and their friends. They have done far more for Burma than the Burmese governments of old ever did and now they have promised the Burmese full self-government. We do not see that there is anything to be gained by blaming the British for faults which lie here in Burmese hearts.
>
> On the whole we have come away from Pang Long feeling much happier about the future. We realize now the size and shape of the problems which face us and can see our way much more clearly. We realize, too, that there is a fund of good fellowship in Burma only wanting to be released by wise leadership, and we hope that all the peoples of Burma, Burmese and Hill peoples alike, will find and support those wise leaders without delay.
>
> For the Hill peoples the safeguarding of their hereditary rights, customs and religions are the most important factors. When the Burmese leaders are ready to see that this is done and can prove how they genuinely regard the Hill peoples as real brothers equal in every sense to themselves, we shall be ready to consider the question of our entry into close relations with Burma as a free Dominion.
>
> In the meantime we hope the good work of brotherly cooperation started at Pang Long will continue under the auspices of the United Burma Cultural Association and we express our very grateful thanks to the Shan Saohpas for giving the Hill peoples this historic gathering.[1]

The next day ex-Premier U Saw also made a memorable and entertaining speech. He spoke for more than one hour, making very concrete suggestions to the Shan, contingent on his party's winning the next election, among which was the offer of a Minister for the Frontier Areas, who would be nominated by the people themselves. Without mentioning his backing of dominion status, U Saw made it clear that he did not visualize total separation from Britain and expected at least to remain within a simple defensive alliance. Some interruptions by the Hsa Htung *myosa* on the behavior of the Myanmar Ba Maw government officials gave the chairman an opportunity to stop the speech when U Saw was in full spate, and he continued it at a later meeting when he spoke for about one and a half hours.

He later elaborated in detail how the Frontier Areas and Myanmar could work together as a united dominion. He also stressed that the people of the Frontier Areas would be granted local autonomy and there would be no interference with their customs and religion. And he elegantly explained how he would take the business and commerce from the British and other foreign firms and place it into the hands of the government-sponsored agencies with the profits to help the farmers or cultivators. He thanked the governor for giving an opportunity to the Myanmar leaders to state their case to the leaders of the Frontier Areas, and he publicly apologized to the Shan on behalf of the people of Myanmar for the misbehavior of Dr. Ba Maw and his men. He also made concrete constitutional proposals, the first ever made to the frontier peoples by a leading Myanmar.

The Shan, Kachin, and Chin discussed among themselves and decided to draft a manifesto declaring that under no circumstances would they federate with Myanmar at the moment, but that instead they wished for self-government on the dominion level, in a "Frontier Areas Federation." The weak link was the Chin delegation, which felt that it was in no position to talk roughly to Myanmar upon which the Chin relied for food. At the same time, even the Chin did not wish to have union with Myanmar now if there was any way of avoiding it.

U Saw's proposals were thoroughly discussed, but the hill peoples still had doubts about all the promises made by the Myanmar leader. That was the crux of all the arguments against union. From every side came instances of broken promises and villainous behavior during the Ba Maw regime. From every side hopes were expressed that the day of union could be postponed until the people of the Frontier Areas had built up a federal organization strong enough to ensure equitable treatment from Myanmar. In short, the frontier peoples were still uncertain and afraid about the future. The Chin and Kachin made approaches to the Shan *saohpa* to see if these would be willing to pay the deficit in administration shouldered in prewar days by the Myanmar government. The Shan showed some signs of agreement to do so but were worried that they would find the burden too great for them.

U Saw, after his speech, talked with other national representatives and answered their questions. Mg San Pe, ex-member of the East Asia Youth League, Taunggyi, asked if there was any difference between the rules on Dominion Status of 1936 and those of 1939. U Saw replied that under the law that came into force in 1942, a country that had attained dominion status had a right either to remain within the British Commonwealth or to secede from it.

Mg Tin Aye, ex-president of the East Asia Youth League and leader of Shan Youth, asked whether Myanmar could get a seat on the UN Security Council. U Saw said yes and that Myanmar would get dominion status before India.

A Kachin representative mentioned the attitude of the Myanmar toward the Kachin in the past and asked U Saw if he could guarantee the welfare of the Kachin, a minority. U Saw replied that there were other minorities such as the Karen, Shan, Chin, Myanmar Muslims, and that the Kachin need not be anxious about this as future relations between the Myanmar and the other indigenous races would be cordial and they would all unite and work together.

U Saw prefaced his speech with the remark that the success of the Pang Long Conference made it clear that the allegation in the White Paper which characterized the peoples of the Frontier Areas as ignorant and backward was erroneous and that he would have liked the prime minister or at least the governor of Myanmar to be present at the conference to remark on the political awakening of the peoples of the Frontier Areas so that independence for these peoples would not be denied them.

He also spoke on the policy of the Myochit Party and urged the representatives present to forget the misunderstanding that had existed in the past between Myanmar and the peoples of the Frontier Areas. He urged unity between the two groups. He quoted the example of the government of the USA where different nationalities were to be found under one government and expressed the view that it would not be difficult to create a similar form of government in Myanmar to include the Frontier Areas. He urged the peoples of the Frontier Areas to decide now to unite with the Myanmar. When Myanmar attained freedom they could decide whether they wished to remain as part of the Myanmar state. If they wanted it, there would be no interference in their internal administration except in important centralized matters like defense, etc. If they were dissatisfied with their inclusion in Myanmar they could secede as the constitution guarantees the right of secession at anytime. That, U Saw said, would be the policy of any party in power, whether Myochit or AFPFL, and added that if the Myochit Party were in the opposition it would adhere to the same policy and recommend it to the party in power.[2] U Saw's speech dominated the conference and impressed the frontier peoples, clearing off half of the suspicious atmosphere. He asked them, "How long, if at all, would the British be prepared to finance the Frontier Areas, on their way to self-sufficiency?" The Chin and Kachin also asked if there was to be no tangible reward for their past loyalty and good service.

The possibility of a Myanmar dominion denying to the Frontier Areas a due share of customs and excise duties was but one of the fears expressed, and on more than one occasion, Mr. H. N. C. Stevenson, director of the Frontier Areas Administration, was asked whether the government could now push ahead with a road from Kamapyu to Papun and Moulmein, and thus open a back door to the sea through what, it was hoped by all, would be a separate Karen area.

On March 28, further meetings among the hill leaders continued. U Saw was asked many questions and he answered and promised that the Myanmar government would do everything to meet the needs of the frontier peoples including a fair share of development and of "revenue." But he could not dispel the deep-seated fear of Myanmar double-dealing. U Saw was able to form a United Myanmar Cultural Society, with the Yawng Hwe *saohpa* as president and himself as secretary. The objective of the Society was to introduce the mutual study of languages, customs, and religions to establish a better understanding and cooperation between all the peoples of Myanmar, but to avoid the inclusion of politics in its constitution. U Saw made a good impression on the leaders of the frontier peoples through his facts and diplomacy. At the farewell dinner on March 28 evening, U Saw, on behalf of the Myochit Party, and Meikhtila U Ba Yin gave encouraging speeches stressing the need to have unity and cooperation until freedom was achieved.

At this conference the Chin delegation strongly stressed their need for the financial assistance from the British until they could stand on their own feet and join the

Federation of Myanmar. They also proposed for the Lushai Hills to be included in the Frontier Areas Administration. The question of the councils was also discussed at length by both Chin and Kachin.

The Kachin delegates were interested mainly in the boundary settlement and the establishment of the Kachin State. They insisted on the inclusion of the Myitkyina and Bhamo Districts in the Kachin State and they were ready to forgo the Katha District. Matters concerning the Shan peoples in Myitkyina and Bhamo and the Kachin people living in Hsen Wi, Mong Mit, and Tawng Peng were thoroughly discussed at the conference.

On the whole, the first meeting of the frontier peoples at Pang Long was successful. All speeches by delegates were constructive and aimed at getting security and cooperation between the Frontier peoples of the hills and the Myanmar people from the plain. But U Nu's speech was generally disliked by the delegates for its bluntness and lack of tact. The Pang Long conference brought the Myanmar leaders and the frontier leaders together for the first time and to have a face-to-face talk which helped clear a lot of misunderstanding. The main conclusions arrived at by the frontier peoples were as follows:

1. To stick together to ensure fair treatment from the Myanmar people.
2. To make no approaches to the Myanmar without prior consultation among themselves.
3. To go in together to join with Myanmar and not as separate units.
4. To build up a strong bloc and to get financial aid from His Majesty's government.

Plans were made to hold another conference at Pang Long the next year and to meet annually in areas like Karen, Kachin, and Chin Hills. The Shan chiefs were to set up a press that might become a mouthpiece of the frontier peoples. Besides the political discussions, the conference also held a cattle show, a plowing exhibit, new inventions in weaving, implement demonstrations, cottage-industry demonstrations, and an arts and crafts show. Discussions dealt with village hygiene, forest preservation, erosion control, and other matters of importance to the people. A film show was also arranged for the conferees and the public. Famous films like *The Battle of Britain*, *The Battle of Russia*, and TVA were shown to the joy of spectators. For the first time the Shan chiefs met with other Frontier leaders and the leaders from Myanmar proper to discuss their future unity and freedom. For the first time also the people's representatives were treated equally with the *saohpa* in political matters and in those shaping the destiny of the future Shan State.

Credit for the success of this conference should go to the *saohpa* of Lai Hka, who took the responsibility to arrange everything and to meet a large portion of the expenses for this meeting. (For more information on the 1946 Pang Long Conference, see appendix 29.)

12

Postwar Political Developments in the Shan States

With the victory of the Allied Forces in 1945, the Second World War came to an end and the British reoccupied Myanmar including the Federated Shan States. Political awakening took place in Myanmar. The Myanmar nationalists, led by General Aung San, greatly inspired by the declaration of the Atlantic Charter and other political statements issued by leaders of the Allied Powers, began to intensify their political activities leading to the demand for independence from the British. Similar developments took place in the Shan States. The Shan chiefs felt that the administrative system of the Federated Shan States that had been created by the British in 1922 did not fit the changing situation in the Shan States. Moreover, the Shan chiefs wanted to take into their own hands the administrative authority exercised by the British officials. They began to see that their personal rule over their states as in the old days would have to change and administrative power shared with representatives of the people. They also realized that representative institutions should be introduced in a new administrative system. Therefore an administrative system must be introduced in the Shan States to meet the new political situation in the states.

Another crucial problem that emerged after the Second World War was how to politically amalgamate with Myanmar proper once independence was granted. Should the Federated Shan States, the Hill Tracts, or the frontier peoples be left alone? Geographically Myanmar proper, the Federated Shan States, and other Hill Tracts and Frontier Areas fell in one category of physiography and all must share the same fate of joy and woes about their political future. The question was how and on what principles? Did all the hill and frontier nationalities want to join in a future federation with Myanmar? Let us see how the Frontier Areas Committee of Enquiry of 1947 did its job to sound out these nationalities about the federation.

The idea of forming this committee was conceived during conversations between His Majesty's government and the Executive Council of the government of Myanmar in London in January 1947, in which it was agreed:

> A Committee of Enquiry shall be set up forthwith as to the best method of associating the Frontier peoples with the working of the new constitution for Burma. Such committee shall consist of an equal number of persons from ministerial Burma nominated by the Executive Council and of persons from the Frontier Areas nominated by the governor after consultation with the leaders of those areas with a neutral chairman from outside Burma selected by agreement. Such committee shall be asked to report to the government of Burma and His Majesty's government before the summoning of the Constituent Assembly to achieve the early unification of the Frontier Areas and ministerial Burma with free consent of the inhabitants of these areas.[1]

The committee was to make an inquiry of all the people who lived in the areas listed in the Government of Myanmar Act of 1935. These areas fell into two parts. Part 1 contained those areas administered by the governor at his discretion and Part 2 those areas administered by the governor in his individual judgment. But the three Karenni states that were not part of the scheduled areas did not come within the purview of the committee. They would be invited to send their representatives to express their views separately.

The administrative links in the scheduled areas as defined in the 1935 Act covered 113,000 square miles and formed about 47 percent of the total area of Myanmar. The population of that time was about 2,400,000, or 16 percent of the total. The main administrative units were as follows.

(1) The Federated Shan States. The Shan States of the British territory were ruled by the hereditary Shan chiefs called *saohpa* under the general supervision of the governor of Myanmar. They possessed quasi-autonomous rights regarding the management of their internal affairs. In 1922 these states were formed into a federation for common subjects and came to be known as the Federated Shan States. But for purposes of convenient administration, the Federated Shan States were divided into northern and southern groups. Within the federation were the notified areas of Taunggyi, Kalaw, and Lashio and the civil stations of Loi Lem and Loi Mwe, which were placed under the direct administration of the government of Myanmar through the federation officials:

a. The Northern Shan States

Area (sq. mi.)	21,400	
Total population		
(a) Federated States	600,000	
(b) Unfederated Wa States	82,614	
Population by Races		
Shan and Lolo Muso	333,960	44%
Palaung-Wa	220,000	28%
Indians, Chinese, and others	93,240	12%
Kachin	71,070	9%
Myanmar group	53,130	7%

Six states made up the northern group, including the Wa State of Mong Lun. The other Wa States which were not included in the federation were brought under the administration only in 1935. Ko Kang, a substate of Northern Hsen Wi with a predominantly Chinese population, was administered by a Chinese *myosa*.

b. The Southern Shan States

Area (sq. mi.)	56,416	
Total population	927,000	
Population by Races		
Shan and Lolo Muso	515,412	55.6%
Karen group	192,108	20.4%
Myanmar group	152,955	16.5%
Palaung-Wa	50,985	5.5%
Indian, Chinese, and others	18,540	2.0%

(2) a. Bhamo District

Area (sq. mi.)	4,148	
Total population	129,000	
Part 1 population	52,000	
Part 2 population	77,000	
Population by Races		
Kachin	49,794	38.6%
Shan	36,765	28.5%
Myanmar group	33,540	26.0%
Indians, Chinese, and others	8,901	6.9%

The Bhamo Part 2 area was a constituency area, represented in the Myanmar Legislature and the Constituent Assembly.

b. Myitkyina District

Area (sq. mi.)	19,762	
Total population	298,000	
Part 1 population	189,000	
Part 2 population	100,000	
Population by Races		
Kachin	157,642	52.9%
Shan, Lolo, Muso	16,586	25.7%
Myanmar group	40,230	13.5%
Indians, Chinese, and others	23,542	6.9%

Myitkyina was represented in the Myanmar Legislature and the Constituent Assembly, but Kamaing township was nonconstituency. The Shan States in the Hkamti Long area were included in Part 1. Katha District was in ministerial Myanmar, but included a small Part 1 area.

(3) a. Chin Hill District

Area (sq. mi.)	10,317	
Total population	186,100	
Population by Races		
Chin	183,786	98%
Others	2,232	1.2%

Kanpetlet Subdivision in the south of the district had close ties with the neighboring Chin population of ministerial Myanmar.

b. Arakan Hill Tracts

Area (sq. mi.)	3,543	
Total population	34,000	
Population by Races		
Chin	25,772	75.8%
Others	4,624	13.6%
Myanmar group	3,570	10.5%

The Myanmar group of the population who were Arakanese Buddhists nearly all lived in the southern tract bordering on the Arakan Division.

(4) a. Salween [Thaı. Lwin] District

Area (sq. mi.)	2,582	
Total population	57,000	
Population by Races		
Karen group	49,020	86.0%
(Tai) Shan	4,389	7.7%
Myanmar	2,223	5.9%
Others	1,311	2.3%

b. Karenni

Area (sq. mi.)	4,519	
Total population	70,000	
Population by Races		
Karen	51,310	73.3%
Shan	13,580	19.4%
Myanmar group	2,600	3.8%
Others	2,450	3.5%

(5) Naga Hill District

Area (sq. mi.) 5,898 [excluding Homalin Part 2 subdivision]

Total population 24,000 + Homalin approximately

Population by Races	Part 1 area only	
Naga	71,736	85.4%
(Tai) Shan	12,264	14.6%

Homalin Subdivision was a Part 2 nonconstituency area more advanced than the rest of the district. In Part 1 the Shan States of Thaungdut and Singkaling Hkamti and the Somra Tract inhabited by the Chin and the Shan were more advanced than the rest of the district, which was inhabited by the Naga tribes. These were the most backward of all frontier people and were brought under the administration only in 1940, and little progress in civilizing them had so far been possible.

Other Part 2 areas

(6) a. Tamu township population 5,870

Tamu township was a small Part 2 nonconstituency area of the India-Myanmar frontier in the upper Chindwin District. Details of the racial composition of the population were lacking, but it was predominantly Shan.

b. Thaton Part 2 area population 218,008
c. Eastern Taungoo population 160,000
d. Kya-in population 59,897
e. Myawady population 8,360[2]

Regarding the geographic and historical background of the Frontier Areas, the physical features of the country, it would be found that the great river valleys of Myanmar proper were surrounded from the northwest to the southeast by an unbroken chain of mountain and hill country covering all land from approaches from India and China except the extreme southeastern approach from Thailand. More than one hundred tribes inhabited these hill areas. The largest of them were Shan, Kachin, Chin, and Karen, and more than 95 percent of the Frontier Areas were dominated by them. There was a diversity of languages, dress, and customs, but there was also an intimate relationship not only between the races of the Frontier Areas but also between them and the Myanmar and the Karen. Most of the races belonged to the Tibeto-Burman language family. They included the Chin, Kachin, Naga, Lahu, and Akha. There was an indication of common ancestry in the languages of the Myanmar, the Chin, and the Kachin. The Shan, however, belonged to a separate language group known as Tai.

The Shan and Myanmar also had close historical and cultural links. In the middle of the eighth century the Shan formed a powerful state called Nan-chao in modern Yunnan and resisted Chinese attempts at conquest until 1253. About 1254 the Nan-chao ruler subjugated certain tribes of Upper Myanmar and had close relations with the kingdom of Myanmar composed of Pyu, a race that later merged with others to form Myanmar.[3]

The Shan kingdom of Nan-chao was ended by the invasion of the army of the Mongolian emperor Kublai Khan in 1253, forcing the Shan to migrate to the south and west. Some of them entered Thailand to found the kingdom of Chiang Rai in 1262,

Chiang Mai in 1296, and Ayutthaya in 1351. These kingdoms were later consolidated to form the kingdom of Siam, or later Thailand. Those entering Myanmar established many states known as *mong* in the northwest, north, northeast, and east of Myanmar. Well-known *mong* of these areas were Hsaung Hsop (Thaungdut), Kale, Waing Hso (Wuntho), Mong Yang, Mong Kwang, Mong Mao, Mong Hsen Wi, Mong Hsi Paw, Mong Nai, Mong Lawk Sawk, Mong Lem, Mong Keng Tung, Mong Keng Hung, and others. Some of these Shan before the Chinese conquest of Nan-chao migrated across northern Myanmar into Assam, where they founded the once powerful Kingdom of Ahom. There is a record of a relationship between the Shan of the Mao Kingdom and the Bagan Kingdom in the marriage between the Shan princess Sao Mon Hla and the Myanmar king Anawrahta (1044–1207). After the fall of Bagan before the Mongol invasion in 1287, three Shan princes dominated Upper Myanmar and the youngest prince named Thihathu became king in 1312, establishing his capital at Pinya. His younger son, Sao Yun, founded another kingdom known as Sagaing in 1315. During this period Shan penetrated into Upper Myanmar. Another wave of Mao Shan invaded the kingdoms of Sagaing and Pinya in 1364. After their departure the two kingdoms were united under another Shan king, Thadominpya, who established the capital of Inwa (Ava). By this time many of the Shan had penetrated into Myanmar, had intermarried, and had become Burmanized Shan.

Another invasion of the Mohnyin (Mong Yang) Shan, led by their chief Sawlon (Sao Long) into Upper Myanmar, took place in 1507. After a long period of attack the capital Inwa fell in 1527 with the death of its king in battle. A large number of the Inwa population took refuge in Taungoo. After the conquest Sawlon put his son, Thohanbwa (1527–43), on the throne of Inwa and left for Mohnyin. Because of his misrule he was assassinated by Mingyi Yannaung and was succeeded by the *saohpa* of Hsi Paw under the title of Hkun Mong (Hkonmaing) in 1543. Although Sao Hkun Mong had plans to consolidate Shan-Myanmar into a united kingdom, he did not live long enough to realize his plan. He was succeeded by a very weak Shan king, Mobye Narapati, who lost the kingdom to the Myanmar king, Bayinnaung, in 1555. Bayinnaung took over all the Shan States under his rule as well as Chiang Mai and Linzin, which belonged to Thailand. The suzerainty of Myanmar kings over the Shan chiefs dated from that period. But the traditional policy of Myanmar kings was not to interfere in the affairs of their feudatory states, and the Shan chiefs were left to rule their own states. Many Shan princes and princesses were brought to the Myanmar court and many Shan married Myanmar princes and princesses and some Shan princesses became Myanmar queens. From then on, Shan levies became the backbone of the king's army and were known for their spearmanship and their skill in fighting on elephants. The Shan preserved their own language and many of them learned Myanmar, and the two races shared many things in common especially religion. The last king of Myanmar, Thibaw, was half Shan. After annexing Upper Myanmar in 1885, the British, as successors to the Myanmar king, also claimed the Shan States as their possession. Many of the Shan chiefs, however, denied the claim, and under a Myanmar prince known as the Limbin prince, tried to resist the British, but they gave up when the Limbin prince negotiated with the British and surrendered.

The relationship between the Myanmar and the Kachin at that time was less close. The Kachin belonged to the Tibeto-Burman language group, but they were latecomers into Myanmar compared with the Myanmar, the Chin, and the Shan. They soon occupied Myitkyina, Bhamo, and Katha Districts and later reached as far south as the Shan state of Keng Tung. The Kachin were scarcely described in the Myanmar chronicles and inscriptions before the fifteenth century, but the Myanmar king Bayinnaung of Taungoo (1551–81) used Kachin levies for his army. The Kachin practiced shifting cultivation in the hills and had their own chiefs, called *duwa*, who administered according to tribal customs. They acknowledged the suzerainty of the Myanmar and the Shan rulers concerned. The armies of King Alaungpaya (1752–60) consisted of Kachin levies. The Myanmar king did not interfere in their internal administration. The suzeranity exercised over the Kachin did not mean more than occasional presents or tribute from them and their occasional service in the Myanmar armies. In some cases, Kachin *duwa* of importance received appointment orders from the Myanmar king. Thus, the Kachin *duwa*, a powerful chief, received his appointment order and his badge of office from King Mindon (1853–78).

The Kachin did not easily submit to the British when they annexed Upper Myanmar in 1885. The British had to send several expeditions to the Kachin Hills to put down the Kachin resistance. Kachin opposition was broken in 1895, and the Kachin Hill Tribes Regulation introduced British administration in 1895. The Kachin were not self-sufficient in the hills and they had always been obliged to maintain contact with the population of the plains through Shan-Myanmar villages in the foothills.

As for the Chin, they had migrated into Myanmar from the Tibetan plateau, settled along the Somra Hill Tracts down to Cape Negrais. The Chin of northwestern Myanmar had contacts with Myanmar at the time of the kingdom of Bagan (1044–1287). There were Chin levies in the armies of King Bayinnaung (1551–81) and of King Alaungpaya.

Legendary history had it that the ancestors of some of the principal tribes ascended the Chin Hills from the Kale-Kabaw and Myitha river valleys. One group went there from the foothill of the Myanmar village of Yezagyo and became the clans now inhabiting the northeast region of Tiddim. Another group went up to Mount Kennedy from the Kale valley. It went up the western slope of Kennedy Peak and settled in Zangpitam above Thuklai village, Siyin Valley. Later it moved to Cimnuai near Saizang village, Sokte area. Its members became the ancestors of the present tribes called Sizin, Sokte, Kamhau, Zo, and Thado.

The remainder moved from the Myitha River valley into the Central Chin country and were the ancestors of the Zanniats, Zahaus, Tashons of Falam, and various tribes of Haka.[4]

The British sent several expeditions to the Chin Hills to put down the Chin resistance forces. The British troops passed by the Kalemyo–Fort White–Tiddiim Road to the Basha Hills or Leisan to encounter the Chin resistance groups. The Chin resisted the advance until they were subdued. It was not until 1892 that the northern people now inhabiting the Tiddim area were disarmed. Down to the south, the various tribes of the Haka area also sternly resisted the advance of the British troops from the Gangaw Valley.

The Chin and the Myanmar had a close relationship, and several Chin could speak Myanmar fluently. The Chin living in the Pakokku, Thayetmyo, Prome, Magwe, and Henzada areas were mostly Buddhist and adopted Myanmar culture and became Myanmarized. Even in respect of the Chin in the Chin Hills, those who lived in the southern portion and the region near the Kale-Kabaw Valley were in close contact with the Myanmar. The Chin, living in the valley and on hilltops, spoke different dialects so that they had to use the Myanmar language as the medium of communication among themselves.

As for the Karen (Kayin) people, they mostly occupied positions in the Southern Shan States and in the hills of Taungoo District. The Karen in the Shan States had a very cordial relationship with the Shan, and those who lived in Salween (Than Lwin) District intermingled with the Shan as well as with other nationalities. They were the earliest settlers in Myanmar and after migrating southward along the hill areas, some streamed down to the plains of the Ayeyarwady Delta and the Tenasserim (Tanintharyi) Division and settled peacefully with other nationalities. The Karen were peace-loving people, shy and aloof; many of them preferred to live in the seclusion of the hills. Those who lived in the hills had their own chiefs. When the British took over Tenasserim the Karen' chief was Sgaw Saw Ku, who surrendered to the British authorities.

As for Karenni (Kayah), their home region comprised the states of Kantarawady, Baw La Ke, and Kyebogyi. Karenni means Red Karen. They had a feudal administrative system like the Shan. They were mostly independent of Myanmar rule, but occasionally sent tribute to the Myanmar kings. King Minkyinyo (1486–1531) once received propitiatory tribute from the rulers of Karenni. The Myanmar kings made no attempt to interfere in their internal affairs unless they became very aggressive, as they did once in 1845. They raided the neighboring Shan States in pursuit of slaves. Once the Myanmar sent an expeditionary force to the Shan States and raided Karenni and did not withdraw until the Karennis submitted. After the trouble, the chief of Kyebogyi received from the Myanmar king recognition as the ruler of a separate state in the Karenni and the title of *myosa*. In 1866 the chief of Kantarawady in Eastern Karenni helped the Myanmar king suppress a rebellion led by the king's son, the prince of Myingun, and in recognition of these services the chief was granted by King Mindon a letter of appointment under the title *myosa* of Kantarawady. In 1881 the chief sent his son, Saohpa, with others to King Thibaw at Mandalay and Saohpa received royal recognition as *kyem-mong*, or heir apparent of the state.

A Myanmar outpost was established at Loi Kaw in 1872 and another at Nammakon in 1873, which was withdrawn in 1876 on the representation of the British government. In 1873 the independence of Western Karenni was guaranteed as follows by an agreement between the British and the Myanmar governments:

> It is hereby agreed between the British and the Burmese governments that the State of Western Karenni shall remain separate and independent and that no sovereignty or government authority of any description shall be claimed or exercised over that state.[5]

After annexing Upper Myanmar in 1885, the British, under the Agreement of 1875, left Western Karenni alone for some time. They tried in 1887 to secure the peaceful submission of the *myosa* of Kantarawady in Eastern Karenni but failed. In 1888 the *myosa* even raided the Shan state of Mawk Mai, which had accepted British suzerainty. The British sent an expeditionary force to subdue the *myosa*. He was deposed and his son Sawlawi was appointed chief of Kantarawady and subsequently continued, under a *sanad*, on the same terms as the chiefs of Western Karenni, of whom there were four at the time, nominally independent, formally recognized as feudatories by the government of India, and presented with *sanad* appointing them *myosa* on terms similar to the *myosa* of Kantarawady. These four states were later reduced to two by amalgamation.

The three Karenni States were never annexed to the British Crown and had the status of feudatories. The chiefs, under the *sanad* recognizing their appointment, were required, among other conditions, to pay an annual tribute and accept and act on any advice given to them by the British political officer concerned.

THE IMPOSITION OF BRITISH ADMINISTRATION IN THE FRONTIER AREAS

The British came to consider the Frontier Areas strategically important, because human migration had been going on constantly and it was very difficult to know when and how immigrants moved from one place to another. Even within the country human movement was difficult to control. In those days nobody knew how many people came down from the top of the mountains to the foothills. For many reasons they kept moving. Perhaps they moved for food, shelter, hunting, looting, and perhaps because of fighting, war, epidemic diseases like smallpox, the plague, diarrhea, dysentery, and perhaps due to famine, political or religious persecution, racial cleansing, and so on. To control the situation a sort of administration became necessary for the ruling authority. Thus the British administration came into existence following 1886. Local advances continued in the far north as late as 1940, when the headhunting Naga tribes were brought under some sort of administration.

In Myanmar proper the British government introduced the Government of Myanmar Act in 1935, which came into force in 1937, and formed a Federated Shan States to introduce reforms in administration in the Shan States. But for the Frontier Areas, nothing much changed materially. They were ruled and administered as part of Myanmar in the traditional ways by local chieftains under the general supervision and control of the governor of Myanmar.

Regarding British administration in the Shan States, four stages may be roughly classified. The first was from 1886 to 1897, when the Shan chiefs voluntarily submitted themselves to the overlordship of the British, and *sanad* including terms of administration and succession were issued. The actual administrative authority was in the hands of the feudal chiefs, the *saohpa*. Two advisers were attached to help the *saohpa* of Hsi Paw and the *saohpa* of Yawng Hwe in their administration and to check what they were actually doing. That became the origin of the system of "assistant superintendents" in the Shan States.

The second stage from 1897 to 1922 was marked by the introduction of local self-government in Myanmar and of the lieutenant governor's council, of which a Shan *saohpa* was a member throughout this period.

The third stage covered the period from 1922 to 1935. During these years a federal form of administration was introduced as a trial. The federation of Northern and Southern States came into effect on October 1, 1922, just one year before diarchy, or government by two joint rulers, was introduced into Myanmar proper. The Federal Council of Shan chiefs, with the commissioner as president, was also introduced. The Shan chiefs had no executive power, but they could express their views on federal and general matters including the federal budget. It was rather like an advisory council and no more. The Myanmar Frontier Service came into existence with the establishment of the federation. Toward the end of this period suggestions were made to create a People's Council.

The last stage was from 1935 to 1942. During these years a series of reforms were introduced, finally resulting in a system of representation of the *saohpa* in the government. The most significant feature of the reforms was the emergence of a small Standing Committee of Chiefs composed of six representatives elected by the main council. Another outstanding feature of this committee was that it could have direct dealings with the governor periodically. Moreover, all federal subjects came under the general direction and supervision of the council.

Although the system of administration was different between Myanmar proper, the Frontier Areas, and the Federated Shan States, the course of events like politics, religion, social, cultural, and especially economic development forged a number of new links between the Frontier peoples and Myanmar during this period. Many trading centers sprang up in the valleys and riverbanks where Myanmar, Shan, Indian, and Chinese merchants settled and built up a considerable development in trade and commerce with the people of the nearby hills and villages. By 1935 trade and contacts developed and people moved into these trade centers to become towns and sites where goods were transacted between the people of the towns and the hill folk, and their relationship with each other became indispensable.

The 1935 Act allowed for the stages of development in the scheduled areas by dividing them into less politically advanced regions, known as Part 1 areas, which were administered by the governor at his discretion, and the more politically advanced Part 2 areas, which were administered by ministers. The governor had a special responsibility over these and could overrule the decision of ministers on these areas. A further division was made in Part 2 between constituency areas which returned members to the Myanmar Legislature in Yangon and the nonconstituency areas.

It was contemplated that as Part 2 areas continued to develop they should, in time, be merged in Myanmar proper. The same course of development was open to Part 1 areas. The Act allowed Part 1 areas to become Part 2 areas as they matured, and Part 2 areas to be merged in ministerial Myanmar, but did not permit the reverse process in either case.[6]

The 1935 Act remained in operation until the Japanese invasion in 1942 and the process of closer association between Myanmar and the Frontier Areas continued. The links between the two were not only commercial but financial. For instance, health, education, and other services were financed in part by the revenues of Myanmar, since all the Frontier Areas, with the possible exception of the Federated Shan States, were in deficit.[7] Moreover, Kachin, Chin, and Karen (Kayin) had all come to regard service in the Myanmar army and police, both financed by Myanmar, as an important source of income.

By the time of the Japanese occupation in 1942, the frontier peoples had become accustomed to many amenities of which they had known nothing before 1886, and which they could not afford to maintain out of their own resources. Thus, both political and economic links had been strengthened between them and Myanmar since the British annexation of 1886.[8]

After the British reoccupation in 1945, it was found that the administration under the 1935 Act did not fit in with the political aspirations of Myanmar. Myanmar nationalism had greatly increased both in strength and in the urgency of its demands, and a similar, though less marked, development had taken place among the frontier peoples, who were anxious to take into their own hands as soon as possible many of the powers formerly exercised by the British. Realization began to dawn on them that the traditional methods of personal rule must be modified by the development of representative institutions. The representative institution must be created whenever necessary. A start was made by creating the Village Council to advise the chiefs on the exercise of their powers. Larger districts were fostered to develop the Domain Councils to which the villages could send their representatives. These councils would play an advisory role at first and an executive role later.

The process of development was quite slow. In 1947 development was at its rudimentary stage. As far as the Shan States were concerned, the absorption in 1945 of the duties of the commissioner of the Federated Shan States, into those of the director of the Frontier Areas Administration, with headquarters in Rangoon (Yangon), and the placing of the Federated Shan States under the charge of two residents, constituted a reversion to the system of administration before 1925, where there was no separate commissioner for the Shan States. This did away with the central executive of the Federated Shan States and the control over federal departments. The *saohpa* therefore formed their own executive councils including the representatives of the people.[9]

Gradually the Frontier leaders who were enlightened began to realize that they were economically and politically less advanced than Myanmar proper. The means of communication was difficult and scarcity of population hindered development in agriculture. Local production, including staple foodstuff and rice, was inadequate and the frontier peoples had to depend on Myanmar proper for the supply of all these needed materials. They appreciated that in order to achieve a higher standard of living they needed a measure of outside assistance, which would have to come from either Britain or Myanmar, and that in the conditions of the modern world, they had certain common interests with Myanmar which precluded a continuance of the prewar arrangements for entirely separate administrations. Nonetheless, the historical fact that the frontier peoples had never experienced interference in their internal affairs was not forgotten, and the desire for a large measure of autonomy was almost universal.

The political events that developed during the Second World War brought the frontier peoples and the Myanmar people together to share the same vision of their future political freedom. More and more contacts between Myanmar and frontier political leaders were made during 1945 and 1946, which led to the two political conferences that took place in the central town of Pang Long in the Shan State, where mutual understanding was achieved. The London Agreement obtained in January 1947 paved the way for the speedy creation of a new constitution for Myanmar. The problem of relations and political unification and understanding between the frontier peoples and the Myanmar acquired a new urgency. It was also made known that the objective of both His Majesty's government and the government of Myanmar was "to achieve early unification of the Frontier Areas and ministerial Myanmar with the free consent of the inhabitants of those areas."[10]

In February 1947 leaders and representatives of the majority of the frontier peoples met members of the Myanmar Executive Council at Pang Long under the terms of paragraph 8 (b) of the London Agreement, and agreed on a form of association during the interim period until the new constitution came into force.[11]

THE PANG LONG AGREEMENT

The terms of the Pang Long Agreement (see appendix 30), which regulated the relationship between Myanmar and the major portion of the Frontier Areas when the Committee of Enquiry began its work, were as follows:

The Pang Long Agreement, 1947

A conference having been held at Pang Long attended by certain members of the Executive Council of the governor of Burma, all *saohpa* and representatives of the Shan States, the Kachin Hills and the Chin Hills.

The members of the conference, believing that freedom will be more speedily achieved by the Shans, the Kachins, and the Chins by their immediate cooperation with the interim Burmese government.

The members of the conference have accordingly, and without dissentients, agreed as follows:

1. A representative of the Hill peoples, selected by the governor on the recommendation of representatives of the Supreme Council of the United Hill Peoples (SCOUHP), shall be appointed a counselor to the governor to deal with the Frontier Areas.
2. The said counselor shall also be appointed a member of the governor's Executive Council, without portfolio, and the subject of Frontier Areas brought within the purview of the executive authority by Constitutional Convention as in the case of Defence and External Affairs. The Counselor for Frontier Areas shall be given executive authority by similar means.
3. The said counselor shall be assisted by two deputy counselors representing races of which he is not a member. While the two deputy counselors should deal in the first instance with the affairs of their respective areas and the counselor with all the remaining parts of the Frontier Areas, they should by Constitutional Convention act on the principle of joint responsibility.
4. While the counselor, in his capacity as member of the Executive Council, will be the only representative of the Frontier Areas of the council, the deputy counselors shall be entitled to attend meetings of the council when subjects pertaining to the Frontier Areas are discussed.
5. Though the governor's Executive Council will be augmented as agreed above, it will not operate in respect of the Frontier Areas in any manner which would deprive any portion of these areas of the autonomy which it now enjoys in internal administration. Full autonomy in internal administration for the Frontier Areas is accepted in principle.
6. Though the question of demarcating and establishing a separate Kachin State within a United Burma (Myanmar) must be relegated for decision by the Constituent Assembly, it is agreed that such a state is desirable. As a first step toward this end, the Counselor for Frontier Areas and the deputy counselors shall be consulted on the administration of such areas in the Myitkyina and the Bhamo Districts as are Part 2 scheduled areas under the Government of Burma Act of 1935.
7. Citizens of the Frontier Areas shall enjoy rights and privileges which are regarded as fundamental in democratic countries.
8. The arrangements accepted in this agreement are without prejudice to the financial autonomy now vested in the Federated Shan States.
9. The arrangements accepted in this agreement are without prejudice to the financial assistance which the Kachin Hills and the Chin Hills are entitled to receive from the revenues of Burma, and the Executive Council will examine with the Frontier Areas counselor and deputy counselors the feasibility of adopting for the Kachin Hills and the Chin Hills financial arrangements similar to those between Burma (Myanmar) and the Federated Shan States.[12]

The agreement not only settled the form of association during the interim period but also enunciated certain principles. These were that the frontier peoples should be entitled to fundamental democratic rights, that they should have the rights to full autonomy in the internal sphere, and that they should be entitled to receive a measure of assistance from the revenues of ministerial Myanmar which were relevant to the decision of the ultimate form of association. The formation of the Supreme Council of the United Hill Peoples (SCOUHP) was also a noteworthy step forward in the establishment of representative institutions among the frontier peoples.

The Frontier Areas Committee of Enquiry was composed of:

1. Chairman. Lieutenant Colonel D. R. Rees Williams M. P.
2. Myanmar members. The Honorable U Tin Tut, CRE, member without portfolio of the Executive Council
3. Thakin Nu, vice president, AFPFL
4. U Khin Maung Gale, AFPFL
5. Saw Myint Thein, Karen Youths' Organization
6. Frontier Areas members. The Honorable Saohpa of Mong Pawn (Shan), counselor to His Excellency the governor for the Frontier Areas, and member of the Executive Council.
7. Sima Sinwa Nawng (Kachin), deputy counselor
8. U Vum Ko Hau (Chin), deputy counselor
9. Saw Sankey, Karen National Union
10. M. B. J. Ledwidge, Myanmar Office, secretary
11. U Tun Pe, B.FR.S, joint secretary
12. Major Shan Lone, OBE, MC, B.FR.S, assistant secretary

Saw Myint Thein joined the committee when it moved to Pyin Oo Lwin (Maymyo) in place of the Honorable U Kyaw Nyein, Home member, who was a member in Yangon, but was forced to resign owing to pressure of other work.

Program of the Committee

- to hear the evidence of all interested parties
- to invite witnesses to testify before the committee
- to select the main body of witnesses through the councils in each area
- to interview individuals and organizations separately
- to allow witnesses from the Arakan Hill Tracts and the Salween (Than Lwin) District to interview in Yangon
- to interview witnesses from other Frontier Areas at Pyin Oo Lwin
- to have a private committee meeting with the chairman and two members for a quorum
- to allow the members' advisers to attend the meetings but without the right to participate in the discussions

Advisers

1. Sao Boon Waat, political secretary to the Honorable Saohpa of Mong Pawn
2. Labang Grong, adviser to Sima Duwa Sinwa Nawng
3. U Thawng Chin Thang, B.FT.S., adviser to U Vum Ko Hau

The Honorable U Kyaw Nyein, who resigned from the committee when it left Yangon, was also permitted to attend certain meetings in Pyin Oo Lwin as an observer. The committee held its first formal meeting in Yangon on March 18, 1947, to hear witnesses as follows:

March 19: Director, Frontier Areas Administration Salween District witnesses
March 21: Saw Marshall Shwin, president of Shwegyin Karen Association
March 22: Director, Frontier Areas Administration
March 24: Arakan Hill Tracts witnesses
March 26: Karen Youths' Organization witnesses

Meetings in Pyin Oo Lwin

On March 27, 1947, the committee moved to Pyin Oo Lwin, and resumed hearing in accordance with the following program:

April 11: Witnesses from
1. Shan States Peoples' Federation Congress
2. Kalaw, Taunggyi, and Lashio. Notified areas and Loi Lem
3. Northern Wa States
4. Ko Kang State

April 12: Witnesses from
1. Southern Wa State
2. Northern Hsen Wi State
3. South Hsen Wi State
4. Tawng Peng State

April 14: Witnesses from
1. Karenni States
2. Mong Mit and Keng Tung states
3. Papun United Karen Organization

April 16: Witnesses from
1. Myitkyina and Bhamo Council Kachin
2. Hkamti Long Shan
3. Kachin Youth League
4. Jinghpaw National Modern Civilization Development Association
5. North Hsen Wi-Mong Mit Kachin

6. Army Kachin
7. Frontier Constabulary Kachin
8. Nepali Association, Myitkyina

April 17: Witnesses from
1. Karen National Union
2. Bhamo AFPFL

April 19: Witnesses from
1. Falam Chin
2. Haka Chin
3. Tiddim Chin
4. Chin Pensioners' Association
5. Kanpetlet Chin
6. Somra Tract (Part 1 area) Chin
7. Thaungdut State (Part 1 area) Shan
8. Singkaling Hkamti State (Part 1 area) Shan
9. Homalin Subdivision (Part 2 area) Myanmarized Shan

April 21: Witnesses from
1. Supreme Council of United Hill Peoples
2. Shan *saohpa*
3. Other southern Shan states
4. Tiddim and Kanpetlet Chin
5. Bhamo (Part 2 area)

Burman community

The committee held a total of twenty-four meetings, seventeen devoted to the hearing of evidence and seven to private deliberations.

After hearing the witnesses who expressed unanimously their desire to take part in the work of the Constituent Assembly, the committee recommended the following be given representation in the Constituent Assembly:

1. The Federated Shan States, including Ko Kang and Mong Pai
2. The Kachin Hills
3. The Chin Hills with the Arakan Hill Tracts
4. The Karenni States
5. The Somra Tract
6. The Salween District
7. The Homalin Subdivision

Regarding the distribution of the seats the committee's recommendations were as follows:[13]

1. Federated Shan States, including Ko Kang and Mong Pai	26
2. The Kachin Hills	7
3. The Chin Hills with the Arakan Hill Tracts	6
4. Karenni	2
5. The Salween District	2
6. The Somra Tract	1
7. The Homalin Subdivision	1
	45

The observations made by the committee were as follows:

1. The witnesses from the Federated Shan States and from the Kachin Hills were strongly in favor of a federated Burma in which the Federated Shan States would form a state or unit and the Kachin Hills another.
2. Witnesses unanimously expressed their desire for the fullest possible autonomy for the states within the Federation and agreed that certain subjects of general scope should be entrusted to the Federation.
3. Representatives from the Chin Hills expressed their unwillingness to federate with Burma Proper but preferred to amalgamate with ministerial Burma. . . . They wanted no interference with their tribal customs and traditions, preferring their chieftains to be allowed to administer their tracts as at present.
4. The witnesses from the Somra Tracts, Thaungdut, Singkaling Hkamti, and the Homalin Subdivision wanted their areas to be incorporated in ministerial Burma and to be given the same constituency and other rights as other areas in Burma Proper.
5. The representatives from the Karenni stated clearly their wish to participate in the Constituent Assembly but did not definitely commit themselves to any view about the entry of the Karenni States into a federated Burma.
6. The present circumstances would call for an elastic interim constitution establishing perhaps a Federal Council that would be somewhat on the lines of a legislature with such subjects as could be allocated to the federal sphere . . . . The Federal Council when established by the Constituent Assembly could then be elaborated into a Senate or a federal legislature.
7. The consensus among witnesses indicated that if there should be a Burma federation, the federal organ should deal with the following subjects:
   (1) External Affairs
   (2) Defence
   (3) Posts and Telegraphs
   (4) Communications
   (5) Currency and Coinage
   (6) Customs
   (7) Titles and Honors[14]

There was a danger that the anxiety of the constituent states for the fullest possible internal autonomy might lead to the constitution of a weak federal or central government that would be the government of Burma which deals with the outside world.

8. *Right of secession.* The majority of the witnesses who favored a federation of Burma asked for the right of secession by the states at any time. Few federal constitutions contained provision for the secession of states . . . if any such right was to be contained in the federal constitution for Burma, it would have to be carefully limited and regulated.

9. *Constitutional safeguards.* The recommendation of the Constituent Assembly relating to the Frontier Areas should be incorporated in the Burma Constitution and in the appropriate act of parliament.
10. *Interim arrangements.* During the transitional period, the Shan counselor or the deputy counselors for the Kachins and Chins should continue in office. The Frontier Areas administration should also continue in this period under the control of the counselor and his deputies. Where possible, administrative officers should be drawn from the indigenous peoples of the Frontier Areas.
11. *States and other territorial units.*
    (1) *The Federated Shan States*
        (a) This Federation should consist of the present states. The notified areas of Lashio, Taunggyi, and Kalaw and the civil stations Loi Lem and Loi Mwe should, for convenience in the administration of the Federation, be incorporated in the states in which they were situated.
        (b) Mong Pai State should continue to be grouped with the three Karenni States for administrative purposes. Its political future should be decided by a committee consisting of representatives of the Shan States Council, Mong Pai, and Karenni.
        (c) The Ko Kang State or substate should remain a substate of North Hsen Wi.
    (2) *The Kachin Hills.* If a Kachin State was to be established as a constituent state in the Burma Federation, the question was whether the Part 1 and Part 2 areas should be amalgamated to form the new administrative and economic unit. Evidence given by representatives of Part 2 areas in Bhamo District indicated probable unwillingness by the Burmese and the Shan-Burmese population of the Part 2 areas to be merged in the new state, particularly as some of these were constituency areas. It was left to be settled by negotiations in the Constituent Assembly. It was agreed that the triangle should be included in the new Kachin State and also Hkamti Long area.

        The Namwan Assigned Tract should also be included in the state, but this inclusion would not of course affect its position as an assigned tract.

Kachin witnesses assured that if Part 2 areas should be united with Part 1 areas to form the new state they should willingly guarantee the rights and privileges of the non-Kachin people and freedom to retain their own customs.

(3) *The Chin Hills.* In view of the doubt about the wishes of the people of the Chin Hills and of the Arakan Hill Tracts in regard to the political future, it must be left for negotiation and decision in the Constituent Assembly.

(4) *The Karenni States.* The representatives of the Karenni States expressed a desire for some form of association with other Frontier Areas. The exact form should be worked out in the Constituent Assembly.

(5) The future of the Mong Pai State had already been referred to in paragraph 11 (b) above.

(6) *The Salween District.* Evidence from the second group of representatives of this district indicated the desire for incorporation in ministerial Burma as an ordinary district but with the rider that wherever possible administrative officers in the district should be Karen.

(7) *The Naga Hills.* External government of some kind was necessary in this area until its people were fit for administering their area as a state in the Burma Federation or a unit in ministerial Burma. Its administration should be either entrusted to the Federal Council or supervised by the government of Burma with Homalin as the headquarters of the Naga Hills. It was also desirable that close liaison should be maintained by the Burma government with the government of Assam, which also had Nagas on its borders, in order that a common policy for the Naga might be worked out and operated by the two authorities.

(8) *The Wa States.* The administration of these areas should be supervised either by the Federal Council or by the government of the Federated Shan States until their people were fit to take over the administration of their own area either as a state in the Burma Federation or as a unit of Burma proper. It was also recommended that the Shan States government rather than the federal authorities would be in the best position to supervise the administration of the Wa States.

Other Areas

- Tamu township, the Homalin Subdivision, and the Somra Tract should be included in ministerial Burma and have full constituency and other rights.

  The Eastern Taungoo, Kya-in, Myawady, and Thaton Part 2 area should be included in ministerial Burma with full constituency and other rights, but negotiations to this end should take place in the Constituent Assembly.

- Thaungdut and Sinkaling Hkamti should be included in ministerial Burma with full constituency and other rights. The *saohpa* in these states should continue to perform their present functions.

- The Homalin Subdivision should be included in ministerial Burma and have full constituency and other rights.
- The Somra Tract should be included in ministerial Burma and have full constituency and other rights.
- The Katha Part 1 area should be incorporated in ministerial Burma and have full constituency and other rights, but this was a matter to be negotiated in the Constituent Assembly. Regarding the wishes of the people of the Shan States over the formation of the federated Burma, common subjects and autonomous and other rights are described in appendices.

EVIDENCE FROM REPRESENTATIVES OF THE SUPREME COUNCIL OF UNITED HILL PEOPLES[15]

Maymyo, April 21, 1947

(1) Saohpa of Yawnghwe, *president*
(2) Saohpa of North Hsen Wi, *vice-president*
(3) U Htun Myint
(4) *Duwa* Zau Lawn, Central Kachin Executive Council
(5) Zau Rip
(6) Chief Pumza Mung, KSM, ATM, Chin Hills
(7) Chief Van Kio
(8) Sang Sam, *secretary*, SCOUHP (interpreter)

1. Chairman:	You gentlemen know the object of our enquiry?
Saohpa of Yawng Hwe:	Yes.
2. Chairman:	Would you let us know the views of SCOUHP as to the future association of the Frontier Areas with ministerial Burma?
Saohpa of Yawng Hwe:	We want to associate with Burma on the condition that full autonomy is guaranteed in our internal administration.
3. Chairman	What about common subjects?
Saohpa of Yawng Hwe:	They are going to be combined with Burma.
4. Chairman	Have you any suggestions as to how these common subjects should be dealt with?
Saohpa of Yawng Hwe:	Subjects like Defence, External Affairs, Currency and Coinage and so on and so forth will be common subjects.
5. Chairman	What form of government do you suggest to deal with them?
Saohpa of Yawng Hwe:	A federal government.
6. Chairman	What is the federal government to consist of?
Saohpa of Yawng Hwe:	It will consist of representatives of Burmese, Shans, Kachins, Chins, and Karens.
7. Chairman	Should it be in a form similar to the United States of America system or will it be in a simpler form of government?
Saohpa of Yawng Hwe:	It is possible that it may be similar to the United States' system.
8. Chairman:	Do you think this country will be able to run this proposed system straightaway? Have you enough

	men able to run a system like that of the United States?
Saohpa of Yawng Hwe:	We consider that we have enough men for this purpose.
9. Chairman:	Can you give us the list of common subjects you suggest?
Saohpa of Yawng Hwe:	These common subjects will consist of External Affairs, Currency and Coinage, Customs, Excise and Railways.
10. Chairman:	And other communications?
Saohpa of Yawng Hwe:	Not other communications.
11. Chairman:	Are these representatives here from the Shan, Kachin, and Chin groups in the SCOUHP?
Saohpa of Yawng Hwe:	Yes.
12. Saohpa of Mong Pawn:	I think the president of the SCOUHP has some proposal as to how we (the SCOUHP) should go into the federal government, that is, concerning the Shan States Council going direct into the Federal Council?
Saohpa of Yawng Hwe:	Yes, here is a diagram of it.
13. Chairman:	I see from your diagram that the Shan, Kachin, and Chin areas are to send representatives to the SCOUHP and SCOUHP itself is to send representatives to the Federal Council. If I understand this diagram correctly, there would be no direct representation of the Shan, Kachin, and Chin areas in the Federal Council. Am I right?
Saohpa of Yawng Hwe:	Yes.
14. U Vum Ko Hau:	Are you considering sending representatives to the Constituent Assembly from the SCOUHP?
Saohpa of Yawng Hwe:	We do not contemplate sending members of the SCOUHP to take part in the Constituent Assembly. Provincial councils from the various areas will do that.
15. Chairman:	Is there anything else the president of the SCOUHP would like to say?
Saohpa of Yawng Hwe:	We have already submitted to the chairman a memorandum of the answers to the questionnaire as determined by the SCOUHP.

The chairman read out the memorandum to the committee as follows:

Part 2, pp. 4–5. Evidence given by the president of SCOUHP 1 to 7 (pp. 4–5)

Evidence Given by the President of SCOUHP

1. Representative members to the Constituent Assembly to be nominated by the provincial councils proportionately on an intellectual basis, irrespective of race, creed, and religion as far as the Hill Areas are concerned.
2. To take part in the Burmese Constituent Assembly on a population basis, but no decision to be effected in matters regarding a particular area without a two-thirds majority of votes of the representatives of the areas concerned.
   (a) Equal rights for all.
   (b) Full internal autonomy for all representatives of Hill Areas.
   (c) Rights of secession from Burma Proper at any time after attaining freedom.
3. It is resolved that due provision shall be made in the future Burmese Constitution that no diplomatic engagements shall be undertaken or appointments made withour prior reference to the Hill States.
4. In matters of common subjects, e.g., Defence, etc., no decision shall be made without the prior consent of the majority of representatives of the Hill States irrespective of Burmese votes.
5. The provision shall be made in the Constitution of the federated Burma that any change, amendment, or modification affecting the Hill States, either directly or indirectly, shall not be made without a clear majority of two-thirds votes of the representatives of the Hill States.
6. When opinion differs on the interpretation of the terms in the Constitution, the matter shall be referred for decision to a bench of the High Court of Judicature at Rangoon comprising the Chief Justice and two other Justices.
7. The total number of the Burmese members in the Federal Cabinet shall not exceed the total number for the Frontier States in the said Cabinet.

President, SCOUHPC/Maymyo
Dated the 21st April 1947

The Shan States Council

1. It shall be called the Shan States Council.
2. Members shall be equally represented on the council from the *saohpa* and the people (thirty-three *saohpa* and thirty-three popularly nominated representatives).
3. For immediate purposes the representatives of the people shall be nominated on an intellectual basis, but election on a population basis shall be the fundamental rule of election.
4. The nomination of the representatives of the people shall be left to the present representatives of the people with the power to call in for advice and assistance anybody having the genuine interests of the Shan States at heart.

5. This council shall be invested with the following powers:
   (a) legislative, (b) executive, and (c) finance.
6. An Executive Committee consisting of eight members (four *saohpa* and four representatives of the people) shall be selected from the council to be in charge of all the departments in the Shan States.
7. The present Executive Committee of the Council of Shan States *Saohpa*, together with two nominated representatives of the people, shall carry on with the work till such time as the Shan States Council and its Executive Committee come into existence as contemplated in questions three and four.
8. The Shan States Federal Fund shall be revived and placed within the sole financial power of the Executive Committee.

(Signed) Hkun Pan Sing, President
Council of Shan States *Saohpa*
Dated Taunggyi, the 15th February 1947

Addition to five above: (d) judicial (The Shan States shall have a separate High Court within the Shan States.)
Addition to six above: If eight members are considered to be too many, four to five main departments can be started with.

(Signed) Hkun Pan Sing
President, Shan States Council
Dated Maymyo, the 21st April 1947

Decisions and Resolutions of the Meeting of the Supreme Council of the United Hill Peoples, held in Yawng Hwe Haw, Yawng Hwe, from 18th to 25th March 1947

Extracts: Meeting No. 3, dated 23rd March 1947

1. Representative members to the Constituent Assembly to be nominated by the Provincial Councils proportionately on an intellectual basis, irrespective of race, creed, and religion as far as the Hill Areas are concerned.
2. To take part in the Burmese Constituent Assembly on a population basis, but no decision to be effected in matters regarding a particular area without a two-thirds majority of votes of the representative of the areas concerned.
   (a) Equal rights for all.
   (b) Full internal autonomy for all representatives of Hill Areas.
   (c) Rights of secession from Burma Proper at any time after attaining freedom.

Emergency SCOUHP meeting held at Yawng Hwe Haw, Yawng Hwe, at 1 A.M. on the 27th March 1947

Present: Saya Zau La
Duwa Zau Lawn
Labang Grong
Captain Mang Tung Nung
Chief Thawng Za Khup
Chief Hniar Kulh
U Vawmthu Mawng
Saohpalong of Yawng Hwe State
Saohpalong of North Hsen Wi State
U Kya Bu

1. It is resolved that due provision shall be made in the future Burmese Constitution that no diplomatic engagements shall be undertaken or appointments made without prior reference to the Hill States.
2. In matters of common subjects, e.g., Defence, etc., no decision shall be made without the prior consent of the majority of representatives of the Hill States irrespective of the Burmese votes.
3. Due provision shall be made in the Constitution of a United Burma that any change, amendment, or modification affecting the Hill States, either directly or indirectly, shall not be made without a clear majority of two-thirds votes of the representatives of the Hill States.
4. When opinion differs on the interpretation of the terms in the Constitution, the matter shall be referred for decision to a bench of the High Court of Judicature at Rangoon comprising the Chief Justice and two other Justices.

(Signed) S.S.Thaike,
President, SCOUHP, Yawnghwe

The Shan States desire the following facts be taken into consideration by FACE [Frontier Areas Committee of Enquiry] in its report to the governments concerned:

(1) The Shan States shall participate in the forthcoming Constituent Assembly, members to be nominated by the Shan States Council on a population basis.
(2) In the Constituent Assembly no decision shall be effected in matters regarding the Shan States or any change, amendment, modification affecting the Shan States in the future Constitution of the Federation without a clear majority of two-thirds of the votes of the members from the Shan States.
(3) Association with Burma shall be on a federal basis with—
    (a) equal rights and status;
    (b) full internal autonomy for the Shan States;
    (c) right of secession from the Federation at any time after attainment of freedom.

(4) Federation on subjects which cannot be dealt with by the Shan States alone such as
   (a) Defence
   (b) Foreign and External Affairs
   (c) Railways, Post, and Telegraph
   (d) Coinage and Currency
   (e) Customs, etc.

   which would be defined as common subjects by the Constituent Assembly.

(5) The selection and appointments of the judges of the Supreme Court to interpret the Constitution should by convention be approved by the majority of the Frontier members of the federal government.

Basic Questionnaire for Witnesses
Shan States

Q. 1. What is the economic position of your area?
A. Fair.
Q. 2. What is the geographic position of your area?
A. . . . .
Q. 3. How have the political desires of the people you represent been discovered, e.g., by council meetings, etc?
A. Pang Long Conferences on two occasions, 1946 and 1947.
Q. 4. Do your people desire union with Burma?
A. No.
Q. 5. If not, do they desire federation with Burma?
A. Yes.
Q. 6. Do your people think that members of the races in the Frontier Areas should send representatives to participate in the work of the Constituent Assembly?
A. Yes.
Q. 7. If the answer to question six is in the negative, what do they propose in respect of the future of the Frontier Areas?
A. . . . .
Q. 8. If the answer to question six is in the affirmative, what do they think should be the total number of representatives of the Frontier Areas in the Constituent Assembly?
A. On a population basis.
Q. 9. How do they divide the total proposed members in your reply to question eight between the several races in the Frontier Areas?
A. Only three races, Shans, Chins, and Kachins recognized.

Q. 10. Do they think that representatives of the Frontier Areas in the Constituent Assembly should be elected in a manner similar to that for Burma Proper? Or do they think elections unsuitable? If so, do they wish to suggest an alternative method?

A. No.—Yes.

Q. 11. Would they regard the entry of Frontier Areas representatives into the Constituent Assembly as involving the inclusion of the Frontier Areas in a United Burma?

A. No.

Q. 12. How do they propose that the Constituent Assembly should settle questions relating to the internal affairs of the Frontier Areas?

A. This question does not arise. Full internal autonomy.

Q. 13. What methods of internal autonomy do they propose, so far as they affect Burma Proper?

A. This question does not arise.

Q. 14. Does Burma declaring for a state outside or inside the Commonwealth make a difference?

A. No.

Q. 15. Do they think that a small committee should be appointed to allocate subjects between the central government of Burma, and the governments of separate states and provinces? Have they any suggestions as to what the common subjects should be?

A. Yes.

Q. 16. Have they any observations to make on boundaries?

A. . . . .

Q. 17. What do they suggest as the legal condition in the new Constitution, i.e., statutory or customary law?

A. Customary law.

Q. 18. What safeguards do they require for the faithful execution by the central government of Burma of any agreements reached?

A. His Majesty's government to be guarantors.

Special Questionnaire

Shan States

Q. 1. What future do you propose for the notified areas of Kalaw, Taunggyi, and Lashio and the civil stations of Loi Lem and Loi Mwe?

A. Go back to their respective parent states.

Q. 2. What future do you propose for the Wa States?

A. We like to welcome them in the SCOUHP, but that is a matter for Was to decide.

It is our desire that Was should be given freedom simultaneously with us.

Q. 3. What future do you propose for Ko Kang State?

A. It has been a substate of North Hsen Wi since prewar days.

Q. 4. What future do you propose for Mong Pai State?

A. It should remain in the Shan States.

EVIDENCE OF WITNESSES FROM THE SHAN STATES[16]
Maymyo, 21st April 1947

1. President and Representatives of the Shan Saohpa

(1) Saohpa of Tawng Peng State, president
(2) Saohpa of Yawng Hwe State
(3) Saohpa of North Hsen Wi State
(4) Saohpa of Lai Hka State
(5) Saohpa of Hsa Mong Hkam State
(6) U Htun Myint
(7) Hkun Hti
(8) U Pyu
(9) Sang Sam (interpreter)

37. Chairman: Have the *saohpa* considered the question of the association of Shan States with ministerial Burma?

Saohpa of Tawng Peng: Yes, we have.

38. Chairman: Would you like to give the committee the views of the Council of *Saohpa*?

Saohpa of Tawng Peng: The views of the *saohpa* are recorded in the statement already submitted this morning.

39. Chairman: Is there anything else you would like to say?

Saohpa of Tawng Peng: We have nothing else to say.

40. Chairman: Actually the Council of *Saohpa* has ceased to exist and in its place the Council of the Shan States, comprising both the *saohpa* and the representatives of the people, has been constituted. Is that not so?

Saohpa of Tawng Peng: Yes.

41. Chairman: Has the new council met?

Saohpa of Tawng Peng: We have not yet met

42. Chairman: How much power has the council?

Saohpa of Tawng Peng: We have not yet drawn up the constitution.

43. Chairman: Is it the desire of the *saohpa* that the representatives to the Constituent Assembly shall be nominated by the council?

Saohpa of Tawng Peng: Yes.

44. Chairman: Is it also their intention that the representatives to the SCOUHP. shall be nominated by this council?

Saohpa of Tawng Peng: Yes.

45. Chairman: Do you gentlemen think that it is better to send representatives from the SCOUHP to the federal

	government rather than direct from the Shan States' Council when the latter is set up?
Saohpa of Tawng Peng:	Yes, the representatives should come from the SCOUHP.
46. The Hon. U Tin Tut:	Is the SCOUHP going to be a subfederation with a government of its own?
Saohpa of Tawng Peng:	Yes, for the Frontier Areas only.
47. The Hon. U Tin Tut	What subjects is it going to administer?
Saohpa of Tawng Peng:	All the common subjects of the Frontier Areas—Kachins, Chins, and Shan States.
48. The Hon. U Tin Tut:	I thought the federal government was to deal with the common subjects. What I am trying to visualize is what the function of this SCOUHP will be.
Saohpa of Tawng Peng:	The SCOUHP is going to deal with the subjects which are common only to the Frontier Areas, i.e., Shan States, Kachins, and Chins.
49. The Hon. U Tin Tut:	Is it going to have subjects different from those of the individual states? Or is it going to supervise the administration of these subjects?
Saohpa of Tawng Peng:	SCOUHP will deal with subjects which are common to the Frontier Areas. As far as purely home affairs are concerned, they will be administered by the states themselves.
50. Chairman	Have you a list of the subjects to be administered by the SCOUHP?
Saohpa of Tawng Peng:	We have not drawn them up yet.
51. Chairman	Is there anything else any of you would like to say?
Saohpa of Tawng Peng:	No, nothing else.
51a. The Hon. U Tin Tut	Is the idea that the SCOUHP will deal with some subjects which are not federal subjects?
Saohpa of Tawng Peng:	They will deal with certain common subjects for the three areas.

[The chairman thanked the witnesses, who then withdrew.]

2. Shan States People's Freedom Congress and Hsi Paw State

(1) Ko Tun Myint [Shan States People's Freedom Congress]
(2) Hkun Saw [Shan States People's Freedom Congress]
(3) U Sein, Hsi Paw State

52. Chairman:	I understand that you, who attend here, are from the Shan States People's Freedom Congress. Is

	that right? Can you tell us something about the Congress?
Ko Tun Myint:	We have reorganized this Congress from March of this year.
53. Chairman:	What are its aims and objects?
Ko Tun Myint:	The unity, freedom, and progress of the people.
54. Chairman:	Is this a movement aimed at *saohpa*?
Ko Tun Myint:	The aim and object of this association is to secure the freedom of the country in cooperation with the *saohpa*.
55. Chairman:	How many members have you in the Congress?
Ko Tun Myint:	136,743 members.
56. Chairman:	Are they paid-up members?
Ko Tun Myint:	Yes, sir.
57. Chairman:	Has your Congress considered the question with which the committee is concerned?
Ko Tun Myint	We have considered it only since we came here.
58. Chairman:	What has been the result of your consideration?
Ko Tun Myint:	We have decided to go into the Constituent Assembly which is going to be held not very many days from now, in Rangoon.
60. Chairman:	Would you like to be represented in the Constituent Assembly?
Ko Tun Myint:	Yes, sir.
61. Chairman:	You mean that you would like the Congress to be represented there, or the Shan people to be represented there?
Ko Tun Myint:	The Shan people.
62. Chairman:	Have you thought out what sort of representation you want; how many members?
Ko Tun Myint:	We propose to be represented in the Constituent Assembly in proportion to the population-on-population basis.
63. Chairman:	As compared with ministerial Burma?
Ko Tun Myint:	Yes, sir.
64. Chairman:	How do you suggest that the representatives should be chosen?
Ko Tun Myint:	We propose that the representatives shall be chosen by the Provincial Council which is going to be formed in the Shan States.
65. Chairman:	So the representatives will really be nominated by the Provincial Council?

Ko Tun Myint: Yes, sir.

66. Chairman: Have you thought out what the eventual outcome should be so far as the association of the Shan States with Burma is concerned?

Ko Tun Myint Yes, sir, we have thought it out.

67. Chairman: What have you in mind about the future association between the two?

Ko Tun Myint As a federation.

68. Chairman: There are many kinds of federation. What kind do you like?

Ko Tun Myint: The common subjects should be dealt with by the central federation, and the rest by the states. The states will have internal autonomy.

69. Chairman: This central federation you are talking about—is that a central body with representatives of ministerial Burma and the Frontier States or is it the Burma Legislative Assembly itself?

Ko Tun Myint: By and by, after the formation of the Constituent Assembly, there might probably be two houses: the Upper and the Lower. The representation to the Lower House will be on the basis of population, and that to the Upper House will be according to territory.

70. Chairman: Are you talking about some federal parliament? Is that what you meant?

Ko Tun Myint: Yes, I mean a federal parliament.

71. Chairman: Do you mean a federal parliament in addition to a parliament for ministerial Burma itself?

Ko Tun Myint: Yes, the ministers from ministerial Burma shall have to be in that federal parliament.

72. Chairman: Do you mean that there should be one parliament for ministerial Burma and one parliament for the Shan States and, in addition, another parliament for the whole, including the Frontier Areas?

Ko Tun Myint: Yes, exactly.

73. Chairman: There are two possible ways, are there not? First you can have a federal system as in the United States of America and secondly you can have your representatives in the Legislative Assembly of Burma Proper. Which do you prefer?

Ko Tun Myint: I prefer the first way.

74. Chairman: Does it make any difference to you whether Burma stays within the Commonwealth or goes out?

Ko Tun Myint: No, sir.

75. Chairman: You do not mind either way?

Ko Tun Myint: No, it does not matter.

76. The Hon. Saohpa of Mong Pawn: With regard to the federal Upper House do you prefer the House to consist of representatives of regions or of nationalities?

Ko Tun Myint: I prefer it to be on the basis of nationality.

77. The Hon. Saohpa of Mong Pawn: What future do you propose for the Wa States?

Ko Tun Myint: We have not thought specially about the Wa States, but we have included them in our consideration regarding the Shan States.

78. Chairman: Should they form part of the Shan States?

Ko Tun Myint: If they should like to be in the Shan States, well, they can be.

79. Chairman: If not?

Ko Tun Myint: Well they can choose to be outside it, but they ought to be given freedom at the same time as the Shan States.

80. The Hon. Saohpa of Mong Pawn: What about Ko Kang State?

Ko Tun Myint: We propose that the Shan States' parliament should consider this question.

81. Sima Sinwa Nawng: Papun District is under the direct administration of the governor. Does your Congress think that the privileges which the Karens, Chins, and Shans have received should also be extended to the Papun District?

Ko Tun Myint: We are prepared to give them every assistance if they should care to take help from us.

82. Sima Sinwa Nawng: If there is a federation, have you thought out how you are going to send your representatives?

Ko Tun Myint: We have thought out what subjects should be handled by this federation.

83. Chairman: What are they?

Ko Tun Myint: Foreign Relations, Defence, Communications and Currency.

84. Chairman: Do you believe that the Burma ministerial government would agree to all these things being dealt with by the Federal Council?

Ko Tun Myint: There is no reason why the ministerial government should not agree to it.

85. Chairman: Well, take the question of finance. The Frontier Areas are 16 percent of the whole in population. Most of the finance at the moment comes from ministerial Burma. Do you see ministerial Burma being prepared to allow finance to be handled by the Executive Council?

Ko Tun Myint: We shall have to settle that question in the Constituent Assembly with the Burmese people.

86. Chairman: Can you tell me something about what you propose? Do you propose that there should be one parliament for the Shan States itself?

Ko Tun Myint: Well, we propose to have a sort of council, not exactly a parliament—but a sort of council.

87. Chairman: For the Federated Shan States?

Ko Tun Myint: Yes, sir.

88. Chairman: Will that council appoint representatives, so far as the Shan States are concerned, to the federal authority?

Ko Tun Myint: Yes, at present we make that proposal.

89. Chairman: A parliament for Burma consisting of a Senate and a House of Representatives, that is what you said. Well, until these are set up do you foresee a Federal Council for Burma, representatives being appointed to it from the Federated Shan States Council?

Ko Tun Myint: It is possible.

90. Chairman: Have you considered the question of the "notified areas" and "civil stations"?

Ko Tun Myint: According to the Congress these will have to be made over to their respective states.

91. U Khin Maung Gale: Which of the nationalities do you think should be represented in the Senate?

Ko Tun Myint: For example, only those peoples who number over fifty thousand will have representatives in the Senate, and not those who do not come up to that number.

92. Chairman: If the council of the Shan States is going to select representatives, that would seem to be on a territorial and not on a nationality basis?

Ko Tun Myint: It depends on the will and pleasure of the Shan council.

93. Chairman: Whether it should be nationality or territorial?

Ko Tun Myint: Yes, sir.

94. U Khin Maung Gale: Just now you talked about a Shan State, a Kachin State, and a Chin State, yet in the composition of the Senate you want representation by nationality. How can you reconcile these two views of representation by territory and representation by nationality?

Ko Tun Myint: The best thing will be representation by nationality, but if that is not possible we shall have to choose the alternative of territory.

95. Chairman: You have suggested nationality but in fact, so far as you have gone, you have worked on a territorial and not a nationality basis.

Ko Tun Myint: We will try and work it out and if that is not possible we shall have to revert to the other.

96. Thakin Nu: Because some other nationalities do not come up to the required number, you will have to work on the territorial basis?

Ko Tun Myint: Some of nationalities do not come up to the required number.

97. Chairman: By internal autonomy, which you mentioned earlier, you meant autonomy on a territorial basis?

Ko Tun Myint: Yes, sir.

98. Chairman: A territorial basis for internal autonomy and a nationality basis for the federal Senate will be very difficult to work out.

Ko Tun Myint: Perhaps so.

99. U Khin Maung Gale: When you ask for internal autonomy you ask on a territorial basis, but when you ask for the representation in the Senate you ask on a nationality basis?

Ko Tun Myint: Yes, sir.

100. Chairman: Hkun Saw, do you want to say anything in addition?

Hkun Saw: In the Frontier Areas there are Shans, Kachins, and Chins. Supposing Shans were represented in the federal Senate by two persons, Kachins and Chins would likewise be represented by two—each race represented by two. There are many tribes in the Shan race but those who are in the Shan States we would consider as Shans in spite of their tribes. The population of Chins, Kachins, and Shans is about equal.

101.	U Vun Ko Hau:	How many principal tribes are there in the Shan States?
	Hkun Saw:	Some of them are different.
102.	U Vun Ko Hau:	Are the dialects the same?
	Hkun Saw:	Some of them are different.
103.	U Vun Ko Hau:	How many different dialects are there?
	Hkun Saw:	I cannot say exactly, but the thirty tribes have some three dialects which are similar.
104.	U Vun Ko Hau:	Can they all understand the Shan language?
	Hkun Saw:	No, some of them do not understand it.
105.	The Hon. Saohpa of Mong Pawn:	Is that the universal language?
	Hkun Saw:	Generally the Shan language is spoken and understood but there are some who do not understand it.
106.	The Hon. Saohpa of Mong Pawn:	When you say two representatives from each area in the federal Senate, how many representatives do you suggest for Burma?
	Hkun Saw:	Burma should be represented by two.
107.	Chairman:	What about you, U Sein? Are you representing Hsi Paw State?
	U Sein:	Yes, sir. I represent Hsi Paw State.
108.	Chairman:	You heard the other representatives. Do you agree with what they have said?
	U Sein:	I agree with them.
109	Chairman:	Is there anything you would like to add to what they have said?
	U Sein:	In the Shan States there may be a number of tribes but all of them are at the same time Shans and most of them speak the Shan language which is almost universal. Shan culture is imbibed by almost all.
110.	Chairman:	Is that all?
	U Sein:	My friends have already spoken.
111.	U Khin Maung Gale:	Are you a member of the Shan States People's Congress?
	U Sein:	Yes, I am a member.
112.	Chairman:	Are you also a representative of the Hsi Paw State? By whom were you chosen?
	U Sein:	I am a representative. I was chosen by the votes of the Hsi Paw State, Advisory Council.
113.	Chairman:	Are you a member of that council?

U Sein: I am a representative. I was chosen by the votes of the Hsi Paw State Advisory Council.

114. Chairman: Is that the official council of the state?

U Sein: Yes, under the direction of the government, it is the "People's Advisory Council."

115. Chairman: But it is the official one set up recently.

U Sein: Yes, at the insistence of the government.

116. Chairman: Anything further that you would like to say?

U Sein I endorse what my friends have said.

[The chairman thanked the witnesses and wished them a safe return journey. The witnesses then withdrew.]

3. Southern Shan States other than Keng Tung

(1) Hkun Hti
(2) U Htun Myint
(3) U Pya (Taungthu)
(4) U Sein Nit
(5) Sang Sam (interpreter)

117. Chairman Have you gentlemen selected your spokesman?

Hkun Hti: I will speak for all of us.

118. Chairman: Whom do you represent?

Hkun Hti: We represent the Southern Shan States.

119. Chairman: By whom were you selected?

Hkun Hti: We were selected by the Shan States' Council.

120. Chairman: But, how can that be when we were told it has not met.

Hkun Hti: Before the Pang Long Conference we had the Shan States *Saohpa* Council, but afterward it was dissolved and a new council was formed. Representatives of the people are also to be on this new council. The Executive Committee of the new council has met and selected us as representatives to this committee, but the full council has not met yet.

121. Chairman: Are the other three witnesses also selected by this Executive Committee?

Witnesses: Yes.

122. Chairman: What is the opinion of the Southern Shan States people on the question of the association of the Shan States with ministerial Burma?

Hkun Hti:	Our views are just the same as those recorded in the statement submitted by the *saohpa* and we have nothing to add to it.
123. Chairman:	Is there anything else any of you would like to say?
Witnesses:	No, all has been said.

[The chairman thanked the witnesses, who then withdrew.]

4. Mong Mit and Keng Tung States

(1) U Shein, Mong Mit State
(2) Sao Sing Zai, representative of the *saohpa* of Keng Tung State
(3) Sai Ling Tip, representative of the people of Keng Tung State

124. Chairman	U Shein, you are the representative of Mong Mit State? Is it in the Northern Shan States?
U Shein	Yes, sir.
125. Chairman	Are you a representative of the people?
U Shein:	Yes, sir.
126. Chairman:	Where and when were you elected?
U Shein:	At Mong Mit on the 23rd of March.
127. Chairman:	Do you know the purpose of this enquiry?
U Shein:	Yes, sir.
128. Chairman:	Will you tell the committee what your people desire with reference to the subject matter of enquiry?
U Shein:	What the masses want is to abide by the decision of SCOUHP to unite with Burma.
129. Chairman:	What exactly do you mean by "unite"?
U Shein:	I mean "federation."
130. Chairman:	What would be the common subjects?
U Shein:	Foreign Relations, Currency and Coinage, Customs, Communications. These are the common subjects.
131. Chairman:	What about Defence?
U Shein:	SCOUHP will decide that.
132. Chairman:	Can you tell us whether your people want the Shan States to be represented in the Constituent Assembly?
U Shein:	We would like to send representatives to the Constituent Assembly.
133. Chairman:	In what numbers?
U Shein:	On a racial basis.

134. Chairman: In what numbers?
U Shein: On a basis of one is to fifty thousand.
135. Chairman: Anything further you would like to say?
U Shein: No, sir.
136. Chairman: Sao Sing Zai, you are the representative of the *saohpa* of Keng Tung State, and your colleague is a representative of the people. Is he not?
Sao Sing Zai: Yes, sir.
137. Chairman: What is the wish of the *saohpa* and the people with regard to the future association of the Keng Tung State with the other Frontier Areas people? In other words, does the Keng Tung State wish to remain in the Shan States Federation?
Sai Ling Tip: Yes.
138. Chairman: What do the people wish with reference to the future association of the Shan States and ministerial Burma?
Sai Ling Tip: It depends on the decision of the Shan States Council.
139. Chairman: Have they got any views on it at all?
Sai Ling Tip: We want internal autonomy and equal rights in the federation.
140. Chairman: Is that in the Shan States Federation?
Sai Ling Tip: Yes.
141. Chairman: Have you got any ideas as to the form of federation?
Sai Ling Tip: Representatives should be sent on a population basis to the Federal Council.
142. Chairman: What subjects should the Federal Council deal with?
Sai Ling Tip: It depends on what the internal government cannot decide.
143. The Hon. U Tin Tut: You mean subjects which the internal government cannot properly deal with?
Sai Ling Tip: Yes, sir.
144. Chairman: Do you wish to send representatives to the Constituent Assembly?
Sai Ling Tip: Yes.
145. Chairman: In what proportion?
Sai Ling Tip: On a basis which is a compromise between a population basis and a racial basis.
146. Chairman: Does Sao Sing Zai agree with what you have said now?

Sao Sing Zai: Yes, sir.

147. Chairman: Sao Sing Zai, your state is very closely associated with Siam (Thailand). Is it not?

Sao Sing Zai: Yes, in everything.

148. Chairman: In fact, it is much easier to get into Siam than into Burma?

Sao Sing Zai: Yes.

149. Chairman: Are you still anxious to remain in the Shan States Federation?

Sao Sing Zai: Yes, for the present.

[The chairman thanked the witnesses and wished them a safe return. The witnesses then withdrew.]

5. North Hsen Wi State[17]

(a) Howa Duwa Hkun Hpung

150. Chairman: What is your name?

Howa Duwa Hkun Hpung: My name is Hkun Hpung.

151. Chairman: You are the representative of North Hsen Wi State?

Howa Duwa Hkun Hpung: Yes, sir.

152. Chairman: North Hsen Wi State is predominately Shan?

Howa Duwa Hkun Hpung: Yes, sir.

153. Chairman: But there is a big Kachin minority there?

Howa Duwa Hkun Hpung: Yes, sir, but more Shans than Kachins.

154. Chairman: Whom are you representing this morning? Are you representing all the people of North Hsen Wi State?

Howa Duwa Hkun Hpung: Yes, I am the president of the Kut Kai Council (which is Kachin) as well as a member of the State Advisory Council (which is Kachin and Shan) and a member of the SCOUHP from North Hsen Wi State.

155. Chairman: You are sent by the council to represent the people of the state?

Howa Duwa Hkun Hpung: I am sent by the chief of North Hsen Wi State.

156. Chairman: By the *saohpa*?

Howa Duwa Hkun Hpung: Yes, sir.

157. Chairman: What is the desire of the *saohpa* and the people of North Hsen Wi State as regards the future of the Shan States?

Howa Duwa Hkun Hpung: The opinion of the people is that Chins, Kachins, and Shans, according to the Pang Long Agreement, should associate themselves with the Burmese government, and these free people should form themselves as a SCOUHP to participate in the Burmese Constituent Assembly.

158\. Chairman: Have you considered the form of association between the people of the Frontier Areas that you mention and ministerial Burma?

Howa Duwa Hkun Hpung: The Frontier Areas people should have equal rights with the Burmese and should also obtain the internal autonomy of their areas.

159\. Chairman: Have you worked out any form of government which could carry out the purpose you have in mind?

Howa Duwa Hkun Hpung: Once freedom is obtained, it is left to the representatives of the Frontier Areas people to work out the form of constitution in the Burma Constituent Assembly.

160\. Chairman: How many representatives do you suggest there should be in the Constituent Assembly for the Frontier peoples?

Howa Duwa Hkun Hpung: There should be representatives in equal numbers of Chins, Kachins, and Shans.

161\. Chairman: Yes, but how many should there be in the Constituent Assembly?

Howa Duwa Hkun Hpung: I cannot say what number at present. It is left to the council to decide.

162\. Chairman: Which council?

Howa Duwa Hkun Hpung: The Shan States Council.

163\. Chairman: Well, the Shan States Council cannot decide for the Chins.

Howa Duwa Hkun Hpung : The SCOUHP Council.

164\. Chairman: SCOUHP Council? When is it going to meet again?

Howa Duwa Hkun Hpung: If necessary, after this Enquiry Committee meeting. We are waiting for the president.

165\. Chairman: Anything else which you would like to say?

Howa Duwa Hkun Hpung: I want to speak on the internal problem of North Hsen Wi State. Before the war, it was one complete state and Ko Kang State was considered a subsidiary state of North Hsen Wi State; but since the war, Ko Kang State has become a separate state. I want all

	the people of North Hsen Wi State, the Kachins, the Chinese, and the Shans, to live together in one state and to participate in the Federated Shan States as well as in the SCOUHP. I leave it to the government to consider this problem.
166. Chairman:	You haven't mentioned the Karens at all. Don't you think they should form part of the SCOUHP?
Howa Duwa Hkun Hpung:	I have not spoken to the Karens yet.
167. Chairman:	Yes, but what do your people think about it?
Howa Duwa Hkun Hpung:	The people's opinion is that the Karens should join us in the SCOUHP.

[The chairman thanked the witness and wished him a safe return journey. The witness then withdrew.]

South Hsen Wi State[18]

(b) U Hme

168. Chairman:	What is your name?
U Hme:	My name is U Hme.
169. Chairman:	Where do you come from?
U Hme:	I come from South Hsen Wi State.
170. Chairman:	Are you a representative of the *saohpa*?
U Hme:	No. I am a representative of the masses.
171. Chairman:	How did the masses select you?
U Hme:	There was a meeting and it was decided to select me as a representative.
172. Chairman:	Where was the meeting held?
U Hme:	At Mong Yai.
173. Chairman:	And when was that?
U Hme:	During the Tabaung Festival in the month of March.
174. Chairman:	And what did they instruct you to say?
U Hme:	The resolution passed at the meeting was that we agreed to the Pang Long Agreement and decided to join the Shan States with ministerial Burma.
175. Chairman:	Do you agree to the federation of the Shan States with ministerial Burma?
U Hme:	Yes, sir.
176. Chairman:	Have you considered what the form of union should be with Burma?

	U Hme:	We want internal autonomy.
177.	Chairman:	And what should be the common subjects?
	U Hme:	Defence, Foreign Relations, and Communications.
178.	Chairman:	Have you thought at all how the form of union should be framed?
	U Hme:	We want to send representatives to the Constituent Assembly.
179.	Chairman:	In what numbers?
	U Hme:	In proportion to our population.
180.	Chairman:	In comparison with ministerial Burma?
	U Hme:	Yes, sir.
181.	U Khin Maung Gale:	What about Finance as a common subject?
	U Hme:	We don't want to have Finance as a common subject in the central government.
182.	Thakin Nu:	Do you know what is known as the British Commonwealth of Nations?
	U Hme:	Yes, sir.
183.	Thakin Nu:	At the Constituent Assembly the question whether we shall remain within or outside the British Commonwealth of Nations will have to be decided. So, if Burma decides to go out of the British Commonwealth of Nations, will your decision to federate with Burma be affected?
	U Hme:	We have asked for permission to send representatives to the Constituent Assembly. We shall abide by the decisions of the Constituent Assembly.
184.	U Khin Maung Gale:	Are you a member of the Shan States People's Freedom Congress?
	U Hme:	No, I am not.

[The chairman thanked the witness and wished him a safe return journey. The witness then withdrew.]

6. Tawng Peng State

(1) Ko Nwe
(2) Ko Pwint

185.	Chairman:	Ko Nwe, you are a representative of Tawng Peng State?
	Ko Nwe:	Yes, sir.

186.	Chairman:	Is Tawng Peng one of the states in the Shan Federation?
	Ko Nwe:	Yes, it is in the Northern Shan States, sir.
187.	Chairman:	Are the Bawdwin Mines in your state?
	Ko Nwe:	Yes, sir.
188.	Chairman:	Are you a representative of the *saohpa* or the people?
	Ko Nwe:	I am a representative of the people.
189.	Chairman:	When were you elected as a representative?
	Ko Nwe:	A meeting was held on the full-moon day of Tabaung, in March, and a resolution was passed to the effect that I should come here as the people's representative.
190.	Chairman:	Where was the meeting held?
	Ko Nwe:	In the town of Nam Sam, the capital of Tawng Peng State.
191.	Chairman:	What are the desires of the people of Tawng Peng State with regard to the future of the Shan Federation?
	Ko Nwe:	We are satisfied with the agreement made at Pang Long and we support it.
192.	Chairman:	The Pang Long Agreement did envisage cooperation with Burma, did it not?
	Ko Nwe:	Yes.
193.	Chairman:	Have you worked out the form of cooperation that you desire?
	Ko Nwe:	We will consider this question only after our council is formed.
194.	Chairman:	Which council?
	Ko Nwe:	The Shan States Council.
195.	Chairman:	The Shan States Council has already been formed, has it not?
	Ko Nwe:	Our aims and objects are for a Federal Council.
196.	Chairman:	Have you considered the question of sending representatives to the Constituent Assembly which is shortly to meet in Rangoon?
	Ko Nwe:	Yes, we have considered it.
197.	Chairman:	What is your decision?
	Ko Nwe:	We have decided that the Shan States Council should elect representatives to the Constituent Assembly.
198.	Chairman:	In what number?
	Ko Nwe :	I do not know.

Ko Pwint:	On a population basis.
199. Chairman	Ko Pwint, are you also a representative from the people of the Tawng Peng State?
Ko Pwint	Yes, sir.
200. Chairman	Were you selected at the same time as your colleague?
Ko Pwint:	Yes.
201. Chairman:	Do you mean by "population basis" one proportionate to the population of Burma?
Ko Pwint:	Yes, sir.
202. Chairman:	Have you any ideas about the form of association between Burma and the Shan States?
Ko Pwint:	We would like to hold elections as in Burma Proper, but we cannot carry them out at present. It is not advisable or suitable at present to have an election.
203. Chairman:	Who would then appoint the representative?
Ko Pwint:	They should be elected by the Shan States Council.
204. Chairman:	Are you talking about representatives to the Constituent Assembly?
Ko Pwint:	Yes.
205. Chairman:	Have you any views on what the form of government should be in order to associate Burma with the Frontier Areas?
Ko Pwint:	We should have equal rights with Burma Proper. We should also have the right of secession if we desire self-determination.
206. U Khin Maung Gale:	If Burma and the Shans were to unite what form do you suggest?
Ko Pwint:	Federation.
207. U Khin Maung Gale:	What subjects do you propose to entrust to the central government?
Ko Pwint:	Defence, Communications, Foreign Relations, and Customs.
208. U Khin Maung Gale:	What about Finance?
Ko Pwint:	Finance and Currency are also to be included.
209. U Khin Maung Gale:	Do you mean that you are going to empower the central government with these subjects?
Ko Pwint	Yes.
210. The Hon. Saohpa of Mong Pawn:	Finance too?
Ko Pwint:	By Finance, I do not mean all finance, I mean currency.

211.	Chairman:	Do you mean by currency the actual coinage issue?
	Ko Pwint:	Yes.
212.	U Khin Maung Gale:	If Burma were to go out of the British Commonwealth of Nations, how would it affect the federation of the Shan States with Burma?
	Ko Pwint:	It will not affect it in any way.
213.	Chairman:	Do you wish to say anything more?
	Ko Pwint:	We want to unite with Burma and have freedom.
214.	Chairman:	Are you a member of the Shan States People's Freedom Congress and your colleague too?
	Ko Pwint:	Yes, sir. We both are members.
215.	U Vum Ko Hau:	Who are the majorities of the laborers in the Bawdwin Mines?
	Ko Pwint:	At present the Indians form the majority and next come the Chinese.
216.	U Vum Ko Hau:	Are these Indians imported from India or are they nationalized Burmans?
	Ko Pwint:	Most of them are imported from India.
217.	Chairman:	For the purpose of working in the mines?
	Ko Pwint:	Yes, sir.
218.	U Vum Ko Hau:	What is the percentage of our own indigenous races working in the Bawdwin Mines?
	Ko Pwint:	The indigenous races from 10 to 15 percent only.

[The chairman thanked the witness and wished him a safe return journey. The witness then withdrew.]

Maymyo, 16th April 1947

7. Kachin of North Hsen Wi and Mong Mit States

(1) Howa Duwa Hkun Hpung, North Hsen Wi
(2) Duwa Zau Bawk, North Hsen Wi
(3) Lashi Gam, North Hsen Wi
(4) Kareng Hkam, ATM, North Hsen Wi
(5) Duwa Zau Ba, Mong Mit.

219.	Chairman:	Are you all representatives of North Hsen Wi State?
	Witnesses:	Four are from North Hsen Wi and one is from Mong Mit.
220.	Chairman:	Have you elected a spokesman to speak for all of you?

	Witnesses:	Duwa Zau Bawk will speak for us.
221.	Chairman:	You all know the purpose of this enquiry?
	Duwa Zau Bawk:	Yes.
222.	Chairman:	What are the views of the North Hsen Wi Kachins on their future position?
	Duwa Zau Bauk:	We want to live cordially with the Shans and to remain in the North Hsen Wi State as a substate under the *saohpa*. We want to have equal rights with the Shans and internal autonomy within our own substate. We want to send our own representatives to the Constituent Assembly on a population basis.
223.	U Vum Ko Hau:	What is the population of the Kachins in North Hsen Wi?
	Duwa Zau Ba:	Over ninety thousand.
224.	The Hon. Saohpa of Mong Pawn	Does that figure include the Kachin population of Mong Mit as well?
	Duwa Zau Bawk:	No, the population of Mong Mit is not included in that.
225.	Chairman:	Is there anything else you four gentlemen would like to say?
	Lashi Gam:	We support the Kachins' claim for a distinct Kachin State in Bhamo and Myitkyina Districts, federated with Burma. This is all I want to say.
226.	Chairman:	Duwa Zau Ba, you come from Mong Mit State?
	Duwa Zau Ba:	I represent the Kachins of Tawng Peng, Mong Mit, and Ko Dong States, sir.
227.	Chairman:	They are minorities in the Shan States?
	Duwa Zau Ba:	Yes.
228.	Chairman:	What are their wishes?
	Duwa Zau Ba:	I have already signed the memorandum demanding a distinct Kachin State. All the Kachins in our area support this claim.
229.	Chairman:	What about your own position? Do you want to stay in the Mong Mit State?
	Duwa Zau Ba:	Yes, we want to stay under the *saohpa* as a substate.
230.	The Hon. *Saohp*a of Mong Pawn:	Do you propose the substate be called "Kachin Substate" or merely "Ko Dong Substate"?
	Duwa Zau Bawk:	We do not want to differentiate between Shans and Kachins; we just want to have a substate.
231.	Chairman:	Is there anything else you would like to tell us?

Duwa Zau Ba: We want to stay in the Shan States with the same status as the Kachins of North Hsen Wi and we support all the statements made by them.

Howa Duwa Hkun Hpung: I have signed the memorandum asking for a Kachin State; but I want to add something to that. In the Shan States, including the Wa and Keng Tung States, there are over one hundred thousand Kachins and for that reason we asked the British government in 1945 to give us a distinct Kachin State in the Shan States. We had no grounds to ask for it, and therefore we do not want to raise the matter again. The people of my area, however, want to support the Kachins' claim for a distinct state in Myitkyina and Bhamo Districts, which areas have never been under anybody. If the non-Kachins in Bhamo and Myitkyina Districts have the same ideas as the Kachins of North Hsen Wi State, there should be no difficulty in the development of social dealings with the people of that area.

232. Chairman: What you mean is that if the Kachins in the North Hsen Wi State are prepared to remain with the Shans, the non-Kachins in the Bhamo and Myitkyina areas should be prepared to live with the Kachins?

Howa Duwa Hkun Hpung: Yes, exactly. The Kachins are backward and are like a younger brother to the Burmans and Shans, and if the Shans and Burmans assist the Kachins in every way, the prosperity of Burma will then be assured. I am a representative of both Shans and Kachins of North Hsen Wi State. What my colleagues have just stated is incomplete. I want to explain further about the separate Kachin State in the Shan States. The most thickly populated Kachin areas are in Tawng Peng, North Hsen Wi, and Mong Mit; we want to have a distinct Kachin State there and have our own local autonomy. But the budget, etc., should be handled by the respective Shan chiefs. That means some will go to North Hsen Wi, some to Tawng Peng, and some to Mong Mit.

233. The Hon. U Tin Tut: Do you want a combination of the three Kachin Substates? For what purpose?

Howa Duwa Hkun Hpung Yes, to preserve the Kachin race. The Kachins of Mong Mit and Tawng Peng are very backward. They have never even seen their *saohpa*. They have just been under the assistant residents all the time and they know nothing. By having a combination of three groups, they can help one another. We have no intention of rising up against the Shan States or anybody.

234. Chairman: From an administrative point of view, they are within three distinct Shan States, are they not?

Howa Duwa Hkun Hpung: Does that mean that we cannot form a Kachin State composed of the areas of the three Kachin Substate?

235. Chairman: I am asking whether the difficulty is that the Kachin areas lie in three different Shan States, no two of which adjoin one another?

Howa Duwa Hkun Hpung: We shall have to settle that in the SCOUHP.

236. Sima Sinwa Nawng: If you send any representatives to the Constituent Assembly should it be from any distinct area, e.g., from Mong Mit or North Hsen Wi or Tawng Peng?

Howa Duwa Hkun Hpung: It should be on a population basis. We do not mind whether it be from Mong Mit or North Hsen Wi or Tawng Peng.

[The chairman thanked the witnesses, who then withdrew.]

Maymyo, 11th April 1947

8. Ko Kang State

(1) Yang Cheje

(2) Yang Kyein Sein

237. Chairman: Well, you two gentlemen are from Ko Kang State, and Yang Cheje, you are the son of the *myosa* of Ko Kang State, is that right?

Yang Cheje: Yes, sir.

238. Chairman: The *myosa* is the hereditary chief, is he not?

Yang Cheje: Yes, he is.

239. Chairman: Is it a fact that most of the inhabitants of the Shan State are Chinese?

Yang Cheje: Of the total population of 40,804; 33,474 are Chinese.

240. Chairman: What are the others?

Yang Cheje: The numbers are: Palaung 3,224; Shans 1,405; Lisu (allied to the Chinese) 720; Myaung (also allied to the Chinese) 649; Kachins 600; and Sino-Shans 96.

241. Chairman: If my understanding is correct, prior to the Japanese occupation Ko Kang was a substate of North Hsen Wi?

Yang Cheje: Yes, it was.

242. Chairman: Has there been any difference since the British reoccupation?

Yang Cheje: It has become a separate state.

243. Chairman: What state is it now?

Yang Cheje: Ko Kang State.

244. Chairman: Does your father now claim to be an independent chief?

Yang Cheje: Yes, sir.

245. Chairman: Has your father any council to advise him?

Yang Cheje: We have not formed a council yet, but we have two or three elders to advise him.

246. Chairman: He claims to be not merely an independent monarch but an absolute monarch as well, is that right?

Yang Cheje: I cannot say, sir.

247. Chairman: Well, now what is the opinion of your father and the elders and, if they have any real means of knowing the will of the people of Ko Kang with regard to the future of the state?

Yang Cheje: If we get internal autonomy and if we have all the rights and privileges of the *saohpa* we should like to abide by the decision of SCOUHP.

248. Chairman: Do you desire to form part of the Shan Federation?

Yang Cheje: If we get internal autonomy we will join.

249. Chairman: What is your father's view on the association of the Shan States with ministerial Burma?

Yang Cheje: If we get what I have mentioned just now, he agrees to whatever federation the Shans choose to join.

250. Chairman: He will abide by the decision of the Council of the Shan States?

Yang Cheje: Yes, sir.

251. Chairman: Supposing he does not get autonomy; supposing the Shan *saohpa* do not agree?

Yang Cheje: Then we won't join the federation.

252.	Chairman:	What would you do then?
	Yang Cheje:	We will convince the *saohpa* of our case.
253.	Chairman:	Supposing you fail to do so?
	Yang Cheje:	We believe that we will succeed.
254.	Chairman:	You make no provision for failure?
	Yang Cheje:	We will try not to fail.
255.	Thakin Nu:	Since Ko Kang is on the Chinese border and since the majority of her population is Chinese, in case of failure, would you like to go over to the Chinese?
	Yang Cheje:	We will join with whatever country gives us internal autonomy.
256.	Chairman:	What do you mean exactly by internal autonomy?
	Yang Cheje:	There should be no external interference in our internal affairs.
257.	Chairman:	Yes, but that is only halfway. What are the common subjects you propose should be dealt with by whatever federation you join?
	Yang Cheje:	Communications, Finance, Defence, and Foreign Affairs.
258.	Chairman:	These are the common subjects?
	Yang Cheje:	Yes, we will abide by whatever decision they make regarding these subjects.
259.	Chairman:	In other subjects you want to run your own affairs.
	Yang Cheje:	Yes, sir.
260.	Chairman:	What do the Kachin minority say?
	Yang Cheje:	Because they are in the minority they would abide by whatever decision we make; when we fought the Japanese they joined us.
261.	Chairman:	Is there any Chinese pressure in your area?
	Yang Cheje:	No pressure at present. But they have been making propaganda.
262.	Chairman:	What sort of propaganda?
	Yang Cheje	Political propaganda.
263.	Chairman:	For what purpose?
	Yang Cheje:	They say that China is good. I do not know what they mean by it.
264.	Chairman:	Who is the gentleman with you, what is his position?
	Yang Cheje:	He is the peoples' representative.
265.	Chairman:	Is he the representative of the three elders?
	Yang Cheje:	No, sir, he does not represent the three elders.
266.	Chairman:	How did the people select him?

	Yang Cheje:	At a meeting.
267.	The Hon. Saohpa of Mong Pawn:	With effect from what date do you consider Ko Kang State separated from North Hsen Wi State?
	Yang Cheje:	I do not know definitely, sir. When my father interviewed the former governor of Burma in India during the war he was told verbally.
268.	The Hon. Saohpa of Mong Pawn:	Has this separation been legalized by the civil government on its return to Burma?
	Yang Cheje:	I do not know, sir, if it was legalized. However, since the time of the Japanese we have been running our own show and the government did not say a word to us.
269.	The Hon. Saohpa of Mong Pawn:	Will your father be content to remain in North Hsen Wi State if he is allowed to manage the affairs of Ko Kang State?
	Yang Cheje:	My father would like to stay in it: we are from a different tribe and our customs are different; and so is our social life.
270.	The Hon. Saohpa of Mong Pawn:	Do you consider yourself still in the Shan Federation at present?
	Yang Kyein Sein:	We have no dealing with the Shan Federation at present and we do not know our position.
271.	Chairman:	Yang Kyein Sein, you are said to be the representative of the people of Ko Kang State?
	Yang Kyein Sein:	Yes, sir.
272.	Chairman:	By whom were you chosen?
	Yang Kyein Sein:	On receipt of a letter from the government the people selected me And sent me here.
273.	Chairman:	How did they make this selection?
	Yang Kyein Sein:	On receipt of the letter from the government and when the people came to know that certain evidence was to be given at Maymyo I was selected.
274.	Chairman:	Yes, but where, how, and when?
	Yang Kyein Sein:	We invited the people and informed them that we had a letter from the government to such and such effect and then they collected and said to me, "You had better go and represent us": and thus I came here.
275.	Chairman:	Where did they collect?
	Yang Kyein Sein:	At Ko Kang.
276.	Chairman:	Is there a town of Ko Kang?

Yang Kyein Sein	At the bazaar.
277. Chairman:	You mean at the bazaar of Ko Kang?
Yang Kyein Sein:	It is a market town—Longkong, also known as Malipa.
278. Chairman:	You just got the people who happened to be in the bazaar together?
Yang Kyein Sein:	Yes, sir.
279. Thakin Nu:	What the chairman means is, did they come for shopping purpose, or did they come for the purpose of discussion on receipt of the letter from the government?
Yang Kyein Sein:	On receipt of the letter we informed the people that such and such was the case and that certain evidence was to be given before the committee. On Market Day they collected at the bazaar, and the selection was made.
280. Chairman:	What did they tell you to say?
Yang Kyein Sein:	No specific instructions were given. But I was told "proceed to Maymyo and answer what the government asks you. You go and ascertain what the questions are."
281. Chairman:	Well, what is your own view on the future of Ko Kang?
Yang Kyein Sein:	Similar to what Yang Cheje has stated, sir. We do not want any external interference in our internal affairs.
282. Chairman:	Would you like to say anything further?
Yang Cheje:	No, sir.

[The chairman thanked the witnesses, who then withdrew.]

Maymyo, 12th April 1947

9. (a) Southern Wa States

(1) Naw Hkam U, Mong Lun State
(2) Sao Naw Hseng, Hsawng Long State

283. Chairman:	Naw Hkam U, are you the chief minister of the Mong Lun State?
Naw Hkam U:	Yes, sir.

284. Chairman:	Is the Mong Lun State one of the thirty-three states in the Shan Federation?
Naw Hkam U:	Yes, sir.
285. Chairman:	Are the people of the Mong Lun State all Was?
Naw Hkam U:	There are Shans as well as Was.
285A. Chairman:	Are there more Was than Shans? Have you any idea about their numbers?
Naw Hkam U:	There are more Was than Shans.
286. Chairman:	Is the *saohpa* or chief of your state a Shan or a Wa?
Naw Hkam U:	He is actually a Wa, but by intermarriages and so on, he has become almost a Shan.
287. Chairman:	What are you yourself?
Naw Hkam U:	I am a Shan.
288. Chairman:	Has the chief of Mong Lun a council?
Naw Hkam U:	Yes.
289. Chairman:	Is that State Council representative of the people in any way?
Naw Hkam U:	Yes, it is a peoples' council.
290. Chairman:	Has that council considered the subject matter of this enquiry?
Naw Hkam U:	Yes.
291. Chairman:	What is the desire of that council with regard to the future status of Mong Lun?
Naw Hkam U:	In the past, we have been in the Federated Shan States and now we are willing to continue to be in them and abide by the decisions of the Shan States Council.
292. Chairman:	Is that the *saohpa*'s view too?
Naw Hkam U:	Yes.
293. Chairman:	Have you any ideas about the form of association between the Federated Shan States and Burma?
Naw Hkam U:	We are not well educated in politics but we are willing to abide by the decision of the Federated Shan States Council.
294. Chairman:	Sao Naw Hseng, is the state of Hsawng Long one of the Wa States?
Sao Naw Hseng:	Yes, sir.
295. Chairman:	Is the Hsawng Long State one of the thirty-three states in the Shan Federation?
	Sao Naw Hseng: No, it is a separate Wa State.
296. Chairman:	Is it administered by the Frontier Areas administration? Have you any British officers there?

	Sao Naw Hseng:	Yes, it is administered by the assistant resident from Mong Lun.
297.	Chairman:	Who is your *saohpa*?
	Sao Naw Hseng:	I represent the chief of Ving Ngun. I am the head of the Hsawng Long State, which is a sort of a substate of Ving Ngun.
298.	Chairman:	Are you also a chief?
	Sao Naw Hseng:	I am a minor chief.
299.	Chairman:	Are the people in your substate Was or Shans? Sao Naw Hseng: All Was.
300.	Chairman:	Is the principal state Wa or Shan?
	Sao Naw Hseng:	It is a Wa State. There is only one Shan village in my state.
301.	Chairman:	Have you a State Council or elders to assist you?
	Sao Naw Hseng:	Yes, there is a State Council.
302.	Chairman:	Have you discussed with the State Council the subject of this enquiry?
	Sao Naw Hseng:	Yes, sir, but I do not know much about politics, I cannot even speak good Shan. I was sent by the chief of Ving Ngun (the principal state) to come here.
303.	Chairman:	What do you want to happen to your state, politically?
	Sao Naw Hseng:	We will abide by whatever decision the government makes in regard to our future.
304.	Chairman:	What does the chief of Ving Ngun think about it?
	Sao Naw Hseng:	I am representing him, and he will say the same thing.
305.	U Khin Maung Gale:	Would you like to go into the Federated Shan States?
	Sao Naw Hseng:	No, Was are Was and Shans are Shans. We would not like to go into the Federated Shan States.
306.	The Hon. Saohpa of Mong Pawn:	If the Shan States prosper, would you not like to prosper along with them?
	Sao Naw Hseng:	I cannot say, because I have no instruction from my chief on this point.
307.	Chairman:	Have you any other instructions?
	Sao Naw Hseng:	I have nothing more to say.

[The chairman thanked the witnesses and wished them a safe return home. He also requested them to convey the committee's greetings to the *saohpa*.]

(The witnesses then withdrew.)

9. (b) Northern Wa States

(1) Hkun Sai

(2) Sao Maha

308. Chairman: We are very pleased to see you and thank you for coming here. Are you representing the people of the Wa States?

Hkun Sai: I come as representative of the chief of Mong Kwang.

309. Chairman: Is that a Wa chieftain?

Hkun Sai: Yes, he is a Wa chieftain.

310. Chairman: What does the chieftain think about the future of the Wa States?

Hkun Sai: The chieftain told me that he had received orders from the government to come and listen to what the committee had to say. When I arrived at Lashio, the resident told me to come here and listen to the committee and what it had to say.

311. Chairman: Do you know anything about the object of this committee?

Hkun Sai: I do not know anything.

312. Chairman: The object of this committee is to find out what the peoples of the Frontier Areas want as regards their political future.

Hkun Sai: As for the future, we would like to remain as in the past, that is, to be independent of other people.

313. Chairman: Do you want any sort of association with other people? What about the Shans? Do you want to join up with them?

Hkun Sai: We do not want to join with anybody, because in the past we have been very independent.

314. Thakin Nu: Don't you want education, clothing, good food, good houses, hospitals, etc.?

Hkun Sai We are very wild people and we do not appreciate these things.

315. Chairman: Do you have any communication with other people, for example, with the Shans and the Chinese? Or do you live entirely by yourselves?

Hkun Sai: We live entirely by ourselves.

316. Chairman: Does the chieftain rule on his own or do the people have any say? Is there any form of council?

Hkun Sai: Yes, we have elders. They advise the chieftain.

317.	Chairman:	Are the elders selected by the tribes?
	Hkun Sai	The chieftain as well as the people agree that they should be elders.
318.	Chairman:	Are the Wa States administered now to some extent by the Frontier Service? Do they have British officers?
	Hkun Sai:	Yes.
319.	Chairman:	Do you want something of the same kind of administration to continue?
	Hkun Sai:	As for the future, I cannot say but now we are working hand in hand with the government.
320.	Sima Sinwa Nawng:	Do you want that to continue?
	Hkun Sai:	I do, at present.
321.	Sima Sinwa Nawng:	Are there any Kachins in the Wa States?
	Hkun Sai:	Yes.
322.	Sima Sinwa Nawng:	How many?
	Hkun Sai:	I do not know.
323.	Chairman:	Do the people of the Wa States know that you are being sent here as their representative?
	Sao Maha:	No.
324.	Chairman:	Sao Maha, who sent you here?
	Sao Maha:	One assistant resident sent me, I do not know his name. I come from Mong Mon.
325.	Chairman:	Do the people of that district know that you have come here?
	Sao Maha:	No.
326.	Chairman:	Do you know what this committee is considering here?
	Sao Maha:	I do not know. I was sent from my state to Mong Mon where I stayed ten days. From there I was sent to Lashio and from Lashio I was sent over here.
327.	Chairman:	What do you want the future position to be in the Wa States?
	Sao Maha:	We have not thought about that, because we are wild people. We never thought of the administrative future. We only think about ourselves.
328.	Chairman::	Have you got any ideas how you would like the Wa States to be administered in future?
	Sao Maha:	No.
	Chairman::	We know that you have come a long way through very difficult country and we are very grateful to you for coming to Maymyo. We are very glad to

meet you. We hope you will take back our greetings to the people of the Wa States.

[The witnesses then withdrew.]

10. Notified Areas

(1) Ko Myat Tun, Kalaw notified area
(2) Ko Ba San, Taunggyi notified area
(3) Ko Aung Nyun, Lashio notified area.

329. Chairman: Ko Myat Tun, are you from Kalaw?
Ko Myat Tun: Yes, sir. I am from Kalaw.
330. Chairman: Have the people of Kalaw considered the subject matter of this enquiry?
Ko Myat Tun: Yes, sir. The Kalaw people have considered it.
331. Chairman: Is Kalaw a notified area?
Ko Myat Tun: Yes, sir.
332. Chairman: Have you had a meeting of the people of Kalaw?
Ko Myat Tun: Yes, sir. We had a meeting.
333. Chairman: Was the meeting a representative one? Was there a large gathering?
Ko Myat Tun: It was a meeting of the whole town.
334. Chairman: What did they decide there?
Ko Myat Tun: In gist, sir, for Burma and the Shan States to be united and for both Burma and the Shan States to get freedom.
335. Chairman: What did they decide about the form of unity between the Shan States and Burma?
Ko Myat Tun: Our aim is that the Shan States should get freedom as much as Burma gets freedom, and go into Burma as part of Burma.
336. Chairman: Do you mean by sending representatives to the Burma Legislature?
Ko Myat Tun: Yes, sir.
337. Chairman: In other words, they would like the Shan States to be part of ministerial Burma, i.e., Burma Proper?
Ko Myat Tun: We propose to send Shan ministers to the Ministry of Burma to work together with other ministers of Burma on a proportionate basis.
338. Chairman: What ministers are you talking about?
Ko Myat Tun: The ministers elected by the Shan States.

339. Thakin Nu:	There are two ways of uniting with Burma. One way is for the Shan States to be united with Burma as a part of Burma and the other is to be federated with Burma. Which does Kalaw want? That is what the chairman wants to know.
Ko Myat Tun:	What I mean to say is for the Shan States to be united with Burma as part of Burma or to be federated with it having in the latter case their own form of government for local and internal affairs and federation with Burma for common subjects.
340. Chairman:	Does that mean that Kalaw wishes the Shan States to be merged with Burma as part of Burma or to be federated with it having in the latter case their own form of government for local and internal affairs and federation with Burma for common subjects?
Ko Myat Tun:	We wish the Shan States to have internal autonomy and to federate with Burma for common subjects.
341. Chairman:	What about the future of Kalaw? What was decided at the meeting about that?
Ko Myat Tun:	To follow in the footsteps of the Shan States; whatever the Shan States get, Kalaw should get.
342. Chairman:	What about its future position? Is it to be merged with the Shan States or to remain separate?
Ko Myat Tun:	To merge with the Shan States.
343. Chairman:	What state do the people of Kalaw want to be in?
Ko Myat Tun:	In Thamakhan (Hsa Mong Hkam), which is the nearest to us.
344. Sima Sinwa Nawng	Previously Kalaw was part of Thamakhan (Hsa Mong Hkam) and it was under the Thamakhan *saohpa*?
Ko Myat Tun:	Yes.
345. Chairman:	That is previous to its becoming a notified area?
Ko Myat Tun:	Yes.
346. U Khin Maung Gale:	Are you a member of the Shan States People's Freedom Congress?
Ko Myat Tun:	No, I am not a member.
347. Chairman:	By whom were you chosen to appear before this committee?
Ko Myat Tun:	By the meeting of Kalaw.
348. Thakin Nu:	Will your decision to federate with Burma be affected if Burma decides to go out of the British Commonwealth?

	Ko Myat Tun:	It does not affect us.
349.	Chairman:	Ko Ba San, you represent Taunggyi?
	Ko Ba San:	Yes, sir.
350.	Chairman:	Is that a notified area?
	Ko Ba San:	Yes, sir.
351.	Chairman:	Have you had a town meeting at Taunggyi?
	Ko Ba San:	Yes, sir.
352.	Chairman:	How many people attended that meeting?
	Ko Ba San:	The whole town, sir.
353.	Chairman:	Did they select you to represent them here?
	Ko Ba San:	Yes, sir.
354.	Chairman:	What was the decision of the people of Taunggyi?
	Ko Ba San:	Firstly, to federate with Burma. Secondly, that Taunggyi should be restored to Yawng Hwe because it was part of Yawng Hwe previously.
355.	Chairman:	Did they go further at all and suggest what form of federation they wish with Burma?
	Ko Ba San:	No, we have not decided.
356.	Chairman:	Anything more you would like to say?
	Ko Ba San	I have nothing to say but I am prepared to answer any questions put to me.
357.	Chairman:	Have you thought yourself about the form of federation between the Shan States and Burma?
	Ko Ba San	I have my personal opinion.
358.	Chairman:	Would you like to express it?
	Ko Ba San	No, sir. I do not like to divulge it.
359.	Thakin Nu:	Why not?
	Ko Ba San:	Because it is my single individual opinion.
	Thakin Nu:	I think you can express it as your individual opinion.
	Chairman:	You are a man of standing in your town and your opinion would be valuable.
360.	U Khin Maung Gale	I think you are a member of the Shan States People's Freedom Congress and you will therefore abide by the decision of the Congress?
	Ko Ba San	Yes, sir.
361.	The Hon. Saohpa of Mong Pawn:	Do you want to say anything about the civil station of Loi Lem?
	Ko Ba San:	Yes.

(Witness produced a document from the people of Loi Lem. This was read out to the meeting by the interpreter, as follows:

"A meeting of the Shan States People's Freedom Congress was held at the Congress premises in Loi Lem and the following decisions were made; 1. To send representatives to the coming Constituent Assembly.; 2. To depute Ko Ba San as representative to the Enquiry Committee which is going to be held at Maymyo."

362.	U Khin Maung Gale:	You represent Loi Lem as well?
	Ko Ba San:	Yes.
363.	Chairman:	I understand that the people of Loi Lem desire to send representatives to the Constituent Assembly. Do they desire to form part of the Shan States?
	Ko Ba San:	They desire to be federated.
364.	Chairman:	What I mean is do they desire to merge with any state? If that be so, what state would that be?
	Ko Ba San:	It would be Lai Kha.
365.	Chairman:	U Aung Nyun, you represent Lashio?
	U Aung Nyun:	Yes, sir.
366.	Chairman:	Have you been appointed by the people of Lashio to represent them?
	U Aung Nyun:	Yes, sir.
367.	Chairman:	We have the minutes of the Lashio town mass meeting held on the 20th March of this year to ascertain the views of the people of Lashio on the subject matter of this enquiry. We notice that 447 people attended the meeting.
	U Aung Nyun:	Yes, sir.
368.	Chairman:	A certain resolution was passed unanimously?
	U Aung Nyun:	Yes, sir.
369.	Chairman:	The question decided was that the people desired to stay within the North Hsen Wi State. Is that so?
	U Aung Nyun:	Yes, sir.
370.	Chairman:	Does it mean that the people want to reenter the North Hsen Wi State?
	U Aung Nyun:	Burma is on the verge of freedom and the same applies to the Shan States. We should like to go into the North Hsen Wi State to get the advantage of this freedom.
371.	Chairman:	Have they given you any other instructions beyond that? Anything about the future association of the Shan States with Burma?
	U Aung Nyun:	No further instructions, sir.
372.	Chairman:	Have you had any instructions other than that mentioned in the minutes?

U Aung Nyun: No, sir. No further instructions.

373. Chairman: Have you any personal views you would like to express?

U Aung Nyun: My personal opinion is that the Shan States should federate with Burma.

[The chairman thanked the witnesses and wished them a safe return home.]

401. Chairman: Who is from the Hkamti Long Area?

Duwa Zau Lawn: U Aung Ba.

402. Chairman: Now, U Aung Ba, you are from the Hkamti Long Area?

U Aung Ba Yes, sir.

403. Chairman: What is the major race in your tract?

U Aung Ba: Roughly, sir, the Shans form the majority of the population, and the minority is Kachin; very insignificant in number are Lisus.

404. Chairman: What are you yourself?

U Aung Ba: I am a Shan, sir.

405. Chairman: Do the Shan majority wish to form part of the Kachin State?

U Aung Ba: Yes, sir.

406. Chairman: Who is from Katha?

Duwa Zau Lawn: Padip La Tawng, sir. He is the representative of Katha and was one of the signatories of the Memorandum. Because I told him that it will not be necessary for him to give evidence, he did not come here, sir.

… … …

2. Thaungdut and Sinkaling Hkamti States

(1) U Ohn Pe (*saohpa*'s representative)
(2) U Maung Than
(3) U Ba Lin
(4) U Ba Pe
(5) U Nyan Paing

766. Chairman: Are you the representatives of Thaungdut State and Singkaling Hkamti State?

Witness: Yes, sir.

767. Chairman: Have you selected a spokesman to speak for you all?

U Ba Lin: Yes, sir. I am the spokesman.
768. Chairman: Are you one of the representatives of the Thaungdut State?
U Ba Lin: Yes, sir.
769. Chairman: Is that a Shan State?
U Ba Lin: Yes, sir.
770. Chairman: Is it surrounded by Chins?
U Ba Lin No, sir. It is not surrounded by Chins.
771. Chairman: Who are your neighbors?
U Ba Lin: We adjoin the Upper Chindwin District on one side.
772. The Hon. U Tin Tut: Are the people there Burmese?
U Ba Lin: Yes, sir.
773. Chairman: Do you adjoin the Somra Tract?
U Ba Lin: Yes, sir.
774. Chairman: Are they Chins?
U Ba Lin: Yes, sir.
775. Chairman: Then you are surrounded partly by Burmese and partly by Chins?
U Ba Lin: Mostly by Burmese. There are also Manipuris on one side.
776. Chairman: Is your state a small Shan State surrounded by other people?
U Ba Lin: Yes, sir. But although we are all Shans we are Burmanized.
777. Chairman: But you were originally Shans?
U Ba Lin: Yes, sir.
778. Chairman: And you have a *saohpa*?
U Ba Lin: Yes, sir.
779. Chairman: Does the *saohpa* administer the state?
U Ba Lin: Yes, sir.
780. Chairman: What is the desire of the people of this state regarding their political future?
U Ba Lin: I will read out their desire.
Chairman: Yes, please.
U Ba Lin: The representatives from Thaungdut and Singkaling Hkamti States should come to the committee and give evidence as follows:

(1) We will unite with Burma Proper with the following rights and privileges:

(a) The government of Burma shall continue to recognize and allow our *saohpa* to administer their respective states.

(b) If either *saohpa* fails to govern his state according to democratic principles, he shall abdicate in favor of one of his relatives.

(c) The *saohpa* shall not move away from the areas which they are administering.

781. Chairman: You mean move away permanently?

U Ba Lin: Permanently, sir.

(d) If there is none in the line of the *saohpa* who is capable of administernig the state, the people shall elect one from the masses.

782. Chairman: Who is to decide whether the *saohpa* is capable or not?

U Ba Lin: We, the masses, and the central Burma government.

783. Chairman: Anything more?

U Ba Lin: That is all, sir.

784. Chairman: Is there anything more you or your friends would like to say?

U Ba Lin: I have nothing more to say, sir.

785. Chairman: What about the Singkaling representatices? Have you anything in particular to say?

Saw Mya Sein: Nothing in particular, sir.

786. The Hon. U Tin Tut Do you want to be represented in the Constituent Assembly?

Saw Mya Sein: No, we do not intend to be.

787. The Hon. Saohpa of Mong Pawn: What about the representative from Thaungdut? Don't you want to send representatives to the Constituent Assembly?

U Ba Lin: No, sir.

788. U Khin Maung Gale: May I ask the *saohpa* U Mya Sein one question? Do you agree with what U Ba Lin has said just now?

Saw Mya Sein: I endorse everything that U Ba Lin has said.

789. Chairman: You are the *saohpa* yourself?

Saw Mya Sein: Yes, sir.

790. Chairman: Anything further you would like to say, *Saohpa*?

Saw Mya Sein: No, sir.

791. U Vum Ko Hau: Are you Shan or Shan-Burman?

Chairman: They said that they were Burmanized Shans.

U Vum Ko Hau: Is that not the same as Shan-Burmans?

The Hon. U Tin Tut: Literally, they said they were originally Shans, but had become Burmans.

792. Sima Sinwa Nawng: What is the Shan population of your area?

	Saw Mya Sein:	About seven thousand in Thaungdut and three thousand in Singkaling Hkamti Long.
793.	The Hon. U Tin Tut:	Is there any other population?
	Saw Mya Sein:	Yes, sir, in Singkaling Hkamti Long there are Nagas and a small number of Kongsai.
794.	The Hon. U Tin Tut:	What are Kongsai?
	Saw Mya Sein:	Chins.
795.	Chairman:	Is the *saohpa* in contact with the Nagas at all?
	Saw Mya Sein:	Yes, we are in contact.
796.	Chairman:	We have not been able to get them here to give evidence. Do they know anything about this committee?
	Saw Mya Sein:	I myself had to come here hurriedly. One day I heard of the committee and the next day I had to leave for Maymyo.
797.	Chairman:	We are told that the Nagas are busy headhunting and that they are not able to devote any attention to other things, even to this committee.
	Saw Mya Sein:	They are addicted to headhunting but I don't know if that is the reason why they have not come here.
798.	Sima Sinwa Nawng:	What about the Lisai Kachins?
	Saw Mya Sein:	They are our neighbors, sir.
799.	Sima Sinwa Nawng:	In Homalin?
	Saw Mya Sein:	They are in the Myitkyina direction.

[The chairman thanked the witnesses, who then withdrew.]

Maymyo, 19th April 1947

3. Homalin Subdivision

(1) U Ba San
(2) U Thein Pe

800.	Chairman:	What are the people of Homalin Subdivision?
	U Ba San:	Nominally they are known as Shans but 75 percent of them speak Burmese and if you eliminated the Burmese language they would not understand each other. There is no such thing as Shan script or literature among us.
801.	Chairman:	Are you originally of the Shan race?

U Ba San:	Our ancestors came from Hkamti Long, but, on account of the danger from the Kachins, they had to migrate down the valley of the Chindwin. Nowadays though we are Shan by descent, we are Burmanized and, in fact, Burmese.
802. Chairman:	What is the view of the people of the Homalin Subdivision on their political future?
U Ba San:	In our customs, and way of living, we are Burmese and we should like to enjoy all the rights and privileges of Burmans, 100 percent.
803. Chairman:	In other words, you mean you would like to be in ministerial Burma?
U Ba San:	Yes, sir.
804. Chairman:	Do you want to be represented at the Constituent Assembly?
U Ba San:	Under the 1935 Act we are scheduled as Part 2 areas and we have no right to vote under that Act. However, we would like to send our representatives to the Constituent Assembly.
805. Chairman:	Would your people like to vote in any elections in Burma in future?
U Ba San:	Yes, sir.
806. Chairman:	How will the representatives to the Constituent Assembly be elected?
U Ba San:	By mass meetings.
807. Chairman:	Not by District Council?
U Ba San:	No, by public meeting.
808. The Hon. U Tin Tut	Have you a district council?
U Ba San:	No, sir.
809. U Vum Ko Hau:	How many representatives do you want to send to the Constituent Assembly?
U Ba San:	It would be better if we could get two representatives.
810. Chairman:	What is the population of your subdivisions?
U Ba San:	We had a census in 1945. According to that census the population of our subdivision is forty-five thousand.

(U Thein Pe submitted a memorandum in Burmese to which he had nothing to add verbally.)

The geographic situation of Homalin township is that it is overrun by hills, and that Shan live in areas on the side of the rivers and streams, and some Chin, who are looking forward to the new Constitution of Burma, live in some hilly portions. He said the Naga wish to remain as such within the boundaries of Homalin township.

The Myanmar political momentum in Myanmar proper after the Second World War, especially around 1946 and 1947, was like the rising tide, and the demand for freedom and independence from the British had become more and more intense and dynamic. Preparations were made and delegations were sent to London to negotiate with the British government the ways in which independence should be granted to Myanmar. But one problem remained to be solved. Should independence be granted to the Myanmar people without the frontier peoples? Would the frontier peoples like to join hands with the Myanmar in their struggle for independence? What would they like to do? To sound them out about the issue of independence a Frontier Areas Committee of Enquiry was formed in 1947 based on the following points:

1. Free intercourse between the people of the Frontier Areas and the people of ministerial Burma without hindrance.
2. Asking the leaders and representatives of the people of the Frontier Areas whether they would like to express their views on the form of association with the government of Burma during the transitional period.
3. Appointing a small group of frontier representatives to advise the governor on the frontier affairs and to have close liaison with the Executive Council.
4. Appointing one Frontier Area representative as executive counselor in charge of frontier affairs.
5. Finding the best method of advancing the common aims expressed by the people of the Frontier Areas.
6. Choosing the best method of associating the frontier peoples with the working of the new Constitution for Burma.
7. Equal representation between ministerial Burma and Frontier Areas in the Enquiry Committee with a neutral chairman.
8. Submission of report of the Enquiry Committee before summoning of the Constituent Assembly.

Some important extracts from the personal interviews with the Shan chiefs, *saohpa*, and Shan representative were presented here to enable the public to know exactly how the Shan people were thinking about the political amalgamation with Myanmar at that time and also about the essential and traditional rights of autonomy in their internal administration.[19] The views they expressed during the question time were simple, frank, sincere, and honest. They were worthy of being taken into serious account in the founding of a sovereign nation, the Union of Myanmar, the home of all the ethnic nationalities who had been living together from time immemorial, sharing prosperity and poverty, joys and woes, and making countless and endless sacrifices for the survival of "our golden homeland."

13

A Second Pang Long Conference and Its Historic Agreement, 1947

In 1946 the first multinational conference was convened at Pang Long in the Central Shan States, to the satisfaction of those who sponsored it and of those who attended it. It was the first meeting between the Frontier Areas representatives and the representatives from Myanmar proper. The delegates to the conference expressed openly, frankly, and sincerely their views, trust and distrust, likes and dislikes, possibility and impossibility, feasibility and unfeasibility on the question of their future political unity that they urgently needed to forge in their demand for freedom, independence, and sovereignty from the British. A British observer who attended the meeting remarked:

> On the whole I think it can be said that the first meeting of the Frontier peoples at Pang Long was a success. All except the Nu speech were moderate and constructive, and discussion gave all present a better idea of the magnitude of the problems confronting them. Undoubtedly it has done a lot of good to the Burmese leaders who visited Pang Long, for they were able to see with their own eyes that in spite of every effort [by] the administration to present the case for union as favourably as possible, the Burmese still have a lot of distrust and dislike to overcome before they can attain this end.[1]

The initial understanding for political unity was obtained between the leaders of the Frontier Areas and the leaders of Myanmar proper. The initial announcement was clearly made known to the British observers and the British officers of the Frontier Areas Administration that the frontier peoples had a "strong will" to unite with the Myanmar peoples from the plain for their future political unity and freedom. Only ways and means and steps were to be found and laid down at the second multinational conference to be held again at Pang Long in February 1947. The Second Pang Long Conference was historic, decisive, and one on which the fate of the country hung. With faith and trust, sincerity and confidence, and strong will, the multinational leaders of the second conference unanimously passed a resolution for unity, based on the historic Pang Long Agreement, in their demand for freedom, independence, and sovereignty from the British, and for that Myanmar was granted independence on January 4, 1948. [The text of the agreement is given in chapter 12 and appendix 30.]

The achievement of historic unity meant the achievement of freedom and the release from colonial bondage, which had lasted nearly a century.

Therefore the Pang Long Agreement was interpreted as a sacred historic document for the "Spirit of Union," which could not be destroyed, dispensed with, disputed, discriminated, dissolved, divided, or eliminated. It was an unforgettable precept of honor which had been pinned to the heart of every citizen and which had brought the unbreakable historic unity of the "Union Peoples" who had shared their historic woes and joys in the course of their history of ups and downs. Anyone who would attempt to violate the principles and the spirit of Pang Long could be termed a criminal. Anyone who would attempt to destroy this historic agreement could be regarded as a traitor. To destroy the agreement meant to destroy the Union. There could be no excuse for such action. Those who initiated the idea to hold the conference, those who sponsored and organized, those who met, and those who helped in every possible way to enable the multinational leaders to meet each other at this conference and to forge the historic Pang Long Agreement, should never be forgotten. We owe them a historic gratitude. Everyone of us should give them a big bow and honor them on every occasion. These initiators and organizers, whoever they were, should be thanked for the sacrifice they made of their time, energy, money, and even lives. They have made history for us, a history of national unity, a history of freedom, independence, and sovereignty, and a history of the Union of Myanmar, which has been recognized by the United Nations Organization since its existence.

It is interesting to see how the Second Pang Long Conference was organized. On the front cover of the invitation was a symbolic figure of the Shan people, the tiger. Then came "1947 Progrmme [*sic*] for Pang Long Pwe." "Pwe" in both Myanmar and Shan means festival. The Pang Long Festival was announced to be held from February 6 to 12, 1947. The organizers used the word *pwe* to indicate that this conference would include political lectures, educational lectures, health lectures, fun fair, trade fair, cultural exhibition, movie shows, and all kinds of amusements to attract people to political as well as social participation, to make the conference livelier and to arouse the political consciousness of the youth and hill peoples of the Frontier Areas. How meals would be served, how guests would be treated and entertained, how the guard of honor would be inspected, how the Shan National Anthem would be played, how the flag would be raised, and how prizes would be offered for the winners of the cattle show were all included in the invitation, reproduced below.

1947.
PROGRMME
FOR
PANGLONG PWE.

လွင်ကာၼ်ထေ့်ထပ်ပွႆးတော်ပြင်လုင်။
ပင်လုံပွဲတော်–အစီအစဉ်။

The Nyaungnankyetthaye Press,
YAWNGHWE.
ညောင်နန်းကြက်သရေစာပုံနှိပ်တိုက်။ညောင်ရွှေမြို့။

FIGURE 13.1. Cover of the 1947 program for Pang Long *pwe*

1947
PROGRMME [*sic*] FOR PANG LONG PWE

လွင်ကာၼ်ထေ့်ထပ်ပွႆးတော်ပြင်လုင်။
ပင်လုံပွဲတော်–အစီအစဉ်။

The Nyaungnankyetthaye Press,
YAWNGHWE
ညောင်နန်းကြက်သရေစာပုံနှိပ်တိုက်။ညောင်ရွှေမြို့။

Notice

I. Tea and meals will be served every day at the following hours:

ၶႆႈၶိင်လေ်ခဝ်ၾၵ်တေလိင်ထွႆးခင်ကာခိင်ကာၼ်တ်ဝ့်ပျတ့်ၶႆႈယဝ်။

လဘက်ရည်၊ ထမင်းစားသုံးချိန်မှာ၊ နေ့စဉ်၊အောက်ဖော်ပြပါအတိုင်းဖြစ်သည်။

Morning tea 07.00 to 08.30 hrs

ခံဆိင်လီးဂင်ခ်ု။

နံနက်လဘက်ရည်ပွဲ။

Breakfast 08.30 to 10.30

ခဝ်ခ်ု

နံနက်စာစားပွဲ။

Tea 14.00 to 20.00

ခံ့ဆိင်

လဘက်ရည်ပွဲ။

Dinner 18.00 to 20.00

ခဝ်ခံ

ညစာစားပွဲ။

II. The invited guests will be given time to deliver lectures, if they so desire, during the lecture hours.

ခိဂ်ထကာခ်မွဂ်ဝ့ံ လိုဝ်းခခ်ေ့ပေျခ်ရှေ့လတ်လိုင်၊ ခ်ုးကတုင်းခိင်ရှေ့လတ်ခခ်း ရှေ့လတ်လိဳယူဝ်။

ဘိတ်မံထကပြုသော၊ ဧည့်သည်များဟောပြောချိန်တွင်၊ ဟောပြောလိုကအချိန်ကန့် သတ်ပေးမည်။

III. Arts and crafts exhibitions, etc., will remain open to all from the 6th February 1947 till the end of the conference during the hours of 10.00 to 16.00 every day.

ကတတ်ပိလ်ျမေ်မိုဝ်း ကခ်ပျဝ့်လိုဝ်းခခ်ေ့တော့်ကဝ်ဂင်ခ်ု ႑႐ခေရိတော႟ုဝ်ခံ ႔ခေရိငေ့လ်ျ ခေ်ဝ့်ယူဂူဝခ်းယဝ်။

လက်မှုပညာ၊အစရှိသော၊ပြပွဲတို့ကို၊ ကောင်စီပွဲတွင်းနေ့စဉ်နံက် ၁၀နာရီမှ၊ ညနေ၄နာရီထိ ဖွင့်လစ်ထားကြောင်း။

IV. Guests who desire their morning tea served in their Tawmaw will please send their own boys for the same.

ခႂ်ႈၶိုင်ၵင်ၶႂ်ႈၶၼ်ႈ၊သင်ဝႃႈဢွၼ်ၵိၼ်တီႈတေႃႇမေႃႇတုဝ်ထဝ်ၵဝ်ၶႅ်လိုင်လႅင်ႉႁုၶႅ်းၽႂ်ႉႁုၶႅ်းမၶႅ်း
ၵဝ်မႈၵိၶႅ်လႆယူဝ်၊

နံနက်လဘက်ရည်ကို၊မိမိတို့တော်မော်တွင်မိမိဘွိုင်များ၊စေလွှတ်ယူဆောင်၍၊သောက်
နိုင်သည်။

V. Meals in the Mess Hall are also available for the public on payment.

ႁုၶႅ်းတင်းလႆၽႂ်ႉသေမဝ်ဝႃႈပေႃႈဢွၼ်ၵိၶႅ်တင်းၵိၶႅ်တင်းယႅ်တီႈယုင်လုင်ထိုင်မႈသိုဝ့်ၵိၶႅ်လႆ
ယူယဝ်

မည်သူမဆို၊အစားအစာများကိုစားပွဲရုံကြီးအတွင်း၊လာရောက်ဝယ်ယူသုံးဆောင်နိုင်သည်။

VI. Please read notice board at the Mess Hall for the events of the day.

ၵတုၵ်လွင်ႁုဝၶႅ်းၶၶႅ်ႈ?ၶိလ်းတေႃႇၸတေႃႇလူၵၶႅ်တ်ဝ့်တီႈၶႂ်းယုင်လုင်ၶၶႅ်ႈသေၵႂ်း။

နေ့စဉ်အစီအစဉ်ကိုစားပွဲရုံရှိ၊နို့တစ်ဘုတ်တွင်ဘတ်ပါ။

6th February 1947

12.00 hrs. Saohpalong's [*sic*] arrival

ထဝ်ၸလေုင်ထဝ်ၶဝ်တေႁွတ်ၸိဝ်မႈတင်းသိင်။

စဝ်ဖလုံများရောက်ချိန်။

14.00 hrs. To appoint the following:

ပုၶႅ်တၸတေလိုၵ်တင်ၶင်ၵၶႅ်ပႈပၸတ်ၶႂ်ႈ

အောက်ပါအတိုင်းရွေးကောက်တင်မြှောက်ရန်။

(1) Reception Committee

ထုံးၶံၶိၵ်

ညှော်ခံကော်မတီ။

(2) Fund and Preparation Committee

ထုံးၵၶႅ်ၶိုင်ပွင်ၵိၵ်လုလ်ၸိုင်ၶႅ်း

ရံပုံငွေနှင့်အစီအမံကော်မတီ။

(3) General secretary and joint secretary for the conference

ၵတုင်ဝုၼ်လုင်လေႃႁႂ်ႇပုးလုလ်ၵတုၼ်းဝုၼ်တပွႆး

အထွေထွေစက္ကရိတေရီနှင့်တွဲဘက်အမှုဆောင်စက္ကရိတေရီ။

(4) Chairmen for lectures

ဂုၼ်းလုင်ပုၼ်တႃႁေႃလတ်။

ဟောပြောခြင်း၏ ချယ်ယာမင်လူကြီး။

20.00 to 21.30 hrs. General discussion of Saohpalongs

ထဝ်ၽေလုင်ၶဝ်ထဝ်လတ်ထႃဂၼ်ႁွင်းၶဝ်ထဝ်

စဝ်ဖလုံများ၏ အထွေထွေဆွေးနွေးခြင်း။

21.30 to 22.30 hrs. To attend the Ceremony of Grand Preparation (Swandawgyi) to be offered next morning

ပုၼ်တႃတေႃဂျီလူဝ်ႈပြေးလုင်ပိၼ်ထဝ်လေႃတင်သွႆးတေႃလုင်။

ဆွမ်းတော်ကြီးကြည်ညိုရန်။

7th February 1947

11.00 to 14.00 hrs. To approve selection of lectures made by Selection Committee

တႁွဵတ်ၵတီၵၼ်ထုိးလိၵ်ႈဝုံလွင်ႁေႃလတ်ၼၼ့်။

ရွေးချယ်ထားသောဟောပြောချက်များအတည်ပြုရန်။

16.00 to 17.30 hrs. Recreation

ၶိုင်လိုဝ်သဝ်

အားလပ်ချိန်။

20.00 to 21.30 hrs. To discuss National Anthem and flag

တလတ်ထႃဂၼ်လွင်ႁုံးၶိုဝ်းတႆးလေႃၵလံတႆးႁဝ်း။

အမျိုးသားသီချင်းနှင့်၊အလံတော်တွက်ဆွေးနွေးရန်။

8th February 1947

10.45 hrs. All to be seated in the Assembly Hall

တေႃလိၶင်တီယူၸႂ်တီယူမၼ်းၶႂ်းယုင်လတ်ထႃဂၼ်

ခမ်းမကြီးအတွင်း၌၊အသီးသီးနေရာယူထိုင်ကြရန်။

10.00 hrs. President will inspect Guard of Honor

ကုဂ်ဂထလုင်တေတုလ်း(ဂတ်,ကွဂ်,ၸေ,ကေါ်ချေ)

ဥက္ကဋ္ဌကြီး(ဂါတ်အောဖအော်နာ)ကိုရှုစားခြင်း။

11.00 hrs. Arrival of president and Executive Committee members

ကုဂ်ဂထလုင်လေ်ဂုၶ်းလုင်ထုံးကၶ်ၶိုင်ပွင်သင်မိုင်းတံးတော်ႁွတ်ၸိဝ်

ဥက္ကဋ္ဌကြီးနှင့်အမှုဆောင်ကော်မတီလူကြီးမင်းများရောက်ချိန်

11.05 hrs. (a) General secretary will declare the opening of the conference

ကတင်းဝု ၶ်လုင်တေၸုလ်ပွံးလတ်ထုဂၶ်။

အထွေထွေစက္ကရီကစီးဝေးပွဲဖွင့်လှစ်ကြောင်းကြော်ငြာရန်

(b) President's address

ကမိင့်ဂုံးလတ်ကုဂ်ဂထလုင်။

ဥက္ကဋ္ဌကြီး၏မိန့်ခွန်း။

11.30 to 12.30 hrs. Lecture No.1, On Cottage Industry

လတ်ၵျေလုလ်ဂၶ်လွင်ဂၶ်ၶေ်းၶုံးၸိုၶ်းၶုံးယေ်း

အိမ်တွင်းလက်မှုလုပ်ငန်းဟောပြောခြင်း။

12.30 to 14.00 hrs. Lecture No. 2, On Improved Methods of Plowing

ဂုံးၵျေလတ်ၶေလွင်ၶေ်းကၶ်ထံၵှ်ထံၶျေးၸှ်ၶိုတ်ပၶ်ၸွ
င်းမိုဝ်လိဝ်ၶုံ့

ခေတ်မှီလယ်ထွန်ယက်ရေးဟောပြောခြင်း။

16.00 to 17.30 hrs. To witness plowing demonstration

ပုၶ်တျတေတုလ်းလွင်ထံၶျေး

နည်းပြထွန်ယက်ခြင်းကိုရှုစားခြင်း။

20.00 to 21.30 hrs. Entertainment

ပုၶ်တျခံခိဂ်တေၵိတ်ဂုံးကံၶၶ်ၵှ်ၵွင်။

တီးမှုတ်သီဆိုခြင်းဖြင့်ဧည့်ခံခြင်း။

9th February 1947

11.00 to 12.00 hrs. Lecture No. 3, On Improvement of Agriculture

ၵျေလတ်လုၺ်လွင်ၽုၵ်သွံႇလွင်ၵၢၼ်ၶိုတ်ၶေၼ်းမိုဝ်လိဝ်ၼႆႉ

ခေတ်မီလယ်ယာစိုက်ပျိုးရေးဟောပြောခြင်း။

12.00 to 13.00 hrs. Lecture No. 4, On the Breeding of Animals

ၵျေလတ်လုၺ်လွင်လိင့်လူႉသတ်တိရိၵ်သၼ်

ကျွဲနွားတိရစ္ဆာန်မွေးမြူရေးဟောပြောခြင်း။

13.00 to 14.00 hrs. Lecture No. 5, On Public Health and Latest Medicines

ၵျေလတ်လုၺ်လွင်ၵုၼ်းဝၼ်ၵုၼ်းမိုင်းၸွႆႈယူႉလီၵိၼ်ဝၼ်လေႃ
လွင်ယၢယၢပေႃမွႆမိုဝ်လိဝ်ၼႆႉ

ပြည်သူ့ကျန်းမာရေးနှင့်၊ခေတ်မီဆေးဝါးအကြောင်းဟောပြောခြင်း။

16.00 to 17.30 hrs. Cattle show

ပွီးၶေၼ်သတ်ဝုဝ်းၵွီး

ကျွဲနွားတိရစ္ဆာန်ပြပွဲ။

20.00 to 21.30 hrs. Discussion on Education

လတ်ထၢဂၼ်လွင်ပိင်ညၢယေး

ပညာရေးဆွေးနွေးရန်။

10th February 1947

11.00 to 12.00 hrs. Lecture No. 6, On Education

ၵျေလတ်ၽိပိင်ညၢယေး

ပညာရေးဟောပြောခြင်း။

12.00 to 13.00 hrs. Lecture No. 7, On the Various Duties of the Indigenous Races of the FSS (Federated Shan States)

ၵျေလတ်ပုၼ်တၢဂၼ်ၶေၼ်းတၢဝုၼ်ဂုၼ်းထၢတိမိုင်းတႆးၶၼ့်

သျှမ်းပြည်ဇာတိသားတို့ လိုက်နာဆောင်ရွက်ရန်ဝတ္တရားများအ
ကြောင်း ဟောပြောခြင်း

13.00 to 14.00 hrs. Lecture No. 8, On Advancement of Buddhist Religion
၄ေါလတ်လွင်လုလ်သါသခေါတ်ါဖြေးပိခ်ထဝ်
ခငိဂ္ဂိဝ်တေဂ္ဂိဝ်ဂ္ဂိင်း ပိုင်းသုံ်ခခေ့်။
ဗုဒ္ဓသာသနာတော်ပွင့်လင်းထွန်းကားရေးဟောပြောခြင်း။

16.00 to 17.30 hrs. Distribution of prizes to the cattle-show winners
ပုခ်တါတေပခ်သူးကတုဂ်ပွိုးခေ်သတ်တိရိသခ်
တိရစ္ဆာန်ပြပွဲဆုရသူတို့အားချီးမြှင့်ရန်။

20.00 to 21.30 hrs. To discuss political problems of the Federated Shan States
လတ်ထါကခ်ျကခေ်လွင်မခ်လွင်မိုင်းပုခ်မိုင်းတိုး
သျှမ်းပြည်၊ပဒေသရာဇ်အရေးဆွေးနွေးရန်။

11th February 1947

11.00 to 12.00 hrs. Lecture No. 9, On the Future Constitution of the Federated Shan States
၄ေါလတ်လုလ်လွင်ပွင်ဝခ်ပွင်မိုင်းမိုဝ်းခါပုခ်တါမိုင်းတိုး၄ဝ်းခခေ့်။
သျှမ်းပြည်အနာဂါတ်အုပ်ချုပ်ရေးဟောပြောခြင်း။

12.00 to 13.00 hrs. Lecture No.10, On Cooperative Societies
၄ေါလတ်လုလ်လွင်တင်းဂ္ဂိတ်းတင်းသင်ကခ်ၽုလ်ဂုင်ပခီလို်
ကခ်ပိခ်သမဝါယမ လို်ခခေ့်
သမဝါယမကုမ္ပဏီတည်ထောင်ဖွင့်လှစ်ရေးဟောပြောခြင်း။

13.00 to 14.00 hrs. Lecture No. 11, On the Uplift of National Spirits of Indigenous Races of the Federated Shan States
တါ၄ေါလတ်ပခ်လွင်ပခ်တင်းခငိဂ္ဂိဝ်ထို်ဂုခ်းထါတိမိုင်းတိုး၄ဝ်း
တေ်ယွင် ယေါယို်ခိုခ်မုးခခေ့်
သျှမ်းပြည်ဇာတိသားတို့၏၊ဇာတိမာန်မြှင့်တင်ရေးဟောပြောခြင်း။

16.00 to 17.30 hrs. Free distribution of clothing to the poor
ပုခ်တါပခ်ခုဝ်းပခ်လိင်းဂုခ်းၽခေ်ခဝ်
ဆင်းရဲနွမ်းပါးသူတို့အား၊အခလွတ်အဝတ်ပေးကမ်းရန်။

19.00 hrs. State dinner followed by entertainment

တၢလိင့်ပွႆးၵိၼ်ၶဝ်ႈ

ညဥ့်စာစားပွဲကြီးကျွေးမွေးရန်။

12th February 1947

06.30 to 08.30 hrs. Offering meals to Sangha and listening to sermons at Laihka Tawmaw

ပင်းၵဝ်သင်ၶႃတေႃႇၶဝ်ထဝ်လေႇ ၵပ်သွႆးယဝ့်ၵႂၢၼ်ၵၢၼ်ထွႆႈတြႃးတေႃႇ
ၾြႃးပိၼ်ထဝ် တီတေႃႇမေႃႇလုင်လိူဝ်းၶႃ။ လဲချားတော်မော်တွင်
သံဃာတော်တို့အားဆွမ်းကပ်တရားတော်နာရန်။

11.00 to 13.00 hrs. General discussion on matters that may be brought forward

လတ်ထၢၵၼ်လွင်လုၺ်ၵိၵ့်ထၵၼ်ပေမိူးမုၼ်းၶၼ့်။

ပေါ်ပေါက်လာသောကိစ္စအရပ်ရပ်များဆွေးနွေးရန်။

13.00 to 15.00 hrs. Farewell lunch

ပွႆးၵိၼ်ၶဝ်ႈၵင်ဝၼ်းယဝ့်ၽေႃတၢၵၼ်

နုပ်ဆက်နေ့စာစားပွဲ။

List of Guests to be Invited to the Pang Long Conference, February 1947

1. His Excellency the governor and family
2. His Excellency's staff
3. Mr. H. N. C. Stevenson
4. Mr. L. R. Ogden, OBE., B.FR.S
5. Mr. J. L. Leyden, B.FR.S
6. US consul general and wife
7. US Information Bureau
8. Chinese consul general
9. Representative in Rangoon of Government of India
10. (to 20)Present governor's Executive Council members (eleven in number)
    (a) U Aung San
    (b) U Ba Pe
    (c) U Mya
    (d) Thakin Mya
    (e) U Saw
    (f) Thakin Ba Sein
    (g) Mahn Ba Kaing

(h) Saw Ba Kaing
(i) U Tin Tut
(j) U Aung San Wei
(k) Sir Maung Gyi

21. (to 23) Karenni chiefs
    (a) chairman, Board of Officials, Kantarawady State
    (b) *Myosa* of Bawlake State
    (c) *Myosa* of Kyebogyi State
24. U Thein Lwin, director of forests
25. Sir Paw Tun, KT, AMT, bar-at-law
26. Sir Htun Aung Gyaw, bar-at-law
27. Sir Mya BU, KT
28. U Pu, BA, bar-at-law
29. U Ba Dun, bar-at-law
30. U Thet Su, DIC, B. Ag
31. U Kim Mein, MBE
32. U Ba Lwin, BA, FRCS
33. U Tint Swe, BA, BL, FR.Hist.S.
34. U Choe, BA, B ED
35. U Kaung, MA (Edin) IES
36. U Hla Pe, BA, BL
37. U Sein, rice miller, Rangoon
38. U Ba Glay
39. U Chit Hlaing
40. Major Shan Lone, A. R. Sinlumkaba, Bhamo District
41. (to 43)Chin representatives (three in number)
    (a) Kamhau chief Pun Za Maung, ATM
    (b) Lunbang chief Hlur Hmung, BEM, ATM
    (c) Mi Er chief Kio Mang, ATM
44. (to 46) Myitkyina Kachin representatives (three in number)
    Care DC Myitkyina
47. (to 49) Bhamo Kachin representatives (three in number)
    (a) Lawdan chief, Care DC Bhamo
    (b)
    (c)
50. The Ko Kang *myosa*, Ko Kang, Care resident, NSS
51. The administrator of Mong Pai State, via Loi Kaw
52. (to 54) The president and two members of the Lower Myanmar Karen representatives
55. (to 57) The president and two members of the AFPFL
58. (to 60) The president and two members of the Myo-Chit Party
61. (to 62) ditto, and one member of Communist Party

63. (to 64)ditto, ditto of Communist Party in Myanmar
65. (to 67)ditto two members of Dobama Asiayone
68. Sir U Thwin, Rangoon
69. BIA U Maung Gyi, Mandalay
70. U Ohn Khin, Rangoon
71. U Pe Khin
72. (to 74) The president and two members of Maha Bama
75. Myama Alin, one editor
76. Thuriya, ditto

A private letter written to Sir Gilbert Laithwaite by Mr. Leyden on February 25, 1947, included the following remarks on the Pang Long Conference of 1947:[2]

> . . . Pang Long was, from my point of view, quite a success as it got the hill people in a position where they could freely express themselves. Aung San and Tin Tut were both very reasonable and patient and answered all questions in a perfectly straightforward manner.

At the First Pang Long Conference U Saw dominated the meetings and the discussions. Many questions were put to him and he skillfully and patiently answered all of them, expressing his sincere views and spirit of accommodation and cooperation with the frontier peoples.

The Second Pang Long Conference was dominated by U Aung San, who answered all the questions put to him factually, patiently, and sincerely. The frontier peoples, including the Shan leaders and representatives, were impressed by his frank straightforward remarks and his honest and sincere spirit of cooperation and concern for the hill peoples to achieve freedom like the Myanmar people. They all believed in him and looked to him as the national leader in whom they could put their trust. Finally, the whole of frontier leaders pledged to cooperate with him and his colleagues. He made a spirited call for unity at the conference. He made a great promise, saying that the Myanmar would never interfere in the internal affairs of the hill peoples. He also assured the hill peoples that they would enjoy the same rights and privileges as the Myanmar.

Addressing a well-attended meeting comprising *saohpa*, *mahadevi*, Jingphaw, and Chin leaders and Mr. A. G. Bottomley, undersecretary of state for the dominions, and other guests and representatives, U Aung San said he had come to Pang Long with two objectives: to secure the unity of all the peoples of Myanmar and to explain what he and his delegation had done about the hill peoples during the London talks. U Aung San pointed out that the world had undergone a great change politically and now it had become necessary for the people of Myanmar to unite. He also said that in a way Myanmar would soon be achieving its independence and that the question of the hill peoples was the only problem remaining to be solved. He also pointed out at the

London talks that the independence of Myanmar could not be real unless and until the hill peoples were also granted independence at the same time.

U Aung San continued to say that the administration of the hill areas would soon be in the hands of the hill peoples' representatives, because Britain would have to give up Myanmar sooner or later and that the hill peoples would have to depend on themselves for that matter. Therefore, unity had now become highly essential. He also remarked that the living standard could be raised to a reasonable level after independence. He said that the hill peoples should not be swayed by threats or praise and must be firm in their pledge for unity. He advised them not to be afraid of anybody, whether white or black, and not to allow themselves to be persuaded by threats or coaxing and they must all say that they wanted independence as Myanmar. If they were to do so today they could get their freedom the next day. In reply to the question put to him by the *saohpa* of Yawng Hwe, U Aung San replied that the hill peoples would be allowed to administer their own areas in any way they pleased and that Myanmar would not interfere in their internal administration. He added that the Shan had the same right to choose their own constitution in the same way as the people could accept the present constitution if they wished to do so, but if they wanted any alterations they were at liberty to do so, and the Myanmar would never interfere in their affairs.

On February 6, 1947, the Shan-Kachin Committee met at Pang Long and made the following decision:

> The Committee was of the opinion that the freedom for the Shans and Kachins would be achieved sooner through cooperation with the Burmese; as such the two races would send in their representatives to take part in the Executive Council of the Burmese government during the transition period, with the following conditions:
>
> 1. Same status, rights, and privileges as enjoyed by Burma on democratic lines.
> 2. The Shan and Kachin members in the Executive Council would be responsible for all their internal affairs and would jointly be responsible for common subjects, e.g. Defence, Foreign Affairs, Railways, Customs, etc.
> 3. This committee supported the demand of the Kachin for their desire to have a distinct separate state.
> 4. The terms of agreement as arrived at between the Myanmar delegates and His Majesty's government are not to be binding on the Shan and Kachin.
> 5. The right to secede after attainment of freedom from Confederation with Burma if and when we choose.

Shan Committee

(Signed)	Hkun Pan Sing	Saohpalong of Tawng Peng State
	Sao Shwe Thaike	Saohpalong of Yawng Hwe
	Sao Hom Hpa	Saohpalong of North Hsen Wi State
	Sao Num	Saohpalong of Lai Hka State
	Sao Sam Htun	Saohpalong of Mong Pawn

Hkun Pung
U Tin E
U Htun Myint
U Kya Bu
Hkun Saw
Sao Yape Hpa
Hkun Htee [Hkun Hti]

Kachin Committee

(Signed) Sinwa Naw, Myitkyina
Zau Rip, Myitkyina
Din Ra Tang, Myitkyina
Zau La, Bhamo
Zau Lawn, Bhamo
Labang Grong, Bhamo

A combined Chin-Kachin-Shan committee met at Pang Long on February 7, 1947, at 9 A.M., as reported:

The Chin delegation, having arrived on the night of February 6, 1947, was welcomed to the meeting. It consisted of:

1. U Hlur Hmung, ATM, IDSM, BEM, Falam, Chin Hills
2. U Thawng Za Khup, ATM, Tiddim, Chin Hills
3. U Kio Mang, ATM, Haka, Chin Hills

1. The terms of the decision arrived at yesterday by the Shan representatives and the Kachin delegation at their meeting at 2:30 P.M. were read out and explained to the Chin delegates, who approved of the decisions and subscribed to them with the following additions, which were unanimously approved by all.
   (a) All rights and privileges as regards central revenue enjoyed by Shans shall also be extended to the Chins and Kachins on a population basis.
   (b) Any deficiency in local finance shall be made good from Burma revenues.
   (c) There shall be formed a Supreme Executive Council of the United Hill Peoples composed of representatives of Shan, Chin, and Kachin which shall have full powers to decide on all matters of policy between the Hill peoples and the government of Burma.

Shan Committee

(Signed) Hkun Pan Sing, Saohpalong of Tawng Peng State
S. S. Thaike
Sao Hom Hpa, Saohpalong of North Hsen Wi State
Sao Num, Saohpalong of Lai Hka State

Sao Sam Htun, Saohpalong of Mong Pawn State
Representative of Hsa Tung *saohpalong*
Hkun Pung
U Tin E
U Htun Myint
U Kya Bu
Hkun Saw
Sao Yape Hpa
Hkun Htee [Hkun Hti]

Kachin Committee

(Signed) Sinwa Naw, Myitkyina
Zau Rip, Myitkyina
Din Ra Tang, Myitkyina
Zau La, Bhamo
Zau Lawn, Bhamo
Labang Grong, Bhamo

Chin Committee

(Signed) U Hlur Hmung, ATM, IDSM, BEM Falam
U Thawng Za Khup, ATM, Tiddim
U Kio Mang, ATM, Haka

The Chin-Shan-Kachin committee at its meeting on February 7, 1947, at 1 P.M., unanimously resolved that a subcommittee of the underlisted members be formed and given full powers to negotiate with the Burmese leaders according to the terms of the decisions of the 6th and 7th February 1947 arrived at by (a) the Kachin-Shan committee and (b) the combined Chin-Shan-Kachin committee:

1. U Kya Bu
2. *Saohpalong* of Mong Pawn State
3. Sin Wa Naw
4. Zau Lawn
5. U Hlur Hming
6. U Thawng Za Khup

On February 7, 1947, at 10 A.M. a combined Chin-Shan-Kachin committee held another meeting and passed a resolution to establish a Supreme Executive Council of the United Hill Peoples as follows:

(a) The representatives to the Supreme Council shall be six each from Shans, Chins, and Kachins.

(b) The meeting of this Supreme Council shall be held within the Shan States, at least twice a year. Nevertheless as the occasion demands, emergency meetings may be held any time.

(c) The locality of the meeting shall be chosen by the Executive Committee of the Council of Shan States *Saohpa*, and people.

(d) The Supreme Executive Council shall be provided with a permanent office and staff, but for immediate purposes the secretariat office and staff of the Shan States Supreme Council shall function as a temporary secretariat of the Supreme Council.

(e) Details about the Constitution and rules of the procedure defining the functions and powers of the Supreme Executive Council as regards the individual sections of the Hill Peoples on the one hand, their union on the other, and finally with the Burma administration were to be deliberated upon by a subcommittee to which the following were nominated:

1. U Kya Bu	Shan Committee
2. Sao Sam Htun	Saohpalong of Mong Pawn State
3. Sinwa Naw, Myitkyina	Kachin Committee
4. Zau Lawn, Bhamo	Kachin Committee
5. U Hlur Hmung	Chin Committee
6. U Thawng Za Khup	Chin Committee

The subcommittee will, after deliberation, draw up a draft for submission to the Shan-Chin-Kachin committee for amendment and final approval and shall have the right to call in any person for advice.

Dated Pang Long, the 9th February 1947
(Signed) Hkun Pan Sing, chairman, combined
Chin-Shan-Kachin committee

A meeting of all the *saohpa* and representatives of the people of the Shan States, held at Pang Long on the February 11, 1947, unanimously decided that the Shan National Day be celebrated on the February 7, every year instead of as previously on the September 7.

It was also resolved that the attached song shall be the National Anthem as a temporary measure and the attached specimen flag shall be the Shan National Flag. The flag shall be a tricolor of yellow, green, and red horizontal bars, with a white ball in the middle, nine inches in radius, or 1 1/2 feet in diameter. The flag shall be 3 feet by 5 feet.

Shan National Anthem:

ၵလံသုံ့သံတ၊ လိုၶ်ၶံးလဝ်လၵ်ျ၊ ၸႂ်တဵးမီးတေႃ်လ၊

ၸွႆ့ပိုင်းလွႆဝ၊လ၊ သူလဝ်ႁဝ်းၶ၊ ၸႂ်မီးလွႆသိတ့်လ၊။

(ၵလၢမ်,သမ့်လၶ်,တ၊, လိူၶ်ၶမ်းလဝ်;လၵ်;ၵျ၊, ၸႂ်;တဵးမီးတေ,လ၊,

ၸွမ့်ပိုင်းလွႆဝ၊,လ၊, သူလဝ်;ႁဝ်းၶ၊; ၸႂ်;မီးလွႆသိတ်;လ၊။)

Shan National Flag

Dated Pang Long, the 11th February 1947
(Signed) Hkun Pan Sing, president,
Council of Shan State *Saohpa*

FIGURE 13.2. Shan national flag

At the meeting of the Shan States, *saohpa*, representatives of the Shan people, Kachin, and Chin, the following were nominated, as a temporary measure, to the SCOUHP (Supreme Council of the United Hill Peoples).

Shan Members

1. *Saohpalong* of Yawng Hwe
2. *Saohpalong* of North Hsen Wi
3. *Saohpalong* of Mong Pawn
4. U Htun Myint
5. U Kya Bu
6. Sao Boon Waat

Kachin Members

1. Sinwa Naw
2. Zau Rip
3. Dinra Tang
4. Padip La Tawng

5. Duwa Zau Lawn
6. Duwa Zau La

Chin Committee

1. U Pam Za Mong
2. U Thawng Tin Lyen
3. U Kio Mang
4. U Sein Lien
5. U Hlur Hmung
6. Mang Ling

Sao Boon Waat proposed and was seconded by U Htun Myint that the *saohpalong* of North Hsen Wi should be president of the SCOUHP. The motion was unanimously carried.

The *saohpalong* of North Hsen Wi proposed and was seconded by U Kya Bu that Sin Wa Naw should be vice-president. The motion was unanimously carried. The headquarters of the SCOUHP would, as a temporary measure, be situated in Yawng Hwe.

The Shan *saohpa* were unanimous in their determination to unite with Myanmar provided they could be assured of internal autonomy. The selection of *saohpa* of Mong Pawn as the counselor for the Frontier Areas was a wise choice.

Regarding the Second Pang Long Conference, the governor of Myanmar, in his letter to the secretary of state for Myanmar, made the following remarks:

> There was an under-current of hostility (shown) by the Saohpas against the Frontier Service and it was obvious that the Saohpas want to run their country in their own way and not to be (controlled) by the Frontier Service. Many Saohpas told me privately that they were prepared to accept European and other officers as advisers until . . . they have acquired sufficient experience to stand on their own.
>
> The Saohpas have commenced introduction of popular representation into their councils, and one of my official meetings at Taunggyi was composed of eight Saohpas and eight representatives from the people. I was impressed with the latter and I can foresee that before many years have passed a great deal of authority will pass from Saohpas to the people. The Saohpas as a whole are not impressive, but provided they are prepared to accept advice for the next few years and are able to attract to the Shan federal council the right type of representatives from the people then I believe that union with Burma will be successful.[3]

The British observer, in his letter to Sir Gilbert Lathwaite, commented:

> The draft of a proposed agreement between the Burma Government and representatives of the Shans, Jingpaws, and Chins has been drawn up, according to a message received from the AFPFL from Pang Long yesterday.
>
> . . . Pang Long was, from my point of view, quite a success as it got the Hill peoples in a position where they could freely express themselves. Aung San and Tin Tut were both very reasonable and patient and answered all questions in a perfectly straightforward manner.[4]

About three hundred persons took part in a demonstration staged on Monday by the students, youth organization, and PVOS. The demonstrations shouted such slogans as "Shan and Myanmar" and within ten years all the golden results would be seen. Aung San very boldly offered the right of secession to the Shan leaders and representatives if their desire and wishes were not fulfilled as promised. Those very fine and sweet words of assurance came like a magic wand touching the nerve centers of all the frontier peoples removing all doubts and suspicions from their minds and electrifying them to shout slogans like "Unity with Myanmar," "Freedom with Myanmar," "Independence with Myanmar," and "Forever with Myanmar." The students and the public joined in the shouting and the whole town of Pang Long echoed with the shouts of the slogans. It was indeed a heart-moving scene from the Pang Long Conference.

When this expected or unexpected message of Pang Long unity and the Pang Long Agreement reached London, the British prime minister, Mr. Clement Attlee, and his colleagues were left with no choice but to reconfirm their decision to immediately grant independence to Myanmar. The date set for the granting of independence was January 4, 1948. February 12, 1947, the date on which the Pang Long Agreement was reached, was declared "Union Day" for all peoples of Myanmar.

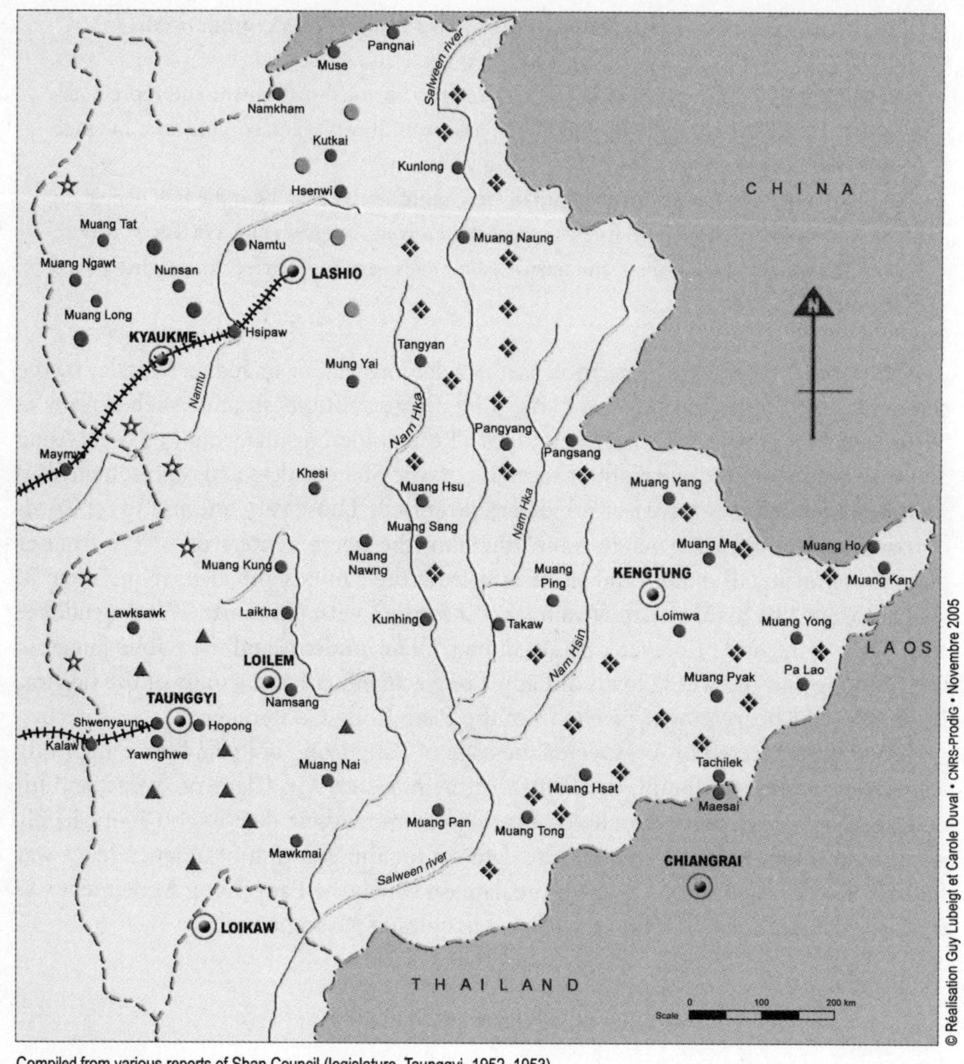

Compiled from various reports of Shan Council (legislature, Taunggyi, 1952–1953)

- ☆ BCP (Burmese Communist Party) or White Flag communists now known as CPB
- ▲ Pa-O rebels allied to the Karen national Defence organization (KNDO)
- ● PVO (People's Volunteer Organization)
- ● Kachin army mutineers and rebels under Captain Naw Seng
- ❖ KMT (Chinese stragglers under General Li)
- - - Occidental limits of the Shan States
- Railway tracks
- ● Town
- ◉ Urban center

MAP 20. Positions of Shan rebels and Kuomintang forces in Shan State, 1949–1951

14

The Kuomintang Incursion into the Shan States

A historic agreement was signed on February 12, 1947, in the little town of Pang Long in the Central Shan States. Under the Pang Long Agreement, the hill peoples, led by the Shan *saohpa* and the leaders of the other national minorities, unanimously voted to join the Myanmar leaders in their struggle for independence from the British. The effect of that historic unanimity hastened the British government to grant Myanmar independence on January 4, 1948. The Myanmar people, together with other national minorities, were very happy and enjoyed the first fruit of their independence after a long wait. The Shan were happier for having had the opportunity to organize the hill peoples to attend the conference and to be able to meet all the expenses of the historic conference. The Shan leaders were also proud of their leading role and efforts to persuade the national minorities and the Shan people to support the resolutions made at the Pang Long Conference and join hands with the Myanmar people in their struggle for independence. The people of this country had been in bondage to British colonialism from 1824 to 1942 and again from 1945 to 1948, and to Japanese fascism from 1942 to 1945. Their experience with both colonialism and fascism was so bitter that it made them forge the political unity they had achieved at Pang Long, which led to their freedom and sovereignty in 1948.

After independence, tranquility prevailed in the Shan States, but only for a short time. The Shan farmers would not have time to enjoy peace, because they had to undertake the tasks of reconstruction and rehabilitation that had affected them during the Second World War. Their sustainable economy of the old days had to be restored. Abandoned farms and rice fields had to be cultivated, new rice fields had to be reclaimed, for the increase in population and unattended citrus, tea, and fruit plantations needed care and attention. Old weirs were repaired and new dams were built. Damaged water wheels were renovated and many new canals were dug. New methods of irrigation were introduced in the hope of expanding wet-rice cultivation. Without national or international aid, the Shan farmers strove hard to restore the normal condition of the local economy and the normal course of life in these remote areas.

Suddenly, to the great surprise and shock of the Shan, Kuomintang soldiers armed with modern war equipment appeared on their doorstep with the grand plan to make Shanland a springboard to reinvade and recapture China from the Red Army. Only then did the Shan realize that the remnants of the Kuomintang soldiers defeated by the Red Army had crossed the border into their peaceful land. The long struggle for power that had taken place between the Communists and the Nationalists had finally come to an end with the defeat of the Nationalists led by Chiang Kai-shek. He and his followers escaped to Taiwan (Formosa) in 1949.[1] The Twenty-sixth and Ninety-third Divisions of Chiang's Eighth Army, which were stationed in southwestern China, were unable to withstand the attack of the Chinese People's Liberation Army in 1949, and had crossed over into the northeastern Shan States.[2] These Kuomintang remnants were led by General Li Mi of the Eighth Army, Lt. General Liu Kuo Chuan of the Twenty-sixth Division, and Major General Mah Chaw Yee and Major General Liu Chin Tsung of the Ninety-third Division.[3] The number of Kuomintang soldiers at the beginning of 1950 was about seventeen hundred and they occupied the northeastern Shan States around Mong Yang in Keng Tung State.[4] By May 1951 the Kuomintang force had increased to two thousand and established bases along the Myanmar-China border in the Ko Kang and Mong Lun states.[5]

FIGURE 14.1. H. E. Justice U Myint Thein, leader of the Myanmar delegation, speaking in the First Committee (*KMT Aggression Against Burma*, 102)

Many new recruits further enlarged the Kuomintang army. Those who could not adjust to the new Red regime fled to join General Li Mi. Some of these new recruits left General Li Mi's army to settle down in the Shan States and later became citizens of the country. Many of the local population were also forced to join the Nationalist camp. Yunnan is a province where many ethnic minorities live, mostly the Tai Neu and Tai Lu people. There are many Tai Neu principalities along the Myanmar-China border. Each of these principalities was ruled by its chief, called *saohpa*. A feudal administrative system was practiced in these principalities. Feudalism was contradictory to Communism and the Chinese Communist authorities targeted the *saohpa* as anti-Communists. The *saohpa* and the Tai Neu people had a rather hard time under the Communist regime. Some of the Tai Neu chiefs joined the Nationalist forces when the struggle for power took place between the two camps. When the Communists took power in Yunnan, they arrested many remaining Tai Neu chiefs and severely punished them for supporting the Nationalists and stripped them of what remained of their autonomous or independent rights. Such influence somehow or other reached the Shan States when the Kuomintang crossed over the border and after a few years the Shan *saohpa* in the Shan States almost suffered the same consequences as their brothers in China. The Chinese Nationalist political organizers launched anti-Communist campaigns down to the level of minority villages along the China-Myanmar border. Many of the local population were enticed into the Nationalist camp with a show of money and gold. A number of Chinese feudal lords threw in their lot with the Kuomintang in the hope of getting back their lands that had been confiscated by the Communist government. A lot of Chinese adventurers or opium smugglers also came to join the Kuomintang troops hoping to do illegal business across the border, and some of them looked forward to making money through smuggling under the cloak of the Kuomintang. From that day onward the volume of opium trade increased rapidly and the growing tide of this trade has continued to this day. There did not seem to be any effective means to stop it. The drug business destroyed the moral character and lives of many young Shan, who were made helpless by the indifference of the national or international human rights organizations. Another method that the Kuomintang generals used to get new recruits was to appeal to the Kuomintang deserters of the Second World War. Thus the Kuomintang troops increased to the point where they dared to challenge both the Red Chinese forces and the Union of Myanmar forces.

The Myanmar government asked the Kuomintang either to leave the Union territory or to surrender. But the Kuomintang was determined to remain in Myanmar and to make its territory a military base to invade mainland China. The Myanmar government did not expect resistance from the Kuomintang to its legal demand for evacuation or surrender. But when the commander of the Union forces in Keng Tung sent an ultimatum to the chief of the Kuomintang force, General Li flatly refused to surrender and warned that he would retaliate with full force if attacked by the Union forces. A few Kuomintang suspects were arrested by the Myanmar intelligence officers in Keng Tung. The Kuomintang general sent a letter demanding the release of the

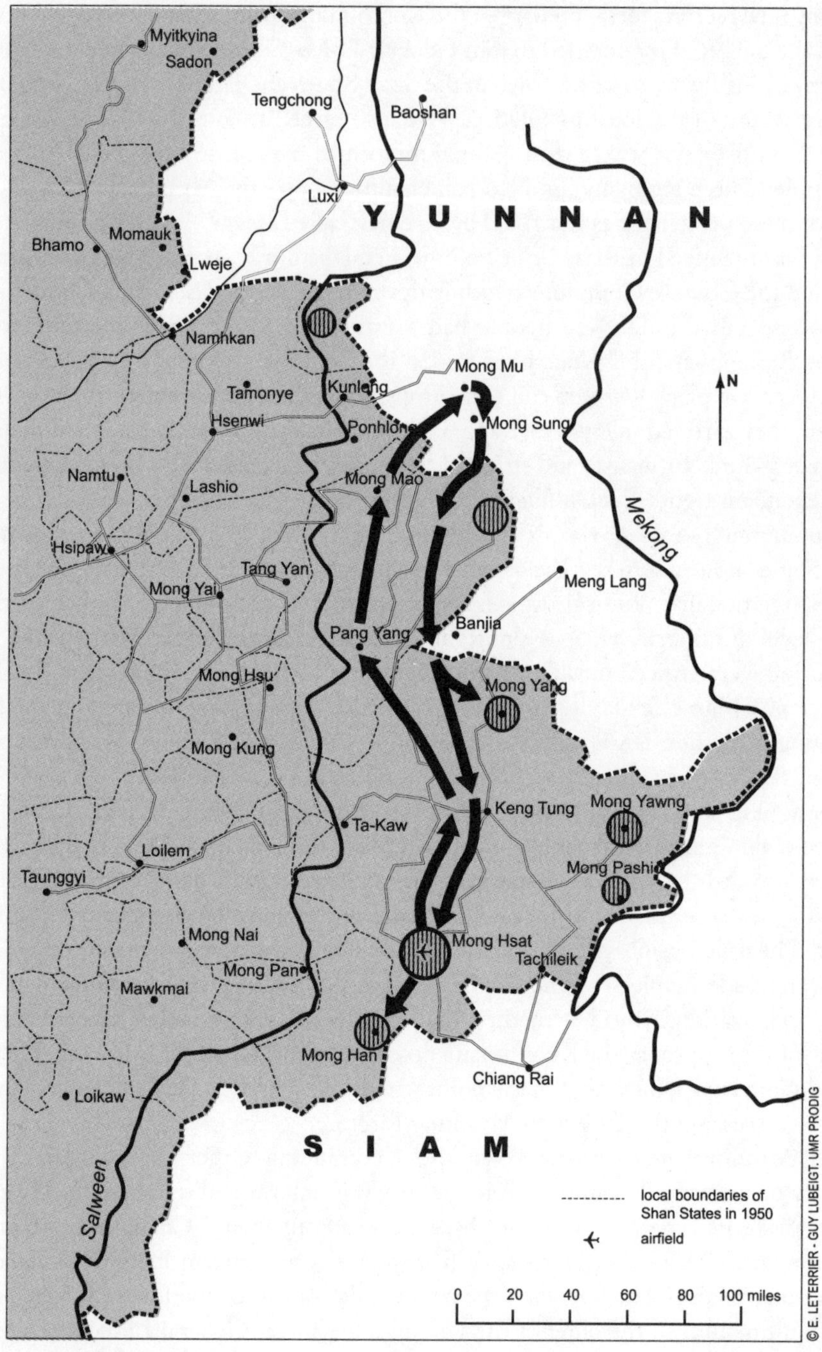

MAP 21. Jungle tracks and strongholds of the Chinese KMT troops during the occupation of eastern Myanmar, 1951–1952

Chinese civilians, saying, "If unfortunately there will be any disastra (disaster) bursted [*sic*] owing to the offensive progress of your men toward Mong Ling–Tachileik, we shall be ready to accept with a spirit of sacrifice and protection; but it is very clear the responsibility of the said occurrence is at your side."[6]

The Kuomintang went so far as to reconstruct the Keng Tung–Tachilek road that led to the Myanmar-Thai border, through which they hoped to get quick military supplies from Thailand. Their plan to withstand any attack by both the Union forces and Red Chinese forces was made very clear at the press interview given by General Lai Iang Sae Tia of the Kuomintang Army while he was in Thailand. He also mentioned his visit to the Nationalist Chinese military attaché in Bangkok.[7]

The Myanmar government had no choice but to launch an attack against the Kuomintang. From June 1950 to December 1951, five operations under the names of Operations Keng Tung (June–July, 1950), Operations Frost (February 1951), Operations Pang Long (October 21, 1951), Operations Mo-gyo (Special Operations), and Operations Ba-yint Naung (Special Operations) (September 15, 1952) were launched against the Kuomintang.[8] About two hundred Kuomintang were captured during the operations.[9] For a short time the tension seemed to subside. General Li Mi went to Taipei to consult with the Nationalist government. The Kuomintang remnants grouped under the command of General Liu Kuo Chuan and carried on their military activities around Mong Hsat, which later became the military headquarters of the Kuomintang. The Union government had inadequate troops to cope with the situation in Mong Hsat. The Union troops also had engagements with the Communist insurgents in the middle and lower parts of Myanmar. The Kuomintang then, for the time being, had a free hand to build up their position in Mong Hsat for the liberation of mainland China through the back door of Yunnan. Kuomintang military bases and fortresses were set up in Mong Hsat, Mong Yang, and Mong Nyent and along the Myanmar-China border. The Kuomintang troops penetrated into Yunnan to recapture some Tai Neu and Lu principalities like Kung Ma, Kangai, Mong Long (Fuhai), and Hsiphsaungbana for a few weeks before they were again driven out by the Red Chinese forces.[10]

Failing to invade, the Kuomintang changed its strategy. It adopted guerrilla warfare tactics and began to make unexpected attacks. A rather fierce clash between the two forces took place near Koolun in Yunnan Province, where 42 Communist soldiers were killed. In September 1953 the Kuomintang launched another military attack, called "ammunition raid," under General Kyu Yen in the area of Ku Yung where about 130 Communists died.[11]

Alarmed by the repeated raids, the Chinese Communists, took measures to strengthen their forces by sending the Forty-fourth Army to Yunnan to repulse any further attack by the Kuomintang. Hearing this news, the Viet Minh government also took measures to strengthen its frontier forces, fearing fighting would spill into its northern territory. The Myanmar government was also alarmed, fearing that the Chinese Communists might enter Myanmar to fight the Kuomintang. Occasionally the Red Chinese took advantage of the Kuomintang issue and entered northeastern Myanmar under the pretext that they came to protect the lives and properties of the frontier peoples from the atrocities of the Kuomintang.[12] The Korean War and the Indochinese War kept the Chinese Communists busy on other fronts in their mainland, but they did not overlook the possibility that they might be stabbed in the back by the Kuomintang. More and more Communist troops were deployed along the frontier principalities of Men Kiu, Mang Hing, Htat Ting, Kaung Kok, and Ywang Kok. Political and propaganda techniques were used to consolidate the local population, just as the Kuomintang had done.[13]

FIGURE 14.2. Kuomintang recruits training in Shan State. (*KMT Aggression Against Burma,* 152)

Propaganda pamphlets were distributed saying that the Chinese Communist troops came to safeguard the local people from the marauding Kuomintang soldiers, as there was no Myanmar force to take care of them. Local tribes along the frontier were organized into Communist camps. The Communist authority announced a reward with big sums of money or gold for anyone who captured Kuomintang soldiers, dead or alive. Any local chief who had been forced to be pro-Kuomintang was to be eliminated and replaced with a Communist protégé.[14] Local militia units were formed and women's volunteer forces were also organized to secure the Communist forces. These paramilitary organizations were placed under Colonel Naw Seng,[15] who commanded a battalion in the Thirteenth Army of the Second Red Chinese Army group.[16]

With the growing tide of Communist military power on the Chinese side of the border, the Kuomintang intensified its military buildup in the Shan States. The Union government sent its request to surrender but the Kuomintang leader ignored it and continued to expand military activities to the western regions of the Than Lwin River and to the Northern Shan States.[17] A new order was issued placing all the Kuomintang forces in all parts of the Shan States under the single command of General Liu Kuo Chuan, who had his headquarters at Mong Hsat. General Lui divided the Kuomintang military area into three sectors: the Eastern Sector with its headquarters at Pang Yang under General Fu Cheng Yang with four thousand Kuomintang soldiers; the

Northeastern Sector, with its headquarters at Lung Htan under General Wang Yu Wai, having about three thousand soldiers; and the Southeastern Sector with its headquarters in Mong Hsat, having one thousand Kuomintang soldiers.[18]

With the Kuomintang military headquarters, bases, and garrisons scattered over the eastern and northern parts of Shanland, the Shan people suffered much. They had to provide food and porters and recruits quite against their wishes. Young men from the military area fled from their homes for fear of conscription. Some fled to west of the Than Lwin River to take refuge in big cities like Taunggyi, Mandalay, and Yangon. Some fled to Laos and Thailand. Many boys went into monasteries to become novices to avoid being conscripted by the Kuomintang. Many unfortunate lads were forcibly drafted into the Kuomintang camps to render military and nonmilitary services. The Shan farmers did not have a peaceful time to cultivate their rice fields and sometimes they were caught in the crossfire between Union forces and the Kuomintang troops. Buffaloes were killed and some farmers were wounded and killed in the midst of fighting. There was no Red Cross Society to take care of them and local dispensaries were not enough to cope with the casualties. There were no compensations or any kind of help for the damages done to their fields, to their villages, to their monasteries, and for the deaths they suffered from fighting between the Union forces and the Kuomintang Army.

The scope of war increased when the Nationalist government of Taiwan openly supplied more arms, ammunition, and other kinds of military equipment.[19] Chiang Kai-shek's government denied that there was a supply of arms, but the letter captured from Chiang Kai-shek to General Li Mi clearly indicated that he was behind the Kuomintang movement in Myanmar. In the letter he said that a big reward would be given to Kuomintang soldiers once they had completed their mission of liberating the Chinese motherland.[20] Reinforcements of new soldiers were flown into Thailand from Taiwan and then to the eastern part of the Shan States. New airfields were built by the Kuomintang in the Mong Hsat area. C-46 planes flew to the new airfield carrying new military equipment. Moreover, Chiang requested the Vietnamese government to release the thirty-five thousand Nationalist soldiers who had been interned by the French government in Indochina after the Second World War. They were to cross over Laos to join the Kuomintang forces in Myanmar. But the French authority in Vietnam refused to comply.[21]

There were also concrete evidences that the arms sent to the Kuomintang forces in Myanmar were made in the United States. Carbines, mortars, and machine guns captured had clear marks of being made in USA.[22] Kuomintang were also reported to have received arms from private American companies in Southeast Asia. The Southeast Asia Corporation and the Bangkok Commercial Corporation, which employed Americans, Thais, and Chinese citizens, were listed as companies supplying military equipment to the Kuomintang troops.[23] The Kuomintang in turn supplied gold, silver, wolfram, opium, and other mineral products of the Shan States.[24]

The Chinese Communist government now turned its full attention to its southwestern front because of the danger. Reinforcements of Communist troops were made along the frontier and people's militia forces were organized. National minorities were brought under tight control for fear of infiltration from the Kuomintang agents, and especially the Tai ethnic people were kept under severe surveillance because of their connection with the Shan in the Shan States.

The Chinese Communist government began to make their accusation against American involvement in Kuomintang affairs. It also charged that an American technical mission was surveying Lampang and Chiang Mai roads in northern Thailand that would connect with the road that led to the Kuomintang bases in eastern Shanland.[25] Moscow came in to join the accusation against the United States, saying that American army men were with the Kuomintang and training them in techniques of guerrilla warfare.[26] The Soviet newspaper *Izvestia* further accused the United States as follows:

> Why is the Kuomintang clique striving so persistently to maintain its units in Burma? The answer is clear: The Kuomintang are not quitting Myanmar territory, because they are supported by the aggressive US circles interested in maintaining and increasing tension in the South East. . . .
>
> The active support of Kuomintang bands in Burma by US ruling circles exposes these circles as the culprits in creating the tense situation in South East Asia as violators of the United Nations decisions.[27]

The *Nippon Times* reported that a clandestine air supply system was set up "between Formosa and northern Myanmar, with the assistance of . . . the Central Intelligence Agency."[28]

When General J. Lawton Collins, the US Army chief of staff, visited Bangkok and Formosa in October 1951, the Communists accused him of making arrangements to help the Kuomintang campaign in Myanmar. The United States government very often denied that there was a connection between the Department of State and the Kuomintang remnants in Myanmar. However, the *New York Herald Tribune* commented that there might not be official help given to the Kuomintang by the American officials but that many private American citizens were involved in the air transportation between Formosa and Mong Hsat could not be denied.[29]

Thailand was another power that actively aided the Kuomintang military campaign in Myanmar. The frequent movements of Kuomintang soldiers and smugglers in and out of Thailand were reported many times, but the Thai authority never acknowledged the truth of the reports. The Thai government also remarked that its police force was patrolling the frontier to prevent border violations by the Kuomintang.

The Kuomintang incursion into Myanmar was at first considered to be a tiny spark from a burning fire. It could have been put out easily but no big power was interested in doing so. Instead they fanned the wind to inflame that little spark of fire to keep burning in the eastern and northeastern part of the Shan States. The power struggle among the big nations took place in Shanland and the Shan States became a theater of war. The first to suffer from the consequences of war were the Shan people. Their enjoyment of a peaceful life after independence was unfortunately very short-lived and misery befell them again.

Another consequence that followed the Kuomintang incursion into the Shan States was the "narcotic explosion" which opened the floodgates to the drug trade. The flow of opium was so swift that it soon flooded over the Shan States, down to Thailand and other parts of Southeast Asia, and finally to the whole world like a torrential rain on a stormy day, bringing social disasters one after another, affecting the health and lives of thousands of youths, causing an alarming shock to the United Nations. The drug war against humanity then began.

During this period, poppies were widely and freely grown. The growers took good advantage of the Kuomintang incursion. Opium extraction became a booming business and a lucrative one. It was a miracle cure for the economic crisis. Drugs and arms became intertwined and a large amount of drug money was used to buy arms and ammunition for the insurgents. The activities of drug dealers and arms dealers brought untold ill effect to civil societies. Smuggling gangs mushroomed everywhere and linked up with other rings of underground international drug dealers. Their secret drug outposts were everywhere and their network of drug operations covered many strategic places in urbanized societies, including many big cities of the world. All known and unknown means of communications and transportation were brought into the network of the underworld drug business. This affected the Shan States and the Shan people very much, especially the youths. The Golden Triangle became the focus of world accusation as the evil place of the Shan States. The war with the Kuomintang was brought to an end through negotiation and diplomacy with the help of the United Nations. But its appendix, the drug war, does not seem to show any sign of coming to an end. It keeps on multiplying with the application of modern technology and science, supplemented by mobile laboratories skipping from one place to another in the vast and wild forests, deep valleys, and rugged mountains of the Shan States. The quality and quantity of drugs developed from opium to heroin to ephedrine to "*ya ma*" and other drugs. They sprang up everywhere, waiting to claim human lives. Many young people have died, and more lives are being affected with the onset of HIV, the twin brother of the drugs. A conversation between two old men in Tachileik will help to paint the picture of the drug-HIV situation of the town. The first old man addressed the second old man, whom he met on the way.

First: How are you today?
Second: Very busy.
First: Why so busy?
Second: Going to the cemetery every day.
First: Why to the cemetery every day? What for?
Second: You see, young people die every day because of the effect of drugs and HIV. So we old people keep busy going to the cemetery to bury the corpses. Young people die so early today because they indulge in

> drugs and sex whereas we old people abstain from touching those. So we live longer than the young people.

The problem of the illegal immigrants that followed the Kuomintang invasion also greatly affected the Shan States. No prohibition, no supervision, no restrictions, and no immigration laws existed to prevent the illegal immigrants brought along with the Kuomintang. Many Yunnanese who did not wish to live under the Communist regime slipped through many points along the border into the Shan States without any difficulty. They hid themselves in forests, valleys, rugged terrain, and remote villages on the slopes of the mountains, engaging in illegal trade and poppy growing. They gradually crept into nearby villages, towns, and cities whenever the situation was favorable and, through various means, to occupy various sectors of the local and national economy, ranging from restaurant owners to top bankers, using the drug money to run all sorts of businesses until most of the important jobs and professions fell into their hands. They worked harder than everybody and their main objective was to attain a high standard of living, which they mostly did. Today every village, every town and every city in the Shan State is booming with new immigrants or new citizens. Nowadays, border-crossing immigrants have become an international problem and there seems to be no effective measure to stop it. We will have to live with it now and in the future.

With moral, political, and military backing from the Nationalist government in Taiwan and from the sympathizers and pro-Nationalist friends around the world, the Kuomintang forces expanded their activities and fortifications throughout the Shan States. Shanland was now transformed from a land of peace and tranquility into a land of war. Once, the mornings in Shan State were greeted by the sweet song of chirping birds, but now not only mornings but whole days were greeted by the echo of firing guns, mortars, cannons, and the explosion of deadly bombs. Everywhere uniformed men with guns slung on their shoulders replaced the farmers on whose shoulders were plows and baskets of paddy. The natural world suddenly changed from bad to worse for the Shan farmers of the region. Now the question was: to whom should they look for their protection and safe living in this remote part of the world?

Kuomintang secret networks were spread far and wide in the Shan States training secret recruits, raising secret funds, and organizing propaganda among native Chinese in Yangon and ethnic people of the Shan States.[30] When these secret agents were arrested it was clear that they were officially authorized by General Li Mi to collect funds from the local Chinese.[31] With aid and supplies coming from pro-Nationalist organizations around the world, the Kuomintang made every effort to speed up their military training programs. General Liu Kuo Chuan issued instructions to local commanders for the reorganization of military units and the distribution of military supplies. The general staff in Taiwan also issued an order to devote military training to guerrilla warfare. In addition to that, psychological and propaganda programs were introduced to win the support of the local people in the Union of Myanmar, particularly the ethnic peoples of the Shan States. Propaganda pamphlets were issued by Mr. Kyi San, chief

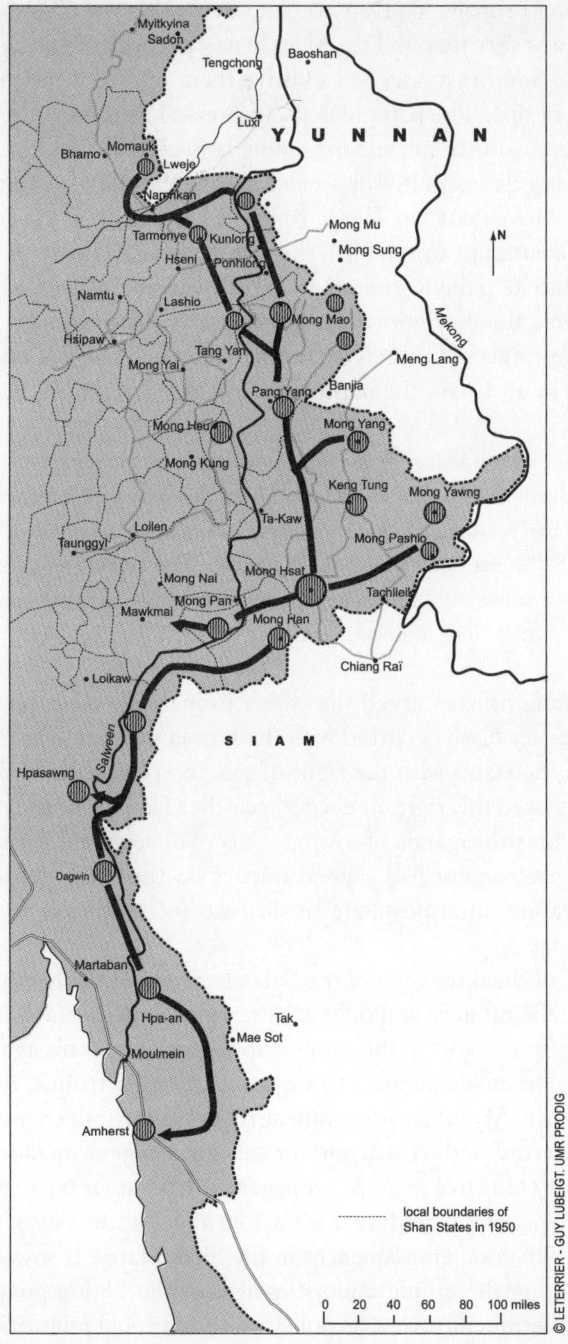

MAP 22. Jungle tracks and strongholds of the Chinese KMT troops during the occupation of eastern Myanmar, 1952–1953

of the Kuomintang Propaganda Department, saying that the Chinese Nationalists had come into Myanmar territory and the Shan States to check the advance of the Chinese Communists into Southeast Asia and to drive them out from the province of Yunnan when the time was ripe. The pamphlet also expressed its regret at having clashed with the Myanmar forces, due to misunderstanding between the two forces.[32]

The Kuomintang also exploited dissension among the ethnic peoples. They organized the "Free Lahu Movement" in Keng Tung area, promising the Lahu people every assistance in their attempt to establish the Lahu autonomous state, and in return the Lahu people had to help the Kuomintang in their campaign against the Communists.[33] Another issue that the Kuomintang exploited was the surrender of administrative power by the *saohpa*, the Shan chiefs of the Shan States.[34] The Kuomintang propaganda statement issued by Li Chaw, the regimental commander, on July 3, 1952, said:

> (II) Try by every means to incite the Sawbwas and Headmen to spread Sedition against the Burmese Government in abolishing the system of Sawbwa Administration by utilizing the recruits, Shan Volunteers, in order to accomplish its intention of governing all the nationalities by the Burmese. The recruiting officers sent by the Burmese Government and the volunteers recruited shall be denied passes issued by us and we shall put all kinds of obstacles in their way.[35]

The Kuomintang officers urged the *saohpa* to maintain their power, and promised to help them in case a clash occurred with the Union government. Furthermore, Shan State was one of the states with the right of secession from the Union of Myanmar.[36] The Kuomintang used this right to encourage other factions of the people to strive for independence. This propaganda of sowing seeds of dissension between the Shan chiefs and the Union government had a great impact on the Shan people and the Union government, creating an atmosphere of distrust and suspicion which disrupted the spirit of Pang Long.

The summary of the discussion of the Subcommittee of the Kuomintang 4,904 Battalion describing the military and political strategies to be pursued in Myanmar[37] gave very clear instruction to stir up the local people to take up arms against the Myanmar troops, to strive for independence, to organize guerrilla troops, to rob government treasuries, to destroy Myanmar government organizations, to encourage the minority tribes to take up arms, and to struggle for self-government or independence, and so on. That was a very effective piece of propaganda. It went far into Yunnan where there were many ethnic peoples including the Tai Neu and Tai Lu. This piece of propaganda did not produce any good consequences in the Shan States. It sowed seeds of distrust and suspicion among the ethnic minorities against the Union government. It might have made the government review its policy on the national minorities living in Myanmar. The policy could have become either rigid or liberal. The Chinese Communist government and the Myanmar government faced a common threat and danger because of this propaganda. The two governments could have consulted together and formulated a common policy on the national minorities on both sides of the borders. Any cultural, literary, or other activity initiated by the national minorities was carefully and seriously watched especially that of the Tai ethnic groups. Because of the Kuomintang propaganda, the Shan people in the Shan State were bound to suffer much more in the years to come even after the Kuomintang evacuated from the Shan State. That was the regrettable part of the intrusion of the Kuomintang into the Shan States. There was no good reason or justification for the Kuomintang troops to forcibly occupy Shanland and to give trouble to its peace-loving people. For the Shan peoples the occupation of Shanland by the Kuomintang meant the disappearance of peace and tranquility, abandonment of farmland, the destruction of plantations, the loss of security and lives. There was no moral and legal justification for the Kuomintang troops to occupy the Shan States, but their intrusion created an endless chain of misery for the Shan people and other ethnic minorities.

To affect the neutral position of the Myanmar government, the Nationalist government instructed the Kuomintang forces to allege that the Myanmar government had signed a secret treaty with the Chinese Communists.[38] This accusation created misunderstanding between the Western bloc and Myanmar, and resulted in serious trouble for the Myanmar government on the international level. While pursuing a propaganda warfare on domestic, national, and international levels, the Kuomintang also pushed the military offensive and directed its forces to attack every weak position on the Union front.[39]

Moreover, the Kuomintang generals tried to win the friendship of the Karen (Kayin) and Mon rebels and to form a common front against the Myanmar troops.[40] The Kuomintang forces in Myanmar announced the formation of an "Anti-Communist National Salvation Army." The scope of their activities expanded not only in Yunnan but also in Myanmar. The Chinese Nationalist chargé d'affaires, Mr. Patric Soong, was so confident that he declared at a press conference that the Kuomintang forces with twelve thousand soldiers were under the direct command of the Nationalist headquarters in Formosa, and that the Kuomintang forces were deployed in undemarcated territory

FIGURE 14.3. Kuomintang recruits in the Shan States in front of a Shan *wat* (temple). (KMT *Aggression Against Burma*, 152)

in Myanmar. He also openly said that the operations of the Kuomintang forces were an extension of the struggle against Communists in Korea, Indonesia, and Malaya.[41]

The Kuomintang intensified its operations against the Myanmar government. It often raided frontier outposts of Myanmar forces and ambushed government officers who were on routine duty. Local chiefs and headmen who refused to render services were arrested and forced to pay ransom money for their release.[42] Communications were very often interrupted and businesses were looted and some citizens were killed. Even members of missionary groups were kidnapped and asked to pay ransom. On February 15, 1953, a Roman Catholic priest and two Buddhist monks were ambushed and killed by the Kuomintang.[43]

Regarding the situation that prevailed in the Shan States, *The Times of India* gave the following remarks:

> Burma's ill-defended border towns are being subjected to savage probes by the so-called Kuomintang spearhead. The Chinese forces are now striking out . . . against the Burmese rather than the Chinese Communists. Kuomintang raids on isolated garrisons and towns are often marked by violence against civilization and murder and loot. The current Kuomintang threat to Burma has provoked, both politically and militarily, a sharp reaction.[44]

The Kuomintang troops, instead of fighting the Communists in Yunnan, spent much of their time and ammunition fighting against Myanmar forces. This caused much suffering of the native people and there was nobody to rescue them. Their native land became not only a ground for propaganda but also a theater of war for the elimination of one group by another. People in the border towns were conscripted and many were forced to work as porters for free. The word "porters" became a catchword of everyday use in the Shan States even up to the present day. These porters were conscripted by both the Union forces and the Kuomintang and had to carry loads of rations, ammunition, and other military equipment. Sometimes they were used as guides and as shields when severe fighting took place. Many were killed in the operations and their deaths were never announced and their families were never informed. They have not returned home up to now but the members of the family still keep praying for their return. Life was so worthless in this part of the world. Such a senseless war should not happen in this remote part of the region where a lot of innocent people lost their lives.

The increase in activities of the Kuomintang brought a reaction from the Chinese Communists, which caused the Myanmar government considerable concern. Pro-Mao Chinese in Myanmar launched a counterpropaganda campaign. Red Chinese–controlled banks used monetary means to exert their influence on the native Chinese in Myanmar. Loans were given only to those who dissociated themselves from the Nationalist Chinese to support the cause of the Chinese Communists.

Communist-sponsored Chinese schools stepped up their political indoctrination of schoolchildren. The Communists took advantage of the Kuomintang issue to knock down once and for all the Nationalist Chinese Associations in Myanmar. Taking the anti-Kuomintang feeling of the Myanmar people as a cover, the Communists secretly intensified their attempt to draw Myanmar into the orbit of the Red Star. *The Nation* in its April 27, 1953, issue warned the government that if strong measures were not taken to stem the tide of Communism, which was steadily rising, it would be impossible to stop the flood in the future.[45] As the paper stated, the secret forces, which were operating within Myanmar—the Chinese Nationalists and the Chinese Communists—could no longer be concealed as the two factions clashed during demonstrations on Chinese New Year's Day.[46]

Communist Chinese subversive agents were extremely active not only inside the country but also outside. Moreover, the Red Chinese also sent Kachin Communist agents to organize armed bands among the non-Communist Kachins on the Myanmar side of the border. They justified their action by saying that they had come to help their kinsfolk who were victims of the Kuomintang aggression.[47] Moreover, hundreds of Communist soldiers of the Forty-third Division of the Red Army were reported to be massing along the northern frontier of the Wa State of the Union of Myanmar. *The Bangkok Post* reported that about six thousand Thai Liberation troops were alerted in the southwestern province of Yunnan.[48] During this time some of the Myanmar Communists also slipped into Red China. The Chinese Communists secretly invited them to seek consultation and to form a common front against the Kuomintang troops. Both the Nationalists and the Communists conducted extensive political and military activities. They called for an all-out war against each other, and the situation became very explosive and threatened to destroy the newly won independence of the Union of Myanmar. Shan State, being the frontline region in this confrontation, suffered most. Schools closed, disrupting the children's schooling. Many villages were deserted. Men fled for fear of being conscripted either as recruits or as porters. Girls and womenfolk fled for fear of forced marriages and rape. *The Times* (London) warned the world of the dangerous situation and of a new world crisis that would take place if the Communist Chinese and the Kuomintang were allowed to continue their activities in this area.[49]

The Beijing government, watching the way in which the Union government handled the Kuomintang problem, began to lose patience and offered to send its armed forces to help the Myanmars clean out the Kuomintang forces. But the Myanmar government declined Beijing's offer.[50]

The slow response of the government to the Kuomintang irritated the public and the Shan people so much that *The Nation* wrote:

> Our Government is no doubt highly embarrassed about the Kuomintang. But I only wish we knew what it is doing about it. I only wish our dear Government will start breaking its habits of secretiveness about such matters of foreign policy. . . . In matters of external relations, especially when some other nations treat us in cavalier fashion, our Government can rest assured that it will have our staunchest support.[51]

The Kuomintang soldiers turned their guns in the wrong direction and committed more and more atrocities in the Shan States. The Kuomintang question, at first insignificant on the stage of Myanmar politics, had now become a burning national issue. The Myanmar parliament became a boiling pot where opposition leaders asked for a debate. U Nu, the prime minister, was accused of muddled thinking and incompetence on the Kuomintang issue. Questions were asked. Who sponsored the Kuomintang? With whose arms was the Kuomintang marauding in the Shan States and Myanmar? Myanmar political leaders in the parliament accused the United States. *The Nation* described the debate as follows:

> It was a wonderful slugging match. The Government speakers accused the BWPP [Burma Workers' and Peasants' Party] of being the "loudspeakers" of the Communists of Burma [Myanmar] who were stabbing the Government in the back whilst the latter was engaged in driving back the Kuomintang aggression. The BWPP alleged that the Government was allowing the Americans to stage-manage things in Burma. It ultimately came to personal blows "you know us and we know you," said the Honorable U Kyaw Nyein."We have given you enough latitude. You be careful."[52]

The Kuomintang issue had indeed served the purpose of the opposition party, strengthened the cause of the insurgents, and eroded the pillar of American-Myanmar relationships. Regarding the Kuomintang question, Mr. Tibor Mende analyzed the situation correctly in an article in *The Reporter*:

> The sooner the Nationalists are taken out of Burmese territory by the Formosa Government, to whose design the American Government is privy, the better it will be for the future Burmese-American friendship.[53]

Anti-American feeling, created by the presence of the Kuomintang and the propaganda of the opposition parties, reached a high point when news of three white men killed with the Kuomintang soldiers appeared in the Myanmar newspapers.[54] Documents, diaries, a family photo, and a group photo found on the dead bodies proved that they were instructors to General Li Mi. Addresses found on them were mostly from New York and Washington.[55]

The Union government spent more than 40 percent of its income for national defense, but that was not sufficient to cope with internal rebel activities. A large portion of the national budget would have to be allotted if the Union forces were to drive out the Kuomintang remnants by military means. In that case a severe strain would be put on the national economy, and many welfare programs would have to be postponed. Moreover, the Kuomintang forces were better armed. The Union government felt that the problem should be solved through diplomatic rather than military means. The good offices of India and the US were sought by the Union government to persuade the Nationalist government to withdraw from the Shan States and Myanmar territory.[56]

The Indian prime minister, Mr. Jawaharlal Nehru, was very cooperative. He assured the Myanmar government of help in every possible way. US help was sought through the American ambassador, Mr. Willian J. Sebald. Mr. Sebald made a very realistic approach to the Kuomintang issue and reported to the State Department to be more flexible and sympathetic or otherwise American prestige in Southeast Asia could be affected. But the State Department did not seem to be much impressed by his report.[57]

The Union government never received concrete assurance from the United States of support to end the Kuomintang involvement in Myanmar. Mr. Sebald's attempt to have the State Department understand the real situation of the Kuomintang in Myanmar was known and appreciated by the government and the Myanmar people. Mr. Sebald earned great respect in Myanmar for his efforts, as did Ambassador Chester Bowles in India.

Myanmar prime minister U Nu met Indian prime minister Mr. Nehru in March 1953 and discussed the means of solving the Kuomintang problem. They realized the unwillingness of the American Republican administration to put pressure on the Kuomintang to withdraw from Myanmar. American policy on the Chinese Communists was very rigid and very pro-Nationalist. The Union government refrained from putting direct questions to the American government on Kuomintang affairs for fear of severing their relationship with the United States. The Myanmar government realized the importance of United States' friendship and American aid.[58] Since 1950 Myanmar had received $31 million from the United States, much of this for the Pyidawtha Welfare Scheme, which was initiated on August 4, 1952.[59] However, this aid, which should have been entirely for the welfare scheme, had been partially diverted to defense because of the increased activities of the Kuomintang. To show its displeasure at the American policy, the Union government terminated US aid to Myanmar. In a note delivered to the American ambassador to Myanmar, the Union foreign minister, Sao Hkun Hkio, stated:

> I am to request under Article V of the Economic Cooperation Agreement, between our two Governments, that the Government of the United States will accept notice that we do not want the aid programme to continue beyond June 30, 1953.
>
> The Government of the Union of Burma, however, wish to put on record their appreciation and gratitude for the materials and service received under the Economic Cooperation Agreement which are of great help to them in implementing their rehabilitation programme.[60]

Economic aid was terminated not because of failure or success, but purely for political reasons. The cancellation hindered the development of the Pyidawtha Welfare Scheme and postponed other economic projects. The government and most of the people, except the opposition party, were unhappy about the termination of aid, which was essential for national economic development. *The Nation* commented on the feeling of the people:

> Quite apart from the pros and cons and the motives and reasons for the decision, most people feel a sense of regret that there is to be no aid, principally because Burma needs foreign aid so badly, and it seems inevitable now that all the really good schemes for the Welfare State will be held up or handicapped because of a lacking of foreign financial and technical assistance.[61]

The opposition party was quite satisfied with the ending of US aid and it boasted, "American aid has gone forever, because we wished it gone."[62] On the international aspect, the termination of American aid to Myanmar meant an ideological victory for the Communist bloc, especially Red China, which welcomed the deterioration of American relationships with any nation in Southeast Asia. The vacuum of economic aid was soon to be filled by the socialist bloc.

The United States did not favorably respond to the diplomatic efforts made by the Myanmar government, which was left with no choice but to bring the Kuomintang problem to the United Nations. The decision was hard for the Union government, for its neutral foreign policy could be affected.[63] Prime Minister U Nu reported to the parliament on March 2, 1953, about the presentation of the Kuomintang problem to the United Nations. He stated:

> We have requested the United States Government . . . to cause the withdrawal of these unwanted forces from our territory . . . the Kuomintang aggressors, far from abandoning . . . are now increasing their nefarious deeds, and we . . . take the matter up to the UNO in spite of the possible consequence . . . and greater complication.[64]

FIGURE 14.4. Mr. James Barrington, U Myint Thein, Mr. Henry Cabot Lodge, and Mr. V. K. Krishna Menon.

Referring to Article 2, paragraphs 2 and 3 of the United Nations Charter, the Union government requested the UN General Assembly to include on the UN agenda its case, entitled "Complaint by the Union of Myanmar Regarding Aggression Against Her by the Government of Formosa."

When the complaint was voted to be included on the agenda, the title was changed to "Complaint by the Union of Myanmar Regarding Aggression Against Her by the Government of the Republic of China."[65]

Dr. Tingfu F. Tsiang, the representative of the Republic of China, rejected the Myanmar complaint, saying," . . . the idea of aggression against Myanmar has never entered the minds of the Chinese government."[66] He also denied that the Kuomintang forces were part of the Army of the Republic of China. On this, the Indian newspaper *Amrita Bazar Patrika* commented:

> How could one believe that over a period of three years the [Nationalist] authorities had no control over their nationals on whom they depended for recovery of the mainland? Moreover, it was unbelievable that any general of the Nationalist army should engage himself in private adventure in other countries without the approval of his government.[67]

The complaint received unanimous support from the Asian-Africa bloc. The Indian delegation leader, Mr. Menon, in supporting the Myanmar case, said:

> There were facts that established the link between the army (KMT) and Formosa . . . the danger was the more serious in that troops had not only invaded Burma but were supporting rebellion stirred up against the legal authorities.[68]

Mr. Bokhari, the Pakistani delegate, and Mr. Paler, the Indonesian delegate, spoke in favor of the Myanmar case and condemned the encroachment of the Kuomintang on Myanmar territory. All representatives from the Middle East gave their approval to the Myanmar complaint. Sir Gladwyn Jebb, the British delegate to the United Nations, remarked:

> The United States had still to give its own view on a case that impinges so clearly on its relations with the Nationalist Chinese regime. . . . Over the past years they had changed from an ill-equipped body of 1,700 men to a force of 12,000 relatively well armed and equipped, and the conclusion could not be escaped that these new weapons and supplies had to come from Formosa.[69]

The United States did not try to defend the action of Nationalist China in the Kuomintang affair. Henry Cabot Lodge, the American delegate, finally stated:

> The US considered as fully justified the Burmese Government's desire to be rid of the Chinese troops. It was a case of a challenge to the national sovereignty of the Union of Burma.[70]

The complaint of the Union of Myanmar was thoroughly debated in the United Nations General Assembly. But the Myanmar resolution was subjected to many amendments before its final adoption. The Myanmar wording of the resolution was accepted by nations that were not connected with the nationalist government. But to those that had diplomatic and close relations with the Nationalist government, the Myanmar wording seemed too direct and extreme. The first amendment to the draft resolution was made by the Argentine delegate, Mr. Ferrer Vieyra; the second amendment was proposed by the Mexican delegate, Mr. Dela Collina. The delegates of Argentina and Chile made the third amendment. The Lebanese delegate, Mr. Arkoal, also proposed an amendment. After a long and exhaustive debate the Mexican draft resolution was finally approved in the First Committee 58 to 0 with the abstention of the Union of Myanmar and the Republic of China. The adopted resolution reads as follows:

> Having examined the complaint by the delegation of the Union of Burma regarding the presence, hostile activities, and depredation of foreign forces in the territory of the Union of Burma; considering that these facts constitute a violation of the territory and the sovereignty of the Union of Burma;
>
> Affirming that any assistance given to these forces which enable them to remain in the territory of the Union of Burma or to continue their hostile acts against a member state is contrary to the Charter of the United Nations;
>
> Considering that the refusal of these forces to submit to disarmament or internment is contrary to international law and usage;
>
> 1. Deplores this situation and condemns the presence of these forces in Burma and their hostile acts against that country;
> 2. Deplores that the foreign forces must be disarmed and either agree to internment or leave the Union of Burma forthwith;
> 3. Requests all states to respect the territorial integrity and political independence of the Union of Burma in accordance with the principles of the Charter;
> 4. Recommends that the negotiations now in progress through the good offices of certain member states should be pursued, in order to put an end to this serious situation by means of the immediate disarmament and withdrawal of the said forces from the territory of the Union of Burma or by means of their disarmament and internment;
> 5. Urges all states:
>   (a) to afford the government of the Union of Burma on its request all the assistance in their power to facilitate by peaceful means the evacuation of these forces from Burma; and

(b) to refrain from furnishing any assistance to these forces which may enable them to remain in the territory of the Union of Burma or to continue their hostile acts against that country;

6. Invites the government of the Union of Burma to report on the situation to the General Assembly at its eighth regular session;[71]

The adopted resolution was presented to the General Assembly for recommendation, and Myanmar was asked to declare its stand on the resolution. The Union delegate, U Myint Thein, voted for the resolution with the following remarks:

> The draft resolution fell short of what we considered to be appropriate and justified . . . my government . . . cannot help but be touched by the obviously sincere and sympathetic attitude taken by the member states to this delicate issue . . . hence, the Burmese government . . . has instructed the Burma delegation to identify itself with the draft resolution now before the General Assembly and to vote for it.[72]

All members of the General Assembly approved the resolution on April 23, 1953, except Nationalist China, which abstained.

The resolution was followed by the establishment, at the initiation of the United States government, of a Joint Committee on the Evacuation of Foreign Troops from Myanmar. The committee consisted of representatives of the United States, Myanmar, Formosa, and Thailand. The US representative was to be the chairman of the committee. Bangkok was chosen as the base of the committee. The first of its meetings was held on May 22, 1953. Agreement was reached at the meeting to evacuate the foreign troops from Myanmar as soon as possible. The first evacuees were old and infirm Chinese soldiers and young lads and the weapons that they laid down were obsolete and unserviceable. This evacuation went on for many months. Myanmar left the joint committee in a fit of frustration. The committee went on for some more months and at the Ninth Regular Session of the UN General Assembly, it was reported that fifty-five hundred foreign troops and one thousand dependents had been evacuated from Myanmar.[73] But it was still far from over. The Kuomintang remnants still roamed about the jungle of the Shan States, forcing the Union government to mount a major operation against them. The Thai government sealed off its borders and disarmed those who slipped through. Finally it was estimated that three thousand Kuomintang troops were still left in the wild region of the Shan States engaged mostly in the drug trade and a variety of other smuggling businesses.

The problem was brought under control with the help of the United Nations, but it had heavily taxed the resources of the newly born independent nation of Myanmar.

CONCLUSION

The incursion of the Kuomintang, the occasional intrusion of the Chinese Communists, sporadic fighting between the two forces, and the introduction of military rule into the Shan States brought in a long queue of bitter consequences, causing great suffering and misery to the Shan and other ethnic people living along the Myanmar-China border of the northeastern areas. Hundreds and hundreds of acres of rice fields were abandoned, plantations of various fruits and crops were untended, villages and small towns were deserted, monasteries, temples, and shrines were destroyed and burned, properties were looted, fowls were stolen, pigs were killed, cattle and buffaloes were taken away without payment. Shan and other ethnic people were forced to move to new settlements, or they fled to other parts of the country or to Laos or Thailand, and communication and transportation channels were cut off. Only military vehicles moved about, but their movement was limited by the inaccessible terrain. Ass, mule, and horse caravans were used as means of transportation. Girls and women were raped and had to accept forced marriages, boys and men were conscripted either as soldiers or porters. Many were wounded and some were killed in the midst of the battles, and some disappeared and up to now nobody knows where they are. Education was disrupted and students had to drop out. Everywhere military barracks were full of men in uniform; they were either Kuomintang or Union soldiers, or Chinese Communists or other insurgent groups. For two or three years this part of the country was heavily dominated by armed forces, national and foreign. The native people who could not or dared not adjust themselves to the new atmosphere or environment had a hard time, and struggled to survive. The peace and tranquility which once prevailed in this area was greatly disturbed by the deadly sound of gunfire, which chilled everyone and frightened birds and animals away from the area.

The Kuomintang and the Chinese Communists accelerated their propaganda machines and bombarded each other with accusations. Worst of all was the effort that tried to split up the ethnic nationalities into various factions and to classify them as either pro- or anti-Communist or Nationalist. All sorts of accusations were also made against the Union government. Seeds of dissension and sedition were sown between the Shan chiefs and the Union army and the Union government by the Chinese Nationalists, destroying the spirit of the Pang Long Conference. The propaganda pamphlets issued by the Kuomintang propagandists contained the following elements:

(a) Based on the principle of annihilation of the public enemy, any territory may be used as a base for anti-Communist operations just as the United States is making use of other countries as its base.

(b) Our battalion is situated between the Myanmar army and the bandits (Chinese Communists). We are being attacked from the South as well as from the North. So militarily we shall resist the Communist bandits in the North. Politically we shall join hands with all political parties of Myanmar especially with the government of Kawthulay and the two parties of Karen and Mon to enhance their power in recognizing their government to achieve the aim and objective of anti-Communism.

(c) National independence shall be the slogan to call the people together so that the Myanmar government will become helpless and surrender without fighting.

(d) Myanmar who are corrupt and accept bribes control the Myanmar government. They oppress the other nationalities.

(e) Assist the hill tribes in striving for independence and in choosing their leaders.

(f) The Myanmar government is doing away with the sawbwa so we must support the Sawbwa of Mong Pan and other states to become independent.

(g) Request moral and material assistance from the overseas Chinese and stir up public opinion against the government.

(h) To be clear about the movement of the enemy, intelligence should be obtained regarding the movement of the Myanmar forces from Lashio to Namkham. At all important points along this route, spies should be posted.

(i) Inspect secretly the topography of the region and determine the holding points along the route. Also find out the places for ambush and plan lines of communication and put up defense work.

(j) The Chinese Communist bandits set up the Myanmar army to drive away the Chinese Nationalist army in the hope of getting Naw Seng and his followers to enter Myanmar and to occupy the North so as to join hands with the Chinese Communists.

(k) The discipline of the Myanmar army is very low; they rape and rob especially our Chinese and other races.

(l) Support the movement of national independence. This shall be the duty of our forces.

(m) Stir up the local people to seize arms and ammunition from the Myanmar (Bamar) soldiers for use in their own defense.

(n) Organize guerrilla troops to disturb the Myanmar army and also concentrate on lightning strikes.

(o) Encourage and support the tribes in the north of Myanmar in their struggle for independence and to establish provincial government.[74]

Many were misled by such propaganda, which brought suspicion, hatred, and noncooperation, and created mistaken racial attitudes, and mistaken views on the concepts of chauvinism and Myanmarization. Many ethnic and national leaders were caught squarely in the propaganda and seemed to lose the spirit of reconciliation, which sensible citizens considered the only solution for the future of the Union of Myanmar. The Chinese Nationalists even ground on their propaganda machine to split up the government into political factions with the pro-Left faction gaining more and more influence on the country and pushing the country to become an arena for an ideological contest between Communism (socialism), militarism, and feudalism. The outdated feudal ideology that dominated the Shan States for centuries lost its grip and finally faded away like a summer mist, leaving Communism, socialism, and militarism as the remaining contestants on the political stage of Myanmar.

The Chinese Communists, not to be outdone by the Nationalists, also revved up their propaganda engine to organize the frontier people and the Myanmars to join their side and to divide them into political factions as did the Nationalists. But the Chinese Communist propagandists did not leave much of a choice for the people, a choice of being pro- or anti-Communist. If they chose the latter, they were bound to be in trouble. The political situation of the country for various reasons went from bad to worse, and later on became so chaotic that the Union armed forces were left with no choice but to take over the country. The politicians were not only unable to stave off the threatening dangers but were split among themselves to the point of irreconcilability. Finally, both the underground and above-ground leftists looked to the Eastern Communist bloc for moral and material support, with the military group seeming to do the same.

The country entered into a new phase of political development with the elimination of feudalism and the emergence of socialist militarism. It brought Myanmar-American relations to an end and the American aid to a stop. The Kuomintang incursion into northeastern Myanmar from 1950 to 1953 was a short period, but it created a series of bad consequences. It changed not only the political face of Shanland but the whole of Myanmar, pushing it into the orbit of the Eastern power bloc and the adoption of a more active neutralism in its relationships with other powers of the world.

The United States had every means to insist on the withdrawal of the Kuomintang troops from the Union of Myanmar. Had such means been used, the Kuomintang issue would not have been brought to the United Nations and the prestige of the United States as well as of Nationalist China would have remained internationally safe and sound. To allow the question to come up before the United Nations incalculably hurt the position of these two nations. As *The Economist* stated: "Their complaint to the United Nations Organization is really a jab at the Americans; it undermines American prestige in Southeast Asia; it calls to question Washington's whole policy . . . for Southeast Asia."[75] If the issue had been solved by the intervention of the United States, as requested by the Union government, much trouble would have been avoided. Relations between the two countries would have improved, and the prestige of the United States in Myanmar would have skyrocketed. Moreover, the economic and political situation of the Union of Myanmar would have been greatly different from what it is today.

15

The Shan State Council

To keep up with changing political conditions after the Pang Long Conference, a new political institution was introduced in Shan State on April 21, 1947. It was called the Shan State Council. The council was comprised of sixty-six members, thirty-three *saohpa* and thirty-three popularly nominated representatives. For immediate purposes, the representatives of the people were nominated on an intellectual basis (that is, chosen by government officials and the upper class), but were later elected on a population basis. The Shan State Council was invested with the powers of legislation, executive, and finance. It was also agreed that an executive committee of eight members, four from the *saohpa* and four from people's representatives, would be selected from the council to be in charge of it and all departments in the Shan States. Under the council was the government of the Shan State, which would carry out all resolutions passed by the council.

Regarding the Shan State Council and the government of Shan State, the Union Constitution provided for them in chapter 9. According to section 154 (1) of the Union Constitution, the Shan State Council was to be composed of all the members of parliament representing Shan State. The *saohpa* who were the members of the council could not become members of the Chamber of Deputies in parliament. But they could become members of the Chamber of Nationalities by right and had to choose among themselves to occupy the seats in the chamber. Those members who failed to get seats in parliament could not become members of the Shan State Council. Any law on any matter the council was not competent to legislate must be recommended and referred to parliament. Moreover, any bill passed by the Shan State Council must be presented to the president for approval and signature. After that the bill was again referred to the Supreme Court for final acceptance. The president could also refer any bill presented to him to the Supreme Court for interpretation as to whether or not it went against the Constitution. The court with its three judges considered the case or matter or bill and gave its decision. If found to be unconstitutional, the bill was returned to the Shan State Council for amendment. If the amendment was rejected the president could decline to sign it. After the pronouncement of the Supreme Court in favor of the bill it was signed by the president and promulgated as an Act. According to section 158 (5) of the Union Constitution, the president could also sign the bill without referring it to the Supreme Court. Provisions of the bill would not be called into question because this was beyond the competence of the State Council. The Act signed by the president was kept in the office of the minister of Shan State. The head of Shan State was empowered to summon and prorogue the State Council as he thought appropriate.[1]

The main aim of the Shan State Council was to lead the Shan State government. The government was headed by a minister appointed by the president on the nomination of the prime minister in consultation with the Shan State Council. He must also be a member of parliament representing Shan State. He was the head of Shan State according to section 160 of the Union Constitution. He had executive power, which he could exercise through officers subordinate to him. He was the sole authority in charge of the administration of Shan State. He could recruit state officers, transfer, post, and discipline them on matters related to public welfare and security without prejudice and with full generosity. The executive authority of the state could be extended to matters over which the State Council had power to make laws under the Union Constitution. But all such matters and the decision of the council were binding on the head of state. All matters related to Shan State, carried out by the head of state, were thoroughly considered and discussed by the council. To assist the head of state in his duties and functions, a cabinet of state ministers was elected by the council at its first meeting after the general election.

The head of state had to prepare an annual report on matters related to Shan State. He made requests, recommendations for the consideration of the council on such measures as he thought fit for the promotion of public welfare. The head of state also prepared an annual budget of the receipts and of the expenditure of the state and presented it to the State Council with recommendations for consideration. If conditions demanded a contribution from the Union, the contribution was made with the approval of parliament and included in the State budget and its terms observed and the budget incorporated in the Union budget. The law determined all matters related to the Constitution of the state, including the powers and duties of the head of state, of the State Council, and of the cabinet of state ministers and their relations to each other and to the Union government.

At its first meeting the Shan State Council found it hard to elect its head of state. The first candidate earmarked by the council was Sao Sam Htun, the *saohpalong* of Mong Pawn, who had been recognized as an architect in the formation of the Shan State Council, in the creation of the Union, and in the drafting of the Union Constitution. Unfortunately he was assassinated on July 19, 1947, together with Bogyoke Aung San and his comrades. The contestants for this supreme post were Sao Hkun Hkio of Mong Mit and U Htun Myint of Lang Hkay. U Htun Myint belonged to the People's Representatives group led by the Shan State People's Freedom League. Under section 160 of the Union Constitution, U Htun Myint was nominated by the prime minister, in consultation with the Shan State Council, as candidate for head of Shan State.

The candidates were put to a vote in the Shan State Council, and U Htun Myint won by eleven to ten votes. He was the first commoner to become the head of the Shan State to the dislike of the *saohpa*, whose prestige was greatly affected by the defeat of their candidate, Sao Hkun Hkio, of Mong Mit. They put great pressure on the prime minister, U Nu, for a change. At first U Nu refused, but later he compromised by appointing U Htun Myint minister of mines and industry and Sao Hkun Hkio was elected head of Shan State by a vote of thirteen to eleven, thus solving the problem.

At its first meeting in February 1948 the Shan State Council proposed forming an Enquiry Committee to deal with the following resolutions:

1. The centralization of Shan State revenue
2. The centralization of police for the stability and security of the whole of Shan State
3. The abolition of gambling for the good of the whole of Shan State
4. The transfer of state officials from one state to another in Shan State
5. The election of the district officers and local and regional officers, or *ne-baing*, through adult suffrage

The democratic process came into play in the formation in the Shan State Council. A power struggle between the two groups in the State Council took place. The first group was led by the *saohpa* and those who supported them; the second group, by the Shan State People's Freedom League and those who supported them. The *saohpa* group objected to the resolution and the formation of the Enquiry Committee. It organized a meeting at Mong Kung, and passed new resolutions which included the following points:

1. Members of the Enquiry Committee should be chosen through an election.
2. The committee should visit every state, not only the notified areas.
3. The duration of the committee should be extended to three years to find out the real views of the people of Shan State.
4. The actions of the committee should be announced to the witnesses one month before the enquiry is made.[2]

The administrative and financial powers of the *saohpa* during the time of the Federated Shan States were controlled by residents appointed by the governor of Myanmar, a decision that didn't sit well with the *saohpa*. Moreover, the 1935 Myanmar Act did not give much administrative power to the *saohpa*. Taking advantage of the outbreak of the Second World War and the withdrawal of the British from Shan State, the *saohpa* began to wield more power than before. When the British reoccupied Shan State, the Shan *saohpa* had already appointed their own district, regional, and local officers, like *myosa*, *ngwehkunmu*, *ne-baing* or *hein* (provinical officer), *ahmatchoke* (chief minister of the state), *akun ahmat* (revenue officer), *taya ahmat* (judical officer), *pu hmong*, *pu kang*, *pu mong* (general petite officer), and *pu kye* (headman).

Taxes and revenue were collected in the respective states and about 10 to 20 percent of the money was used for salaries and about 75 percent for personal purposes, causing dissatifaction among the public. The district officers who collected taxes and revenue were paid 10 percent of the collection. Judicial powers were also handled by the *saohpa* ranging from second-class magistrates to session judges.

The division of powers regarding administration and finance was not well defined as yet between the *saohpa* and the Shan State Council. For example, in the matter of finance, revenue, and budget, two systems coexisted. One was controlled by the Shan State central government and the other by the respective *saohpa*. The *saohpa* had to prepare their own state budget annually, which was again subject to the approval of the assistant resident.

To maintain law and order in their states, the *saohpa* had to keep their own police force. Salaries and uniforms were to be provided. But the police could not trespass on any neighboring state without the approval of the ruling chief of state. After independence this system did not fit the times. People began to urge a change to suit the new environment. Reforms must be introduced in all aspects of administration, especially in revenue and taxation. A system of uniformity became a necessity in all aspects. At the begining every state was administered by the *saohpa*, who was required to contribute 25 percent of his revenue to the Shan State government. Most failed; only Keng Tung State could fulfill the obligation. The situation in many parts of Shan State was not peaceful, and insurgency disrupted the collection of revenue. The cost of administration could not be met, owing to many factors and insufficiency of the revenue. In some states a large part of the revenue was depleted through mismanagement. Therefore many members of the Shan State Council felt the need for centralization and uniformity of the system in the collection of taxes and revenue. It became of prime importance for Shan State.

> The next important reform to be introduced in the Shan State was the uniformity of laws for the whole of the state. In this regard section 92 (2) of the Union Constitution precribed: Each State Council shall have power exclusively to make laws for the State or any part thereof with respect to any of the matters enumerated in List ii of the said schedule (hereinafter called "the State Legislative List").[3]

Without uniformity of laws that could be applied to the whole country, it would be very difficult to deal with criminal cases. A criminal could take refuge in another or a neighboring state. Sometimes permission had to be sought from the state concerned if the police had to pursue a criminal suspect. In such cases, a delay could take place, which would give the criminal a good chance to escape.

Democratization in selecting or electing district or local officers was another important reform to be introduced in Shan State. Before the Second World War such officers were directly appointed by the feudal chief of the state and they were mostly hereditary. The new reform required these officers to stand for election through adult suffrage and to familiarize the people with the democratic system. The new system helped to choose people of prominent ability for administrative posts. Some of the feudal chiefs showed their displeasure with the new system, but the people welcomed the change.

Judicial function was another important matter for the Shan State. Section 133 of the Union Constitution read:

> Justice throughout the Union shall be administered in courts established by this Constitution or by law and by judges appointed in accordance therewith.[4]

This section was applied to Shan State and judicial courts established to carry out proper judicial functions in Shan State. In this matter the judicial powers of the *saohpa* had to be clearly defined, candidates fit for judicial posts recruited, and the legal system equally applied throughout the Union for the benefit of the people. The administrative power of the officer or *saohpa* also properly defined the extent of the injudicial powers. Courts with qualified judges had to be established throughout Shan State to implement the judicial system in which everybody could stand equally before the law without prejudice to race, rank, color, and sex.

The fourth point of reform was to have a uniform system of transfer for all officers in Shan State. Before 1947, before the emergence of the State Council, all state officers were appointed by the *saohpa*. These officers could not be transferred from their first appointment. For lack of challenging cases or problems, such officers were likely to commit bribery and corruption. New knowledge and new experiences in administration would be accumulated as officers moved from one place to another and into new social and cultural environments. They would improve their ability to judge judicial affairs and their dealing with peoples. Justice would prevail through government officers because justice went along with them. The spread of justice and the uniformity of the administrative system would go along with officers transferred from one state to another throughout the Union.

The abolition of gambling was the most important social factor in Shan State. The state had been badly infected with the disease for many centuries and it had become a social ill, destroying the Shan moral character. Gambling was a major cause of the corruption of state officers. It destroyed the integrity of good people. People were trapped into moral corruption because of gambling. Gambling lured young people into prison. Farmers lost their plantations and rice fields because of gambling. Gambling invited stealing, looting, cheating, lying, and even killing. It led to corruption, loss of money, loss of moral character, and loss of property. It also caused the separation of wife and husband, parents and children, and disintegration of families and even societies. The abolition and reduction of gambling became a necessity. Gambling could hinder the economic and social developments needed by the Shan people. It was a stumbling block to the educational development of children, a social poison for youths. Many people ran into debt because of gambling. It caused great misery to the people by damaging their health. In the old days gambling was always a part of every festival, either religious or social. Like opium smokers whose nerves are paralyzed, people were hynotized by gambling and lost their strength for economic or social activities. They all drowned in a sea of gambling. People called for reform and for gambling to be eradicated from the soil of Shanland.

The reforms introduced by the Shan State Council became a political question and the Shan people became divided into two camps—those who supported reforms and those who objected. Demonstrations were staged, slogans were shouted. The level of political knowledge of the Shan people was quite low at that time. They had been under feudal rule for so long that their knowledge of politics did not go beyond the feudal boundaries. Those who were politically more enlightened and conscious wanted quick reform to catch up with the changing times. There were also those who were conservative and whose political views were not acute enough to accept the change toward modern development.

A Southern Shan State resident from Taunggyi named U Htun Aung made the following remark on June 15, 1948:

> From the administrative point of view the centralisation of the Shan State Government is most essential for the smooth and efficient running of the administrative machinery and for the unification of the whole of Shan State, but as such a change will directly affect the position of the Saohpas there may be strong reactions from them and their followers against such a move unless the Saohpas themselves come to the final agreement with full understanding and consent to the proposal. In my opinion the Saohpas and the Shan State people should be given more time to fully grasp the significance of such a proposed change of the Constitution and also to enable them to think out for themselves the advantages or otherwise contemplated by the proposal.[5]

After the Second World War, anticolonial activities began to spread all over Southeast Asia. In Myanmar a new political ideology based on Marxist socialism also began to take root everywhere, including in Shan State. Feudalism, which had existed in eastern Myanmar in Shan State, could not survive in isolation. The wind of Marxist socialism blew too hard for the feudal institution to withstand. The people of Shan State were divided into two camps. One was antifeudalist and the other one was profeudalist. The profeudalist force consisted of the *saohpa* and their followers, mostly peasants. The antifeudalist group was comprised of intellectuals, businessmen, and the middle class. The profeudalist *saohpa* camp refused to see the changing conditions that were shaping the destiny of the future world. They were very reluctant to accept the program of reforms that might affect their feudal institution. On the other hand, the antifeudal camp wanted a quick change to meet the requirements of modern conditions. They felt that feudalism must go—and quickly. The two views were irreconcilable. The die was cast and the struggle between the two forces began. The Shan State government, which was newly established, was given the role of substituting for the feudal administration, which was still controlled by the feudal chiefs. The old civil servants of the colonial days could not adjust to the new environment that had developed in Shan State. The newly appointed civil servants of the Shan State were torn between feudal administration and Shan State government. Most of the civil servants of both groups foresaw the trouble that might befall the Shan State in the near future unless the situation was handled with great care. Gambling had become a special tool that the antifeudal group made good use of to knock off the feudal system. Because of gambling the Shan people suffered much. Gambling had been part of the feudal system since its existence. Another target of criticism against feudalism was the festivals, or *pwe*, that took place in all parts of Shan State. Gambling and *pwe* became twin points of criticism against the profeudal group. The antifeudal group saw these as social evils that should immediately be eradicated from the Shan State. The feudal chiefs refused to yield to the demand, because gambling and *pwe* were their sources of revenue. Political tension increased, and the stability and unity of the people were greatly affected, because they had no common ground on which to unite for the higher objective of development. Most of the statesmen of the time favored the introduction of a quick program of centralized administration to solve the problem. An assessment made by U Htun Aung, a veteran administrator, is worth considering.

He suggested gradual change, giving the *saohpa* enough time to think about adaptation, and the introduction of reforms to meet the needs of the times. Regarding gambling and *pwe*, U Htun Aung gave a balanced view, saying they were traditional practices. The *pwe*, he said, was important for the Shan people, because it served not only as a convenient rendezvous for them but also as recreation. It served as an occasion for social intercourse and trading as well as for exchange of information. Gambling, he said, was an evil thing for the Shan people. But it was a source of revenue for the feudal society, which had no modern industries and business, and did not increase crime in the Shan State. He cautioned that the amalgamation of states was a very delicate problem that should be handled with skill and patience, since nothing short of rebellion could be expected. He recommended a five-year timetable that would settle the state's problems.[6] The suggestions were sound and good but beyond the reach of the statesmen of that time.

Independence was attained and the government of the Shan States was formed in Yangon. Sao Hkun Hkio of Mong Mit became the head of the Shan State and U Ba Ni of the same state became his secretary.

A mountain of problems was waiting to be solved by the new government. The first was how to replace the British style of administration with a native one. New boundaries of the Shan State with the Kachin and Kayah States and with Mandalay Division would have to be redemarcated. Responsible officers of the pre-independence period who handled the combined departmental affairs of the Kachin, Shan, and Kayah states would have to be readjusted and reallocated to fit in with the new setup. To solve these complicated problems a conference between ministers and secretaries of the Shan, Kachin, and Kayah states was convened at Taunggyi on July 3, 1948.[7] Under the agreement reached at the conference, the Shan State government retained the following posts:

1. Chief medical officer
2. Chief veterinary officer
3. Chief mechanical transport officer
4. Liaison officer
5. Legal adviser or advocate
6. Principal education officer
7. Principal forest officer
8. Chief works officer was also retained but terminated on September 30, 1948

Concerning the management of the State Finance and Revenue Department, additional posts were created and more officers were appointed. It was also agreed that all proposals involving references to the Finance and Revenue Ministry of Myanmar would be transmitted through the Ministry of Shan State.[8]

On local administration, the *saohpa* still retained most of their administrative power. They were still reluctant to give up their traditional privileges and rights. In some places they and their subordinate officers committed malpractices and the head of the Shan States had to order them to keep an Advisory Council to assist in their local administration. But many of them refused. Another strict order was issued on July 24, 1948, by Sao Hkun Hkio, the head of Shan State, directing the *saohpa* to establish an Advisory Council without fail to avoid further mismanagement in their administrative affairs.[9] Assistant residents were appointed by the Shan State government to look into the state's affairs run by the feudal chiefs. The *saohpa* also claimed the right to be consulted on the appointment of assistant residents and other government officers. They even wanted them to be classified as selection grade officers in the government. Any government officer who passed through their state should call upon them and consult them on handling local administrative affairs concerning their states.

Another problem that came to the notice of the Shan State government was the creation of a Kachin substate in Tawng Peng State. It was finally decided to settle the problem in Yangon between the Kachin leaders and the head of Shan State assisted by the *saohpa* of Tawng Peng and Hsen Wi.

Mostly the *saohpa* were unable to adjust themselves to the administrative policy laid down by the Shan State government. They stuck to their traditional rights to which they had been accustomed for centuries. The government did not have much choice but to carry out the administrative centralization for all of the Shan States.

It passed a series of Acts to enforce centralization. The first Act, passed in 1948, fixed the monthly salaries of the chairman at K. 1,250, the vice chairman at K. 450, and the ministers of the Shan State Council at K. 1,100. Moreover, all of them were forbidden to engage in trade and business of any kind that might affect their prestige and integrity.[10]

An Act was also passed confirming the power of the Shan State government to make any law in the interim period before the election. Another Act was passed dealing with the members of the council and the Shan State minister, and the Union Constitution section 162 (1), (2), (3), clarified and confined the power of the Shan State Council.[11]

The Act also confirmed the right of the State Council members to draw their daily and traveling allowances as members of parliament and whenever assigned state duties.

On January 13, 1949, a special conference was convened in Mong Nai and important resolutions were passed requesting all *saohpa* and residents to observe and implement them. The resolutions included handing back the civil stations of Loi Lem and Loi Mwe to their owners, Lai Hka and Keng Tung states. The second resolution agreed to open a Chinese consulate in Lashio. The third resolution dealt with the boundary question with China. The Myanmar-China boundary in the region of Wa State, as agreed upon in 1941 by the Chinese government (Nationalist) and his Majesty's government, was to be demarcated in the next opening session with the cooperation of the Chinese government. Another resolution dealt with frontier security and considered the following towns strategic and important: Lashio (with airport), Nam Hkam, Kyu Kok, Hsen Wi, Mong Yu, Kun Long, Muse, Tang Yan, Keng Tung, Mong Phyak, and Tacheleik (as land stations). Another resolution was passed concerning talks with the Chinese Embassy in Yangon on the regulation of the entry of seasonal laborers, caravan traders, and petty traders. A plan to build an airstrip in Keng Tung by the Union government at the cost of K. 347,000 was also agreed to. A plan to open new telecommunication offices at Aung Ban, Kalaw, Taunggyi, Hsi Paw, Kyaukme, Lashio, Nam Hkam, and other isolated areas was also agreed to. The conference also put on its agenda the creation of a separate cadre for the forest service and the allocation of the forest royalty for Shan State. The conference also considered the renewal of the lease held by the Myanmar Corporation Limited in Nam Tu, which was going to expire on December 13, 1949. The conference passed a resolution requesting the War Office to increase Union military police posts in Shan State to reinforce security along the frontier. The final resolution concerned the issue of two Shan companies to be absorbed into the Shan battalion with sanction from the president. It was also agreed to absorb that Shan battalion into the Union armed forces.

There were other Acts that should be extended and applied to Shan State. They were:

1. Myanmar Army Act
2. Myanmar Navy Act of 1947
3. Myanmar Volunteer Air Force Act of 1941
4. Myanmar Air Force Act of 1947
5. Myanmar Industries Act
6. Myanmar Press Registration Act
7. Myanmar Press Emergency Power Act
8. Buddhist Women's Special Marriage and Succession Act
9. Sea Custom Act
10. Land Custom Act
11. Public Utilities Protection Act of 1947
12. Essential Supplies and Services Act of 1947
13. Control of Export and Import Act of 1947

14. Public Property Protection Act of 1947
15. Saving Certificate Act
16. Penal Code Act of 1947
17. Women's Compensation Act of 1923
18. Trade Union Act of 1924
19. Trade Dispute Act
20. Mines Act of 1924
21. Cooperative Society Act

Finally the right to collect land customs was vested in the residents of Shan State.[12]

After the Pang Long Conference, political awakening rapidly took place, and the role of feudal chiefs diminished. But they made their last struggle. Most of the antifeudal forces began to ally themselves with the Shan State People's Freedom League. The struggle between profeudalists and antifeudalists took a bitter turn. The profeudal group staged demonstrations in some areas where the Enquiry Committee toured. But the world political situation would not permit feudalism to survive. New forces of antifeudalism equipped with the new ideology of socialism began to gather more and dynamic forces from other parts of Shan State and Myanmar proper. A historic change was waiting at the doorstep of Shan State, but the last hardship would have to be overcome for the new era to set in.

At this juncture the insurgency problem crept in and peace was greatly disturbed in Shan State. Soon after independence, the Union of Myanmar witnessed the appearance of the Shan State's enemies like the Red Flag Communists led by Thakin Soe, the Mujahid, the White Flag Communists led by the Thakin Than Htun, who had about twenty-five thousand followers at that time, and the People's Volunteer Organization (PVO). They were all antigovernment forces who believed in achieving power through armed struggle. The most serious threat to the government came from the Karen (Kayin) National Defense Organization (KNDO). In a way the newly formed Myanmar government was surrounded by enemies. The situation in Myanmar became precarious, communication to parts of Myanmar was cut off, and Yangon, the capital of the country, was in a very critical position. The unstable situation in Myanmar affected the Shan State administration too. Communication by rail and road between Myanmar and the Shan State was cut off. The capital of Shan State was very insecure. Remnants of the KNDO and PVO roamed Southern Shan State and attacked police stations and outposts.

Lashio, the Northern Shan State capital, was briefly occupied by the PVO on March 16, 1949,[13] and the resident of Northern Shan State, Sao Boonwat, was taken prisoner. The treasury was looted and prisoners and political detainers were freed. At that time, the head of Shan State, Sao Hkun Hkio, was in Lashio but he did not come to the notice of the PVO.[14] Sao Hom Hpa, the *saohpalong* of Hsen Wi, with his volunteer levies came down to recapture Lashio from the rebels' hands. Sao Hom Hpa later became special commissioner of Northern Shan State. In those states occupied by the rebels the administration ceased to function. During this multicolored insurgency the *saohpa*, the people, and the Shan government remained loyal to the Union. At that time Prime Minister U Nu faced appalling difficulties and had to cut the salaries of government servants. The civil servants in Yangon and throughout the Union called a strike, but officers in Northern Shan State and in Southern Shan State remained loyal to the Union government and worked hard to enable it to function.

Taunggyi was occupied by the KNDO on August 13, 1949. The Shan State government was caught unprepared and no effective resistance could be made by the Union military police force. Clearly there was no coordination between the *saohpa* and the Shan State government to take joint action against the KNDO. While Taunggyi was under occupation, Sao Kyaw An was the resident but could do nothing except to hide for his safety. The KNDO insurgents were led by Saw Wida, Naw Seng, and S. Thein, and the treasury in Taunggyi was looted. Criminals and political detainers were freed from prison. Naw Seng stayed a week in Taunggyi and went up with his troops to Lashio, passing through Loi Lem, Lai Hka, Mong Kung, and then to China. He reached Lashio on August 28, 1949. The Union military police put up no resistance and some of them even joined the KNDO. For some time the KNDO came and went without hindrance. They occupied Taunggyi for over three months and evacuated only on November 23, 1949.[15] The morale of the Shan people was low and the prestige of the Shan State government was greatly affected. The states that were situated on the way to Loi Kaw like Mawk Mai, Mong Pawn, Sam Ka, Nam Hkok, Nawng Mon, Wan Yin, Hsi Seng, and Yawng Hwe were mostly affected by the KNDO insurgents. Highways to Loi Lem, Loi Kaw, and Northern Shan State were rife with robberies and sometimes murders, and motor cars with passengers had to travel in convoys under heavy escort.

Under such political conditions in Shan State, the State Council meeting had to be convened and the government stationed in Yangon. Sao Hkun Hkio called an urgent council meeting to assess the situation in Shan State. The first agenda discussed at the meeting was the budget of Shan State. The insurgents had taken 35 lahks from the state's treasuries, leaving the Shan State budget in clear deficit. The council members also discussed the transfer of the Shan State government back to Taunggyi. To keep the Shan State goverment in Yangon was more expensive; it was too far away from Shan State affairs, which needed to be attended to at close range. The people began to lose confidence in the Shan State government because they had been left at the mercy of the insurgents.

There was also a very heated debate at the council meeting over the purchase of the Ching Tsong Palace in Yangon. U Htun Aye, the then Shan State minister for education and social services, proposed buying the palace. The reasons he gave were that it could be used as a residency for the State Council members as well as for those who worked in the Shan State government who had to leave their home in Shan State. It could also be used as a hotel for traders and merchants of Shan State who came to do their business in Yangon and for students who came to pursue their further studies in Yangon. Moreover, the building could also be used as a meeting place of the Shan State government since the unsettled situation prevented its move to Taunggyi. Council members U Khin Maung Latt and U Htun Myint strongly objected to the proposal and the argument became very heated on both sides. Finally a vote was taken. Six members voted for the purchase and five against it.[16] So the Ching Tsong Palace was bought for K. 150,000, which was allotted for its renovation.

THE MILITARY ADMINISTRATION

Owing to the chaotic situation in Shan State, the Union government, in consultation with the Shan State government and the Kachin State government, introduced a bill for the military administration in Northern Shan State and part of the Kachin Hills on November 23, 1949. The president, in proclaiming the bill, said:

> I, the President of the Union of Burma, in exercise of power vested in me by Section 2, declare that Martial Law shall be enforced in the Kachin Hill Tracts of Northern Hsen Wi and the Kodaung Hill Tracts of Mong Mit State.[17]

The proclamation was followed by another order called Military Administration Proclamation No. 13 of 1949. It said:

> I, *Maha Thiri Thu Dhama*, Lieutenant General Ne Win, Supreme Commander, Union Armed Forces, do hereby give notice to all concerned that, with effect from this date, the said areas, namely the Kachin Hill Tracts of North Hsen Wi State and the Kodaung Hill Tracts of Mong Mit State, shall, until such time as may be hereafter announced, be administered for general, police, and judicial purposes by and under my direction.
>
> I direct that all officers of the Government of the Union discharging general and police administration duties shall act under my direction in all matters within their jurisdictions.
>
> I further direct that all Courts and Tribunals now existing in the area aforesaid shall cease forthwith to exercise the jurisdiction and powers vested in them and that, instead thereof, the following classes of Courts with respective powers as defined below be established:
>
> (a) Superior Military Courts of Criminal Jurisdiction which shall have power to try all offences and to pass any sentence authorized by law; and
>
> (b) Inferior Military Courts of Criminal Jurisdiction which shall have power to try any offences not punishable with death and be competent to pass sentence of imprisonment not exceeding seven years or whipping or fine.[18]
>
> Ne Win,
> Lieutenant General
> Supreme Commander, Union Armed Forces
> Dated Rangoon, the 6th December 1949

To help carry out the military administration, U Hkun Seng, assistant resident of Kut Kai; U Zaw Latt, Shweli Amat, Nam Hkam; and U Kareng Kham, ATM, Kut Kai Amat were appointed judges of inferior Military Courts of Criminal Jurisdiction in the Shweli area of North Hsen Wi State. The situation improved and the government decided to withdraw the military administration on June 1, 1951.[19]

Keng Tung was another area that felt the effects of the KNDO insurgency. Communication between Keng Tung and Taunggyi was also cut off. The Shan State government sent U San Lu, the minister for transport and communication, to Keng Tung to counter the propaganda of the KNDO. He could not go to Keng Tung by road, owing to the disruption of communications and had to go through Thailand. The people were caught in the propaganda of the KNDO, which came through on the Taungoo radio. The government officers lost control over the population. The people also lost confidence in the government, seemed to be in favor of the KNDO, and moved to welcome them. The Chinese bandits took advantage of the unsettled situation and raided some of the villages in the border area. This chaotic situation in Keng Tung was reported by U San Lu to the head of Shan State on September 20, 1949.[20] It became necessary for military administration to be introduced in Keng Tung. Proclamation No. 17 was issued, placing Keng Tung and Tachileik under military administration on August 7, 1950.[21] Judges for superior and inferior courts were also appointed, and Hpaya Kwan and U Win were made judges of superior and inferior courts respectively. Sao Hkun Suk, the personal assistant to the *saohpalong* of Keng Tung, and Sao Ywat Mong, the *ahmatchoke* of Keng Tung, were appointed first-class magistrates for the military administration area. After one year the situation improved and the military administration was withdrawn on August 1, 1951.

It became important that Taunggyi should be rescued from the KNDO rebels. Shan levies were organized from the states of Mong Kung, Kehsi Mansam, Mong Nawng, Mong Shu, Mong Pan, Mong Lun, Mong Nai, and Mawk Mai to reoccupy Taunggyi. The irregular forces called levies were not well armed and the soldiers were conscripted without any training. They were ineffective in fighting against the KNDO insurgents.[22] For all that, Taunggyi was reoccupied, the situation improved, and communication with Yangon resumed. The question arose as to how to disband the levies. What kinds of compensation or gratuity or allowances should be given to those who served and who lost their lives in action against the KNDO?[23] There was no clear announcement from the authorities. The people, especially the Shan youths, were discontented with the way the authorities handled the problem. They sent their complaints to the head of Shan State, who did not have much choice but to plan a program to solve the problem. To divert the attention of the Shan youths and to take measures against any invasion of Taunggyi and Shan State, in the future the head of Shan State proposed to form a Shan battalion for self-defense.[24] Under this program all *saohpa* levies were to be absorbed into the Shan battalion and equipped and organized along the lines of the army to meet the needs of the day. Sao Hkun Hkio sent the following message to U Tin, minister of finance and revenue of the Union government:

> I found it necessary to mobilize the local people in order to combat and repel the insurgents. This mobilization was undertaken after discussion with the Supreme Commander, Lieutenant General Ne Win, who agreed that I should take all the steps possible in the matter. The expenditure on administration and food etc. has hitherto been met by the Shan State government. In order to regulate the position of these state levies, the Permanent Secretary was approached to sanction the raising of the battalion of levies for the Shan State, but in view of the War Office's recent policy to effect the gradual fade-out of irregular units, he found that request incompatible with the declared policy and accordingly could not issue the necessary sanction and suggested that the state levies be classified as civil defence force and should approach the State Board for necessary funds.[25]

On the other hand, the *saohpa* began to see that the old type of administration could not continue. They finally agreed to keep a State Advisory Council in their administration. They had to change to meet the needs of the people or, at least, to take democratic practices into consideration. They also agreed to accept the advice of the people for the future improvement of their administrative machinery. The *saohpa* also realized the need of the people's cooperation in the future, and the *saohpa* of Lai Hka, Mong Kung, urged the people not to cooperate with the KNDO insurgents.

Most of the people in Shan State were uneducated and in danger of falling into the trap of the enemy's propagada. So it became necessary for the Shan State government to publish newspapers in Shan, Pa-O, and Myanmar languages to counter the enemies' propaganda. Two newspapers appeared. One was called *Mai Song Mong Tai* in Shan and *Khit Hme Shan Pyi* in Myanmar language. The first issue came out in Shan on April 2, 1946, sponsored by E. G. N. Kinch, a retired chief education officer, and U Po Hla, deputy inspector of schools. It was later managed by Sao Sai Mong and Resident U Htun Aung and became the propaganda mouthpiece of the Shan State government. The paper had the following objectives:

1. To increase the general knowledge of the public on domestic and national affairs
2. To encourage the public to read Shan newspapers
3. To enhance the confidence of the people in the government
4. To serve as a means of communication between the government and the populace

The Shan State Council was created and the voice of the Shan people was heard in the Shan State Council. Administration in Shan State was to follow the prescription in *The Shan State Manual* and to accord with the visions mentioned in chapter 9 of the Union Constitution.[26] At the meeting in May 1947, there were thirty-three representatives of the people and thirty-three *saohpa*. The matter was discussed of selecting twenty-two members from the Shan State Council to draw up a constitution for Shan State that would conform with the Union's Constitution.[27]

Relations between the *saohpa* and the representatives of the people were cordial before the attainment of independence, but became strained when the Shan State government came into existence. Criticism of the *saohpa* by the Shan State People's Freedom League became strong and bitter, and the *saohpa* who were not politicians showed their dislike and displeasure. The league went so far as to ask the liberal *saohpa* to give up their power as had the maharajas in India. The powers of the *saohpa* were to be clearly defined and their status spelled out in the state constitution. The league also suggested that the role of the head of Shan State and the state ministers should be not only to advise but to take initiatives. It felt that the emergence of a state constitution was very important, and an eight-member committee was formed to draw up a state constitution. The Constitutional Committee consisted of:

1. Saohpalong of Sam Hka, chairman
2. U Htun Myint (Taunggyi)
3. U Htun Aye, minister of health and social services
4. U Kya Bu
5. U Po Khin Pa-O
6. Pangmi *saohpa*
7. One adviser
8. Secretary U Sang Sam

THE PA-O IN SHAN STATE

A variety of national races live in Shan State and the Pa-O are one of them. The Pa-O people originally lived in Hsa Tung in southeastern Myanmar. They are affiliated to the Kayin people. They moved to Southern Shan State during Alaungpaya's time. They first settled around Nam Hkok, Nawng Mon, and Hsi Seng and they established their first town, Hsa Tung, taking the name of their original home. Gradually their population increased and they became one of the dominant national races in Southern Shan State. The Pa-O are religious and work very hard, engaging in agriculture and plantation, especially in *thanatpet* plantation. They use the leaves of *thanat* trees to roll the cheroots, which are the popular cigarettes of the local people. They had their representative in the Shan State Council. In September 1950 they formed their own political front, the Pa-O National Association. In the old days they also had their feudal chief, Sao Hkun Kyi, who was a Pa-O and a *saohpa* who ruled Hsa Tung Hsi Seng. He was an enlightened chief and his political outlook during the anticolonial period was quite well known. He wrote a short account, "The Mistakes Committed by the *Saohpa*" (*Sawbwa Amar Taw Pong*). After independence, antifeudalism among the Pa-O became so strong that some of them went underground to form an antifeudalist insurgency group. The aboveground people urged them to return to the fold. The first president of the Pa-O National Association was U Po Khin and the secretary was U Pyu. Both of them became members of the Shan State Council and the antifeudalist forces of Shan State. They called for the end of feudal administration and the adoption of democratic practices in Shan State.[28]

On December 11, 1950, about four thousand Pa-O, led by Bo Hein Maung, demonstrated in Taunggyi to express their desire for democracy. The Pa-O representatives met the head of the Shan State and expressed their grievances.

THE CREATION OF EASTERN SHAN STATE

Up to this period Shan State had been comprised of two parts, Northern and Southern. But the chaotic situation after 1948 demanded that Southern Shan State be divided into two parts called Southern Shan State and Eastern Shan State.[29] The eastern part consisted of Keng Tung, Ko Kang, Mong Lun, and the Wa states, all lying on the eastern side of the Than Lwin River, and only Mong Pan was situated west of it.[30]

Eastern Shan State was considered very important from the strategic point of view. It was necessary that proper civil administration be introduced and programs promoting culture, the economy, education, and health be launched, especially in the Wa States. The Supreme Commander Ne Win was consulted and he gave his consent.[31]

A new resident was appointed to handle the administrative affairs of Eastern Shan State. U Hkun Shelli, a veteran administrator with much experience, was chosen resident of Eastern Shan State.[32] He was well respected and well liked by the people of that region.

Keng Tung was the biggest state of Eastern Shan State. In the old days the *saohpa* administrative system was firmly rooted, but the administrative system of Keng Tung was divided into two parts. One part was administered by the *saohpa* himself and the other by the Shan State government. The resident was not to interfere in the internal administration of the *saohpa*. But on behalf of the Shan State government, he could deal with such matters as customs and immigration. Cordial relationships had to be maintained with Thailand, China, and Laos. Special attention had to be paid in introducing the new administration in the Wa area. Another underdeveloped area was the district of Ko Kang. Communication was also difficult. It was placed under a special commissioner in Lashio. No assistant resident was posted there. As for the State of Mong Lun, the assistant resident stationed in Mong Yang had to take charge of Mong Lun's administrative affairs. The main duty of the assistant resident was to promote economic, social, and educational programs of the State of Mong Lun.

The Wa States, although not densely populated, was a critical area. It had been a bone of contention in the Border Commissions of British Myanmar and China, which met often to settle border problems. During the war and the British reoccupation, the area was not properly administered and was beyond the control of the central government. Wa State was ruled by petty chiefs whose loyalty sometimes went to China and sometimes to the Shan chiefs and the Myanmar government. When Shan State was administratively divided into three parts, the Wa States were included in Eastern Shan

State, and the Shan State government took care to see that it was properly administered. The head of the Shan State government often urged the resident and assistant resident to tour Wa State to see that administration was in proper order. The resident of Eastern Shan State also served as adviser to the *saohpa* of Keng Tung. The resident was also given judicial power and was the session judge and district judge. Section 30 of the District Procedure Code said, "The State Government, in consultation with the High Court, invests . . . the magistrate of the first class with power to try as a magistrate all offenses not punishable [by] death or [by] imprisonment for life or [by] imprisonment for a term exceeding seven years."[33] The resident was also assigned to look after revenue, treasury, and general administration. Before the proper administration could function, Shan State encountered another problem following that of the KNDO. Northeastern Shan State was invaded by Kuomintang forces, gravely affecting the lives and security of the people of the area. About three thousand Kuomintang troops infiltrated into the Wa States and demanded food supplies from every village. On May 8, 1952, Kyu Kok was set on fire and people's livestock and some houses were burned and some lost their lives.[34]

To cope with the deteriorating situation in Shan State, a conference composed of civil and military officers was held in Kalaw on March 12, 1951. Assessments were made of security and the situation during the KNDO occupation, the participation of the police force, the civil officers, and the public, and finally the role of the army in Shan State security was also discussed and planned. Levies were to be organized for local defense but must be well disciplined and not misuse their firearms. They should also be familiar with the changing tactics used by the insurgents. The insurgents avoided head-on clashes with the government forces and mostly used guerrilla tactics. The special commissioner emphasized the need to have full cooperation between the civil and the military to successfully carry out the scheme of security. Since the Shan State government was kept in Yangon at that time, it was very difficult to put the scheme of security into operation. The government was stationed far from the people and was not well informed of a situation that needed quick action. Lack of personal contact with the local chiefs and the local administrators was a deficiency of the Shan State government.

At the sixth session of the meeting held in August in Taunggyi, U Khin Maung Latt proposed the shift of the Shan State government from Yangon back to Taunggyi so that the government could have close contact with the people in an emergency. The government stayed so far from Shan State that the Shan people did not even know it existed. They thought that the office of the resident was the Shan State government. A resolution was then passed to transfer the Shan State government back to Taunggyi. The actual transfer was made on May 2, 1951.[35] It was a period of four years after independence that the Shan State government came back to its native place, Taunggyi.

THE FIRST ELECTION

The first election was held in Shan State and of twenty-five seats, nineteen were filled and the remaining six could not be filled, owing to instability in the areas. They were all representatives of the people. Twenty-five representatives to the Chamber of Nationalities were elected from among the *saohpa*.

The people of Shan State had their first experience of voting to elect their representatives. It was their first taste of democracy. Sao Hkun Kyi was elected chairman of the Shan State Council and U Po Kyaw became the vice chairman. Sao Hkun Hkio was elected head of Shan State and he formed the state cabinet with the following members:

1. U M. Zau Latt	Minister of public works
2. U Yee Tip	Minister of information
3. Sao Maung	Minister of education
4. Sao Htun Aye	Minister of home affairs
5. U Hla Shein	ICS retired, minister of finance and revenue
6. U Tin	ICS retired Minister of mines and cooperation

The new cabinet had to tackle a lot of problems. The situation in Shan State was still chaotic and security was very bad. Travel between states could not be done safely because the highways were infested with insurgents, dacoits, and robbers. Both government officers as well as the general population had to travel from Taunggyi to Loi Lem in convoys with heavy escorts. Telephone lines were cut off by the insurgents and could not be easily replaced. Every headman was instructed to inform the government if strangers were putting up in the local area. The Chinese from Yunnan came down en masse as traders or refugees with their pack animals. Shan State Council member U Htun Aye proposed that the government take some measures to check the flow of illegal immigrants into Shan State. Ko Kang was a region dominated by the Chinese because of its location on the Myanmar-China borders. There were also Shan, Kachin, Lishaw, Miao, Loila, Muso, and Palaung, but they formed an insignificant minority. The majority were Chinese from Yunnan province. Ko Kang was a far-flung region and communication at that time was very difficult, preventing the Shan State government from effectively enforcing its administration and laws. Ko Kang sent its tributes to Hsen Wi and sometimes to the Myanmar government. The *saohpa* of Hsen Wi appointed a *myosa* from the Yang clan, a descendant of a wealthy Chinese family of Yang Chang. This Chinese *myosa* was later promoted to *saohpa* of Ko Kang like other Shan *saohpa*. When the Second World War came the Yang family helped to provide transport for both Chinese and British troops on a business contract, and the head of the Yang family, Yang Win Ping, became very wealthy. When the British evacuated to India, he went along, and when the British reoccupied Shan State he came to Ko Kang to be its administrator with the title of ATM.

After independence, in 1951 the president of the Union of Myanmar made Ko Kang a separate substate in Shan State. Yang Kyin Sai, who was later *saohpa*, was appointed *saohpa* of Ko Kang for two years and his term could be renewed on condition he proved satisfactory. His brother Yang Kyin Sein came down to Yangon to set up a private bank and business. He came to live on University Avenue and became a member of parliament representing the Ko Kang constituency. Many armed groups were also around that region engaged mostly in the drug business. Sometimes they looted and murdered and often tried to challenge the state power. At that time Ko Kang had 120 circles and 440 villages. Taxes were collected by the *saohpa* and his subordinate headman, especially the Sin Ye.

As the situation around 1951 was going from bad to worse the head of Shan State had to take some positive measures. For that, military forces were essential. The head of Shan State then sent a message to U Tin, the minister of defense, saying:

> From the reports received from time to time I am of the opinion that the internal situation in the Shan State is on a downward trend . . . more military and semimilitary forces be released on duty in the Shan State so that the insurgents . . . be finally crushed.[36]

Naw Seng entered China to organize Communist activities along the border, which became a cause for concern to the Shan State government. The insurgents intended to create unrest and instability in Shan State, paving the way for the growth of Communism. It became important to arrest the deteriorating condition in Shan State and to prevent the Communists from getting a foothold. It would also mean danger to Shan State. The Kuomintang from the eastern flank of the Than Lwin would come in to strike the Communists and Shan State could become a battleground for international war. Shan State, having a border with China, Laos, and Thailand, could have border problems at any time anywhere unless careful attention was paid. Border crossings had taken place in the past and had continued in the present and would perhaps continue in the future unless both parties took preventive measures. Criminals, drug traffickers, and smugglers could create border problems and danger for the countries concerned.

Meanwhile, the political power struggle between pro-*saohpa* and anti-*saohpa* groups continued, and no positive steps could be taken by either side to eliminate the other. The deteriorating situation dragged on, wasting much time and energy. Security measures should have been in the forefront but little attention was paid to them. The Communists on one side and the Kuomintang on the other intensified their propaganda warfare as well as armed clashes, making Shan State more insecure than ever before and paved the way for the military to step in and introduce a military administration in Shan State.

MILITARY ADMINISTRATION

The civil administration became ineffective owing to the intensified activities of the multi-colored insurgents, as well as the Kuomintang. Communication and transportation were cut off and the whole Shan State was insecure. The president of the Union, in view of insurgent activities and the danger to public tranquility and the lives of the people, made a declaration on September 13, 1950, in accordance with the Union Constitution of section 94 (1). It read:

> I, Agga Mahatharay Sithu U Ba U, the president of the Union of Burma, therefore declare that under the Union Constitution Act 94 (1) a state of emergency exists in the Shan State because of the insurgency which threatened the stability of the Union of Burma.[37]
>
> U Ba U
> President of the Union of Burma

The Shan State government had no choice but to accept the military administration. A mass meeting was held by the head of Shan State, Sao Hkun Hkio, on October 28, 1952, at the Taunggyi Olympic Sports Ground.[38] About five thousand people attended. Sao Hkun Hkio explained that the situation was very critical and necessitated a military administration with the approval of parliament. Colonel Aung Gyi, who attended the meeting, explained at length how Myanmar was plagued by political turmoil and racial strife with insurrection. He also emphasized the urgent need to prevent the country from falling into the hands of the insurgents and to launch offensive warfare against them. He said that from now on the army would take responsibility to clear away all the insurgents in the Shan State. He also implied that those who practiced racial discrimination would be considered enemies and that only Pa-O (Taung Hsu) people would be regarded as friends. He said the army was not involved in politics and its only aim was to look after the welfare of the people.

Bo Khin Maung Gale, the minister of home affairs, then officially transferred the Shan State administration into the hands of General Ne Win, the supreme commander of the armed forces. The general promised that the army would not act in a dictatorial manner and would cooperate with the local administration. But he said that the Shan police and the government police would be amalgamated. The army would also handle criminal cases and civil cases would be left to the civil department. He also pointed out that there should not be any bloodshed to end feudalism in Shan State.

The actual military administration began on December 1, 1952.[39] Following the military takeover, judicial, security, and police departments were also run by the military authorities. Colonel Saw Myint, commander of the Fourth Light Infantry Brigade, stationed at Kalaw, was given charge of the military administration. A Military Coordination Committee was formed composed of:

1. Colonel Saw Myint	Commander of the Fourth Light Infantry Brigade, Kalaw
2. Sao Htun Aye	State minister of health
3. U Ba Ni	Secretary of the Shan State government
4. U Nyi Pu	Commissioner, Taunggyi
5. U Thoung Pe	Resident of Taunggyi
6. U Ba Aye	Deputy inspector general of police

The committee was invested with executive power and its main responsibility was to implement the smooth running of the military administrative machinery. The committee held its first meeting on May 6, 1953, and passed four resolutions. The first one dealt with civilian arms licenses. These were to be controlled by and issued with the approval of the military administration. The second resolution specified that the military administration was to be informed when opium was sold to foreigners. The third resolution specified that the transport of liquor from one place to another should be under the control of the military administration. The last resolution assigned escorts to military officials touring in Shan State.

For the convenience of the military administration, Southern Shan State was divided into the following districts:

District No. 1 consisted of Taunggyi, Kalaw, and Pindaya and Ywa Ngan, Hsi Seng, and Lawk Sawk.

District No. 2 comprised Loi Lem, Mong Nai, Lai Hka, Mawk Mai, and Mong Kung. Each district had one resident and, if needed, an additional resident was appointed. Experienced officers from Myanmar proper were employed at the expense of the Union government. An order was issued about correspondence with the military administration. All letters must be addressed to the supreme commander of the Armed Forces through the Home Ministry. Official letters must be written either in Myanmar or in Shan but not in English.[40]

All government officers on tour were required to report to the military authority. The insurgents intensified their propaganda against the government. They tried to provoke racial hatred among the nationalities in Shan State. The Coordinating Committee drew up a plan to counteract the propaganda. Officers from Myanmar proper were asked to carry out this counterpropaganda more efficiently.

In the beginning, the military administration did not run smoothly in some areas in Shan State. Shan State had three administrative systems—the Shan State government, the *saohpa* administration, and the military administration. In some places they made no adjustments to fit in with each other. Sometimes misunderstandings and hitches occurred because of different orders from different sources.

The report of the special commissioner, Sao Hom Hpa, submitted to the Shan State government through the secretary, U Ba Ni, ran as follows:

> Mong Kung *saohpa* and his state officers came to me and complained about the difficulties and the situation of his state, saying that the military administration officers could not do or help them in certain matters, [because] they had received no instruction from their superior. And there were lots of misunderstanding and lack of cooperation among them.
>
> The *saohpa* and his state officers were rather difficult to hand over their state to the government without delay. I think the *saohpa* and his officers had tried their best to maintain law and order. But the police had been controlled by the military administration and there was a lack of cooperation. It seems that they could not carry on the administration.[41]

The *saohpa* and the people were troubled at the installation of the military administration in Shan State. They were not accustomed to it. The state officers and the *saohpa* had to adjust themselves to the new administration. But the people were bound to cooperate with whoever came to administer them. In their lifetime they had been under various rules: the feudal chiefs, the British, the Japanese, the Shan State government, and now the military, but none of them had been democratic.

In the meantime efforts were being made by some of the *saohpa* and enlightened politicians. There were three groups of *saohpa* at this time. One group consisted of those who saw the changing conditions and realized that they would have to give up their power. The second was comprised of those who would like to stick to their traditional right to rule. The third did not care much about what happened.

Sao Hom Hpa, the Hsen Wi *saohpalong*, had a liberal view of the Shan State administration of the future. At the Pyidawtha meeting held on November 12, 1953, he proposed that the *saohpa* should relinquish their traditional administrative power and introduce reforms in Shan State.[42] He suggested that Shan State be reorganized and redivided into more governable administrative districts. He also proposed that after relinquishing their traditional administrative powers, the *saohpa* and their families should be given suitable gratuities and pensions. All *saohpa* state officers should be transferred to the Shan State government to become its servicemen. Because most of the *saohpa* and their relatives were poor, he proposed that gratuities and pensions should be given to them to enable them to adjust to the new environment. He hoped that his proposal would be adopted by 1955–56.

A summary of his proposal is as follows:

1. The *saohpa*'s financial allowance should be calculated according to the prewar standard when the country was in normal condition.
2. All retired *saohpa*, apart from those who were the members of the House of Nationalities, should be given preference to join the government service in any department which they deem fit, without affecting their pensions.
3. The pensions to the heir apparents called *kyemmong* and their close relatives were also to be fixed and granted accordingly.

4. With regard to the *saohpa*'s relatives those who are willing and able to join the government service should be accepted.
5. The government should support the children of the *saohpa* and their relatives for their education.
6. The *saohpa* and their relatives should have the full privilege and enjoy a small estate in their respective states or anywhere in Shan State where they have chosen to stay.[43]

Some people did not like the scheme and campaigned against the feudalists, accusing them of trying to maintain their outdated institution. There were also all sorts of elements known and unknown, declared and undeclared, secretly and openly encouraging the end of feudalism, even by force of arms, if necessary.

The internal situation, coupled with the Kuomintang incursion and the Communist encroachment, went from bad to worse. Taking advantage of the chaotic situation, the Intha, a lake-dwelling people, formed a United Inlay Association on December 7, 1952, with Sao Kyaw as its president.[44] Its general objectives were to establish unity among the Inthas, to live peacefully, to try to eliminate injustice in Shan State, to encourage the development of democratic administration, and to bring democracy to Shan State. Political parties were also nurtured by the military administration to multiply the forces of antifeudalism.

The Shan State government underwent a lot of difficulties in this period. It had to try to survive amid contesting elements of antifeudalism, profeudalism, the military, and foreign elements of Communism and the Kuomintang. The government faced a financial deficit almost every year as shown below:

Financial Year	Income	Expenditure
1948–49	937,000	1,114,000
1949–50	1,465,000	12,975,000
1950–51	1,541,000	13,342,000
1951–52	1,917,000	13,494,000
1952–53	2,342,000	17,312,000
1953–54	2,354,000	19,237,000
1954–55	2,798,000	21,112,000[45]

The figures clearly showed that the Shan State government faced a deficit budget almost every year because expenditure exceeded income. The Union government had to subsidize it to make up for the deficits.

In the colonial days the Shan chiefs had had to contribute 25 percent of their income to the British government as the federal contribution, which came to Rs. 906,00 yearly. After independence, the contribution was raised from 25 percent to 40 percent. The following figures show the contributions by the *saohpa* from 1948 to 1954.

1948–49	62,000
1949–50	485,000
1950–51	261,000
1951–52	531,000
1952–53	389,000
1953–54	183,000[46]

The *saohpa* should have contributed more, but because of the insurgency, in some areas taxes and revenue could not be collected. *Saohpa* were accused of pocketing the lion's share of the revenue.

By 1953 the army had gathered its forces to strike against the insurgents in Shan State. Keng Tung was the first target, then came Wa State and Ko Kang. Kayah State including Moe Bye (Mong Pai) up to Mong Kung was the third target. The last target included Lawk Sawk to Pyin Oo Lwin.

During the military administration, those who broke the law of security and opposed the military administration were arrested. Prominent figures like Ahmatchoke Sao Maung of Hsa Mong Hkam, the Pa-O leader U Pyu, U Kyaw Sein, and U Htun Ya were held in custody for a long time.

During the military administration, Moe Bye (Mong Pai) State was transferred from Shan State to Kayah State.[47] Moe Bye had belonged to Shan State since the old days, but it was situated near the border of Kayah State and was inhabited mostly by the Padaung people. During the feudal age Moe Bye was ruled by a Shan *saohpa*.

With the situation greatly improved on September 10, 1954, military administration was officially withdrawn from Shan State. The Shan State government resumed its functions. Criminal and civil courts functioned as before; the police force, which had been centralized, was taken over by the Shan State government.[48] All security measures now fell into the hands of the Shan State government. Headmen were elected by adult suffrage in accordance with democratic practice. Taxes and revenue were collected by officers of the Shan State government. The government set up a new plan of administration. The Shan State was divided into five districts, thirteen subdivisions and thirty-two townships to ensure the smooth running of the administrative machinery. More assistant residents and township officers were appointed to take up administrative duties from the *saohpa*. News and rumors of *saohpa* relinquishing their power spread over Shan State, but no official announcement was made.

On January 6, 1955, an All-Myanmar Pa-O Convention was held in Taunggyi. About fifteen hundred Pa-O representatives attended the convention, and a resolution asking for a separate state was passed.[49] The liberal Pa-O opposed the resolution, causing a split among the Pa-O, and a new organization called Pa-Ah-Ma-Sa came into existence.[50] It was led by Bo Kyaw Win and Hein Nanda.[51]

The forces of antifeudalism in Northern Shan State became more dynamic and the following resolutions were passed at a meeting held at Hsi Paw by the peasants as follows:

> as proclaimed by Sao Hkun Hkio . . . be brought into force within this year. . . . Section 10 of the Shan State Customary Law which was diametrically opposed to the Constitutional law of the Union be rectified within the framework of the code of criminal procedure. . . . the existing land system which was worse than feudalism be abolished and the cultivators be given land as in Burma (Myanmar) Proper. . . . agricultural loans be given to the farmers in time and that agriculture banks be opened in places where there were farmers. . . . gambling be forbidden in places where agricultural loans were given so that loans might be utilized on genuine farming expenses. . . . Federated Shan State administration be withdrawn and replaced by the central government as speedily as possible . . . election of Thugyi (headmen) and tax collectors be held before 1956. . . . exemption from Thathameda tax.[52]

Gradually, public participation in the affairs of state began to take root. Political campaigns on reforms and on abolition of feudal administration took place everywhere. The time had come for the feudal chiefs to transfer their power to the Shan State government.

The Shan people gradually became enlightened and political parties were formed to contest the elections and to choose people's representatives to the Shan State Council and to the parliament. The following parties were in existence in Shan State:

1. Shan State People's Organization (SSPO)
2. Union of the Shan State People's Organization (USSPO)
3. Shan State Peasants' Union (Ya Ta La Sa)
4. Pa-O National Organization (Pa-Ah-Ma-Pha)
5. Pa-O National Association (Pa-Ah-Ma-Sa)
6. Shan State Hill People's Organization (SSSPO)

Elections were held and the number of candidates elected was as follows:

Party	House of Representatives	House of Nationalities
SSHPO	14	25
Ya-Ta-La-Sa	2	
USSPO	4	
Pa-Ah-Ma-Pha	1	
Independent	4	

In the elections the *saohpa* party, SSHPO, gained the majority, and at the first meeting it proposed to open an Intermediate College in Taunggyi with the Shan language as one of the optional subjects. A proposal for opening two agricultural banks was also made. One was to be in Taunggyi and the other in Lashio. A democratic election was held to choose people's representatives, but in some places this did not go smoothly or transparently. A few cases of murder and torture occurred in some areas because of political jealousy.

After the elections a cabinet was formed with the following as state ministers:

1. Sao Hkun Hkio — Head of state
2. Sao Pye — Deputy head of state and minister for interior
3. Sao Man Hpa — Minister for health and education
4. Sao Hkun Aung — Minister for information and unity for indigenous races
5. M. Zaw Latt — Minister for finance and revenue
6. U San Lu — Minister for soil conservation
7. U Po Hmone — Minister for public works and irrigation[53]

At the meeting of the Ninth Session of the Shan State Council, the question of the budget was hotly discussed. The Shan State government was in trouble because of budget restrictions. U Po Hmone, the member of parliament from Hsi Paw, explained that during the British period, the Shan States received revenue from the Customs, Myanmar Railways, Forest Department, Post and Telecommunications in an appropriate ratio. Now, the Shan State government had been receiving aid of 120 to 149 lakhs from the Union government for some eight years since independence. With the introduction of the income tax, the Thathameda tax was abolished in Shan State and the right of collecting the income tax was granted.

Border crossing posed a constant problem for the Shan State government especially in the Wa States. Clashes between the Wa and the Chinese took place very often. Because of the repressive measures taken by the Red Chinese, about one thousand Wa crossed the Chinese border into Myanmar. They belonged to the Sandon Lawa of Myanmar. They had often crossed and recrossed the border in the past, causing a problem. Other minorities like the Yawyin, Atzie, Lahu, and Tai Nua also freely crossed the border into the Wa areas.[54] Reports of a clash between the Chinese Communists and the Wa over the question of taxation was also received by the Shan State government. The Wa had refused to pay taxes and a fight took place, killing some of the Chinese tax collectors. Troops were brought in to suppress the rebellion and many Wa crossed over into Myanmar. Mongma and the nearby villages were burned and razed, and many refugees fled into Myanmar. The Wa tribesmen gathered for reprisals, posing a big cause for concern for the Shan State government and the Union government.[55] Those who had been supported by the Communists fled to join the Kuomintang, making things more complicated for Shan State as well as for the Union of Myanmar. Chinese youths who spoke Myanmar were sent as intelligence servicemen to the border area to spy for them.[56]

To mend the deteriorating situation, a friendly conference between Myanmar and the People's Republic of China was held at Mongshi on December 14, 1956.[57] Eighty-five delegates from Shan State attended the meeting and, as a gesture of reconciliation, Red Chinese soldiers were evacuated from the territory.[58]

In 1957 rumors spread among the public that Shan State would be separated from the Union after the ten years provided in the Constitution in 1958. The rumors alarmed many people and shocked many political parties in Shan State and Myanmar proper as well. People kept asking: Would Shan State really secede from the Union? Would the Shan people opt for separation? Would the disintegration of the Union be possible? Would there be any means to safeguard the Union? Would there be any political solution for that or would the armed forces be used if separation actually came? Would the constitution really permit Shan State to secede from the Union as provided? What would be the responses from the statesmen, from the politicians, from the legalists, from the constitutional advisers, from the officers of the armed forces, and finally from the public as a whole? It was another turning point in Myanmar's post-independence political history and a test of the first democratic constitution and the parliamentary system that was in operation.

Chapter 10 of the Union Constitution provided the following sections and subsections for the right to secede from the Union:

201. Save as otherwise especially provided in this Constitution or in any Act of Parliament made under Section 199, every State shall have the right to secede from the Union in accordance with the condition hereinafter prescribed.

202. The right of secession shall not be exercised within ten years from the date on which this Constitution comes into operation.

203 (1). Any State wishing to exercise the right of secession shall have a resolution to that effect passed by its State Council. No such resolution shall be deemed to have been passed unless not less than two-thirds of the total number of members of the State Council concerned have voted in its favour.

(2). The Head of the State concerned shall notify the President of any such resolution passed by the Council and shall send him a copy of such resolution certified by the Chairman of the Council by which it was passed.

204. The President shall thereupon order a plebiscite to be taken for the purpose of ascertaining the will of the people of the State concerned.

205. The President shall appoint a plebiscite Commission consisting of an equal number of members representing the Union and the State concerned in order to supervise the plebiscite.

206. Subject to the provisions of this chapter, all matters relating to the exercise of the right of secession shall be regulated by law.

It was difficult to exercise the right of secession. All democratic steps would have to be systematically and strictly followed. The words, the phrases, the language used in the sections and subsections of chapter 10 regarding the right of secession were very well chosen, well coined, and expressed with all democratic ideals in the best English, by the best legal experts of the nation (Myanmar) led by U Chan Htun Aung, who was trained in the best institution abroad. Theoretically the constitution looked good and sound and democratic, written within a short period of time to meet the needs of the urgent situation. At that time nobody would have imagined the evil consequences that might arise from these sections of chapter 10.

Many questions then arose regarding this chapter.

1. Would the constitution work?
2. Would it be practically implemented when the time arrived?
3. Would it be suitable to the autocratic environment of Myanmar?
4. Would it be possible to accept it even though the terms in chapter 10 were so democratic?
5. Who was responsible for putting chapter 10 in the Union Constitution?
6. Why did they put chapter 10 in the constitution?
7. Did they not foresee the evil consequences that might arise from chapter 10?

Rumors of secession continued, spreading across the whole of Myanmar and the world. There were people who would like to put more oil on the burning fire. They took the issue into their hands and helped to spread the rumors, adding their views however irrelevant. Newspapers, national and local, both in English and in Myanmar, helped to fan the flames. News spread that Shan villagers were administering charms and tattooing themselves for immunity against weapons and getting ready to fight; secret meetings were held to organize people for self-defense; secret talks were made with foreign embassies; assistance had been garnered from SEATO. On June 26, 1957, local newspapers, both in English and in Myanmar, published the news of how Shan State would secede from the Union and become a future United States air base.[59] To counter the alarming news the head of Shan State on July 6, 1957, called a press conference to refute the allegation. Some news was sensational, some made up, some just propaganda, and most just false and groundless. But it widened the gap of trust and confidence between nationalities, sowing more misunderstanding, and bringing on political miscalculation beyond repair. The Shan *saohpa* became targets of criticism and were accused of being nasty separatists. The Shan State government was also blamed for not taking any measures to stop the rumors and for not declaring its official stand on this issue.

The first political group to officially pick up the issue was the All-Myanmar Shan National Organization in Yangon. U Ba Khin, president, U Ba Aye, secretary, and U Win Maung, organizer, were the executive members of the organization. Its members were mostly Shan who had lived in Yangon since British times. They gave a press conference at the reporters' office in Yangon on July 24, 1957, at twelve noon. At the conference they expressed their desire that Shan State should not be separated from the Union. U Ba Khin said separation from the Union would not serve the purpose of anyone, citing the example of India and Pakistan and also the proverb, "Divided we will fall and united we will stand." They finally suggested that the Shan State should stay in unity with the Union.[60]

JAPANESE WAR REPARATIONS AND THE SHAN STATE GOVERNMENT

The Myanmar government and the Japanese government signed a peace treaty in 1957 and Japan agreed to give war reparations to Myanmar worth $20 million plus economic aid worth $20 million.

The Union government agreed to share the war reparations with the Shan State government. When the Myanmar delegation went to Japan to finalize the War Reparations Agreement, Sao Man Hpa, Shan State health and education minister, and some Shan representatives were also included. The members of the Shan State Council and parliament gave their approval to mostly accept laboratory equipment and machinery that might be useful to the Shan State's development program. But in practice, luxury goods and cars (Prince sedans and Toyota jeeps) were included in the war reparations. The cars were allotted to ministers and selection grade officers, who had to pay 5 percent of their salary for them.[61]

In the meanwhile the situation in Shan State was that the *saohpa* could no longer continue to exert their authority. Ways and means to peacefully transfer their power to the Shan State government had to be sought.

A committee was formed to draw up a plan for compensating the *saohpa*, with the following members:

1. Sao Hkun Hkio	Saohpalong of Mong Mit
2. Sao Shwe Thaik, Aggamahatharaysithu Aggamahathiri Thudama	Saohpalong of Yawng Hwe
3. Sao Hom Hpa, Thadomahathraysithu	Saohpalong of Hsen Wi
4. Hkun Pan Sein, Mahathraysithu	Saohpalong of Tawng Peng
5. Sao Htun Aye	Saohpalong of Hsa Mong Hkam
6. Sao Pye, Thraysithu	Saohpalong of Mong Nai
7. Sao Kya Saing	Saohpalong of Hsi Paw
8. Yan Kyin Sai	Saohpalong of Ko Kang
9. Sao Num	Saohpalong of Lai Hka[62]

A political split in the AFPFL took place on April 30, 1958, which affected the political stability of the whole country. The AFPFL was, in fact, the only solid political party that had been running the country since independence in 1948.[63] It split into a faction known as AFPFL (Clean), led by U Nu and U Tin and another named AFPFL (Stable) led by U Ba Swe and U Kyaw Nyein. An election was held and a vote taken within parliament which the Clean AFPFL won and U Nu became prime minister again. But politically the country deteriorated beyond control and U Nu handed over the reins of government to General Ne Win on October 28, 1958.[64]

The split of the AFPFL and the fall of U Nu's government also greatly affected Shan State. The Shan State government led by Sao Hkun Hkio had to resign in accordance with section 120 (1) of the Union Constitution which stated:

> If the Prime Minister at any time resigns from the office, the other members of the Government shall be deemed to have resigned from the office. . . .[65]

In place of Sao Hkun Hkio, the Shan State Council unanimously chose Sao Hom Hpa to be the head of Shan State. He formed a new government composed of:

1. Sao Hom Hpa — Head of state
2. Sao Man Hpa — Minister of home religious, judicial, and rehabilitation
3. U Pyu (Pa-O) — Minister of information and unity of indigenous races
4. U Zaw Latt — Minister for finance and revenue, soil conservation and national planning
5. U San Hla Baw — Minister for agriculture, forest, veterinary, mineral, transportation, industrial, and cooperatives[66]

Soon after the formation of the new Shan State government, a new Security Council of the Shan State was formed with Sao Hom Hpa as president, Sao Man Hpa as vice president, the deputy inspector general of police, and a representative each from the Fourth, Sixth, and Ninth Brigades as members. The secretary of the Shan State government also acted as secretary of the Shan State Security Council. The council had the following objectives:

1. Security
2. Peace and tranquility
3. Welfare of the people

A new administrative system was introduced to be more or less in line with the military setup as follows:

1. Southern Shan State Command, consisting of Taunggyi and Loi Lem districts and Eastern Shan State.
2. Northern Shan State Command, consisting of Kyaukme and Lashio districts and a special northeastern district.

A commissioner was placed in each of the commands.[67] The formation of the Shan State Security Council indicated that the political situation was not getting better. The split of the main political party, AFPFL, in Myanmar proper made the situation worse than one could expect.

The secession problem became a political cyclone, blowing wild over the Shan State. The political leaders of Shan State could not ignore it and they realized the necessity of amending the constitution as prescribed in chapter 11, Amendment of the Constitution, which stated:

> 207. Any provision of the Constitution may be amended, whether by way of variation, addition, or repeal, in the manner hereinafter provided.
>
> 208. (1) Every proposal for an amendment of the Constitution shall be in the form of a Bill and shall be expressed as a Bill to amend the Constitution.

(2) A Bill containing a proposal or proposals for the amendment of the Constitution shall contain no other proposal.

209. (1) Such Bill may be initiated in either Chamber of Parliament.

(2) After it has been passed by each of the Chambers of Parliament, the Bill shall be considered by both Chambers in joint sitting.

(3) The Bill shall be deemed to have been passed by both Chambers in joint sitting only when not less than two-thirds of the then members of both Chambers have voted in its favour.[68]

Regarding the proposal for amending the constitution by the Shan State government, the chapter that follows will give a detailed account.

The subject that always dominated the political stage of the Shan State Council was the ending of the feudal institution, which involved the surrender of hereditary feudal administrative powers to the Shan State government. Finally the *saohpa*, feeling the pressure of the times and of the national and international situation, agreed to transfer their feudal powers to the Shan State government by democratic means, as will be described in the coming chapter.

16

The Transfer of Feudal Power to the Shan State Government

Before the establishment of the independent Republic of the Union of Myanmar, the Shan hill region located to the east of the Union of Myanmar was known as the Federated Shan States. The Federated Shan States was set apart from ministerial Myanmar for administrative purposes and was under the direct rule of the British governor of Myanmar through a commissioner and thirty-three hereditary chiefs, or *saohpa*. Forests and public works were administered by the federal chiefs, and the *saohpa* themselves administered their states under customary laws and local practices and traditions.

Under the administrative system, the governor had authority and power over the enactment of laws and general administration, and the Myanmar Legislative Assembly had no authority whatsoever over the Federated Shan States and over the *saohpa* who ruled their states.

Within Myanmar the hill region was less developed all round than Myanmar proper, which had much advanced in development. The British believed that the Federated Shan States could not be included in the parliamentary system; the same went for other regions such as the Kachin Hills, the Naga Hills, the Triangle Area, the Hukaung Valley, the Salween (Than Lwin) District, and the unfederated Shan areas of occupied parts of Myitkyina and Chindwin districts. The plea put forward for this separate treatment was that these areas were not sufficiently advanced politically to take part in the representative government granted to Myanmar proper. Thus the jurisdiction of the Myanmar parliament did not extend to the areas listed above.

The Aung San–Attlee Treaty was signed in London in January 1947, and it was followed by the conference at Pang Long in Lai Hka State, in Central Shan State, which would become a symbol of national unity. Bogyoke Aung San headed the AFPFL leaders and, with leaders of the hill region, conducted the Pang Long Conference successfully, making great efforts to this end. On February 12, 1947, the day that became Union Day, unity was achieved among the national races of the country. All leaders of the hill regions and Myanmar unanimously agreed to create a union so that the people from the plain and from the hills became one single entity, and it was to be declared to the world. The Pang Long Conference and the creation of the Union ushered in a new era in the history of independent Myanmar.

THE CONSTITUENT ASSEMBLY

On April 7, 1947, a Constituent Assembly was formed to draw up a constitution under the provisions of the Aung San–Attlee Treaty. The Assembly convened and held sessions from June 9, 1947, to September 24, 1947. During this period it drew up a constitution to create the Republic of the Union of Myanmar.

The constitution had 14 chapters and 234 articles. In it, Shan State, Kachin State, Kayin State, Kayah or Karenni State, all of which were hill regions, were organized as part of the Union of Myanmar with complete local autonomy regarding culture and social matters and economic affairs. They were given the right to form their own cultural, social, and economic organizations and to freely govern themselves.

During the sessions of the Constituent Assembly, the leaders of Shan State demonstrated beyond all doubt their unity of purpose and identity of outlook with the leaders of Myanmar proper and were able to show the world the strong national unity that existed at that time. One of the architects in the creation of the Republic of the Union of Myanmar was Sao Sam Tun, *saohpalong* of Mong Pawn, who was assassinated together with Bogyoke Aung San on July 19, 1947, before they could witness the fruition of their efforts—the declaration of the Sovereign Independent Republic of the Union of Myanmar, on January 4, 1948.

THE SHAN STATE GOVERNMENT

From 1948 the Shan State government was provided for in section 160 of the Constitution of the Union of Myanmar, which stated:

> A member of the Union government to be known as the minister for the Shan State shall be appointed by the president on the nomination of the prime minister acting in consultation with the Shan State Council from among the members of parliament representing the Shan State. The minister so appointed shall also be the head of the Shan State for the purposes of this constitution.

Soon after Myanmar became independent, the maharajas of India who ruled over states consisting of many cities renounced their prerogative rights, and surrendered their states and power to the people in ceremonies held for the purpose.

The *saohpa* of the Shan States within the Union of Myanmar, desiring to move with the times in working for the advancement of the people, and opening the way for the development of a democratic way of life, unanimously decided to renounce their hereditary executive powers and privileges. This decision was made public through a press conference held on October 25, 1952. The head of the *Saohpa* Association, Sao Hkun Hkio (head of Shan State), said that the decision to renounce their hereditary administrative and executive powers stemmed from the desire that they had been entertaining for quite some time to give full democratic rights to the people. They felt that the benefits and advantages accruing to a democratic way of life should be made available to the people to the fullest extent.

In accordance with this desire, and to show it in practice, all *saohpa* of Shan State declared that they would surrender all their administrative powers. In appreciation, the government of the Union of Myanmar agreed to give the *saohpa* and their families a lump-sum pension.

Following the agreement during the administration of General Ne Win on March 9, 1959, at the emergency meeting of the Shan State Council held at the House of Nationalities, the minister of home affairs, Shan State government, Sao Hman Hpa, *saohpalong* of Mong Shu, tabled a proposal to amend section 154 (2). The council's resolution on the amendment of the bill read:

> That this council recommends the amendment to the Constitution that the provisions of section 154 (2) remain in force until the expiry of the next term of parliament to be elected at the forthcoming general election.

In explaining the resolution on section 154 (2) Sao Hman Hpa said that it conformed with the times and that ten years had gone by and section 154 (2) was no longer in accord with the changing times and therefore had to be revised. To become a representative of the Chamber of Deputies or Chamber of Nationalities such a person must be elected in accordance with the democratic system

At present the twenty-five seats in the Chamber of Nationalities selected by the thirty-three unelected *saohpa* made it difficult to consider that they represented the will of the people. According to the statement, not allowing *saohpa* to become members of parliament constituted a loss of privileges.

Therefore, the home minister explained, in order to allow people of the Shan State to stand for election to the Chamber of Nationalities and also to permit *saohpa* to be elected to parliament, it was necessary to abrogate section 154 (2).

The proposal was supported by U Kyi Myint, representative of Keng Tung; U Nyunt Maung, representative of Pang Tara; U Htun Ya, representative of Sam Ka; U Htun Aye, representative of Nam Hkam; and U Ba Htun, representative of West Hsi Paw. Although Maha Devi Sao Hearn Hkam of Hsen Wi put up a proposal for the revision, it had no support, and therefore the council adopted the revision concerning Section 154 (2). The corresponding provision for Kayah State was in section 183 (1) of the constitution, which read:

183 (1) Even if parliament enacted any other acts:

(a) The *saohpa* of Kantarawady, Baw La Ke, and Kyebogyi must be elected representatives of Kayah in the Chamber of Nationalities.

(b) When Mong Pai becomes part of Kayah State, in accordance with the above proposal, the representative of Mong Pai must represent Kayah State in the Chamber of Nationalities.

(c) *Sawpya* and *saohpa* cannot become members of parliament.

SUBMISSION TO THE PARLIAMENT

The section 154 (2) revision was adopted by the council. It was necessary to put it up to parliament. Accordingly, Sao Hom Hpa, the Shan State minister, submitted to parliament on March 12, 1959, the draft of the second amendment to the constitution:

1. (i) The act shall be known as an act for the second amendment to the Constitution of the Union of Myanmar.

   (ii) This act shall become effective from the last date of the dissolution of the second parliament.

2. Sections 154 (2) and 183 (1) shall be nullified by this act.

The head of Shan State, Sao Hom Hpa, explained at great length the reason for putting up the proposal that had been decided by the Council of Shan State and Kayah State.

The proposal was discussed and supported by U Ba Nyein, representative of Monywa, Pa-Ma-Nya-Ta; Thakin San Myint, representative of Tha Nat Pin, AFPFL (Stable); U Tun Aye, representative of Nam Hkam; and Thakin Chan Htun, representative of Tatar U, AFPFL (Clean). Although Sao Hearn Hkam, Maha Devi, representative of Northern Hsen Wi, tabled an amendment proposal, it was withdrawn when the head of Shan State clarified the situation, and this second amendment was ratified by parliament.

RATIFICATION BY THE CHAMBER OF NATIONALITIES

Although parliament ratified the draft of the second amendment to the Union Constitution, the Chamber of Nationalities had to ratify it also. Therefore Minister Sao Wunna presented the amendment to the Chamber of Nationalities on March 16, 1959.

Sao Hkun Hkio, *saohpa* of Mong Mit, explained in four parts how the *saohpa* would relinquish their power as contained in the proposal made by Minister Sao Wunna. Dr. Sein Ban, representative of North Hinzada, AFPFL (Stable), and Thakin Thein Maung, representative of Ma U Pin, AFPFL (Clean), supported the proposal in the Chamber of Nationalities, and it was ratified.

RATIFICATION BY THE TWO HOUSES OF PARLIAMENT

Since the draft of the second amendment to the Union Constitution had to be ratified by a joint session of the two houses of parliament, the Chamber of Deputies and the Chamber of Nationalities, the proposal was put up to the session, held on March 17, 1959.

In the joint session, the head of Shan State, Sao Hom Hpa, presented the draft for discussion.

The proposal was discussed by U Tun Aye, representative of Nam Hkam, and U Tin Ko Ko, representative of North Yawng Hwe. It was then put to the vote in the joint session. Of 366 representatives, 318 voted for the motion, exceeding two-thirds of the representatives. Therefore the chairman of the session declared the draft amendment ratified.

Following the ratification, the foundation for the people's administration of Shan State was laid and signed at Taunggyi on April 24, 1959. An impressive and auspicious ceremony was held in Taunggyi, the headquarters of the Shan State government, to mark the transfer to the government of the hereditary rights and administrative powers of the thirty-three *saohpa* of Shan State. The first to sign the agreement was the *saohpalong* of North Hsen Wi, who was also the head of Shan State, followed by other *saohpalong*.[1]

Among the dignitaries who witnessed the signing were U Myint Thein, chief justice of the Union; U Khin Maung Pyu, minister for home affairs; ministers and officials of the Shan State; twenty-five deputies representing Shan State constituencies; and Colonels Tin Maung, Thein Doke, and Khen Za Mung.

LIST OF *SAOHPALONG* WHO SIGNED THE AGREEMENT

1. Thadomahathraysithu Sao Hom Hpa	North Hsen Wi
2. Aggamahathraysithu Aggamahathiri Thudhamma Sao Shwe Thaike	Yawng Hwe
3. Sao Sai Long	Keng Tung
4. Sao Kya Saing	Hsi Paw
5. Sao Hkun Hkio	Mong Mit
6. Thraysithu Sao Pye	Mong Nai
7. Mahathraysithu Sao Hkun Pan Sein	Tawng Peng
8. Sao Kyi	Mong Kung
9. Sao Hso Hom Hpa	Hsen Wi South (Mong Yai)
10. *Thraysithu* Sao Num	Lai Hka
11. Sao Hkun Sa	Lawk Sawk
12. *Mahathraysithu* Sao Hkun Kyi	Sam Ka
13. *Thiripyanchi* Sao Shwe Kyi	Mong Pan

14. *Wunnakyawhtin* Sao Mun Laik	Mong Lum
15. Sao Hso Hom, BA (Hons)	Mong Pawn
16. *Mahathraysithu* Sao Tun E	Hsa Mong Hkam
17. *Thraysithu* Sao Shwe Hmun	Kehsi Mansam
18. *Thiripyanchi* Sao Moe Kyaw	Loi Long (Pang Laung)
19. *Thiripyanchi* Sao Hkun Aung	Baw
20. *Wunnakyawhtin* Sao Hman Hpa	Mong Hsu
21. Yan Kyein Saing	Ko Kang
22. Sao On Maung	Mong Nawng
23. Sao Hkun Nyun	Sa Koi
24. Sao Sein Nyun	Wan Yin
25. Sao Hkun Saung	Kyone
26. Sao Hkun Yee	Ye Ngan
27. Sao Win Kyi	Pang Tara
28. Sao Htun Sein	Pwe Hla
29. Sao Hkun U Kyamaing	Pang Mi
30. Sao Thoung Shwe, Kyamaing (signed by Sao Lun On)	Nam Hkok-Nawng Wawn
31. Sao Aung Myint (signed by Daw E Thant)	Hsa Htung
32. Sao Htun Hpa, Kyamaing (signed by Sao Bo Hkam)	Mawk Mai
33. Sao Hkun Oh, Kyamaing (signed by Nang Shwe Oo)	Ho Pong

THE SHAN STATE COUNCIL EMERGENCY MEETING

After the signing ceremony the Shan State Council held an emergency meeting in the Council Room in Taunggyi on April 27, 1959, at 11 A.M. The meeting was presided over by Mahathraysithu Sao Hkun Kyi, *saohpalong* of Sam Ka. It was attended by twenty-one *saohpalong* including Thado Mahathraysithu Sao Hom Hpa, head of state, Sao Hkun Hkio, *saohpalong* of Mong Mit, and Mahathraysithu Sao Hkun Pan Sein, *saohpalong* of Tawng Peng, and ministers and officials of the Shan State government.

The chairman declared the meeting open, and the home minister, Wunnakyawhtin, Sao Hman Hpa, put up a proposal that the council accept the general allowance provided by the Union government as commuted pension regarding the renunciation of power by the *saohpa*. The proposal was thoroughly discussed, accepted, and confirmed by U Tun Aye, MP, Nam Hkam; Sao Hearn Hkam, the *mahadevi* of Yawng Hwe, North Hsen Wi; and U Tun Ya, MP, Sam Ka.

The home minister made another motion and the council agreed to ratify the agreement between the Shan State government and the *saohpa* handing over to the people all the powers enjoyed by the *saohpa*. U Tun Aye, MP, Nam Hkam, and U Tin Ko Ko, MP, North Yawng Hwe, discussed and then approved it.

The council also adopted another proposal introduced by the home minister, Sao Hman Hpa, recommending that in the interests of Shan State, the *saohpa* shall transfer their administrative and judicial powers to the Shan State government and that the council shall approve, in accordance with section 161 (1) of the Constitution of the Union of Myanmar, of such authority resting with the head of Shan State, or with whosoever he may appoint on his behalf to exercise such powers. On matters falling within the jurisdiction of the Union of Myanmar it was agreed that these be dealt with by the Union government on its behalf and in the best interests of the Shan State government.

The minister of finance and revenue, U Zau La, also proposed that since it was not possible at that time at fixed equal rates of taxation for all areas in Shan State, a Committee of Advisory on Financial Matters be formed to review the fixing of a uniform rate of taxation. The motion was adopted after a discussion made by U Tun Aye, MP, Nam Hkam.

Finally the council dealt with supplementary budget estimates for the financial year 1958–59 introduced by Minister Zau La. It was approved under the head "43 Supplementary Grants for Pension" to allot 26,063,100 kyats after discussion by U Tun Aye. The meeting was then adjourned.

The final ceremony for the renunciation of hereditary rights by the *saohpa* of Shan State in favor of a democratic government and the foundation-laying ceremony for people's administration held on April 29, 1959. The Union president, U Win Maung, who was taking a vacation at his summer residence in Pyin Oo Lwin (Maymyo), flew to Heho on March 28, 1959, at 9 A.M. and was received by U Myint Thein, the Union chief justice; U Khin Maung Pyu, minister of home affairs and information; Sao Hom Hpa, head of Shan State; Brigadier General San Yu; and various state officers. Bouquets were offered to the president by Shan, Bama, Kayin, Pa-O, and Palaung beautiful damsels.

The president and his entourage motored to Taunggyi and on the way big crowds of people from townships and villages, and including schoolchildren, lined the road to welcome him. In Taunggyi, pavilions were built and people from various associations and organizations including the Taunggyi Municipality Fire Brigade, government officials and all sorts of musical and dance troupes happily welcomed the president. Flowers were offered by the Taunggyi ladies. Students lined the streets waving Union and Shan flags and shouting slogans to welcome the president.

The prime minister, General Ne Win, arrived in Taunggyi from Kalaw by car on April 28, 1959, at 3 P.M. and put up at Brigade Command No. 4. U Tin, Speaker of the Chamber of Deputies of the Union government, arrived at Heho by special plane on April 28, 1959, at 8:45 A.M. accompanied by leaders of AFPFL (Stable) and AFPFL (Clean).

U Shwe Mya, chief secretary, and U Khin Maung Gyi, secretary to the ministry of information, also attended the ceremony establishing people's administration in Shan State.

On April 28, 1959, at 7 P.M. a state dinner was hosted by Sao Hom Hpa in honor of the laying of the foundation for people's administration in Shan State. The dinner was attended by the Union president, U Win Maung, Prime Minister General Ne Win and Mrs. Ne Win, the Union chief justice, U Myint Thein, the Speaker of the Chamber of Deputies, U Tin, *saohpa* of Shan State, official guests from the Shan State government, guests from the Union government, and officials from the military administration.

The ceremony establishing a people's administration was held on the State Football ground in Taunggyi. Speeches were delivered by the Union president, the prime minister, and the head of the Shan State.

At 6:50 A.M. troops were ready for the military demonstration, official guests from both the Union government and the state government were present. *Saohpa* and their Maha Devi, including their children and relatives, also attended. Responsible officials from the Myanmar army and members of parliament were also present in the state pavilions. At 6:57 A.M. the Union prime minister, and General Ne Win (Thadothiri Thudhamma) arrived and all stood up to welcome him.

At 7 A.M. the Union president arrived and was welcomed by Lt. Colonel Aung Zin to inspect the guard of honor.

The first to deliver the speech was President U Win Maung, followed by the head of Shan State, Sao Hom Hpa, and then Prime Minister Ne Win.

In his address the president said that throughout the thousand years of Shan State history, that day stood out as the most significant and auspicious because it marked the first successful stage in ushering in popular government throughout Shan State. That success, he emphasized, was due partly to the will of the Shan people and partly to the democratic spirit shown by the *saohpa* themselves.

The president praised the Shan chiefs for taking part in the framing and enactment of the Union Constitution. The constitution, he said, was based on fundamental human rights and it provided for a socialist economy within a democratic framework aimed at all-round development and progress for every citizen.

The president also remarked that it was quite in keeping with the spirit of the constitution that the Shan chiefs, having the best interests of the people at heart, should have voluntarily renounced the hereditary rights of administrative, judicial, and revenue supervisory powers and thereby paved the way for a changeover to a representative government for Shan State. The changeover, he declared, was also consistent with the spirit of the new era of progress with its special emphasis on democracy.

The president also observed that Shan State was to witness that day the introduction of a new type of administrative machinery. It was his fervent prayer that the change in the administrative system might be accompanied by the corresponding change for the better and an improvement in the economic and social conditions of the people.

"From today onward," he emphasized with family spirit and manner, "let us work together for the mutual benefits of Shan State and the Union. Let's try to safeguard the Union Constitution and independence. Let us join hands together as brothers of the same family and defend our Union from being encroached upon by the offenders."

The president then called for all-out efforts to promote mutual welfare between Shan State and the Union of Myanmar. His four wishes were as follows:

> May the Shan State develop and be prosperous.
> May the Union live long.
> May independence be strong and firm.
> May democracy be firmly established.

After that Prime Minister Ne Win delivered his address. He said that the ceremony marked the triumph of the Union over one of the most difficult hurdles in the course of its race toward the goal of democracy. But the democracy that the Union was striving for, he pointed out, was not the kind that could be stretched and distributed at will but a real democracy as provided for in the preamble to the Union Constitution, which states:

> We, the people of Burma including the Frontier Areas and the Karenni States (the Kayah State), determined to establish in strength and unity a sovereign independent state. To maintain social order on the basis of the eternal principles of justice, liberty, and equality and to guarantee and secure to all citizens. Justice, social, economic, and political; liberty of thought, expression, belief, faith, worship, vocation, association and action; equality of status, of opportunity and before the law. In our Constituent Assembly this tenth day of Thadingyut waxing, 1309 BE (twenty-fourth day of September 1947 AD) do hereby adopt, enact, and give to ourselves this Constitution.

The prime minister remarked that this by itself clearly indicated acceptance of democratic principles by the Shan peoples. He said that in fact the age-old feudalism which had remained in practice until that day was directly connected to the spirit of the constitution and, consequently, certain sections of the constitution needed to be modified.

General Ne Win explained how the necessity for the modifications arose, pointing out that when the British government granted Myanmar its independence, the plan had been to maintain the status quo of what was known as the Hill Tracts. Failing this, it had intended to absorb these areas into the British Commonwealth. Being simple-minded, the inhabitants of what were known as the Shan States within the Union were deceived into believing that Myanmar proper had nefarious designs on them.

The prime minister went on to say that to allay those suspicions and fears Bogyoke Aung San had included special safeguards in the constitution for the *saohpalong*, guaranteeing them continued exercise of their special rights and privileges. The same had been done for the *sawphya* of the Kayah State. Bogyoke Aung San, the prime minister said, had intended that the time would come when the state would realize that these provisions in the constitution were anomalous and that it would accordingly take steps to keep up with the times. Subsequent events showed that Bogyoke Aung San's intentions had been fulfilled.

Although much might be said against the way the *saohpalong* had administered their states and felt and acted in the past, relinquishing their hereditary rights was a praiseworthy act, General Ne Win declared. Had the *saohpalong* clung on to their rights, political and administrative problems would have beset Shan State and the Union, but by this present move, they had circumvented these problems. For such magnanimous gesture, the prime minister added, the *saohpa* and *sawphya* should be enshrined in history.

Regarding the future role of the *saohpa*, he expressed the hope that they would, in close cooperation with the people, actively assist with capital and brains in the economic, social, and industrial development of Shan State and of the Union as a whole. He also hoped that the people of Shan State would not be disrespectful to the *saohpalong*, because they no longer wielded power.

In conclusion General Ne Win urged the people of the Shan State to keep alive the Pang Long spirit kindled by Bogyoke Aung San, to foster Union consciousness, to destroy separatists and traitors to the Union, to eschew racialism, and to forward the progress and prosperity of the entire Union.[2]

On April 29, 1959, the head of the Shan State, Sao Hom Hpa, also delivered an address noting that the *saohpalong* had helped to draw up the constitution and were aware that Myanmar was to be a socialist state. Hence, in 1952, the Shan State government, headed by the *saohpalong* of Mong Mit, had made plans to relinquish their powers, though these had not come about at that time.

Now that within the short space of a few months, all powers had been given up to be replaced by a new administrative system, Sao Hom Hpa gave the assurance that the *saohpalong*, being public-spirited, would continue to work hand in hand with the Shan masses and strive more than ever for the benefit of the Union.

He urged whichever government came up in the future to strive hard to improve the administrative machinery so that it would be able to deal with the states in great momentum.

AGREEMENT BETWEEN THE SHAN STATE GOVERNMENT AND THE *SAOHPA*

This agreement is made on the 24th day of April 1959 between the government of the Shan State represented by its head and the *saohpa* of Mong Nai State, hereinafter referred to as the *saohpa*.

Whereas in the immediate and the best interests of the Mong Nai State and its people as well as of the government of the Shan State, the *saohpa* of Mong Nai State is desirous that the administration of the said state should be vested solely in the government of the Shan State without any reserve of power, authority, or jurisdiction in favor of the said *saohpa*.

And whereas the government of the Shan State and the government of the Union of Myanmar welcome the said transfer of power, authority, and jurisdiction.

It is hereby agreed as follows:

Article 1

The *saohpa* of the Mong Nai State hereby transfers to and vests in the government of the Shan State all his powers, authority, and jurisdiction in relation to the government of his state as from the 24th day of April 1959.

Article 2

In consideration of the said transfer the *saohpa* shall be entitled to receive as his commuted pension an outright payment of the sum of K 6,62,385 (Kyats six lakhs sixty-two thousand three hundred and eighty-five only) free of all taxes.

The amount so paid is intended to cover payments by the *saohpa* to his relatives of such sums of money and in such manner as he may think fit in lieu of pension received by them prior to this agreement. The said amount is also intended to cover expenses for the maintenance of the *saohpa*'s personal bodyguards (if any) maintained by him.

Article 3

Without prejudice to any future amendment to the Constitution of the Union of Burma, the *saohpa* shall be entitled to enjoy the use of the title of *saohpa*.

Article 4

The *saohpa* shall, subject to law, be entitled to the full ownership, use, and enjoyment of all his private properties, *e.g.*, *haw*, private houses, paddy fields, gardens, plantations, arms, etc., belonging to him on the date of this agreement as distinct from the properties, *e.g.*, offices, schools, jails, lock-ups, bungalows, hospitals, other buildings, lands, etc., of the Mong Nai State.

The *saohpa* will furnish the government of the Shan State before the 22nd day of April 1959 with an inventory of all the immovable property held by him as his private property.

Article 5

No inquiry shall be made by or under the authority of the government of the Shan State and no proceedings shall lie in any court in the Shan State against the *saohpa* in respect of anything done or omitted to be done by him in bona fide exercise of his powers, authority, or jurisdiction as *saohpa* or under his authority as such during the period of his administration of the Mong Nai State.

Article 6

Except for the previous sanction of the government of the Shan State, no criminal proceedings shall be instituted against any person in respect of any act done or purported to be done in the exercise of his duties as a servant of the Mong Nai State before the day on which the *saohpa* transfers the administration of the said state to the government of the Shan State.

Article 7

1. The government of the Shan State hereby guarantees *either* the continuance in service of the permanent members of the Mong Nai State Services on such conditions as are not less advantageous than those under which they were serving before the 1st June 1952 or the payment of them of reasonable compensation.

2. The government of the Shan State further guarantees the continuance of pensions and leave salaries sanctioned by the *saohpa* to members of the Mong Nai State Services who have retired or proceeded on leave preparatory to retirement, before the 1st June 1959.

In witness whereof the head of the Shan State for and on behalf of the government of the Shan State and the *saohpa* on behalf of himself, his heirs, and successors have hereunder set their hands at Taunggyi the day, month, and year first above written.

(Signed) Sao Hom Hpa,
Head of the Shan State
(For and on behalf of the Government of the Shan State)

(Signed) Sao Pye,
Saohpa of the Mong Nai State

OBSERVATION

The age-old feudal institution that had been operating in Shan State for more than a thousand years came to an end on April 29, 1959. It was too old to survive and too outdated to fit in with the changing political conditions of the twentieth century. Since the beginning of the twentieth century, the world had been ideologically in great conflict. Capitalist imperialism which had dominated the international political stage was in decline. A struggle between Nazism-fascism and capitalist imperialism led to the outbreak of the Second World War. Soon after the war, the world itself came under the influence of the newly emerged ideology of Marxist socialism, especially in the world of the have-nots.

In Southeast Asia a number of newly independent countries, included in the sphere of the have-nots, riding on the rising tide of the new ideology, turned against the evil influence of the old ideology and got themselves ready to accept the new Marxist-socialist ideology, the only alternative they believed would help to free them from the bondage of colonialism and promote the progressive way of life for the people. For many centuries the people of Southeast Asia were exploited by capitalist-imperialistic institutions in the fields of economy and politics. For them old institutions must go and new institutions based on the principles of Marxist socialism must be introduced for a trial.

Myanmar, after the Second World War, was a fertile ground for the growth of Marxist socialist ideology. Many Myanmar patriotic youths of the day were heady with Marxist ideology. They hoped to save the Myanmar people from the bondage of colonialism under the banner of this ideology. The Myanmar people, especially the politicians who professed a Marxist socialist ideology, were divided into two groups, the extremist and the liberal.

The liberal group successfully strove for national unity with the national races within the country to get independence from the British. The radical or extremist group, which believed independence could be achieved only through armed struggle, went underground to be known as the Myanmar (Burma) Communist Party (BCP), giving a lot of trouble to the country and sapping the strength of the nation to a great extent.

The liberal group, after achieving independence, adopted a democratic parliamentary system with socialist objectives for a trial. The trial failed after a decade and the political party of the AFPFL split into two factions, Stable and Clean. Other political parties danced around the split and involved themselves in the same game of power politics, further deteriorating the parliamentary system.

Politics became personal and factional and lost its national characteristics, weakening the country in all aspects, especially political.

The BCP and other insurgent groups took advantage of the political turmoil to ravage the country and disrupted the peace. Parliamentary democracy was then in its last stage of survival.

The only force in the Union that remained united and intact was the Union Armed Forces, Myanmar Tatmadaw. Its role became very prominent and important as the political situation of the country deteriorated.

Now, let us take a glance at the eastern region of the Union of Myanmar, called Shan State. What happened there? Shan State also could not avoid being affected by the split of the AFPFL. The *saohpa*, the ruling chiefs of Shan State, as well as the politicians split into different factions as happened in Myanmar proper.

The thirty-three *saohpa* who dominated politics in Shan State had never been able to unite into a single force that could mediate in Myanmar politics. They were not dynamic and quick enough to introduce reforms in their own states to meet the need of all-round development of modern times. Moreover, the feudal ideology could not match the growing forces of socialism or Communism or militarism and it was bound to be replaced. The Shan State people suffered much politically, economically, and educationally under the feudal administration for many years. The question was: who should they look to?

The incursion of the Kuomintang into Shan State added more trouble than the people could bear. The Kuomintang encroached on a large portion of Shan State after their defeat in the Chinese mainland and regrouped to use Shan land as a springboard to reinvade the mainland. They also recruited the native people for their troops, harassing the villagers to serve as porters, robbing and looting the properties of the nearby towns and villages, raping and committing adultery against married women and human trafficking, smuggling out prohibited goods like jade, precious stones, silver, gold, and other metals. Worst of all was the narcotic trade, which led to the growing of more poppies, the extracting of more opium, and the manufacturing of more heroin tablets which greatly affected the moral character and health of the Shan people. Many native youths became addicted to drugs and brought concern to their parents.

During the Kuomintang occupation, Shan State knew no peace. Fighting took place everywhere between the Chinese Communists, the Kuomintang, and the Union Forces, causing death and destruction to many native people. Very often the people were caught in the crossfire between two or three opposing forces and many lost their lives without being noticed by national or international humanitarian organizations.

The Kuomintang propaganda machinery also ground hard. Thousands of propaganda pamphlets were distributed, creating racial hatred, misunderstanding, mistrust, suspicion, ill-feeling, discrimination, and chauvinism between the Shan and Myanmar leaders including military officials and some sections of the public. Many leaders lost their sense of reconciliation and impaired the "Pang Long spirit" or the "Union spirit" that was once cherished by the Shan people. The Kuomintang propaganda did irreparable harm to the Shan leaders and the people. It urged Shan State to separate from the Union of Myanmar. It encouraged other national minorities to set up autonomous states and pick up arms to fight against the Union Armed Forces. The Union Armed Forces had shifted its attention to the Shan State and established a military administration to protect the people and to ensure peace and security. A new budget was allotted to buy arms and to fight against the Kuomintang.

On the other hand, the Chinese Communists moved more of their troops to the border areas to counterattack the encroachment of the Kuomintang. Very often the Communist soldiers crossed over into Shan State territories in pursuit of the Kuomintang. They also tried to organize the other ethnic peoples along the border to join their militia forces as did the Kuomintang.

Soon after the Second World War, the Shan State became peaceful and the Shan people began to put efforts to their work of rehabilitation. But for reasons they did not understand, their peaceful homeland had become a battleground of foreign forces. Imagine how much the Shan people suffered from the indiscriminate fighting that took place in their homeland. In this situation there was no way the feudal chiefs could help. It was beyond their power to help solve the problem. The feudal institution could not match the modern political and military conditions. In fact it had become defunct. It needed to be abolished. But how? By peaceful means or by force? The parliamentary system in Myanmar was in crisis and, in its final trial, it chose to resolve the issue of fuedalism in Shan State by peaceful means. Missions were sent to Malaysia and India to study how the feudal system was maintained or abolished. The Indian example was adopted and the maharajas were given lump-sum pensions for relinquishing their prerogative administrative powers.

The ceremony relinquishing power ended and the majority of the Shan people were happy and welcomed the new era of democracy that had been ushered into the Shan land. But they did not actually know much about the nature and function, the bittersweet taste of democracy. Still, they all hoped to find something better than feudalism. There were also those who disapproved of their Shan chiefs taking a lump-sum pension. They felt that the hereditary power of administration should not be exchanged for money. After all, all these powers derived from the people, so why should the *saohpa* take the money? They had been extracting money from the people through all sorts of taxation, for a long time. They had led luxurious lives for many years and that was enough. Some Shan youths, on behalf of those people, went to some of the feudal chiefs and put the matter straight to them. All sorts of vague reasons and answers were given to them. The Shan youths pressed on, saying that the pension should be contributed voluntarily to building institutions of higher learning and hospitals for the people. But all these appeals and requests were fruitless, to their great disappointment.

In retrospect, the addresses given by the three great statesmen—the president, the prime minister, and the head of Shan State—contained many fine, beautiful, and impressive words about democracy, national unity, safeguarding the constitution and the Union, destroying separatists and traitors, striving toward progress and prosperity, peace and security. But all these magnificent words, including the constitution and democracy itself, were buried on March 2, 1962, by a coup d'état, only three years after the *saohpalong* of Shan State had surrendered their hereditary rights and powers in exchange for democracy. The foundation of people's administration also disappeared from Shan land. The Shan people could do nothing except pray for democracy to come back soon.

Commuted Pensions for *Saohpalong*

State	Commuted pension based on the maximum annual revenue for 15 years	Commuted pension based on average forest royalty for 15 years	Total amount of commuted pension	Payment of commuted pension in accordance with the 88th meeting of cabinet
	Kyat	Kyat	Kyat	Kyat
1. Sa Koi	13,815	15	13,830	50,000
2. Pang Mi	33,585	...	33,585	50,000
3. Kyone	46,200	...	46,200	50,000
4. Sam Ka	120,780	...	120,780	120,776
5. Wan Yin	122,445	...	122,445	122,438
6. Baw	136,680	6,990	143,670	143,666
7. Mong Pai*	144,585	...	144,585	144,581
8. Ye Ngan	155,670	360	156,030	156,026
9. Pwe La	157,350	...	157,350	157,350
10. Nan Kok Nawng Won	191,745	...	191,745	191,741
11. Mong Pawn	215,040	...	215,040	215,044
12. Pang Laung	239,070	...	239,070	239,070
13. Ho Pong	250,125	...	250,125	250,125
14. Hsa Htung	262,620	2,355	264,975	264,968
15. Kehsi Mansam	263,595	...	263,595	263,595
16. Mong Hsu	264,030	...	264,030	264,023
17. Pang Tara	270,135	...	270,135	270,139
18. Ko Kang	332,520	...	332,520	332,524
19. Mong Pan	365,890	41,955	407,845	407,846
20. Mong Nawng	372,975	10,005	382,980	383,021
21. Hsa Mong Hkam	378,915	79,350	458,265	458,258
22. Mawk Mai	390,465	18,240	408,705	408,709
23. Lawk Sawk	413,670	13,605	427,275	427,279
24. Mong Lun	447,510	...	447,510	447,506
25. Mong Nai	640,140	22,245	662,385	662,385
26. South Hsen Wi	948,105	17,805	965,910	965,914
27. Lai Hka	979,875	14,610	994,485	994,481
28. Mong Kung	1,050,375	28,695	1,079,070	1,079,066
29. Yawng Hwe	1,245,870	2,205	1,248,075	1,248,075
30. Mong Mit	1,313,512	451,170	1,764,682	1,764,683
31. Tawng Peng	1,702,665	2,235	1,704,900	# 1,867,914
32. Hsi Paw	2,763,960	109,920	2,873,880	2,873,881
33. North Hsen Wi	3,463,920	62,985	3,526,905	3,526,910
34. Keng Tung	5,060,493	540	5,061,033	5,061,035
Total	24,758,327	885,330	25,643,657	25,863,029

* (Kayah State)

Inclusive of K 163,012 commuted pension based on average mineral royalty for fifteen years.

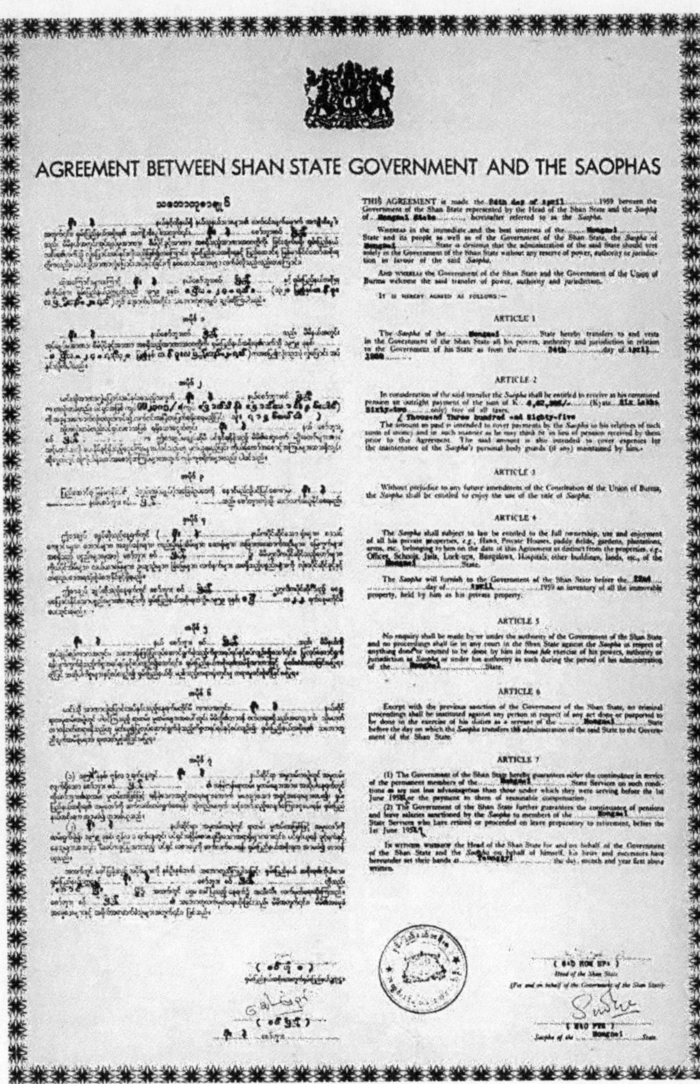

AGREEMENT BETWEEN SHAN STATE GOVERNMENT AND THE SAOPHAS

THIS AGREEMENT is made the 24th day of April..........1959 between the Government of the Shan State represented by the Head of the Shan State and the *Saopha* of Mongnai State.......... hereinafter referred to as the *Saopha*.

WHEREAS in the immediate and the best interests of the.......Mongnai.......... State and its people as well as of the Government of the Shan State, the *Saopha* of Mongnai..............State is desirous that the administration of the said State should vest solely in the Government of the Shan State without any reserve of power, authority or jurisdiction in favour of the said *Saopha*.

AND WHEREAS the Government of the Shan State and the Government of the Union of Burma welcome the said transfer of power, authority and jurisdiction.

IT IS HEREBY AGREED AS FOLLOWS:—

ARTICLE 1

The *Saopha* of the.......Mongnai..........State hereby transfers to and vests in the Government of the Shan State all his powers, authority and jurisdiction in relation to the Government of his State as from the..........24th.............day of April.... 1959........

ARTICLE 2

In consideration of the said transfer the *Saopha* shall be entitled to receive as his commuted pension an outright payment of the sum of K. 6,62,385/-........(Kyats Six Lakhs Sixty-two.......Thousand Three hundred and Eighty-five only) free of all taxes.

The amount so paid is intended to cover payments by the *Saopha* to his relatives of such sums of money and in such manner as he may think fit in lieu of pension received by them prior to this Agreement. The said amount is also intended to cover expenses for the maintenance of the *Saopha's* personal body guards (if any) maintained by him.

ARTICLE 3

Without prejudice to any future amendment of the Constitution of the Union of Burma, the *Saopha* shall be entitled to enjoy the use of the title of *Saopha*.

ARTICLE 4

The *Saopha* shall subject to law be entitled to the full ownership, use and enjoyment of all his private properties, *e.g.*, Haws, Private Houses, paddy fields, gardens, plantations, arms, etc. belonging to him on the date of this Agreement as distinct from the properties, *e.g.*, Offices, Schools, Jails, Lock-ups, Bungalows, Hospitals, other buildings, lands, etc., of the ....Mongnai..............State.

The *Saopha* will furnish to the Government of the Shan State before the 22nd.... ....day of.......April..............1959 an inventory of all the immovable property, held by him as his private property.

ARTICLE 5

No enquiry shall be made by or under the authority of the Government of the Shan State and no proceedings shall lie in any court in the Shan State against the *Saopha* in respect of anything done or omitted to be done by him in *bona fide* exercise of his powers, authority or jurisdiction as *Saopha* or under his authority as such during the period of his administration of the.......Mongnai..............State.

ARTICLE 6

Except with the previous sanction of the Government of the Shan State, no criminal proceedings shall be instituted against any person in respect of any act done or purported to be done in the exercise of his duties as a servant of the ....Mongnai..........State before the day on which the *Saopha* transfers the administration of the said State to the Government of the Shan State.

ARTICLE 7

(1) The Government of the Shan State hereby guarantees either the continuance in service of the permanent members of the.......Mongnai..............State Services on such conditions as are not less advantageous than those under which they were serving before the 1st June 1959 or the payment to them of reasonable compensation.

(2) The Government of the Shan State further guarantees the continuance of pensions and leave salaries sanctioned by the *Saopha* to members of the ....Mongnai.......... State Services who have retired or proceeded on leave preparatory to retirement, before the 1st June 1959.

IN WITNESS WHEREOF the Head of the Shan State for and on behalf of the Government of the Shan State and the *Saopha* on behalf of himself, his heirs and successors have hereunder set their hands at.......Taunggyi..........the day, month and year first above written.

(SAO HOM HPA)
Head of the Shan State
(For and on behalf of the Government of the Shan State)

(SAO PYE)
Saopha of the.......Mongnai..........*State*

FIGURE 16.1. Agreement between the Shan State government and the *saohpa*.

17

Proposal for Revising the Constitution

The quasi-federal constitution that had been put to the test in Myanmar thirteen years after independence failed to meet the needs of the ethnic nationalities who lived in the states of the Union.

The states' representatives gathered in Taunggyi, the capital of Shan State, in 1960 and expressed their dissatisfaction with the failure of the constitution to meet their needs. They pointed out the articles and clauses in the constitution that required amendment, and the reasons for amending them. They believed that all the crises that had arisen from the weak constitution could be resolved only by establishing a truly federal state system, in which Myanmar proper would be one of the component states, just like the others. In accordance with the then existing law, the proposal for amending the constitution would have to be approved by the parliament. Therefore, after the Chamber of Deputies of the parliament of the Union of Myanmar had passed the resolution for amending the Union Constitution, the Shan State government took the first active step in the matter. Even before the government established the Union of the Committee for Constitutional Amendment, the Shan State government convened a meeting on November 7, 1960, in Taunggyi, to obtain a wide variety of views on constitutional amendment.

The following delegates were invited to the meeting

1. Members of parliament representing Shan State
2. Two representatives from each constituency of Shan State
3. Three representatives from each political party of Shan State
4. Signatories to the Pang Long Agreement from Shan State
5. Former members of the Constituent Assembly representing Shan State
6. Other interested persons from Shan State[1]

Before the formal meeting was convened, a preliminary discussion on constitutional amendment was held in the office of the head of Shan State, Sao Hkun Hkio, on November 5, 1960.

The following independent observers and representatives of political parties attended the discussion:

1. Sao Hkun Hkio, head of Shan State
2. Thraysithu Sao Pye
3. Mahathraysithu Sao Htun E
4. Thiripyanchi Sao Hkun Aung
5. U Than Pe
6. U Si Ta
7. Thiripyanchi Sao Shwe Hmon
8. U Hla Pe
9. U Phyu
10. U Kyaw Sein
11. U Htwe Lon
12. Mr. Feroz Khan
13. U Aung Than
14. U Htun Ohn
15. U Lun
16. U Chit U
17. U Tin E
18. U Htun Pe
19. U Hkun Hti
20. Wunnakyawhtin U Thaung Pe[2]

At this meeting those present, realizing that much time would be required to draw up amendments to the constitution, decided that the *saohpa* of Hsa Mong Hkam, Sao Htun E, should make a motion at the meeting on November 7 for the formation of a scrutiny committee. They also decided that Thraysithu Sao Pye would be chairman, that the Shan State Council secretary, Sao Kya Sone, would be secretary, and that three representatives from each political party and from the Saohpa's Association, as well as five independent representatives proposed by U Tin E, would be members of the committee.[3]

At the meeting held at Sa-Myein Yeiktha[4] Building in Taunggyi, the participants decided to form a committee that would study matters about the constitutional amendment.

The Scrutiny Committee for Constitutional Amendment was then formed with the following members:

1. Sao Pye, Shan State Council		Chairman
2. Sao Hkun Aung	(Ya-Ta-Sa-Nya-Pha)	Member
3. U Hme	"	"
4. Sao Ywat Mong	"	"
5. Sao Shwe Thaike	(Saohpa's Association)	"
6. Sao Man Hpa	"	"

7. Sao Kya Seng	"	"
8. Sao Shwe Hmon	(Ya-Pa-Nya-Pha)	"
9. U Htun Ohn	"	"
11. U Htun Aye	(Ya-Pa-La-Pha)	"
12. U Hkan	"	"
13. U Aung Than	"	"
14. U Lun	(Ya-Pa-Nya-Pha)	"
15. U Soe Maung	"	"
16. U Chit U	"	"
17. U Pyu	(Pa-Ah-Ma-Pha)	"
18. U Hla Pe	"	"
19. U Kyaw Sein	"	"
20. U Htun Pe	(Independent)	"
21. U Hkun Hti	"	"
22. U Htun Myint	"	"
23. U Hkun Naung	"	"
24. U Yee Yao	"	"
25. Sao Kya Sone	"	Secretary[5]

The main task of the committee was to study and give suggestions concerning amendments to the constitution.

At its first meeting the committee decided to co-opt the following persons to the committee:

1. Sao Man Hpa
2. U Kya Bu
3. Dr. Ba Nyan
4. Sao Htun E
5. U Hkun Sam Myat
6. Sao Kyaw Khaung
7. Sao Hso Hom (*saohpa* of Mong Pawn)[6]

The committee was renamed the "(Shan State) Steering Committee for the Amendment to the Constitution of the Union of Myanmar."

The committee first considered the principles on which the constitutional amendment should be based. It therefore studied the principles laid down by the government concerning amendments to the constitution. These principles were:

1. To examine the provisions of the Constitution of the Union of Myanmar; and, without impairing its existing principles, to amend any provisions that contained insurmountable difficulties in their execution, if any such provision exists.
2. To amend those provisions found to be detrimental to democracy, but in so doing not to infringe upon the basic principles of the constitution.

3. To amend those provisions found to be detrimental to the perpetuation of the Union and to national unity and in so doing, to give priority to the perpetuation, solidarity, and unity of the Union.

In studying the principles for constitutional amendment, the steering committee could not define "existing principles" and so it could not begin its work on constitutional amendment.[7]

When the delegates from Shan State arrived in Yangon to attend the meeting of the committee held on December 22, 1960, they asked Dr. E Maung, the minister of justice, about the principles for amending the constitution.[8]

He answered: "Do not bother about principles. It is all right, so long as our Union of Myanmar remains a democratic state, and does not become a Communist or a fascist state."

At this meeting with Dr. E Maung, Sao Shwe Thaike presented to the committee a letter containing his personal views on constitutional amendment. He wrote:

> During the practical application of the Constitution of the Union of Burma for the past thirteen years, it was found that the constitution permitted the practice of racism . . . it appeared that Burma Proper had not become a constituent state of the Union, but had taken the place of the British in the administration of the constituent states. It also appeared as if these states did not join together in a voluntary union but were brought into subordination of Burma Proper. These constituent states had to request Burma Proper to provide for their needs. There is not a single right of self-determination given to the states by the constitution, and all administrative matters have had to be undertaken in accordance with the wishes of the Union government.[9]
>
> As no financial powers were given to the states, nothing could be done for their development; for example, as only Kyats 125 lakhs had been allotted as annual contribution to the Shan State, it appeared that the Shan State deserved only that amount, and no more. The Shan State had no voice in matters concerning the benefits accruing from the finances of the Union government. All other states were also in the same position.[10]
>
> According to the principle of federation, Burma Proper should be one of the constituent states and enjoy only those rights that the other states enjoyed. But because, under the present constitution, Burma Proper exercised the power and rights of the Union government, which are greater than those enjoyed by the states, the states are dissatisfied. No one in the states has the intention of destroying the Union. If Burma Proper becomes a constituent state of the Union, on an equal footing with other states, the dissatisfaction will gradually disappear. Therefore a true federal constitution should be drawn up in all sincerity."[11]

Having received an answer from Dr. E Maung to their questions about constitutional amendment, the Shan State steering committee was able to continue its work. It studied the constitutional provisions about judicial, administrative, and financial matters. And to clarify matters about administration, the committee met with such former Shan State officials as ex-Secretary U Nyo, Resident U Thaung Pe, Shan State Government Adviser Sithu U Tin, and U Hla Shein and discussed matters about their administrative experiences. From such studies the committee concluded that a partial amendment to the constitution would be inadequate and that a revision of the entire constitution was necessary. None of the representatives of the political parties in the steering committee could give suggestions about the guiding principles for constitutional amendment. Therefore the committee decided to base its work on the articles written by U Htun Myint (Taunggyi) in the *Botataung* newspaper under the title "The Federal System We Want."[12]

Work was carried out in accordance with the decision, and then the committee passed the following resolution on January 24, 1961:

> That the provisions for equal rights and opportunities between the various states and nationalities are not adequately prescribed in the present Constitution of the Union of Burma. The steering committee has therefore agreed that to ensure equal rights and opportunities for all, the constitution should be revised in accordance with the principles of a truly federal constitution.
>
> The steering committee has decided that in redrafting the constitution in accordance with genuine federal principles, the following basic requirements for ensuring equality shall be included:
>
> 1. Establishment of a Burmese state;
> 2. Assignment of equal powers to both chambers of the Union parliament;
> 3. Each state shall be represented by an equal number of representatives in the Chamber of Nationalities;
> 4. The following departments shall be vested in the Central Union, and all other powers, rights, and entitlements shall be transferred to the states:
>   (a) Foreign Relations
>   (b) Union Defense
>   (c) Union Finance
>   (d) Coinage and Currency
>   (e) Post and Telecommunications
>   (f) Rail, Air, and Water Transport
>   (g) Union Judiciary
>   (h) Collection of Custom duties at Seaports.
> 5. Union revenue shall be distributed equally.[13]

After laying down the above principles for amending the constitution, the steering committee formed a subcommittee with U Htun Myint (Taunggyi), *saohpa* of Mong Pawn Sao Hso Hom, Sithu U Tin, U Kyaw Sein, U Kya Bu, and U Hla Shein as members. On the instructions of the committee, the members of the subcommittee

FIGURE 17.1. Shan State Steering Committee for the amendment to the Constitution of the Union of Myanmar, February 22, 1961.

Seated left to right: Sao Kyaw Khaung, M.P. Ya-Ta-Sa-Nya-Pha; Thiripyanchi Sao Hkun Aung (*saohpa* of Baw) minister for information, Ya-Ta-Sa-Nya-Pha; Mahathraysithu Sao Htun E (*saohpa* of Hsa Mong Hkam) Ya-Ta-Sa-Nya-Pha; Thraysithu Sao Pye (*saohpa* of Mong Nai), chairman, chairman of the Shan State Council; Agga Mahathraysithu Agga Mahathirithudhamma Sao Shwe Thaike (*saohpa* of Yawnghwe) Saohpa's Association; Sao Yawt Mong, minister for public works, Ya-Ta-Sa-Nya-Pha; Thraysithu Sao Shwe Hmon (*saohpa* of Kehsi) Ya-Pa-Nya-Pha;

Standing left to right: U Htun Myint Galay (Independent); U San Mya, M.P. Ya-Pa-Nya-Pha; U Htun Ohn, Ya-Pa-Nya-Pha; U Hkun Hti (Independent); Sao Kya Sone, secretary, secretary of the Shan State Council; Sithu U Tin, (adviser on administration matters) present by invitation; U Khan, Ya-Pa-La-Pha; Sao Hso Hom (*saohpa* of Mong Pawn) Ya-Ta-Sa-Nya-Pha; U Aung Than, Ya-Pa-La-Pha; Sao Kya Seng (*saohpa* of Hsipaw) Saohpa's Association; Mahathraysithu U Kya Bu, retired principal agricultural officer, Shan State; U Hkun Sam Myat, parliamentary secretary, Ya-Ta-Sa-Nya-Pha; U Sang Sam, secretary, Shan State government, present by invitation.

went to Yangon, collected and studied data and materials relating to constitutional matters, and submitted a report to the steering committee.[14] After studying it and making numerous additions, amendments, and changes, the committee produced the document, "The Proposed Amendments to the Constitution of the Union of Myanmar, submitted by the Shan State." The document was approved by the State Convention, held on February 25, 1961, in Taunggyi.[15]

The document was presented in four parts:

1. Historical Background
2. The Shan State After the Second World War
3. The Defects and Difficulties that the Shan State Has Encountered in the Practical Application of the Constitution of the Union of Myanmar
4. The Establishment of a Truly Federal Union

Part 1 gave a condensed account of the migration of the Shan people into Myanmar and of Shan-Bamar relations up to the end of the Second World War. Part 2 comprised an account of postwar Shan State, the Pang Long Conference of 1946, the Aung San–Attlee Agreement, the Pang Long Conference of 1947, the Pang Long Agreement, the Frontier Areas Enquiry Commission, the AFPFL Convention, and the participation of Shan State in the Constituent Assembly. In relating how the constitution was drafted and approved by the Constituent Assembly, the document drew attention to the second of the seven directives concerning the constitution proposed by General Aung San:

> Within the Union, the individual states established by the constitution shall enjoy the powers of autonomy prescribed by the constitution. The document submitted by the Shan State said that this statement was but a general principle for the formation of the Union. Moreover, in putting forward the directives relating to the constitution in the Constituent Assembly there was criticism that:
>
> General Aung San himself had introduced the constitution drafted by the Preliminary Convention of the AFPFL to the Constituent Assembly "as a basis for discussion" and so it is quite apparent that some effort had been made to classify the constituent states into several levels.[16]

But the following reasons were given for accepting the constitution at the time:

1. Unfortunately, the national leaders headed by General Aung San were assassinated before the Constituent Assembly could complete its task. The whole country went into mourning. The fraternal national races became even more united.
2. The representatives of the colonialists approached the representatives of the Shan State and warned them that the situation in Burma was very bad, and that they should go home. They also tried to create divisions by promising the Frontier Areas more financial assistance for economic development should they decide not to federate with Burma, but would remain separate.

3. But the representatives of the Shan State, who had already committed themselves to achieving independence by cooperating with Burma Proper, were not to be swayed. They carried on participating in the work of the Constituent Assembly.
4. The representatives of the Shan State who participated in the Constituent Assembly were (1) politically immature; (2) had no understanding of legislative processes; (3) were preoccupied with the prospect of total independence within one year; (4) were trying to exhibit a united front after the loss of their leaders through political assassination. Therefore they casually accepted the provisions of the constitution.
5. They accepted General Aung San's exhortation to trust the spirit rather than the letter of the law. They never dreamed that after having gained independence, those considered as brethren might bring pressure on them by resorting to precise and literal interpretations of the constitution.
6. The Shan representatives were at the time in deep mourning over the assassination of their national leaders; were eager to gain freedom as speedily as possible in accordance with the guidelines laid down by their leaders; never entertained the thought that their own brethren would begin pressuring and bargaining against them after freedom had been obtained; never realized that by allowing Burma Proper to be combined with the Union government instead of being established as a constituent state; failed to understand that by allowing the separation of powers to be conducted according to the Canadian model, the Shan State would also lose its dignity and autonomy.
7. For the reasons stated above, the *saohpalong* of Tawng Peng, on behalf of the representatives of the Shan State, warmly supported the constitution.[17]

Part 3 of the Shan State document discussed in detail some of the provisions of the constitution and offered suggestions on the manner in which these might be revised. The discussions began with the use of the expression "Frontier Areas" in the preamble, which referred to people who are "citizens of Myanmar, including the Frontier Areas and the Karenni States." The document suggested that the use of the expression Frontier Areas should be revised as it sounded "derogatory and should therefore be replaced by the words "The Shan State, the Kachin State, the Kayin State, the Kayah State, and the Chin State." Since General Aung San had openly declared at the preliminary AFPFL convention that it was not appropriate to establish a unitary state,[18] the document suggested that the idea of a federal state formed with autonomous constituent units should be clearly stated in the preamble.

The document contained a further suggestion that section 8 of the constitution should be deleted. The section states: "All powers, legislative, executive, and judicial, in relation to the remaining territories of the Union of Myanmar shall, subject to the provisions of section 180, be exercisable only by, or on the authority of, the organs of the Union."[19]

The reason given for such deletion was that the section provided Myanmar proper with the right to exercise these powers of the Union in its own interests and that acceptance of a true federation would necessitate the deletion of this section. If this section did not exist, Myanmar proper would be just another state. In that case, it would experience firsthand the extent to which the constitution limits the powers of the states.[20]

The document also criticized the ambiguities in the definition and practical usage of the word "state" in section 9 of the constitution. The section states: "In this chapter[21] and in chapters 3[22] and 4[23] the term 'state' means the executive or legislative authority of the Union or of the unit concerned according as the context may require."[24]

The Shan State document pointed out that since the meaning of the term "state" was ambiguous in some places, it was not clear at all whether it referred to the constituent states, to Myanmar proper, or to the Union; that in the application of certain important provisions of the constitution the term "state" did not appear to mean the constituent state and consequently Shan State was denied some of the rights which it should have enjoyed; that although the meaning of "state" seemed to be clear in English, it did not appear to include the constituent states in its Myanmar usage; that as the Union government interpreted "state" at its own convenience the constituent states had no power to act on fundamental human rights, and that sections 42,[25] 43,[26] and 44[27] appeared to be beyond the jurisdiction of the constituent states.[28]

The amendment committee also discussed sections 23 (4) and 23 (5) and criticized the manner in which they were put into practice. The two subsections stated:

> (4) Private property may be limited or expropriated if the public interest so requires, but only in accordance with law, which shall prescribe in which cases and to what extent the owner shall be compensated.
>
> (5) Subject to the conditions set out in the last preceding subsection, individual branches of national economy or single enterprises may be nationalized or acquired by the state by law if the public interest so requires.[29]

In referring to the economic rights in the above section and subsection, the document clarifies that only the Union government could exercise them and that Shan State could not. If Shan State needed anything, the Shan State ministry, on behalf of the Union government, had to issue the order in the *Gazette*. In carrying out its duties, the Shan State government had to buy whatever commodities it needed, just like ordinary people, and this state of affairs diminished its dignity. In contrast, when the Union government departments wanted to acquire anything from Shan State, they could use the executive power vested in the Union government, without the need to consult the state government. This privilege amounted to a complete disregard for the state government. An example of this conduct may be seen in the supply of hydroelectric power from Lawpita to Upper Myanmar proper. The power was transmitted by cables erected across Shan State, using pylons built on Shan land. The land, belonging to the people who had originally cleared it for their own use, was expropriated by the Union government, which paid no compensation for using it. Moreover, the Union government failed to give prior information to the Shan State authorities about such matters.[30]

The amendment committee pointed out the defects that were found in section 30:

1. The state is the ultimate owner of all lands.
2. Subject to the provisions of this constitution, the state shall have the right to regulate, alter, or abolish land tenures or resume possession of any land and distribute it for collective or cooperative farming or to agricultural tenants.
3. There can be no large landholding on any basis whatsoever. The maximum size of private landholding shall, as soon as circumstances permit, be determined by law.[31]

In this section it would appear that the "state" meant the Union government. In stating that the state was the ultimate owner of all lands, the section was vague about whether this implied that the "state" meant Myanmar proper or the constituent states. It was also not clear whether land in Myanmar proper belonged to Myanmar proper, or whether land in the constituent states belonged to the respective states. If the "state" was interpreted to mean Myanmar proper, then it would seem that all lands within a constituent state would belong also to Myanmar proper. Therefore Shan State appeared to have no right to carry out land reform and land resettlement within its area. Thus the rights enjoyed by Shan State before independence, regarding the transfer of land title for the Shan, surrender of title and of succession, protection of landownership, and enactment of regulations on land had all been lost for the people of Shan State.[32]

The amendment committee also pointed out that Shan State suffered from the defects in section 31, which were similar to those of section 30, and which state:

1. By economic and other measures the state may help workers to associate and organize themselves for protection against economic exploitation.
2. The state shall protect workers by legislation intended to secure to them the right of association, to limit their hours of work, to ensure to them the right to annual holidays, and to improve working conditions, and, as soon as circumstances permit, to provide them with schemes for housing and social insurance.[33]

According to section 31, only workers at the Bawdwin Mines in Shan State were entitled to the rights provided by law. Other workers in Shan State did not enjoy the same rights as those given to workers in Myanmar proper. Although the Shan State government wanted to protect the rights of its workers, it had no power to do so.[34] The committee's document also criticized section 91 concerning the formation of regional organizations in the constitution, which states:

> Provision may, however, be made by law on principles of regional autonomy for delegating to representative bodies of such regions as may be defined in the law, specified powers in administrative, cultural, and economic matters. A law embodying such provisions shall determine the rights, powers and duties of such representative bodies and their relations to the parliament and the Union government.[35]

The document stated that the powers conferred by section 91 were not given to the state councils. This affected the dignity of the councils, in the establishment of representative local authorities within the states. It was most unsatisfactory for the Shan State that only the Union parliament could confer on the representative local authorities powers relating to administrative, cultural, and economic matters. Such a situation was tantamount to creating a parallel government within Shan State.[36]

Section 92 (3) of the constitution stated: "Any State council may, by resolution, surrender any of its territories or any of its powers and rights to the Union."[37]

Under this section, the state council could, by a decision, surrender its territories and its powers to the Union of Myanmar. However, the parliament had no power to grant any part of Myanmar proper or any of its powers to the states. Under genuine federal principles, the central Union government would be empowered to deal with matters pertaining to the states, and in wielding such powers, it should act only with the concurrence of the states. No state should surrender its territories or powers without the agreement of all the other states. If one compared the Union Legislative List and the State Legislative List, one would find that the powers reserved to itself by the Union were lopsidedly in its favor. If the states were to surrender any more territories or power to the Union, they would be left with nothing. According to the present legislative lists, the states could have no reason to surrender any of their rights.[38]

In its proposed amendments to the Union Constitution, Shan State clearly expressed its dissatisfaction with section 93, which read:

> The powers exercisable by the Union, by reason of the entry in the Union Legislative List, relating to the regulation of forests, mines, and oil-fields and mineral development, shall be subject to the condition that before the issue of any certificate, license, or other form of authorization, for the exploitation, development, or utilization of any forest, mine, or oil-field, the issuing authority shall consult the Union minister of the state concerned.[39]

According to the above stipulation, the Union government controlled the right of extraction and use of the mineral, forest, and petroleum products of value belonging to the states. Although in such matters consultation must be made with the Union minister of the state concerned, the decisions of the Union authorities were ultimately final. The authority for the extraction and use of these natural resources should reside in the state government concerned.[40]

The document also criticized the defects of section 94 (1), which states:

> Notwithstanding anything in section 92, if the president has declared by proclamation (in this constitution referred to as a "Proclamation of Emergency"), that a grave emergency exists whereby the security of the Union is threatened, whether by war or internal disturbance, or that a grave economic emergency affecting the Union has arisen in any part of the Union, the parliament shall have power to make laws for a

state or any part thereof with respect to any of the matters enumerated in the State Legislative List.[41]

The document stated that from experience gained during the military administration in the Southern Shan State, the term "president" referred only to the Ministry of Defense, the Home Ministry, and other ministries of the Union government. The document pointed out that nowhere was it mentioned that in proclaiming an emergency, the president must first get either the Shan State Council's or the Shan State government's consent.[42]

The document also discussed section 96, which states:

1. All revenues from the sources enumerated in the Fourth Schedule to this constitution shall form part of the revenues of the state in or by which they are raised or received.
2. All revenues other than such as are assigned to the states by the last preceding subsection shall form part of the revenues of the Union:

   Provided that the Union may make such grants or contributions from its revenues in aid of the revenues of the units as it may determine to be necessary on the recommendation of any board or other authority appointed for the purpose.[43]

Section 96 provided for the revenues of the governments of the constituent states to be supplemented by grants from the revenues of the Union government, if recommended by either a board or any other authority formed for this purpose. In this provision it would appear that the states had no right to receive such revenues, but that Myanmar proper granted such "aid" to the states out of sheer generosity. In reality, however, this so-called aid granted to the states consisted of revenues to which both the states and Myanmar proper were entitled, and which should be proportionately shared by them. The word "grant" should not be used. Therefore, the granting of the proportionate share of the revenue, to which the states are entitled, should not require the prior recommendation or approval of any "body" or "authority."[44]

The document also discussed section 122 of the constitution under which it would appear that the states could not establish industries or factories within them. Section 122 reads:

Subject to the provisions of this constitution, the executive authority of the Union extends:

(a) to the matters with respect to which parliament has power to make laws and
(b) to the governance, in accordance with the provisions of any treaty or agreement in this behalf of any armed forces not raised in the Union that may, with the consent of the government of the Union, be stationed in the Union or placed at its disposal.[45]

According to this section, it would appear that every matter over which parliament had the right to legislate would come under the administrative authority of the Union government. If this section were to be read in conjunction with the Union Legislative List, it would appear that since the states had no executive authority over matters relating to forests, petroleum, and mines, the state governments had no right to set up industries and factories within their own territories.[46]

The document also discussed sections 128 and 131. Section 128 provides that: An auditor general shall control on behalf of the Union all disbursements and shall audit all accounts of moneys administered and authorized by the parliament and the state councils.[47]

Section 131 provides that the auditor general shall submit to the Chamber of Deputies, at such periods as may be determined by law, reports on the accounts of the Union and the states.[48]

Thus, according to sections 128 and 131, all disbursements made on behalf of the state councils were administered and audited by the auditor general acting for the Union government. In this context, it would appear that appropriations and expenditures authorized by the state councils were subject to scrutiny and supervision by the Union government. The document assigned the state to appoint the auditor general and made him responsible only to the state council. Again the requirement to present a report on the state budget to the Chamber of Deputies would make it appear that the state governments were subservient to the Finance Committee of the Chamber of Deputies. In fact the State Budget Report should be submitted only to the state council. Only the Finance Committee appointed by the state council should have the power to penalize the state government for any misuse of its finances.[49]

The document also proposed that the word "council" mentioned in section 154 (1) be replaced by the term "State Legislature." The section states: "All the members of the parliament representing the Shan State shall constitute the Shan State Council."[50]

The document pointed out that the word "council" was an English term, and therefore it would be more suitable to use the words "State Legislature."[51]

The document also cited the difficulties in implementing section 160, which states:

> A member of the Union government, to be known as the minister for the Shan State, shall be appointed by the president on the nomination of the prime minister, acting in consultation with the Shan State Council, from among the members of the parliament representing the Shan State. The minister so appointed shall also be the head of the Shan State for the purposes of this constitution.[52]

Administrative difficulties were bound to occur, since a prime minister could not be expected to appoint a person he did not like to his cabinet.[53] The only solution to this problem was to create a true federal Union. Problems might also arise because the prime minister, in accordance with the decision of the Supreme Court of the Union, could appoint as head of state a Shan member of parliament who did not enjoy the support of the state council.[54]

The document also discussed the difficulties resulting from section 162 (1), (2), and (3).

The section states:

> 1. Subject to the provisions of this constitution, the executive authority of the state extends to the matters [over] which the state council has power to make laws, and in all such matters the decision of the council shall be binding on the head of the state.
> 2. The head of the state shall consult the state council on all other matters relating to the state.
> 3. In order to facilitate the communication of the decisions and the views of the State council to the head of the state, the council shall, at its first meeting after a general election, elect from among its members or otherwise, a cabinet of state ministers to advise the head of the state [on] his functions.[55]

Since section 162 (1) stated that in exercising his executive powers, the head of the state must do so in accordance with the decisions of the state council, this requirement would appear that the council should remain in permanent session, an impracticable stipulation.

The stipulation in subsection (3) was also impracticable, since it empowered the council to select members of the state government, whether the head of the state agreed to such a choice or not, and it was difficult to define the extent of the powers entrusted to the members of the state government. It was impossible to guess what the term "other matters" referred to.[56]

The document next discussed section 164 (2). The section states:

> Subject to any conditions that may be imposed by the Union in respect of any contributions from the Union, the state council shall have power to approve the budget of the state; and to enable the president to satisfy himself that the conditions have been duly observed, such budget shall be incorporated in the Union budget.[57]

In this matter the document pointed out that only the money in excess of the sum to which the state was proportionately entitled should be considered a "grant." The amount to which the state was entitled proportionately from Union revenues should not be bound by special procedures or regulations, although such regulations might be made about a genuine "grant."[58]

The document further discussed section 219, which states:

> All timber and mineral lands, forests, water, fisheries, minerals, coal, petroleum, and other mineral oils, all sources of potential energy and other natural resources shall be

> exploited and developed by the Union; provided that, subject to such specific exceptions as may be authorized by an act of parliament in the interests of the Union, the Union by an act of parliament may grant the right of exploitation, development, or utilization of the same to the citizens of the Union or to companies or associations, at least 60 percent of the capital of which is owned by such citizens.[59]

Under this section, all timber and mining lands, forests, water, fisheries, minerals, coal, petroleum, and all natural resources of energy or electricity located within the state were to be exploited and developed by the Union government. There would be fairness and justice only if the forests, mining lands, coal, petroleum, and all other resources located in Myanmar proper were to be exploited by a true federal government and the revenues and the profits so gained were shared by Myanmar proper, the Shan State, the Kachin State, the Kayah State, and the Karen State.[60]

The document also pointed out the dissatisfaction caused by the inclusion of section 222 in the constitution, which says:

> In this constitution, unless the context otherwise requires, the following expressions have the meanings hereby respectively assigned to them, that is to say:"Unit" means (a) any state forming a constituent unit of the Union of Burma; (b) all the territories of the Union of Burma not forming part of any state.[61]

According to this section, Myanmar proper could be regarded as merely another constituent unit of the Union. But in practice, not only was Myanmar proper not regarded as a constituent state but worse still, under the name "Union government" it exercised all the powers that only a truly federal government should enjoy. The states thought that Myanmar proper had unjustly held power over them in its role as the Union government. This was the cause of dissatisfaction among the states.[62]

The Constitutional Amendment Committee also discussed some other sections of the constitution and proposed amendments. The few provisions included on the Union Legislative Lists under the Third Schedule–List 1 which caused discontent in Shan State are:

> 1. Defense: that is to say, the defense of the Union and of every part thereof, including generally all preparations for defense as well as all such acts in times of war as may be conducive to its successful prosecution and to effective demobilization after its termination, and in particular—
>   (1) the raising, training, maintenance, and control of naval, military, and air forces and employment thereof for the defense of the Union and the execution of the laws of the Union and the states.
>   (2) ......
>   (3) ......

(4) Local self-government in cantons, the constitution, and powers within such areas of canton authorities, the regulation of house accommodation in such areas, and the delimitation of such areas.

(5) Arms, firearms, ammunition, and explosives.[63]

On the use of the armed forces to uphold the laws of the Union and the states during the period which ended in the recent general elections, there had been dissatisfaction throughout the Union, due to defective administration, inexperience, and ineptitude in administration and political machinations.

The armed forces were stationed in Shan State, but owing to a lack of understanding, unpleasant difficulties had arisen. The document pointed out that since law and order had now been restored in Shan State, the powers entrusted to the army for maintaining peace and security should now be reviewed, so that the army and the civil authorities could carry out their functions along clearly demarcated lines. In this way, both would serve the interests of the Union in a closer and more cordial manner.

As regards subparagraph (4), difficulties had been encountered by the creation of cantons in Shan State. The Shan State government had not yet approved or signed any agreement concerning certain areas expropriated for these cantons. The establishment of cantons was a system devised by the British and was now outmoded. This system had created problems for the urban population.

Regarding subparagraph (5), the document stated that the Shan State government had to assume responsibility for maintaning peace and security, but it had no modern weapons; various insurgent groups and dacoits had better weapons than the government. Wrong ideas had prevailed in certain quarters among the higher authorities about the provision of arms and ammunition to Shan State. Although the Shan State government was responsible for maintaining public order, it had no authority to buy arms and ammunition for the police force. After the *saohpa* had relinquished their powers, the police force had been enlarged, but without arms it could not carry out its duties effectively.

The document also cited discontent in Shan State with the following points found on List 1 of the Third Schedule:

2. External Affairs:
   - (2) Entering into agreements with the United Nations Organization without consulting the states
   - (3) Participating in international conferences, associations, and other bodies and implementing decisions made there
   - (5) Entering into and implementing treaties and agreements with other countries
   - (6) Regulating trade and commerce with foreign countries
   - (7) Acquiring foreign loans
   - (16) Maintaining import and export across customs frontiers as defined by the Union government

3. Communications:
   - (11) Posts and telegraphs, telephones, wireless, broadcasting, and other like forms of communication
4. Finance:
   - (1) Loans on credit of the Union
   - (2) Duties of customs including export duties
   - (4) Taxes on the sale of goods
   - (6) Taxes on income
   - (9) Estate duty and duties on succession to property
   - (10) Excess profits tax
   - (11) Savings banks
   - (12) Stamp duty on bills of exchange, checks, promissory notes, and other documents
5. General:
   - (4) Acquisition of property for the purpose of the Union
   - (11) Public debt of the Union
   - (13) Civil Law and Procedure, including the laws relating to: infants and minors; adoption; transfer of property; trusts and trustees; contracts; arbitration; insolvency; actionable wrongs; lunacy.
   - (16) Newspapers, books, and printing presses
   - (23) Electricity
   - (28) Planning
   - (31) Standard weights and measures
   - (32) Opium, except for excise duties thereon
   - (34) Development of industries where development under Union control, decided by Union law to be expedient in the public interest
   - (35) Cooperative societies
   - (36) Regulation of forests, mines, and oil-fields (including labor and safety in mines and oil-fields) and mineral development
   - (37) Migration within the Union

The document pointed out that on foreign affairs the states had not been consulted when the Union entered into agreements or treaties with the United Nations Organizations and its agencies for aid and grants. Therefore, in carrying out such agreements, difficulties had arisen for Shan State. The document explained that such agreements should be ratified not only by parliament but by the state council after prior consultation and the approval of the state government. Similarly, in drawing up regulations on trade and commerce with foreign countries, the Shan State government should be allowed to participate in the matter. As regards foreign loans, it would appear that the states had no right to take such loans. But they should be permitted to procure foreign loans, in accordance with the requirements of state finances. The document also stated that export and import duties collected across customs frontiers should be considered revenues of the Shan State government and be included on the State Revenue List.[64]

Regarding communications, the Shan State government had installed and operated wireless stations in towns which were headquarters of the district commissioners, as well as in certain towns which served as headquarters of assistant residents, and in police stations that were considered important. The Shan State government should have the right, under the constitution, to operate such wireless stations without having to pay license fees to the Union government. In the field of broadcasting, the Shan State government believed that it should be given the right to broadcast programs to promote the education and culture of the Shan people. Such broadcasts would be in harmony with democratic principles as envisaged in the constitution. They would also help develop education and culture in the Union.[65]

On financial matters, such as the payment of loans, the states had an indirect responsibility. Therefore, state governments should first be consulted, and ratification of loan agreements should receive the prior confirmation of the state councils. In making decisions for the use of such loans, care should be taken, so that the money would be spent on projects indispensable to the states, and thus the states should be allowed to borrow money for such purposes.

The document also suggested that states should share proportionately the money gained from customs duties. If export duties were collected on goods from Shan State, the entire amount should be turned over to the state after deduction of expenses. What was happening was that export duties were collected at Yangon and appropriated by the Union government. Export duties collected in Shan State were similarly taken by the Union government. Before the Second World War, these export duties were received by the Shan State government.

Shan State should collect taxes on commodities and trade to be used by its government. It expressed dissatisfaction with the income tax, since the state civil servants had to pay tax to the Union government and not to the Shan State government. The state government believed that income taxes collected in the state should be given to the state government. The same may be said of excess profit taxes. This document also pointed out that if companies were allowed to operate savings banks, the Shan State government should also be given the same right. Stamp duties on promissory notes and other negotiable instruments should be given to the Shan State government.[66]

The section titled "General" empowered the Union government to acquire property for matters relating to the Union. The State Legislative List had no similar provision, implying that the state had no power to acquire property. This right should be included on the State Legislative List. Regarding debts incurred by the Union, the Shan State government should not be made liable to repay any portion of such debt, because under the present constitution there is no fairness in the allocation of the Union government expenditure. The Shan State government should be made to contribute proportionately to the repayment of such debt only when a truly federal government was established. The document also suggested that the administration, jurisdiction, and powers regarding Civil Law should be given to Shan State, in the same way as in Criminal Law. The Shan State government should also have the right to establish printing presses. The document pointed out that under existing law, the Shan State government had no right to establish a government printing press.[67]

Shan State was still facing electricity problems and was dissatisfied with the supply of electricity within its area. Electric power was supplied to towns such as Meiktila, Myingyan, Kyaukse, and Mandalay, but although Taunggyi was the capital of Shan State, it had been bypassed. Only when the matter was brought to the attention of the Union government was Taunggyi electrified. Large and small towns in Eastern and Northern Shan State remained without electricity. Therefore, in places where the Electricity Supply Board was unable to supply power, the Shan State government should be permitted to supply it.[68]

"Planning" should have been included on the State Legislative List, but it was not. The Shan State government felt that, as regards weights and measures, it should have been allowed to standardize them for Shan State, in conformity with principles set down by the Union government.

Opium was an important subject for Shan State. People engaged in the cultivation, manufacture, and sale of opium were quite numerous in areas of Shan State east of the Than Lwin River. Although such activities relating to the production and sale of opium were undesirable, they were difficult to eradicate for lack of suitable crops that could be used as substitutes. At present because of the threat posed by the military operations of the Kuomintang, the Shan State government must continue to administer opium cultivation in accordance with existing laws, since this was the only way by which the problem could eventually be solved.[69]

Regarding section 34 "General," Shan State had been able to establish industries in the state only a few months ago, because of a misinterpretation declaring that Shan State had no power to set up industries. To ensure greater clarity, this subject should be included on the State Legislative List.

Cooperatives were also very important for the economy of Shan State. But by using them for political purposes, a successful enterprise for the people had been brought into disrepute. Therefore cooperatives should be administered by the Shan State government.

Section 36 of the Union Legislative List 1 reads: that as regards the regulation of forests, mines, and oil-fields and mineral development. According to sections 93 and 122, the Shan State government had no administrative power to regulate such matters. On the regulation of forests, Shan State used to administer them in its own right before independence. After independence it had had to surrender this administrative power. The Union government maintained that it would administer the forests and that after deducting administrative and other expenses, it would hand over the surplus money, if any, to Shan State. As the revenue received from the forests of Shan State amounted to about three million kyats, this arrangement must be objected to.

As for migration within the Union, when it involved migration from Myanmar proper to the states, or from one state to another, the prior consent of the government of the receiving state should be obtained.[70]

The State Legislative List 2, mentioned in the Third Schedule of the constitution, gave power to the states only in connection with the expenditure of revenues. As this power was found to be insufficient, dissatisfaction with the following points on the State Legislative List 2 was also mentioned:

2. Economic Affairs:
   (1) Agriculture; cattle pounds and the prevention of cattle trespass
   (2) Land; land revenue; land improvement, and agricultural loans; colonization; encumbered and attached estates; treasure trove.
3. Security:
   (3) The administration of justice; constitution and organization of all courts subordinate to the High Court, and fees taken therein, preventive detention for reasons connected with the maintenance of public order; persons subject to such detention
   (4) Jurisdiction and powers of all courts subordinate to the High Court on any of the matters enumerated on this list.[71]

Paragraph (1) under the heading "Economic Affairs" mentioned only agriculture, so it appeared that the Veterinary Department was not within the jurisdiction of the Shan State government. The question whether this department was or was not included on the State Legislative List had arisen previously. Therefore it was highly desirable that in determining divisions between the lists, the demarcation should be more clearly defined.

Paragraph (2) dealt with land, land improvement, and agricultural loans. Because of its unfavorable financial situation, the Shan State government could not provide agricultural loans, except for emergency loans, for extremely poor farmers. As a result the farmers had to rely on cooperatives and agricultural banks for loans. But either because of rivalry between these two bodies, or because of the scarcity of village cooperatives and agricultural banks, only 5 percent of farmers in Shan State who annually needed loans were likely to get them. If this state of affairs continued, even at the end of twenty years, the farmers of Shan State were unlikely to enjoy facilities equal to those of their counterparts in Myanmar proper. Therefore in accordance with the principles prevailing in Myanmar proper, the Shan State government should administer the cooperatives and agricultural banks within the state.

Relating to paragraphs (3) and (4) under the heading "Security," the appointment of judges in Shan State was still under discussion in the Supreme Court. But care must be taken to ensure that existing rights were not lost in the process.[72]

A study of Schedule 4 of the State Legislative List and the State Revenue List would show that the departments under the jurisdiction of Shan State on the Legislative

List, besides those of forests and excise, were departments of expenditure rather than revenue. In the annual allocation of revenues by Myanmar proper, Shan State received less than its fair share, owing to the sacrifices being made in the interests of the smaller states. Thus in the present circumstances, since the annual budget deficit of Shan State ranged from 25 million to 30 million kyats, the state government's income was no longer sufficient. Clearly the Shan State government would achieve effective administration and satisfactory development and establish a sound economy only when the Union government returned to the state government some of the revenues it had collected and appropriated for itself.[73]

The document also cited the following points that had become the cause of general dissatisfaction with certain sections of the constitution:

1. The Pang Long Agreement was the basis for creating the Union. But the parliament, the Union cabinet (Council of Ministers), and important senior and junior Union civil servants, seem to have forgotten or have been indifferent to the agreements and guarantees made in that historic document.
2. The sections in the constitution are interpreted very one-sidedly.
3. There is an assumption that in carrying out matters included on the Union Legislative List it is unnecessary to consult the state governments.
4. The Union civil servants have a very low opinion of the states.
5. They do not even accord state ministers the requisite respect.
6. In carrying out government functions (including financial ones) they act in a very biased and domineering manner.
7. The states do not receive the assistance they are entitled to.
8. In dealing with matters on the Union Legislative List within Shan State, Union government departments disregard the Shan State government.
9. They interfere in the politics and administration of Shan State.[74]

Part 4 of the document contained a proposal for the "Establishment of a Truly Federal Union" with the following headings:

1. The Structure
2. Distribution of Rights and Powers
3. Establishment of Parliament
4. Distribution of Union Revenues and Finance
5. Complete Autonomy for the States

Concerning the structure, the document stated that even at the time when drafts of the constitution were submitted to the Constituent Assembly for ratification, U Chan Htun had explained that a federal structure had been adopted due to unavoidable circumstances. But in adopting the federal structure, the true federal types such as those of the United States of America and Switzerland were not considered models for the Myanmar constitution. Instead, the Canadian type, which U Chan Htun considered moderate, was adopted. U Chan Htun stated: "Our constitution, though in theory federal, is in practice unitary." The reasons for framing such a constitution were:

> The chapters setting up the states, together with the concession of a right of secession (under stringent safeguards), were inserted to assuage the doubts of the Frontier leaders, rather than to meet actual or administrative requirements; a form of atonement for age-old suspicion of the Burmese which the Hill people could not at once discard.[75]

However, the frontier leaders' desire for a true federal structure was not due to suspicions of the Bamar, as U Chan Htun erroneously supposed, but was based on the principle of the right of self-determination for any nation or race. In the Union of Myanmar that was established, individual states were formed for the people of the Frontier Areas, such as Shan State, Kachin State, Kayah State, and Kayin State. But no separate state was established for Myanmar proper. Instead, it was established as an entity governed by the central Union government. This structure of the Union under the constitution was thus the cause for suspicion on the part of the frontier peoples. As it was also not in conformity with the principle of equality, it was feared that this structure could one day become the cause of the breakup of the Union. Therefore to ensure stability and equality, it was urged that in revising the constitution, Myanmar proper should be established as one of the constituent states.[76]

Regarding the distribution of powers, the frontier leaders expressed the desire that it be done in accordance with the true federal constitution. The distribution of power under the present Union Constitution was contrary to the wishes of the frontier leaders. In practice, the states had been given enumerated powers and the Union residuary powers. Although Myanmar proper was not a constituent state, it held all the powers of the Union government, which should not be the case. Thus the frontier peoples were dissatisfied because they believed that the Bamar had a monopoly on power. Therefore they suggested that in revising the constitution, the true federal principle must be followed, with the central government being given only those powers concerning subjects common to all, while allowing the states to retain all residual powers.[77]

The Union parliament was established with two houses, the Chamber of Nationalities and the Chamber of Deputies. But the Chamber of Nationalities did not enjoy the same powers as the Chamber of Deputies. The states also did not have the right to send an equal number of representatives to the Chamber of Nationalities. Since the Union government was responsible only to the Chamber of Deputies, the Chamber of Nationalities had little influence and as such could not defend the rights of the states. In revising the constitution, the Chamber of Nationalities must be given powers equal to those of the Chamber of Deputies and every state should also have the right to send an equal number of members to the Chamber of Nationalities.[78]

Concerning the Union revenues and budget allocations, the document on the "Proposed Amendments to the Union Constitution" stated:

> Of the revenue apportioned to the states under section 96 (1) of the constitution, apart from the revenue on lands and forests, all the rest do not amount to anything. The revenues collected are inadequate even for the current expenditure of the states. The states have to depend on the grants from the Union provided under the exception to section 96. The states have been unhappy with the way the revenues are distributed [since] the date of independence. No definite financial policy has been laid down up to now. That is why, when the new truly federal constitution is drawn up, the question of distributing revenues must be considered in depth, and enacted explicitly.[79]

On complete autonomy for the states, the document on the "Proposed Amendments to the Union Constitution" put forward the following suggestions:

> 1. The right of every constituent state, including the Burma State which shall be established, to complete autonomy shall be spelled out in the new constitution. The constitution shall require that there be no interference by the central government or by any other state in the internal affairs of any state.
> 2. Since the revised new Constitution of the Union of Burma will be of the genuine federal type, the states shall each have their own constitution, their own State Legislative Assembly, their own separate government, and their own distinct and separate judiciary and courts of law, provided that these state institutions are not inconsistent with the Central Union Constitution.
> 3. For those peoples who lack the qualifications for forming a state, national areas shall be established, and guarantees for the protection of their national rights shall be entrenched in the new constitution.[80]

U Tun Aye (Nam Hkam), who was a member of the Steering Committee as a representative of the Ya-Pa-La-Pha, did not attend any of the meetings at which the document on the "Proposed Amendments to the Union Constitution" was drafted. He also did not sign this document, because he disagreed with its contents.[81] After the drafting was completed, the Steering Committee submitted the document for adoption to the All States Conference, held in Taunggyi on February 25, 1961. A small committee, composed of Sao Shwe Thaike, the *saohpa* of Hsa Mong Hkam Sao Htun E, Sao Kyaw Khaung, U Hla Pe, U Soe Maung, and U Hkun Sam Myat, was formed and entrusted with the responsibility of discussing the document with Dr. E Maung, the minister for judicial affairs.[82]

18

The All States Conference at Taunggyi

SCRUTINY COMMITTEE FOR THE STATES AND THE FEDERAL ISSUE

The document suggesting revision of the Constitution of the Union of Myanmar submitted by Shan State was discussed by the Scrutiny Committee at its meeting at the New Secretariat on Kanna Road, Yangon, on March 15, 1961.[1] A draft for revising the constitution was presented by the Kayin State minister, Dr. Saw Hla Tun. The discussion, however, was primarily based on the document submitted by Shan State. Sao Shwe Thaike, the *saohpa* of Hsa Mong Kham, Sao Htun E, and Shan State minister Sao Hkun Aung explained the proposals in the document.

They pointed out that the constitution was drafted to limit the powers of the states,[2] and for that reason difficulties were encountered during the past thirteen years in economic development and administrative matters. To overcome those difficulties, it had become imperative that a true federal constitution be drafted. On this matter all political parties in Shan State had been consulted at the Taunggyi Conference.[3]

The revision of the constitution was further discussed at the special meeting of the States Scrutiny Committee on March 20, 1961.[4] At that meeting the *saohpa* of Hsa Mong Hkam again explained that the document submitted by Shan State was made in all sincerity and without any external influence to prevent the Union from disintegrating.[5]

Though differences over the Shan document emerged among the states' leaders, the majority agreed to accept it. Dr. Saw Hla Tun supported the document, but suggested that solutions be sought to deal with the difficulties that might arise in revising the constitution. He presented to the chairman of the meeting the Kayin State resolution, passed and signed by the Kayin State leaders, supporting the document submitted by Shan State.[6]

Minister for Kayah State Sao Wunna suggested forming a committee composed of the representatives of all the states to work collectively and unitedly in order to achieve success in revising the constitution.

U Sein of Kayah State also spoke in favor of the document, urging that the constitution be revised immediately while the opportunity was favorable.[7]

Kachin minister Duwa Zau Rip asked for more time as the situation in his state, at that time, was unfavorable for revising the constitution. U Zan Hta Sin of Kachin State suggested forming a committee to study the draft for constitutional revision presented by Shan State and the other states. He said the most difficult problem faced by the states was financial. U Sein Toe, finance minister of the Kachin State, was in favor of the document presented by Shan State, but suggested that the views of the other small states should also be considered on whether they would accept a true federal system or not.[8]

U Zahre Lian, the Chin minister, said the Chins had no state but were making an effort to achieve one. He doubted that Shan State would get all that it had asked for in its draft and suggested that it should have focused on getting sufficient financial contributions and transferring certain powers to the states. He announced that he would put the Shan State document to the Chin Council for consideration and would give a reply later.[9]

Captain Mang Tung Nung, parliamentary secretary of the Chin Affairs Ministry, spoke in favor of the document. Although he supported the present constitution in principle, as difficulties had gradually begun to appear in its implementation, he thought it was time to remove those sections of the constitution that limited the powers of the states.[10]

To further discuss the principle of a true federal system as presented by Shan State and to revive the Supreme Council of the United Hill Peoples that had been formed in 1947, the leaders of the states agreed to hold an All States Conference in Taunggyi. Shan and Kayah states took responsibility for convening the conference.[11]

MEETING BETWEEN PRIME MINISTER U NU AND STATE LEADERS

Just before the All States Conference was held, Prime Minister U Nu met with the Speaker of the Chamber of Nationalities Sao Hkun Kyi, Union Minister for Shan State Sao Hkun Hkio, ex-President Sao Shwe Thaike, Parliamentary Secretary of Shan State Ministry U Hkun Sam Myat, Kayah State Minister Sao Wunna, and the representatives of Shan and Kayah states from the Chamber of Deputies and the Chamber of Nationalities. The prime minister discussed with the state leaders matters relating to the document proposing revisions of the constitution, as well as the insurgency in Shan State. U Nu said that problems should be solved through sincere discussion and that external military assistance should not be sought for solving internal problems. He also asked the attendees about the veracity of reports that some politicians in Shan State were instigating the Shan insurgency, and that foreign influence helped draft the document. The Shan State representatives denied both allegations. U Nu promised that on his return from China he would go to Shan and Kayah states for further discussions to help solve the problems within the states.[12]

U Nu returned from Yunnan on April 16 and on the afternoon of April 17 met with Shan State officials in Lashio. In the evening he had discussions with the *saohpa*, members of parliament, and leaders of Shan State parties. During the discussions a Shan representative gave his view that if a Federal Council, as desired by Shan State leaders, was created and entrusted with full powers, the political problems of Shan State would disappear. U Nu declared that he would not yield to any demand under the threat of arms or the creation of violent upheavals. He added that there was no problem that could not be solved amicably, through friendly negotiations at the table.[13]

DISCUSSIONS BETWEEN PRIME MINISTER U NU AND SHAN STATE REPRESENTATIVES

U Nu arrived in Keng Tung on April 18 and held discussions with civil and military officials, political leaders, and *saohpa*. At the dinner he hosted, he said that the leaders of Myanmar proper did not practice chauvinism, nor did they have expansionist intentions. He said no problem could not be solved fraternally at a face-to-face meeting.[14]

U Nu arrived in Taunggyi again on April 21 and met on the morning of April 21 with Shan State ministers and Shan State government officials. At the meeting the *saohpa* of Hsa Mong Hkam, Sao Htun E, presented the situation in Shan State. He also drew the prime minister's attention to the timely help given by Shan State to the Union during the critical period of insurgency in 1948–49. He urged the prime minister not to believe the rumors spread by certain people. He assured him that Shan State would never try to break up the Union.[15]

At the meeting U Nu revealed that he had received an important letter from Singapore. The letter said a representative of a foreign organization was to be stationed in Bangkok to direct and assist the Shan State revolution, and to get foreign assistance to enable Shan State to secede from the Union. U Nu knew who the culprit was and had decided to arrest him, but Sao Hkun Hkio had made a personal request not to carry out the arrest. Consequently the arrest was postponed.[16] U Nu also urged his audience not to believe the allegation that the Bamar were practicing chauvinism over the Shan people. He said that there were the Lahu, E-Kaw, Palaung, Danu minorities in Shan State, and these people were also worried that the Shan people might also practice chauvinism over them and oppress them. He said it was better not to entertain any idea of "the major race as against the minor one."[17]

Brigadier Aung Gyi, who also attended the discussions, noted that Shan State had not only political and administrative problems but military problems. He asked the *saohpa* to speak out if they had any grievances. He said there were good soldiers in the army, as well as bad ones. Battles had to be fought in Shan State because the number of Shan insurgents had risen day by day, and being a citizen of the Union, not because he was a Bamar, he was responsible for safeguarding the Union. He said news had been received from the Thai authorities that Shan insurgent leaders had gone to Bangkok to seek arms. The brigadier warned that the situation in Shan State could get worse if the insurgency remained unchecked. He urged the *saohpa*, therefore, to cooperate with the army to bring the insurgency to a speedy end.[18]

On April 21 Prime Minister U Nu held discussions with *saohpa*, members of the Chamber of Deputies and the Chamber of Nationalities, leaders of various political parties, independent politicians, members of the Steering Committee for the Revision of the Constitution, and the ministers of the Shan State government at the Government Guest House in Taunggyi.

During the discussions the *saohpa* of Mong Nai, Sao Pye, presented the document proposing the revision of the constitution, with explanations. After that, Saohpa Hkun Pan Sing (Tawng Peng), Sao Htun E (Hsa Mong Hkam), Sao Hso Hom (Mong Pawn), Sao Hkun Aung (Baw), U Po Hlaing (Ya-Ta-Sa-Nya-Pha), U Htun Aye (Ya-Pa-La-Pha), U Aung Than (Ya-Pa-La-Pha), U Kyaw Sein (Pa-Ah-Ma-Pha), U Lun (Pa-Ah-Nya-Pha), U Htun Pe (Independent), and U San Mya (Independent) presented their views, pointing out that the revision was based on the principles laid down by the Union government and drafted collectively by the leaders of Shan State. They explained that a true federal constitution needed to be drafted because the present one lacked strong guarantees for the states and the national minorities. Therefore a draft for a true federal constitution had been prepared to perpetuate the Union, prevent the country from becoming Communist or fascist, and avoid the undermining of democracy. The revision document had been carefully drafted in the spirit of Pang Long, involving no foreign interference and having no intention to secede from the Union.[19]

U Htun Aye (Ya-Pa-La-Pha) was the only person at the discussions against the proposals for revising the constitution submitted by Shan State. He argued that as long as the insurgency was still rampant in Shan State, and as long as the *saohpa* still enjoyed the privilege of being members of parliament without having to contest a seat in the elections, the revision of the constitution should not be considered.[20]

He went on to say that just before U Nu and Shan State leaders met on April 29 in Taunggyi, the Ya-Pa-La-Pha had given a press conference, and that he, U Htun Aye, had said that although he was then in favor of revising the constitution in principle, he doubted that implementation was possible until the insurgency in Shan State was eliminated and the members of parliament could be elected by the people.

U Nu said that most people, including himself, suspected that some *saohpa* were, somehow or the other, aiding the insurgents. He would like the Shan State government to condemn the insurgents in order to dispel these doubts and suspicions.[21]

On the evening of April 21, discussions were held between the army officers led by Brigadier San Yu[22] and the representatives of Shan State.[23] The purpose was to enable Shan State representatives to voice their dissatisfaction with the army, frankly and openly. The representatives complained that voters who had supported the "Clean AFPFL" in the 1960 general elections had been abused by the soldiers, that suspects had been arrested, tortured, and killed, making some others go underground, and that some women had been harassed by the soldiers. San Yu replied that should there be any cause for complaint in the future, the representatives should communicate with the brigade commanders and discuss matters with them frankly and openly, at any time. He urged them to trust the army, cooperate with it, and seek its help at all times.[24]

PRESS CONFERENCE BY PRIME MINISTER U NU

On his return from Taunggyi, U Nu held a press conference in Yangon on April 25. At the conference he revealed the details of the letter he had received from Singapore about the request for foreign help made by a prominent person[25] from Shan State. U Nu said the document revising the constitution submitted by Shan State was discussed at the cabinet meeting, held on April 24. The cabinet had decided that the document would be discussed at a face-to-face meeting which should lead to a solution. This would be done only on condition that *saohpa* and political leaders made a declaration denying their links with the Shan insurgents.[26]

ALL STATES CONFERENCE AT TAUNGGYI

On June 8, 1961, Shan and Kayah states convened an All States Conference at the Sa Myein Yeiktha in Taunggyi to discuss the document revising the constitution submitted by Shan State and to reconvene the Supreme Council of the Organization of the United Hill Peoples. Representatives of Myanmar and the Ya-Pa-La-Pha were not invited.[27]

The conference was attended by delegates from Kachin, Kayah, Kayin, and Shan states and the Chin Special Division, and also from the Mon and Rakhine areas, to whom U Nu had promised statehood. There were altogether 226 delegates and 104 observers. Shan State had 130 delegates and they were in the majority; the Chin and Rakhine areas had only 5 delegates each. Of the heads of states, only the Kayah State minister, Sao Wunna, could attend the conference.[28] Dr. Saw Hla Tun, the Kayin State minister, was abroad on a tour to study small industries and modern techniques of farming.[29] Sao Hkun Hkio, Shan State minister, could not attend the opening ceremony, because he was in Geneva attending the Fourteen-Nation Conference on Laotian Affairs, but he returned on June 8, the day the conference was convened.[30] Kachin Minister Sama Duwa Sinwa Nawng and U Zahre Lian (Chin), who believed that the true Federal Principle was not feasible,[31] boycotted the conference.

Minister Sao Wunna acted as chairman of the conference and gave a short account of the history and objectives of the Supreme Council and the reasons for its revival. Then he continued:

> The states had joined hands with Burma Proper to achieve independence. Therefore, we must continue to strive for the perpetuation and development of the Union. We

> will never accept any attempt to weaken, destabilize, or cause the disintegration of the Union. We will not be contented with mere verbal condemnation. We will have to fight, unitedly, for the eradication of any such attempt. Similarly, we should be aware of our responsibility to totally eliminate any attempt to sow seeds of dissension between Burma Proper and the states, and among the states themselves, and also to prevent any violence. The states are like younger brothers, while Burma Proper is like an elder brother. Therefore, if the states have any demands to make, they should be made on good grounds and in a family spirit. Violent means or armed rebellion should not be entertained even in thought. Success will not be achieved, especially in this Union, if high-handed tactics are used. We should not take advantage of the opportunity to force others into a corner. Such devious means with evil intentions will adversely affect the good will of the other party, in which case neither side will benefit. In conclusion I would like to request you all to deliberate at this conference with a sense of unity and good will for the benefit of the whole Union.[32]

The opening address by Sao Wunna was followed by the speeches of Shan State delegate Sao Htun E, Rakhine delegate U Maung Oo Kyaw, Kayin State delegate U A. Soe Myint, Mon delegate Nai Hla Aung, Chin delegate Captain Mang Tung Nung, Kayah State delegate U L. Aung Sein, and Kachin State delegate U Zan Hta Sin. Most of the speeches recalled the spirit of the Pang Long Conference held in 1947, and its significance was expressed in such slogans as "Pang Long Conference and the Union are inseparable," "The birth of the Union was made possible by the Pang Long Conference," "Pang Long is an important pillar of unity for the nationalities."

The delegates declared that the objectives laid down at that conference had, however, not come about. Conditions in the states had not developed as they should have during the thirteen years of independence.

The delegates felt the time was now ripe for analyzing the problems of the states, and to find ways of perpetuating the Union, which had its birth at the Pang Long Conference.[33]

A committee comprising the following persons was formed to supervise the Taunggyi All States Conference:

1. Sao Htun E (Shan), member of the panel of chairmen
2. U Hla Pe (Shan), member of the panel of chairmen
3. Sao Hkun Aung (Shan), member of the panel of secretaries
4. U Maung Oo Kyaw (Rakhine), member of the panel of chairmen
5. U Tha Dun (Rakhine), member of the panel of chairmen
6. U Maung Maung (Rakhine), member of the panel of secretaries
7. Nai Hla Maung (Mon), member of the panel of chairmen
8. Nai Ngwe Thein (Mon), member of the panel of chairmen
9. Nai Thein Maung (Mon), member of the panel of secretaries
10. Captain Mang Tung Nung (Chin), member of the panel of chairmen
11. U Kyin Shin Htan (Chin), member of the panel of chairmen

12. U Hla Nyein (Kayah), member of the panel of chairmen
13. U L. Aung Sein (Kayah), member of the panel of chairmen
14. U Chit Maung (Kayah), member of the panel of secretaries
15. U A. Soe Myint (Kayin), member of the panel of chairmen
16. Saw Po Aung (Kayin), member of the panel of chairmen
17. U Saw Paul Paw (Kayin), member of the panel of secretaries
18. Duwa Zau Lawn (Kachin), member of the panel of chairmen
19. Howa Duwa Hkun Hpon (Kachin), member of the panel of chairmen
20. Duwa Nang Zing La (Kachin), member of the panel of secretaries

STATES UNITY ORGANIZATION

The supervisory committee met on June 9 and discussed the formation of a States Unity Organization. The conference passed a resolution comprising the following objectives:

1. The perpetuation of the Union
2. The right of self-determination for the states
3. The promotion of friendly relationships among the Union nationalities
4. The protection of human rights
5. The development of all ethnic minorities in each state
6. The making of concerted efforts in dealing with matters relating to the states[34]

These objectives were thrashed out by the Shan delegates U Htun Pe, U Kyaw Sein, U Htun Ohn, U Tha Zan, U Sao Aung Hpu; Kachin delegate Duwa Lawang Li; Kayah delegate U Saw Thein; and Rakhine delegate U Ba Phyu at 2:00 P.M.[35]

A committee for establishing the States Unity Organization was formed on June 10:

1. Sao Hkun Aung	Shan State information minister
2. U Kyin Shin Htan	Chin
3. Nang Zing La	Kachin
4. U Hla Pe	Shan
5. U Tha Dun	Rakhine
6. U A. Soe Myint	Kayin
7. U Chit Maung	Kayah
8. U Nai Thein Maung	Mon
9. U Htun Pe	Shan (secretary)
10. U Nyunt Pe	Shan (secretary)[36]

As the discussions on the States Unity Organization continued until June 11, the Taunggyi All States Conference was unable to convene on schedule.[37]

Differences of opinion arose about the formation of the States Unity Organization and seven delegates from the Kayin National Organization, Saw Norton Bwa, Mahn

Aung Than, Mahn Nyunt Maung, Saw Ba Lin, Mahn Aye Maung, Mahn Htun Yone, and U Moe Tha left Taunggyi on June 11.[38]

The AFPFL Kayin delegate U A. Soe Myint resigned from the panel of chairmen and U Saw Paul Paw resigned from the panel of secretaries on June 12, objecting to the strong political implications embodied in the formation of the States Unity Organization. But they continued to attend the conference.[39]

Finally the delegates agreed to form the States Unity Organization on June 12.

THE ARRIVAL OF THREE MINISTERS IN TAUNGGYI

Minister Sao Hkun Hkio returned to Yangon from Geneva on June 8. Before leaving for Taunggyi, he met with Ministers U Zahre Lian and Sama Duwa Sinwa Nawng at his residence. They discussed the document revising the constitution and the question whether to attend the Taunggyi conference, which they decided to attend.[40] After the meeting, Minister Sama Duwa Sinwa Nawng told reporters that he had originally decided not to attend the conference, because the head of Shan State would not be present. Now that he had been invited by the head of Shan State, he would attend. Minister U Zahre Lian gave the same reason for attending the conference.[41] Minister Sao Hkun Hkio, Minister Sama Duwa Sinwa Nawng, and Minister U Zahre Lian arrived in Taunggyi on June 13.[42]

The supervisory committee of the States Unity Organization met on June 13 at 9:00 A.M. with Sao Wunna as chair. Matters on the formation of a provisional executive committee and finance committee were discussed. When the All States Conference convened at 2 o'clock in the afternoon, Sao Hkun Hkio, minister for foreign affairs and head of Shan State, acted as chairman. Kachin State Minister Sama Duwa Sinwa Nawng and Chin Division Minister U Zahre Lian attended the conference. The formation of the States Unity Organization, its objectives, and work programs were ratified. A discussion was also held about the formation of an executive committee of the States Unity Organization, which comprised the following persons:[43]

1. Sao Hkun Hkio, president
2. Sao Wunna, vice president
3. One Kachin representative, vice president
4. Sao Htun E (Saohpa of Hsa Mong Hkam), secretary
5. U Hla Pe(Pa-O), joint secretary
6. Sao Hkun Aung (Saohpa of Baw), information officer
7. One Kayah representative, treasurer
8. U Tha Dun (Rakhine), auditor
9. Three Kachin representatives, reserve EC members
10. Two Chin representatives, reserve EC members
11. One Rakhine representative, Reserve EC member
12. Two Mon representatives, Reserve EC members

13. Two Kayin representatives, Reserve EC members
14. Four Shan representatives, Reserve EC members

The Constitution of the States Unity Organization stipulated that the organization was to be composed not only of Shan, Kayah, Kayin, and Kachin states which already existed within the Union of Myanmar, but also of the representatives of the Mon, the Rakhine, and the Chin Division, which had all the characteristics and qualifications of statehood, and which were attaining statehood. The States Unity Organization was to be steered by a supervisory committee composed of six representatives from each state.[44]

The objectives of the organization were:

1. To try to the utmost to perpetuate the Union
2. To give to the states within the Union the right to self-determination and to exercise this right freely
3. To promote friendly relations between national minorities in the Union, irrespective of race or religion
4. To protect and defend national equality within the Union and the enjoyment of human rights in accordance with the principles of world democracy
5. To strive for the development of all national minorities within the states
6. To solve all problems relating to the member states of the organization in a concerted manner[45]

The political program of the States Unity Organization was as follows:

1. To protect and defend with the help of the people the perpetuation of the Union against any element that might threaten the independence of the Republic of the Union of Myanmar
2. To maintain the nation's neutral policy on the basis of the five Principles of Peaceful Coexistence
3. To unitedly defend the full right to self-determination of every national minority in the states from encroachment by all subversive elements
4. To strive to the utmost for the cultivation of friendship between national minorities and to resist narrow nationalism and chauvinism
5. To unitedly strive for full equality and for democratic rights of every national minority in the Union
6. To strive to the utmost for the political, social, and economic development of all nationalities in the states
7. To unitedly seek redress for grievances and suffering of any national minority in the states within or outside of parliament[46]

The economic program of the States Unity Organization was as follows:

1. To establish a system of national economy free from foreign monopoly and control

2. To establish a modern agricultural system
3. To establish industries owned by nationals within the states
4. To encourage a cooperative system of collective production and collective trade
5. To have the right to determine how the raw materials underground and aboveground in the states would be used by the national minorities
6. To render mutual and reciprocal help to one another in interstate economic matters[47]

The principles embodied in the social policy of the States Unity Organization were as follows:

1. To raise the standard of living of the people in the states
2. To preserve, safeguard, and promote the culture, customs, traditions, and literature of the national minorities
3. To upgrade to the utmost programs for the physical fitness and public health of the people of the states
4. To establish universities and vocational schools and institutes
5. To maintain and protect the traditional judicial system of national minorities which does not in any way hamper modern development[48]

On June 13, the day the States Unity Organization was formed, the Ya-Pa-La-Pha issued a statement saying that although each state had expressed grievances at the conference, no redress could be offered, because no political party from Myanmar proper had been invited; that because of this one-sided presentation of the grievances, problems could not be solved, and more misunderstanding could take place.

The statement made an appeal to consider the condition of the Shan masses when other states and national minorities asserted their legitimate rights at the Taunggyi Conference, which had originated owing to the *saohpa*'s dissatisfaction with the surrender of their powers.[49]

DISCUSSIONS ON THE SHAN PROPOSAL

The States Unity Organization was formed on June 13 and the document revising the constitution was taken up at the conference on June 14. The Supreme Council for the Supervision of the Taunggyi All States Conference met on the morning of June 14. It opined that if a true federal system proposed by Shan State was to be adopted, a new constitution would have to be written. But as parliament had the power only to amend the constitution and not to write a new one, it would not be possible to propose the Shan Principle in parliament. It was possible, however, to declare it an objective. Sama Duwa Sinwa Nawng objected to the proposal. At this juncture, the panel of chairmen, including Sama Duwa Sinwa Nawng, agreed that no resolution would be passed on the

Shan proposal but that discussion alone would take place, and this continued in the evening.[50]

Sao Hkun Hkio acted as chairman of the conference on June 14 at 2:00 P.M. The *saohpa* of Mong Nai, Sao Pye, the *saohpa* of Hsa Mong Hkam, Sao Htun E, and U Kya Bu explained matters relating to the document revising the constitution submitted by Shan State.[51] They pointed out that the representatives from all parties in Shan State had been invited to discuss the revision of the constitution and that the Shan proposal had emerged out of these discussions. Sao Pye said a Steering Committee had been formed and responsibilities assigned to it. The committee was to receive and consider proposals from individuals. A true federal system was agreed upon on the basis of majority opinion.

Sao Pye continued:

> After the true federal principle had been agreed upon, we started work on it. The work could not be done within a day or two, nor was it done superficially. We took the time, and we took due care and caution, so that no public criticism would arise. We also took care to avoid the disintegration of the Union and to promote its perpetuation. It was undertaken with good will and in all sincerity on our part.[52]

Sao Pye also explained that after the draft had been made by the Steering Committee, a conference had been convened that had adopted the draft. He also revealed how U Htun Aye (Nam Kham), a member of the Steering Committee, had commented on the draft but had not endorsed the Shan proposal.

He also said that the Shan Principle was the best one, that only fools and the insane would reject it. U Htun Aye had stated, only outside the Conference Hall, that the Shan proposal was too premature. Sao Pye went on to say that it was regrettable that newspaper reports had accused the *saohpa* of aiding the insurgents. The Shan proposal aimed only to secure the rights that were due to the states and the enjoyment of such rights, nothing more and nothing less.[53]

The *saohpa* of Hsa Mong Hkam, Sao Htun E, then explained in detail how the Shan Principle emerged, and why the Taunggyi All States Conference had been held. He pointed out that the need to revise the constitution arose out of the treaty concluded between the People's Republic of China and the Union of Myanmar for the demarcation of their common boundary; how the government had laid down the principles for revising the constitution; how Shan State leaders had discussed the matter of revision in November 1960; how a Steering Committee was formed by Shan State; how Dr. E Maung had remarked that any revision was acceptable so long as Myanmar did not become a Communist or fascist state; how the Steering Committee had written the draft after gathering facts and evidence for the amendment and after interviewing those persons who had held responsible positions in the Shan State administration; how the conference was held and how the draft presented by the Steering Committee was confirmed; how the confirmed draft was submitted to the Committee for the

Amendment of the Constitution, led by Dr. E Maung, on March 11, 1961; how he, Sao Htun E, had been surprised when asked by Prime Minister U Nu at the meeting between Shan State leaders and U Nu, held at the prime minister's residence, whether the Shan Principle was free from foreign influence; how the assurance was given to U Nu that there was no involvement of foreign influence in the draft; how Shan State leaders had expressed their opinion on the Shan Principle to U Nu on his return from China and during his visit to Shan State; how at that time, U Nu accepted the principle without any reservation, and had said he would consult his colleagues in Yangon; and how U Nu had assured the Shan State leaders that any problem would be discussed in a brotherly spirit. On the accusation that the Shan Principle was drawn up under foreign influence, the following clarifications were given:[54]

> Now we have been accused of acting under foreign influence. From the beginning we have been working with good will for the perpetuation of the Union. We also foresee that the disintegration of the Union will lead us back into slavery again. We view this prospect very seriously. We will work with all the good will that is possible. Some people misunderstand our motive and think that we are taking advantage of the insurgency in the Shan State. The reports of insurgency were not made until 1959 and 1960. There have been reports of insurgency since 1946 and these flames of insurgency came to the Shan State in 1949 from Burma Proper. The flames did not die, but started burning a little in Mong Pan in 1955, culminating in violence in 1958 and 1959. It is unthinkable that people would believe that we have taken advantage of the insurgency. We have no wish for armed insurgency. We have no wish to kill our brothers and sisters. We wish with heart and soul for peace, and consequently believe that our present constitution cannot be relied upon to deal with such matters. And we have now laid down the groundwork for its revision.[55]

In presenting the Shan Principle, U Kya Bu recounted the historical struggle to secure independence after the Second World War. He related how the opportunity was secured to discuss the question of independence for Myanmar between Bamar political leaders and the leaders of the Hill Regions, for the first time, at the Pang Long Conference in 1946. The conference was made possible by the host, Sao Num, the *saohpa* of Lai Hka, who took all the responsibilities, and also by the cooperative leadership of the *saohpa* of Mong Pawn, Sao Sam Htun, the *saohpa* of Yawng Hwe, Sao Shwe Thaike, the *saohpa* of Mong Nai, Sao Pye, and others. U Kya Bu pointed out that the Shan State Federated Council, composed solely of *saohpa*, and which was only advisory, was dissolved and that a new Shan State Council had been formed, made up of an equal number of *saohpa* and representatives of the people, with full administrative, judicial, and legislative powers. U Kya Bu related that the letter demanding the formation of the new council was signed by twenty leaders, including himself, before being sent to the authorities concerned. Therefore, he said, he could not be accused of being a protégé of the *saohpa*.[56]

He also reminded his listeners about what Bogyoke Aung San had said at the mass meeting in Taunggyi in December 1946: "Let us join hands to fight for independence. Therefore, the Bamar who are in Shan State should not insult the Shan, should not take undue advantage, and should not bully them."[57]

U Kya Bu said that while the Pang Long Conference was taking place in 1947, *saohpa* and the people's representatives joined hands and abolished the Shan State Federated Council and established a new council, with full powers, with half of the members made up of *saohpa* and the other half of people's representatives. He also reiterated that the Taunggyi conference was held in good faith, without foreign influence, and with the sincere intention of perpetuating the Union.

While the conference was in session, Sama Duwa Sinwa Nawng fell ill, running a temperature as high as 105° F, and was advised by Dr. Ba Nyan, brother of U Kya Bu, to forgo that day's meeting. But Sama Duwa Sinwa Nawng ignored the advice.

U Kya Bu told the meeting that before Bogyoke Aung San arrived at the Pang Long Conference, the Shan, Chin, and Kachin delegates had agreed to join hands with the Bamar to get independence. He pointed out that the Hill peoples had played a very important role in striving for the emergence of the Union.[58]

When Bogyoke Aung San came to the Pang Long Conference, the leaders of the hill peoples presented him with a Federal Principle they had agreed on. Bogyoke accepted the proposal in principle. But the national leaders were assassinated while the constitution was still being written, and the hill leaders were in great distress. In view of the political emotions at that time, it was difficult to foresee how conflicting interpretations of the constitution would arise later on.

National leaders, including U Nu himself, had said that independence was so important that if the constitution had some defects, they could meet again after independence to discuss the matter on the basis of give and take like real brothers. Consequently, the constitution was confirmed and accepted although the signatories knew that what they had asked for had not been written into the constitution.[59]

U Kya Bu said that after thirteen years of experience, it was not only the Shan who had come to discover the defects of the constitution but U Chan Htun, the constitutional adviser himself, had said that the 1947 Constitution was unitary in practice and federal in theory. Nobody was to be blamed for this defect. More important now was to revise the unitary constitution so that it would become a true federal one, in accord with the original objectives laid down at the Pang Long Conference.[60]

As regards the concern by some states over financial difficulties once a true federal system was established, U Kya Bu pointed out that the financial condition of some of the thirteen colonies which constituted the United States of America at the time of its establishment might perhaps not have been as good as those of the states constituting the Union of Myanmar. A study of the USA would show that it included not only very large states like Texas, with an area of 67,339 square miles and a population of about 6 million, but also very small states like Rhode Island, with an area of 1,214 square miles and a population of 713,346.[61] Hence the states within the Union of Myanmar, said U Kya Bu, need not fear having to face financial difficulties.

After the three Shan State representatives had explained the proposal known as the Shan Principle, U Zahre Lian was the first to speak against it. He reminded the delegates of the objectives of the Committee for the Amendment of the Constitution, led by Minister Dr. E Maung. These objectives stated that in amending the constitution "the basic principle underlying [it] should not be affected in any way." But the document presented by Shan State asserted: "In amending the constitution today, it will not suffice merely to amend and substitute the defective clauses. The constitution will work only when the whole constitutional system is changed into a new and true federal one."[62]

That showed clearly, said U Zahre Lian, that Shan State intended to draft a new constitution. If the amendment proposal could not be submitted to the coming session of parliament in August, the implementation of the amended constitution would not be possible. If such a situation arose, he said, the states would suffer.[63]

He noted that although the Shan Principle sounded easy enough, it would not be so in the actual implementation. In the Shan proposal the following subjects were to come under the jurisdiction of the Union government:

1. Foreign Affairs
2. Union Defense
3. Union Finance
4. Coinage and Currency
5. Posts and Telegraphs
6. Railways, Airways, and Waterways
7. Union Judiciary
8. Ports and Duties

The rest of the powers were to be transferred to the states. The expenditures incurred by seven out of these eight departments exceeded their earnings. Only the Ports and Duties Department gained sufficient income from duties collected. As such it would be impossible for the federal government to support the states if a true federal system were to be introduced.[64] "In my view," he said, "it is impossible for the Chins to accept the Federal Principle. It does not mean that the minority people do not want a federation. What I would like to point out is that the time is not yet opportune for such a system."[65]

Then he continued:

> U Kya Bu, in his presentation, had made a comparison with the United States of America, and stated that at its founding the standard of the thirteen American states was not as high as that of our present states. This may be true if the comparison is made in terms of the standard of the delegates attending this Conference. But in reality the rural people from the Shan State or the Kachin State or Burma Proper, have not yet reached the level of the American people at the time of its founding.[66]

The third point that U Zahre Lian discussed was the formation of the Bamar state. He said:

> The proposed principle submitted by the Shan State includes the question of forming a Bamar State. I do not think it is right to pass a resolution at this conference simply on the basis of our agreement on the proposed principle. It will not be right if this proposal is decided by us alone. It is better to have the views of the Bamar delegates when dealing with the question of forming or not forming a Bamar State. I do not think it is correct to pass a resolution demanding the formation of the Bamar State at this conference, where the Bamar delegates are not included.[67]

He continued:

> Even if a true federal principle is accepted by the government, I do not think that parliament has the authority to implement it. I do not know much. . . but I do not think that parliament can enact such a revision. In my opinion the parliament should be dissolved and a Constituent Assembly[68] should be convened on the issue whether there is agreement or disagreement on the Federal Principle. That is why the issue is a very difficult one. As I have said, although this problem appeared to be easy its implementation will be difficult.[69]

U Zahre Lian also said:

> As I have said, if a true federal system is established, it will be difficult for us Chins. I also think that it might be difficult for the Kachin State as well. Because if the federal system is introduced, it involves the plain regions in the Part (1) 40[70] and Part (2)[71] areas which the former colonialists had annexed. If the people living in the plain regions do not agree to be part of the Kachin State of the Federated Kachin State, what shall we do?[72]

He continued:

> Do we need to revise the present constitution? Yes, we do. I am not satisfied with it either. There are a lot of grievances. However, there is no need for an immediate solution. We will have to find a kind of constitution upon which we all can agree. . . . That is what the panel of chairmen should do, and they should put it up at the coming conference for confirmation. That is the proper procedure and one that I would like to suggest.

In conclusion, he suggested that a resolution should not be passed on the Shan Principle, but that a new proposal should be drafted.

After U Zahre Lian had discussed the matter, U Zan Hta Sin, the former minister for Kachin State, spoke in favor of the Shan proposal. He drew attention to the directives issued by Bogyoke Aung San at the Constituent Assembly during the drafting of the constitution in which Bogyoke Aung San had said: "All powers and rights of the Sovereign Independent Republic of Myanmar and its component states and government organizations are derived from the people."[73]

U Zan Hta Sin continued: "We have come here not according to our own wishes. We have been elected and given the mandate to discuss state affairs, and that is why we are here. Those who are not members of parliament are people also chosen by their respective organizations as representatives."

He also explained that the present constitution was incompatible with the times. The peoples of the states would like to have a much higher form of government. Therefore a federation was demanded in accordance with the wishes of the people.[74]

Regarding the formation of a Bamar state, he said:

> In the resolution there is an offer of a Bamar State for the Bamars. It is not appropriate to pass such a resolution without the Bamar representatives. That is true, I agree with the minister. . . . The offer should not be forced upon the Bamars without their consent. It is merely a suggestion. . . . When a true federal system is established it is impossible not to have the Bamar State. . . . If we make a comparison between the Hill people and the states on the one hand, and Bamar Proper on the other, in terms of population and areas, the Bamar State represents more than half. At present we are only urging for the formation of a Bamar State. When a true federal system emerges in response to our demand, they will have to take it irrespective of the wishes of the Bamars. We will not have to compel them. . . . I want to make it clear that when the Federal Principle is demanded, then a problem will occur.[75]

On whether parliament had the right to pass a resolution revising the constitution, U Zan Hta Sin said:

> Regarding [that] question . . . , I am not a legal expert, but from what I understand, parliament has the authority to do so. This authority is vested in the members of parliament. Members of the Chamber of Deputies and members of the Chamber of Nationalities come to attend the parliament, not of their own free will, but in accordance with the will of the people. They are elected by the people. . . . That is why I believe that the present members of parliament have the authority to decide upon a constitution based on the Federal Principle. . . . My view [is] that any amendment to the constitution can be made, in part or in whole, in this parliament.[76]

The Chin representative, U Kyin Shin Htan, continued the discussion in support of the Shan Principle. He was taking part in the discussion, in place of Captain Mang

Tung Nung, who was ill, and spoke as a representative of the Chins. He said: "What I wish to discuss is not quite in line with what has just been stated by U Zahre Lian, our minister." He noted that when the Pang Long Agreement was signed, and the hill peoples had joined hands with the Bamar for independence, the objectives were to enjoy equal opportunities together and to ensure the Union would be preserved. But these two objectives had not yet been fulfilled, because the existing constitution had not been drawn up in accordance with the principles of the Pang Long Agreement, but had been drafted in a form embodying both unitary and federal features.[77]

Regarding U Zahre Lian's remarks that it was still too early to implement a true federal system, U Kyin Shin Htan said: "Let me say this. Before the British came, we had been living independently."[78]

He continued:

> I do not think an endorsement of the Shan State proposal in its entirety is necessary. I think a mere proposal in support of a true federal system would be sufficient. We do not intend to discuss the proposal in detail at this very moment, so a resolution or a confirmation of the proposal should not be made at once. What we are endorsing now is support for a true federal system and not its details.[79]

Sama Duwa Sinwa Nawng was the next person to speak. He began by saying that it was only Shan State that could convene such important meetings as the Pang Long Conference, which gave birth to the Union, and the present conference. Shan State also had a historic tradition of holding conferences on problems of national importance. Because the holding of such conferences was very exhausting, it would be worthwhile only if resolutions beneficial to all citizens of the Union could be passed by them.[80]

He added:

> Now we have heard about all the weaknesses of the unitary system. As for ourselves, we do not wish to condemn either the unitary or the federal state. Both systems might be good depending on the needs of various countries. We have established for ourselves a unitary form, and now that we want to change it into a federal union, let us weigh the pros and cons for such a change. There might be a lot of benefits. We . . . do not [oppose] the federal system.[81]

Regarding the procedures for amending the constitution:

> There may be different procedures. . . . But no constitution in the world has provided for the drafting of a new constitution. That does not mean, however, that a constitution cannot be amended. There are proper procedures for doing that, and we must abide by [them].[82]
>
> Chapter 2 of the constitution gives parliament the authority to make such amendments. Regarding this power, chapter 2 states: "Any provision of the constitution may

> be amended, whether by way of variation, addition, or repeal in the manner hereinafter provided." This shows that the present parliament has the power to amend the constitution. But it is a different matter when a new constitution is to be written. It would then require a different procedure altogether.[83]

Sama Duwa Sinwa Nawng continued his discussion by saying that he had found nothing in the Myanmar constitution, or in the constitution of other countries, that gave parliament the mandate to write a new constitution. However, he said, there were two methods by which a new constitution could be written. The first method was, when due to changing conditions, the present constitution became impracticable and the government announced a new policy and accordingly drew up a new constitution. The other method was, when the government did not approve of the first method, by forming a federal party, allowing it to contest the elections, and then writing a new constitution. Such a precedent occurred in France under President Charles de Gaulle, when the incumbent government, finding that the then constitution was impracticable, dissolved parliament and declared that a new election be held for a Constituent Assembly, to draw up a new constitution.[84]

Because the present parliament had no authority to draft a new constitution, he said, it would be a waste of time to ask for a true federal constitution, particularly when the outcome was not so certain. Sama Duwa Sinwa Nawng therefore suggested that the following amendments be made in the present constitution:

1. The prevailing opinion being that the State government had no authority in matters relating to rights of landownership, such rights should be granted to it.
2. Authority to operate electricity, mining, and industries should be granted to the State government.
3. The assumption that subjects not on the State Legislative List in the present constitution are on the Central Legislative List should be dispelled and subjects not on the Central Legislative List should be included.
4. The State Legislative List should be expanded.[85]

After Sama Duwa Sinwa Nawng had made his comments on the Shan proposal, Duwa Zau Lawn, former minister of the Kachin State, who, like U Zan Hta Sin, was a member of the Kachin National Congress, continued the discussion. He said:

> Concerning the question whether a resolution to adopt a true federal system should be passed or not, the Union ministers for the Kachin State and the Chin Special Division have counseled against [its passage] on the grounds that it would be premature. We do not think it is premature; in fact we think it is long overdue. Leaving aside the question of feasibility and the length of time involved, we should just consider that we want a true federal union. This is our intense desire and our objective. Once this desire is fulfilled we will be greatly gratified and the country will be peaceful and prosperous. For these reasons we support the proposal to establish a true federal system at this conference.[86]

He went on to state:

> Having had our proposal accepted, we must next find ways and means to achieve this objective. We understand that we cannot achieve this objective all on our own, but would need the support of the Bamars who form the majority or that of the leaders of the prominent political parties within the Union, and some of the leaders who represent the masses. We need to discuss the matter with them on a give-and-take basis. At this juncture, if these people hold any good will toward us, then they will accept this proposal.[87]

He added:

> There is no intention whatsoever to cause the disintegration of the Union or to disrupt its unity. There is no such intention of beating the drum or raising our hands to kill one another. Political parties and political leaders of Burma Proper have been preaching the policy and program for the perpetuation of the Union, the solidarity of the Union, and the unity of the national minorities. We too want these objectives achieved. We support the same policy and program. We believe that [they] can be achieved only when a true federal system is established.[88]

Duwa Zau Lawn next pointed out that Kachin State had already requested that the Constitutional Amendment Committee consider some of the points suggested by Sama Duwa Sinwa Nawng regarding the possibility of redressing the grievances of the states by amending the present constitution. The committee had obliged by agreeing to amend only one point regarding the selection of the state chairman. Duwa Zau Lawn said he doubted that parliament would allow the redress of all the grievances.[89]

By the time Duwa Zau Lawn finished his discussion, it was six o'clock in the evening and the time allotted for it had run out. The remaining delegates were each given ten minutes to speak. The chairman, Sao Hkun Hkio, also requested the delegates to focus only on whether they were in favor of or against the Shan proposal. Bonpauk Tha Kyaw and Nai Ba Saw (Mon) endorsed the Shan proposal after a brief discussion.[90]

U A. Soe Myint requested a further five minutes more than his allotted ten minutes so that he could discuss the Shan proposal fully. He said: "I have nothing much to say regarding the principle proposed by Shan State. It has been presented with all the historical facts and evidence from the past. We also know what the principle entails, and we dare not say that it is an impossible principle."

But he struck a note of caution by drawing the delegates' attention to the saying: "One man's meat is another man's poison."[91] He cited a passage in the document which stated that no sufficient directives on the equality of the states and national minorities were guaranteed in the present constitution of the Union of Myanmar.[92] He said he supported the document on that point. He also pointed out the differences in the historical background of the Shan and the Kayin people. He noted that the Shan document included no suggestions for redressing the grievances of Kayin State. Therefore, he said, to accept everything proposed by Shan State could create certain problems for the Kayin.[93]

He declared that it was correct to say that the states had very limited rights and powers. He said it would be the proper thing to do if the defects and deficiencies could be removed by granting certain rights to the states. No doubt the present constitution had some weaknesses, but the state councils were free to manage their own affairs. The head of state had the greatest authority to manage state affairs. Moreover, he was a minister, a member of the Union cabinet. Members of parliament had every right to criticize and to amend any law or act concerning the country. U A. Soe Myint said he was quite satisfied with the present Union Constitution.[94]

U A. Soe Myint, who had himself participated in the Kayin armed struggle from 1947 to 1953, cautioned the delegates in his concluding remarks:

> Even before the question of the federal system arose, a struggle for an independent Kayin State had been waged for five or six years. But what did it achieve? We have had to face severe repression. We have finally been made to realize that the Kayin people cannot do whatever they wanted to do on their own. We must consider each matter from all angles. We must not act blindly, but only after due consideration. Since we have to live together with other people, we must also consider whether they can or cannot accept what we are doing. We have returned to the legal fold to work with the government.[95]

After U A. Soe Myint, Duwa Zau Lawn continued the discussions. He said: "Now what I understand from the speech of the Kayin leader U A. Soe Myint is that the Shan proposal is quite good and quite favorable, but the pros and cons of whether the proposal should be accepted or not must be weighed carefully."[96]

He continued:

> But there is one encouraging fact. A resolution was passed at the meeting held in the Hall of the Kayin State Council on March 18, 1961, at 11:00 A.M. on Saturday at No.1 Saya San (Hermitage) Road[97] Yangon, and which was attended by all Kayin members of parliament. The resolution agreed to the proposal for revising the constitution as originally submitted by the Scrutiny Committee. I point this out because I want everybody to know how the Kayin members of parliament felt about the proposal for constitutional amendment.[98]

After Duwa Zau Lawn, U Zahre Lian continued his discussion:

> I would like to make a clarification here. I do not want any statement issued that might imply my consent to the proposal for revising the constitution submitted by the Shan

> State. My point is that it will be a good thing to draft a resolution which we can all pass, after due discussion. Now the principle proposed by the Shan State might be good for the Shan State, but it could be bad, for example, for the Chin State. Perhaps a better principle could emerge. I would like to endorse the proposal of the Kachin delegates, which asks for more powers for the states.[99]
>
> . . . [If] we support [the Shan] proposal and pass a resolution at this conference endorsing it, that would be tantamount to using undue pressure.[100]

He explained that if pressure were used the states would face difficulties in implementing the proposal. He suggested that a fresh proposal, on which all could agree, should be drafted for presentation.[101]

After the delegates of the various states had finished their discussions, the chairman of the conference, Sao Hkun Hkio, concluded the session by saying that if one looked at the points of discussion, one would find no differences of views about the objectives. But there were, of course, differences of opinion about the implementation of the objectives. This was because some of the delegates were from the government organizations, and some from nongovernment organizations, and hence it was quite natural for these differences of views to arise. As the situations in the various states were not the same, there could also be differences of views in matters of detail.

Then he said: "This evening, after the discussion, I would like to request the delegates to arrive at a consensus on this principle without going into details. I also can see the difficulties we are facing. It does not matter how the Federal Principle is drafted. It is not a resolution. I ask only for a consensus."[102]

Sao Hkun Hkio asked the delegates to raise their hands to show their approval or disapproval of the Federal Principle. Sama Duwa Sinwa Nawng, U Zahre Lian, and U A. Soe Myint did not do so and remained neutral.[103] Sama Duwa Sinwa Nawng and U Zahre Lian were dissatisfied with the action of Sao Hkun Hkio because they thought that he had broken the original pledge he had given them that the purpose of the meeting was not to pass any resolution on the Shan Principle, but only to have a discussion.[104]

When the Supervisory Council for All States met on June 14 at 7:00 P.M. U Zahre Lian did not attend. Sama Duwa Sinwa Nawng attended the morning session and again spoke out about his dissatisfaction with the request for a show of hands to express approval of the Shan Principle.[105]

To reconcile the differences of opinion that had arisen during the conference, the Supervisory Council held another meeting on June 15. U Zahre Lian put up another proposal for revising the constitution, but it was rejected without discussion. As for the proposal put up by Sama Duwa Sinwa Nawng, the council decided to discuss it at the meeting on June 16. The panel of chairmen also passed a resolution to put up the amendment proposal based on the Shan Principle at the conference on June 16. U Zahre Lian again asserted that the Kachin, Chin, and Kayin delegates from the political parties in power could not agree to the resolution. Sama Duwa Sinwa Nawng and U

Zahre Lian did not attend the final day of the conference on June 15, but returned to Yangon from Taunggyi.[106]

THE FINAL DAY OF THE TAUNGGYI ALL STATES CONFERENCE

The Taunggyi All States Conference ended on June 16, 1961, and passed five resolutions:

1. To unitedly strive for the perpetuation of the Union of Myanmar, for the development of the states, and for the equality of all national minorities, the conference unanimously passes a resolution for the formation of an All States Unity Organization.
2. As the present Constitution of the Union of Myanmar does not contain sufficient provisions for the equality of states and national minorities, and also with the desire for the perpetuation, and out of consideration for the good of the Union of Myanmar, it is deemed that a revision of the constitution has become necessary. Therefore:
   (a) The conference unanimously agrees to endorse in principle the proposal for revising the Constitution of the Union of Myanmar;
   (b) A request will be made to revise the Constitution of the Union of Myanmar, based on the principle proposed by Shan State.
3. The conference expresses the desire that a National Convention, composed of all nationalities in the whole Union, be immediately called at an appropriate place to ensure the development and prosperity of the Union of Myanmar; for better and closer relationship of the peoples of the states within the Union; for consultation with one another on the question of equality of all the citizens of the Union.
4. This conference passes a resolution urging the Union government to immediately create new states within the Union that meet the requirements of statehood, to fulfill the strong desire of the Mon, Rakhine, and Chin nationalities.
5. The conference passes a resolution denouncing the Kuomintang forces which are committing armed aggression against the Union, and earnestly praises the Armed Forces which are driving out the KMT forces with might and main.[107]

After passing these resolutions, the conference formed an Interim Executive Committee of the All States Unity Organization with the following members:

1. Sao Hkun Hkio (Saohpa of Mong Mit)	Chairman
2. Sao Wunna (head of Kayah State)	Vice chairman
3. Duwa Hkun Hpong (leader of Kachin State)	Vice chairman
4. Sao Htun E (Saohpa of Hsa Mong Hkam)	General secretary
5. U Hla Pe (member of parliament)	Joint secretary
6. U Soe Maung (Ah-Pa-Nya-Pha)	Joint secretary

7. Sao Hkun Aung (Saohpa of Baw)	Information officer
8. U Hla Nyein (representative of Kayah State)	Treasurer
9. U Tha Dun (Rakhine representative)	Auditor
10. Saw Ba Yin (representative of Kayin State)	Member
11. Saw Thin Sein (Kayin representative)	Member
12. Duwa Zau Lawn (representative of Kachin State)	Member
13. Duwa Nang Zing La (representative of Kachin State)	Member
14. U Maung Oo Kyaw (Rakhine representative)	Member
15. Captain Mang Tung Nung (Chin representative)	Member
16. U Kyin Shin Htan (Chin representative)	Member
17. Nai Ngwe Thein (Mon national leader)	Member
18. Nai Ba Saw (Mon national leader)	Member
19. Sao Pye (Saohpa of Mong Nai)	Member
20. Sao Num (Saohpa of Laikha)	Member
21. Sao Sai Long (Saohpa of Keng Tung)	Member
22. U Chit Maung (representative of Kayah State)	Member
23. Sao Shwe Hmon (Saohpa of Kehsi Mansam)	Member

The All States Unity Organization formed by the Taunggyi All States Conference had Kachin, Kayah, Kayin, Chin, Rakhine, Shan, and Mon representatives as members. On the other hand, Sama Duwa Sinwa Nawng, U Zahre Lian, and U A. Soe Myint did not endorse the resolutions passed by the conference for revising the Constitution of the Union of Myanmar.

19

The Federal Principle

ARRIVAL OF SHAN STATE REPRESENTATIVES IN YANGON

After the All States Conference ended in Taunggyi, Sao Pye, the *saohpa* of Mong Nai and chairman of the Shan State Steering Committee for the Revision of the Constitution, traveled down to Yangon, arriving on June 26, 1961. He was accompanied by Sao Num, the *saohpa* of Lai Hka, Sao Shwe Hmon, the *saohpa* of Kehsi Mansam, U Hkun Hti, U Tun Myint (Taunggyi), U Htun Pe, U Kyaw Sein, U Mya Min, U Than Htay, and U Than Pe. The purpose of their visit was to explain to the prime minister and other political leaders of Myanmar the resolution of the Taunggyi All States Conference.[1] Before meeting with the prime minister, the Shan representatives—comprising Sao Pye, the *saohpa* of Mong Nai; Sao Num, the *saohpa* of Lai Hka; Sao Shwe Hmon, the *saohpa* of Kehsi Mansam; Sao Htun E, the *saohpa* of Hsa Mong Hkam; U Kyaw Sein; and U Htun Pe—went on July 1 to the Pyidaungsu (Union) Party Headquarters, in accordance with their program to informally explain the Federal Principle to the political leaders. They met with the former secretary-general, Thakin Kyaw Dun, and explained to him how the Federal Principle had come about. They said that the principle, which was adopted by the Taunggyi Conference, should not be regarded as a Shan proposal but as a principle that had been agreed upon, proposed, and adopted by all parties and all races at the conference. Sao Htun E, the *saohpa* of Hsa Mong Hkam, explained that the principle was drafted at the urging of the people, under the leadership of the *saohpa*. It did not arise as a consequence of the relinquishing of the traditional powers by the *saohpa*, which meant that they would no longer be able to elect members of parliament (Chamber of Nationalities or the upper chamber) from among themselves, from the next general elections onward.[2]

Thakin Kyaw Dun was aware that the states had grievances, but he believed that these arose from personal conflicts. He therefore saw no need to revise the constitution merely to resolve problems that had arisen out of personal conflicts. He urged them to resolve the problems in a "family spirit" by conciliation, not by vindictiveness. He was confident that an acceptable solution could be found.[3]

The Shan State representatives, U Htun Myint (Taunggyi), U Nyunt Pe, U Mya Min, U Hkun Hti, U Htun Pe, and U Kyaw Sein, went to the residence of U Aung Than, president of the People's Progress Party, and met with its leaders on July 1. They agreed that the culprit for all the grievances of all the states, including Shan State, was the AFPFL government that had been in power for ten years. The AFPFL government had been guilty not only of chauvinism in relation to the national races but of maladministration, giving rise to the problems concerning the national races.[4]

On July 2 the Shan State representatives, Sao Pye, *saohpa* of Mong Nai; Sao Num, *saohpa* of Lai Hka; Sao Shwe Hmon, *saohpa* of Kehsi Mansam; Sao Htun E, *saohpa* of Hsa Mong Hkam; U Kyaw Sein, and U Htun Pe, went to meet the party leaders of the People's Volunteer Organization (PVO) led by Bo Po Kun, Bo San Maung, Bo Ohn Tin, and Bo Aung Naing. They stated that Shan State was not going to secede from the Union, and that its representatives had come to Yangon to dispel the mistrust and the misunderstanding held by the Bamar toward the people of Shan State. The leaders of the PVO replied that they wanted unity, not dissension among the national races of the states and the nationals of Myanmar proper, and that their views on the Federal Principle had been expressed in their message, which was sent to the Taunggyi All States Conference.[5]

On July 4 the Shan State representatives went to meet the party leaders of the Anti-Fascist People's Freedom League (AFPFL), at the Bow Lane home of Bo Khin Maung Gale on Po Sein Road. At the meeting were Sao Pye, Sao Shwe Hmon, and U Than Pe from the Shan State Representative Group, and Bo Khin Maung Gale, Thakin San Myint, and Thakin Chit Maung (Myan Aung) from the AFPFL. Sao Pye explained that the Union government had appointed a Constitution Revision Committee, and that the committee chairman, Minister Dr. E Maung, had stated that the Shan State representatives could bring forward any amendment to the constitution, so long as such amendment would not turn the nation into a Communist or fascist state. Consequently, the suggestions for revising the constitution in accordance with the Federal Principle had been submitted by Shan State. Shan State did not intend to secede from the Union. If it had such intention, it could have done so in 1948, 1949, and 1950, when the Myanmar government was beset with insurrection all over the country. In demanding the federal system, Shan State was not trying to put pressure upon the government, but was merely using the opportunity to present a plan for revising the constitution. Dr. E Maung also said that no external machinations were involved.[6]

On July 5 the Shan State representatives went to meet the president of the Union, U Win Maung, to explain the Federal Principle to him. President U Win Maung urged that in discussing the Federal Principle, patience and "the family spirit" should be exercised.

The Shan State representatives also met with Bo Min Gaung and Bo Let Ya, who also replied in the same words as those used by the president.[7]

On July 6 the Shan State representatives met with the members of the Internal Peace Committee led by Sayagyi Thakin Kodaw Hmaing and former brigadier Kyaw Zaw. The meeting began with the presentation of a "Bangkok" *pasoe* (Bamar male undergarment) by the Shan leaders as a gift for Sayagyi Thakin Kodaw Hmaing. Then U Htun Myint (Taunggyi) explained how the decisions of the Taunggyi All States Conference had come about and how the Federal Principle had originated. Sayagyi Thakin Kodaw Hmaing then gave the following words of advice. He said Shan and Bamar had a tradition of unity in their fight against the expansionist colonialists and that while there was yet time, everyone should work for the good of the country. Whether the Shan or the Bamar were at fault, he urged that the slate be wiped clean, and prayed that all work together to promote peace and unity. Former brigadier Kyaw Zaw then presented the views of the Internal Peace Committee. He said that the Federal Principle had been born of the grievances against the expansionist colonialists, the misrule of the *saohpa*, and maladministration. He believed it was right for the national races to seek equality and the right to self-determination because that was the natural thing to do. But he warned that the Chinese Kuomintang and SEATO were stirring up trouble within Shan State and it was important to oppose certain Shan insurgents who were colluding with them. He feared that hatred would develop between the Shan and the Bamar, and urged that chauvinism be discarded.[8]

On July 7 the Shan State representatives met with Prime Minister U Nu for a discussion that lasted two and a half hours. At the meeting were Minister Sao Hkun Hkio, Minister Sao Wunna, U Ohn (*saohpa* of Hsa Mong Hkam), Sao Htun E (*saohpa* of Lai Hka), Sao Num (*saohpa* of Kehsi Mansam), Sao Shwe Hmon (*saohpa* of Mong Nai), Sao Pye, U Than Htay, U Mya Min, U Than Pe, U Hkun Hti, U Nyunt Pe, U Kyaw Sein, U Htun Myint (Taunggyi), and U Htun Pe. Sao Htun E, the *saohpa* of Hsa Mong Hkam, presented the decisions of the Taunggyi conference. He stated that the conference was not concerned in any way with secession from the Union. Neither was there any involvement of the expansionist colonialists. The Federal Principle had evolved from the invitation to the states by the Constitution Revision Committee, headed by Judicial Minister Dr. E Maung, to bring forward any suggested amendment to the constitution desired by the states. Prime Minister U Nu replied that he was willing to accept the resolution calling for the convening of a national conference (one of the decisions of the Taunggyi conference). On the proposed amendment of the present constitution in accordance with the Federal Principle, however, he had already entrusted the matter to the Advisory Committee headed by Dr. Ba U, so he merely promised he would ask the committee to present its report as soon as possible.[9]

On July 8 Sao Htun E, U Kyaw Sein, and U Nyunt Pe, representatives from Shan State, went to meet the minister for finance and revenue, Thakin Tin. Sao Htun E recounted how the Federal Principle came about. The minister said that restructuring the Union in accordance with the Federal Principle would not benefit the states and would only adversely affect them. Looking into the state budgets, he said the annual revenue collected in Shan State was only 6 million kyats, and Myanmar proper had to subsidize the Shan State budget to the tune of 12.5 million kyats annually, in addition to capital grants. As one who had participated in drawing up the 1947 Constitution, he informed the meeting that at a time when none of the states could stand on their own feet, a deliberate decision had been taken to reject the Federal Principle and to draw up the 1947 Constitution under which Myanmar proper would continue to make sacrifices to help the states for as long as they could not stand on their own feet. If, under the Federal Principle, Myanmar proper were to become another constituent state, it would no longer be able to grant assistance to the Shan, Kachin, Chin, Kayin, and Kayah states.[10]

The Shan State representatives also met with U Ba Swe, the president of the AFPFL, on July 8. At the meeting U Ba Swe said that speaking for himself and not for the AFPFL, he supported the Federal Principle but did not like the circumstances under which it came into being. The discussions, lasting about three hours, covered not only the federal issue but also the need to avoid communal clashes and divisions.[11]

PRESS CONFERENCE BY PRIME MINISTER U NU

After meeting with the representatives of Shan State, Prime Minister U Nu held a press conference on July 11. At the conference were Minister Sao Hkun Hkio and the representatives from Shan State; Minister Dr. E Maung, Minister Bohmu Aung, Chief Secretary U Shwe Mya, Secretary U Win Pe, Inspector General of Police U Bo, Deputy Inspector General of Police U Ba Aye, and Pyidaungsu Party Organizer U Ohn. U Nu spoke on the Federal Principle:

> I have studied the Shan proposal myself and . . . I found that the Shan representatives could not be blamed for what they have been doing. The Shan representatives, having drafted the proposal, had invited the minorities, who were agreeable to it, and they made decisions, which they have put before the government. Thus they cannot be blamed for what they have done.[12]
>
> They have merely acted in accordance with the government's invitation to bring forward any suggestions for amending sections of the constitution that present difficulties in their actual implementation. The government had been considering making amendments to the constitution during the present session of parliament, and had decided to invite suggestions. When a group of people, with the permission of the government, drew up a resolution [declaring] what they wanted and presented it to the government, they were only exercising their democratic rights. We are not angry with the drawing up of the Shan proposal. But there have been some misconceptions on the issue within the country. I myself had one or two misconceptions, which were subsequently dispelled, after two meetings with Sao Hkun Hkio, when clarifications were made. At my meeting with him, I said that drawing up the Shan proposal and inviting those who agreed to support it was perfectly legal. But after submitting

> the proposal, to threaten that they will fight if we do not amend the constitution as proposed, would be going beyond the bounds of democracy. No one in authority in the Shan State has ever said that they would fight if the constitution was not amended in accordance with the Shan proposal. Only one or two irresponsible persons had done so. I had merely said that we should try to ensure that things do not go beyond the pale of democracy by allowing one or two such irresponsible individuals to declare that the Shans would fight if their proposal was not accepted. Sao Hkun Hkio, in reply, had requested the government to prosecute such irresponsible persons in accordance with the law.[13]
>
> We, as well as the Shans, do not follow the policy of "give us what we want or we fight." Both parties have adopted the traditional method of settling disputes peacefully, as within a family.
>
> I would like to give the same advice I gave to Sao Hkun Hkio and his colleagues, not only to the minority groups such as the Rakhines, Mons, Kachins, Kayins, Kayahs, and Chins but also to Bamars. Everyone, I assume, would want to prevent the breakup of the Union. This desire of every citizen to prevent the disintegration of the Union can be achieved only when the minorities and the Bamars strive together, in unity, for the preservation of the Union.

In order to do so, the principle to be observed is:

> The minority groups, such as the Shans, Kayins, and Kayahs, should avoid doing things their own way on matters relating to the Union without regard for the Bamars. The Bamars and the minorities must consider the aspirations of both sides, thereby ensuring the stability of the Union. If the Bamars proceed to do whatever they want, then the Union will inevitably break up. If we want our Union to endure, it will not do to act only in one's own interest; we must consult one another and try to find solutions. If we wish our Union to endure, please do not try to oppose one another. Let us try to resolve our differences in a family spirit. Let me warn both the minorities and the Bamars about this issue. Do not be alarmed at the mention of the Shan proposal. We will take care of it in the "family spirit."

After U Nu had given the above clarification, a journalist asked Sao Hkun Hkio for his views on the military's statement about the Shan insurgency. He replied: "The revision of the constitution has nothing to do with the Shan insurgency. So if you ask me about the Shan insurgency in the context of the revision, I cannot give you an answer."[14]

The journalist explained that his question was concerned only with the Shan insurgency. Sao Hkun Hkio said:

> The Shan insurgency did not arise from our activities in respect of the revision of the constitution, but started when Naw Seng occupied Taunggyi in 1949. These days

> the *saohpa* are blamed for whatever happens in the Shan State. At that time the *saohpa* had weapons and men. So if they had taken up arms for the sake of secession during those days, the Union, as we know it, might no longer be in existence. Now that the *saohpa* have given up their powers, it would be madness to take up arms. We are always working in full consultation and in concert with the Tatmadaw.[15]

Another journalist asked: Wouldn't it be a good idea to first deal with the elimination of the insurgency, so that suspicions that there was some connection between the *saohpa* and the insurgency could be dispelled?

Sao Hkun Hkio replied: "Are we to suspend the Federal Principle until all insurgents, including the Communists, have been wiped out?"

Asked whether any thought had been given to the issuing of a statement that Shan State would not secede from the Union, Sao Hkun Hkio replied that this matter had also been discussed with General Ne Win during the talks held earlier concerning the surrender of powers by the *saohpa*. During those talks it was pointed out that since the *saohpa* would be contesting the general elections under the same rules as everyone else, from 1964 onward the question of secession was no longer their sole concern. Sao Hkun Hkio said that in the present circumstances the answer remained the same.[16]

STATEMENT BY THE REPRESENTATIVES OF SHAN STATE

At the press conference called by Prime Minister U Nu on July 11, a statement expresssing the point of view of the Shan State representatives about the Federal Principle was distributed to those present. The statement presented the details about how the representatives of Shan State had arrived in Yangon to clarify the Federal Principle to the president of the Union, the prime minister and his cabinet, the leaders of the Pyidaungsu Party, the AFPFL, the National United Front, the leaders of the Internal Peace Committee headed by Sayagyi Thakin Kodaw Hmaing and former brigadier Kyaw Zaw, journalists and writers. The statement also explained how the Shan State representatives had met and briefed the leaders of various political parties about the drawing up of the Federal Principle, guided by the objectives of promoting friendliness and harmony among the national races, the granting of equal rights to every national race, thus ensuring the stability of the Union. The statement pointed out how, during those discussions, the leaders of the political parties had received the clarification with interest, and made their own suggestions in a brotherly manner, which had pleased the Shan State representatives. Because the representatives were able to clarify not just the Federal Principle but also the Taunggyi All States Conference and the States Unity Party which resulted from the conference, as well as the new party's objectives, the Shan State representatives now believed that they had dispelled mistrust, suspicions, and misconceptions about the Federal Principle and the States Unity Party, and that the understanding between Myanmar proper and Shan State had been enhanced.[17]

The Shan State representatives were confident the people would come to appreciate that, in drawing up the Federal Principle, no foreign machinations were involved, that the Shan had merely publicized, with sincere intentions, their grievances at being deprived of what was due to them, based on human democratic rights. That Shan State had committed itself, in a brotherly manner and in the family spirit, to working patiently within democratic bounds, for its right to equality, until the entire Union came to accept that right. In working for its rights, Shan State, since it abhorred the use of force, had declared that it would never consider taking up arms, now or in the future.

The statement was signed by Sao Hkun Hkio, Sao Pye, Sao Htun E, Sao Num, Sao Shwe Hmon, U Htun Myint, U Hkun Hti, U Than Htay, U Htun Pe, U Than Pe, U Nyunt Pe, U Mya Min, and U Kyaw Sein.[18]

THE FEDERAL PRINCIPLE AND THE YA-PA-LA-PHA STAND

While the Shan State representatives were in Yangon to hold discussions with the leaders of the political parties, U Htun Aye (Nam Kham), U Ohn Pe, U Tin Ko Ko, U Kyaw Zaw, U Htan Ywet, and U Pe Myint of the Ya-Pa-La-Pha (Shan State People's Liberation Party) also came down to Yangon to present their stand on the Federal Principle, by issuing press statements and holding press conferences.[19] The Ya-Pa-La-Pha statement, issued on July 13, contained the following points:

1. Today, in the Shan State, when the relatives of the *saohpa* who have given up their powers, and their trusted lieutenants and their former retainers are taking up arms in order to secede from the Union and to establish a separate feudal state;
2. When those insurgents and armed combatants (who actually are lackeys of the Thais and of the KMTS) are rampaging through the states;
3. When the powers of the Shan State government are held by Sao Hkun Hkio and a small group of *saohpa*, without having had to go through an election;
4. The Ya-Pa-La-Pha very strongly objects to the "*Saohpa* Principle" which has been presented in the guise of the Federal Principle.[20]

The statement also criticized the Federal Principle as being an untried system in the world and impracticable. The Ya-Pa-La-Pha also claimed that the Shan armed insurgency came about within months of the surrender of powers by the *saohpa*; that at the beginning, the objective was to prevent the *saohpa* from surrendering their powers, but that later the objective was to secede from the Union and to establish a separate Shan state, for which purpose anti-Bamar propaganda was disseminated. The first formal call for secession had been made in 1957, when the Shan-language weekly publication of the *Saohpa*'s Association, *The New Shan State*, began its "hate Bamar campaign."[21] Toward the end of 1957, at a meeting in Mong Yai, a resolution was passed calling for Shan State to secede from the Union when the ten-year constitutional period had lapsed. The meeting was held at the home of Sao Maung, vice chairman of the Shan State Council and member of Sao Hkun Hkio's Shan State United Hill Peoples' Organization. The chairman at that meeting was U Po Hmon, the minister for public works in Sao Hkun Hkio's Shan State government. The statement alleged that the tiny spark emitted at the meeting developed into a conflagration in Shan State after the *saohpa* gave up their powers.[22]

The Ya-Pa-La-Pha also claimed, at its July 13 press conference, that the Federal Principle that emerged from the Taunggyi conference was proposed by a mere handful of *saohpa*; that the people of Shan State knew nothing about the matter; that the *saohpa* were unhappy at having to give up their powers and as a result had come up with the Federal Principle; that the insurgency in Shan State was watched, engineered, and organized by the state government; that the Shan insurgents were in league with the Kuomintang and were receiving assistance from foreign sources; that the Shan insurgents were trying to win over the Kachin youth by drawing their attention to the Bamar proposal to make Buddhism the state religion. U Htun Aye and his party further claimed that the Shan State government had put forward the Federal Principle because they would no longer be able to do as they pleased in the 1964 elections. U Htun Aye said that seven Ya-Pa-La-Pha members had been killed by Shan insurgents and that the Ya-Pa-La-Pha Party was actively assisting the Myanmar army in Shan State.[23]

In disputing these accusations leveled against the *saohpa* by U Htun Aye and party, Sao Htun E, the *saohpa* of Hsa Mong Hkam, declared that the fact that the leaders of Shan State had time and again condemned the Shan insurgents clearly demonstrated that there was no connection between the Shan *saohpa* and the Shan insurgents; that just because there were relatives and former retainers of certain *saohpa* among the insurgents it could not be construed that the Shan *saohpa* supported the insurgency.[24] If such assumptions were to be accepted, one might argue that General Aung San was to blame, because his wife's brother-in-law, Thakin Than Tun, happened to be the leader of the Communist insurgents. The claim that the Federal Principle was the brainchild of the *saohpa* alone was also untrue, as the people of Shan State had approved it. Furthermore, Shan State did not contemplate seceding from the Union. In fact, the Federal Principle was drawn up to strengthen the Union to make it more enduring. It was through the efforts of the *saohpa*, in defiance of the wishes of the expansionist colonialists, that the 1947 Pang Long Conference had been successfully held. During 1949–50, when the Union was on the brink of disaster, the *saohpa* remained loyal to the Bamar, thus saving the Union from disintegration. Again when the governing AFPFL Party split into two, the *saohpa* did not take sides, but merely urged both faction leaders, U Nu and U Ba Swe, to work for unity.[25]

THE FEDERAL PRINCIPLE AND THE REPORT OF THE GOVERNMENT ADVISORY COMMITTEE

While Shan State representatives and the members of the Ya-Pa-La-Pha Party were in Yangon trying to win over the people to their point of view on the federal question, the Union government referred the matter to the advisory committee with Dr. Ba U as chairman, Dr. Thein Maung, U Ohn Pe, and U Chit Thaung as members. The terms of reference were:

> To examine the demands made by the Shan State people and their government and, after consulting the leaders and representatives of the people of the states and Burma Proper, to give advice and suggestions on what steps should be taken in the future.[26]

On receiving the reference from the government on April 27, 1961, the advisory committee invited the head of Shan State, Sao Hkun Hkio, to give his advice. He was the first person to hold discussions with the committee on July 22, 1961, followed by the other heads of state and representatives of state governments and leaders and representatives of various political parties in the states and in Myanmar proper.[27] The *Report of the Government Advisory Committee on the Amendment of the Constitution*, as proposed by the Shan State government and its people, was submitted on January 8, 1962.[28]

The report first dealt with the nine grievances as listed by the Shan State government and its people, and presented the committee's comments and advice on each grievance as follows:

Grievance No.1: In dealing with the states, the Union ministers and their officials ignore the spirit and the letter of the Pang Long Agreement.

The committee's advice on this charge was:

> In making the charge the Shan State government and its people seem to overlook the legal position of the Union ministers and their officials in dealing with the states: they are bound by the Union Constitution. Under the constitution, the Union ministers and their officials cannot interfere in the administration of state subjects. In fact, the Union ministers and their officials do not seem to have the intention of interfering in the administration of state subjects.
>
> It may be that in administering the Union subjects in the states, the Union ministers and their officials did not go into full consultation with the State government concerned. It is true that the consultation is not called for under the constitution, but by way of social morality, the state concerned should be consulted or informed before a measure is taken.
>
> The alleged grievance can thus be removed by an understanding between the Union government and the State government concerned.

Grievance No. 2: Interpreting the constitution is done one-sidedly; i.e. it is interpreted to the disadvantage of the states and to the advantage of the Union government.

The committee's report commented on this grievance:

> In interpreting an act or a rule, differences of opinion arise even among judges. If the states think or feel that the constitution is not interpreted by the Union government correctly, they have the remedy at hand. They can have recourse to section 151 of the constitution.[29]

Grievance No. 3: In administering the Union subjects in the states, the Union government does not consult the state government concerned.

The advisory committee commented on this grievance as follows:

> Constitutionally and legally the Union government is not bound to consult a State government in administering a Union subject in that state, but out of courtesy and out of political expediency, the State government concerned should at least be informed, if not consulted, of what the Union government intends to do.

Grievance No. 4: The Union government officials look down upon the states.

The view of the committee was as follows:

> There is generally a black sheep in every flock not only in Myanmar but all over the world. Because of one black sheep, other sheep should not be condemned. In any event, we understand that the Union government has already taken steps to see that the Union government officials, both military and civil, pay proper regard not only to State governments but to their people as well.

Grievance No. 5: Union government officials do not pay due respect to state ministers.

The report's comment on this matter was:

> We do not think that Union government officials intentionally and deliberately treat State ministers with disrespect. It may be that their manners and behavior in dealing with State ministers are somewhat casual. In any event, this matter can be settled administratively.

Grievance No. 6: On administrative matters, including finance, the Union government takes a one-sided view.

The committee's views on this grievance were:

> As we pointed out above, the impression seems to prevail, as the result of the difference of angle from which one looks at the matter in question. This in turn is due to the difference of opinion in interpreting the constitution. This matter can easily be solved by discussion between the Union government and the State government.

Grievance No. 7: The states do not get assistance to which they are entitled.

The report made the following observation:

> Judging by what has transpired in the course of discussion, this grievance seems to refer mainly to the issue of Japanese reparations. At the beginning of the payment of the reparations, the Shan State did not get a share. It may be that the reparations were, at the beginning, applied to works which needed immediate attention. Later the Shan State was given a share. If the states made representations to the Union government about the nonreceipt of shares which they feel they are entitled to, out of monetary aid or assistance rendered by foreign countries, we are sure the Union government will promptly and sympathetically take their representations into consideration.

Grievance No. 8: In administering subjects set out on the Union List in Shan State, the Union government departments do not consult the Shan State government.

The committee's view on this matter:

> Constitutionally and legally, the Union government departments are not under any obligation to consult the Shan State government about administering the Union subjects in the Shan State, but as pointed out above, they should do so out of courtesy and political expediency. This matter can be settled administratively to the satisfaction of everybody concerned.

Grievance No. 9: Interference in Shan State politics and administration.

The committee reported on this matter as follows:

> Neither in the Shan State government's blue book, nor in the course of discussion with the Shan State ministers or with the political leaders and representatives of the Shan State people, is there any indication [of] who interferes in Shan State politics and administration. If there is any such interference as alleged, it should be brought to the notice of the Union government or of the prime minister. We are sure steps will be taken at once to put a stop to it.

After the committee had given its views on the grievances of Shan State, it addressed the constitutional question. It expressed its views on federation and a true federal government as follows:

> Federation means an association of independent states for certain common purposes, in which the member states retain a large measure of their original independence. As the association is free and voluntary, member states, in law, are free to leave the Union if they wish to.
>
> . . . the Federal Principle consists in [dividing] power in such a way that the powers to be exercised by the general government are specified and the residue is left to the regional governments. It is not enough that general and regional governments should each be independent in its own sphere; that sphere must be marked out in a particular

> way. The residuary powers, as they are called, must lie with the regional governments. On this view a government is not federal if the powers of the regional governments are specified and the residue is left to the general government.[30]

After quoting from K. C. Wheare's book, *Federal Government*, the report presented brief studies of the constitutions of the United States of America, Australia, Canada, South Africa, India, and Switzerland, and concluded that no true type of federal government exists. Even if there was one on paper, in actual practice it tended to become a unitary government.[31]

The advisory committee noted that the Shan State government and its people had not explained what was meant by a true federal government in their blue book, and expressed its belief that the Shan proposal hinted that the idea of a true federal government was like the federal government of the United States of America. The report continued:

> The American form of federal government is excellent both in form and on paper. It is the ideal type of federal government. But what is it like in practice? As pointed out above, "federation" means an association of independent states on a free and voluntary basis. As the association is free and voluntary, any member state can leave the federation at any time it chooses. But when this theory was put to the test, it failed. (20)

The report gave the historical evidence of the failure of the theory:

> When a dispute arose between the Northern States and the Southern States in the middle of the nineteenth century (1861–65) over the slave question, the Southern States threatened to secede from the Federation. To prevent their secession, President Abraham Lincoln declared war. If secession had been allowed, it would have broken up the Union, resulting in the ultimate destruction of the whole nation. (20–21)

The report went on:

> Since then the federal government has been encroaching on the sphere of the State government, in the name of national welfare and safety. The governors of states, at one of their annual conferences, lamented that they had now become puppets in the hands of the federal government. What thus became clear was that, though in theory the American form of government is federal, yet in actual practice it is gradually becoming unitary. (21)

Such were the comments of the advisory committee, complete with quotations from Wheare's *Federal Government* and Anderson's *The Nations and States: Rivals or Partners?* On the Federal Principle, the committee further presented its findings: "In the interviews with the advisory committee, the heads of state, members of State governments and a great majority of the leaders and representatives of political parties of various states did not insist on the federal form of government as hinted indirectly in their 'blue book.'"[32]

The committee, however, did not consider that federation as suggested in the blue book would strengthen or solidify the Union, and the report accordingly stated:

> Under such a structure there will not, and in fact can not, be a strong and stable government. There will be constant bickering and quarrel within the federal government. Similarly, there will be a constant quarrel and clashes between the two houses. The Union will thus break up in no time. The federal form of government as proposed in the Shan State government's blue book thus is not only impractical and impracticable but eventually will lead to the breakup of the Union. The Shan State government's proposal for a federal form of government cannot, for these reasons, be accepted. (26–27)

The advisory committee then stated its view that the three essential characteristics of a true federation were present in the present Constitution of the Union of Myanmar:

> The three essential characteristics of a true federation are (1) association of free states on a voluntary basis; (2) the right to secede; and (3) the right to complete autonomy. So far, two essential characteristics out of the three are present. They are (1) association of free states on a voluntary basis and (2) the right to secede.
>
> Now if we look at the Legislative List, we shall find that there is a division of subjects between the Union government and the State governments. Each government is supreme and independent in its own sphere. One cannot encroach upon the sphere of the other. That fact also conforms with the third characteristic for a true federal system.
>
> Since the three essential features of a true federal system are present in the Union of Burma, it would be proper to accept the Union as a federal union rather than as a unitary state. (28–29)

On the charge that the Union government interferes in the administration of state subjects the report stated: "As in the administration of other state subjects, when examined properly and thoroughly, it is found that there is no interference on the part of the Union government and if there is any, it is capable of being corrected administratively." (29)

The report continues:

> In fact, what the Shan State government and its people and what other State governments and their people feel most sore about is their helplessness in relation to their own land, their own forests, their own mines, their own minerals, and their inability to start to work any industry in their own state.
>
> All they know and feel is that they are not allowed to participate in the distribution of their own land and in the working, regulating, and developing of their own forests

> and mines. In this respect their feelings of frustration are real and intense. We must do something to allay their feelings; otherwise, they may become desperate and endanger the stability of the Union. . . .
>
> Whatever it may be, we must now find a solution, firstly, to satisfy the desire of State governments and their people to participate in the working and regulating of their resources, and secondly, to enable the Union government to keep control over these natural resources so that they may not be wasted or damaged. The only way out we can think of is to have a Concurrent Legislative List. Into this list all subjects of controversy shall be entered. Both the Union government and the State governments shall have legislative powers over these subjects. Where there is a conflict between the State law and the Union law, the latter shall prevail over the former. The Union government will generally deal with policy, whereas the State government will generally deal with its natural resources, such as land, forests, mines, petroleum, and other mineral oils in its own state. The Union government will deal with land, forests, mines, petroleum, and other mineral oils situated in Myanmar Proper. The kind of Concurrent Legislative List we have in mind is similar to the one we herewith attach as annexure "A." (31–34)[33]

Regarding other suggestions in the blue book, on the question of amending some or deleting others of the provisions of the constitution, namely the preamble and nineteen specific sections, the advisory committee was in favor of amending only sections 30, 91, 93, and 219. Sections 30, 93, and 219 dealt with land, forests, mines, minerals, petroleum, and other mineral oils, and as a result the committee recommends that these sections be placed on the Concurrent Legislative List. Regarding section 91, the committee's report stated:

> The leaders of the Shan State have complained that if parliament delegates part of its legislative powers to representative bodies within a state, it will mean setting up "a state within a state," causing confusion, friction, and bickering between the State Council and the local bodies. It appears, in our opinion, that there is a good deal of truth in the view held by the Shan State leaders. When the State Council had no control over a representative or local body within its state in matters of legislation, it will amount to the setting up of two rival bodies in a state.
>
> We should, therefore, like to suggest amending this section in such a way as to give powers to a State council or a State government to check, control, and approve, on behalf of the parliament and the Union government, all rules, regulations, and bylaws passed by local bodies. (38)

Regarding the Shan State proposal in the blue book to make Myanmar proper a constituent state (section 222), the view of the advisory committee was as follows:

> The Shan State government and its people say that according to section 222, Myanmar Proper should be a state accorded with all necessary characteristics similar to other states.
>
> If we look at the constitution of the German Empire before the First World War, we shall find that the Prussian government was, more or less, the German government and the Prussian chancellor was the German chancellor. Our constitution is somewhat analogous to the constitution of the German Empire of those days.
>
> The Union government is the government that rules Myanmar Proper. It is therefore not necessary to set up a separate government for Myanmar Proper, thereby entailing enormous cost and administrative difficulties. As it is, the constitution is working smoothly and amicably. It is therefore not necessary to make Myanmar Proper a state as suggested.

The committee then set out its recommendations under three headings:

1. Constitution
2. Redress for the alleged administration grievances
3. Conduct to be observed in the social and official relations between the Union officials on the one hand, and the State officials and the State people on the other

The recommendations on the constitution were:

> We cannot recommend the adoption of the type of federal government as proposed by the Shan State government and its people, as it is impracticable. It contains features which will inevitably lead to the breakup of the Union in the foreseeable future.
>
> On the other hand, our type of government, in the circumstances prevailing now, is the ideal [one]. It has all the essential characteristics of a federal government, being an association of states on a voluntary basis; the states other than Kachin and Kayin have the right to secede under certain specified conditions; and all states have the right to enjoy autonomy. The Union of Myanmar clearly has all the three requisites of a true federal state. (43)

But the Shan State government and the governments of other states complain that they have no complete autonomy; they are denied the right to manage, regulate, and develop their own natural resources such as lands, forests, mines, minerals, and the right to set up industries. To redress this complaint the advisory committee recommended the introduction of a Third Legislative List called the Concurrent List. To that list it recommended the transfer from the Union List subjects relating to lands, forests, mines, petroleum, oil fields, and industries and other subjects that may be controversial.

It also proposed that the Union government should deal with matters of policy applicable to the whole Union, and that the state governments should implement that policy in their states. The Union government will also deal with the management and development of lands, forests, mines, minerals, and petroleum oil fields in Myanmar proper. (43–44)

The recommendations on redressing the alleged grievances were:

1. Though constitutionally and legally the Union government is not bound to inform the states of what it intends to do in the states about the administration of the Union subjects therein, yet if the Union government does so out of courtesy, it will not only remove possible misunderstanding but improve official and social relations between the two.
2. A certain proportion of local men, if qualified and efficient, may be appointed to both the senior and junior ranks of the Union Services operating in the states. (46)

The recommendations on social and official relations between the Union officials and state officials and state people were as follows: "Union government officials, both civil and military, serving in the states may be instructed to deal with the state officials and state people in a brotherly manner and to pay due regard to state ministers." (47)

The advisory committee's report quoted above, containing both the English- and Myanmar-language versions, was submitted to the Union government on January 19, 1962.[34] Since the committee included among its members Dr. Ba U, Dr. U Thein Maung, former chief justice of the Union, and U Ohn Pe, former justice of the High Court, it could be said that the views of the committee on the Federal Principle carried legal weight, but it could not be said with any certainty that the committee's recommendations would have to be accepted.

AMENDMENT PROPOSED BY THE CONSTITUTION REVISION COMMITTEE

On January 20, 1962, one day after the advisory committee submitted its report, Sao Hkun Hkio and Dr. Saw Hla Tun went to meet Prime Minister U Nu at three o'clock in the afternoon. At this meeting Sao Hkun Hkio and party urged that the constitutional amendments relating to the states, proposed by the Constitution Revision Committee headed by Dr. E Maung, should not be introduced at the coming February session of parliament, but should be deferred.[35] The constitutional amendments were objected to by Sao Hkun Hkio and Dr. Saw Hla Tun.

These amendments were:

1. If the president considers that the head of state is acting unconstitutionally in administering the state, he shall take over the power of the state.
2. If the prime minister has to appoint the person selected by the State Council, as the head of state, the head of state shall not be accepted as a minister in the Union cabinet.[36]

Prime Minister U Nu promised not to introduce the constitutional amendment at the coming session of parliament. Instead, he said he would convene a national conference to discuss the revision of the constitution.

THE FEDERAL PRINCIPLE OF THE STATES UNITY ORGANIZATION

At 4:00 P.M. on January 20, 1962, eight representatives of the States Unity Organization met with Prime Minister U Nu: Sao Hkun Hkio, Dr. Saw Hla Tun, Sao Htun E (Hsa Mong Hkam), U Tha Tun (Rakhine), Nai Ba Saw (Mon), Captain Mang Tung Nung (Chin), U Hla Nyein (Kayah), and U Chit Maung (Kayah).[37] U Nu told them that the federal issue would be discussed at the national conference.

The document submitted by the States Unity Organization contained the following sections: (1) Introduction, (2) Why we want a true federal constitution, (3) What sort of federal government shall we devise? and (4) Conclusion.[38]

The introduction gave a brief account of the All States Conference held in Taunggyi, and how the conference gave birth to the States Unity Organization. Chapter 1 noted that since the Union of Myanmar was populated by Bamar, Shan, Kayin, Chin, Rakhine, Mon, Kayah, and other people, the long-term stability of the country, as well as the attainment of peace and welfare, depended on the cooperation, in a loving brotherly spirit, among the various national races. Such cooperation demanded national unity, and national unity could be achieved only if one national group gave the others equal powers and treated one another with respect, love, and consideration. The document recalled that when General Aung San was alive, the Union had been united because the general had gone about the task of promoting unity in the correct way, but that the unity he had been able to achieve had since then been loosening day by day. The document added that the Kachin, Chin, Shan, and Kayah had, from the very beginning, wanted a true federal government and had stated this before the Frontier Areas Committee of Enquiry. The document quoted the *Report of the Frontier Areas Committee of Enquiry* to substantiate this point. Furthermore, in presenting his seven-point directives to the Constituent Assembly, General Aung San had said, for points 1, 2, and 4:

1. The constitution shall be a constitution for a sovereign, independent republic to be known as the Union of Myanmar.
2. The individual states established by the Constitution of the Union of Myanmar shall enjoy autonomy as prescribed in the constitution.
3. . . .
4. Adequate safeguards shall be embodied in the constitution to protect the rights of the minorities. (6)

At the time the draft constitution was being submitted to the Constituent Assembly, the constitutional adviser, U Chan Htun, had also said: "I am here to explain whether our constitution is to be a federal or a unitary [one]. We may hold a very strong belief that the unitary constitution is superior, but in the present circumstances we shall have to establish a federal type in accordance with the directives." (7)

This made it very clear that the desire for the federal constitution was not something that had just arisen, but had been present since the struggle for independence, as claimed by the States Unity Organization.

Thus, at the time of the formation of the Union, General Aung San had declared that the constitution must be a federal one, and U Chan Htun, the constitutional adviser, had also explained to the Constituent Assembly that the Union of Myanmar had to be a federal union. Yet, ten years later, at a meeting between U Chan Htun and Professor Hugh Tinker, U Chan Htun is said to have declared: "Our constitution, though in theory federal, is in practice unitary." (8) The States Unity Organization document quoted those words from Tinker's book *The Union of Burma*.[39]

Regarding the acceptance of the 1947 Constitution by the national races, the document said that because of the assassination of General Aung San and the other leaders, the whole country was then in great distress and in mourning. At the same time the national races were eager to gain independence as speedily as possible. Under these circumstances, they failed to discuss the constitution with the seriousness it deserved. Instead, they credulously and casually ratified it because they:

1. believed that the constitution would be a truly federal constitution
2. believed that the constitution was better than the Canadian Constitution
3. had no knowledge of Constitutional Law
4. trusted completely the directives laid down by the national leader General Aung San
5. believed that should the constitution turn out to be, in any way, defective, the defects could later be remedied in a family spirit (7)

Regarding the difficulties encountered by the states, the document stated:

> After the proclamation of independence, the leaders of the states found that, under the constitution in force at the time, they were unable to carry out economic, political and administrative matters in the interest of various people in their own states, to the extent that they desired, due to interference by Myanmar Proper, which had usurped the powers of the Union. The people in the states were also having to suffer considerably, because of the economic, political, and administrative oppression of Bamars. (8)

In analyzing those difficulties, the document noted that the basic problem was that the present constitution, instead of having separate governments, had the central government of the Union serving as a government for both Myanmar proper and the whole of the Union. It declared: "That is why we consider it to be tragic that General Aung San's directives concerning the establishment of a true federal government perished at the same time that the general expired." (8)

The states expressed their feelings in the document:

> The constitution that is in force denied [our] rights to autonomy. It also failed to provide equality. All the powers of the Union have been completely usurped by Myanmar Proper, thus transforming the constituent states into vassal states.
>
> The people of the states had to struggle bitterly against the domination and oppression by Myanmar Proper. Because of the lack of autonomy and the lack of equality, the national unity built up by General Aung San has steadily deteriorated. This is indeed a bad sign for the Union. (8)

On the type of federation to be established, the document stated in chapter 2:

1. To ensure that the Union of Myanmar becomes a true federal union, it must be based on the national stand that all the states coming together to form the union are equal. Therefore a true federal union cannot be a combination of Myanmar Proper and the states. Myanmar Proper must first be established as a state, after which a true federal union of states should be formed.
2. As the usurpation of the central powers of government by Myanmar Proper means a lack of equality, thereby creating dissatisfaction, we strongly desire the removal of this dissatisfaction by establishing a Union of Myanmar with Myanmar Proper as one of the constituent states. (9)

The document also presented the view of the States Unity Organization on parliament's powers to amend the constitution:

1. We sincerely believe that under the Constitution of the Union of Myanmar, the present parliament has the power to establish Myanmar Proper as a constituent state.
2. Under section 222 (a) (B) of the Constitution of the Union of Myanmar, the meaning assigned to the expression "unit" already covers Myanmar Proper, and all that needs to be done is to designate Myanmar Proper as a constituent state of the Union.[40]
3. In order to make the change to the status of Myanmar Proper, it will be necessary to amend the constitution. We believe that such amendment can be effected under part 11–New States. Section 199, and in the manner amendments to the constitution were made previously in parliament, under chapter 11.[41]

DISCUSSIONS ON THE FEDERAL PRINCIPLE

The Union cabinet (Council of Ministers) met on February 13, 1962, and decided that neither the Federal Principle submitted by the States Unity Organization nor the draft of the Appointment of the Heads of State (Constitutional Amendment Act) would be submitted at the session of parliament to be convened on February 15. Instead it planned to convene a national conference to deal with the matter. The plan was opposed by Minister Sao Hkun Hkio and Minister Sama Duwa Sinwa Nawng, who argued that the question of amending the constitution should be determined by a cabinet decision.[42] Sama Duwa Sinwa Nawng wrote to Prime Minister U Nu on February 19 urging a reconsideration of the cabinet decision. The minister also told newspaper correspondents that convening a national conference instead of the cabinet making a decision when it was fully competent to do so, could create a bad precedent.[43]

Since the Chamber of Deputies was to meet on February 15 and the national conference was to be held on February 24, the leaders of the states who were already in Yangon held preliminary meetings among themselves. Of these meetings, the meeting of the Committee to Study the Problems of the States, held on February 12, was attended by state ministers, the minister for Chin affairs, and members of the States Unity Organization. The meeting discussed the Draft Constitutional Amendment Act, the Federal Principle submitted by Shan State, and the Federal Principle submitted by the States Unity Organization. The meeting accepted all the draft amendments, with two exceptions: the amendment enabling the president to take over the power of the states; and the amendment denying heads of states membership as ministers in the Union cabinet. In discussing the Federal Principle, however, differences of opinion arose, and therefore no decision could be reached. Minister Sama Duwa Sinwa Nawng and U A. Soe Myint repeated the objections they had raised at the Taunggyi Conference against the complete revision of the constitution. They argued that it was possible to empower states to deal with their own agricultural lands, forests, and minerals as they deemed fit, without changing the constitution. However, most of the attendees spoke in favor of the Federal Principle, and so they agreed to continue the discussions at the national conference.[44]

A meeting of the executive committee of the States Unity Organization was held on February 13, chaired by Minister Sao Wunna. It discussed the Federal Principle, with reference to the constitutions of the United States of America, Canada, and Australia. Thereafter, the organization decided to appoint a committee of eleven members to prepare a draft for the executive committee, and to request U Sein and U A. Soe Myint to serve as legal advisers, in addition to the present legal adviser, U Tin Ohn.[45]

The organization met again on February 18 with Duwa Zau Lawn in the chair. It decided that discussing the Draft Constitutional Amendment Act would merely distract attention from the Federal Principle, and that therefore the States Unity Organization should discuss only the Federal Principle at the national conference, and exclude all other subjects. It further decided that only state representatives who were not government servants should present the views of the states at the national conference and that heads of state should take no part in the discussion.[46]

The Shan State Steering Committee for the Revision of the Constitution of the Union of Myanmar also met on February 18. It elected U Htun Myint (Taunggyi), U Kya Bu (Shan), U Kyaw Sein (member of parliament), Sao Htun E (Hsa Mong Hkam), Sao Hso Hom (Mong Pawn), and U Soe Maung (People's United Party) as representatives of Shan State to the national conference.[47] Similarly, the States Unity Organization elected U Kya Bu (Shan), U Sein (Kayah), U Tha Tun (Rakhine), Duwa Zau Lawn (Kachin), Nang Zing La (Kachin), and Mon Ngwe Thein (Mon) as States Unity Organization representatives to the national conference.[48]

While the parliament was in session, the national conference to discuss the Federal Principle began meeting at 6:00 P.M on February 24, in the Main Hall of the Myanmar Broadcasting Service on Pyay Road in Yangon. Prime Minister U Nu presided over the meeting. As chairman of the meeting, he sat at the top end of the hall flanked by members of the Government Advisory Committee, Dr. Ba U, U Thein Maung, U San Nyunt, and U Chit Thaung.

Among the attendees were Thakin Tin, Dr. E Maung, Bo Tin Maung Gyi, U Saw Lu Lu, U Ba Maung, and U Chit Pe from the Union Party; U Kyaw Nyein, Thakin Tha Khin, Bo Khin Maung Gale, U Shein Htang, and Mahn Mya Sein from the AFPFL; Widhura Thakin Chit Maung, Bo Mya Thway, Bo Aung Naing, U Tun Aung Kyaw, U Kyaw Nyein, and U Aung Myint of the National United Front.

Representatives from the states also arrived at the conference, dressed in their colorful national costumes.[49]

PRIME MINISTER U NU'S ADDRESS

After the master of ceremonies had announced the conference's agenda on the Federal Principle, the prime minister gave his address on item 3 of the agenda, emphasizing the following points:

> Gentlemen: We are gathered here today to discuss the Federal Principle presented by the States Unity Organization. As the head of the government I have the duty to reveal my views on the federal issue, but it is not yet my turn to speak, so I shall not give my view tonight. I shall do so in due course.
>
> Gentlemen: The agenda for our discussion is as follows: Tonight, after my opening speech, the head of the Shan State, Sao Hkun Hkio, will present the Federal Principle. His presentation will be seconded by (1) Duwa Zau Lawn, Kachin State representative; (2) Captain Mang Tung Nung, Chin Special Division representative; (3) U Htun Myint (Taunggyi), Shan State representative; and (4) U Sein, Kayah State representative.

> After these two items on the agenda have been presented, the discussion will be prorogued until 6:00 P.M on Thursday, March 1. The reason for proroguing the discussions is to give the leaders of the NUF, the AFPFL, the Ya-Pa-La-Pha, the Union Party, and the members of the Government Advisory Committee sufficient time to properly study the speeches of the head of state Sao Hkun Hkio, Duwa Zau Lawn, Captain Mang Tung Nung, U Htun Myint, and U Sein in support of the Federal Principle.
>
> Gentlemen: When we resume our discussions at 6:00 P.M on Thursday, March 1, in this very same place, one representative from each of the following parties, namely (1) NUF, (2) AFPFL, (3) Ya-Pa-La-Pha, (4) Union Party, will present the views of his party on the Federal Principle.
>
> After the representatives of the political parties have had their say, Agga Maha Thiri Thudhamma Dr. Ba U will present the views of the Government Advisory Committee.
>
> Gentlemen: After all these representatives have spoken, a committee will be formed with (1) six members from the States Unity Organization, (2) three members from the NUF, (3) three members from the AFPFL, (4) three members from the Ya-Pa-La-Pha, (5) three members from the Union Party, and (6) the members of the Government Advisory Committee.
>
> I myself will chair this committee. After the committee has discussed all issues that need to be discussed with regard to the Federal Principle, the committee will report to the national conference all agreements arrived at. Any issue that cannot be resolved will also be reported.
>
> Gentlemen: I propose that this conference hold further discussions on what should be decided in connection with the Federal Principle only after the committee's report has been studied. [50]

U Nu then spoke at length on the importance of having a stable and enduring Union:

> The problem to be discussed here, beginning from today, is none other than the problem of ensuring a stable and enduring Union. It is my firm belief that if we, the founders of the Union, cannot resolve this problem during our regime, no other regime will be able to do so, and I am sure, gentlemen, that you all share my view on this matter. If our Union were to collapse, neither the people of the states, nor the people of Myanmar Proper, will benefit in any way. I firmly hold the view that everybody will stand to lose, and I am sure you all hold the same view too.
>
> I would like to urge all present here, who are the founders of the Union, not to lose sight of the responsibility we bear in trying to resolve this very important problem.

Regarding the way the discussions were to be conducted, U Nu said:

> There are, roughly, two ways in which discussions can be held. One is discussion between enemies and the other between members of a family. A family discussion is different from a discussion between enemies. In a family discussion the members of a family, brothers and sisters, present what each of them wants, and in so doing there may be differences of opinion, but such differences will be overcome by a give-and-take attitude on the part of each party.
>
> Our present discussion must be a family discussion. Each of you, gentlemen, and each of us, who are members of the family of our Union, must put all our views on the table. In so doing, there will, of course, be differences. After that, to ensure benefit for ourselves, for our children, and for our Union, we will have to negotiate till we reach an agreement which will resolve those differences.

On the objectives of the discussions, he said: "We wish to seek, hand in hand with you, gentlemen, the best means of ensuring the stability of the Union, the preservation of our independence, and the preservation of our democracy."

On the manner in which the above objectives were to be achieved:

> In seeking the best means of ensuring unity, independence, and democracy, I would like to call the attention of both the people of Myanmar Proper and the people of the states to one very important point, and this is none other than that the means we are seeking must satisfy the three conditions set out in the eternal principles of Loka Pala, namely, that they must be just, independent, and equal.

U Nu concluded his speech. "Let us all try our utmost to ensure that our sovereign and independent Union does not revert to the extremely ugly status of a vassal state or a slave state."

PRESENTATION OF THE FEDERAL PRINCIPLE BY SAO HKUN HKIO

After Prime Minister U Nu concluded his speech, Minister Sao Hkun Hkio presented the Federal Principle as chairman of the States Unity Organization.[51] He recounted the history of how the present Union came into being, beginning with the Pang Long Conference of 1947. He began by speaking about the Pang Long Agreement that led to the establishment of a Union based on the three major principles: (1) equality of opportunity, (2) autonomy of the Frontier Areas, and (3) the right to secede from the Union after gaining independence. After the Pang Long Agreement had been signed, witnesses testified before the Frontier Areas Commission of Enquiry that the Union should be established on the basis of those three principles. The preliminary convention of the AFPFL, held in May 1947, had adopted the arrangement of granting equality to the minority nationalities and of establishing a true federal Union built on the basis of that equality. Minister Sao Hkun Hkio also summarized the seven directives that General

Aung San had delivered in the Constituent Assembly during its deliberations on the question of drawing up a suitable constitution. Then he described the circumstances surrounding the adoption of the present constitution:

> The political situation at the time was very confused, the entire nation was mourning the assassination of General Aung San and the other leaders, and the struggle for independence had become one burdened by sorrow, so we resolved that we had to prevent outsiders from interfering in our country's affairs by hastily adopting the constitution, without criticism, in the Constituent Assembly.

Minister Sao Hkun Hkio then presented the experiences of the states during the period after independence:

> At the time, all the people of the various states had harbored within our breasts the great aspiration that the Union of Myanmar we believed in was about to gain independence; that once independence was gained, we would all be able to create progressive and developing states; and that a Union composed of such progressive states joined together would come into being. However, in striving, hand in hand, with "Big Brother Burma Proper" along the fourteen-year period of independence, we have come to realize that our aspiration to autonomy was not entirely fulfilled.
>
> We have now come to realize that we have not been given the power to work to the utmost for the development of our states.

And the reason for this was:

> Our Union, instead of representing all the states, was seen to primarily represent only the areas of Bamars, which had come to be known as Burma Proper.
>
> The states being denied equality with Burma Proper lacked the opportunity to work, to their utmost ability, for their own development, and so progress had not been achieved to the degree that one would have expected to achieve. The reason for this state of affairs is that, in establishing the Union, the national races who possessed the attributes to form states, like the Shans and the Kayahs, formed the constituent states—the Shan State and the Kayah State—while the people of Burma Proper did not form a state on the basis of equality with other states.
>
> If the spirit of the Pang Long Agreement and the directives of General Aung San concerning the equality of all constituent states had been observed in implementing the Union, the Union government would have been one that represented all the states.
>
> Today, instead of forming a state for Burma Proper, the authorities had decided to retain the Union government as the government of Burma Proper, and the powers of the Union and those of Burma Proper had been treated as being one and the same. Due to this fact, our nation has gradually deteriorated from being a federal union to that of a unitary state. This is why we of the states now entertain increasing suspicion, day by day,

of the good faith of the government in Burma Proper. And as these suspicions have multiplied, we have now come to publicly express the dissatisfaction felt by the states with Burma Proper. We have now come to realize that the Union, as presently constituted, is not the kind that will promote national unity, nor is it likely to be a Union of equals.

The third point raised by Minister Sao Hkun Hkio concerned the inconsistencies within the constitution in force.

If one compares the preamble of the present Constitution of the Union of Burma with the sections of the constitution which are supposed to have been drawn up on the basis of the preamble, one will discover many inconsistencies. Although the preamble clearly sets out the eternal principles of justice, liberty, and equality, the fact that the sections which follow contain just the opposite of these eternal principles has been the cause of our sorrow. This fact has also been the motivation that has further strengthened our desire to have the constitution revised. As an example of the inconsistencies in the constitution, allow me to point out that under section 222, Burma Proper is a constituent "unit" like the other constituent states, but under section 8 it has come to dominate over the other states by exercising the powers of the Union, and this has given rise to real grievances by the states.[52] In truth, the essence of this section is that, although Burma Proper should be a constituent state within the Union, it has in fact taken over the powers and authority of the Union, thus convincing us, the people of the states, that Burma Proper is using these powers to lord it over the states of the Union.

The final point dealt with the establishment of the federal union.

I would like to present on behalf of the States Unity Organization the form of union we desire. This will involve:

1. The establishment of Burma Proper as one of the constituent states
2. The granting of equal powers to the two chambers of parliament
3. The sending of an equal number of representatives from each state to the Chamber of Nationalities
4. The voluntary granting of certain restricted powers to the Union government by the states and retention of all reserve powers by the states.

Commentary by Duwa Zau Lawn

The first speaker to support Minister Sao Hkun Hkio's presentation was the Kachin State representative Duwa Zau Lawn, who spoke in support of the presentation by the chairman of the States Unity Organization.[53]

Let me tell you why the people of the states are at present so dissatisfied, aggrieved, and suspicious of the people of Burma Proper. It is because (1) the present constitution differs considerably from the constitution envisioned in the directives of our national leader, General Aung San; and (2) because the form of the Union government that the national races of the Frontier Areas such as the Shans, Kachins, and Chins desired, a desire which they had, time and again, expressed to the Bamar leaders during the period before and after independence, differed so much from their aspirations that it has become the cause for anguish and dissatisfaction.

The form of Union the national races desired was embodied in the Pang Long Agreement, reached between General Aung San and the leaders of the minorities, that after independence, the Union would be based on the principle of equality.

The representatives of the Shans and the Kachins also testified before the Rees-Williams Frontier Areas Committee of Enquiry in 1947 that they desired autonomy for their states within the Union, but that they were willing to cede certain departments which concerned all the states to the central government of the Union.

Before we gained our independence, due to the divide-and-rule policy of the English expansionists, we, the minority races, distrusted the Bamars. So when General Aung San called upon us to struggle for independence together, we were quite undecided about the matter. But at a meeting in Myitkyina on November 29, 1946, between the national leader General Aung San and Kachin leaders, and then at a meeting between the general and the minority leaders in Pang Long, trust between the Bamars and the minorities was slowly built up. We studied the directives for drawing up the constitution delivered at the preliminary convention of the AFPFL by General Aung San, and this combined with our observations that the general's national policy was correctly based on: (1) equality of all national races; (2) full autonomy for all national races; and (3) protection of the rights of the national races. We completely changed our views and decided to put our trust in the Bamar leaders led by General Aung San. We managed then to forge an unprecedented unity within the entire country. When the Constituent Assembly was convened to draw up the constitution, our trust went so far as to leave everything to the Bamar leaders.

While the Constituent Assembly was in progress, General Aung San and some of his colleagues were assassinated by a group of evil people. The constitution that was finalized after the assassination was not in accord with the correct national policy laid down by the general, and as we gradually found out, it did not accord with the principle that we, the minorities, desired.

In recounting the difficulties encountered by the states under the present constitution, Duwa Zau Lawn pointed out:

In the fourteen years that the constitution has been in existence, we have faced all sorts of difficulties. We have found that it is inadequate and deficient. This is because the present constitution did not embody the basic principles originally agreed upon. It has not lived up to our expectations; the essence of a federal union had been lost; and it is like a dish of food without salt, bland and tasteless.

When we first gained our independence, we, the minority peoples, were overjoyed and confidently believed that we were now masters of our own destinies, that we would now be able to do our utmost for the economic development of our states. We had high hopes. But as one year followed another after independence, we found that the actual conditions fell far short of our aspirations. We became aggrieved and dissatisfied. Consequently, our relations with people from Burma Proper deteriorated. We began to gossip among ourselves that the majority Bamars were oppressing the people of the states by restricting our freedom, interfering in our internal affairs, and practicing hegemony.

Regarding how the states were being dominated by Myanmar proper under section 8 of the constitution, Duwa Zau Lawn had this to say:

Although under section 222 of the constitution, Burma Proper is merely another constituent "unit" in the Union, we have seen that it has been dominating the other states by virtue of section 8. This section has created two classes of people: the superior and the inferior, as it had handed over undue powers to the Bamars. This fact is the antithesis of the principle of equality, and is incompatible with correct national policy. If we study the present constitution not only from the legal and the administrative points of view, but also from the national point of view, we will find that it no longer has a national character, and as a result, national unity has steadily eroded. Furthermore, in the case of the Kachin State, its constitutional provisions differ from those of the other states in that they provide for the protection of the rights of other different races.[54] This provision is not conducive to national unity but, on the contrary, engenders racial disharmony.

Duwa Zau Lawn then concluded his speech: "Our call for a 'truly federal' union is not to stir up racial tensions, nor are we demanding a 'confederation.' We have presented our demand for a 'true federal union' because we firmly believe that is the only means by which national unity can be regained."

Commentary by Captain Mang Tung Nung

After Duwa Zau Lawn had spoken in support of the Federal Principle introduced by Minister Sao Hkun Hkio, the next speaker was Captain Mang Tung Nung, the representative of the Chin Special Division.[55]

We have established a Union of Burma because we are in favor of a federal system. When in September 1947 a draft constitution, apparently establishing a federal union, was proposed in the Constituent Assembly, we all voted for it without fuss. We had believed that we would be able to implement the constitution on the basis of federal principles. But things did not [happen] the way we had hoped for and believed in. After encountering problems over a [long] time we have come to realize that our constitution does not conform to the type of federal union we had in mind.

We had believed that we would have a constitution, whereby the minority peoples of the states and the people of Burma Proper would enjoy equal rights and power, but the situation in the states under the present constitution has fallen short of our expectations and we have come to realize now that our present constitution does not uphold the Federal Principle.

When we look into what has happened during the fourteen years since independence, we see that the right to self-determination of the peoples of the states and Frontier Areas is about to disappear.

In today's Union of Burma, the "union spirit" has plummeted and it is difficult to perceive that "bond of affinity" that should exist in our Union. In defining the constituent units of the Union, the constitution does not use the words "the states and Burma Proper." There are only two types of units: (1) the states and (2) the remaining territories. What we nowadays refer to as Burma Proper is, in truth, just another unit within the Union. But since the only unit that can wield the powers of the Union happens to be Burma Proper, dissension and discord have risen among the constituent units of the Union. Now that these disagreements and dissatisfaction have multiplied, who is to provide the solution? Without solutions, these problems will escalate to the extent that could affect our national unity. I would like to request all of you to give serious consideration to this matter.

On the question of the basis on which the constitution should be revised, he said:

Our view is that in revising the constitution, we would like to make it a truly federal one. Unless this is done, the problems will persist. We believe that the "spirit" and "philosophy" of the Union must correspond exactly with the provisions laid down in the Union Constitution, without any discrepancies. How can one expect continued stability while carrying on with the existing inequality between the states and Burma Proper? Could one expect to find the essence of democracy in such a situation? We fear the answer is "No!" Therefore we would like to support the proposal, and my advice is that we should scrap the distinction between states and Burma Proper, and make our Union a union of equal states by turning Burma Proper into a state like the others. I believe that this will dispel all suspicions of inequality.

It is only by accepting the principle of a union of states as I have set out, will there emerge a true federal union, in which the states equally share the executive, judicial, and legislative powers, and transfer to the central Union government only certain necessary, specific powers.

Commentary by U Htun Myint

The third speaker in support of the Federal Principle was U Htun Myint (Taunggyi), who said:[56]

> Burma had striven for decades to free itself from the status of a British colony, through various stages of struggle, beginning with the days of Wunthanu [love of one's own race] movement, up till the days of General Aung San. Burma had, in stages, made demand after demand, starting with the demand for self-government, called "home rule," to the final demand for total and unconditional independence. If one looks at these demands from the point of view of the Myanmar nationals, the demands will certainly be regarded as fully justified. On the other hand, from the point of view of the colonialists, they would, without doubt, appear to be unlawful demands. The struggle for independence by the Myanmar nationals on the one hand, and the desire of the British to preserve the colonial status of Burma on the other, of course, advocated very different points of view. I do not wish to claim that our situation today fits exactly the example I have just given. The example concerned relations between a colonialist-expansionist regime and Myanmar nationals struggling to free themselves from political bondage. In our own case, it is a relationship between members of the same family, seeking equality. So the relationships are very different. However, the feelings that we have today must be the same as those held by the Myanmars in the colonial days, and I present this example to you simply because I wish to highlight those sufferings. The essence of the true Federal Principle that we have proposed is equality. To put our demands in the simplest terms, we are saying: "Let us all—Bamars, Shans, Kachins, Chins, Kayins, Kayahs, Mons, Rakhines—brothers in the same family, treat one another equally, and let us enjoy everything equally.
>
> I don't know how some people have interpreted the "true Federal Principle" so as to lead them to flatly reject the idea. Such outright rejection, when viewed from the perspective of the feelings we presently endure, could only be interpreted as declaring: "We cannot accept you as equals, and we will not share the fruits of independence equally with you." Such blatant rejection by newspapermen, or politicians, or legal experts from Burma Proper could only be interpreted as a refusal to accept us as the equals of Bamars and a refusal to share the fruits of independence equally. Yes, every time our elder brothers, the Bamars, callously reject our true Federal Principle, we are deeply hurt, just as the Myanmar nationalists must have felt every time the British authorities rejected their demands for independence.

On the close relations that had existed between Shan and Bamar, U Htun Myint said:

> We Shans, like the Bamar nationals, used to have our own country, our own people, and our own sovereignty. The relations between the Shans and the Bamars throughout history have had moments [of] enmity, as well as moments of amity and friendship. Racially the Shans are more closely related to the Thais, but in their actual

> relationships, the Shans have been closer to the Bamars. Both the Bamars and the Shans have been enslaved by the British and have had to suffer together, under British domination.
>
> The Shans and the Bamars achieved independence by struggling together. And just as the Bamars would not like to get rid of one master merely to have another, so the Shans also would not like to shake off one form of slavery and then suffer another.

Then to show that the Shan had always wanted a true federal government even during the struggle for independence, he said:

> In the same way that the Shans joined forces with the Bamars to attain independence, they had joined hands, on an equal footing with the independent Bamars, to form the Union. From 1945 till 1947 when the Constituent Assembly was convened, we, the Shans, made it very plain that we would take our independence with the Bamars and that we would like to form a Union under a "true Federal Principle," and the documents that provide evidence of those aspirations are still in existence.

U Htun Myint continued:

> [Regarding] our submission of the Shan proposal, some persons will ask: "What sort of madness has made you Shans to suddenly press for these further demands that you call the 'true Federal Principle'?" Some others will ask: "Who are the people who have set you up to make such demands? Whose machinations are behind these demands?" When we hear such questions we are deeply hurt.

On the Shan support for the constitution at the Constituent Assembly U Htun Myint said:

> Some people have said: "Didn't the Shan representatives participate in the drawing up and approval of this constitution at the Constituent Assembly?" Yes we did. At the Constituent Assembly we, the representatives of the Shan State, did participate in the drawing up and the approval of the constitution. But please let me explain further the circumstances under which such approval was given.
>
> We, who participated in the work of the Constituent Assembly as representatives from the Shan State, had absolutely no political experience at the time. I also admit, with complete honesty, that we knew nothing about matters of legislation. We participated in the Constituent Assembly, not so much to carry out legislative business, as because we firmly believed that just as it would be meaningless for Burma to gain independence without the Frontier Areas, so it would be just as meaningless to put forward the case of the Frontier Areas without Burma Proper being included. This belief made us strive for an independent Union, hand in hand, and on an equal footing with Burma Proper. Our priority was to free ourselves from the domination of the

> expansionist-colonialists. We sincerely believed that once the yoke of the expansionist-colonialists had been overthrown, there would be no need to make special demands between kindred people.

U Htun Myint then related what General Aung San had said at the Constituent Assembly:

> I can still hear, to this day, the words of our revered and trusted leader, General Aung San, spoken at one of the committee meetings while we were carrying out our duties in the Constituent Assembly. When the constitutional adviser U Chan Htun presented a host of provisions of the draft constitution which he and his office had prepared, General Aung San remarked: "U Chan Htun, it won't do for you to go into such lengthy details right now. A proposal containing broad principles will suffice. Once we have gained our independence, we can put into effect whatever we need by enactment in parliament. In the manner in which you are going about the business, at such great length, how can the task be completed in two or three months' time?"

Then to make the point that the present constitution was approved solely because of their trust of and love for General Aung San and the leaders of the AFPFL, U Htun Myint said:

> We love and respect General Aung San and the leaders of the AFPFL, and just as we loved and respected them, [so] we trusted them completely. General Aung San's stand was that there was no need to draw up a lengthy and detailed constitution. He suggested that a constitution that contained the broad principles and the necessary elements would be sufficient. Once independence was achieved, adjustments would be made in accordance with the circumstances and the time. That was the trend of General Aung San's thinking. Since we had complete trust in General Aung San and the leaders of the AFPFL we placed our whole future entirely in their hands. Some Shan State representatives at the time, fearing such an outcome as we are now facing, wanted to engage the services of a foreign constitutional expert.[57] We fought against the proposal because we felt that such an action would be taken to mean that we were suspicious of the motive of the AFPFL.

After the assassination of General Aung San, the Constituent Assembly carried on with its work but, according to U Htun Myint, the constitution that took shape was not the kind that the general had envisioned. He said:

> It was very clear that it diverged completely from the principles laid down by General Aung San. If the present constitution is compared with the draft constitution drawn up by the preliminary AFPFL convention, it will be seen that there are a vast number of differences.

U Htun Myint went on to explain that although the constitution differed from the type preferred by General Aung San, the Shan State representatives accepted it because they still trusted and relied on the Bamar leaders led by the prime minister. He said:

> After General Aung San was assassinated we continued to place our trust in the Bamar leaders headed by Prime Minister U Nu. We did not give much attention to the contents of the constitution, because we didn't understand them too well. To this day, we still hold the belief that by adhering to the directives of General Aung San and by working in accordance with the spirit instead of the letter of the constitution, we can still achieve our aim. It was in this spirit and the trust we had in the Bamar leaders, about which I have described, that we accepted the constitution.

On the experiences after independence, U Htun Myint said:

> When we came to put the constitution into practice after independence, we found that the family spirit shown at the Constituent Assembly had disappeared completely. The good will that had been present behind the wording of the constitution also seems to have disappeared. It was only when the precise interpretations of every word in the constitution were made and implemented that it dawned upon us that our expectations were absolutely wrong. Day after day our grievances became more and more pronounced. Whenever we put forward demands for our rights, we got the constitution shoved down our throat. The result was that we, of the states, were relegated to the situation where we were evermore dependent on the good will of the party in power in Burma Proper. We were reduced to the status where we would be able to breathe freely only by such dependence. We have been reduced to the status of vassal states in relation to Burma Proper.

Regarding finance, he said:

> We are completely tired of having to rush around with palms extended, begging for revenue to which we are entitled, but which has been redesignated as "grants" to be distributed as largess by Burma Proper. There have been innumerable instances where, because those "grants" were delayed, the administration in the states had encountered difficulties. With regard to the distribution of these "grants" some persons have likened us to goods wagons being dragged along in tow by Burma Proper acting as the locomotive engine. I wish to say to those persons, "Our true Federal Principle means that you do not need to drag us along at such great sacrifice to yourselves. Uncouple us and let us go free. Your best efforts to drag us along for thirteen whole years have got us nowhere near our objectives. Leave us to go our own way and depend on our own efforts.

Regarding the revision of the constitution:

> Like the saying, "Once bitten twice shy" we have learned the lesson that putting our trust in the good will of a leader or a political party will no longer suffice. After all, men and political parties are mortal. We have now come to realize that we will have to draw up a constitution that will protect our rights, a constitution drawn up in precise terms so that there can be no ambiguity.

Then to emphasize that mere amendments of a few sections of the constitution would not suffice, he said:

> At first we believed that it might be possible to limit the revision to changing a few sections of the constitution, but when we studied the constitution, bearing in mind the practical difficulties we have encountered, we found that the sections were complementary to one another. We then realized that the whole constitution itself would have to be rewritten. That is why we have submitted the proposal that would alter the very basis of the constitution. The question may be asked, "Can't we just change the Revenue List to give you Shans more rights?" The answer to that is "Most probably, Yes!" But this will not cure the root cause of our malady. It will be merely a palliative. Since the root cause will remain, further problems will keep cropping up. We sincerely believe that our true Federal Proposal is the correct remedy that will remove the root cause of the illness.

He then presented the four basic points on which the "true Federal Proposal" was based:

1. Establishment of a Bamar State
2. Equal powers to the two chambers of parliament
3. Equal number of state representatives in the Chamber of Nationalities
4. Central powers to be strictly limited, with the reserved powers going to the states

U Htun Myint explained these four basic points:

> With regard to the establishment of a Bamar State, we should remember that just as we cannot live in a vacuum, [so] a federal union cannot exist without equality. Until the question of the establishment of a Bamar State is completely resolved, the rest of the revisions we have proposed, such as those regarding the parliament, and the revision of the division of powers, will not be resolved. The reason for my saying so is that when the leaders of Burma Proper look at any problem or subject, they are unable to see it from the point of view of a state. They see it from the point of view of Burma Proper, which controls the levers of power of the central government.

> Today there is no need to argue over the merits of a unitary or a federal state. For, as far as we are concerned, there can be no other type of government than a federal one. I am sure everyone will accept that our constitution today is not a true federation.
>
> A federal union should be a union of states, so our Union of Burma should also be a union of states. But the Constituent Assembly, which brought forth our constitution, had to labor under very peculiar circumstances. No wonder, we created a peculiar federal union, the likes of which are not to be found elsewhere in the world. We established states, like the Shan State, the Kachin State, and the Kayah State, but instead of establishing a Bamar State, we let it amalgamate with the central government. Due to these prevailing circumstances, we ended up adopting this very peculiar constitution. We had hoped then that the constitution would work.
>
> In adopting the constitution in this manner, we, the representatives of the Shan State, are also to be blamed. But two matters of overriding importance occurred at the time which affected our performance. One was the assassination of our leaders, who were irreplaceable, which caused us great sorrow; and the second was our determination to get independence within one year, in accordance with the line laid down by our leaders. These two overriding considerations prompted us to accept the present constitution without making further demands.

Then U Htun Myint explained the experience of thirteen years under the present constitution:

> We have had practical experience in implementing this unique and peculiar constitution during the past thirteen years. We, as members of the Constituent States, have become more and more disenchanted with this constitution. The fact that Burma Proper and the states are not equal has become clearer with each passing day. To highlight this inequality I shall cite but one single example concerning governmental power. Because the Shan State is designated as a state, it is under the Union government in all matters relating to the subjects that have been transferred to the Union government.
>
> Burma Proper, on the other hand, although a unit of the Union, has not been designated as a state, but has been amalgamated with the Union government, so with regard to all those subjects that were transferred to the Union or central government, our Shan State has in fact fallen under the authority of Burma Proper. In other words, Burma Proper, which has taken control of the central powers of the Union, is now lording it over the states. Leaving aside the constitutional aspect, this point in itself is sufficient to show very clearly that there is no equality between the states and Burma Proper.
>
> That is why in presenting our Federal Principle, in order to ensure equality, we have insisted on including the establishment of Burma Proper as one of the constituent states as the first requirement.

Then going on to the division of powers, U Htun Myint said:

> Our present Union is not a true federal union, but rather a loose type of union akin to Canada. We have tried that Canadian type of division of powers for thirteen years. We no longer want this type of federation. That is why we have come forward with our proposal for a true federal union like the USA, Switzerland, and Australia, where the federal or central powers are enumerated and the remaining powers reserved to the states.

Then referring to the demand for the granting of equal powers to the two chambers of parliament, U Htun Myint explained:

> The reason for having two chambers of parliament is to ensure that each chamber will act as a check and balance on the other. Therefore it follows logically that the two chambers should enjoy equal powers. In a federal union the existence of two chambers of the legislature is a necessity. Since a union is made up of constituent states, which naturally is based on territorial constitutions and population, the two chambers of the legislature not only serve as a check and balance on each other, but the second chamber also takes on the additional duty of preserving and protecting the rights of the states. In a federal union, because there is a disparity in the size of the population and the territory among the states, the application of democratic principles of one person = one vote, could lead larger states dominating over the smaller ones. Hence the second chamber is usually constituted, not on a population basis, but with the same number of representatives for each state, regardless of whether the population is large or small.

Turning to the question of finance, U Htun Myint said:

> The greatest problem every federal union in the world faces is sharing the federal revenue. If this problem is so difficult to resolve in other countries, we should not be so naive as to expect that the same problem can be solved easily in our own country. However, we considered that at least a basic principle by which the division should be made needs to be established. A union is normally established by constituent states coming together, voluntarily and by mutual consent.
>
> Then by unanimous agreement, certain powers are surrendered to the Center, while the states retained the remaining powers to administer themselves, in the manner best suited to them. This is the basic idea of a federal union. Hence federal revenue should also be allocated accordingly. Ideally, the Center should be able to manage on its own revenues, and the states should also be able to do so on their own. The Center and the states should not have to be dependent on one another.
>
> However, the fact is that states are very different from one another. They are not equal in terms of productive forces, as well they do not have the same amount of or the same natural resources. That is why there has to be provision for financial assistance from the Center to the less developed states. At the same time it is the duty of the

> Center to modernize and develop them. Therefore, in considering the allocation of Union revenues, we should not be constrained by narrow parochial views. We should not also lose sight of the fact that the Union of Myanmar is set to march along the path toward the goal of a socialist society. We must bear in mind that in order to achieve this objective, we will have to draw up numerous economic development projects, and that we, the people of all the states, will have to bear the responsibility of providing the funds required for all those projects.

Then U Htun Myint talked about the way the constitutional amendments should be carried out:

> Some persons are of the opinion that our demands cannot be accommodated under the law as it stands. We do not wish to get into any arguments on points of law. As General Aung San used to remark, "Law is like a telescope and it is adjustable." He also used to say, "Law is not gospel truth." Laws are made by men, so there is no reason why men cannot change them. We do not wish to argue here whether it is possible or not possible to change the law. We are more concerned with whether there is the good will to make the change.
>
> If we all agree that there is a need to change the constitution, the constitutional experts will always find a way to draw up the amendments to the constitution within the limits imposed by the law. Here I would like to present an example. Formerly, the British parliament had no act providing for the granting of independence to Myanmar, and I am quite certain that no advisory committee appointed by the British government would have recommended that Burma be granted independence. However, when the granting of independence to Burma became unavoidable, the British constitutional experts used the existing law, which was the Government of Burma Act 1935, to create an interim government with full powers, and to convene a Constituent Assembly.

Commentary by Kayah U Sein

After U Htun Myint had spoken in support of the Federal Principle, the last person to speak in favor of it on February 24 was Kayah U Sein.[58]

Mr. Chairman and Respected Leaders,

> The Union of Burma was established on the basis of justice, liberty and equality by agreement between the leaders of the Frontier Areas and those of the Bamars, headed by General Aung San. In principle, the path laid down by our leaders was a fully democratic one. But as the chairman of the States Unity Organization and Representatives have made clear in their presentations this evening, the principles of justice, liberty and equality have been abused during the past thirteen years.

He also said:

> The Union of Burma, established by the sweat, blood, and determination of leaders General Aung San, Sao Sam Htun, the *saohpa* of Mong Pawn, Thakin Mya, Mahn Ba Khaing, Sayagyi U Razak, Deedok U Ba Cho, and U Ba Win, on the basis of national unity, justice, and liberty, is no more in existence in its true form. It has now been transformed. It does not need any imagination to see that. It makes us wonder whether our Union is almost at the point of breaking asunder.

Then Kayah U Sein talked about how, after the *parinibbana* (demise) of the Lord Buddha, when it was considered that circumstances had arisen which might lead to the disappearance of the Buddha's religion, the First Buddhist Council was held within three months of the Buddha's *parinibbana*. After that, whenever it was considered that impurities had crept into the teachings of the Buddha, kings who took on the title of Sasanadayaka (Promoter of Religion) would undertake to organize *sanghayanas* (councils)to bring the teachings back in line with what the Buddha had taught. King Mindon convened the Fifth Buddhist Council and the Sixth Buddhist Council was held in Yangon during the time when U Nu was the prime minister. U Sein said: "Just as the Pitaka, or the Teachings of Buddha, were constantly restored to their original purity by the Sanghayanas, so also our constitution should be reviewed in consultation with the leaders of the states to accord with the true Federal Principle laid down by our leaders."

After Kayah U Sein's presentation, the conference concluded for the day with refreshments being served to the delegates.

THE SECOND DAY OF THE CONFERENCE ON THE FEDERAL PRINCIPLE

The conference continued for a second day, on March 1, at 6:00 P.M. It resumed with Prime Minister U Nu in the chair, presenting the agenda. He explained that as the discussions which were about to take place were very important, it would be inappropriate to rush through them in a single day. To give other representatives and people from the country time to study the discussions, the conference decided that on March 1 only one representative each from the NUF and the AFPFL would present their opinions. The conference would resume on March 7.[59]

Commentary by Thakin Chit Maung

In accordance with the above agenda, the first speaker, Thakin Chit Maung, representative of the National United Front (NUF), spoke for an hour as follows:[60]

> The edifice of unity and friendship among all peoples established by the architect of the Union, our national leader General Aung San, is today in a very precarious state.

If we cannot preserve this edifice for even one single generation, we are certainly going to be recorded in history as children who do not know how to respect and cherish the inheritance passed down to us by our parents. I myself subscribe to the view that it is with a feeling of remorse that we are now holding this conference with the representatives of all our national races, in fervent family spirit, so as to be able to shoulder our duty to maintain the edifice of unity and friendship in good shape, before it is too late. (1–2)

Presenting the view of the NUF, he said:

All the national races in our Union are dissatisfied and restless because they are all greatly aggrieved. The Bamars are dissatisfied in their own way, as are the Kayins and the Shans. They are no longer able to contain their grievances. I consider that the first great problem we should seriously tackle is to find out the cause of all this dissatisfaction. I believe that the call for a truly federal constitution also arose out of this general feeling of dissatisfaction.

He gave the NUF's perception of how this general dissatisfaction should be tackled:

An inquiry into this problem, if it is to be confined only to legalistic matters and amendments to the constitution, will not be comprehensive or complete. (2)

The basis of our dissatisfaction and distrust of one another did not arise recently. It is an evil that has accumulated over many years, beginning from the days of feudalism and colonialism. It is important for us to have drawn the conclusion that this problem is the result of the manipulation of the feudalists and the colonialists, both in the old and in the new form, whose policy is to sow seeds of dissension among our national races, so that we will hate one another like enemies. (3)

Next Thakin Chit Maung presented his views on how to tackle the problem:

If we forget this historical fact, and go on accusing one another as if we were enemies, the problem will never be resolved. If we keep looking for enemies in our own camp and not in the enemy's camp in the belief that "this problem is caused by Bamars" or "the Kayins" or "the Shans" and persist in treating one another like enemies, and blaming one another, we will ultimately bring about the disintegration of the Union, which is the goal of our enemies. Let me state very clearly here that we will encounter even greater dangers and difficulties than we are facing today if we go on making enemies of friends. (3)

The architect of our Union, General Aung San, built up the friendship and unity between our various peoples during our days of servitude by identifying the colonialist-expansionists as the enemy. In building up national unity during the days when we were under the Japanese fascists, he identified the fascist ideology as the enemy. At the end of the Great War, in the bitter struggle for national liberation, he targeted the

> British expansionists as enemies. This correct method of pinpointing the real enemy, in building up national unity, bore fruit on February 12, 1947, in the form of the historic Pang Long Agreement. This lesson from history bears testimony to the fact that knowing the real enemy will produce the correct solution. (4)

Thakin Chit Maung went on to talk about the dangers of manipulation by the expansionists:

> The colonialist-expansionists have frequently attempted to assassinate national leaders of the world who have identified them as the real enemy. For the same reason, General Aung San and our leaders who had achieved the unity of our national races have fallen victim to the colonialist-expansionists and their henchmen. The unity forged with the blood and sweat of our leaders was strong enough to enable us to achieve national independence, much to the displeasure of the British colonialist-expansionists. The latter continued to undermine our national unity by various means. I still recall vividly the words of one of the world leaders of the colonialist-expansionists, the former British prime minister, Sir Winston Churchill, who when the Labour government submitted the Burma Independence Bill to the British parliament, expressed his opinion that the granting of independence to Burma would inevitably lead to strife; and after he had pronounced those threatening words, using his own authority and through the help of his agents Tulloch and Campbell, and his henchmen within the country he was able, within one hundred days of independence, to foment insurgency in Burma that involved all races and all strata of society.[61] It was due to this British strategy that the national unity built up by General Aung San had disintegrated, and a civil war had broken out, causing much bloodshed among the national races. Since then we had lost sight of the real enemy, and had started to look upon one another as enemies. The more we lose sight of the real enemy, the more we seem to bring about bloodletting among ourselves. (4–5)

Thakin Chit Maung then went on to speak about how the AFPFL was responsible for the general situation now prevailing in Myanmar.

> According to modern political treatises, every democratic government is responsible for what happens in the country. The AFPFL government was responsible for ten years of turbulence during the insurgency. The government, being unable to distinguish between the real friends and the real enemies, used drastic single-party authoritarian and militaristic methods to suppress the dissidents.
>
> In the name of worldwide "democratic practice" all kinds of violence and suppressive measures, together with vote-rigging, were committed in both Burma Proper and the states. (7)
>
> In the economic and social fields too, the rule applied was that "those who are not with us are enemies to be treated with disregard, and those who are with us shall be regarded as a privileged class, whether they be from Burma Proper or from the states. (7)

Then to prove that the colonialist-expansionists were intruding into the country taking advantage of the breakdown of national solidarity and unity, Thakin Chit Maung said:

> When we had descended to that level, national solidarity and unity started breaking down, and as in the saying, "when cattle stray from the herd they get devoured by the tiger" we found that the American expansionists and their stooges, the Kuomintang (KMT) Army of aggression had blatantly invaded and seized large areas of the eastern and northern parts of the Union. But because we were in a weakened state, due to the divisions among ourselves, the AFPFL government turned to the enemy as to a friend and sought assistance to resolve the problem. It had to lie to the United Nations by declaring that "unknown" armed foreign troops were on Burmese soil. At this juncture, the military bloc known as SEATO, which was led by the American expansionists, instead of withdrawing became even bolder, openly penetrating into the ranks of national races, including certain Burman, Kachin, Shan, and Mon groups that had taken up armed struggles. They raised familiar specters among these groups by saying: "Are you not afraid of Burmese chauvinism?" or "Are you not afraid of Communism?" and then went on to establish strong bases for a colonialist counterrevolution by providing arms and funds to those dissidents. (7–8)

Thakin Chit Maung then went on to express his view that the present problems had not been caused by the constitution. He said:

> Is it because the constitution has not been a truly federal constitution that the nation had been driven to such a sorry plight? Or is it the manipulation of the American expansionist gang that has been fomenting trouble all over the world, combined with the misguided actions of those in government, that has driven us to the present crisis? Though we should have seen through the problem and explained it to the public, we failed to do so. Now the proposal has been made that a truly federal constitution should be brought into being, by amending the present constitution. This problem has not suddenly come out of the blue, but is just another manifestation of the problem that has existed in the lengthy course of our history. This problem has two facets. One represents the view of the unsophisticated national races who earnestly believe that all these problems arose because of the failure to set up a truly federal union. The other represents the view of the expansionists who, lurking in the dark forests, stealthily instructed their minions to ask for a truly federal union and to secede if the demand was not met. These are the two facets of the proposal we see clearly, as one and the same. (10–11)

Thakin Chit Maung then went on to present the NUF's ideas for bringing about a solution to the problem.

> That is why we must thoroughly discuss and try to resolve, with extreme patience and unflagging zeal, and in a family spirit, the proposal for a true federation put forward on behalf of the public and the unsophisticated national minorities. But with the expansionists who are threatening the independence of the Union, we must confront the problem decisively. (11)

Commenting on the idea of a federal union, Thakin Chit Maung said:

> The wording "A federal union is a federation of states coming together on the basis of equality" is the description generally given in all political science texts. However, in the actual implementation of this theory, each federal union in existence in the world today has been influenced by its own economic and social circumstances and its varied history, and as a consequence, there is a variety of federal unions today. Although the basis of every federal union is similar, the actual characteristics of each are quite different. History makes this quite evident. Therefore, just because the theory says so, it does not always have to follow that everything must be in exactly the same form in every country. It is because of these historical evidences that our founding fathers, General Aung San and the other leaders, have with great foresight created our present Union, wherein all the different national races can live together in accordance with our needs, and be united in keeping with our historical trends. (13)

Thakin Chit Maung continued:

> We should recount how at the May 1947 Preliminary Conference of the AFPFL, when our solidarity was at its peak, the draft constitution that was drawn up and presented by the "Triple One" (One Hundred and Eleven) Committee had reflected our actual needs and had resulted from a consensus of those present. Allow me to present the history of those times. We must now review objectively why, at that time, a Burma State was not created. Was it through our ignorance or was it an act of omission, or was it due to sufficient historical, political, and economic reasons that made it clear a Burma State was unnecessary? And we must examine scrupulously whether it was because Burma Proper was not made a constituent state that the principal characteristics of our federal union had disappeared, or whether although the federal union, as created, was theoretically correct, the problem arose because of external machinations, compounded by the misconception and wrongdoing of the ruling government? These are questions we must go into extensively. From the start, using Burma Proper as a nucleus, we have had to form a Union of States unequal in development, size, and population—a legacy left behind by the expansionist feudal regime. Under these circumstances, it is imperative that Burma Proper take on the onerous task of leadership in creating a Union wherein all enjoy equal political, economic, and social rights. Only then would we be fulfilling the historic goal of founding the Union. Because we have lost sight of this goal, we have failed to raise all our national races to the same level of development. (13–15)

To state it quite clearly, we need to remedy this deplorable state of affairs wherein the Union is faced with multifarious political, economic, financial, and military problems, endless blood-letting among brethren due to hatred, distrust, and suspicion toward one another instead of love and trust. Under these circumstances, it would not do to "fence off our own yards" and part in hatred and feelings of mistrust, lest our Union be doomed. (15–16)

But even more frightening is the prospect that if we were to establish a "true federal union" with gaps and loopholes at a time when the American SEATO military bases have intruded into Burma Proper and among the national races through various means, our Union could suffer the ignominious fate of being drowned in shallow water. (16)

The unity and stability of the Union must certainly be built on a firm and stable economic structure at its foundation, and the adoption of clear-cut economic measures. The economic policy for the entire Union must be one of equality and shared responsibility. Burma Proper must not only provide unwavering leadership but also be selfless in granting equality. In establishing a modern economy, it is imperative that the Kachin, Kayah, Chin, Mon, and Rakhine States, which cannot yet stand on their own feet, would have to be developed together with Burma Proper on a mutual development basis. (16–17)

At present, the prevailing economic situation is so different from the economic policy enshrined in the constitution, it is no wonder that there is great unrest. As regards government economic concerns, nothing substantial has been achieved. In such circumstances, should the national races box themselves in, in enclosures representing narrow nationalism, and should one race continue to dominate over the leadership within the Union, it would only hasten the economic collapse of the Union.

In this manner, splits and rifts would occur at the very foundation of our Union, leading in the end to its disintegration. No amount of effort will be able to save it. As each state embraced capitalism, socialism, or feudalism, and began jostling and attacking one another, we would certainly be inviting foreign intervention in our affairs. (17–18)

Thakin Chit Maung then suggested:

Only if we are able to implement with united efforts the three consecutive Five-Year Development Plans, on the basis of mutual development, would we be able to build hopes for the future of Burma Proper and that of the constituent states. Further I would like to comment on the level of literature, art, science, and culture of our brethren from the nationalities, which remains regrettably low. To raise that level through various development projects, Burma Proper must lead the way, by showing a spirit of self-sacrifice and extending of assistance so that development will take place uniformly, between the states and Burma Proper. In this matter there is a real need for Burma Proper, even at its own expense, to extend assistance to the states for their social and cultural development, through assistance projects. In view of this consideration, there

> should be no differentiation between Burma Proper and the states, otherwise the states would suffer immensely. (18–19)

Thakin Chit Maung gave his views on national security:

> I wish to further present a matter of the utmost importance. This is none other than the problem of the national defense of our Union. No major country of world power can, as yet, guarantee world peace and security. They can only talk about prospects for peace. More than in any other area, the countries of Southeast Asia, which had for a long time been the stronghold of the imperialists and where today foreign military bases like those of SEATO are being established, one must be ever vigilant to defend oneself from military incursion. In the light of this fact, one can gauge how important political and military unity is in the defense of the Union. (19)

Thakin Chit Maung next spoke about the problems of leadership, chauvinism, narrow nationalism, and the danger of imperialism encountered in every country that had been formed as a federation of several nationalities. His analysis was as follows:

> In every country in the world, whether it be unitary or federal in form, where different national races are involved, one group inevitably becomes dominant, either through sheer numbers or through greater capabilities. This dominant group has to provide leadership for the development of the remaining national races. At this juncture, it is very important to distinguish between leadership and chauvinism. Leadership is essential. In China it was the Hans, and in the Soviet Union it was the Russians who had provided leadership in the various revolutions. When the imperialists plan to take over a country, they will do their best to sow seeds of discord and dissension between the dominant race and the other national minorities. When they became estranged from the dominant race, the minority races become victims of the imperialists who propagate the concept of chauvinism and narrow nationalism for their own purposes. If we are to set up a truly federal union at such a time, the imperialists will surely foment animosity between Burma Proper and the states. (20)

Thakin Chit Maung then went on to explain that a constitution for a nation should be framed only when national unity is at its peak.

> According to the lessons from world history, we find that constitutions are generally drawn up at the peak of national unity, as a symbol to mark a revolutionary change. Constitutions have never been successfully drawn up in times of disunity, animosity, hatred, and discord. This is the lesson one learns from world history. Even if constitutional changes are formulated at such times, not only will they fail but they will also create rival combatants for power. Therefore, I repeat that at this time, when our

> Union is in such dire straits, it would be a grave error to try to amend our constitution from its very foundations. (21)

Thakin Chit Maung described the three major points on which the NUF's view differed from that of the All States Organization regarding the true Federal Principle. He said:

> Our Union is a federal union formed by constituent states with Burma Proper as a nucleus. We strongly believe that that model was chosen as the most suitable type in view of our political, social, economic, and cultural history. The Union was formed with Burma Proper as a nucleus with the intention of providing a center for unity and leadership. In practical terms, some of the states have been recognized as states throughout history, while others at this moment are still in transition toward achieving statehood. Others are trying to acquire attributes of statehood. Yet again, other national minority groups are still living amidst other communities with their political, economic, and social identities still in their initial stages.
>
> All along our history, Bamars have always led in the struggle for independence due to their superior numbers as well as their capability. In view of the existing economic and social situation, the Bamars must assume the leadership. It is also Burma Proper's historic duty to guide the nation politically in the future. It was in these circumstances that in framing the present constitution, the Union was based on Burma Proper as the center of unity and leadership. We (NUF) therefore believe that the present constitution represents the federal type that is most suitable for us in the present period of history and the existing circumstances. (23–24)

Thakin Chit Maung then dealt with the complaints of the leaders of the states that they were being dominated by Burma Proper and treated like vassal states. He said:

> Our brethren, the leaders of the states, are of the opinion that Burma Proper has appropriated for itself the powers of the Union government and dominated the states and the national minorities, treating them like vassal states. For this reason they have demanded a true federal union, wherein all states will have full internal autonomy and equal status with Burma Proper. They would like a Union like the United States, Switzerland, or the Soviet Union. In other words, they want a new constitution to make our Union into a kind of federation. But there is a great difference between the circumstances under which the United States, Switzerland, and the Soviet Union had evolved and those under which our own Union was conceived and brought into being. At this juncture, let me retrace a bit of history. (23–24)

He then gave a brief history of the United States and drew the following conclusions:

> The states which came together to form the United States of America were, originally, sovereign independent states. They then formed themselves into a confederation. But when they found that this form of union was not satisfactory for them, they had to form a federation. It can be seen from their history that the move was from decentralization to centralization; that is, from loose centralization to tight centralization. The system of real presidential executive was adopted by the USA, in which the president became the center of unity and leadership for the United States. Therefore we should firmly accept that in every union in the world, there must be a symbol which in essence serves as a center of unity and leadership. (26)

On the example of Switzerland:

> Switzerland started as several small sovereign independent states or cantons. In the face of common enemies those small cantons formed a confederation which was a very loose one. The small cantons, having enjoyed their sovereign independence which they dearly cherished throughout their long period of history, would not achieve a union beyond a confederation until 1848. The confederation was not much of a success. (26–28)
>
> A civil war broke out in Switzerland in 1846. It was only at the end of the civil war in 1848 that the present constitution of Switzerland was drafted. In 1848 the Swiss Diet drew up the present constitution. The constitution was a piece of legislation that tried to reconcile the traditional with the model methods of forming a Union of States. It will be seen that it is a blending of a confederation and a federation, drafted under the prevailing circumstances, to suit the needs of the cantons. It can also be seen in this constitution that the Swiss Confederation, which began with sovereign independent cantons, has slowly moved toward centralization as well. (29–30)

Regarding the history of the Soviet Union, Thakin Chit Maung said: "The principle of the dictatorship of the proletariat and socioeconomic structure is the basis of unity and leadership in the Soviet Union" (30). He continued:

> To sum up, our Union, formed around Burma Proper as the center, is clearly the best form at this juncture, whether we view it in the light of the history of how federal states in the world are formed, or through the concept of the center of unity and leadership. (31)

Next he touched on the second point of difference between the NUF's stand and the Shan proposal:

> The second point of difference is one of standpoints. In considering the problem of the nationalities within our Union, we believe that the most urgent priority, the "order of the day," is not the matter of making Burma Proper a constituent state but to create states for the national races who deserve to have their own states, and to promote the right to autonomy for those nationalities who already have their own states. The

> standpoint of the leaders of the states is that all problems will be solved by making Burma Proper a constituent state. Thus there is a difference of standpoints. (34)

Regarding the third point of difference:

> The third point of difference between us is the question of approach. We believe that so long as the maneuvers of foreign imperialists and the internal insurgency are not brought to an end, the problem of the nationalities and the serious political, economic, financial, and military problems of the country will not be remedied. Therefore our approach should be that of resolving the above problems as the first priority. And secondly to resolve all problems peacefully through a united effort. The approach of our brethren from the states is that, in accordance with the true Federal Principle, the first priority is to build fences and to create states on a true Federal Principle and secondly, to solve all problems on the basic principle of equality. (34–35)

He then made a forecast that though under the present circumstances it was not yet possible to implement a true federal constitution, a time would come when a "Socialist Republic of the Union of Burma" would be established and a true federal constitution could then be framed. He said:

> There is one argument I would like to present. The question may be raised: "Is the Union of Burma never going to be worthy of a truly federal constitution?" I would like to state that there will certainly come a time in our Union's future history when Burma Proper and the states will be truly equal. That time is none other than the time when we are able to establish a Socialist Republic of the Union of Burma. I believe that time will be when we have established a socialist society where there is no longer any political, economic, or social exploitation of man by man, class by class, nationality by nationality; in other words, after we have staged this socialist revolution, a truly federal union will be born, just as our struggle for national independence had brought forth our present Union Constitution. Believe me, that day is not far off. (35–36)

Thakin Chit Maung said that although the NUF considered it was not yet time to change to a truly federal constitution at this juncture, the party acknowledged that the present constitution had certain defects, that it needed to be remedied immediately. His suggestions for amending the constitution included:

- Giving the state representatives full powers, such as those enjoyed by ministers, in the central Union government
- Upholding the principle of state autonomy; establishing a Union Planning Commission and State Planning Commission, in order to draw up concrete and separate plans, and to coordinate them for the exploitation and production of natural resources within the Union and the states
- Establishing a fund for the development of the Union and prescribing proce-

dures contributing toward proper deposits and withdrawals from the fund
- Making special grants to the states, by the Union
- Establishing separate civil services for the Union and the states; allotting to the states a larger quota of foreign assistance grants and from the Japanese war reparations to ensure the quickest development
- Upgrading the State Councils to the status of State Legislatures
- Allowing the heads of state to be freely elected by the State Legislatures
- Allowing the State budgets to be enacted freely and the division of revenue between the Union and the states to be determined strictly through consultations
- Including such items as agricultural lands, forests, mines, oil wells, establishment of industries, presently included on List 1–Union Legislative List, and such other items as may be agreed upon, on a new List 3
- Drawing up a concurrent list and allowing the states to deal with those matters freely, so long as their actions do not contravene Union policy
- Giving freedom of action to the states in such matters as workers' rights, and reform, and the democratization of local administration
- Appointing states' representatives on an equal footing to all social and economic boards and corporations set up by the central government
- Allowing the states to set up, separately, broadcasting stations to broadcast in their own languages for the purpose of educating their people in accordance with central Union government policy
- Prescribing clear directives concerning the elimination of all feudalist, chauvinist, and militarist oppression, and promoting the full democratic rights of the people in all the states and the Union, and the establishment of a Socialist Republic of the Union of Myanmar (38–40)

Finally, Thakin Chit Maung summarized the NUF's views on the subject of "amending the constitution in accordance with the true Federal Principle":

1. In view of the present situation, internal as well as external, our country will become more like a confederation if we adopt the true Federal Principle, and we believe that this will steadily lead, not to national solidarity but to disintegration. Therefore we do not support it.
2. We acknowledge that during the fourteen years the present constitution has been in force, the ordinary people in the states and in the Union have suffered greatly due to imperialistic machinations as well as from the misguided actions of our own government. We sympathize with our people for their suffering and support the view that every effort must be made to amend the constitution so as to remove the flaws that have led to such sufferings. But any amendment should be made strictly within the framework of the present constitution.
3. A true federal form of government based on capitalism can only be true in form, but not in essence. If we desire a federal Union which is true in form and in essence,

we must march toward the goal of creating a Socialist Republic of the Union of Burma.

4. We accept this national conference as a forum for the free exchange of views between participants. We do not accept it as a venue where decisions are made by the use of pressure on one another.
5. The discussions presented here should be reviewed by the authorities concerned, and then a Union Solidarity Conference should be called in 1963, where further discussions should take place before the final decisions are made. (41–43)

Commentary by U Ba Swe

That same evening, after Thakin Chit Maung had presented the NUF's views on the Federal Principle, U Ba Swe presented the AFPFL's views:[62]

> I sincerely believe that we shall be making a very big mistake if we heedlessly rush into the act of changing the very basis of the constitution, in the framing of which our national leader General Aung San himself took a leading part, and which was thoroughly discussed before it was unanimously approved. But by so saying I do not imply that we are against holding a national conference such as the present one, where we can discuss things in an intimate and brotherly manner. If any misunderstanding exists, it is indeed very important to discuss those matters in a family spirit. I firmly believe that if we set about resolving our problems in the family spirit, with love and understanding, there will be no problems within our Union of Burma that cannot be resolved.

After giving the AFPFL's views on the proposed constitutional amendments, U Ba Swe described how the nationalities within the Union of Myanmar belonged to the same family, and had become disunited due to the machinations and the sowing of seeds of discord by the imperialists during the colonial period, and how these nationalities had joined hands to achieve independence.

> I also believe that in solving our problems, we should approach them in line with the conditions in the Union of Burma, and attempt to find appropriate measures accordingly. One might then ask whether a study of the experiences of other countries in the world should be ignored. To such a question I would like to honestly admit that the developments and experiences of other countries also need to be studied.

U Ba Swe pointed out that the United States, Switzerland, Australia, and Canada which had adopted the federal system, had a great number of immigrants. Then he declared that since the Soviet Union and the Union of Myanmar had completely different political systems, there was no need even to consider the Soviet Constitution.

He said:

> My brother delegates may well ask "Are the Soviet Union and some other Communist countries formed as federal states because of the presence of immigrants as well?" I will answer to the point. The manner in which political leadership is exercised in Communist countries is very different from the way we do it here in a parliamentary democracy. Hence we do not need to consider how things are run in Communist countries.

U Ba Swe went on to explain why the Union of Myanmar had been formed after independence:

> Historically the Chins, Kachins, Kayins, Mons, Kayahs, Rakhines, Shans, and Bamars are a family of national races who had lived in close relationship with one another within this country. So the question might be asked: "Why was a sovereign state established, not on a unitary but on a federal basis, after independence?" The answer to that is clear. Our family had lived under the British colonial rule, quite literally, divided. We were not only physically separated but also, by policy, encouraged to suspect and distrust one another so that when we got together to establish a new state after independence, we were like complete strangers to one another. That is why we had to create a federal state though we were inclined toward a unitary type.

U Ba Swe then related how nations with a federal government had been progressively moving toward the unitary form due to their experiences:

> If we closely study the countries of the world which at present have the federal form of government, we will see that the views they held regarding the federal form at the time of forming the federation have since undergone considerable change. Although the form remains federal, we will see that in the actual division of political power there has been much leaning toward the unitary type. Why have the people who had once preferred a federal government changed their attitude? It was because, when a federal union was established, the people of the states were found to be quite obsessed with self-interest and a narrow outlook, and they wanted to retain as much power as they could. But once they started implementing the federal constitution, they came to realize that in practice, the division of power led to its fragmentation, so much so that the central government, which had to take responsibility for the entire Union, became very weak and ineffective. Gradually, the central government found itself without adequate power to upgrade and improve the Defense Forces to a level that could ensure the security of the nation; and found itself without the means to develop the economy, or provide all the necessary social services for the people. The result was that the country became backward and completely helpless. Because they wish to avert such a fate, those countries, though retaining the federal form, have been surrendering more and more power to the central government.

U Ba Swe gave his views on federal unions:

Generally speaking, there are two types of federal unions. One strictly limits the powers of the central government and assigns the residual powers to the states; the second type restricts the powers of the states and assigns the residual powers to the federal government. Under the first type, the central government is weak and the states powerful; under the second type, the states are weak and the central government is strong. When we study all the federal unions that are in existence in the world today, we will see that federal states of the first type are perceptibly changing into the second type, by way of constitutional amendments or by decisions of the Supreme Court or by administrative procedures. In other words, the trend is to increase the strength of the federal authority by increasing the powers of the federal government. This is the correct path for the federal system, which people are now accepting, having realized the reality. This is the period when national security and the economy of the nation are considered of paramount importance. That is why the states are now willingly transferring their powers to the federal government in order to make it more effective.

U Ba Swe then spoke about whether a Bamar constituent state should or should not be established:

I am quite prepared to willingly accept the transformation of Burma Proper into a Bamar constituent state if it can be shown that such a step is a logical one to take. However, since I do not believe such is the case, I would like to urge that Burma Proper not be made into a constituent state but be retained under direct central government control as provided under the present constitution. Burma Proper is more developed than the other states due to its geographical position. We did not establish a Bamar constituent state, because we felt that a highly developed Burma Proper should also participate in assisting in the development of the underdeveloped states. We believe that we made the right decision by not transforming Burma Proper into a constituent state because of this very special circumstance. If we had made Burma Proper into a state, things could very well have turned out quite differently. Burma Proper could well have refused to assist in the development of other states, by claiming that it was a state just like any of the others. Selfishness could have manifested itself if the Bamar constituent state insisted on spending all its resources solely on itself to the exclusion of all the other states. The powers assigned to the central Union government would, as a consequence, become less effective. The Bamar State would demand additional powers, just like the states are doing now. Therefore the Union Legislative List, the State Legislative List, and the Third Legislative List in the present constitution schedule would be very different from what they are now. In such an eventuality, the central Union government would become a weak, ineffectual one. If the Bamar constituent state were to unrestrictedly spend all its natural resources and its revenue on its own construction and development projects, we fear that other states would stagnate in the same misery they have endured under the British regime. Our Union would then undoubtedly begin to disintegrate. That is why I believe that our previous

> measure in not making Burma Proper into a constituent state is the most correct and logical thing to do.

To strengthen his argument, U Ba Swe gave the example of the United States of America, noting that the federal system was moving toward tight central control:

> When the thirteen colonies first came together to form the United States of America, they were convinced, at the initial stage, that each individual state should be free to do what it liked, within the Union. However, due to the circumstances, the form of federalism in the United States has since changed to such an extent that today the president of the United States enjoys almost dictatorial powers during his four-year term. In other words, the states in the US have become just nominal. We can see that the greater share of powers is now invested in the US president. In other words, the United States has been transformed from a true federation into a federal form that leans toward a unitary state. The various federal unions in the world are also, quite perceptibly, moving in the same direction, so I would like to urge that we should not go against the historical tide and drag our nation back into the past.

U Ba Swe pointed out that although the USA and the Union of Myanmar were both established as federal unions, there was one significant difference between them:

> I would like to present to you another difference existing between the United States and our Union.[63] If you look at the United States you will notice that there is not much disparity between the states, whereas it is not so in our Union of Burma. There is a great difference in size and in population among our various states. Some are extensively large and others are relatively small. This is due to the fact that the states in the Union of Burma are [governed] not on a regional basis as in the United States but on the basis of ethnic communities.
>
> It was because of this great divergence in size and population among the various units that when it came to establishing the Chamber of Nationalities we did not prescribe an equal number of representatives from each state. This fact is well known to all our brethren who had served in the Constituent Assembly. However, we made sure that the number of representatives of each state in the Chamber of Nationalities was fixed in such a way that each state was given a greater number of representatives than it would have been entitled to if the decision had been made on a population basis. According to this unique solution prevalent in our Union, the combined representatives of all the states outnumber the representatives of Burma Proper in the Chamber of Nationalities. As regards the Chamber of Deputies, the universal practice is to allocate seats strictly on a population basis. However, in our own peculiar situation, we have not followed that practice. It can be quite clearly seen that we have, with the objective of favoring the states, allocated more seats to them in the Chamber of Deputies than they would have been entitled to if representation had been strictly made on a

population basis. This special distinction makes our Union quite different from other federal unions. Another characteristic which distinguishes our constitution from those of other federal unions is that our constitution provides for State ministers to sit in the central or federal cabinet. We have studied other federal constitutions but we have not seen any that gives such rights to their constituent states. It is only in the Union of Burma, due to its own special circumstances, that the right to sit in the central cabinet is given to the state ministers.

U Ba Swe then presented the views of the AFPFL on the matter of granting equal powers to the two chambers of parliament:

We have accepted the fact that our constitution has provided for a parliament of two chambers, namely, the Chamber of Deputies and the Chamber of Nationalities. In allocating powers to these two chambers, under our constitution both chambers enjoy equal powers in all matters with the exception of the selection of the prime minister, and in the matter of money bills. If we study the constitutions of those countries in the world that have bicameral legislatures, we will see that these powers are always entrusted only to the Chamber of Parliament whose members are elected from the entire nation on a population basis. This is the practice of all states in the world that accept the system of parliamentary democracy wherein the government is responsible to the parliament. There is no other alternative. In our nation, although the prime minister is elected by the Chamber of Deputies, our states are in no way at a disadvantage, because the ministers for the states are automatically entitled to a seat each in the Union cabinet. My brother delegates are well aware that in no other federal union is this privilege granted to their states.

U Ba Swe went on to say that the constitution of the Union of Myanmar was indeed a true federal constitution.

I would like to present here the answer to the question: "Is our present constitution genuinely federal?" The British governor presided over Burma until we adopted the Constitution of the Union of Burma on January 4, 1948. At the time we formed our Union, no threats or coercion were involved. No one can deny that it was a completely voluntary Union. In the tradition of federal unions, our constitution laid down in detail the responsibilities of the Union government and those of the states. Further, a Supreme Court was established, with responsibility for interpreting the constitution in any dispute arising out of the division of powers between the Union and the states. These characteristics that I have mentioned are the primary characteristics of a true federal union. I therefore wish to declare that since the characteristics in our Constitution are in consonance with the true federal principles, the Union of Burma is a true federal union. Regarding whether the residual powers should be vested in the Union or in the states, the federal unions in the world differ from one another. Depending on each nation's situation, it is up to each country to decide where the residual powers should be vested. I have never before heard the argument that just because the residual powers are vested in the central government, the federal constitution has become imperfect. It is only now that I have heard such an absurdity.

U Ba Swe made one more point before delivering his conclusion:

> Brother delegates! I would like to say something about the right of secession. That right was accepted by the Americans at the time of the establishment of the United States of America, but today it is no longer invoked. As early as one hundred years ago the right of secession became something undesirable, and as such was opposed and defeated by President Abraham Lincoln. A civil war was waged to enforce that right contained in the American Constitution. It is because he effectively deleted that undesirable right of secession that Lincoln is recognized as a historic figure by the world today. But in making this presentation, I am not in any way suggesting that we should revoke the right of secession clause from our constitution. I firmly believe that a right given at the beginning of our nationhood should in principle never be taken away.

In conclusion U Ba Swe said:

> Brother delegates! It has been but fourteen years since we have had the chance to work hard, hand in hand together again as members of a family. During this period of working together there have inevitably been some misunderstandings. But these misunderstandings can, as I have said, be resolved if we seek solutions in a family spirit. In our dealings with one another, there have been mistakes, poor judgment, and uncivil attitude on the part of certain individuals. But our Union of Burma should not be wrecked merely because of the inconsiderate actions of a few individuals. We should again in a family spirit seek out the wrongdoers and try to dispel the misunderstandings within our Union, by reeducating, reprimanding, or even taking further effective action against those found guilty of such conduct. Brother delegates! Just as some of our constituent states are undeveloped and backward, so also are certain areas within Burma Proper. We must put forth our utmost effort to develop those underdeveloped areas so that every part of our country will become equally developed. If we join hands in this task, there can be no doubt that we will achieve success.

When U Ba Swe, the last speaker scheduled to speak on the second day of the national conference, had concluded his speech, Prime Minister U Nu, the chairman of the conference, gave a concluding address in a joyous voice. He also announced the adjournment of the conference till March 7. After that Attorney General U Ba Swe, Minister Dr. E Maung, the AFPFL's U Ba Swe, U Kyaw Nyein, Thakin Tha Khin, and Bo Khin Maung Gale came up to Thakin Chit Maung to congratulate him on his speech. U Kyaw Nyein remarked: "So, even you Communists are not free from chauvinism." And Bo Khin Maung Gale, in an amiable vein, said: "Your speech was quite good, but you couldn't give a speech without taking a swipe at us, could you?" Thakin Chit Maung replied: "Well, we couldn't very well pretend that the people of Burma Proper were completely innocent. Don't you think it is best to admit it, if we are at fault?" U Ba Swe supported Thakin Chit Maung on that point. The delegates then moved into the Reception Hall to partake of refreshments and left the Myanmar Broadcasting Station at 8:30 P.M.[64]

THE UNION PARTY'S VIEW ON THE FEDERAL PROPOSAL

According to the agenda of the national conference, Minister Dr. E Maung was to have presented the Union Party's view on the Federal Proposal on March 7. But because the army staged a coup on March 2, he did not get an opportunity to deliver his speech although it had already been printed.[65]

According to the printed speech, Minister Dr. E Maung would first have made the point that the stability and durability of the Union was a matter of the gravest importance for every national race within the Union, and a problem that concerned every citizen in the Union of Myanmar. If the proper solution to this problem was not found, the Union could collapse. And if it collapsed, no national race would be exempt from the fate of returning to a condition of servitude. And that is why it was of such vital importance to find a correct solution to the problem. He then gave a brief background description of the present constitution, from the Pang Long Conference to the time when the drafting was completed, during which fourteen resolutions were submitted at the AFPFL's preliminary preparatory conference and General Aung San's seven-point directive was in fact merely the first seven of those fourteen resolutions submitted at the preliminary conference. Therefore though the constitution might appear to differ from the directive, if one looked at the seven-point directive alone, a study of the entire fourteen resolutions submitted at the preliminary conference would show that the constitution was in full consonance with the seven-point directive.[66] (9–18)

The Union-States Subcommittee held a meeting on June 23, 1947. The second meeting, held on June 24, 1947, was chaired by General Aung San himself. The minutes of the meeting were later confirmed by the next meeting, held on June 25, 1947. An extract from the minutes read:

> [Owing] to the peculiar conditions of the constituent states within the Union of Burma, no other federal type could exactly match the needs of the Union. The subcommittee therefore agreed to draft a constitution, incorporating such features of federal constitutions of countries like the United States, Switzerland, and the USSR as were relevant to the needs of the Union of Myanmar. (26–27)

The Union-States Subcommittee held further meetings on June 25 and 27 and on July 1, 4, 8, 10, and 12, 1947, to discuss matters concerning the states. On the division of powers between the Union and the states, the subcommittee agreed on July 15 to accept the recommendations of the Ad Hoc Committee on the division of powers between the Union and the states, and also agreed that the unlisted or residual powers be assigned to the Union. The fact that the recommendations of the Ad Hoc Committee had been accepted was put on record in the interim report of the Union-States Subcommittee, issued on July 17, 1947.

Dr. E Maung's printed speech went on to make the point that General Aung San and his senior colleagues had thrashed out the basic principles that should form the basis of the constitution, and indeed had drafted them before seven of them were assassinated.

This fact, the speech said, was supported by the records of the Constitution Drafting Committee of the Constituent Assembly. The interim report of the subcommittee, which was chaired by General Aung San, stated clearly that all problems concerning the Union and the states had been discussed and settled by the subcommittee.

Regarding the establishment of a constituent state for Myanmar proper, as called for by the federal proposal of Shan State, Dr. E Maung declared that since the drafting of the constitution was under the leadership of General Aung San, this matter had been thoroughly considered and a decision had been taken, as shown by the following extract:

> The *saohpa* of Yawng Hwe, the *saohpa* of Mong Pawn, and Sama Duwa Sinwa Nawng requested a clarification on certain points, and General Aung San, Thakin Mya, U Ba Cho, and U Chan Htun explained those matters at length. Everyone unanimously agreed in principle to promulgate the constitution in accordance with the draft drawn up by the AFPFL preliminary conference, i.e. that in the Union of Myanmar, soon to be established, apart from Burma Proper all the other states would have separate administration and governments, but because Burma Proper, in contrast to the other states, being much larger in area, in population, and more advanced in its economic development, and also because of financial and human resources constraints on the part of the states, a separate legislature and government would not be set up for Burma Proper. Instead the Union legislature and Union government would also serve as the legislature and government of Burma Proper. (26–27)

To show that the division of powers between the central Union government and the states had also been discussed and decided upon while General Aung San and the other leaders were still alive, the speech went on to state:

> On the division of powers, after the powers of the states had been enumerated, it was agreed to assign the residual powers to the central government. This fact proves that

> General Aung San and the leaders of Burma Proper and of the states did not accept the idea of assigning only the powers concerning common subjects to the Union government and leaving the residual powers to the states. (28)

On the granting of equal powers to the two chambers of parliament the speech noted that the idea was rejected even while General Aung San and his colleagues were still alive:

> The third section of the proposal of the leaders of the states entitled "The True Federal Principle" dealt with the granting of equal powers to the two chambers of parliament. This point, as is well known, was also thoroughly considered by General Aung San and the leaders from Burma Proper as well as the leaders from the states, and the following decisions were taken for the reasons shown below: I have already presented this decision to the conference earlier, but with the chairman's permission, I would like to present again a summary of the report. The report states, firstly, that the Chamber of Deputies must take responsibility for the central government. This fact proves that our leaders never had any intention of granting equal powers to the chambers of parliament. The reason given was that to do so would mean involving so many political parties and many national races that no government responsible to both chambers could ever hope to be stable. Another reason given was that members of parliament in the Chamber of Deputies were being elected from the constituencies drawn up on a population basis, whereas in the Chamber of Nationalities, sparsely populated states and minority peoples were given favored treatment through larger representation than they would be entitled to on a strict population basis. Thus the fact that our leaders have granted greater powers to the Chamber of Deputies is very much in accord with democratic practice. It is clear that General Aung San and the other leaders rejected the granting of equal powers to the two chambers even from those early days, in order to promote democracy and the stability of the Union. (28–29)

On the question of the sharing of revenue:

> The procedure in which revenue is presently shared shows that Burma Proper has to shoulder a lot of the responsibilities of the states. But the leaders of Burma Proper understand and accept that Burma Proper must shoulder the burden [of developing] the states. Because of the acceptance of this fact the prime minister has devised the system of sharing the revenue in proportion to population. I shall be presenting, at an appropriate time, the amount of money from the revenue of Burma Proper that is being spent on the states. I would like to report, through the chairman, that the present way in which the revenue is being shared means that for every kyat spent on Burma Proper, the states received no less than one kyat each. (30–31)

The speech went on to declare that the views of the Union Party did not in any way mean the total rejection of the problems submitted by the leaders of the states, that from the time the Federal Proposal first arose, the Union Party government had given full attention to the situation in the states and the desires of their people, and that in the cases where these desires could be granted, the government had acted with dispatch. (31–32)

Dr. E Maung, in conclusion, clarified the stand of the Union Party on the proposal put forward by the States Unity Organization:

> The Union Party, in view of its objective of promoting democracy and the stability of the Union, cannot accept the proposal known as "The True Federal Principle" put forward by the chairman of the States Unity Organization, because.
>
> (a) It differs radically from the principles embodied in the Constitution of the Union of Burma, as laid down with wisdom and foresight by General Aung San and leaders from Burma Proper and from the states.
>
> (b) It contains elements opposed to the principles of democracy which General Aung San and the leaders of Burma Proper and of the states, in their wisdom, had wished to nurture and promote.
>
> (c) It contains elements that could lead to the breaking up of the Union, and is therefore at variance with the concept of promoting the stability and durability of the Union, desired by General Aung San and the leaders of Burma Proper and of the states.
>
> (d) The Union government is already doing its utmost, in a family spirit, to assist the states wherever it was appropriate and possible.

However, although the Union Party cannot accept "The True Federal Principle," the party believes that the recommendations of the Government Advisory Committee, which have been submitted after serious discussion and careful consideration on this matter, will promote the stability and the economic development of the Union, and are in consonance with the principles of justice, equality, and liberty. (33–34)

20

The Coming of the Coup d'État

Within a few hours of the end of the second day of the All Nationals Conference on the Federal Proposal, held on March 1, 1962, army units from the Mingaladon Headquarters entered Yangon at midnight.[1] Their purpose was to stage a coup d'état. Thus early in the morning of March 2, 1962, they occupied all departments and offices of strategic importance. The army also arrested ministers of the Pa-Hta-Sa (Union Party) government, the president of the Union, the chief justice of the Union, the heads of the constituent states, and the *saohpa*.[2]

A few days before the army units advanced into Yangon, some of the members of the Armed Forces High Command had made preparations for the takeover of state power. To facilitate the takeover of state power, a member of the Armed Forces High Command who was involved in plotting the coup even made preliminary inquiries about the stand of the Union Military Police Battalions.[3]

Some members of the Armed Forces High Command had made urgent arrangements for staging the coup d'état as early as the end of the first day (February 24, 1962) of the All Nationals Conference. On February 27, 1962, the commanding officers concerned were assigned responsibilities to mount a coup d'état by the high officials of the Armed Forces, and to occupy strategic places, to arrest the ministers of the Pa-Hta-Sa government, the president, the chief justice, the heads of the constituent states, and the *saohpa*. Although the tasks were assigned, the time and date for the assumption of state power were not made known to the commanders.[4]

On February 28, 1962, the commanding officers who were to carry out the coup d'état received their orders, and placed their units on alert. That very night, the verbal orders to begin the operation were given by the high authorities of the Armed Forces. The commanding officers responsible for the operation consulted among themselves and decided to stage the coup on March 2, 1962, the operation to begin on March 1, at midnight. These arrangements were also known to the director of Military Intelligence Service and the commanding officers of the Signal Corps. But the officers in charge of the coup operation kept the information to themselves and briefed neither their subordinate officers nor their men.[5] The troops were alerted only for a "military operation."[6]

CARRYING OUT THE COUP

On March 1, 1962, at about 11:00 P.M. the military units that would roll into Yangon were briefed on the impending coup by the operation commanders, and all army personnel involved were ordered to stand by. All the subordinate officers were each assigned their respective duties and the military units finally entered Yangon at midnight.[7]

Military units were ordered to proceed to the Mingaladon Airport Communications Station, the Yangon broadcasting station, the Telegraph Office, the Parliament Building, the Office of the Police Commissioner, the Union Military Police Headquarters, the Union Bank, the Central Railway Station, the Yangon Port, police stations, the residences of the ministers in Windermere Park, the Shan State Guest House in Windermere Court, Golden Valley,[8] the prime minister's residence on Pyidaungsu Lane, Sao Shwe Thaike's residence at the corner of Kokine and Goodliffe Roads,[9] the residence of Chief Justice U Myint Thein on Kaba Aye Pagoda Road, and the Kayah State Guest House on Fraser Road,[10] which were surrounded.[11] At about 2:00 A.M. the army units arrested Prime Minister U Nu, who lived on Pyidaungsu Lane Goodliffe Road; Minister Dr. E Maung; Sao Pye, *saohpa* of Mong Nai, who lived on Pyay Road at 7½ mile, and Sao Ohn Maung, *saohpa* of Mong Nawng. At about 3:00 A.M. other ministers, U Raschid, Thakin Tin, Thakin Tin Maung, U Thwin, U Ba Saw, Dr. Saw Hla Tun, Sao Hkun Hkio, Sao Wunna, Nai Aung Tun, U Ba Myaing, and Parliamentary Secretary Kayah U Sein, President U Win Maung, who was living at his new house on Inya Road, Chief Justice U Myint Thein; as well as U Kya Bu, U Soe Maung, U Lun, U Chit U, U Htun Myint (Taunggyi), who were staying at the Kayah State Guest House; and Shan *saohpa* and members of parliament from Shan State and the Speakers of the Chamber of Deputies and the Chamber of Nationalities were arrested.[12]

When the members of the government were arrested, it was explained to them that the army had seized power, and they were asked to surrender all the arms in their possession.[13] At the time of his arrest, Chief Justice U Myint Thein asked to see the arrest warrant, and the officers were nonplussed and had to refer the matter to the commander of their units. The commander personally went to U Myint Thein's house to inform him of the army's seizure of state power, and of his arrest by the army units.[14]

Since the police on security duty at the residences of the ministers had been informed in advance that they must not offer any resistance when army units arrived, the arrest of the ministers went off smoothly, without any incident.[15] But when army units arrived at the residence of the *saohpa* of Yawng Hwe, Sao Shwe Thaike, at the corner of Kokine and Goodliffe Roads in Yangon, they were met with gunfire. Upon their arrival the troops shouted out in the Shan language to the security guards not to resist. But as the guards opened fire, the troops returned fire, and Sao Shwe Thaike's seventeen-year-old son, Sao Myee Myee Thaike, died from bullet wounds in the head and leg. There were no other casualties.[16] Concerning Sao Myee Myee's death, his elder brother Sao Tzang (Eugene Thaike) went to report to the Yankin police station that at about 2:00 A.M. on March 2, 1962, that unknown men in uniform had entered their house and opened fire, killing Sao Myee Myee Thaike alias Sao Hso Hpa. The Yankin police station opened a murder case under section 302 of the Penal Code.[17]

The army expressed its regrets at the death of Sao Myee Myee Thaike. The chairman of the Revolutionary Council, General Ne Win, sent a message to the *saohpa* and *mahadevi* of Yawng Hwe, which was delivered by Colonel Saw Myint in person. The message read: "I understand that your son Sao Myee Myee lost his life at dawn on March 2, when army personnel arrived at your residence to perform their duties as directed by the Revolutionary Council. For this unexpected tragedy, members of the council as well as myself are deeply sorry."[18]

At that time the *mahadevi* Sao Hearn Hkam was away in England, so Colonel Saw Myint delivered the message of condolence to Sao Shwe Thaike's eldest son, Sao Hseng Hpa.[19] The Revolutionary Council also sent a wreath to the funeral of Sao Myee Myee Thaike, held on March 4, 1962.[20]

The list of persons arrested by the Revolutionary Council on the morning of March 2, 1962, included:

1. President U Win Maung
2. Prime Minister U Nu
3. Minister Thakin Tin
4. Dr. E Maung
5. U Raschid
6. U Ba Saw
7. Thakin Tin Maung
8. U Thwin
9. Sao Hkun Hkio
10. Sao Wunna
11. Dr. Saw Hla Tun
12. U Zahre Lian
13. U Ba Myaing
14. Nai Aung Tun
15. Chief Justice U Myint Thein
16. Speaker of the Chamber of Deputies Mahn Ba Saing
17. Speaker of the Chamber of Nationalities Sao Hkun Kyi
18. Saohpa of Yawng Hwe Sao Shwe Thaike
19. Saohpa of Mong Nai Sao Pye
20. Saohpa of Lai Hka Sao Num
21. Saohpa of Hsa Mong Hkam Sao Htun E
22. Saohpa of Keng Tung Sao Sai Long

23. Saohpa of Kehsi Mansam Sao Shwe Hmon
24. Saohpa of Baw Sao Hkun Aung
25. Saohpa of Pang Long Sao Moe Kyaw
26. Saohpa of Pangtara Sao Win Kyi
27. Saohpa of Ywa Ngan Sao Hkun Yee
28. Saohpa of Mong Pan Sao Shwe Kyi
29. Saohpa of Sam Hka Sao Hkun Nyunt
30. Saohpa of Mong Lern Sao Mohn Leik
31. U Hkun Hti
32. Sao Mahn Hpa (member of parliament for North Hsen Wi)
33. Sao Aung Hpu (member of parliament for East Loi Lem)
34. U San Myat (member of parliament for Loi Lem)
35. U Chit (member of parliament for South Loi Lem)
36. U Yee Yao (member of parliament for North Keng Tung)
37. U Hkun Naw (member of parliament for West Keng Tung)
38. U Pyu (member of parliament for Mong Pawn)
39. U Kyaw Sein (member of parliament for Hsa Mong Hkam)
40. U Lun (member of parliament for Sam Hka)
41. U M. Zau Latt (member of parliament for Kut Kai)
42. U Sein (Kayah)
43. U Htun Myint (Taunggyi)
44. U Kya Bu, Hkun Myat Hpu
45. U Soe Maung
46. U Chit U
47. U Than Tin
48. U Tin Aung[21]

The two persons who were not arrested on March 2, 1962, were Bohmu Aung, who was in Ngapali on holiday, and President-elect Sama Duwa Sinwa Nawng, who was in a village in Myitkyina District, where his grandparents and parents had been living all their lives.[22]

Of those arrested, apart from Dr. Saw Hla Tun and U Zahre Lian, there were no others from the Kayin State, the Chin Special Division, or the Kachin State.[23] Most of those arrested on the morning of March 2 were first sent to the Yangon broadcasting station near Windermere Park, where they were temporarily accommodated. The army units kept them in the hall in the broadcasting station, where only the night before, the All Nationals Conference on the Federal Principle had taken place. But at about 6:00 A.M. those under arrest were sent to Mingaladon on trucks accompanied by a motorcade of armed guards. The weather that morning was cloudy with drizzling rain. Troops and tanks stood guard along the road to Mingaladon.[24] In Mingaladon the detainees were kept together at the Yan Gyi Aung Garrison Cinema Hall, and were served with Indian *nan roti* and tea.[25]

Shortly thereafter, Mahn Ba Saing, Sao Hkun Kyi, U Ba Saw, Dr. Saw Hla Tun, U Zahre Lian, U Ba Myaing, and Sao Mahn Hpa were released. General Ne Win met them briefly at the Dagon Guest House and informed them that they had been arrested by mistake.[26]

Among those interned in Mingaladon U Win Maung, U Nu, U Myint Thein, Thakin Tin, Sao Hkun Hkio, U Raschid, and Sao Wunna were isolated and placed under heavy guard. They were divided into two groups and detained at the training encampment[27] near Yan Gyi Aung Cinema Hall.[28]

The name of Sao Kya Seng, *saohpa* of Hsi Paw, was not included on any list of persons detained by the army. But according to his *mahadevi*, Thusandi, he was arrested in Taunggyi and taken to Ba Htoo Myo Military Academy, where he was incarcerated, but managed to have a letter smuggled out to his *mahadevi*. The army sent a letter to the *mahadevi* denying that Sao Kya Seng was ever arrested. But he was never seen again after the coup.[29]

ANNOUNCEMENT OF THE FORMATION OF A GOVERNMENT BY THE CHIEF OF STAFF (DEFENSE SERVICES)

Early on the morning of March 2, 1962, rumors had spread that the army had taken over state power. This was later confirmed when the Myanmar broadcasting station interrupted its Kayin program, and the chief of staff (Defense Services) General Ne Win's announcement was made at 8:25 A.M. that the Myanmar Armed Forces had assumed state power. Only then did the people of Yangon come to learn about the coup.[30] The announcement made by the chief of staff was as follows:

> In order to put a stop to the extremely grave situation that has befallen the Union, the Armed Forces have taken over the government. . . .
>
> The people of the country should not feel disturbed, but should continue to carry on with their work, normally and peacefully.
>
> Government employees should also continue to carry out their duties as before. Education officers and students, especially, should not allow the present developments to interfere with their work, but should go ahead with the examinations which are being held.
>
> We promise to do our best for the health and prosperity of the people."[31]

That same morning the Myanmar broadcasting station announced that a Revolutionary Council of the Republic of the Union of Myanmar had been formed. Headed by General Ne Win as chairman, the council consisted of sixteen members.

1. Brigadier Aung Gyi
2. Commodore Than Pe
3. Brigadier T. Clift

4. Brigadier Tin Pe
5. Brigadier San Yu
6. Brigadier Sein Win
7. Colonel Thaung Kyi
8. Colonel Kyi Maung
9. Colonel Maung Shwe
10. Colonel Than Sein
11. Colonel Kyaw Soe
12. Colonel Saw Myint
13. Colonel Chit Myaing
14. Colonel Khin Nyo
15. Colonel Hla Han
16. Colonel Tan Yu Saing[32]

On the morning of March 2, another announcement was made about the formation of a new government. The allocation of the portfolios of the new government was as follows:

1. General Ne Win	Chairman, Revolutionary Council; Ministry of Defense Finance and Revenue; and Judicial Affairs
2. Brigadier Aung Gyi	Ministry of Trade Development and Industries
3. Brigadier Tin Pe	Ministry of Agriculture and Forests; Cooperatives and Commodity Distribution
4. Commodore Than Pe	Ministries of Education and Health
5. U Thi Han	Ministry of Foreign Affairs; Labor; Housing; and Mines
6. Colonel Kyaw Soe	Ministry of Home Affairs and Immigration
7. Lieut. Colonel Ba Ni	Ministry of Transport and Communications[33]

The announcement also said that ministries which would be combined, and the names of the ministers who would take charge of those combined ministries would be announced later.[34] Those persons entrusted with responsibilities by the Revolutionary Council would take on the duties at their respective ministries on the afternoon of March 2, 1962.[35] On March 5, 1962, the names of the combined ministries and their ministers were announced. They were:

General Ne Win	Prime Minister's Office; National Planning Ministry
Brigadier Aung Gyi	Ministry of Supplies
U Thi Han	Public Works and Reconstruction Department to be combined with Ministry of Housing
Colonel Kyaw Soe	(a) Ministry of Regional Democratization and Local Bodies (b) Religious departments under the Ministry of Religious Affairs and Social Welfare

	(c) National Registration Department to be combined with the Immigration Ministry
Colonel Saw Myint	(a) Relief Rehabilitation Ministry
	(b) Social Welfare Department to be placed under the Ministry of Social Welfare and Religious Affairs
Lt.-Colonel Ba Ni	Department of Transport to be placed under the Ministry of Roads and Communications[36]

FORMATION OF THE SUPREME COUNCILS FOR THE STATES

After the formation of the government, the Revolutionary Council announced the abolition of the Shan State Council, the Kachin State Council, the Kayin State Council, the Kayah State Council, and the Chin Affairs Council, with effect from midday March 3, 1962. The Revolutionary Council set up the Shan State Supreme Council with U Tun Aye (Nam Kham) as chairman, and U Kyaw Zaw, U Ohn Pe, U Tin Ko Ko, and Colonel Maung Shwe as members.[37] Not only had the chairman of the Supreme Council, U Tun Aye (Nam Kham), rejected the creed of the *saohpa*; he had also opposed, all along, the Federal Principle advocated by Shan State. The secret Military Intelligence Unit Report revealed that U Tun Aye (Nam Kham) had led the movement to unite the Ya-Pa-La-Pha (Shan State People's Federation League) and the Shan State United Hill Peoples' Organization into a single political organization which would accept the directives of the AFPFL. But the effort to form a single All Shan State Organization did not came about, since the Shan State United Hill Peoples' Organization led by the *saohpa* became a separate body. Although his efforts failed, U Tun Aye (Nam Kham) continued to maintain close relations with the AFPFL central organization under the leadership of U Ba Swe.[38] At the time of the AFPFL split, U Tun Aye, together with the Ya-Pa-La-Pha members U Tin Ko Ko (member of parliament for North Yawng Hwe) and U San Hla Baw (member of parliament for Mong Mit), supported the AFPFL (Stable faction) and tabled [placed on the agenda] a no-confidence motion against the Clean AFPFL. In the general elections held in February 1960, U Tun Aye failed to get elected to parliament.[39] While he was waiting for his turn to give his views at the All Nationals Conference concerning the Federal Principle, the Revolutionary Council had seized state power.[40] In appointing U Tun Aye as chairman of the Shan State Supreme Council, the Revolutionary Council chairman General Ne Win said:

> You've never had a chance to show what you can do. I am now giving you the opportunity to serve your country by making you chairman of the Revolutionary Council in the Shan State. Go and do your best. If you fail just hang yourself.[41]

On the same day the Kachin State Supreme Council was formed with U Ding Ratang[42] as chairman and U Tun Yin and Colonel Lun Tin as members.[43] The Kayin State Supreme Council[44] was formed with Dr. Saw Hla Tun as chairman and Saw Pho Aung, U A. Soe Myint, Saw Chit Than, and Colonel Thaung Kyi as members.[45]

On March 4, 1962, the Revolutionary Council established the Kayah State Supreme Council with U A. Mya Lay as chairman and U Saw Thein, U Bu Rae, U Thaing Than Tin, and Colonel Maung Shwe as members.[46] On March 9 the Revolutionary Council formed the Chin Affairs Council with U Zan Kho Liang as chairman and U Phut Pa, U Tin Zam, U Vam Thu Ha Shim, and Lt.-Colonel Saw Maung Tun as members.[47]

POLITICAL PARTIES AND THEIR POSITION UNDER THE NEW REGIME

Despite the announcements about the arrest of the government ministers and political leaders, the seizure of state power on March 2, 1962, the formation of the Revolutionary Council, the establishment of a new government, and the declaration by the chief of staff (Defense Services), the people went about their business as usual.[48] But the original arrangement to hold the Ba-Ta-La-Sa Conference, at which U Kyaw Nyein of the Central AFPFL. Organization was to give an address about imports, had to be canceled owing to the sudden change in the political situation.[49]

At the Pa-Hta-Sa (Union Party) headquarters on Pyay Road in Yangon, many junior leaders came to ask about the arrest of the government ministers. On the same day an emergency meeting was held for consultations about the situation. The general secretary of the Union Party, Thakin Kyaw Dun, U Than Sein, Bo Tin Maung Lay, Bo Tin Maung Gyi, and Saw Lu Lu attended this meeting. U Than Sein voiced his suspicions about the order banning members of parliament from the Parliament Buildings. He also talked about the surprise of the Union Party members of parliament at the abrupt change in the political situation. The general secretary of the party, Thakin Kyaw Dun, appeared to be disturbed but made no comment.[50]

EXPLANATION BY THE CHAIRMAN OF THE REVOLUTIONARY COUNCIL

General Ne Win, the chairman of the Revolutionary Council and head of the new government, arranged to meet with five representatives from each of the three political parties—the Union Party, the AFPFL, and the NUF—at the Defense Services' Dagon Guest House, at 10:00 A.M. on March 4, 1962. Therefore the executive committee members of these three parties held their own meetings to select their representatives to that meeting.[51]

As arranged, General Ne Win met with the Union Party leaders Thakin Kyaw Dun, Bo Tin Maung Gyi, Saw Lu Lu, and Bo Aye; AFPFL leaders U Ba Swe, U Kyaw Nyein, Bo Khin Maung Galay, U Khin Maung Latt, and U Tun Tin; and NUF leaders Thakin

Chit Maung, Bo Pho Kun, Bo Mya Thwe, Bo Aung Naing, and U Aung Myint on the morning of March 4. The general discussed the current general situation, noting that commodity prices had spiraled, that law and order had deteriorated, and that on the federal issue extreme tension made the seizure of state power imperative. He further stated that political parties would be consulted. Because the present constitution could be easily manipulated, it had become necessary to draw up a new one. Ne Win concluded by saying that this would be done in consultation with the Union Party, the AFPFL, and the NUF Party Central Organizations.[52]

The NUF expressed its approval of the policy and program adopted by the Revolutionary Council, as explained by General Ne Win. It therefore proclaimed that it would cooperate with the council in carrying out its work program.[53]

BRIGADIER AUNG GYI'S PRESS CONFERENCES

On March 7, 1962, Revolutionary Council members Brigadier Aung Gyi and Information Minister Colonel Saw Myint held a press conference at the Dagon Guest House. At the conference Brigadier Aung Gyi said:

> The seizure of state power usually takes place due to political and economic causes. In Myanmar the reasons for the seizure of state power were not only economic or political but religious as well as the issue of federalism. The Revolutionary Council did not seize power by force, because we wanted power. This can be clearly seen from the fact that about two years ago, power had been returned to the people's government.
>
> Because of the crisis caused by the federal issue, power had been seized for the second time in order to safeguard the state. Myanmar is a small country. It is not proper for such a small country as Myanmar to be divided into several states. It is true that our constitution provides for the right of secession ten years after gaining independence. If we take the example of Scotland, it had made several attempts to secede from England over the past one hundred years or so, yet it is still part of the United Kingdom until now.
>
> In Myanmar, fifteen years after independence, the situation was such that the cry for secession has grown louder and louder, day by day. But look at what is happening in neighboring countries like Laos and Vietnam. We cannot allow such a situation to take place in our country. It is true that political dissatisfaction has grown to such a proportion that no one can now resolve it peacefully. Shans and Kayahs are demanding secession.[54] Even the smallest of our states, the Kayah State with a population of 87,000 wants to be independent.

Furthermore Brigadier Aung Gyi said that U Nu had allowed political, economic, and religious problems to grow until they had become unmanageable. He criticized U Nu's failure to maintain discipline within his own party.[55]

Aung Gyi again met with the press on March 9 at the National Defense College, on Signal Pagoda Road, Yangon. The meeting was attended by the information minister, Colonel Saw Myint, Lt.-Colonel Lwin, Lt.-Colonel Bo, and the psychological warfare deputy director, U Saw Oo.[56] In reply to queries about the seizure of state power, Brigadier Aung Gyi said:

> Whether democracy is successful or not is not the problem. Due to conditions that had threatened to bring about the state's disintegration, measures to safeguard it had to be taken. Had the problem been handled with firmness, disorders would not have been so bad. Because the government had been too magnanimous, narrow nationalistic ideas had sprung up. As in the epidemics of plague and cholera, preventive measures have been taken at the earliest possible time. Anything could have happened, if one had waited until the end of the national conference at the broadcasting station. If the states were not given what they wanted, there would be secession and conflict. It is impossible to continue to show magnanimity, as it would lead to the same conditions that existed in 1948.[57]

Brigadier Aung Gyi continued:

> The Shan affair is but the latest manifestation of the innermost thoughts of the feudalist reactionaries, whose demand for federalism is nothing less than an expression of narrow nationalism and a mania for statehood. In the past fifteen years of our independence, if the *saohpa* had meant well and had been sincere, they would not have allowed gambling dens to exist, but would have promoted agricultural, health, and educational plans for the welfare of the Shan peoples.
>
> Instead, what have they done? They collected taxes from the people and with the proceeds lived in luxury. Have they built a single school? The *saohpa* have taken a big share of the compensation given by the government, but they have not spent a single pya for the people. Ko Kang District in the Shan State has been regarded as an alien entity. Wa District has been considered underdeveloped. Ministers have not visited the region, not even once. The Paos have been in revolt for the past seven years because they did not want the feudalists. The *saohpa* want to secede from Myanmar Proper in order to ensure the supremacy of feudalism in their districts. This sort of idea is unthinkable and unacceptable in the world community.[58]

Brigadier Aung Gyi commented that the *saohpa* had become reactionaries because of the weakness of the constitution. The Federal Principle was a camouflage to enable the feudalists to maintain their influence. The twenty-five seats reserved for the *saohpa* in parliament were a means to protect the feudal system.[59]

SECRET REPORT ON THE POLITICAL MOVEMENTS IN THE SHAN STATE

A secret report entitled "Shan State Political Movements and the Origins of the Federal Principle," compiled by the No. 2 Military Intelligence commander on the orders of the director of Military Intelligence, gave the reasons for the seizure of state power by the Revolutionary Council.[60] The report stated that in December 1956 at the conference held in Mong Yai town, which was attended by some *saohpa*, a decision was made to secede from the Union and to form a Shan Republic. This was how the problem of the secession of Shan State from the Union originated. A meeting held in Lashio in 1957 and attended by the Yawng Hwe *mahadevi* and some *saohpa* decided that Shan State must secede from the Union. The agitation for secession proved to be effective when a bulletin in the Shan language was issued by the White Tiger Press in the town of Hsi Paw. In 1957 a meeting was held at the home of the *saohpa* of Tawng Peng in Lashio, and discussed that it would be difficult for Shan State to secede from the Union by democratic means, so the only alternative was to stage an armed rebellion.[61]

The secret report disclosed that after the AFPFL split on May 18, 1958, a meeting took place at the home of the head of Shan State, Minister Sao Hkun Hkio. At this meeting Sao Hkun Hkio told the *saohpa* and members of parliament from Shan State that the AFPFL split was an important event. He advised that it was imperative to arrive at serious decisions. Explicit demands must be made about the grievances of the states. Such demands must be made not only by an individual state for itself but unanimously by all the states. The attention of the Myanmar political leaders was focussed on the Shan. Sao Hkun Hkio went on to comment that this was a time of great significance, and that a committee should be formed to present its demands to U Nu.[62]

The political weakness caused by the split of the AFPFL gave the *saohpa* who wanted to secede from the Union the opportunity to prepare for an armed revolt. The report said that in April 1959, *saohpa* from Shan State had to surrender their powers. The Union government compensated these *saohpa*, but they were not satisfied. The most dissatisfied was the *saohpa* of Yawng Hwe, who had not attended the ceremony to mark the surrender of power because of his dissatisfaction. He even said that the *saohpa* had sold out Shan State by surrendering their powers. Even before the surrender of their powers, some *saohpa* had held secret talks with senior and junior administrators of their districts, and had hidden weapons and organized their people in preparation for action. After the *saohpa* surrendered their powers in November 1959, Shan insurgents began to appear and demanded that administrative power be restored to the *saohpa* as the *saohpa* would be replaced by Bamar in the administration of the simple Shan people; the insurgents had agitated the armed forces to oppose the Bamar principle of being the master race and to avoid servitude under the Bamar; the strength of the Shan insurgents had grown owing to racialist organizations, and in some regions they had made alliances with the KMT; opium had been exchanged for arms and ammunition from the KMT, some of which had been bought from Thailand. Some Shan insurgent leaders had lived on the Thai side of the border and moved freely over the border and tried to get weapons from SEATO. In 1960–61 the Shan people had been organized using slogans for the secession of Shan State and the setting up of a Shan Republic. The number of armed insurgents had increased to four thousand and they had supported the demand for the Federal Principle, which had been adopted by the *saohpa* and their cohorts as their political objective. In conclusion, the report said that the *saohpa* had contended that they supported the just and lawful struggle waged by the insurgents for freedom from slavery under Myanmar proper.[63]

The report indicated that the Shan insurgents and *saohpa* were unanimous in their demand for secession or the redrafting of the constitution on the basis of the Federal Principle, as provided for under section 202 of the constitution. The *mahadevi* of Yawng Hwe, Sao Hearn Hkam, who participated in the conference held at Mong Yai, which called for the secession of Shan State, left for Thailand via Myawady, and assumed leadership of the Shan insurgents.[64]

The report also disclosed that when the AFPFL split, the Shan State United Hill Peoples' Organization (Ya-Ta-Sa-Nya-Pha), led by the Shan State *saohpa*, put to the AFPFL (Clean) the following demands:

(a) Shan State nationals living within the Union should be given full autonomy or be given complete rights of self-determination; in other words, some of the sections in the constitution which could be given various interpretations should be changed so that the true rights and privileges of Shan State pertaining to administration, finance, etc. will be guaranteed specifically by these sections.

(b) Although the constitution had not granted any rights or privileges to the state concerning the matters on the Union List, Union ministers concerned should consult the Shan State government when such matters are implemented in Shan State.

(c) Since the entire population of Shan State is dissatisfied with the existing relations between the army and the Shan State government—

   (1) The army should show due regard in its dealings with the Shan State government;

   (2) The army must avoid seizures of land, housing, commandeering of vehicles, and interference in the administration. Apart from military operations, the request for the needs of the army should be made through the Union Defense Ministry. If there is reason, at times, to carry out important matters, the leaders of the army in Shan State should personally make a request to the Shan State government and if such request is not granted, then they should appeal to the Shan State government through the Union Defense Ministry. Absolutely no one in the army should indulge in politics.

(d) No one in the army should indulge in politics. A spirit of fair-mindedness toward ethnic minorities should be instilled in the armed forces. In the formation of the armed forces, the states must be given separate units in proportion to those of Myanmar proper.

(e) Representatives of Shan State must be included either in the Union Defense Council or in the General Staff.

(f) When the state subsidies or contributions are given to Shan State, on the basis of population or of area, an explicit principle must be laid down. A meeting of the States Subsidies Board held annually is unsatisfactory. Instead a meeting of this board should be convened whenever issues arise over big or small financial matters concerning Shan State.

(g) Subsidies for the Shan State government must be given in time.

(h) If it is necessary to cut foreign exchange already allocated to the Shan State budget, it should be done in consultation with the Shan State government. The Shan State government must issue licenses for the import of machinery when necessary for Shan State.

(i) When the Union government does not intend to take foreign loans, it should consult the Shan State government.

(j) Shan State must be allowed to have a share in any internal or foreign joint venture entered into by the Union government.

(k) If the Union government receives foreign aid, Shan State is to be given a fair share.

(l) In the interest of the financial well-being of Shan State, it must be allowed to establish industries with the assistance of the Union government.

(m) Shan State nationals must be included when state scholars, friendly missions, and diplomatic representatives are sent abroad.

(n) The Union government must not in any way interfere directly or indirectly in the politics of Shan State.

(o) If there is a dispute concerning any problem between any Union ministry and the Shan State government, a decision must be given by a special committee headed by the prime minister, and including the deputy prime minister.[65]

The secret report revealed that to maintain their power, the leaders of the AFPFL (Clean) had promised to comply with those demands.[66]

The report said that Dr. E Maung replied, "So long as it is not a Communist state or a fascist state, you all can draft any constitution you like in accordance with democratic principles." The head of Shan State, Sao Hkun Hkio, invited Shan *saohpa*, representatives from political organizations, independent individuals, signatories of the Pang Long Agreement, and the Shan members of the Constituent Assembly to a conference held on February 22, 1962. The conference resolved that:

1. Despite the spirit of the Pang Long Agreement, parliament, the Union cabinet, and important senior and junior officials have ignored it in practice.
2. The constitution has been interpreted one-sidedly.

3. In carrying out matters relating to Union laws, the Union government deemed it unnecessary to consult the state governments.
4. Civil Service personnel of the Union government had a low opinion of the states;
5. There was disrespect for state ministers;
6. Government matters (including finance) has been carried out tyrannically and one-sidedly;
7. No assistance due to Shan State has been received;
8. The Shan State government has been ignored by the Union government departments in implementing matters in accordance with the Union law;
9. There has been interference in Shan State politics and administration.

On November 7, 1961, a Steering Committee for the Revision of the Constitution was formed consisting of thirty members, with Sao Pye as chairman and Sao Kya Sone as secretary. The committee directed all Shan political organizations to put forward principles they favored, but none of them could produce specific principles for the revision. U Htun Myint (Taunggyi) then presented his Federal Principle containing the following basic points:

1. Forming the Bamar state
2. Granting equal powers to the two chambers of parliament
3. Sending an equal number of representatives to the upper chamber
4. Granting residual powers to the states
5. Distributing the Union budget

The Federal Principle presented by U Htun Myint had been adopted by the All Shan State Conference on February 25, 1961. It was readily accepted by the *saohpa* who had previously approved it. Shan, Kayah, Kachin, Kayin, Chin, Mon, and Rakhine, etc. had taken part in the All States Conference, at which five proposals were presented and adopted. These were:

1. To form a States Unity Organization
2. To draft a revised Union Constitution
3. To hold a Union national conference
4. To establish Mon, Rakhine, and Chin states
5. To oppose imperialism

On February 24, 1962, an All Nationals Conference was held at the Myanmar broadcasting station in Yangon to continue discussions about the Federal Principle, approved by the All States Convention. At that convention, the chairman of the States Unity Organization, Sao Hkun Hkio, proposed that every state should have equal privileges within the federal system, which provides for the right of enactment. On the implementation of the Federal Principle U Htun Myint (Taunggyi) said:

> We, the nationals of the states, are very much united in favor of the principle of a true federal union (Federal Principle). We all have passed a firm resolution to go forth without hesitation with the implementation of the Federal Principle. We wish to announce here that the Shan State would strive unceasingly by any means to obtain this Federal Principle. The principle of a true federal union, now called the Shan Principle, is being presented and demanded in a family spirit. We are acting in a family and in a democratic manner. If we fail to achieve it by such means, we will inform the people of the Shan State that we will have to turn to the last resort: in accordance with the right granted in chapter (10) of the constitution, the Shan State would have to secede from the Union. If after secession, we were to offer to set up a true federal union, would the Bamar leaders still refuse to offer us equal treatment? In that case, we will willy-nilly have to use force. As a Myanmar expression goes, if our earnest proposal for marriage, presented in traditional fashion with flowers, bananas, coconuts, and whatnot, is rejected, we will have to carjack the bride (Federal Principle). Down with Bamar chauvinism![67]

Taunggyi U Htun Myint's statements were disclosed in the secret report on political movements in Shan State.[68] Army leaders in Myanmar also believed that due to political instability, there were indications of the Union falling apart and that if the Federal Principle was granted, the Union would disintegrate, spurred on by foreign instigation. There were fears that if the Union disintegrated, Myanmar would lose its independence. And even if independence wasn't lost, the army leaders believed that political and economic problems would arise.[69]

DIFFERENT VIEWS ON THE COUP

A certain ex-army officer who had served for a long period in Shan State and had known some *saohpa* well said that some *saohpa* had intended to secede from the Union; that after the Federal Principle had been achieved, a road between Tachileik and Taunggyi would be built and Shan exports would be sold via that road to the country across the border; that with the money thus gained, arms and commodities would be bought; that financial help would be sought from SEATO and the Thai government; and that after secession was granted and the Tatmadaw had left Shan State, arrangements had been made for the Shan insurgents to take the responsibility for guarding Shan State.[70]

He went on to state that many Tatmadaw officials were worried about the prospect of the Union disintegrating because of the Federal Principle, and that if they stood by despite the imminent threat, they would be blamed for it in the future.[71] Therefore, to prevent the Union from disintegrating and to solve other political problems, the military carried out a coup on the morning of March 2, 1962.[72]

However, former Prime Minister U Nu did not believe that the Federal Principle would lead to the dissolution of the Union, or that the political situation was beyond control. He said the majority of the people also knew that the political situation was controllable, that the demand for a Federal Principle was not a cause for concern, and he himself had arranged and carried out the Conference of the Nationalities.[73]

At the conference it was arranged: (1) that the proposal for the Federal Principle was to be introduced by the head of Shan State, Sao Hkun Hkio, and to be discussed and supported by the Kachin State representative Duwa Zau Lawn, the Chin Special Division representative Captain Mang Tung Nung, the Shan State representative U Htun Myint (Taunggyi), and the Kayah State representative U Sein; (2) that the proposals and matters relating to the discussions were to be studied carefully by the representatives of the NUF, the AFPFL, the Shan State Freedom League, the Union Party, and members of the Government Advisory Committee; (3) that one representative each from the NUF, AFPFL, Shan State Freedom League, Union Party, and Government Advisory Committee would express views on the Federal Principle; (4) that a committee would be formed comprising six members from the All States Unity Organization, and three members each from the NUF, the AFPFL, the SSFL, the Union Party, and members from the Government Advisory Committee; (5) that U Nu was to chair that committee, which would discuss matters relating to the Federal Principle and, finally, to report to him on any agreement reached from the discussions.[74]

U Nu said that while the committee was deliberating, he would set out his views on the Federal Principle at the appropriate time.[75] Before the conference could end, however, the Revolutionary Council carried out its coup. Therefore he did not have the opportunity to express his views on the Federal Principle. Only in 1990, or twenty-eight years after the coup, did it become possible to find the text of U Nu's views on the Federal Principle. Excerpts include:

> Delete that chapter in the constitution which provides for the right of secession. Don't keep it. You keep asking for more power, saying that you were not given enough. When the English were here, we asked for ninety-one departments. . . . the ninety-one departments were given to us. Well, we thought that the ninety-one that were given to us, out of one hundred departments, were a lot . . . but in reality, they amounted to zero; the real meat was the seven departments . . . that the English held on to. I do not know if you feel the same about the present situation. If you do, just say so! If you want more powers, we will discuss the matter in a brotherly way. After discussion we will willingly hand over to you all that you demand, without stint and without heartburn. Just delete the chapter on the right to secession. We will add on more powers to the schedule and lists as mentioned by you.[76]

Thus, U Nu had planned to make his views known to the representatives of the states. If he had had the chance to state them during the conference, the delegates from the states might have accepted them.[77] Sao Hkun Hkio himself, the head of Shan State and president of All States Unity Organization, had said there should be no cause for worry about the proposals and demands put forth at the conference, that this matter had already been discussed with U Nu, and that the request for the Federal Principle was merely a move to give more powers to the states.[78] Prime Minister U Nu himself said that there was no need to worry about the conference, because there was already a solution to the issues.[79]

The representative from Kayah State who had supported the Federal Principle proposed by the head of Shan State, Sao Hkun Hkio, said the Federal Principle which they had asked for was definitely not going to cause the disintegration of the Union, and that they had, at that time, not the slightest intention of seceding. All they wanted was to live in their own house, in a big compound that was Myanmar.[80]

It has been said that a person who had served as the defense minister in the Union Party government related that the reason why the army staged the coup on March 2, 1962, might have been due to the fact that some of the army leaders had come to know of the discussions held by the leaders of the Union Party to reduce the power and authority of the army. The Union Party leaders, in the course of their discussions, said that in the newly independent states and the small developing countries, the strength of the army was often very big, leading to the frequent occurrences of military coups. In the light of these facts the leaders of the Union Party discussed among themselves how best to reform Myanmar's army. They discussed whether the posts of the top army officers should be rotated every three years or whether some of these officers should be retired. The Union Party leaders also discussed the idea of not keeping a standing army, but instead give military training to everyone who has come of age, and to conscript them into military service, if required. The defense minister stated that the army officers probably got wind of these discussions among the Union Party leaders and had used this as an excuse to stage the coup.[81] In an interview with the defense minister in August 1990, he made the following statement:

> During my tenure of office as defense minister we had discussed the matter of moving the National Service Act in parliament. At that time Brigadier Tin Pe went to the districts spreading the news that the present defense minister was about to destroy the army[82] and that in accordance with the National Service Act, everyone who had reached the age of eighteen, male or female, must render military service up to the age of forty-five . . . Military training would be made compulsory . . . part of the army, about fifty thousand strong, would be retained as an Army Training Corps . . . . The rest of the army officers would be absorbed into the district administration, the NCOS would be absorbed into rural defense and administration. . . . Some of the surplus officers would be pensioned and those who were not of pensionable age and had adequate educational qualifications would be sent abroad to pursue studies which would help in the reconstruction of the country. . . . Brigadier Tin Pe had first called up the army officers and told them that he would not stand by and watch the army being destroyed, and that something had to be done. . . . When I was in the Wa region, Colonel Maung Shwe, the division commander, told me that his officers had asked for an interview with the defense minister. I agreed to comply with the request, and met

> with the two hundred army officers. These officers inquired about the National Service Act. I explained to them all about the Act, and I also told them that, at the moment, the strength of the insurgents had dwindled down to about three thousand to four thousand strong, and that these were now desirous of joining the legal fold. . . . When the army officers heard my explanations they were relieved, and said that the National Service Act was not destroying the army; on the contrary, it was making the whole of the Union into an army and as such, there was no reason to object to the National Service Act. . . . This fact was agreed to, twice at the OC[83] conference, and twice by the COs[84] at the latter's conference. At this juncture, Brigadier Tin Pe, while he was in Pathein, had lamented that the defense minister had destroyed the army at Lashio, as well as Taunggyi. . . .
>
> As Brigadier Tin Pe went about spreading such rumors, I had to give all the necessary explanations. . . . In spreading such rumors Brigadier Tin Pe may have been genuinely worried about the matter of the army's power being reduced and the size of the reduction.
>
> I spoke to U Hkun Hti and others about this matter and they agreed that the coup was not staged because of the Federal Principle, but it was done due to the army's anxiety over the curtailment of its power and size. The army had to find an excuse to seize power and stalwartly prevent the curtailment of its power and reduction of its size. It had therefore used the federal proposal as an excuse to justify the coup.[85]

One of the Shan leaders who had asked for the Federal Principle to be implemented made the following remarks about the March 2, 1962, coup:

> He [U Nu] came and questioned us about the amending of the constitution. In reply to his question, I asked how much of the constitution we could amend. . . . Does amendment mean just juggling around words, terms, and sections? To what extent can the amendments be made? Tell us how far the changes can go. Then because he informed us that we could change anything, so long as the [basic] principles were not damaged, we had discussed thoroughly what these principles were. We were all in agreement about this . . . at Taunggyi. . . . We ourselves and the *saohpa* and the people's representatives . . . agreed on what the basic principles should be. We believed that they were contained in the preamble to the constitution . . . to be more specific, these basic principles are the seven guiding principles that General Aung San laid down at the Constituent Assembly. The *saohpa* said: "Well, in that case, to make sure, let's ask Prime Minister U Nu. . . ." So the *saohpa* of Hsa Mong Hkam, Sao Htun E, took the responsibility of going down to Yangon to make inquiries of U Nu. "What are the principles [of the constitution] that cannot be changed? Please explain to us. . . ." and Thakin Nu said: "Rather than ask me about this, go and ask the Judicial Minister U E Maung. We have appointed him chairman regarding this matter." Sao Htun E went and asked U E Maung, and U E Maung replied: "As long as the country does not turn into a Communist state, a fascist state or a dictatorship, you can change the constitution

> from the beginning to the end." Having got the green light from U E Maung, the Shan State put up a Federal Principle. . . . There were no such things as SEATO or imperialist influence; we were merely going to amend the constitution according to [U E Maung's] suggestions, and when we were about to do so, some newspapers—*The Nation*, the *A-Htauk-Taw*, the *Bama-Khit*—and the AFPFL headed by U Kyaw Nyein cried out that the Union was about to collapse, that the Shan State was about to secede; and when this matter gained prominence in the newspapers, U Nu stated that "the situation had become a bit bad, just a little bit, though it isn't because of us. So to thrash this thing out to everybody's satisfaction, let's have a seminar, like a national conference." And so from February onward, when the seminar was convened, we all came down from the Shan State and the Kachin State. Meanwhile we held a meeting among ourselves on March 1 and the delegates put up the principle, which had become the principle of all the states. While the proposal was still being debated and before the matter was resolved, the army staged the coup on March 2. The Shan State proposal served as the best excuse for the coup, but it was not the real reason for the coup.[86]

However, Brigadier Tin Pe (retired), one of the participants in the planning of the coup, said that the main reason why the coup took place on March 2, 1962, was the anxiety over the possibility of the Shan State seceding from the Union, and to prevent the danger of secession, the Armed Forces had begun secretly planning the coup from November 1961 onward.

THE VIEWS OF THE NEWSPAPERS

On March 4, 1962, two days after the Revolutionary Council staged the coup, *The Guardian* newspaper, published in London, stated:

> It is doubtful whether the initial impetus of army rule could have been maintained much longer. Burma's inherent difficulties were beginning to regain the point, when General Ne Win handed over power, and not all the undeniable deterioration since then has been due to the elected government's defects, grave as they may have been. The army may discover this, now that it takes up responsibility again . . . above all, the army will have to show that it can do better than U Nu in dealing with the discontents of the minority peoples in Burma.[87]

The Times said in an editorial:

> General Ne Win has done it again, although he has not arranged an invitation or stepped constitutionally into power as he did in Burma in October 1958. This time General Ne Win has not got the cover of being a constitutional prime minister. He will therefore have to justify his action, though that may be difficult when so many Burmese

> have suffered from the tyranny of political bosses. He will have to expound his policies, and from what is known of him, they are likely to be sensible and moderate. But he will be up against a national image, well projected and well filled by U Nu. And the Burmese take to military rule less easily than Pakistanis. He is unlikely to return powers to the politicians as readily this time as he did last.[88]

The *Herald Tribune*, published in New York, said:

> There is . . . every reason to believe that the General does not intend to set up a permanent military dictatorship . . . and by the same token, short testimony to his present sincerity stating that the military coup was needed to end a "vastly deteriorating situation" in Burma. General Ne Win has also demonstrated that army rule can inspire a considerably higher degree of efficiency in the Burmese public services than civilian government. It remains to be seen whether he can tackle the root problems of Burma—the painfully slow recovery from war-time disruptions, the even slower pace of industrialization, the persistence of rebellion in the hill country, the threat of external and internal Communists, . . . Burma needs more than a caretaker, more than the idealism of U Nu. It needs hard work and statesmanship of a higher order and General Ne Win seems to be the only man who can now provide them.[89]

The Nation newspaper, published in Myanmar, had this to say in its editorials:

> To what extent the events of March 2 were influenced by hostility shown and belligerency expressed at the National Seminar on Federalism can at present only be guessed at. But it would seem that the army had in its possession certain facts sufficiently disturbing for it to adopt the stern measures it has. . . . At any rate, it is domestic trouble that seemed to be the main threat and the conviction of the Revolutionary Council is apparently that both the parliamentary system and those who worked it in this country have failed.[90]

ANALYSIS BY DR. BA MAW

Making an analysis of the coup in *The Nation* on March 9, 1962, Dr. Ba Maw, prewar prime minister and wartime head of state, declared that there were three reasons for the coup.

The first was that, although the politicians in power had used revolutionary slogans and promises during the struggle for independence, they had refused to carry on the revolution after independence even though they had continued to use revolutionary slogans for effect. This had created a general feeling of frustration and betrayal and a dangerous tension because the revolutionary spirit had kept on smoldering beneath the surface, kept alive by the revolutionary slogans which were being used for effect.

The second reason was that although U Nu had plenty of religious faith and an irreproachable national spirit, he lacked a firm, positive political faith and, unable to keep on a fixed course, his government fell back on substitutes, expedients, makeshifts, and day-to day decisions which created the problems leading to its downfall. Together with this, there was a loose use of the word "democracy" which created havoc, with the people coming to believe that democracy meant the right to live and act as one pleased, with maximum rights and minimum obligations, and without any duty to help the country to progress. This made progress nearly impossible and U Nu's government lost the ability and the will to govern.

The third reason was that, without deep-rooted political convictions, the government was unable to impart conviction and driving force to the people. U Nu tried to replace political faith with religious faith and superstitious observances, which defied the laws of history and proved disastrous. There was a general failure of all the postwar plans, but the real failure [lay] in the people who worked the plans.

Together with this analysis, Dr. Ba Maw sounded a note of warning to the new Revolutionary Council which had taken power: that it must fulfill the revolution of rising expectations; that it must win the consent and support of the people and emerge as a people's revolution; and that it must build the foundations for a true and well-protected democracy, making all further seizures of power historically unnecessary and, therefore, impossible. (See appendix 42.)

CONCLUSION

As a consequence of the events related above—the Communist emergency, the insurrection of certain ethnic minorities, the intrusion of foreign forces like the KMT, the problems regarding the federal system, the split in the AFPFL—the situation in the Union of Myanmar by the beginning of 1962 had become precarious, leaving only the armed forces as a strong and unified force and capable of staging a coup, which the military leaders believed would wipe out the evils that had been created by the squabbling politicians and restore the stability of the nation.

The most significant consequence of the coup was that it left the country without a constitution, the backbone of the country, from 1962 to 2007, and, much more than that, it made it very difficult for Myanmar to return to the road to democracy.

Appendixes

List of Appendixes

I

Table of Mung-Mau *Tsaubwa*

No.	Name	Relationship to Predecessor	Commencement of Reign AD	Length of Reign Years	Remarks
1	Kun-lai	...	568	Cx 21342 13445 70	Religious era 1111 or 70 years previous to Myanmar era.
2	Ai-Dyep-That-pha	Son	638	40	Religious era 1181 Died heirless.
3	Kam-Pong-pha	...	678		Son of Chau-Kun-Jun.
4	Kam-Sap-pha	Son	...		The reigns of nos. 3 & 4 are said to have aggregated about 25 years, but no date is given for no. 4.
5	Kam-Sip-pha	Younger brother	703	50	
6	Ni-Fa-maung	Son	753	40	
7	Chau-Khun-pha	"	793	44	
8	Chau-Kai-pha	"	834	34	
9	Chau-Han-pha	"	868	33	
10	Chau-Tau-pha	"	901	32	
11	Chau-Pwot-pha	"	933	27	
12	Chau-Won-pha	"	960	23	
13	Chau-Hon-pha	"	983	12	
14	Chau-Hau-pha	"	995	19	
15	Chau-Lip-pha	"	1014	21	This date is uncertain to about three years.
16	Khun-Kwot-pha	Relation	1035	15	Of the race of Tai-pong of Yun-lung.
17	Chau-Tai-pha	Son	1050	12	
18	Chau-Lu-lu	"	1060	19	
19	Chau-Sang-mwun	"	1081	15	
20	Chau-Sang-yaw	"	1096	7	

21	Chau-Tai-pha	Younger brother	1103	9	
22	Chau-Shen-Nga	Son	1112	11	
23	Chau-Lu-Chu	Younger brother	1123	14	
24	Chau-Nga-Chu	"	1137	8	
25	Chau-Khun-ming	Son	1145	18	
26	Chau-Khun-Kum	"	1163	8	
27	Chau-Tai-Pum	"	1171	17	
28	Chau-Tai-Lung	"	1188	15	
29	Pam-Yau-Pung	"	1203	7	His younger brother, Fu-San-kang, became *Tsaubwa* of Momiet and founded the Asam line of *tsaubwa*.
30	Chau-Ai-Mo-Kang-Neng	Relation	1210	10	A descendant of Kwun-Su of Maing-Nyaung.
31	Chau-Kwam-pha	Son	1220	30	The Soo-Kam-Pha of Pemberton. His younger brother was Sam-Lung-Kung-Maing or Sam-Lung-Pha, the conqueror.
32	Chau-Piu-pha	"	1250	32	
33	Tai-Peng or Chau-Kam-pha	"	1282	3	
34	Chau-Wak-pha	"	1285	30	Probably the founder of the present town of Mung-Mau.
	No king	...	1315	9	
35	Ai-Puk	Son of no. 34	1324	6	
	No king	...	1330	9	
36	Chau-Ki-pha or Tai-Pong	Relation	1339	7	
37	Tai-Lung	Son	1346	50	
38	Tau-Lwei or Chau-Tit-pha	"	1396	19	
39	Chau-Ngan-pha	"	1415	30	

	No king	...	1445	3	
40	Chau-Lam-Kon-Kam-pha		1448	13	Said to be an uncle (probably descendant of an uncle) of Chau-Wak-pha, no. 34, and nearest remaining relative of Chau-Ngan-pha, no. 39.
41	Chau-Hum-pha	Son	1461	29	
42	Chau-Kaa-pha	"	1490	6	
43	Chau-Pim-pha	"	1496	20	Surnamed Kyie-poi-pei-ma.
44	Chau-Hum-pha	"	1516	88	
45	Chau-Poreing	"	1604	...	Of Theinni

SOURCE: Sao Saimong Mangrai, *The Shan States and the British Annexation*, app. 2.

2

Table of Mogaung *Tsaubwa*

No.	Name	Relationship to Predecessor	Commencement of Reign AD	Length of Reign Years	Remarks
1	Sam-Lung-pha	...	1215	13	Otherwise Sam-Lung-Kung-maing, son of no. 31 of Mung-Mau.
2	Chau-Kam-pha	Nephew	1228	20	This was his father's name which he assumed; his real name was Noi-San-pha.
3	Chau-Kun-law	Son	1248	60	
4	Chau-Pu-Reing	"	1308	36	
5	Chau-Tei-pha	"	1344	2	
6	Pwa-Ngan-maing	"	1346	15	
7	Kun-Tau-pha	"	1361	20	
8	Chau-Hung-pha	"	1381	30	
9	Chau-Pin-pha	"	1411	35	
10	Chau-Si-pha	...	1446	50	Surnamed Chau-Kwon-pha. He was brother of Chau-Ngan-pha (no. 39) Mung-Mau.
11	Chau-Kaa-pha	...	1496	24	Surnamed Chau-Kyek-pha
12	Sam-Lung-paw-maing	...	1520	6	Otherwise Chau-Sui-fin. Here the Mau line breaks off.
13	Chau-Sui-kwei	...	1526	32	Surnamed Chaupeng
14	Chau-Hum-pha	Son	1558	6	
15	Chau-Kaa-pha	"	1564	19	
16	Chau-Kon-kam	"	1583	8	
17	Chau-Hum-pha	"	1591	14	He became temporarily independent of Myanmar.

18	Chau-Tit-pha	...	1605	21	Surnamed Chau-Kaa-maing, and probably a grandson of Chau-Hum-pha (no. 44) of Mung-Mau. Here the Mau line recommences.
19	Chau-Sain-Lung	...	1626	3	The country administered by
	No king	...	1629	10	Chau-Tit-pha's queen, no. 20.
20	Lang-Chu-paw	...	1639	12	Dowager queen of Chau-Tit-pha.
21	Cheing-Lung-Ho-Hup	Adopted	1651	12	Said to be a minister's title.
22	Chau-Sui-Yaw	Son	1663	10	
23	Chau-Sui-kyek	...	1673	56	Said to have been a grandson of Chau-Hum-pha (no. 44) of Mung-Mau.
24	Chau-Hum	Son	1729	10	Born at Ava and called by the Myanmar Chau-Maung-pu.
25	Haw-Seing	"	1739	9	
26	Haw-Kam *Again* Haw-Seing	Son ...	1748 1765	17 3	
27	Maung-Kiaw	Son?	1768	3	A Myanmar. His Shan name was, perhaps, Haw-Kam.
28	Maung-Piu *Again* Haw-Seing	Brother ...	1771 1775	4 2	
	No king	...	1777	8	
29	Chau-Yaw-Pan-Kyung	...	1785	11	Was captured by the Myanmars in 1185 BE or AD 1796.

SOURCE: Sao Saimong Mangrai, *The Shan States and the British Annexation*, app. 3.

3
The Diagram for a Proposed Culture System of the Tai Peoples

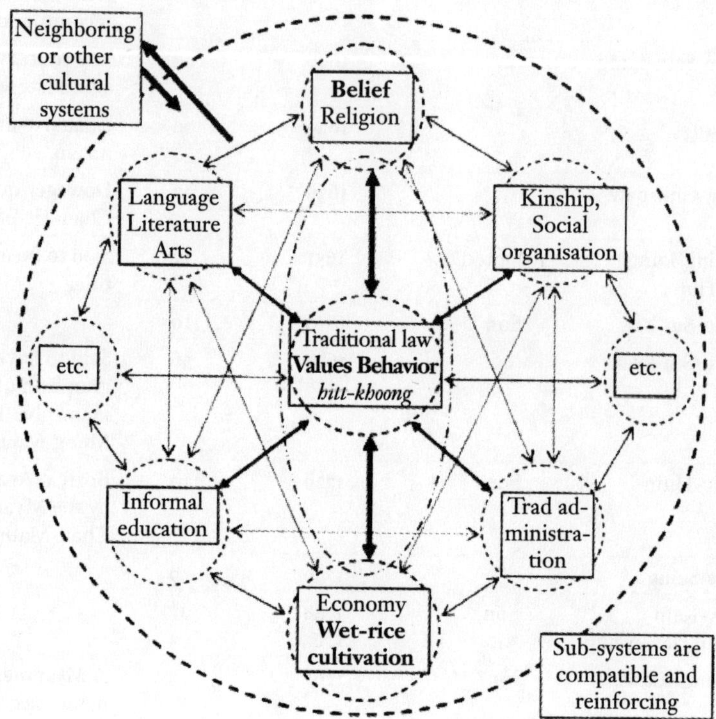

Remarks on the Diagram:

The system comprises the typical way of living and behavior as well as the complete collective knowledge in a wet rice cultivation and water culture system, which I call the "*baan-müng*" system.

This is only a very rough diagram of the general structure of the cultural system of the Tai peoples.

Each of the sub-systems presented here are interlinked with every other sub-system. Many other conceivable and existing sub-systems as well as interlinkages are left out here and must be included in a more comprehensive diagram.

Interlinkages are communication lines and interactions.

SOURCE: Oliver Raendchen, "The Design for a Proposed Cultural System for the Tai People," *Tai Culture* (Berlin: SEACOM, vol. 7, no. 2)

4

Chiefs of Myinsaing and Pinya, 1298–1364

Name	Year of Accession AD	Relationship to Predecessor	Remarks
Athinhkaya		Brother	
Yazathinkyan	1298	Usurpers	The three Shan brothers
Thihathu	1312		The youngest of the three Moved to Pinya
Uzana	1324	Stepson	Son of Kyawswa 1287–98 of Pagan
Ngasishin	1343	Half brother	
Kyawswa-nge	1350	Son	
Narathu	1359	Brother	Ruled only three months. Murdered by successor, Thadominbya, 1364–8
Uzana Pyaung	1364		

SOURCE: G. E. Harvey, *History of Burma*, 365.

5

Chiefs of Sagaing, 1315–1364

Name	Year of Accession AD	Relationship to Predecessor	Remarks
Sawyun	1315		Son of Thihathu the Shan brother 1312–24
Tarabyagyi	1323	Stepbrother	Murdered
Shwetaungtet	1336	Son	
Kyaswa	1340		
Nawrahtaminye	1350	Brother	
Tarabyange	1350	Brother	Son of Sawyun 1315–23
Minbyauk Thihapate	1352	Brother-in-law	Murdered by his stepson Thadominbya 1364–68

SOURCE: G. E. Harvey, *History of Burma*, 366.

6

Chiefs of Inwa, 1364–1555

Name	Year of Accession AD	Relationship to Predecessor	Remarks
Thadominbya	1364	Murderer	Descendant of Thihathu, the Shan brother 1312–24. Founded Ava 1364
Nga Nu	1368	Usurper	Paramour of Saw Umma, reigned only a few days
Minkyiswasawke	1368		Descended from both the Pagan dynasty and the Shan brothers
Tarabya	1401	Eldest son	Reigned seven months, made love to a *nat thami* fairy in the forest, lost his reason and was murdered by an attendant
Nga Nauk Hsan	1401	Murderer	
Minhkaung	1401		Son of Minkyiswasawke 1368–1401. He hesitated to accept the throne, so his younger brother Theiddat killed a cousin claimant and made him accept it
Thihathu	1422	Son	Murdered at instigation of Queen Shin Bo-me
Minhla-nge	1426	"	Poisoned by her son, Son of Tarabya 1401 Descended from Narapati-sithu 1173–1210 and Nagsishin 1343–50
Kalekyetaungnyo	1426		
Mohnyinthado	1427		
Minrekyawswa	1440		
Narapati	1443		
Thihathura	1469	Son	
Minhkaung	1481	"	
Shwenankyawshin	1502	"	
Thohanbwa	1527	Brother	Son of Sawlon the Mohnyin conqueror, murdered

Hkonmaing	1543		*Sawbwa* of Hsi Paw
Mobye Narapati	1546	Son	*Sawbwa* of Mobye (Mong Pai)
Sithukyawhtin	1552		Shan lord of Salin who seized Ava and was overthrown by Bayinnaung in 1555

SOURCE: G. E. Harvey, *History of Burma*, 366.

7

Chiefs of Hanthawaddy (Pegu)

Capitals: Pegu (825–1057), Martaban (1287–1363), Donwun (1363–9), and Pegu (1369–1539, 1740–7)

Name	Year of Accession AD	Relationship to Predecessor	Remarks
Thamala	825		Founded Pegu. Down to 1057 the dates (unattested) are those given in *Shwemawdaw Thamaing*
Wimala	837	Brother	
Atha	854	Nephew	
Areindama	861		
A monk	885		
Geinda	902		
Migadeippagyi	917		
Geissadiya	932		
Karawika	942		
Pyinzala	954		
Attatha	967		
Anuyama	982		
Migadeipange	994		
Ekkathamanta	1004		
Uppala	1016		
Pontarika	1028		
Tissa	1043		1057–1287 Pegu is subject to Pagan
Wareru	1287		Shan adventurer, ruled Martaban from 1281 and Lower Myanmar from 1287. Murdered
Hkun Law	1296	Brother	Murdered
Saw O	1310	Nephew	
Saw Zein	1324	Brother	Murdered by Shan guards
Zein Pu	1331	Murderer	Murdered at instigation of Queen Sandaminhla
Saw E Gan Gaung	1331		Nephew to Saw Zein.Poisoned by his wife, the dowager Sandaminhla, for looking at a concubine

Binnya E Law	1331		Son of Hkun Law
Binnya U	1353	Son	Moved to Pegu
Razadarit	1385	"	
Binnyadammayaza	1423	"	Poisoned by successor
Binnyaran	1426	Brother	
Binnyawaru	1446	Nephew	Son of Lady Shinsawbu, Razadarit's daughter
Binnyakyan	1450	Cousin	
Mawdaw	1453	"	Murdered his son and seems to have been murdered
Lady Shinsawbu	1453		Razadarit's daughter. In 1460 she handed over to Dammazedi, who was not of the blood
Dammazedi	1472	Son-in-law	Grandson of Lady Shinsawbu
Binnyaran	1492	Son	Driven out by Tabinshwehti in 1539
Takayutpi	1526	"	

SOURCE: G. E. Harvey, *History of Burma*, 368.

8

The Dynasty of Pagan, 1044–1287

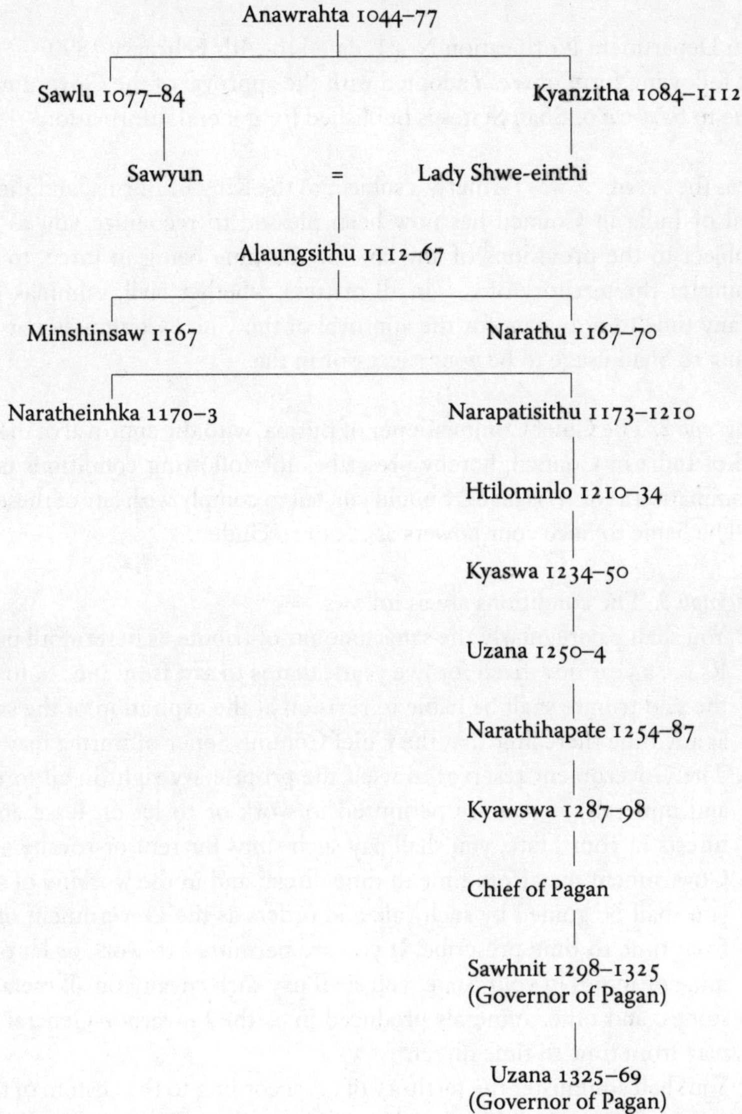

On the female side the family passes into the Shan princes who ruled Ava for the next two centuries.

SOURCE: G. E. Harvey, *History of Burma*, 365.

9

Form of *Sanad* Granted to *Sawbwa*

Foreign Department Notification No. 1, dated the 4th February 1890.

The following form of *sanad* adopted with the approval of the Government of India for issue to *Sawbwa* of Shan States is published for general information:

Whereas the . . . of . . . was formerly a subject to the King of Burma, and the Governor-General of India in Council has now been pleased to recognize you as . . . of . . . and, subject to the provisions of any law for the time being in force, to permit you to administer the territory of . . . in all matters, whether civil, criminal, or revenue, and at any time to nominate for the approval of the Chief Commissioner a fit person according to Shan usage to be your successor in the . . .

Paragraph 2. The Chief Commissioner of Burma, with the approval of the Governor-general of India in Council, hereby prescribes the following conditions under which your nomination as of . . . is made. Should you fail to comply with any of these conditions you will be liable to have your powers as . . . of rescinded.

Paragraph 3. The conditions are as follows:

1. You shall pay regularly the same amount of tribute as heretofore paid, namely, Rs . . . a year now fixed for five years, that is to say, from the . . . to the . . . and the said tribute shall be liable to revision at the expiration of the said term, or at any time thereafter that the Chief Commissioner of Burma may think fit.
2. The Government reserves to itself the proprietary right in all forests, mines, and minerals. If you are permitted to work or to let on lease any forest or forests in your State, you shall pay such sums for rent or royalty as the Local Government may from time to time direct; and in the working of such forests you shall be guided by such rule and orders as the Government of India may from time to time prescribe. If you are permitted to work or let on lease any mine or mines in your State, you shall pay such royalty on all metals, precious stones, and other minerals produced in as the Governor-General in Council may from time to time direct.
3. You shall administer the territory of . . . according to the custom of the country, and in all matters subject to the guidance of the Superintendent of the Shan States; you shall recognize the rights of the people and continue them in the same and on no account shall you oppress them or suffer them in any way to be oppressed.
4. You shall maintain order within the territory of . . . and keep open the trade routes within that territory. Should traders or caravans be attacked within

the boundaries of the said territory, you shall pay such compensation as the Superintendent of the Shan States may fix.

5. You shall, if the Superintendent of the Shan States so desires, keep an agent, who shall reside at the headquarters of the Superintendent, and who shall keep him informed concerning the conditions of the territory of . . .
6. In case of a dispute arising connected with any other part of the Shan States, you shall submit the matter to the Superintendent of the Shan States and abide by his decision. Should any inhabits of . . . commit raids on any place outside the limits of . . . , you shall pay such compensation as the Superintendent of the Shan States may fix.
7. If the Government wishes at any time to make a railway through the territory of . . . , you shall provide land for the purpose, free of cost, except that of the compensation adjudged to the actual occupiers of occupied land, and shall help the Government as much as possible.
8. Opium, spirits, or fermented liquor, and other articles which are liable to duties of customs or excise when imported by sea into Lower Burma, or when produced in any part of Upper Burma to which the Regulations of the Governor-General in Council apply, shall not be brought from . . . into Lower Burma or into any such part as aforesaid of Upper Burma, except in accordance with rules made by the Government and on payment of such duties as may be prescribed in those rules.
9. You shall deliver, upon the requisition of an officer of the Government, any criminal who takes refuge in the territory of . . . ; you shall aid officers of the Government who pursue criminals into the said territory; and in the event of offenders from the said territory taking refuge in any place beyond the limits of that territory you shall make representations of the matter to the authorities concerned.
10. You shall not exercise criminal jurisdiction over European British subjects; in the event of any criminal charge being brought against any such person, you shall make representations of the matter to the Superintendent of the Shan States.

SOURCE: *The Shan State Manual*, 1925.

10

Form of Order of Appointment Issued to *Myosa* and *Ngwegunhmu*

Whereas you have been a subject to the King of Burma, and have now been recognized by the Chief Commissioner *myosa*/*ngwegunhmu* of Burma as of . . . , you will be permitted to retain your office, and at any time to nominate, for the approval of the Chief Commissioner, a fit person to be your successor, *myosa*/*ngwegunhmu*
provided that you observe the following conditions which are hereby prescribed with the approval of the Governor-General of India in Council;

1. That you collect and pay into the treasury of the Superintendent, Shan States, at his headquarters, the revenue assessed by his orders from time to time on the persons or property of the residents in your territory.
2. That opium and other articles which are liable to duties of customs or excise when imported by sea into Lower Burma or when produced in any part of Upper Burma to which the Regulations of the Governor-General in Council apply, shall not be brought from . . . into Lower Burma or into any such part as aforesaid of Upper Burma, except in accordance with rules made by the Government and on payment of such duties as may be prescribed in those rules.
3. That generally, in all matters connected with the administration of the territory under your charge, you shall obey any law or laws that may be made applicable to it by the Government and conform to such rules, orders, or instructions as may from time to time be made or issued by the Chief Commissioner or the Superintendent, Shan States, or any of his Assistants for your guidance.

SOURCE: *The Shan State Manual*, 1925.

II

Sanad Granted to the *Sawbwa* of Kengtung

Whereas by a *sanad*, dated the 10th day of February 1890, Sao Kawn Hkam Hpu of Kēngtūng was, subject to the conditions therein contained, recognized by the Governor-General of India in Council as *Sawbwa* of the State of Kēngtūng; and whereas the said Sao Kawn Hkam Hpu died on the 12th day of April 1896; and whereas you, Sao Kawn Kiau, *intaleng* of Kēngtūng, have been selected to succeed the said Sao Kawn Hkam Hpu as *Sawbwa* of Kēngtūng, the Chief Commissioner of Burma hereby notifies you that the Governor-General of India in Council has been pleased to recognize you as *Sawbwa* of Kēngtūng, and subject to the provisions of any law for the time being in force and to the conditions hereinafter set forth, to permit you to administer the territory of Kēngtūng in all matters, whether civil, criminal, or revenue, and at any time to nominate, for the approval of the Chief Commissioner, a fit person according to Shan usage, to be your successor in the *Sawbwa*ship. Should you fail to comply with any of the said conditions, you will be liable to have your powers as *Sawbwa* of Kēngtūng rescinded.

For the purposes of this *sanad* the States of Mong Pu, Mong Hsat, Hsen Yawt, and Hsen Mawng shall be considered as forming part of and as included in the territory of Kēngtūng.

The said conditions are as follows:

1. In recognition of the loyal conduct of the late *Sawbwa* and as a mark of favor, the Governor-General of India in Council is pleased to exempt the State of Kēngtūng from payment of any tribute for a period of five years from the 1st January 1897. The tribute payable by the State of Kēngtūng shall be fixed at the expiry of the term for which all tribute is hereby remitted, that is, on the 31st December 1901.
2. You shall abstain from communication with States outside British India. Should necessity arise for communication with such States, you shall address the Superintendent of the Southern Shan States through the Assistant Political Officer at Kēngtūng.
3. The Government reserves to itself the proprietary right in all forests, mines, and minerals in the State of Kēngtūng. If you are permitted to work or to let on lease any forest or forests in the said State, you shall pay such sums for rent or royalty as the Local Government may from time to time direct; and in the working of such forests you shall be guided by such rules or orders as the Government of India may from time to time prescribe. If you are permitted to work or let on lease any mine or mines in the said State, you shall pay such royalty on all metals, precious stones, and other minerals produced therein as the Governor-General in Council may from time to time direct.
4. You shall administer the territory of Kēngtūng according to the custom of the country, and in all matters subject to the guidance of the Superintendent of

the Southern Shan States. You shall recognize the rights of the people and continue them in the same, and on no account shall you oppress them or suffer them in any way to be oppressed.

5. You shall maintain order within the territory of Kēngtūng and keep open the trade routes therein. Should traders or caravans be attacked within the limits of the said territory, you shall pay such compensation as the Superintendent of the Southern Shan States may fix.
6. You shall, if the Superintendent of the Southern Shan States so desires, appoint an agent, who shall reside at the headquarters of the Superintendent, and who shall keep the Superintendent informed of the condition of the territory of Kēngtūng.
7. In case of a dispute arising connected with any other part of the Shan States, you shall submit the matter to the Superintendent of the Southern Shan States, and abide by his decision. Should any inhabitants of the State of Kēngtūng commit raids on any place outside the limits of the said State, you shall pay such compensation as the Superintendent may fix.
8. If the Government wishes at any time to make a railway through the territory of Kēngtūng, you shall provide land for the purpose free of cost to the Government, except the cost of the compensation as judged to the actual occupiers of occupied land, and shall help the Government as much as possible. The Government may without further notice resume all jurisdictions over and in respect of all lands used or required for railway purposes.
9. Opium, spirits, or fermented liquor, and other articles which are liable to duties of customs or excise when imported by sea into Lower Burma, or when produced in any part of Upper Burma to which the Regulations of the Governor-General in Council apply shall not be brought from the State of Kēngtūng into Lower Burma or into any such part as aforesaid of Upper Burma, except in accordance with rules made by the Government and on payment of such duties as may be prescribed in those rules.
10. You shall deliver, upon the requisition of an officer of the Government, any criminal who takes refuge in the territory of Kēngtūng. You shall aid officers of the Government who pursue criminals into the said territory; and in the event of offenders from the said territory taking refuge in any place beyond the limits of that territory, you shall make representations of the matter to the authorities concerned.
11. You shall not exercise criminal jurisdiction over any European or American or any servant of the Government. In the event of any criminal charge being brought against any such person, you shall make representations of the matter to the Superintendent of the Southern Shan States.

Dated the 24th April 1897

SOURCE: *The Shan State Manual*, 1925.

12

Sanad Granted to the *Sawbwa* of Hsipaw (Thipaw)

Whereas by a *sanad*, dated the 13th March 1889, Hkun Hseng (Hkun Saing) of Hsipaw was subject to the conditions therein contained recognized by the Governor-General of India in Council as *Sawbwa* of the State of Hsipaw; and whereas the said Hkun Hseng died on the 8th day of May 1902; and whereas you, Sao Hke (Saw Hke) of Hsipaw, have been selected to succeed the said Hkun Hseng as *Sawbwa* of Hsipaw, the Lieutenant Governor of Burma hereby notifies you that the Governor-General of India in Council has been pleased to recognize you as *Sawbwa* of Hsipaw, and subject to the provisions of any law or order for the time being in force and to the conditions hereinafter set forth, to permit you to administer the territory of Hsipaw in all matters, whether civil, criminal, or revenue, and at any time to nominate for the approval of the Lieutenant Governor a fit person according to Shan usage to be your successor in the *Sawbwa*ship.

Should you fail to comply with any of the said conditions, you shall be liable to have your powers as *Sawbwa* of Hsipaw rescinded.

For the purposes of this *sanad* the subStates of Mong Long, Mong Tung, and Hsum Hsai shall be considered as forming part of and as included in the territory of Hsipaw.

The conditions are as follows:

1. You shall pay regularly the tribute of Rs. seventy thousand a year now fixed for five years, that is to say, from the 1st December 1902 to the 30th November 1907, and the said tribute shall be liable to revision at the expiration of the said term or at any time thereafter the Lieutenant Governor of Burma may think fit. If within the said period the State is relieved in whole or in part of the charges connected with the appointment of adviser to the Hsipaw *Sawbwa*, you shall pay such additional sum as tribute, not exceeding such charges, as the Lieutenant Governor may think fit.
2. The Government reserves to itself the proprietary right in all forests, mines, and minerals. If you are permitted to work or to let on lease any forest or forests in your territory, you shall pay such sums for rent or royalty as the Local Government may from time to time direct; and in the working of such forests you shall be guided by such rules or orders as the Government of India or the Local Government may from time to time prescribe. If you are permitted to work or let on lease any mine or mines in your State, you shall pay such royalty on all metals, precious stones, and other minerals produced in Hsipaw as the Governor-General in Council may from time to time direct.
3. You shall administer the territory of Hsipaw according to the custom of the country and in all matters subject to the guidance of the Superintendent, Northern Shan States. You shall recognize the rights of the people and continue

them in the same, and on no account shall you oppress them or suffer them to be oppressed.

4. You shall maintain order within the territory of Hsipaw and keep open the trade routes within that territory. Should traders or caravans be attacked within the boundaries of the said territory, you shall pay such compensation as the Superintendent of the Northern Shan States may fix.
5. You shall, if the Superintendent of the Northern Shan States so desires, keep an agent, who shall reside at the headquarters of the Superintendent, and who shall keep him informed of the condition of the territory of Hsipaw.
6. In case of a dispute arising connected with any other part of the Shan States, you shall submit the matter to the Superintendent of the Northern Shan States, and abide by his decision. Should any inhabitants of Hsipaw commit raids on any place outside the limits of Hsipaw, you shall pay such compensation as the Superintendent of the Northern Shan States may fix.
7. If the Government wishes at any time to make further railways through the territory of Hsipaw, you shall provide land for the purpose free of cost, except that of the compensation adjudged to actual occupiers of occupied land and shall help the Government as much as possible. The Government may without further notice resume all jurisdiction over and in respect of all lands used or required for railway purposes.
8. Opium, spirits, or fermented liquor, and other articles which are liable to duties of customs or excise when imported by sea into Lower Burma, or when produced in any part of Upper Burma to which the Regulations of the Governor-General in Council apply shall not be brought from Hsipaw into Lower Burma or into any such part as aforesaid of Upper Burma, except in accordance with rules made by the Government and on payment of such duties as may be prescribed in those rules.
9. You shall deliver, upon the requisition of an officer of the Government, any criminal who takes refuge in the territory of Hsipaw. You shall aid officers of the Government who pursue criminals into the said territory; and in the event of offenders from the said territory taking refuge in any place beyond the limits of that territory, you shall make representations of the matter to the authorities concerned.
10. You shall not exercise criminal jurisdiction over any European or American. In the event of any criminal charge being brought against any such person, you shall make representations of the matter to the Superintendent of the Northern Shan States.

Dated the 29th April 1906

SOURCE: *The Shan State Manual*, 1925.

13

Sanad Granted to Khin Maung of Mong Mit, 1905

Whereas the State of Möng Mit was formerly a *Sawbwa*ship subject to the King of Burma; and whereas by a *sanad*, dated the 10th April 1889, Saw Maung, ex-*Sawbwa* of Nyaung Hwe, was, subject to the conditions therein contained recognized by the Governor-General of India in Council as *Sawbwa* of Möng Mit, and was thereby to be permitted to administer the territory of Möng Mit for a period of five years; and whereas in 1892 the administration of the State of Mong Mit was resumed by the Government, and the State has since been administered as a subdivision of the Ruby Mines District; the Lieutenant Governor of Burma hereby notifies you, Khin Maung of Möng Mit, that the Governor-General of India in Council has been pleased to recognize you as *Sawbwa* of Möng Mit, and, subject to the provisions of any law or order from the time being in force and to the conditions hereinafter set forth, to permit you to administer the territory of Möng Mit in all matters, whether civil, criminal, or revenue, and at any time to nominate for the approval of the Lieutenant Governor a fit person according to Shan usage to be your successor in the *Sawbwa*ship.

Should you fail to comply with any of the said conditions, you shall be liable to have your powers as *Sawbwa* of Möng Mit rescinded.

The conditions are as follows:

1. You shall pay regularly the tribute of Rs. twenty thousand a year now fixed for five years from the 1st April 1905, and the said tribute shall be liable to revision at the expiration of the said term or at any time thereafter the Lieutenant Governor of Burma may think fit.
2. The Government reserves to itself the proprietary right in all forests, mines, and minerals. If you are permitted to work or to let on lease any forest or forests in your territory, you shall pay such sums for rent or royalty as the Local Government may from time to time direct; and in the working of such forests you shall be guided by such rules or orders as the Government of India or the Local Government may from time to time prescribe. If you are permitted to work or let on lease any mine or mines in your State, you shall pay such royalty on all metals, precious stones, and other minerals produced in Möng Mit as the Governor-General in Council may from time to time direct.
3. You shall administer the territory of Möng Mit according to the custom of the country and in all matters subject to the guidance of the Superintendent. You shall recognize the rights of the people and continue them in the same, and on no account shall you oppress them or suffer them to be oppressed.
4. You shall maintain order within the territory of Möng Mit and keep open the trade routes within that territory. Should traders or caravans be attacked within the boundaries of the said territory, you shall pay such compensation as the Superintendent may fix.

5. You shall, if the Superintendent so desires, keep an agent, who shall reside at the headquarters of the Superintendent, and who shall keep him informed of the condition of the territory of Möng Mit.
6. In case of a dispute arising connected with any other part of the Shan States, you shall submit the matter to the Superintendent, and abide by his decision. Should any inhabitants of Möng Mit commit raids on any place outside the limits of Möng Mit, you shall pay such compensation as the Superintendent may fix.
7. If the Government wishes at any time to make further railways through the territory of Möng Mit, you shall provide land for the purpose free of cost, except that of the compensations adjudged to actual occupiers of occupied land, and shall help the Government as much as possible. The Government may without further notice resume all jurisdiction over and in respect of all lands used or required for railway purposes.
8. Opium, spirits, or fermented liquor, and other articles, which are liable to duties of customs or excise when imported by sea into Lower Burma, or when produced in any part of Upper Burma, to which the Regulations of the Governor-General in Council apply shall not be brought from Möng Mit into Lower Burma or into any such part as aforesaid of Upper Burma except in accordance with rules made by the Government and on payment of such duties as may be prescribed in those rules.
9. You shall deliver, upon the requisition of an officer of the Government, any criminal who takes refuge in the territory of Möng Mit. You shall aid officers of the Government who pursue criminals into the said territory; and in the event of offenders from the said territory taking refuge in any place beyond the limits of that territory, you shall make representations of the matter to the authorities concerned.
10. You shall not exercise criminal jurisdiction over any European or American. In the event of any criminal charge being brought against any such person, you shall make representations of the matter to the Superintendent.

SOURCE: *The Shan State Manual*, 1925.

14

Sanad Granted to the *Sawbwa* of Singkaling Hkamti

Whereas the State of Singkaling Hkamti was formerly a petty subject to the King of Burma, and the Governor-General of India in Council has now been pleased to recognize you as *Sawbwa* of Singkaling Hkamti, and, subject to the provision of any law for the time being in force to permit you to administer the territory of Singkaling Hkamti in all matters, whether civil, criminal, or revenue, and at any time to nominate for the approval of the Chief Commissioner a fit person according to Shan usage to be your successor in the *Sawbwa* ship.

Paragraph 2. The Chief Commissioner of Burma, with the approval of the Governor-General of India in Council, hereby prescribes the following conditions under which your nomination as *Sawbwa* of Singkaling Hkamti is made. Should you fail to comply with any of these conditions, you shall be liable to have your powers as *Sawbwa* of Singkaling Hkamti rescinded.

Paragraph 3. The conditions are as follows:

1. You shall pay regularly the tribute of Rs. one hundred a year now fixed for five years, that is to say, from the 1st April 1892 to the 30th March 1897, and the said tribute shall be liable to revision at the expiration of the said term, or at any time thereafter that the Chief Commissioner of Burma may think fit.
2. The Government reserves to itself the proprietary right in all forests, mines, and minerals. If you are permitted to work or to let on lease any forest or forests in your State, you shall pay such sums for rent or royalty as the Local Government may from time to time direct; and in the working of such forests you shall be guided by such rules and orders as the Government of India may from time to time prescribe. If you are permitted to work or let on lease any mine or mines in your State, you shall pay such royalty on all metals, precious stones, and other minerals produced in Singkaling Hkamti as the Governor-General in Council may from time to time direct.
3. You shall administer the territory of Singkaling Hkamti according to the custom of the country, and in all matters subject to the guidance of the Deputy Commissioner, Upper Chindwin, you shall recognize the rights of the people and continue them in the same; and on no account shall you oppress them or suffer them in any way to be oppressed.
4. You shall maintain order within the territory of Singkaling Hkamti and keep open the trade routes within that territory. Should traders or caravans be attacked within the boundaries of the said territory, you shall pay such compensation as the Deputy Commissioner, Upper Chindwin, may fix.

5. You shall, if the Deputy Commissioner, Upper Chindwin, so desires, keep an agent, who shall reside at the headquarters of the Deputy Commissioner, and who shall keep him informed of the condition of the territory of Singkaling Hkamti.
6. In case of a dispute arising connected with any other States, you shall submit the matter to the Deputy Commissioner, Upper Chindwin, and abide by his decision. Should any inhabitants of Singkaling Hkamti commit raids on any place outside the limits of Singkaling Hkamti, you shall pay such compensation as the Deputy Commissioner, Upper Chindwin, may fix.
7. If the Government wishes at any time to make railways through the territory of Singkaling Hkamti, you shall provide land for the purpose free of cost, except that of the compensation adjudged to the actual occupiers of occupied land, and shall help the Government as much as possible.
8. Opium, spirits, or fermented liquor, and other articles which are liable to duties of customs or excise when imported by sea into Lower Burma, or when produced in any part of Upper Burma to which the Regulations of the Governor-General of India in Council apply, shall not be brought from Singkaling Hkamti into Lower Burma, or into any such part as aforesaid of Upper Burma, except in accordance with rules made by the Government and on payment of such duties as may be prescribed in those rules.
9. You shall deliver, upon the requisition of an officer of the Government, any criminal who takes refuge in the territory of Singkaling Hkamti. You shall aid officers of the Government who pursue criminals into the said territory; and in the event of offenders from the said territory taking refuge in any place beyond the limits of that territory, you shall make representations of the matter to the authorities concerned.
10. You shall not exercise criminal jurisdiction over any European or American. In the event of any criminal charge being brought against any such person, you shall make representations of the matter to the Deputy Commissioner, Upper Chindwin.

SOURCE: *The Shan State Manual*, 1925.

15

Sanad Granted to Sao Hpa Hkan of Lokkun in Hkamti, 1915

Sanad granted by the Lieutenant-Governor of Burma

TO SAO HPA HKAN OF LOKKUN IN HKĀMTI

WHEREAS by a *Sanad* dated the 10th day of November 1911 Sao Nwe Ai of Lokkun in Hkāmti was recognized by the Governor-General in Council as *Sawbwa* of Lokkun in Hkāmti AND WHEREAS the said Sao Nwe Ai died on the 8th November 1914, AND WHEREAS you, Sao Hpa Hkan, have been selected to be the successor of the said Sao Nwe Ai as *Sawbwa* of Lokkun in Hkāmti, the Lieutenant-Governor of Burma is hereby pleased to recognize you as *Sawbwa* of Lokkun in Hkāmti.

RANGOON:
Dated the [illegible] *August 1915.*

Lieutenant-Governor of Burma.

16

List of Shan and Karenni States during the British Regime (with classical names where available)

In order of precedence of state rulers

States	Classical names
I. *Sawbwa*	
1. Kēng Tūng	Khemarata Tungaburi
2. Hsi Paw	Dutawadi
3. Mōng Nai	Saturambha or Nandapwa
4. Yawng Hwe	Kambawsarata
5. Tawng Peng	Pappatasara
6. South Hsen Wi	Siwirata or Kawsampi
7. North Hsen Wi	"
8. Mōng Mit	Gandhalarata
9. Mōng Pai	
10. Lawk Sawk	
11. Lai Hka	Hansawadi
12. Mawk Mai	Lawkawadi
13. Mōng Pan	Dhannawadi
14. Mōng Pawn	Rajjawadi
15. Mang Lun	Jambularata
16. Kantarawadi	
17. Samkā	
18. Mōng Kung	Lankawadi
II. *Myosa*	
19. Nawng Wawn	Pokkharawadi
20. Mōng Nawng	Nandawadi
21. Mōng Sit	Amalgamated with 12
22. Kehsi Mān-sām	
23. Maw Nāng	Amalgamated with 34
24. Loi Lōng	
25. Hsa Htung	
26. Wan Yin	
27. Ho Pong	
28. Nam Hkôk	
29. Sakôi	
30. Mōng Hsu	Hansawadi
31. Keng Lun	Amalgamated with 22
32. Bawlakè	

33. Kyètbogyi	
34. Hsa Mōng Hkam	
35. Maw	
36. Pwèhla	
III. *Ngwegunhmu*	
37. Ye Ngan	
38. Pāngtara	
39. Pang Mi	
40. Loi-ai	Amalgamated with 34
41. Kyauk Ku	Amalgamated with 10
42. Loi Maw	Amalgamated with 4
43. Kyone	
44. Nam Tok	Amalgamated with 9[1]

1. Being compiled

SOURCE: *The Shan State Manual*, 1925, 220, app. 2.

17

Memorandum of the Federated Shan States

Issued September 1930, prior to the London Roundtable Conference

Introductory Letter

To the Right Honorable Wedgwood Benn, DSO, DFC, MP,
H.M. Secretary of State for India

Sir,

We have the honor formally to report our presence in England as representatives from the Federated Shan States.

We had intended to ask you to grant us an interview informally to discuss the position of the Shan States and their Chiefs, but as we feel that we should not, perhaps, be capable of expressing our aims as clearly as we could wish at an interview, we venture to ask you to consider this memorandum.

It is not to be deemed in any way as a memorandum which would have reached you through the proper channels, but simply as a short note of the feeling and aspirations of the Federated Shan States.

Memorandum

of the

FEDERATED SHAN STATES

by their Representatives

The Sawbwa of Mongmit State

and

The Sawbwa of Yawnghwe State

London, December, 1930

London:

[illegible], Ltd., Printers, Blackfriars Road, S.E.1

Cover of Memorandum of the Federated Shan States,
issued in Semtember 1930 in advance of the London Round-table Conference

Origin and Terms of our Appointment

At a meeting of the Chieftains held at the Council Hall, Taunggyi, on the 7th of September 1930, it was resolved, *inter alia,* (a) that the Government should be moved to allow two delegates to attend the roundtable conference to represent the interests of the Federated Shan States; (b) that in the event of the Government's declining our request for representation, two Chiefs should be delegated to attend at London during the period of the roundtable conference, so far as possible to watch over the interests of the States, and to seek an opportunity to lay before His Majesty's Government the aim and desires of the Chiefs. In accordance with these resolutions, telegrams were sent to H.E. the viceroy, H.E. the Governor of Burma, and the Right Honorable the Secretary of State for India. A reply from H.E. the viceroy, dated the 11th September 1930, regretted that it was not possible to include the names of the Federated Shan States' representatives among the delegates to the roundtable conference. A reply from H.E. the Governor of Burma, dated the 28th September 1930, informed the *Sawbwa* that, although they were unable to be represented at the conference, His Excellency, after full consideration, had no objection to the representatives proceeding to England, but that they should take no official action until the question of the separation of Burma had been settled.

The representatives chosen by the Council of Chiefs to present their views were the *Sawbwa* of Mong-Mit and the *Sawbwa* of Yawnghwe, who therefore arrived in England on the 26th October 1930.

Aim of the Representation

1. It is the aim of the present delegation, by the presentation of this memorandum, to draw the attention of His Majesty's Government to the whole position of the Federated Shan States. The Chiefs feel that the present moment is an opportune one to present their memorandum. They would have done so at an earlier date, but they felt that their loyalty to His Majesty's Government demanded their giving the fullest possible trial to the working of the Federation. They are disappointed by the fact that, far from having their powers and status gradually increase, they find themselves in a much worse position than they were in pre-Federation days. Their people still regard them as kings, the present administration deprives them of every right save in an advisory or consultative capacity, and the respect of their subjects is lessened thereby. The status of the Shan States was clearly set out in the speech of H.E. the marquis of Dufferin and Ava, the then viceroy, at a durbar at Government House, Rangoon, on the 24th February 1886. For this purpose it is desired, in a short historical summary, to review the history of the country; its rule, prior to the annexation of Upper Burma in 1886, and in the interregnum between annexation and the Federation of the 1st October 1922. It is wished to call attention to the manner in which the Federation came into being, and the anomalies of its present administration. After the presentation of this memorandum it may be found possible to have a personal interview to learn the views of H.M.'s Secretary of State for India.

2. To determine so far as may be possible at this juncture what the position of the Federated Shan States is likely to be in the event of the separation of Burma from India. This matter, the Chiefs feel, is one that intimately concerns them and that portion of Upper Burma which comprises their states, and on which they hold views that they feel should be considered simultaneously with the question of the separation of Burma. It was for this reason that the Chiefs primarily requested representation at the conference.

3. To review the present administration with particular reference to tariffs, customs, income tax, etc., and to discuss presently and urgently needed reforms suggested by the Chiefs as to legislative and executive powers; and to secure for all the several States a fair and proper share of their own portion of the mines and forests.

4. To draw attention to the reference to the Shan States on page 82 of vol. 1 of the Report of the Indian Statutory Commission. It is felt that the attitude of the *Sawbwa* has been misunderstood. The policy of the *Sawbwa* is distinctly progressive, and they feel that the designation of their States as "backward tracts"—while the term may be relative—rather conveys the wrong impression.

5. To present to the Government the ultimate aim and ideal of the Shan States to attain the dignity and status of an independent State under the Crown with the same constitution as the Indian States.

6. To discuss the revision of the *sanad* as they now appear in *The Shan State Manual* and to determine the status of the Chiefs. It is desired to recall the promise made to the Chiefs at various times by His Majesty's Government and its representatives, and to request the consideration of the restoration to the Shan rulers of their ancient rights, titles, and dignities.

7. In the event of the separation of Burma from India, to define the relationship of the Shan States to the paramount power, and the financial and economic relation between the Shan States, Burma, and India.

As representatives officially designated by our brother Chiefs to present the views of the rulers, we beg leave to hope that this memorandum may be granted the earnest consideration of His Majesty's Government.

We desire also to give expression to the absolute loyalty and devotion of the Chiefs of the Shan States to the throne and person of His Majesty the King-Emperor.

And we have the honor to be, sir,

Your Most Obedient Servants,
Sao Hkin Maung, Sawbwa of Mong-Mit State
Sao Shwe Thaike, Sawbwa of Yawnghwe State
Representatives of the Federated Shan States

Historical Summary

Preannexation

In preannexation days there was a marked difference between Burma Proper and that portion of Upper Burma known as the Shan States.

The history of the relationship between the two countries is too lengthy to enter into in detail, but it should be pointed out that in the vicissitudes of Burma's history, the State had at one time supremacy over Burma (notably between the 13th and 16th centuries of the era).

At the time of annexation, Burma had in some measure gained ascendancy over the Shan States (this was not till the reign of King Mindon), but they were never treated in the slightest degree as a territorial possession of Burma.

It is true that the Shan Chiefs made an annual present of gold and silver flowers to the Burmese kings—more in the nature of a gesture than anything else—and it was the custom of the Burmese rulers to return presents of equal or greater value to the Shan Chiefs. During this latter period the Chiefs of the Shan States still ranked as kings in their own right. Whereas the rulers of Burma were known as the Kings of the Rising Sun, the rulers of the Shan States were known as the Kings of the Setting Sun. This is a fact admitted by the surviving Burmese scholars of the Mandalay Palace. (See Harvey's *History of Burma*, page 270, and appendix 17.)

The right of the Shan Chiefs to rule their own State independent of Burmese control has never been questioned.

When Great Britain annexed Upper Burma, she had no intention of proceeding northward as far as the Shan States, had it not been for the then Yawnghwe *Sawbwa* at whose invitation Great Britain entered into the Shan country and absorbed it into the Empire. The attitude of the then rulers was entirely submissive, and there was no question of any conquest by force of arms.

Interregnum Period—Between Annexation and Federation

During the first negotiations with the *Sawbwa* after the annexation, Her Majesty's Government treated the Chiefs as sovereigns in their own right (*vide* Memorandum of Conference between the *Sawbwa* of Hsipaw, the Chief Commissioner of Burma, and the Chief Secretary, dated the 4th February 1887, appendix 7).

The question of treaty between Her Majesty's Government and the *Sawbwa* eventually resolved itself into the Shan States becoming incorporated in British India, whereby the *Sawbwa* became subjects of the Crown.

Federation era—1st October 1922

1. The constitution of the Federation was framed and complete before the Chiefs were formally consulted, and the Chiefs were compelled to assent to the new constitution at a single meeting at Taunggyi with His Honor, Sir Reginald Craddock, the then Lieutenant Governor of Burma.

The Chiefs of the Shan States accepted the new constitution as an experiment with every good will, expecting that the provisions would be enforced in a sympathetic spirit, and that their powers would be gradually increased.

But the Chiefs feel that a sympathetic interpretation of the present constitution is impossible while it be not administered by officers thoroughly acquainted with the customs of the Shan States. At present the Shan States are burdened with officers whose experience previous to their services in the Shan States has been spent in Burma or elsewhere, and who came to the States with preconceived ideas that render it difficult for them to appreciate our system of Government.

The appointment in recent years of officers unfamiliar with our ways has done much to make our relationship with our own people more difficult.

2. The Shan Chiefs' desire to define their attitude toward their relationship with a separate Burma. It is clear that their States have never been treated as essentially part of Burma. In a letter to the Chief Commissioner of Burma from the Secretary to the Government of India, Home Department, dated from Simla, the 16th August 1886, the Secretary acknowledged that the Shan States did not form part of the population under direct Burma rule (see appendix 14). In pre-Federation days tribute was always paid direct to the Government of India and not to the Government of Burma, and the administration of the two countries has been not only distinct but completely different. The Shan peoples are a race proud of their ancient independence, and with totally different characteristics from the Burmese.

The Shan States, however, would not object to a federal form of Government with Burma in the future constitution of Burma, if the following points are recognized and allowed: (a) that there will be no interference with the affairs of the individual States; (b) that their ancient rights, customs, religions, and privileges will remain unaltered unless and until modified by mutual consent; (c) that it will be more or less on the same lines as proposed in India between Indian States and British India; (d) that the hereditary rights of the Chiefs shall be acknowledged and safeguarded by the British Government.

In a speech delivered on the 24th February 1886, at a durbar held at Government House, Rangoon, the then viceroy (H.E. the marquis of Dufferin and Ava) made the following statement:

"I am very interested in the Shan nationality. Her Majesty's Government is most anxious to make you, and not only you, but all inhabitants of the Shan States, feel how desirous we are to gain their confidence, to cultivate their good will, and to do everything in our power to promote their trade and advance their general interests. You will be doing the Government a real service if you take any opportunity which you may have through your relations with the Shan States of making their rulers and the inhabitants of those States understand that the British Government is fully determined to respect their independence, to abstain from all interference with their internal affairs, and to maintain the same friendly relations which existed between them and the late Burmese Government." (page 169, Government publication of the speeches of H.E. the marquis of Dufferin and Ava, appendix 11.)

In asking for an independent status the Chiefs would like to draw attention to the position of the Karenni States which was recognized in 1875 as an independent State, and while their importance can in no way be compared with [that] of the Shan States, they have still preserved their independence (*vide* page 237 of *The Shan State Manual*, 1925).

It is desired to emphasize that the Shan States are and have always been part of British India and not of Burma.

3. The administration of the Federation as it stands leaves the Chiefs as merely titular and practically deprives them of all opportunities to govern their own States as through countless centuries they have governed, wisely and benevolently, for the happiness of their subjects and the good of the allied Shan States.

The Chiefs feel that with the advice and assistance of the political officers they have the capability, and should be given the opportunity, to govern their own States with wider powers than are at present given them.

The legislative and executive powers of the Chiefs under the present system are mainly purely nominal, and they feel that they should be allowed full freedom in civil and criminal administration and in matters appertaining to revenue. And in affairs generally they should be allowed to govern their States independently.

That their capacity fits them for doing so is proved by the satisfied condition of the people when the Chiefs had absolute power.

Under the present Federation, the council is purely a consultative and advisory body, and its resolutions are not binding. Under the proposed reforms, although the Chiefs should have full control in their own States, there shall be nevertheless a Central Council of the Chiefs with power to deal with all matters affecting the welfare and prosperity of the Shan States as a whole.

4. On page 82 of volume 1 of the Indian Statutory Commission it is stated that "the commission met a number of the principal *Sawbwa* from the Shan States, and they appeared to be very well contented with their present system of administration."

It is true that at that time the commission was informed that the *Sawbwa* were content with the system of administration, but they went on to point out that the actual administration left much to be desired, and presented a memorandum to the commission calling attention to the reforms they desired to be put into operation. No mention of the actual desires of the *Sawbwa* was made in the report of the commission.

The report goes on to say that the States and the people were "backward" and "the areas unfit to participate in a constitution on representative lines suitable for Burma Proper."

The Simon Commission did not visit the areas of which it speaks, and has no personal knowledge of the progressive state of the Shan country.

5. The ultimate ideal of the Federated Shan States is to acquire its own independence under the Crown. It has an important geographical position as a Buffer State; it is bounded on the north and northeast by China, on the east by French Indochina, and on the southeast by Siam. Its position, therefore, in the defense of the North-East Frontier

of Burma is strategically all-important. It has an area of about 56,000 square miles, and a population of about 1,500,000. It is a rapidly developing country with vast natural resources in mineral wealth and forests. Its rulers are enlightened and progressive, and anxious to develop their own states on modern lines. While the powers they have enjoyed from the very beginning of the Shan States' existence are curtailed by the operation of the Federation, their own efforts to improve the country are necessarily seriously restricted.

The restoration of wider powers to the Chiefs would operate to the benefit of the states and to the empire in the larger cultivation and development of the sources of the natural wealth, and in fitting the states to acquire the same measure of independence as the Indian States.

6. The Chiefs desire a revision of their own status. At the time of the incorporation of the Shan States into British India, the Chiefs lost many of their ancient dignities.

A letter from the Government of India to the Secretary of State for India, dated from Simla the 19th October 1886, and signed by the then viceroy and five other members of the Government, reiterated that the "rights and dignities of the Chieftainship" should be recognized, and likened the Shan *Sawbwa* to the native princes of India (appendix 15).

It was again promised in a speech by His Honor, the then Lieutenant Governor of Burma (Sir Reginald Craddock), at a durbar held at Taunggyi on the 22nd March 1920, that "the special powers, rights, and privileges which you [Shan Chiefs] have enjoyed in the past must be conserved for you in the future" (appendix 18).

The original designation of the *Sawbwa* was "maharajah *sawbwagyi*." That this was their ancient title there is no question (*vide* Sir J. G. Scott's *Gazetteer for Upper Burma and the Shan States*, and the Royal Patent Commands). It is requested that this title should be revived.

7. In the event of the separation of Burma from India under a new constitution, and the claim of the Shan States to be treated independently of Burma being successful, it is desired that our political relations with the paramount power be through H.E. the Governor of Burma or H.E. the viceroy of India, but not through the double channel.

8. On the economic relations of the Shan States with other States, it is requested that the Shan States should have the same powers in their external affairs as any other independent Indian State.

9. It is impossible to know what attitude Burma, in the event of separation, will adopt to the railways, posts, telegraphs, etc., the advantage of which the Shan States now enjoy. Owing, also, to the geographical position of the Shan States, it is possible that they may be called upon to defend the North-East Frontier of Burma.

Any question, therefore, of the Chieftains' rights to impose tariffs and customs must be reserved.

The Shan Chiefs claim also a share of such central revenue as receipts from customs, income tax, and others as may be allotted to Burma in future, such share to be calculated in proportion to the revenue, population of the States, and value of produce imported to the Shan States.

The Chiefs desire it to be understood that from time immemorial they have governed their States always for the good of their people, and all new schemes are first explained to their subjects, whose views are always earnestly and carefully considered. This has always been the custom of all the Shan Chiefs.

If the Chiefs attain the powers for which they ask, they wish to assure His Majesty's Government that they will govern their States with the same consideration they have always had for the opinion of their people and the welfare of their States.

10. The Chiefs desire that they be given the same privileges and status as the rulers of the States in India, as the same was promised to them in the various declarations quoted above.

11. The reforms suggested by the Chiefs in relation to internal affairs are as follows:

a. That unless a special high commissioner be appointed for the Shan States, H.E. the Governor of Burma should act as such, and be appointed chairman of the Council of the Chieftains in the same manner as H.E. the viceroy acts as chairman of the Chamber of Princes. The senior Chief should be elected vice-chairman, with power to act as chairman should the high commissioner for any reason be unable to attend.

b. Any matter of finance and assessments should be administered solely by the Chiefs without dictation by the British officers, but only assessments should be made that have regard for the welfare of the people.

c. At the present time the contributions to the Federation by the Shan Chiefs amount to 50 percent of their revenue, out of which the Federation pays for the Departments of Public Works, Education, Medical, and Agriculture, while the Chiefs are responsible for maintaining local administration, including the allowances of the Chiefs and their staffs.

   The Chiefs should contribute only 12½ percent of the revenues of the States, the average to be based on the revenue of the past five years, and the Chiefs should readjust the average at the expiry of every five years.

   The figure of 12½ percent is based on the 25 percent paid by the Chiefs before the days of the Federation. Out of that 25 percent, the Government invariably returned half of the sum (i.e. 25 percent paid by the Chiefs as tributes) to enable the Chiefs to administer the public works and generally to develop the country. The proposed contribution will be the same as in pre-Federation days.

d. As to the forests, mines, and minerals, the Chiefs claim that 50 percent of the revenue thereof should be granted to the respective States concerned as their share, and that 50 percent should be credited to the Federation for the upkeep of the establishment.

e. Lines of communication (e.g. roads and bridges), an important factor for the development of the States, should be left to the public works of the Federation, but civil building of an administrative nature, markets, courthouses, etc., should be left to the States themselves.

f. The Education Department would be administered as in pre-Federation days, i.e. control by individual States but under the supervision of the Federation Education Department.
g. The Medical and Public Health Department of each State should be within their own province of control and supervised by the Central Medical Federal Department, whose advice would be sought and suggestions carried out, particularly during epidemics.
h. On the question of agriculture within the State, this should be left to the Chiefs under technical supervision. The Chiefs are also prepared to conduct their own Veterinary Department.
i. As to the criminal jurisdiction, the procedure to be adopted should be specially considered, subject to the rights of the Chiefs being recognized.
j. As to the civil administration, it is proposed that no alteration should be made.
k. So far as the legislature is concerned, the same modification of the customary laws which are now in force should remain as it is, but so far as Local Regulations and bylaws are concerned, these should be in the absolute discretion of the Chiefs of the individual States.
l. Section (k) shall also apply to the Myelat States, which do not now enjoy the privilege of administering the customary laws.
m. The State budget shall be prepared by the Chiefs and be considered final.
n. The *sanad* at present in force in the Federated Shan States should be revised to conform with the alterations—both in tribute and in status—suggested in the memorandum.
o. Attention should be drawn to the fact that under paragraph 9 of the prefatory note to *The Shan State Manual*, in the case of those Chiefs entitled to a salute, the right of succession is recognized by the viceroy of India, and the Governor of Burma has no jurisdiction. In the event of the separation of Burma from India, all Chiefs will require a definition of their rights as regarded succession which will not be derogatory to their status.

SOURCE: *Memorandum of the Federated Shan States*, 1930.

18

The Military Administration Order, No. 3. Order of the Military Administration Concerning the Establishment of the Shan States Administration Office

(Gunseimei Dai San-go, Shanshū Seichō Kaisetsu ni Kansuru Gunseikan Meirei)

Issued by the Superintendent of the Military Administration, November 14, 1942

I. The Shan States Administration Office shall be established on November 25, 1942.

II. The organization and jurisdiction of the Shan States Administration Office are as described in a separate document, "Organizational Regulations for the Shan States Administration Office."

III. The high commissioner shall execute military administration in accordance with the "Governing Principle for the Occupied Areas Under the Hayashi Army Group" and the following summary. He shall also take over the military administration from the corps commander—Kiku, Tatsu, and Tate Corps—in their respective jurisdictional territories.

- a. In executing military administration in the Shan States, simple and plain measures shall be taken and the existing traditional method shall be adopted. Especially in administering the territories under the control of the Shan minor chiefs, the existing system, for the time being, shall be utilized. Efforts must be made to avoid interfering in matters concerning local administration and to win popular support in order to facilitate the execution of a successful military administration.
- b. Regarding industry, special measures must be taken to expedite the exploitation of essential resources in order to establish a self-supporting foundation of the Greater East Asia Sphere.
- c. Priority policy shall be adopted in administering financial affairs and special efforts must be made to secure a firm financial foundation.
- d. It is essential to improve the welfare of the people by promptly taking preventive measures against epidemics.

Separate Document: "Organizational Regulations for the Shan States Administration Office"

- a. The Shan States Administration Office shall be established at Taunggyi.
- b. The army group commander and the superintendent of the military administration shall have direct control over the following matters:
    1. public relations;
    2. appointment and dismissal of chiefs;
    3. currency, banking, and taxation;
    4. railroad and aviation;
    5. developing sources of electric power;

6. telegraphic communication;
7. the management of Bawdwin and Mawchi mines;
8. personnel affairs.

c. There shall be a high commissioner in the Shan States Administration Office. The high commissioner shall, under the order of the superintendent of the military administration, carry out military administration within his jurisdiction. But he shall obtain approval from the superintendent in administering the following matters:
   1. financial planning;
   2. exploiting essential resources;
   3. postal services;
   4. disposal of enemy properties;
   5. whenever important changes in the existing administrative method are made;
   6. other matters deemed important.

d. Under the Shan States Administration Office, the high commissioner's office, and the following departments with their respective chiefs and necessary personnel shall be established:
   General Affairs Department;
   Domestic Affairs Department;
   Police Department;
   Economics Department;
   Transportation Department.
   The department head shall, under the order of the high commissioner, assume the responsibility for departmental duties.

[e. Omitted by the translator.]

f. The Superintendent Department, with a chief and necessary personnel, shall be established under the Shan States Administration Office. The chief of the Superintendent Department shall, on the order of the high commissioner, direct superintendents under his command, and guide and supervise the rule of the Shan Chiefs.

g. A Court of Justice, with a chief justice and necessary personnel, shall be established under the Shan States Administration Office. The Court of Justice shall have final jurisdiction over cases tried by the chief or mayor of the municipality under the direct control of the high commissioner. The chief justice shall, on order of the high commissioner, administer judicial matters in general and supervise the judicial administration of mayors.

h. There shall be a mayor in the municipality under the direct control of the high commissioner. The mayor shall, on the order of the high commissioner, administer municipal affairs. The mayor shall administer judicial matters for municipal residents.

i. There shall be a Shan Chiefs' Council under the Shan States Administration Office.

[j. Omitted by the translator.]

SOURCE: Frank N. Trager, ed., *Burma: Japanese Military Administration, Selected Documents, 1941–1945*, 203–205. Reprinted with permission of the University of Pennsylvania Press.

19

Governing Principle for Enforcing the Military Administration in the Shan States
(Shanshū Gunsei Jisshi Yōkō)

Issued by the Deputy High Commissioner, the Shan States Administration Office,
November 25, 1942

I. General Principles

a. The Shan States Administration Office shall be established at Taunggyi in order to execute military administration in the Shan States. The Shan States Administration Office shall be under the direct control of the superintendent of the military administration in Burma.

b. The Shan States Administration Office shall have jurisdiction over the old Federated Shan States (for the time being, the territories east of the Salween River shall be excluded) and Karenni States. The above states shall be simply called "the Shan States."

c. Military administration of the Shan States shall be executed in accordance with the "Governing Principles of the Occupied Areas Under the Hayashi Army Group."

II. Military Administrative Organ And Its Jurisdiction

d. The Shan States Administration Office shall consist mainly of Japanese officials and shall carry out a sound military administration. At lower level organizations in local areas Japanese officials shall be posted in positions of leadership. For all other positions natives shall be posted.

e. Military administration authorities in local areas shall utilize the authority of chiefs and their ruling mechanism to the utmost in order to reduce the burden of the army group and to achieve the objectives of the military administration. Regarding the rule of chiefs, presuppose that there will be reforms in the future. Any magnification of the chief's authority should be discouraged and reasonably regulated.

f. The army group commander and the superintendent of the military administration shall have direct control over the following:

1. Matters concerning public relations;
2. Appointment and dismissal of chiefs;
3. Currency, banking, credit systems, and taxation;
4. Railroad and aviation;
5. Developing sources of electric power;
6. Telegraphic communication;
7. Management of Baldwin and Mawchi mines;
8. Matters concerning personnel affairs.

g. The high commissioner shall, on the order of the superintendent of the military administration, carry out military administration within his jurisdiction. But he shall obtain approval from the superintendent of the military administration in administering the following:
    1. Matters concerning financial planning;
    2. Exploiting essential resources;
    3. Postal service;
    4. Disposition of enemy properties;
    5. Whenever important changes in the existing administrative method are made;
    6. Other matters deemed important.

h. Regarding defense of the area, the high commissioner shall be under the direction of the corps commander of the respective jurisdictional areas.

III. Governing Principle For Enforcing The Military Administration

i. . . . natives of the states must be guided so as not to let them lose their hopes for the future.

j. In executing military administration in the Shan States, simple and direct measures shall be taken and existing traditional methods shall be adopted. Efforts must be made to avoid interfering in minor matters concerning local administration except when there is a matter of exceptional unreasonableness or a matter which is disadvantageous or detrimental to achieving the objective of the military administration.

k. Special consideration shall be given to the capabilities of the ruling chiefs. Chiefs shall be given guidance and the existing superintendent system shall be strengthened in order to achieve efficiency within the military administration.

l. When employing natives for the military administration organization, first preference shall be given to Burmese. Strenuous efforts must be made to avoid employing Indians, but if employment of Indians is inevitable, the number must be held to a minimum.

m. In maintaining public peace and order, the existing police system shall be utilized and strengthened. For the time being a native army shall not be organized for maintaining peace and order.

n. The existing judicial system shall be utilized. The chief justice shall have final jurisdiction over cases tried by the chief, the mayor of the municipality under the direct control of the high commissioner, and the superintendent. But the judicial power of the chief shall not prevail over Japanese and their corporate bodies. Trials of Japanese and their corporate bodies shall be in accordance with regulations decided upon by the army group commander.

o. Priority policy shall be adopted in administering financial affairs and special efforts must be made to secure a firm financial foundation.

p. Regarding education, a plan must be made to spread the Japanese language. Major emphasis of education shall be placed on primary and technological educations.

[q. Omitted by the translator]

r. It is essential to improve the welfare of the people by promptly taking preventive measures against epidemics.

s. With regard to industry, special measures must be taken to expedite the exploitation of essential resources in order to establish a foundation of self-sufficiency for Greater East Asia. Furthermore, measures for maintaining a fair balance of supply and demand of resources shall be established and thorough and unified resource research shall be undertaken.

t. Land transportation shall be promptly completed in order to facilitate the maintenance of public peace and order and the procurement and distribution of resources.

SOURCE: Frank N. Trager, ed., *Burma: Japanese Military Administration, Selected Documents, 1941–1945*, 203–205. Reprinted with permission of the University of Pennsylvania Press.

20

Regulation of Duties in the Shan States Administration Office

(Shanshū Seichō Fukumu Kitei)

Issued by the Deputy High Commissioner, the Shan States Administration Office, November 25, 1942

ARTICLE I The present regulation shall describe detailed duties of the Shan States Administration Office.

ARTICLE II There shall be a high commissioner in the Shan States Administration Office. The high commissioner shall under the order of the superintendent of the military administration administer the Shan States.

ARTICLE III The high commissioner's office and the following six departments shall be established in the Shan States Administration Office:

General Affairs Department;
Domestic Affairs Department;
Police Department;
Economics Department;
Transportation Department;
Superintendent's Department.

Duty regulations of the high commissioner's office and departments shall be in accordance with departmental regulations of the Shan States Administration Office.

ARTICLE IV The chief secretary of the high commissioner's office and the department chiefs shall, under the orders of the high commissioner, control the high commissioner's office and their respective departments.

ARTICLE V Civil officials of higher rank who are attached to the high commissioner's office and departments shall, under the order of the chief of the high commissioner's office and departmental chief, carry out their respective duties.

ARTICLE VI Civil officials of junior rank and below, attached to the high commissioner's office and departments, shall, under the order of their superiors, carry out their respective duties.

ARTICLE VII A court of justice shall be established in the Shan States Administration Office. The chief justice shall, under the order of the high commissioner, control the judicial administrative duties in the Shan States.

ARTICLE VIII There shall be a mayor in the municipality under the direct control of the Shan States Administration Office. The mayor shall, under the order fo the high commissioner, administer municipal affairs. The mayor shall, under the order of the chief justice, administer judicial matters under his jurisdiction.

ARTICLE IX In order to supervise the rule of the chiefs, there shall be head superintendents, superintendents, and assistant superintendents. There shall be one Head Superintendent in the Northern Shan States, Southern Shan States, and Karenni States, who shall carry out supervisory duties in his jurisdictional region. Superintendents shall, under the order of the Head Superintendents, carry out their respective duties. Assistant Superintendents shall, under the order of the Superintendent, carry out their respective duties.

ARTICLE X There shall be a Shan Chiefs' Council under the Shan States Administration Office. The Shan Chiefs' Council shall be a channel through which the government delivers its instructions to the people and the people's appeal to the government.

ARTICLE XI If necessary, the Shan States Administration Office may employ nonregular members of its staff. The treatment of the nonregular members shall be the same as that of civil officials.

ARTICLE XII The high commissioner may establish duty regulations. But he shall report the established duty regulations to the superintendent of the military administration.

SOURCE: Frank N. Trager, ed., *Burma: Japanese Military Administration, Selected Documents, 1941–1945*, 203–205. Reprinted with permission of the University of Pennsylvania Press.

21

Departmental Regulation for the Shan States Administration Office

(Shanshū Seichō Bunka Kitei)

Issued by the Deputy High Commissioner, Shan States Administration Office, November 25, 1942

ARTICLE I The present regulations shall describe departmental regulations for the Shan States Administration Office.

ARTICLE II The chief secretary of the high commissioner's office shall administer the following affairs:

1. Matters concerning planning and execution of policies in accordance with the basic policy of the military administration;
2. The disposal of enemy properties;
3. Departmental coordination;
4. Important questions concerning public relations.

ARTICLE III The General Affairs Department shall administer the following:

General Affairs Bureau

1. Matters concerning personnel and services of civil and military officials;
2. The receiving, dispatching, arranging, and preserving of documents;
3. The safekeeping of classified documents and general books;
4. Compilation of the battle journal and history pertaining to the military administration;
5. Safekeeping of seals of the Shan States Administration Office;
6. Counterespionage within the Shan States Administration Office, air defense, and precautions against disasters;
7. Control of the Shan States Administration Office;
8. Reporting of the conduct of personnel as regards their duties in the Shan States Administration Office;
9. Quartering and supplying;
10. Matters that are not managed by other departments and bureaus;
11. Other general affairs.

Investigation Bureau

1. Matters concerning the mobilization of resources and industrial labor;
2. Propaganda and intelligence;

3. The collection, arrangement, and preservation of various kinds of materials;
4. Statistical matters.

Accounting Bureau
1. Matters concerning accounts and payments;
2. Personnel.

ARTICLE IV A Domestic Affairs Department shall administer the following:

Financial Bureau
1. Matters concerning budget;
2. Taxes;
3. Monopolies and other publicly operated businesses;
4. Matters concerning currency policy;
5. The regulation of capital, credit, and banking organizations;
6. Bonds and other securities.

Education Bureau
1. Matters concerning the status and duties of teachers;
2. Diffusion of the Japanese language;
3. Regulation of educational systems and the training of teaching staff;
4. Religion;
5. Questions concerning social and cultural policies.

Sanitation Bureau
1. Matters concerning basic measures for prevention of epidemics;
2. The prevention of epidemics and malaria;
3. Medical establishments;
4. The training of doctors, sanitation supervisors, and nurses;
5. Questions concerning the preservation of health and sanitation.

ARTICLE V The Police Department shall administer the following:

Police Affairs Bureau
1. Matters concerning the establishment of protective measures for police organizations;
2. The status and duties of police officials;
3. The training of police officials;
4. Supervision and direction of police in Chiefs' domains;
5. Personnel consultation;
6. The protection and guidance of released convicts;
7. Questions concerning organization, supervision, and direction of the Vigilance Corps.

Public Peace Bureau
1. Matters concerning crime prevention, search and seize, and criminal arrest;
2. Ideological control of speech, published works, and related material;
3. Protection of Japanese residents and control of foreigners;
4. Control of businesses;
5. Control of transportation;
6. Air defense and disaster prevention;
7. Control of guns, gunpowder, and other dangerous objects;
8. The control of factories, mines, and workshops.

ARTICLE VI The Economics Department shall administer the following:

Mining Bureau
1. Matters concerning the planning and management of mining;
2. The investigation and exploitation of mineral resources;
3. Direction and supervision of mining proprietors;
4. The investigation and development of electric power resources.

Commerce and Industrial Bureau
1. Matters concerning the planning and execution of commercial and industrial policies;
2. The direction and supervision of entrepreneurs and commercial organizations;
3. Price control;
4. The regulation of supply and demand of resources.

Forestry Bureau
1. Matters concerning the improvement and increase of forestry products;
2. Forestation;
3. The direction and supervision of forestry organizations.

Agriculture Bureau
1. Matters concerning the direction, promotion, and processing of agricultural products;
2. The direction and supervision of agricultural organizations;
3. Direction and promotion of stockbreeding.

ARTICLE VII The Transportation Department shall administer the following:

Land Transportation Bureau

1. Matters concerning the management and supervision of the land transportation system;
2. The guarding of the land transportation system.

Postal Service Bureau

1. Matters concerning postal service in general;
2. Telegraph, telephone, and other communications establishments.

Public Works Bureau

1. Matters concerning improvement of roads and rivers;
2. Construction of public works;
3. Waterworks and sewerage systems.

ARTICLE VIII The Superintendent Department shall administer the following:

1. Questions concerning liaison and control of regional administration;
2. Direction and supervision of administrations within the municipality under direct control (of the high commissioner);
3. Direction and supervision of chiefs and administrations;
4. The Shan Chiefs' Council.

ARTICLE IX Regulations for the court of justice and municipality under direct control (of the high commissioner) shall be established by the chief justice and mayor, respectively. These regulations shall be sent to the high commissioner (for approval).

ARTICLE X. Duty regulations for superintendents shall be established by the chiefof the superintendent department and the head superintendent. These duty regulations shall be sent to the high commissioner (for approval).

SOURCE: Frank N. Trager, ed., *Burma: Japanese Military Administration, Selected Documents, 1941–1945*, 203–205. Reprinted with permission of the University of Pennsylvania Press.

22

Detailed Duty Regulations for Superintendents
(Kantokukan Fukumu Saisoku)

ARTICLE I The following duty regulations shall describe detailed duties of superintendents (including assistant superintendents) in the Shan States.

ARTICLE II The main aim of the superintendents shall be to see that the major purport of the Hayashi Army Group commander's "Proclamation to the Shan States," issued on June 4, 1942, be realized.

ARTICLE III In supervising, the superintendent shall first establish a plan and then obtain approval from the chief of the Superintendent's Department.

ARTICLE IV The superintendent may if necessary demand of the chiefs the submission of relevant documentary evidence and objects. He may also, while carrying out his duties, investigate related questions.

ARTICLE V When the superintendent dispatches instructions or memorandums pertaining to questions which demand special attention he shall make two copies, of which he shall keep one and send the other to the chief concerned. The superintendent shall request reports from the Chiefs concerning the disposal of related matters.

ARTICLE VI Whenever there are questions demanding special attention or when exceptional cases arise, the superintendent shall execute the matter according to the directions of the high commissioner of the Shan States via the chief of the Superintendent's Department. If there is an emergency case demanding instant disposal, the superintendent shall report directly to the high commissioner in order to receive proper directions as concerns that matter.

ARTICLE VII Whenever an urgent situation develops in his jurisdiction, the superintendent shall promptly report a summary of the situation to the high commissioner of the Shan States. In reporting the above matters, he will keep close contact with other official organs.

ARTICLE VIII The duty of the superintendent shall consist in making a report on the tenth of every month to the chief of the Superintendent's Department. The report shall consist of the following;

1. Questions concerning the dispatching and absence of officials and other matters relating to their duties;
2. Details for receiving important visitors and interviews with them;
3. Disasters and other unforeseen events;
4. Other matters deemed important.

SOURCE: Frank N. Trager, ed., *Burma: Japanese Military Administration, Selected Documents, 1941–1945*, 203–205. Reprinted with permission of the University of Pennsylvania Press.

23

Judicial Ordinance for the Shan States

(Shanshū Saibanrei)

Issued by the Commander of the Mori Army Group, July 7, 1943

ARTICLE I Jurisdictions for the Shan States Courts and the Shan Chiefs: The Shan States court shall have jurisdiction over both civil and criminal cases and noncontentious cases in the Shan States and the Karenni States except as in the following clauses 1 and 2. The chiefs' courts shall have jurisdiction over both civil and criminal cases and noncontentious cases in the Shan and the Karenni States except all clauses stated below:

1. Cases triable by the general court-martial of the Japanese Imperial Forces;
2. Cases triable by the special court-martial of the Japanese Imperial Forces;
3. Civil cases between Japanese subjects (or Japanese corporate bodies), or between Japanese subjects and non-Japanese subjects;
4. Criminal cases in which Japanese subjects are accused of criminal offenses.

ARTICLE II The Establishment, Abolition, Judicial Territory, and Types of Shan States Court:

The Shan States court shall be divided into two types: the Court of First Instance and the High Court. The establishment, abolition, and judicial territory shall be determined by the high commissioner of the Shan States. [He] may establish a High Court branch in order that it may carry a portion of the judicial matters dealt with by the High Court.

ARTICLE III Court of First Instance:

The Court of First Instance shall have, except for matters under the jurisdiction of the High Court, jurisdiction over the first hearing on both civil and criminal cases. It shall, moreover, deal with noncontentious cases. There shall be a judge and elders in the Court of First instance. The judge may pass judgment on any noncontentious case and civil case, without any limitation on the value of the involved claims. The elders may have jurisdiction over any civil case where the claim value is less than 100 rupees. The judge shall have jurisdiction over criminal cases, but the extent of his jurisdiction shall be designated by the high commissioner of the Shan States.

ARTICLE IV High Court:
The High Court shall review the judgments of the Court of First Instance and the chiefs' courts. The High Court shall also have final jurisdiction over cases. The High Court shall have jurisdiction over the first and second trials of the types of cases stated in clauses 3 and 4, article I. There shall be judges and a chief justice in the High Court and the chief justice shall be selected from among the judges in the High Court.

ARTICLE V The Single Judge System:
A single judge shall administer justice in the Shan States court.

ARTICLE VI Court Clerks:
There shall be court clerks in the courts. There shall be a chief clerk in the High Court who shall be selected from among the clerks in the High Court.

ARTICLE VII The Right of Criminal Investigation for the chief justice of the High Court, senior judge of the branch court of the High Court, and the head superintendents and superintendents.
The chief justice of the High Court, the senior judge of the branch court of the High Court, head superintendent, and the superintendent in their respective areas shall be regarded as district criminal judges according to the Code of Criminal Procedure.

ARTICLE VIII Enforcement and Supervision of the Judicial Administration: Judicial administration shall be supervised according to the following rules:
1. The high commissioner of the Shan States shall supervise the Shan States courts and the chief's courts;
2. The chief justice of the High Court shall supervise the High Court, branch courts of the High Court, and all other inferior judicial organs;
3. The senior judge of the branch court of the High Court shall supervise the respective branch courts and all lower courts under his jurisdiction;
4. The senior judge of the Court of First Instance shall supervise the court staff under his jurisdiction.

ARTICLE IX The Application of Japanese Codes:
Japanese codes shall be used as much as possible in the trial of cases stated in clause 2, article 4. But as far as legal procedure is concerned, discretionary measures shall be taken.

ARTICLE X Adoption of the Existing Judicial Codes:
All customary laws and the existing judicial codes stated in article 4 of the Military Ordinance No. 6, "Matters Concerning the Provisional Measures of the Judiciary System," July 7, 1942, shall be regarded as being revised so far as they conflict with the provisions of the present ordinance.

ARTICLE XI Effective Date:
The effective date for the present ordinance shall be determined by the high commissioner of the Shan States.

ARTICLE XII Enforcing Areas:
The present ordinance shall be enforced in both Shan and Karenni States.

ARTICLE XIII The Abolishment of the Mayor's Courts:
The mayor's courts existing before the enforcement of the present ordinance shall be abolished as follows:

Mayor's courts in Taunggyi, Lashio, Kalaw, Loilem, and Mawchi. All cases under trial by the mayor's courts before the enforcement of the present ordinance shall be transmitted as they are to the Courts of First Instance in their respective jurisdictions. The decisions already passed down by the mayor's courts shall be regarded as being passed by the Courts of First Instance in their respective jurisdictions.

ARTICLE XIV The Abolishment of the Existing Shan States Court:
The Shan States Court existing before the enforcement of the court stated in the above clause shall be, in accordance with the nature of the cases, transmitted as they are to the High Court and the Courts of First Instance in their respective jurisdictions. The decisions already passed down by the existing states courts shall be regarded as being passed either by the High Court or by the Courts of First Instance in their respective jurisdictions.

ARTICLE XV Matters Essential for Enforcement:
The matters essential for enforcing the present ordinance shall be determined by the high commissioner of the Shan States.

SOURCE: Frank N. Trager, ed., *Burma: Japanese Military Administration, Selected Documents, 1941–1945*, 203–205. Reprinted with permission of the University of Pennsylvania Press.

24

On the Question of the Reversion of the Shan States

(Nihonkoku Birumakoku Kan Dōmei Jōyaku Teiketsu No Ken Shinsa Iinkai)

Held at Imperial Palace, July 29, 1943

Meeting of the Deliberative Committee on the Conclusion of a Treaty of Alliance Between Japan and Burma.

Meeting held at Imperial Palace on July 29, 1943.

Committee chairman: Suzuki
Committee members: Tojo, Prime Minister and Army Minister
Shimada, Navy Minister
Ando, Home Minister
Aoki, Greater East Asia Minister
Shigemitsu, Foreign Minister; and others

[On the question of the reversion of the Shan States]

When this question was raised, Hideki Tojo, the prime minister, replied that he was considering the concession of some parts of the Shan States to Thailand and the remaining Shan States to Burma in the future, in order to encourage Thailand and Burma to cooperate closely with Japan in prosecuting the war (p. 13).

On the reversion of the Shan States to Thailand, Minami Jirō, a member of the committee, raised the question whether the territory in question would be the territory east of the Salween River. In reply to this question, Hideki Tojo, the prime minister, stated that since many Chief's domains were located on both sides of the Salween River and he did not wish to divide those domains, he was considering assigning Kengtung and Mongpan States to Thailand and the remaining Shan States to Burma at the appropriate time.

SOURCE: Frank N. Trager, ed., *Burma: Japanese Military Administration, Selected Documents, 1941–1945*, 203–205. Reprinted with permission of the University of Pennsylvania Press.

25

Meeting of the Deliberative Committee on the Conclusion of a Treaty between Japan and Thailand Concerning the Territories of the Thai Government in the Malay and Shan Regions

(Marai Oyobi Shan Chihō Ni Okeru Taikoku No Ryōdo Ni Kansuru Nihonkoku Taikoku Kan Joyaku Teiketsu no Ken Shinsa Iinkai)

Held at Imperial Palace, August 18, 1943

Members present at the meeting:
- Hara, president of the Privy Council
- Suzuki, vice president of the Privy Council, and the committee chairman
- Tojo, prime minister and army minister
- Aoki, Greater East Asia minister
- Shigemitsu, foreign minister; and others

Mr. Shimizu, a member of the committee, asked whether Burma was dissatisfied with the Japanese approval of Thailand's annexation of the two Shan States, . . . In reply to this question, Premier Tojo related the circumstances when he had made the proposal (p. 2) during his interview with Ba Maw at Singapore and Phibun at Bangkok during his trip south. He stated that although Ba Maw had shown no sign of dissatisfaction with Thailand's annexation of the two Shan States, uneasiness might be entertained by the natives, and that therefore both should be left to be considered in Japan's future policies.

SOURCE: Frank N. Trager, ed., *Burma: Japanese Military Administration, Selected Documents, 1941–1945*, 203–205. Reprinted with permission of the University of Pennsylvania Press.

26

Treaty between Japan and Thailand Drafted by the Plenary Session Minutes of the Plenary Session on the Conclusion of the Treaty Regarding the Territories of the Thai Government in the Malay and Shan Regions

(Marai Oyobi Shan Chihō Ni Okeiu Taikoku No Ryōdo Ni Kansuru Nihonkoku Taikikukan Jōyaku Teikestsu no Ken)

Held at Imperial Palace, August 18, 1943

Members present at the meeting:
Hara, president of the Privy Council
Suzuki, vice president of the Privy Council
State ministers:
Tojo, prime minister and army minister
Aoki, Greater East Asia minister
Shigemitsu, foreign minister; and others

The following is the text of the treaty between Japan and Thailand drafted by the plenary session:

ARTICLE I The Japanese government agrees to recognize the annexation by the Thai government of the Kelantan, Trengganu, Kedah, Perlis States and their attached islands.

ARTICLE II The Japanese government agrees to recognize the annexation by the Thai government of the Kengtung and Mongpan of the Shan region.

ARTICLE III The Japanese government agrees to terminate its administration, now being executed over the above areas, within sixty days after this treaty takes effect.

ARTICLE IV The boundaries of the areas stated above in articles 1 and 2 shall be based on the boundaries that exist as of the date of this treaty.

ARTICLE V Detailed matters essential for enforcing this treaty shall be negotiated anddecided upon by the respective authorities of the two governments.

ARTICLE VI This treaty shall take effect on the date of signature.
In witness thereof, the following representatives of the respective governments have signed this agreement. The two copies of this document

have been drawn up in the Japanese and Thai language on [the date of signature].

SOURCE: Frank N. Trager, ed., *Burma: Japanese Military Administration, Selected Documents, 1941–1945*, 203–205. Reprinted with permission of the University of Pennsylvania Press.

27

Minutes of the Plenary Session on the Conclusion of the Treaty between Japan and Myanmar Concerning the Territories of Burma in the Shan and other Regions

(Shan Chihō tō ni Okeru Birumakoku No Ryōdo Ni kansuru Nihonkoku Kan Jōyaku Teiketsu No Ken)

Held at Imperial Palace, September 22, 1943

Members present at the meeting:
Hara, president of the Privy Council
Suzuki, vice president of the Privy Council
State ministers:
Tojo, prime minister and army minister
Aoki, Greater East Asia minister
Shigemitsu, foreign minister; and others

Report of Mr. Suzuki, vice president of the Privy Council:

... in order to induce Burma to increase its war effort and cooperation toward Japan, Japan decided to recognize Burma's annexation of the Shan States. In an interview with Ba Maw during his trip south, Prime Minister Tojo declared that Japan was considering action on the above matter. Furthermore, the Japanese ambassador to Burma recently reported that the Burmese government desired the earliest possible annexation of the above region to Burma. He also reported that Japan's approval and recognition should coincide with the Burmese celebration of their independence on the 25th of this month. This would be a most effective way to lift the morale of the Burmese people in support of the war effort. Consequently, the Japanese government decided to adopt the above measure and proceeded to negotiate with the Burmese government. Both governments finally agreed on the present treaty provisions.

Treaty provisions:

"Treaty between Japan and Burma concerning the territories of Burma in the Shan and other regions."

The Japanese and Burmese governments, resolving to prosecute successfully, in close cooperation, the common war against the United States and Great Britain, and establish a Greater East Asia based on high moral principles, have agreed as follows:

1. The Japanese government agrees to recognize the annexation by the Burmese government of the Karenni State, Wa State, and the whole of the Shan States with the exception of both Kengtung and Mongpan States.
2. The Japanese government agrees to terminate its administration, now being executed over the above areas, within ninety days after this treaty takes effect.

3. Detailed matters essential for the enforcement of this treaty shall be negotiated by respective authorities of the two governments.
4. This treaty shall take effect on the date of signature.

SOURCE: Frank N. Trager, ed., *Burma: Japanese Military Administration, Selected Documents, 1941–1945*, 203–205. Reprinted with permission of the University of Pennsylvania Press.

28

The Speech of the Governor

Pang Long, March 26, 1946

First of all let me say, both for myself and on behalf of those who come with me, how grateful I am to you for this invitation to visit Pang Long. It is now four years since I was last in the Shan State, four years which I think we can all say have imposed on us great and varied trials. There is ample evidence of what the war in Taunggyi and elsewhere, the scars of battle where the guerrillas fought the Japanese on the mountain ridges, the mine craters on the roads, and the bull-pitted walls in those old buildings that still stand.

I know from the reports of my officers that scarcely a single Shan town survived the storm of bombings, first by the Japanese and later by the United Nations. I know that many areas have been ravaged and plundered by the enemy till scarcely a household possesses even a fowl. Yes, war has brought to you, even more than to many other parts of war-torn Burma, misery, poverty, and strain.

But there is something else I have also been told about, something that indeed I could not fail to hear about, and that is the vigor and determination with which the people of the Shan States are rising above their troubles and fighting their way back, by hard work and hard thought, to normal conditions. This very meeting at Pang Long in itself demonstrates this resurgent spirit, for here you are gathered together, representatives of every circle and of every race in the Shan States, not only to decide and place before me what you feel to be your needs for the future, but also to see, and this task is much more important, what you can do for yourselves.

Evidence of the revival of your normal life is already by no means lacking. New houses are springing up everywhere and many of the gaps of war devastation have disappeared. I was delighted to hear how many carts there were on the roads and to note that you still had at least some of your good cattle left. I was delighted also to hear that you have undertaken an increase in food production without delay and that the wheels of your trade are already beginning to move steadily.

Above all I am most reassured to find that, in spite of the want and restlessness which the war has left in its train, the Shan States are still virtually free from bloodshed and violent crime. There is no keener symptom of malaise in the body politic than crime, and it can be held to the credit of the social stability of the Shan peoples, and of the strength and quality of their social institutions, that freedom from this worst of economic brakes has been secured in so short a period of peace.

Trade and prosperity can be nurtured only in security, both of the individual and of the community, and I must congratulate most sincerely all those concerned in this signal victory over one of war's most evil aftermaths.

And now I know you will be wanting to hear what the Government's plans for your future are.

The officers of my Frontier Areas Administration have not been idle during the past years. Many of them have spent much of this period actually in Burma, studying the progress of the war situation on the spot and reporting on political and economic developments. On the basis of these reports we have prepared for the approval of His Majesty's Government plans for the development of the Frontier Areas in every aspect of life, from the constitutional to the economic.

First of all I will deal with the constitutional position.

You will have seen in His Majesty's message to the peoples of Burma that it is the intention of His Majesty's Government for the time being and until the hill people themselves elect to join with the rest of Burma, to keep the administration of the Frontier Areas, as it was in the past, under the direct control of the Governor.

It is the hope of His Majesty's Government and indeed of all of us who have the well-being of Burma at heart that the time will come soon when you will wish to unite with Burma, in a form acceptable to both contracting parties, in a strong and prosperous union.

You will have heard in the Burmese press that the people of Burma themselves are most anxious to include you with themselves in a fully self-governing Burma. I hope that you will give this matter your earnest and dispassionate consideration, so that you can study the advantages to be gained from such a closer unity, not only to Burma but also to yourselves.

Since my return in October I have been reassured to notice in the Burmese press comments on your problems a much greater sense of responsibility and restraint toward the Frontier Areas now than there ever was in the past. This is a good and happy omen. Much of the misunderstanding of the past years was due, I feel sure, to a lack of knowledge of and respect for each other's feelings and troubles, and it will be one of the first duties of my new Frontier Areas Administration to see that adequate publicity is given in both directions in the future.

In the meantime many steps are to be taken in the reform of your internal administration, and I am very pleased to announce that, as a result of representations received from the Shan Chiefs themselves, my Frontier Areas Administration has issued instructions for the immediate formation in every State of State Advisory Councils representative of the races living therein. I am much impressed by this progressive desire of the Chiefs to modify their traditional rule and bring it more into line with modern practice, and I am sure that these new councils will evolve as the years go by into fully representative institution in which the will of the people can make itself known and felt in the administration of their land.

In order to bring a more concentrated attention to bear on Frontier problems the administration of the Frontier Areas as a whole has been reorganized so that the head of it is now in direct contact with the Governor on the one hand and with the residents of the Frontier districts on the other. You will appreciate the difference that this change will make in the speed and efficacy with which your problems can be placed before the Governor.

You will no doubt have noticed another change, that in the designation of the officers of the Frontier Administration serving in the districts. Superintendents have become Residents and Assistant Superintendents Assistant Residents. Now there is a great significance behind this change of name. We are not trying to dress old wolves in new sheep's clothing! The new designations signify and will remain a constant reminder to you of a real change in policy, a change from our direct superintendence of your affairs, as of old, to the aid and advice in running your own affairs, which is our present aim.

You will have heard that I propose to establish, in all subdivisions and districts in the Frontier Areas, Advisory Councils to the district officers. My purpose in forming these councils is not simply to give an empty semblance of responsibility for local self-government. The aim and duty of my officers will be to train these councils to accept responsibility, so that in the years to come they may take over, item by item, all those spheres of local government that are suitable to their status in the administrative hierarchy.

This will, I am sure, provide ample scope for the ventilation of public opinion and enable you to bring your best brains to bear on your problems.

Personally I am confident that these councils will soon become a powerful force for the development of your hills. The peoples of the Shan States have shown in the past that their traditional self-government was a real and well-organized system. They have demonstrated that wisdom in administration is by no means the prerogative only of men of letters, and that by the use of "elder statesmen" in the shape of their village elders they have been able to maintain a very high level of orderly tranquility and justice in the life of the people. But the increase in education and contact with the outer world in the past few years have brought with them the inevitable craving for novelty in government, for slogans, for publicity drives, for five-, ten-, and fifteen-year plans about every imaginable subject. Not all of these new desires are good, but you cannot and must not ignore their existence. For your own peaceful and successful progress you must begin now to graft the new on to the old before the old dies, leaving the new without roots and without strength. That is what evolution means. That is how sound constitutions grow up with the people.

And now for your economic future.

In my address to the Kachins at Myitkyina, I spoke to them of our plans to set in motion as soon as possible geological and agricultural surveys in the Frontier Areas to find ways and means of increasing the prosperity and, through that, the revenue-producing capacity of your land.

These plans are designed to raise the national income and in that way to raise the ability to pay the taxes which alone can give you the schools, the hospitals, the traveling dispensaries, the agricultural experimental stations, and all the other public services you so ardently desire.

You will realize, I am sure, that the basis of all administrative research and progress, and of all public service, is taxation. The lower the taxable capacity of any country, the lower level of its public services must remain. It is no good blinding yourselves to this fundamental fact of government.

At the same time it is no good shying away from development simply because it may result in increased taxation, as has been the case in many hill areas in the past. There have actually been instances when valuable new cash crops have been refused because their production might be taxed; there have been cases when assistance toward irrigated cultivation has been refused because such fields might be subjected to land revenue. How shortsighted it all is! Would you not, all of you, much rather pay a thousand rupees a year tax on an income of Rs. ten thousand than Rs. ten in tax on an income of a hundred? Of course you would!

We are not unoptimistic about the prospects of practical and profitable results from these surveys. For example some of the Chiefs have already got small mining projects in view, while others have, at their own expense, carried out agricultural experiments whose results will be of great value to you all. The proposed surveys will expand and collate the information at our disposal and enable us to coordinate our plans in all economic spheres. For example, there are a number of areas in which it is hoped to increase irrigated cultivation and so preserve the land at present used for "taungya" for more useful purposes such as orchards and fuel and timber reserves. Of these areas we shall aim at developing those nearest to other industrial projects which can absorb their products.

As soon as the communications systems in Burma are restored we shall endeavor to apply to our local agricultural marketing problems many of the improved methods of packing and refrigeration which the war has developed and so increase and improve the trade with Burma in soft fruits, vegetables, and other farming products of the hills for which there is strong and increasing demand in the plains. This type of trade, in particular, lends itself to cooperative effort, and it is my earnest hope that the formation and development of agricultural and marketing cooperatives will be given first priority among the problems to which you will turn your attention.

In this connection I was much pleased to hear of the revival of the Erosion Committee and to know that it has already begun its work. This antierosion work is one of the most important projects undertaken by the Federation, and I hope that it will receive your pressing attention and support in the future. Like the rest of Burma you depend very largely on your agriculture, and you cannot afford to allow your land to go to ruin because of bad or wasteful methods of cultivation or collection of forest products. Remember always that the land is your life. The wise use of your land is and always will be the foundation of all other economic activities.

And now let me turn to matters concerning your health. Our proposals for an increase in medical facilities include increased teaching facilities for nurses at Dr. Seagrave's hospital in Nam Hkam and an improved mobile service of surgical and medical teams. With the recent opening at Nam Hkam of a large new class of student nurses from all States these plans have already got under way and it should not be long before results are evident.

These plans, I must emphasize, deal largely with the treatment and cure of disease after it has occurred. This is not enough. We must also aim at the prevention of disease, which means coordinated action of many kinds. It means improvement of diet to increase resistance against disease, it means building better and more hygienic houses, maintaining cleaner villages, and destroying the carriers of disease—the flies that spread dysentery and cholera, the rat-fleas that spread plague, and, above all, the malaria-carrying mosquito.

The war has improved, as indeed war always does improve, our knowledge of and means of destroying disease carriers of all kinds. It has produced the wonder drug penicillin, of which I hope great things in our campaign against the greatly increased venereal disease in Burma; it has produced the new insecticide DDT, which has enabled us to fight a war through devastated cities, jungles, and swamps with fewer epidemic diseases that were the normal peacetime lot of eastern lands before the war. Perhaps most important of all, it has produced new cures and preventives for malaria, for this disease is by far the most widespread and destructive in your land.

All of these new weapons against disease will be brought into use in the Shan States as soon as adequate civilian supplies are available, but you will realize that they alone cannot win the battle. You must also help. You must keep the villages clean and sanitary, you must grow the eatables to improve your diet, you must build the better houses in which your children can grow up strong and healthy.

Here again I would like to repeat what I said to the Kachins in Myitkyina. So much more can be done if you will save whatever public money is available for use only on those things which you cannot do for yourselves. For instance, if you want a dispensary in your village, build the accommodation for it yourselves by voluntary effort and save money for equipment and medicines. If you want a small local hospital, build it yourselves and contribute in kind the food and vegetables needed for the patients. In this way you can save enough to pay the salary of a ward servant or a compounder, and get better medical service much more easily.

The same principles apply to the increase of educational facilities throughout the Shan States. If village tracts and circles will take from the State and Federation the burden of providing building for schools and food for students, no doubt the number of schools, especially primary schools, could immediately increase throughout the whole area. A detailed plan for educational improvement in the Shan States which provides for technical as well as academic training is at present under consideration by the Frontier Areas Administration.

But here I want to talk to you about a particular aspect of adult education—the training of craftsmen. No country that is not yet fully industrialized can afford to neglect its cottage handicrafts. Yet in the Shan States I hear of skilled crafts dying out because no new pupils are being trained. This will never do. You could improve your incomes in many ways if you gave some thought to improve marketing and increase production. Take, for example, the small painted figures of the various hill peoples which are produced in Mong Nai. These would find a very rapid sale in any center where there are foreign visitors. Much less competent work is sold readily in Rangoon by hawkers traveling from door to door. You may think this is just a small thing, but I can assure you that it is by utilizing every small way of building up your resources that you can soon raise them to an appreciable figure. Other examples I might give include improved manufacture of the striking Keng Tung lacquer bowls, the hand painting for export of the light Northern Shan Hkamauks, and the production of pipe tobacco at Lang Hko. All these minor village industries could be turned into very paying propositions on a moderate scale. Here is one way in which you could put your State and Regional Councils to immediate use. Make them collecting centers for information on cottage industries and technical improvements. If you know of a better way of doing the ordinary daily things that the Shan must do to live, publicize it through your councils and give your fellow men the benefit of your inventive skill. If by any chance your invention is a process worth protecting by patent rights, your councils can bring the matter to the notice of the resident, who will help you to go through the proper procedure. It is a grave mistake to suppose that councils have only political and administrative functions. They can be made use of in a hundred ways, and I advise you to exploit them to the full.

I will not keep you longer. I came here to give my blessing to your deliberations and to wish you every success in your reconstructive effort. I know you will make many demands on the administration, and these we will do our best to meet with the resources at our disposal. But the Governor cannot perform miracles.

I would like to impress upon you once again the need for developing and using to the full the natural self-reliance and inventive ingenuity which is the heritage of all hill peoples. Far too many peoples in this world, especially those for whom their physical environment has made life easy, are apt to sit back and wait for others to do things for them. Far too many peoples sit in idleness and apathy and wait for their Governments to do something for them, forgetful of the fact that it was never possible for any Governments to do anything successfully without the wholehearted and vigorous cooperation of the people.

Let your aim be to ask for nothing from the administration, either of the State or of the Federation or Burma, which you can do for yourselves with your own skill, brains, and energy. In that way such assistance as can be given to you will be of tenfold value and you will extract from every anna of your revenues the last pie of value. I sincerely hope that out of this meeting there will arise concrete proposals not only for action by the administration to better your lot, but for you yourselves to undertake by way of self-help. Therein lies the real key to national resurgence and national progress—therein lies the key to prosperity and happiness and self-respect.

SOURCE: Frontier Areas: Relations Between Frontier Areas and Ministerial Burma; Pang Long Conference, June 9, 1945–May 14, 1947. X/592 [IOR: M/4/2811].

29

Report on the Political Discussions at Pang Long

Burma no. 14 Government House, Rangoon, April 30, 1946
(Secret)
To The Right Honorable Lord Pethick-Lawrence,
His Majesty's Secretary of State of Burma
(Secret) Appendix D

Political Discussions at Pang Long

Of the many Burmese leaders invited to Pang Long only a few were able to turn up. With the exception of U Lun, His Excellency's executive councilors canceled their visit on hearing that. His Excellency was not going. U Tin Tut, who was to have flown to Meiktila and gone on from there with me, did not turn up. Saw and his men were present in strength, and also the AFPFL, which though not invited by the *Sawbwa*, arrived at the invitation of the Youth League!

I arrived at Pang Long on the 26th March too late for the morning meeting, and thereby missed the welcoming address and replies by various leaders. Of these, three were noteworthy. One by a Kachin, whose competence astonished even Saw, one by Saw, which was remarkable for its good humor and good manners, and one by Thakin Nu, which has created a storm. Nu's speech took the form of a diatribe against the British couched in immoderate terms, and it was a grievous shock to the *Sawbwa*, who were incensed at having one section of their guests publicly insulted by another at a meeting of this nature. But the results of the Nu speech have been all to the good, as it put the other Burmese leaders, including Saw, on the defensive. Saw remarked to me later in the evening that he had noticed a distinct change of attitude by the Shan following the speech. Nu's speech also had a deep effect on both the Chin and Kachin delegations, who expressed their displeasure both at its immoderateness and at its lack of good taste in the circumstances in which it was delivered. Their opinion of the AFPFL delegation fell to zero, while Saw's stock rose correspondingly by virtue of his very different attitude.

On the morning of the 27th a further meeting was held at which Saw delivered a speech of more than an hour, making certain very concrete suggestions to the Shan, contingent on his party's winning the next election, among which was the offer of a minister for the Frontier Areas or parts of the Frontier Areas (analogous to the Secretary of State for Scotland), who would be nominated by the people themselves. Without mentioning specifically his backing of dominion status, Saw made it clear that he did not visualize total separation from Britain and expected at least to remain within a single defensive alliance. He was interrupted by the Hsahtung *myosa* on the subject of the behavior of the Ba Maw Government. Burmese officials afforded the chairman an opportunity to stop the speech when Saw was in full spate, and he continued it at a meeting in the evening, when he spoke for about one and a half hours.

At that meeting he elaborated on ways and means by which he thought the Frontier Areas and Burma could work together as a united dominion. He stressed that the various parts of the Frontier Areas would be granted local autonomy and that there would be no interference with their custom or religion. He played rather cleverly on the need to take business and commerce away from British and other foreign firms, and put it into the hands of Government-sponsored trade concerns, which would give the profits to the cultivator. Very wisely he did not elaborate on this. He publicly acknowledged the Burmese leaders to state their case to the leaders of the Frontier Areas, and publicly apologized to the Shan on behalf of the people of Burma for the misbehavior of Ba Maw and his men. That is one side of the story. Saw made a very good personal impression. He also made the first concrete constitutional proposals ever made to the Frontier peoples by a leading Burman. There is no doubt that his views will be given very serious consideration.

Now for the other side of the picture. Between Saw's morning and evening speeches I had a long discussion of more than two hours with the Shan, Kachin, and Chin leaders at Pang Long. I was first of all told that the leaders of all the hill peoples had decided among themselves to draft a manifesto declaring that they would not under any circumstances federate with Burma at the moment, but that instead they wished for self-government, *on the dominion level*, for a "Frontier Areas Federation." The weak link was the delegation from the Chins, who felt that they were in no position to talk too roughly to Burma, on which they rely for food. At the same time even they do not wish to have union with Burma now if there is any way of avoiding it.

The Saw proposals were discussed at some length and it was clear to me that he might have carried the day if only the hill peoples had been able to feel the least confidence in Burmese promises. That was the crux of all the arguments against union. From every side came instances of broken promises and villainous behavior during the Ba Maw regime. From every side hopes were expressed that the day of union could be postponed until the people of the Frontier Areas had built up a federal organization strong enough to ensure equitable treatment from Burma. In short the frontier peoples are still very uncertain and afraid about the future. The Chins and Kachins made approaches to the Shan *Sawbwa* to see if these last would be willing to pay the deficit in administration shouldered in prewar days by the Burma Government. The Shan showed some sign of agreement to do so but were worried in case they would find the burden too great for them. Taken by and large this meeting broke up convinced that union now was not possible, but still not clear as to how a separate Frontier Areas Administration could live.

Saw had asked a question which frightened them all: "How long, if at all, will the British be prepared to finance the Frontier Areas on their way to self-sufficiency?" I was tackled straightly about this and obviously could give no reply but that the matter "was still under consideration by His Majesty's Government." The Chins and Kachins asked if there was to be no tangible reward for their past loyalty and service.

The possibility of a dominion Burma denying to the Frontier Areas a due share of customs and excise duties was but one of the many fears expressed, and on more than one occasion I was asked whether Government could now push ahead with a road from Kamapyu to Papun and Moulmein, and thus open a back door to the sea through what, it is hoped *by all*, will be a separate Karen area.

On the 28th Saw had a further meeting with the hill leaders at which he answered very adroitly all the questions they put to him. These followed roughly the line of the doubts expressed to me, and though Saw had all the answers, saying, among other things, that no responsible Burmese Government would deny the Frontier Areas a fair "development" share of the revenues, he could not dispel the deep-seated fear of Burmese double-dealing. He was, however, able to form a United Burma Cultural Society, with the Yawnghwe *Sawbwa* as the President and himself as a Secretary. This society has as its objects the mutual study of languages, customs, and religions with a view to bringing about a better understanding between all the people of Burma. At the insistence of the *Sawbwa* politics is specially barred by the consideration of the society.

Saw made some fairly pointed remarks about Thakin Nu's speech during his talks and let it be known that he disapproved, but even he could not miss the opportunity to have a dig or two at the good old British lion. The Nu speech undoubtedly created still greater distrust of the Burmese. The general line of argument was that if Nu could speak like that about the British, who, the hill tribes at any rate feel, *have* done something for Burma, what would he say about the hill peoples themselves if piqued by them? That he occupies a prominent position in the AFPFL was regarded as proof that the Burmese people were not yet capable of selecting responsible persons for responsible posts, and that for that reason promises by Burmese leaders, however able, were not worth the breath wasted upon them, because at the next election the Burmese might put in men of the likes of Thakin Nu.

At the farewell dinner in the evening the two Burmese speakers, both of the Myochit Party, An Saw and Meiktila U Ba Yin, again stressed unity and the need for freedom.

On the 29th morning before I went away I had another long interview with the Chin and Kachin Chiefs. The Chins said very little about the separation problem beyond expressing a hope that the British Government would give them financial support till they could get on their own feet and thus could withstand enforced inclusion in the Burmese orbit. They brought up an interesting point, and that is the alleged desire of the Lushais of the Lushai Hills of Assam to come in under the Frontier Areas of Burma. This is perhaps an echo of the Reid proposals.

The question of the councils was discussed at length by both Chins and Kachins, and there is no doubt whatsoever that the subdivisional and district councils will fill a much-felt want and should do a lot to ease the political aspiration now burgeoning in the hills. I noticed a strong tendency by the Chiefs to try and scoop the council, a tendency which will be resisted strongly in areas that have a large number of nonpatrician notables. I was asked by a member of the Chin delegation if the Government intended to give the "plebs" a voice in the future councils.

The Kachins spoke mainly on boundary settlement. They reiterated their claims to the Myitkyina and Bhamo Districts and said that if they could get these they would sacrifice the Kachin Hills in the Katha District. Obviously they felt very deeply on this question and more than one present said that if the British let them down over this they would have no other option but to take up arms to gain their ends. Only one mentioned a more craven alternative. This man said that some felt that without Myitkyina and Bahmo towns the Kachin Districts would have no hub and would therefore never develop. He added that if we did not propose in the end to give the Kachins Myitkyina and Bahmo it would be better for them to enter the Burmese orbit straightaway rather than to fight and antagonize them now only to have to give way to them and be subjected to their spite in the end. This suggestion was shouted down by others present with an anxiety which seemed to indicate that there was some real weight behind it. The Kachin elders reported that the AFPFL had been sending delegations around all the villages visited by Mr. Wilkie, instructing them what to say and in some cases giving them already prepared petitions to sign and deliver. In many cases they said that villages which had already opted for inclusion in the Frontier Areas had since been presented to ask for their first option to be canceled. The Hsenwi *Sawbwa* and the other northern Chiefs are reported to be sending emissaries to canvass the Shan of the two northern districts to persuade them to join the Kachins, so that there can be a solid Kachin-Shan bloc stretching all the way from the Federated Shan States to the Chindwin River. The Kachins of the northern Shan States have told the *Sawbwa* that unless the Shan of Myitkyina and Bhamo agree to remain in Kachin Districts there, the Kachins in three Northern Shan States of Momeik, Tawngpeng, and Hsenwi will demand separation from the Shan States and inclusion in the Bhamo Kachin Hills.

On the whole I think it can be said that this first meeting of the Frontier peoples at Pang Long was a success. All except the Nu speech were moderate and constructive, and discussion gave all present a better idea of the magnitude of the problems confronting them. Undoubtedly it has done a lot of good to the Myanmar leaders who visited Pang Long, for they were able to see with their own eyes that, in spite of every effort by the administration to present the case for union as favorably as possible, the Myanmar still have a lot of distrust and dislike to overcome before they can attain this end.

The main conclusions that the Hill people drew from their discussions were:

1. that they must obviously stick together if they are to ensure fair treatment for all by the Myanmar
2. that no racial group should make approaches to the Myanmar without prior information to and discussion with the other Frontier peoples
3. that if the Frontier peoples desire to join with Burma they should all go in together and not as separate units
4. that the most potent danger to their plans to build up a strong bloc is the possibility that His Majesty's Government may not finance their rehabilitation.

Plans are under way to hold a similar meeting at Pang Long next year, and to meet each year in a different area, *e.g.*, Karen, Kachin, Chin Hills. In the meantime the Shan Chiefs have collected a considerable sum to found their own press, which they propose to make the mouthpiece of the Frontier Areas.

Though the political discussion occupied most of the attention of the leaders, the meetings were by no means mainly political. Cattle shows, plowing exhibitions, implement demonstrations, and an arts and crafts exhibit formed the background to a series of practical talks on village hygiene, forest preservation and erosion control, and other matters of importance to the people. Several clever inventions to save labor in weaving were on view and I have no doubt the exchanges of views and information which took place were of the utmost value. From this practical aspect the Pang Long meeting was a revelation to the Myanmar visitors, several of whom commented on it to me.

Now that we have something to go on, it should be possible to organize "hot-house" training courses for headmen to coincide with future meetings and to organize propaganda dissemination on a Frontier Areas–wide scale.

As it was, the propaganda people did not do too badly. Hendershott was present with *The Battle of Britain*, *The Battle of Russia*, and *TVA*—all very useful films, especially the last. Our own film unit was also there.

One fact was very prominent. The *Sawbwa* were making a great bid to reestablish their prestige before the people. On the whole, I think they were successful, though the lavish display of wealth given by the Laikha *Sawbwa*, notorious for his drunkenness and his women, may have supplied ammunition for the Youth League, who appear at the moment to be leading the opposition to traditional rule.

(Signed) H. N. C. Stevenson, Director,
Frontier Areas Administration

SOURCE: Frontier Areas: Relations Between Frontier Areas and Ministerial Burma; Pang Long Conference, June 9, 1945–May 14, 1947. X/592 [IOR: M/4/2811].

30

The Pang Long Agreement, 1947

Dated Panglong, the 12th.
February 1947.

THE PANGLONG AGREEMENT, 1947.

A Conference having been held at Panglong, attended by certain Members of the Executive Council of the Governor of Burma, all Saohpas and representatives of the Shan States, the Kachin Hills and the Chin Hills :

The Members of the Conference, believing that freedom will be more speedily achieved by the Shans, the Kachins and the Chins by their immediate co-operation with the Interim Burmese Government :-

The Members of the Conference have accordingly, and without dissentients, agreed as follows :-

1. A Representative of the Hill Peoples, selected by the Governor on the recommendation of representatives of the Supreme Council of the United Hill Peoples (SCOUHP), shall be appointed a Counsellor to the Governor to deal with the Frontier Areas.

2. The said Counsellor shall also be appointed a Member of the Governor's Executive Council, without portfolio, and the subject of Frontier Areas brought within the purview of the Executive Council by Constitutional Convention as in the case of Defence and External Affairs. The Counsellor for Frontier Areas shall be given executive authority by similar means.

3. The said Counsellor shall be assisted by two Deputy Counsellors representing races of which he is not a member. While the two Deputy Counsellors should deal in the first instance with the affairs of their respective areas and the Counsellor with all the remaining parts of the Frontier Areas, they should by Constitutional Convention act on the principle of joint responsibility.

4. While the Counsellor, in his capacity of Member of the Executive Council, will be the only representative of the Frontier Areas on the Council, the Deputy Counsellors shall be entitled to attend meetings of the Council when subjects pertaining to the Frontier Areas are discussed.

5. Though the Governor's Executive Council will be augmented as agreed above, it will not operate in respect of the Frontier Areas in any manner which would deprive any portion of these Areas of the autonomy which it now enjoys in internal administration. Full autonomy in internal administration for the Frontier Areas is accepted in principle.

6. Though the question of demarcating and establishing a separate Kachin State within a Unified Burma is one which must be relegated for decision by the Constituent Assembly, it is agreed that such a State is desirable. As a first step towards this end, the Counsellor for Frontier Areas and the Deputy Counsellors shall be consulted in the administration of such areas in the Myitkyina and the Bhamo Districts as are Part II Scheduled Areas under the Government of Burma Act of 1935.

7. Citizens of the Frontier Areas shall enjoy rights and privileges which are regarded as fundamental in democratic countries.

8. The arrangements accepted in this Agreement are without prejudice to the financial autonomy now vested in the Federated Shan States.

9. The arrangements accepted in this Agreement are without prejudice to the financial assistance which the Kachin Hills and the Chin Hills are entitled to receive from the revenues of Burma, and the Executive Council will examine with the Frontier Areas Counsellor and Deputy Counsellors the feasibility of adopting for the Kachin Hills and the Chin Hills financial arrangements similar to those between Burma and the Federated Shan States.

Shan Committee.	Kachin Committee.	Burmese Government.
Saohpalong of Tawngpeng State.	(Sinwa Naw, Myitkyina)	[signature] 12/2/47
Saohpalong of Yawnghwe State.	(Zau Rip, Myitkyina)	
Saohpalong of North Hsenwi State.	(Dinra Tang, Myitkyina)	
Saohpalong of Laihka State.	(Zau La, Bhamo.)	
Saohpalong of Mong Pawn State.	(Zau Lawn, Bhamo)	
Saohpalong of Hsamonghkam State.	(Labang Grong, Bhamo)	

Representative of Hsahtung Saohpalong.

(Hkun Pung)

(U Tin E) (U Htun Myint)

(U [illegible]) ([illegible])

([illegible]) (Hkun Htee)

Chin Committee.

(U Hlur Hmung, ATM, IDSM, B.K.M., Falam.)

(U Thawng Za Khup, ATM, Tiddim.)

(U Kio Mang, [illegible])

31

Letter to the Commander of the Myanmar Army in Kengtung

Top Secret Ex. Doc. 1

June 8, 1950
Tachilek

To The Commander of the Burmese Army in Kengtung

Dear Sir,

I have been informed that you have your men in Kengtung seized more than one thousand Chinese overseas residents, and also put our representee [representative] in custody: it certainly makes my men extremely irritated. I am unable to know your management is reasonable and still I hear that you will send a troop of your men to station at Tachilek? very soon. Therefore, in order to protect the lives and properties of our Chinese overseas in Tachilek, I am here to acknowledge you the following statements, and expect you kindly grant me an answer as quick as you can:

1. Since Northeastern China already becomes as anti-cummunism [anti-Communism] group, and all my men have been counted the most anti-cummunism [anti-Communism] fighters, we are not going to make any belligerency between your men and my men. If any problem occurs, we must [resolve] it peacefully.
2. To prevent the expansion of the exaggerated state in Kengtung I ask you to release either my representee [representative] or Chinese overseas immediately.
3. If there be any good idea of yours, please adopt it in concession bween [between] you and me.
4. No procession of your troop would be allowed to pass Mongling-Tachilek before we have come to a resolution.
5. If unfortunately there will be any disastra [disaster] owing to the offensive progress of your men toward Mongling-Tachilek, we shall be ready to accept with a spirit of sacrifice and protection; but it is very clear the responsibility of the said occurrence is at your side, my dear commander!

I am eagerly expecting a swift answer with clear statements of yours.
I am,

Yours most faithfully,
The Commander of the anti-cummunism [anti-Communism]
Camp in Kengtung,
Major General Lee

SOURCE: *Kuomintang Aggression Against Burma*, 139–141.

32

Summary of a Press Conference on the Kuomintang Military Situation in Northeastern Myanmar

News synopsis by *Lak Mueang,* Thai newspaper

Following the tense situation in the North due to the presence of the Chinese 26th Army near their border, the Interior Ministry is now considering the suitability of declaring a state of emergency. A clear picture of the situation was given during a press interview by a Chinese general who has commanded operations against the Burmese forces, and who is now on an unofficial visit to Bangkok.

He is General Lai Iang Sae Tia. The interview, given to many news representatives, was held at a place which cannot be disclosed. This is what he said. The Kuomintang troops have clashed with the Burmese force and have established themselves at Tha Khilek because the Burmese soldiers resorted to intimidation in order to disarm the Chinese units. Fighting has therefore broken out, and for safety measures Tha Khilek has to be occupied for the time being. Asked whether the Kuomintang troops will proceed to Taiwan, the general remarked: "What's the use? Those in Taiwan are now thinking of quitting the island. Besides we would have to face hardships during the journey, all to no purpose."

To a reporter's query whether the twenty-thousand-strong 26th Army intends to continue fighting with the Burmese force, General Lai Iang replied that a three-point demand is now being negotiated with the Burmese military authorities, *viz.*

(1) All Chinese merchants numbering many thousands arrested by the Burmese soldiers shall be liberated. (2) A guarantee must be given by the Burmese authorities that they will definitely terminate fighting with the Chinese army. (3) The Burmese soldiers shall be withdrawn from the vicinity of the area where the Kuomintang troops have established themselves.

Speaking of the possibility of Chinese Kuomintang troops violating Thai territory, General Lai Iang emphatically declared that this would definitely not take place. The purpose of the Chinese army's presence is to protect the Chinese population in the area, and when an opportunity presents itself, the 26th Army will move back to Yunnan to resume fighting with the Chinese Reds. On the other hand, if the Burmese troops persist in harassing the 26th Army, fighting with the Burmese will have to go on to the bitter end and incidentally this will spell the immediate occupation of Chiengtung.

Explaining the purpose of his trip to Bangkok, the general said he was visiting the Chinese military attaché, an old friend of his. He also wanted to obtain instructions from the Chinese Government in Taiwan what further actions should be taken by his army.

SOURCE: *Kuomintang Aggression Against Burma*, 142.

33

Places and Names of Operations by the Union Armed Forces against the Kuomintang Troops, June 1950 to November 1952

Operations Kengtung

(June to July 1950)

On June 17, 1950	Union forces attacked and occupied WAN MUN NANTA (ML 0802) KMTs out on L of C between milestone 81 and 82 on Kengtung/Tachilek highway, but their attempts were frustrated by our own troops. Casualties: 80 KMTs dead and 1 captured alive.
On June 27, 1950	Junior forces attacked and occupied WAN NA YAO (ML 1305).
On July 7, 1950	Union guerrilla forces attacked and occupied WAN AIHSAM (ML 1301) and consolidated the surrounding areas.
On July 14, 1950	Union forces occupied MANG KO (LU 9687).
On July 15, 1950	Union forces occupied MONG HO PUNG (LU 9687).
On July 21, 1950	Union forces advanced and occupied TA CHI LEIK. KMTS approximately 1,800 withdrew toward MONGHSAT (LU 1585), MONG KWAN (LU 5573) MONG TUN (LU 4375) and established HQ at MONGHSAT (LU 1585). Casualties: Enemy, 81 killed, 160 captured. Own troops, 17 killed, 2 missing.

Operations Frost

(Commenced February 13, 1951)

Union forces reoccupied TANG YANG (LD 2123) and cleared surrounding areas across Salween. KMTs withdrew toward WA States and MONGHSAT (LU 1585). Two spearheads from TANG YANG advanced east up to Salween, and conducted mopping-up operations west of Salween in South Hsenwi States.

Operations Pang Long

(Commenced October 21, 1951)

In August 1951 Union forces sent out special reconnaissance patrol into WA State and KENG TUNG State.

On October 21, 1951	Union forces fighting columns advanced toward NAM MUN.
On December 23, 1951	Union forces fighting columns advanced toward KAWNG-PYAT (SU 8393) area, and cleared all KMT nests and hide-outs.

On December 15, 1951	Union forces fighting columns cleared KMTS from PIN-LONG area. KMTS withdrew toward east and southeast.
On November 29, 1951	Union forces cleared KMTS up to KAWNG-PYAT (SU 8393) area.
On December 24, 1951	Union forces completed mopping up operations in PANG-YANG area. Casualties: Enemy, 67 killed, 7 captured. Own troops, 3 killed, 1 missing.

Operations Mo-gyo (Special operations)

(1952)

In March 1952	Union forces fighting columns cleared areas northeast of KYUHKOK.
On May 11, 1952	Union forces fighting patrols clashed with KMT forces between MONG-YU and KYUHKOK.
On May 19, 1952	Union forces fighting columns cleared areas L of C KENG-TUNG / TAUNGGYI.

Operations Ba-yin-naung (Special operations)

(Commenced September 15, 1952)

On July 7, 1952, Union forces fighting columns operated in LOKIAN area and MONGPING area. Casualties: Enemy, 31 killed, 13 captured. Own troops, 2 wounded.

First Phase

On September 15, 1952	Own troops conducted operations near WAN-HPIT (LO 8794). KMTS from WAN-HPIT withdrew toward north.
On September 14, 1953	fighting took place between Union forces and KMTS 2 miles west of MONG-PIN (LO 8943). On same date the Local Chief organized armed guerrilla groups to fight against KMTS.
On September 15, 1952,	Union forces from MONG-PIN (LO 8943) attacked and occupied surrounding areas.
On September 16, 1952	Union forces followed up and attacked retreating KMTS at WAM-NAO (LO 8981). On same date 300 KMTS attacked MONG-PIN (LO 8943) but were repulsed. KMTS retreated toward south.
On October 1, 1952	KMTS attacked Union forces outpost near MONG-PIN but were repulsed.
On October 9, 1952	Union forces encountered KMTS at milestone 84 / 85. Fighting took place. Operations BA-YIN-NAUNG cleared KMT nests near MONG-PING.

Second Phase

Three hundred KMTs attacked Union forces at MONG-PING on November 18, 1952, 0915 hours. Own troops resisted for two days and repulsed the attack.

On November 23, 1952 — BAF planes carried out air strikes on MONG-PU-AWN (LO 9565) and WAN-HWI-HSUM (LO 9368). Union forces fighting columns advanced south of MONG-PIN and cleared the areas. Casualties: Enemy, 46 killed, 17 surrendered. Own troops, 1 killed, 4 wounded.

NOTE: The local operations conducted by local commander and the ambushes made by Union forces are not included in above operations. Operation Maha, which is still being conducted, is also excluded.

SOURCE: *Kuomintang Aggression Against Burma.*

34

Letter of Encouragement from Chiang Kai-Shek to the Kuomintang in Northeastern Myanmar

To Director Li and through him to all rank and file of the national army stationed at Yunnan and the armed forces of the local anti-Communists

The past two years were the darkest period of our Nationalist Chinese and it was also the time for hard struggle for [them]. The dark period has now begun to transit into a bright period. January of the year before last, after I withdrew from the Government of the Chinese Communists, at the instigation of the Soviet bandits [things] started madly to disturb the tranquility in every part of the whole country. The whole continent of China fell into their hands at the end of the year after last. Many of the unscrupulous and shameless military as well as civil officers surrendered on bended knees. They discarded their loyalty and went over to the bandits. But all of you have been able to stick to your firm determination to uplift the banner of blue heaven and white sun in the most difficult environment and condition to have a life-and-death struggle with a great number of traitors and bandits, to break into pieces the political structure of the Chinese Communist bandits, to defeat the secret scheme of their military operation, and to enhance the national aspiration of the Nationalist Chinese so as to preserve the quality of revolutionary militants. Your revolutionary spirit of unyielding and unceasingly fighting though suffering defeat after defeat will go down in the glorious history of the Chinese nation with praise and tears and also point out the lifeline that leads to the road of existence and freedom, to the compatriots of the whole Chinese nation.

In order to comply with the demand of the people of the whole nation and to add to the power of the whole nation to fight against the Communists, I have resolutely and daringly taken up again from March last year the [presidency] so as to shoulder the burden together with all the patriotic Chinese and the loyal and brave officers and men the responsibility of resisting Russia and the Communists.

For the last one year at the base of renaissance-Formosa there has been a marked progress in every direction. The revolution of administration and the stability of economy have made Formosa a beacon shining into the darkness of the continent. The adequate power of our naval, military, and air force may be regarded as the strongest in Asia for anti-Communists. Once the preparation has been completed the counterattack will be started. On the other hand, the Chinese people who live under the regime of the reign of terror of the Chinese Communist bandits and traitors have already wakened up and have joined in the activity of anti-Communists. The number who are equipped militarily and are in a position to fight against Communism has now increased up to one million six hundred thousand. They strike at the Chinese Communist bandits wherever they meet and have a life-and-death struggle with those bandits of Mao.

Though the Communist bandits make use of the weapons of terror to do away with the anti-Communist elements, the power of this armed people has, on the contrary, made the anti-Communists stronger and stronger, and so the fight goes on and the number becomes greater and greater though they have been mowed down.

Although you are living under the most difficult conditions, you are not fighting the operation alone. There are in the continent over one million six hundred thousand brave fighters of the nation to support you and numerous numbers of compatriots who do not wish to be slaves to help you besides the naval, military, and air forces in free China to fight on your side. Before long our forces to counterattack the mainland shall join hands with you. It is hoped that you will increase and preserve to the utmost your fighting power in order to prepare for assistance in the counterattack. Lastly, may I inform all the brave fighters of all the rank and file that owing to the difficulty of communication the government has not been able to send a great quantity of supply. But the policy of government to promote the power of the armed people in the continent to fight against Communism has already been fixed. After the Nationalist Army has fought back to the continent, all the armed forces of the anti-Communist organization shall enjoy the same privileges as those enjoyed by the regular army. The families of the fighters who fell in the battle against the Communists shall be rewarded by the government. For the sake of saving yourself, your nation, and your country and in order to fulfill the secret mission of anti-Communists and resistance to Soviet Russia, you, my beloved soldiers of the revolution, shall be sincerely united together and stick to all the hardship to struggle for the winning of the final victory.

Chiang Chung Cheng
(Chiang Kai-Shek)
Dated 5th January of 40th Republican year (1951)
Circulated to all ranks immediately.
(Seal) Twan Yu Wun

SOURCE: A/2423, UNGA, Eighth Session, July 22, 1953, 3–4.

35

Letter from a Kuomintang Soldier to Chinese in Yangon Asking for Supplies and Recruits

To Elder Brother Chi Chai, Chi Song, Wei Lin, Swee Wu, Sin Chuan, Kuo Ho, Ching Tung, Hwee and Foo Chun

It has been very long since I took leave from you all. I hope everything is fine with you. I must thank you for all the copies of the first number of the *Freedom Daily* newspaper sent through Kengtung. They reached me all right, please don't worry about it. Your spirit and courage in working for the cause of our country and people are to be greatly admired. Mr. Lu has already been engaged as subeditor. I am sure all of you in Rangoon will be glad to assist him as much as you can. I regret to say that when Wei Lin and Kuo Ho came to Kengtung I could not meet them, because it is a pity I had to go to the front. Sometime ago I sent a letter care of instructor Mr. Lo of Gai Sin Piao Pang (musical club). I wonder if he has received it.

Now the Nationalist Army in Yunnan has started to counterattack. So far it proceeds rather smoothly. This, though, is a sporadical engagement of the counterattack on the mainland. The "paper tiger" of the Red Chinese has been pierced through and as our army advances, many of the Communists have come over to our side. Recovery of the province of Yunnan will take place before long. *Supply of arms and ammunition and uniforms has been transshipped by air from Formosa for the first time*. When any airdrome has been repaired, the plan of full operation on the enemy will be carried into effect. When the time has come, your paper will be informed of good news for you to publish a supplementary sheet and I hope I shall be able to work for your paper.

When all of you have time in Rangoon, will it be possible for you to organize some sort of comfort movement so as to encourage and increase the morale of our troops. In the rainy season what will be useful to our army is soap, rubber shoes, and towels. Sometime ago the Overseas Chinese in Thailand collected a quantity of these things and sent them over here by air. As these things are sent over here by air, the quantity is not enough for distribution. It is to be regretted that the problem of communication is hard to solve. However, I am sure all of you will try your best to send us a quantity of these things. With your reputation and your position a great response will be given by the general public once you set the ball rolling. Should you comply with this request it is hoped that the work would be started straightaway. It would be excellent if it reaches there before the rain. *This army has established a training school to train workers militarily and politically. We would like you to send us candidates for such training as many as you can find them*. When recovery has been made in the mainland, the army will push forward, but the rare person with ability to administrate will be urgently required. The ideal personnel for such work will be those who can administrate and those who also have a good military knowledge. Obviously, personnel with such qualification will be highly appreciated.

Is the Ta Lu singing troupe still in existence?

Please engage some of those who can teach military songs and send them here. For such help we shall be very grateful to you. *If the students of the Chung Tuck High School are not afraid of the hardship of military life and are willing to take up work in the army they are welcome. Can Mr. Kan Shin, the headmaster, try to work it out? We are very anxious to train his students for the work of taking over the administration.*

If your paper is not working at a loss please send more copies to the troops at the front. When they are in the midst of a shower of bullets a cigarette or a copy of a newspaper nearby will be a great comfort to them. How is brother Tau Chi? Is he all right? I hope he will be able to come over here to help in the smooth running of administration. Wang Hun of the *Central Daily News* is working under old Li in a certain place in Yunnan. There is not a third person belonging to the journalist circle serving in this kind of work. It is hoped that brother Tau Chi will not miss this opportunity but come together with some friends over here to work together for the great cause. Hoping to get a reply from you soon and wishing you all in good health.

Your younger brother,
Pei Feng
July 5, a place in Yunnan

N.B. Please excuse me for not writing to all of you one by one. My address: care of Min Seng Medical Hall, Kengtung. Regarding the matter which was entrusted to me by elder brother Chi Chai, I had already sent a special letter, because I have been ordered to accompany the army to carry out certain work and I was unable to go to Formosa.

Please ask brother Swee Wu to send a copy of photo taken at the Ning Nyang Hwi Kuan for my souvenir.

SOURCE: *Kuomintang Agression Against Burma.*

36

Instruction from a Kuomintang General to Local Commanders to Cooperate and Help the *Saohpa* and Headmen in Their Campaign against the Union Government

3074 REGIMENT (Substitute for telegraphic service)
Subject: As per letter
Addressed to: Commander of "Chung" Battalion
Enclosed: Nil
No. Fa Ching/134
Dated 3–7–41 (1952)
Place of issue: Khong-mu-dan

I. According to the telegram from 6180 Regiment No. Mu Mon/124

1. According to confidential report, the Burmese Government is at present recruiting volunteers from all the places. This seems to be the preparation to fight against us.
2. This army and all the sections under it should adopt the following policy to oppose it:
   i. Every section must try to find out the number of the volunteers recruited by the Burmese Government army at its local headquarters, and the manner in which it recruits.
   ii. Try by every means to incite the *Sawbwa* and the Headmen to spread sedition against the Burmese Government by propagating that the Burmese Government is abolishing the system of *Sawbwa* administration by utilizing the recruits, Shan volunteers, in order to accomplish its intention of governing all the nationalities by the Burmese. The recruiting officers sent by the Burmese Government and the volunteers recruited shall be denied passes issued by us and we shall put all kinds of obstacles in their way.
   iii. All the above instructions are to be complied with and report on its results.

(Signed) Li Chaw
Regimental Commander
(Signed) Liu Chin
Assistant Regimental Commander
Duly complied with.
(Signed) Chang Chai Jen

SOURCE: A/2423, UNGA, Eighth Session, July 22, 1953.

37

Summary of the Subcommittee's Discussion of the Kuomintang 4904 Battalion's Military and Political Strategies in Myanmar

Subject 1. What we should do prior to being attacked by the Burma army

Seal of the 4904 Battalion

1. Fundamental principle:
   a. Based on the principle of annihilation of the public enemy of the human race, any place in any free country may be used as a base for anti-Communist operation in the same way as the United States is making use of other countries as its bases.
   b. Our battalion is situated in between the Burmese army and the bandits (Chinese Communists). We are being attacked from the south as well as from the north. So militarily, we shall resist the Communist bandits on the North. Politically we shall join hands with all political parties of Burma specially with the Government of Kawthulay and the two parties of Karen and Mon to enhance their power in reorganizing their Government to achieve the aim and object of anti-Communism.
   c. National independence shall be the slogan to call the people together so that the Burmese Government will become helpless that it will surrender without fighting.
2. Procedure:
   a. The Burmese Government is controlled by the Burmese who are corrupted and who accept bribery. They oppress other nationalities.
   b. By assisting the hill tribes to strive for independence and to choose their leaders.
   c. The Burmese Government is doing away with the *Sawbwa* so we must support the *Sawbwa* of Mong Pan and other states to become independent.
   d. To request assistance morally and materially from the Chinese overseas and to stir up public opinion against the Government.
3. Military preparation:
   a. To be clear about the movement of the enemy, intelligence should be obtained regarding the movement of the Burmese forces from Lashio to Namkham. In all important points along this route, spies should be posted.
   b. To inspect secretly the topography of the region and to determine the holding point along the route and also to find out the places for ambush and to plan lines of communication and to put up defense work.
   c. To fix the signal and to devise ways and means for concentration and disbursement of the troops and also allot time and place and route.
   d. To inform all concerned that the military order shall strictly be observed. Offenders shall be severely punished.

4. Political side:
   a. The Chinese Communist bandits set up the Burmese army to drive away the Chinese Nationalist army in the hope of getting Naw Seng and his followers to enter Burma and to occupy in the North so as to join hands with the Chinese Communists.
   b. The discipline of the Burmese army is very low; its soldiers rape and rob especially our Chinese and other races.
   c. To support the movement for national independence. This shall be the duty of our forces.
5. The discipline of an army:
   a. To make known to all the tribes that we shall not interfere with them in any way except the Burmese and ins and outs of the Government organization.
   b. To take note that good impression on the people of the locality shall be left by our army after having passed through it.
   c. When any furniture or things are required they should be borrowed politely and also ask through the headman of the place for help.
6. Personal preparation:
   a. Each individual should lightly be equipped and be ever ready on the move.
   b. All the unimportant documents should be singled out and destroyed from time to time.
   c. Arms and other things should be examined and cleaned before using them so as to avoid any obstruction.

Subject 2. How we should retaliate when we are being attacked by the Burmese army

1. Strategy:
   a. To avoid a frontal fight, to bypass from the flanks and attack from their back and try to seize the important position and to rob the Government treasury and stores of money and things.
   b. To stir up the local people to seize arms and ammunition from the Burmese soldier for the use of their own defense.
   c. To avoid our responsibility by making use of the names of the enemy of the Burmese Government such as Burmese Communists or followers of Naw Seng for the attack.
   d. Our aim is directed at the Burmese Government. We should, therefore, avoid stirring up bad feelings among the Burmese.
2. Tactics:
   a. Find out the direction in which the Burmese army is moving and then select an advantageous position for ambush.
   b. Organize guerrilla troops to disturb the Burmese army and to concentrate on lightning strikes.
   c. Appoint liaison officers in every detachment so as to assist commanding officers in giving orders in the combined attack.

d. The combination must be good. Movement must be swift and secret. The number and the insignia of each troop should be changed every now and again.
e. If the Burmese army is too strong we should retreat again and again so as to make it become careless that we may start our lightning attack from the rear and to go into the heart of its position.
f. If we attack we should give the Burmese army very severe punishment. Otherwise we should not attack at all.
g. The order to fight should be carried out to the utmost.
h. Once the fight starts we should have no more regard for the Burmese Government. All the Burmese organizations should be destroyed.

3. Supplies:
a. Supplies shall be obtained locally but we must avoid [antagonizing] the people and try to get supplies voluntarily.
b. Should you borrow arms and ammunition from the people of the locality see that you do not stir up hatred.

Subject 3. What we should do after the fighting is over

a. When war is over we should make propaganda that we were attacked by the Burmese army and that we are in no way responsible for the fight.
b. Make propaganda that the Burmese army has in fact committed rape and robbery.
c. Encourage and support the tribes in the north of Burma to struggle for independence and to establish provisional government.
d. To investigate the merits and demerits of the troops taking part in the fight and give reward and punishment accordingly and also to comfort and console the people of the locality.

SOURCE: A/2423, UNGA, Eighth Session, July 22, 1953.

38

Instruction from the Kuomintang Generals to Local Commanders to Attack Every Weak Position of the Union Armed Forces

Top secret

To Li Chun Ching,
(This instruction must be destroyed after reading for compliance)

Since the Burmese forces have started their offensive on our troops we must be able to check them before they become too strong.

They have a very good understanding with Communist bandits of Mao and they are now being influenced greatly by the Communist bandits.

Therefore to make our plans successful we must create trouble between these two Governments.

From now on you and your men must make all attempts to attack the weak outposts of the Burmese troops, in the disguise that you are Mao's Communist bandits and also propagate that Mao's Communist bandits have invaded Burma.

This information must be kept very secret and made known to officers only.

Destroy the document immediately.

From
Yang Tar Hpont
Seal of the No. 2 guerrilla group
of West Yunnan Salvation Army

SOURCE: *Kuomintang Aggression Against Burma*, 159.

39

Order from a Kuomintang General to Local Commanders to Aid the Karen Rebels in Their Campaign against the Union Government

Anti-Communist and Country Saving Army No. 3074 Regiment
Issued instead of telegraphic service No. Fa Mi/176, dated November 1, 1941 (1952)

Telegraphic instruction received from Mr. Chiu

I. Clause 4 of the principal points of the propaganda as issued under telegram "I.U." is amended as follows:

> As the Burmese Government is sticking to the wrong principles, our army shall positively support the political parties (except the Communist) especially the Kawthulay Government and Karens and Mons and to assist them as much as we can so that they may become strong enough to achieve their aim of reorganizing the Government and to work together with us for the object of anti-Communism.
>
> The amendment is requested to be made accordingly and to carry out propaganda to this effect in full.

II. The instruction issued under No. Fa Mi/174 of this HQ is to be amended and carried out accordingly.
To The commander of the "Chung" battalion

(Signed) Li Chao
Region Commander

Already complied with and made known to all concerned.

(Signed) Chang Chai Jen

SOURCE: A/2423, UNGA, Eighth Session, July 22, 1953.

40

Representatives who Attended the 79th Scrutiny Committee Meeting for the States

March 15, 1961, Six-Storied Office, Strand Road, Yangon

1. Sao Wunna, Kayah State Minister
2. Dr. Saw Hla Tun, Kayin State Minister
3. U Zahre Lian, Chin Affairs minister
4. Sao Tun Aye, Shan State Government Health and Education Minister
5. U Sein Toe, Kachin State Finance Minister
6. Sithu Saw Buttler, Secretary, Kayin State Ministry
7. Mr. K. F. Hoe, Secretary, Shan State Ministry
8. Mr. D. J. W. Bartlett, Secretary, Kayah State Ministry
9. Sao Shwe Thaike, Member of the Chamber of Nationalities
10. Sao Hkun Aung, Shan State Government National Solidarity and Information Minister
11. Maha Tharaysithu Sao Htun E, Saohpalong of Hsa Mong Hkam
12. Maha Tharaysithu Sao Nge Du, Chairman of Kayah State Council
13. Sao La Wi, Parliamentary Secretary, Kayah State Ministry
14. Sithu U Hla Shein, Consultant (finance), Shan State Government
15. U Myint Htoo, Legal Adviser for the States
16. U Ba Maw, Secretary, Kachin State Government
17. Captain Mang Tung Nung, Parliamentary Secretary, Chin Affairs Ministry
18. U A. Soe Myint, Parliamentary Secretary, Kayin State Ministry
19. Maha Tharaysithu U Sein
20. Sao Kyaw Khaung, Member of Parliament
21. U Soe Maung, Representative of Inn People's Unity Party
22. U Hla Pe, Member of Shan State Council
23. Sao Shwe Hmon, Saohpalong of Kehsi Mansam

In this meeting Kayah State minister Sao Wunna acted as chairman and Kayah State Ministry secretary Mr. D. J. W. Bartlett acted as secretary.

SOURCE: *The Nation* (Rangoon), March 21, 1961.

41

Representatives who Attended the Special Scrutiny Committee Meeting for the States

March 20, 1961, Six-Storied Office, Strand Road, Yangon

1. Dr. Saw Hla Tun, Kayin State Minister
2. U Zahre Lian, Chin Affairs Minister
3. Sao Shwe Thaike, Member of the Chamber of Nationalities
4. Sao Htun E, Saohpa of Hsa Mong Hkam, Shan State
5. U Sein Toe, Finance Minister, Kachin State Government
6. U Sit Han, Finance and Revenue Minister, Shan State Government
7. U Hme, Planning Minister, Shan State Government
8. U Tom Hmon, Secretary, Chin Affairs Ministry
9. Mr. K. F. Hoe, Secretary, Shan State Ministry
10. Mr. D. J. W. Bartlett, Secretary, Kayah State Ministry
11. Sao La Wi, Parliamentary Secretary, Kayah State Ministry
12. Duwa Htain Baing La, Parliamentary Secretary, Kachin State Ministry
13. Captain Mang Tung Nung, Parliamentary Secretary, Chin Affairs Ministry
14. U A. Soe Myint, Parliamentary Secretary, Kayin State Ministry
15. U Hkun San Myat, Parliamentary Secretary, Shan State Ministry
16. Duwa Zau Rip, Kachin State Government Minister
17. U Soe Maung, Representative of Inn People's Unity Party
18. Maha Tharaysithu U Sein
19. U Myint Htun, Legal Adviser for the States
20. U Hla Pe, Member of the Shan State Council
21. U Zan Hta Sin, Member of the Kachin State Council
22. Saw Po Aung, MP for South Hlaingbwe constituency, Kayin State

At this meeting member of the Chamber of Nationalities Sao Shwe Thaike acted as chairman and Kayah State Ministry secretary Mr. D. J. W. Bartlett acted as secretary.

SOURCE: *The Nation* (Rangoon), March 21, 1961.

42

The Military Takeover in Myanmar: An Analysis by Dr. Ba Maw

One week after the military coup, the old-time politician Dr. Ba Maw made the following remarks.

> It is too early yet to speak either for or against the military takeover, which has set up a revolutionary regime in Burma, nor would it be fair to do so.
>
> We shall have to wait and see. We can, however, do one thing now. We can profitably look for the causes of the failure of the late government, for there can be no doubt that government failed and so opened the way for what has happened. Some of the basic causes seem apparent. But before saying more, I wish to point out the need to deal with them historically, that is, to be as objective as possible and to keep all partisanship and bias out. That is how I will try to give my own views.
>
> The first cause and perhaps the most basic of all is the fact that U Nu, who led that government, is, by temperament as well as conditioning, not a revolutionist. To begin with, he does not have political interest enough, let alone the single-mindedness and dedication of a revolutionist. I do not think he himself will deny this. He made no bold approach to the countless problems that the present revolutionary epoch poses in every newly independent country. The result was that in Burma, which recently won her independence with revolutionary slogans and promises, U Nu and his government refused to carry on the revolution that would give the people something really new and better and more abundant. In fact, conditions have become much worse than before. This has created a general feeling of frustration and betrayal. The politicians in power had used big revolutionary words during the struggle for independence when they were trying to win that power, but once they got it, they scrapped the revolution and became as slow- moving and self-seeking as any past colonial administration. However, although the revolutionary spirit had died in them, it kept on smoldering below the surface in the country as a whole. In fact, the revolutionary slogans that they continued to use for political effect helped to keep that spirit alive. All that built up a dangerous tension, which has now produced its consequences. During this critical period, one of the least revolutionary leaders of Burma rode on the crest of the revolution; even more, following his own religious obsessions, he tried to use various devices and opiates to stem this tide of our national revolution, and even to push it right back into the past. Since independence, Burma has lain paralyzed by this anomaly. It has blocked the natural outlets for her growing urges during a revolutionary period and thus prepared the way for those urges to break through anyhow.

None of the past revolutionary governments really understood that independence is only the beginning of a national revolution and far from being its end. The armed forces have at least demonstrated that they understand this crucial fact by starting the task now before them with a Supreme Revolutionary Council. They have shown a true sense of the spirit of the times.

Revolution is still a magic word among the Burmese. The present rebellions sustained by their revolutionary names and slogans, which have gone for years, prove it. With a clear understanding of the times, the rebels exploited the word, while those in power forgot, or tried to do so. And now the armed forces are going to do what the short-sighted political parties failed to do. The Burmese, it seems, are going to get a revolution to satisfy their "rising expectations" without either turning to Communism or joining the rebellions.

The next cause, as I see it, of U Nu's downfall is his lack of a firm, positive political faith during a period when such faith and passion are overrunning every country, especially the new ones. They constitute the real driving force in the present age of narrow and passionate beliefs. Not possessing such a faith, U Nu has lacked its impelling force; and also its clear-cut ideas. He has plenty of religious faith, as we all know. His personal character is irreproachable. So is his national spirit. But, unfortunately, all that is not enough for a political leader leading his people in a time of revolutionary action. Not having a decisive policy to keep him on a fixed course, his government fell back on substitutes, on expedients, on makeshifts, and on day-to-day decisions, changing and chopping and sailing with the wind most of the time. It was this that created for the government a good deal of the problems that led to its downfall.

The trouble in a way started with the overwhelming vote U Nu won at the last general election. It was won without any declaration of a clear party policy of program, as such things are understood in a democracy. This victory which was obtained without any election promises that matters being given made U Nu believe that it was a personal mandate to act according to his own will, and he thoroughly did so. It also made him so sure of his security in power that he took no precaution against any possible threat to it. He has paid dearly for these blunders.

Next, there was the havoc played by that word democracy used so loosely that it became a mockery. U Nu and his men do not bother about what John Strachey has called the "Plimsoll line" of democracy, namely, the level of development, political, social, economic, educational, and so on below which a democracy [can function] democratically. Instead, democracy, as U Nu made the people believe, came virtually to mean the right to live and to act as one pleases, with maximum rights and minimum obligations, worst of all without any duty to progress or help the country to progress. It was almost a return to the jungle. This alone made any real progress nearly impossible, or at least so slow and meager as to be self-defeating. Thus,

U Nu's government, floundering in cloudy abstractions, lost its ability and even its will to govern.

The last cause followed from the others. Not having any deep-rooted political convictions, such as for instance their Communist enemies have, the government and its party were unable to import a similar conviction and its driving force to the people. This largely accounts for our postwar frustration so far, for what an important American paper has described as Burma's "painfully slow recovery from wartime disruptions, the even slower pace of industrialization." U Nu tried to replace political with religious faith and all sorts of superstitious observances. Politically, it has proved to be very shortsighted and disastrous. It defied the laws of history, especially during a revolutionary period. Thus all our postwar plans have generally failed. The real failure was in the people who worked the plans. They lacked the kind of revolutionary faith that has moved mountains in Soviet Russia and China, and postwar Germany and Japan. I have already explained why they lacked this faith.

A Seizure to End All Seizures

This causal analysis, if correct, should be a warning and a guide to all of us. As its name promises, the new Revolutionary Council will have to see the Burmese revolution through as a part of what Adlai Stevenson has called the revolution of rising expectations in Asia.

Again, this is not only a revolutionary age, but a people's age as well in which the consent of the people must in the end prevail so the council must also strive to win that consent and support for their revolution. It must ultimately emerge as a people's revolution.

Finally, the present seizure of power must make all further seizures historically unnecessary, and therefore impossible. It can do this by building the foundations for a true and well-protected democracy to follow the revolution. In this way it must be a seizure to end all seizures in future.

Like war or rebellion or any other form of direct notion, a military intervention or domination in a democracy is never a good thing. There must be the strongest historical necessity to purify it.

SOURCE: *The Nation* (Rangoon), March 9, 1962.

Notes

Chapter 1

1. Lao, Law, Hkun, Lu, Tai-long, Tai-noi, Tai-no, Tai-man, Tai-mao, Tai-hke, Tai-toi, Pu-tai, Pu-nong, (or nung), Pu-man, Pu-ju, Pu-chei, Pu-en, Pu-yloi, Pu-sui, P'o, Pa, Shui Han or Hwa Pai-i, Pai-jen, Yu jen, P'u-man, Pai, Hei or Hwa Tu-Tao, Nung or Lung-jer. Sha-jen, Hei or Pai Sha-jen, Minchia, and Shui-chai-chung-chai. J. George Scott and J. P. Hardiman, *Gazetteer of Upper Burma and the Shan States, part 1, vol. 1* (Rangoon: The Superintendent, Government Printing, Burma, 1900, 187–188). In subsequent references this work will be referred to as *GUBSS*.

2. Ahom, Ai-lou, Aiton, Black Tai (Tai Dam), Buyi, Caolan, Chuang, Chung-cha, Chung-chia, Cung, Daeng (Tai), Dai, Dam (Black Tai), Dahong, Dioi, Don (Tai), Giay, Hen Payi, Khanti, Kham, Jang, Khao (Tai), Kharn (Tai), Khun, Lai (Tai), Lam, Lanna, Lao, Lao-long, Loi, Lgng, Lue, Luong, Man, Mao, Neua, Ngeo, Nhang, Noi (Tai), Nong, Nora, Nu, Neu, Nung, Pai-yi, Phaké, Phunan, Phu-Thai Po-ai, Pong, San-chay, San-chi, Shan, Siamese, Song, Tai, Tay, Thai, Tho, Turung, Yai (Tai), Yuan, and Zhuang and Zuang Dai. Dr. Nomal Chandra Gogoi, "Tai, Thai and Dai: Origin, Evolution and Dissemination of Tai Culture in China and Southeast Asia with Special Reference to the Ahoms of Assam." Mangshi, Yunnan, The International Conference on Comparative Studies on the Dai Culture in the Four Rivers Valleys in Yunnan Province, 2003.

3. Arthur P. Phayre, *History of Burma* (London: Wanstead, 1967), 6–7.

4. Dr. Laufer's note to Rev. H. I. Marshall, January 6, 1920, referred to by Marshall in his book, *The Karen People of Burma: A Study in Anthropology and Ethnology.* (Columbus, Ohio: University of Columbus, 1920), 6.

5. Dr. Lila Gogoi, *The Tai Khamti on the North-East (New Delhi:* Omsons Publication, 1970), 3.

6. W. W. Cochrane, *The Shans*, vol. 1 (Rangoon: Superintendent, Government Printing, Burma, 1915), 6.

7. Cochrane, *The Shans*, 7.

8. Ibid., 8.

9. Leslie Milne, *Shans at Home* (Bangkok: White Lotus, 2001), 5.

10. Cochrane, *The Shans*, 8.

11. Ibid., 10.

12. William Clifton Dodd, *The Tai Race* (Cedar Rapids: The Torch Press, 1923), 6.

13. Ch'ang-chu, *Hua-yang-kuo-chih*, chapter 2, 2.

14. Ibid., chapter 1, 3 (a).

15. Ibid., chapter 1, 2 (a).

16. Ibid., chapter 3, 1 (b).

17. Ibid., 7 (b).

18. Ibid., 2 (b).

19. Chen Yi Sein, *Ancient Tai*, 26.

20. Ch'ang-chu, *Hua-yang-kuo-chih*, chapter 3, 2 (b).

21. Tan I, *Hou-han-shui-chih: Lieh-chuan*, chapter 76, 18 (a); chapter 77, 25 (a).

22. Likhit Hoontrakul, *The Historical Records of the Siamese-Chinese Relations* (Bangkok: Debsriharis Law Office, 1953), 91.

23. G. H. Luce, "The Tan (AD 97–132) and the Ngai-Lao," *Journal of the Burma Research Society*, vol. 14, part 2, 1960, 209.

24. Ibid., 24–25.

25. Cochrane, *The Shans*, 24–25.

26. Sao Saimong Mangrai, *The Shan States and the British Annexation* (Ithaca, New York: Cornell University, 1965), 22.

27. Likhit, *The Historical Records*, 91–96.

28. W. A. R. Wood, *A History of Siam* (Bangkok: Chalermnit Book Shop, 1924), 34.

29. G. H. Luce, "The Early Syam in Burma's History," *The Journal of the Siamese Society* (*JSS*), vol. 46, part 2 (November 1958), 125.

30. N. Elais, *Introductory Sketch of the History of the Shans in Upper Burma and Western Yunnan* (Calcutta: The Foreign Department Press, 1876), 8.

31. Prince Chula Chakrabongse, *Lords of Life: A History of the Kings of Thailand* (London: Alvin Redman, 1960), 18.

32. Elais, *Introductory Sketch*, 26–27.

33. *The Hsen Wi Chronicle.*

34. Pu Loi Hom and Pu Loi Tun. "The Founding of Mong Kawng." *Golden Jubilee Shan State Magazine* (Yangon: The Taunggyi Association, 1997), 182–186.

35. Elais, *Introductory Sketch*, 19.

36. *GUBSS*, part 2, vol. 1, 194.

37. Elais, *Introductory Sketch*, 124.

38. Ibid.

39. Ibid.

40. *The Hmannan Mahayazawintawgyi*, vols. 1 and 2 (Yangon: Department of Information, Ministry of Information, 1972), vol. 1, 61–75, 138–141, 144–156; vol. 2, 23–26, 89–95, 121–127.

41. Elais, *Introductory Sketch*, 17.

42. Oliver Raendchen, "The Design for a Proposed Cultural System for the Tai People," *Tai Culture*, vol. 7, no. 2.

Chapter 2

1. "Summary of Findings," *The Socialist Republic of the Union of Burma, Ministry of Home and Religious Affairs* (Yangon: Immigration and Manpower Department, 1987), 1–9.

2. *Encyclopaedia Britannica, A New Survey of Universal Knowledge*, vol. 19 (London: Encyclopaedia Britannica, Ltd., 1786), 914.

3. H. L. Chibber, *The Geology of Burma* (London: Macmillan and Co. Limited, 1984), 29–30.

4. "Shan States, Kareni, Chin Hills and Pakoku Chin Hills," *Imperial Gazetteer of India* (Calcutta: Superintendent of Government Printing, 1908), 308.

5. *GUBSS*, part 2, vol. 2, 635.

6. Chibber, *The Geology of Burma*, 42.

7. Stamp L. Dudley, *An Intermediate Commercial Geography* (London: Longmans Green and Co. Limited, 1963), 36.

8. Chibber, *The Geology of Burma*, 260.

9. "Shan States," *Imperial Gazetteer of India*, 336.

10. Oliver Raendehen, "Social Aspects of the Ban-Mong System of the Tai Dam in Northern Vietnam," *Proceedings of the Sixth International Conference of Thai Studies, vol. 1* (Chiang Mai, Thailand: October 14–17, 1976), 428.

11. Personal interview with Hein Pyinnya of Hsi Paw, May 18, 1997.

12. Personal interview with Long Hkun Maha Wan of Lashio, April 5, 1996.

13. Personal interview with Long Loi Mu in Mong Yai, March 3, 1996.

14. Personal interview with Sao Nwe Mao Hkun Ban Pang Long, Putao, Hkamti Long, May 4, 1996.

15. Personal interview with Long Hkun Hkam Leng, Ban Se U, Hsen Wi, June 6, 2004.

16. Personal interview with Ching Hsang Kaung of Manhai, Hsi Paw, Northern Shan State, April 4, 1996.

17. Personal interview with Long Lai Sai Heing of Manpong, Mong Yai, Northern Shan State, June 6, 1998.

18. J. W. Grant, *The Rice Crop in Burma* (Rangoon: Superintendent, Government Printing and Stationery, Burma, 1949), 22–23.

19. Personal interview with Long Sang Hkam Leng of Muse, Northern Shan State, July 19, 1996.

20. Personal interview with Long Ywat Hkam Hein of Mong Nai, Northern Shan State, September 8, 1996.

21. J. S. Furnival, *Introduction to the Political Economy of Burma* (Rangoon: People's Literature Committee and House), 1957, 16.

22. J. E. Spencer, *Shifting Cultivation in Southeastern Asia* (Los Angeles: University of California Press, 1966), 25.

23. Personal interview with Long Hkam Lai of Heho, Southern Shan State, July 17, 1996.

24. Personal interview with Long Sang Men of Panglong, Central Shan State, July 17, 1996.

25. Personal interview with Long Loi Hkam Hein of Namhkam, Northern Shan State, June 6, 1997.

26. Personal interview with Nai Kyaung Loi of Muse, Northern Shan State, March 3, 1996.

27. Personal interview with Sai Hsae of Yawng Hwe, Southern Shan State, January 1, 1996.

28. Personal interview with Long Hkun Htee of Loilem, Central Shan State, July 19, 1996.

29. *Report on the Administration of Burma for the year 1935–36*, 10.

30. Personal interview with Sai Hkam Leng of Lang Hko, Southern Shan State, February 2, 1996.

31. J. W. Grant, *Burma Fruits and Their Cultivation* (Rangoon: Superintendent, Government Printing and Stationery, Union of Burma, 1961), 111.

32. Personal interview with Long Hkun Pwint of Nam Hsan-Loi Long, Northern Shan State, July 7, 1996.

33. Personal interview with Pa Nang Ont of Mong Yai, Northern Shan State, September 19, 1996.

34. "*Shan State, 1983 Population Census*," *The Socialist Republic of the Union of Burma*, Ministry of Home and Religious Affairs (Rangoon: Immigration and Manpower Department, 1987), 1–2.

35. F. T. Moreland, *The Forests of Burma* (London: Green & Co., Ltd., 1944), 54.

36. Alex Rodger, *A Handbook of Forest Products of Burma* (Rangoon: Superintendent, Government Printing and Stationery, Burma, 1963), 11.

37. C. B. Smales, *A Sample Key to One Hundred Common Trees of Burma* (Rangoon: Director of Public Relations, Burma, 1945 [repub.]), 13.

38. "Shan States," *Imperial Gazetteer of India*, 33.

39. Personal interview with Long Sang Pan of Mong Yai, Northern Shan State, May 3, 1996.

40. Personal interview with Long Loi Su of Tang Yan, Northern Shan State, August 17, 1996.

41. Personal interview with Long Hkam Lin of Yawng Hwe, Southern Shan State, May 3, 1996.

42. Moreland, *The Forests of Burma*, 13.

43. Personal interview with the Hkamti Shan, Sao Nwe Gam Pi in Putao, September 26, 1976.

44. J. Russel Andrus, *Burmese Economic Life* (Stanford: Stanford University Press, 1948), 122.

45. Personal interview with Long Loi Hkam of Nam Lan, Hsi Paw, Northern Shan State, May 29, 1997.

46. Personal interview with Long Soi Hkam Ngan of Nam Hkam, Northern Shan State, September 30, 1997.

47. Sylvia Fraser-Lu, *Burmese Lacquerware* (Bangkok: The Tamerind Press, 1996), 135–140.

Chapter 3

1. Phayre, *History of Burma*, 77.
2. Ibid., 78.
3. D. G. E. Hall, *A History of South-East Asia* (London: Macmillan & Co. Ltd, 1964), 148.
4. *The Hmannan Mahayazawintawgyi*, vol. 1, 3rd Edition (Yangon: News & Periodicals, Government Information Department, 1992), 396.
5. Hall, *A History of South-East Asia*, 149.
6. *Ibid.*, 34.
7. Ibid., 155.
8. Phayre, *History of Burma*, 82.
9. Ibid., 85.
10. Ibid., 92.
11. Ibid., 93.
12. Ibid., 94.
13. Hall, *A History of South-East Asia*, 153.
14. *The Hmannan Mahayazawintawgyi*, 376.
15. Ibid., 67.
16. Ibid., 75.

Chapter 4

1. *Report on the Administration of the Shan States for the year 1887–88*, Parliamentary Paper, February 20, 1896.
2. Ibid.
3. *GUBSS*, part 1, vol. 1, 284.
4. Ibid., 286.
5. Ibid., 290.
6. Ibid., 290–291.

Chapter 5

1. J. George Scott, "The British Shan States," *The Asiatic Quarterly Review*, July 1889, 6.
2. Maung Maung Tin, *Konbaungset Yazawun*, vol. 3 (Rangoon: Letimandy Press, 1967), 613–614.
3. Clarence Hendershot, "The Conquest, Pacification and Administration of the Shan States by the British, 1886–1897," typed manuscript, unpublished, 17.

4. Taw Sein Ko, *Hluttaw Hmattan* (Rangoon: Government Printing and Stationery, 1960), 179–180.

5. Sir Charles Crosthwaite, *The Pacification of Burma* (London: Frank Cass & Co. Ltd., 1968), 43.

6. *GUBSS*, vol. 1, part 1, 291.

7. Sao Saimong Mangrai, *The Shan States and the British Administration* (New York: Cornell University, 1965), 107.

8. Scott, *"The British Shan States," The Asiatic Quarterly Review*, 8.

9. Ibid., 9.

10. *Upper Burma Proceedings*, Foreign Department, October 14, 1886, proceeding no. 3, enclosure 2 (3) 19.

11. Scott, "The British Shan States," *The Asiatic Quarterly Review*, 11.

12. Hendershot, "The Conquest," 22.

13. *Upper Burma Proceedings*, Foreign Department, May 10, 1886, proceeding no. 2, 19–20.

14. Hendershot, "The Conquest," 23.

15. *Upper Burma Proceedings*, Foreign Department, October 14, 1886, proceeding no. 3, enclosure 1.

16. File no. 61 A / 1886, *Thibaw Sawbpa* (memo).

17. Scott, "The British Shan States," *The Asiatic Quarterly Review*, 17–18.

18. *GUBSS*, part 2, vol. 1, 184.

Chapter 6

1. File no. 604, 1886, National Archive Department, Shan State. *Upper Burma Proceedings*, Expedition, December 1880, vol. 2664 A.

2. *Report on the Administration of the Shan States for the year 1887–88*, 103–106.

3. Charles Crosthwaite, *The Pacification of Burma* (London: Frank Cass, 1968), 60.

4. *Letter from Chief Commissioner to Superintendent* May 24, 1887; Obituary in *New Burma*, January 1933.

Chapter 7

1. *Letter from Superintendent, Southern Shan States to Chief Commissioner*, January 30, 1888. File no. 88, 1888, Taunggyi.

2. *Letter from Scott to Superintendent, Shan States*, June 22, 1888.

3. "A Dashing Exploit," *St. James's Gazette*, July 3, 1888; "A Dashing Exploit," *The Echo*, August 18, 1888.

4. *Telegram from Chief Commissioner, Rangoon, to J. George Scott*, received at Fort Stedman on May 15, 1888.

5. *Letter from Scott to Superintendent, Shan States*, June 22, 1888.

6. *Report on the Administration of the Shan States for the year 1887–88*, section 42.

7. *Administration of Burma*, 1887–88, 14.

8. *Letter from Scott, Officiating Superintendent, Southern Shan States, to Keng Tung Chief, June 15*, 1889. File no. 59, 1884, Taunggyi.

9. *Letter from Scott to Chief Commissioner*, March 27, 1890.

10. Ibid., September 19, 1892.

11. *Government of India to Chief Commissioner*, October 21, 1892.

Chapter 8

1. *Southern Shan States Report of 1889–90*, section 2.

2. *Hildebrand to the Commander of Siamese Troops*, January 28, 1889.
3. *GUBSS*, part 1, vol. 1, 398.
4. *Southern Shan States Report of 1889–90*, section 5.
5. Ibid., section 7
6. Ibid.
7. *Report of Leveson sent to Chief Commissioner by the Superintendent of the Southern Shan States*, May 1, 1893.
8. *Letter from Superintendent Hildebrand to Chief Commissioner*, March 23, 1893.
9. Hendershot, "The Conquest," 137.
10. *Letter from Hildebrand to Chief Commissioner*, March 25, 1893.
11. *Letter from Chief Commissioner to Government of India*, May 22, 1893.
12. *Lord Rosebery to the Queen-Empress*, July 26, 1893; Hendershot, "The Conquest," 140.
13. *W. W. Warry to Chief Commissioner*, May 10, 1893
14. *Telegram from Government of India to the Chief Commissioner*, March 21, 1895.
15. *Letter from Chief Commissioner to Superintendent, Southern Shan States*, March 22, 1895.
16. Ibid., April 21, 1895.
17. *Letter from Stirling to Superintendent, Southern Shan States*, June 15, 1895.
18. Ibid., September 28, 1895.
19. *Government of India to Chief Commissioner*, January 21, 1896.
20. *Letter from Stirling to Superintendent, Southern Shan States*, May 1, 1896.

Chapter 9

1. *GUBSS*, part 1, vol. 1, 190.
2. Ibid., 191.
3. *Blue book, Burmah*, 1886, 266.
4. *Memorandum of the Federated Shan States by Their Representatives*, appendix no. 2, London, December 1930.
5. *Chief Commissioner to Government of India*, December 9, 1885.
6. Keng Lum was omitted by Political Department Notification No. 24, dated May 20, 1926; Kyawk Ku was omitted by Political Department Notification No. 13, dated February 10, 1928; Loi Maw was omitted by Political Department Notification No. 14, dated February 16, 1928. Loi Ai was deleted by Political Department Notification No. 20, dated April 22, 1930. Namtok was omitted by Political Department Notification No. 31, dated August 19, 1930. Loi Lem has since ceased to be a notified area.
7. As amended by Political Department Notification No. 16, dated March 24, 1930.
8. *The Shan State Manual* (Rangoon: Government Printing and Stationery, 1933), 10–13; *Political Department Notification* No. 16, dated May 5, 1923.
9. File no. 264 B–28. Note of a discussion on Shan States matters on December 13, 1924, at Taunggyi, 16, National Archives Department, Acc. No. 7714, 1/1 (B).
10. These orders were:
    (a) Federated Shan States Law and Criminal Justice Orders (1926). *The Burma Gazette*, June 28, 1926. Political Dept., dated June 21, 1926, No. 33.
    (b) Shan States Law and Criminal Justice Orders (1894). *The Burma Gazette*, July 13, 1895, 1, Political Dept., dated July 13, 1895, No. 33, 262–268.
    (c) Shan States Civil Justice Orders (1900). *The Burma Gazette*, May 19, 1900, Political Dept., dated May 16, 1900, No. 3, Rule 1–3, 5–6, 372–73.
    (d) Shan States Civil Justice (Subsidiary) Order (1906). *The Burma Gazette*, December 1, 1906, Political Dept., November 23, 1906, No. 23, Rule 1–4, 835–36.

11. File no. 96534, Proceedings of the Twelfth Session of the Federal Council of the Shan Chiefs, held in Taunggyi from February 24 to March 1, 1934. 9 NAD Accession No. 5054, 1/1(A).

Chapter 10

1. U Ohn Kin, *Burma Under the Japanese* (Lucknow: Lucknow Publishing House, 1947), 12.
2. Hall, *A History of South-East Asia*, 774.
3. John Leroy Christian, *Burma and the Japanese Invader* (Bombay: Thacker & Co., Ltd., 1945), 351.
4. U Maung Maung, *Burmese Nationalist Movements* 1940–1948 (Edinburgh: Kiscadale Publications, 1989), 50.
5. *Burma During the Japanese Occupation*, vol. 1. (Rangoon: Intelligence Bureau Government of Burma, 1943), 8.
6. Clarence Hendershot, "Role of the Shan States in the Japanese Conquest of Burma," *The Far Eastern Quarterly* 2 (May 1943), 254.
7. Ibid., 256.
8. Frank N. Trager, *Burma: Japanese Military Administration, Selected Documents, 1941–1945* (Pennsylvania: University of Philadelphia, 1971), 226–230.
9. Ibid., 226–280.
10. T'ien Ju-K'ang, *Religious Cults of the Pai-i Along the Burma-Yunnan Border* (Ithaca, New York: Cornell University Press, 1986), 5.
11. David Henley, "A Forgotten Invasion: Thailand in Shan State, 1941–45," http://www.cpamedia.com/history/thailand_in_shan_state/
12. *Burma During the Japanese Occupation*, 27.
13. U Maung Maung, *Burmese Nationalist Movements*, 90.

Chapter 11

1 "*Appreciation of Pang Long Conference*" by the Kachin Elders, appendix C of *Political Discussions at Panglong*, by H. W. C. Stevenson, April 30, 1946, 13.

2. *Summary of speeches made by U Saw at the Pang Long Conference*, 1946.

Chapter 12

1. *Frontier Areas Committee of Enquiry 1947*, Report Presented to His Majesty's Government of the United Kingdom and the Government of Burma, part 1 (Rangoon: Superintendent, Government Printing and Stationery, Burma, 1947), 1.
2. *Frontier Areas Committee of Enquiry*, 2–6.
3. Ibid., 6–7.
4. Ibid., 9–10.
5. Ibid., 11.
6. Ibid., 14.
7. The Shan States were self-supporting before the war, if the Federated Shan States are taken into account. This fund was created in 1922 and maintained by contribution from the states and from the Fund of Burma and by receipts from mineral forests. From 1937 the contribution from the central revenues of Myanmar was not a gift to finance a deficit, but a carefully calculated allotment of what was due to the States in consideration of revenue accruing to the central government from taxation of commercial activity in their territories (e.g. the entire petrol tax accrued in the first place to central revenues, although much petrol was consumed by transport operation in Shan States). The fund has been in abeyance since 1941, but articles 8 and 9 of the Pang Long Agreement foreshadow its renewal.

8. *Frontier Areas Committee of Enquiry*, 14.
9. *Ibid.*, 15.
10. Ibid., 16.
11. Ibid.
12. Ibid., 16–17.
13. Ibid., 24.
14. Ibid., 28.
15. Ibid., 3–46. The six unintroduced speakers in this transcript are members of the Frontier Areas Committee of Enquiry (FACE). Three of them represent Ministerial Burma (namely U Tin Tut, U Khin Maung Gale, and Thakin Nu) and the other three represent the Frontier Areas (namely U Vum Ko Hau, Sima Hsinwa Nawng, and U Sein).
16. Ibid., part 2, 12–23.
17. Ibid., 22–24.
18. Ibid., 24–25.
19. *Frontier Areas Committee of Enquiry*, part 1, 1–30, part 2, 1–43.

Chapter 13

1. "Political Discussion at Pang Long," *Second Pang Long Conference*, appendix D (Secret), February 1946, 16.
2. The text of the historic agreement made at the conference is given in chapter 12. See appendix 30 for the facsimile of the agreement.
3. *Letter from Governor of Burma to Secretary of State for Burma*, February 22, 1947. (File copy, B/F FA. 1252, 1947)
4. *Private letter from Mr. Leiden to Sir Gilbert Lathwaite*. Dated February 25, 1947.

Chapter 14

1. Werner Levi, *Modern China Foreign Policy* (Minneapolis: University of Minnesota), 1953, 267.
2. Andre Roth, "The Crucial Role of Li Mi," *Eastern World* (February 1952), 32.
3. *Burma Weekly Bulletin*, May 6, 1953.
4. *New York Times*, March 7, 1953.
5. *Kuomintang Aggression Against Burma* (Rangoon: Ministry of Information, Government of the Union of Burma, 1953), 10.
6. See appendix 31.
7. See appendix 32.
8. See appendix 33.
9. *Kuomintang Aggression Against Burma*, 9.
10. "The Free Thai Movement," *Eastern World* (January 1945), 18; *Burma Weekly Bulletin* (Rangoon), May 6, 1953.
11. *The Nation* (Rangoon), June 29, 1953.
12. *The New York Times*, July 13, 1953.
13. *The Nation* (Rangoon), July 12, 1953.
14. Ibid., July 12, 1953.
15. Naw Seng was a Kachin captain (a Myanmar [Bamar] citizen) who served in the British Army during the Second World War and won the Myanmar (Bamar) Gallantry Medal. After Myanmar obtained its independence, he served in the Union Army. In 1949, he joined the Karen revolt against the Union government and later escaped into Red China, where he became a colonel in the Thirteenth Army of the Communist Chinese.

16. *The Nation* (Rangoon), January 6, 1953.
17. *The New York Times*, February 24, 1953.
18. *Burma Weekly Bulletin.* (Rangoon) March 11, 1953.
19. "Burma Incident," *New Republic*, February 11, 1952, 8.
20. See appendix 34.
21. *The New York Times*, February 20, 1953.
22. *The New York Herald Tribune*, February 22, 1952.
23. *The New York Times*, August 23, 1953.
24. The northeastern part of the Shan States, especially Ko Kang and Mong Lun, is well known for its opium production. This area came under the control of the Kuomintang, who could easily smuggle out opium to Thailand. Wolfram and other minerals were extracted from the Mawchi mine in Kayah State, which for a time fell into the hands of the Kuomintang.
25. *China Monthly Review*, March 1952, 243.
26. Pleshakov, "The Aggression Against Burma," *New Times* (Moscow) No.17, April 22, 1953, 12.
27. Y. Osipov, "What Is Behind Kuomintangites' Aggression in Burma," *The Current Digest of the Soviet Press* 5, no. 38:17, October 31, 1953.
28. Quoted in *Burma Weekly Bulletin* (Rangoon), May 27, 1953, 59.
29. *The New York Herald Tribune*, March 22, 1952.
30. See appendix 35.
31. *The Nation* (Rangoon), March 19, 1953.
32. Ibid., July 1, 1953.
33. The Lahu are another ethnic group living in the outlying area of Keng Tung State. These people at that time earned their living through opium plantation and trade, which gave them closer business ties with the Kuomintang.
34. There were about thirty-three feudal Shan chiefs, *saohpa*, ruling over the thirty-three principalities of the Shan States since before and during the British administration in Burma. After Myanmar obtained its independence the Union government tried to abolish the feudal system and to bring the *saohpa* under a centralized government of the Shan States. But there were basic disagreements between the *saohpa* group and the Union government on how the surrender of administrative power should be implemented.
35. See appendix 36.
36. See section 201, chapter 10 of *The Constitution of the Union of Burma* (Rangoon: Government Printing and Stationery, reprinted 1957), 56.
37. See appendix 37.
38. *The Nation* (Rangoon), April 22, 1953.
39. See appendix 38.
40. See appendix 39.
41. *The Times* (London), March 30, 1953.
42. *The Nation* (Rangoon), April 2, 1953.
43. *The Times* (London), February 24, 1953.
44. *The Times of India*, February 28, 1953.
45. *The Nation* (Rangoon), April 7, 1953.
46. Ibid., October 4, 1953.
47. Ibid., February 14, 1954.
48. *The Bangkok Post*, June 29, 1953.
49. *The Times* (London), April 1, 1953.
50. *The New York Times*, February 26, 1953.

51. *The Nation* (Rangoon), February 25, 1953.
52. Ibid., March 8, 1953.
53. Tibor Mende, *The Reporter*, May 12, 1953, 8–12.
54. *The Nation* (Rangoon), March 27, 1953.
55. *The New York Times*, November 27, 1953.
56. Ibid., March 9, 1953.
57. *The Nation* (Rangoon), March 31, 1953.
58. Virginia Thompson, "Burma and Two Chinas," *Foreign Policy Bulletin*, May 15, 1953, 32: 1.
59. *Burma Weekly Bulletin* (Rangoon), December 1953.
60. *The Nation* (Rangoon), March 29, 1953.
61. *The Nation* (Rangoon), April 5, 1953.
62. *The Nation* (Rangoon), March 30, 1953.
63. Maung Maung, *Grim War Against KMT* (Rangoon: Nu Yin Press, 1953), 24.
64. *KMT Aggression, Translation of the Honorable Prime Minister's speech in the Chamber of Deputies* (Rangoon: Government Printing and Stationery, 1953), 2.
65. A/2374, 7th Session, UNGA, March 26, 1953.
66. A/2375, 420th Meeting of the Plenary Session of the UNGA, March 31, 1953.
67. *The Amrita Bazar Patrika* (India), April 25, 1953.
68. A/2375, A/C. 42 AC. 1/2 43, A/C. 1/2 44 Rev. 2, A/C. 1/2 45, UNGA, 7th Session, 1st Committee, 61st Meeting, April 22, 1953.
69. A/2375, A C. 1 / L, 42, UNGA, 7th Session, 1st Committee, 609th Meeting, April 20, 1953.
70. A/2375, A / C. 1 / 2, 42, A / C–1 / 43, UNGA, 7th Session, 1st Committee, 609th Meeting, April 21, 1953.
71. Frank M. Trager et al., *Burma's Role in the United Nations*, 1948–55 (New York: Institute of Pacific Relations, 1950), 12.
72. Ibid.
73. Dr. Maung Maung, *Burma in the Family of Nations* (Amsterdam: Djambatan Ltd., International Educational Publishing House, 1956), 150.
74. See again appendix 37.
75. "Burma Accuses Chinese Nationalists," *The Economist* 160, 7: 72, April 11, 1953.

Chapter 15

1. *The Constitution*, 44.
2. F.N. 106. S.G. (A) 48, *Meeting of the saohpa held at Mong Kung*, May 30, 1948.
3. *The Constitution*, 25.
4. Ibid., 35.
5. F.N. 339. S.G. (J) 48 (a), *Appointment of the Shan State Committee of Enquiry.*
6. Ibid.
7. F.N. 118. S.G. (A) 48, *Minutes of the meeting held in the office of the Resident of the Southern Shan State.*
8. Ibid.
9. Order issued on July 24, 1948, by the Shan State government.
10. F.N. 80. S.G. (J) 49, *Distribution of the Shan State Acts.*
11. *The Constitution*, 45.
12. F.N. 53 S.G. (A) 49, *The Report Given to the Shan State Council by the Head of the Shan State.*

13. F.N. 204 S.G. (A) 49, *Insurgency in Southern Shan State.*

14. F.N. 92 S.G. (A) 49, *The Report of Sao Boonwat on the Occupation of Lashio.*

15. Hugh Tinker, *Union of Burma.* (London: Oxford University Press, 1957), 49.

16. After the purchase, the Ching Tsong Palace was renamed Kanbawza Palace. It became the property of the Shan State government but it was later taken over by the revolutionary government.

17. Special Order No. 6, 1949, issued by the president of the Union of Burma on November 23, 1949; F.N. 31 S.G.(A) 49, Military Administration Proclamation Affecting the Northern Shan State, SN 1.

18. *Notification of the Government of the Union of Burma, Ministry of Judicial Affairs, Judicial I Branch,* December 6, 1949.

19. F.N. 271 S.G. (A) 50, Proposal for the withdrawal of military administration.

20. F.N. 340 S.G. (A) 49, Confidential Report to the Head of State.

21. F.N. 231 S.G. (A) 50, Military Administration in Keng Tung and Appointments of Judges of Superior and Inferior Courts; F.N. 57 S.G.(A) 50, Inquiry into the conduct of the state officials in connection with recent insurgent activities in Shan State.

22. F.N. 127 S.G. (A) 50, *Confidential Report* .

23. F.N. 293 S.G. (A) 50, *Confidential File, Raising of one battalion of levies in Shan State.*

24. Ibid.

25. Ibid.

26. *The Constitution,* 43.

27. *Meeting Minutes of the Sixth Session of the Shan State Council,* held in May 1947.

28. F.N. 144 S.G. (A) 52, *Meeting Minutes of the Sixth Session of the Shan State Council.*

29. F.N. 264 S.G. (A) 50, *Meeting Minutes of the Sixth Session of the Shan State Council.*

30. F.N. 297 S.G. (A) 50, *Meeting Minutes of the Sixth Session of the Shan State Council.*

31. F.N. 264 S.G. (A) 50, *Meeting Minutes of the Sixth Session of the Shan State Council; Notes on discussion of the Eastern Shan State.*

32. F.N. 297 S.G. (A) 50, *Confidential File. The Head of State's Special Instruction to the Resident of the Eastern Shan State.*

33. F.N. 297 S.G. (A) 50, *Confidential File. Special Instruction of the Head of Shan State in the Administration of the Eastern Shan State.* S.N. 2. A letter from U Ba Ni to U Hkun Shelle

34. F.N. 90 S.G. (A) 51, *Confidential File. Chinese Movement in Wa States.* S.N. 24.

35. F.N. 28 S.G. (A) 51, *Record of the Shan State Council meeting held from July 31, 1950, to August 9, 1980, Sixth Session. Insurrection in the Northern Shan State.*

36. Ibid.

37. *Burma Gazette,* October 1952, 36.

38. *Record of the Second Historical Importance of the Shan State,* 1 (in Myanmar).

39. U Htun Myint (Taunggyi), *The Saohpas and the Shan State.* Shwe Aye Sar Pay No. 3 (Rangoon: Thamada Press, 1952), 33.

40. F.N. 240 Ya Pa (A) 53, *Appointment of Officers in Military Administrative Areas* (in Myanmar).

41. F.N. 63 Ya Pa (A) 53, *Report on General Matters Concerning Saohpa and Their Relatives* (in Myanmar)

42. (1) F.N. 247 Ya Pa (A) 53, *Meeting Minutes of Pyidwtha Project for the Shan State:* November 12, 1953. (2) F.N. 177 Ya Pa (A) 53, *Transfer of Administrative Power and Plan and How to Solve the Saohpa Problem* (in Myanmar).

43. Ibid.

44. F.N. 17 Ya Pa (A) 53, *Report of the Insurgency in the Southern Shan State* (in Myanmar)

45. *Budget Report of the Head of the Shan State at the Sixth Session of the Shan State Council Meeting held at Kanbawzq School, Main Hall*, on July 26, 1954, on Monday at 11 A.M. (in Myanmar).

46. *The Union of Burma, Record of the Shan State Council Meetings*, from 1 to 8 (Yangon: Government Printing House and Stationery, 1955), 7.

47. *Record of General Conference of the Shan State Council from 1 to 9* (Yangon: Government Printing House and Stationery, 1953).

48. F.N. 241 Ya Pa (A) 54, *Meeting Minutes of Officers of the Shan State government*

49. F.N. 119 Ya Pa (A) 55, *Annual Report of District Resident*, 1955 (in Myanmar).

50. Pa-Ah-Ma-Sa, *Pa-O National Unity Organization.*

51. F.N. 113 Ya Pa (A) 56, *Annual Report of Wunna Kyaw Htin U Nyo, Tuanggyi District Resident 1956* (in Myanmar).

52. F.N. 173 Ya Pa (A) 55, *Demand put up by the peasants of Hsi Paw.*

53. *Record of the First Conference of the Shan State Council from 1 to* 7.

54. F.N. 185 Ra (Aa) 57, *Migration of the Wa and Other Nationalities into Burma*; *The Nation* (Rangoon), September 19, 1956.

55. F.N. 209 Pa (Aa) 58, *Incidents that took place in the eastern and special northern districts of Shan State* (in Myanmar).

56. F.N. 47 Ra (Aa) 57, *Report submitted to the Shan State government on Chinese Incursion into Burma.*

57. *Record of Shan State Council, Second Conference.* File (2), 62.

58. Ibid.

59. *Record of the Third Conference of the Shan State Council (Hluttaw)*, File no. 2, 5. (in Myanmar).

60. *Report of Special Intelligence Officer*, July 24, 1957 (in Myanmar).

61. *Record of the Fourth Session of the Shan State Council Meeting*, File no. 5 (from 1, 2, 3, 4, and 5), 5 (in Myanmar).

62. F.N. 217 Ra (La) 57, *Compensation for Saohpa.*

63. U Sein Win, *The Split Story* (Rangoon: the Guardian Press, 1956), 44.

64. *Burma Gazette*, November 1958.

65. *The Constitution*, 33.

66. *Record of Special Meeting of Shan State Council, Union of Burma*, November 7 to 11, 1958, 7. (in Myanmar).

67. *Record of the 6th Shan State Council Meeting after Second General Election*, 100. (in Myanmar).

68. *The Constitution*, 57

Chapter 16

1. *Burma Weekly Bulletin*, May 21, 1959.

2. *Ibid.*

Chapter 17

1. U Htun Myint (Taunggyi), *Shan State, [a component] of Equal Status Within the Union* (Rangoon: Myanmar Byuha Press, 1960); Meeting Minutes of the "All States Conference," held at the Sa-myein Yeiktha Building, Taunggyi, Southern Shan State (Rangoon: Doh-Ta-Wun Press), 1960.

2. Record of the Shan State Committee for the Amendment to the Union Constitution, Universities Central Library, typescript.

3. Meeting Minutes of the meeting for the Amendment to the Union Constitution, held on

November 5, 1960, at 10:00 A.M. in the office of the head of the Shan State in Taunggyi. Records of the Shan State.

4. Now called Sa-Myein Yeiktha.

5. Minutes of the "All States Conference," 43; "Proposed Amendments to the Union Constitution" submitted by the Shan State (Rangoon: Doh-Ta-Wun Press), 31–32.

6. "Proposed Amendments to the Union Constitution," 32.

7. Minutes of the All States Conference, 43–44.

8. Minutes of the All States Conference, 44; *The Hanthawaddy Daily*, December 23, 1960.

9. Ibid.

10. Ibid.

11. Ibid.

12. Ibid.

13. "Proposed Amendments to the Union Constitution," 1.

14. Personal interviews 0122, 0137, History Dept. (Research), Y.U.

15. "Proposed Amendments to the Union Constitution," 1; Minutes of the All States Conference, 45.

16. "Proposed Amendments to the Union Constitution," 14.

It can be maintained that the criticism resulted from the fact that the draft constitution approved by thePreliminary Convention of the AFPFL mentioned the constituent units that were to be formed as part of the Union of Myanmar. These constituent units were divided into three categories—Union State, Autonomous State, and National Areas. Thus there appeared to be discrimination in the status of the constituent units, but when General Aung San presented the constitution in the Constituent Assembly, he had altered some provisions in the draft constitution approved and accepted by the Preliminary Conference of the AFPFL. "At first the proposal I was to make was the one decided upon at the AFPFL Convention. But on reading the proposal, I found that it needed revision ... so I altered these provisions ... so it could not be held that we had already decided clearly as to which states would be included in the Union. In the proposal presented at the AFPFL Convention, we did mention these states, but we did so without having given much thought to it. However, after some reflection, we believed that since these units would automatically be included in the Union, we have made no mention of the constituent states and have now made only a general statement." *Proceedings of the Constituent Assembly of Myanmar*, vol. 1, *Meeting Minutes*, No. 4 (Yangon: Myanmar Government Printing Press, 1947), 73–83.

17. "Proposed Amendments to the Union Constitution," 14–15.

18. Ibid., 15–16.

19. *The Constitution*, section 8.

20. "Proposed Amendments to the Union Constitution," 16–17.

21. Chapter 2, Fundamental Rights.

22. Chapter 3, Responsibilities of the State for Peasants and Workers.

23. Chapter 4, Directives of State Policy.

24. *The Constitution*, section 9.

25. Section 42: The state shall direct its policy toward giving material assistance to economic organizations not working for profit. It shall give preference to cooperative and similar economic organizations.

26. Section 43: All useful arts and sciences, research and cultural institutes and the study of Pali and Sanskrit shall enjoy the protection and support of the state.

27. Section 44: (1) The state shall direct its policy toward operation of all public utility undertakings by itself or local bodies or by peoples' cooperative organizations. (2) The state shall

direct its policy toward exploitation of all natural resources in the Union by itself or local bodies or by peoples' cooperative organizations.

28. "Proposed Amendments to the Union Constitution," 17.

29. *The Constitution*, section 23 (5).

30. "Proposed Amendments to the Union Constitution," 17.

31. *The Constitution*, section 30.

32. "Proposed Amendments to the Union Constitution," 17–18. Although land, land revenue, and loans for land development were included on the Constituent State Legislative List, it was stated that the 1953 Agricultural Land Nationalization Act covered all land in Myanmar (1953 Agricultural Land Nationalization Act, chapter1, paragraph 2).

33. *The Constitution*, section 31.

34. "Proposed Amendments to the Union Constitution," 18.

35. *The Constitution*, section 91.

36. "Proposed Amendments to the Union Constitution," 18.

37. *The Constitution*, section 92 (3).

38. "Proposed Amendments to the Union Constitution," 18–19.

39. *The Constitution*, section 93.

40. "Proposed Amendments to the Union Constitution," 19.

41. *The Constitution*, section 94.

42. "Proposed Amendments to the Union Constitution," 19.

43. *The Constitution*, section 96.

44. "Proposed Amendments to the Union Constitution," 19.

45. *The Constitution*, section 122.

46. "Proposed Amendments to the Union Constitution," 20.

47. *The Constitution*, section 128.

48. Ibid., section 131.

49. "Proposed Amendments to the Union Constitution," 20.

50. *The Constitution*, section 154.

51. "Proposed Amendments to the Union Constitution," 21.

52. *The Constitution*, section 160.

53. "Proposed Amendments to the Union Constitution," 21.

54. When the AFPFL split into Stable and Clean factions, Dr. Saw Hla Tun and U Zan Htar Sin from the Stable faction resigned as ministers. In their places U Nu appointed U Saw Lu Lu as Karen State minister and Duwa Zau Rip as Kachin State minister, without prior consultation with the state councils concerned. The Union president asked the chief justice whether U Nu's action was legal or illegal. Thereupon the justice minister, Dr. E Maung, gave the following explanation, which was accepted by the Supreme Court. He explained that under section 115 of the Union Constitution, the cabinet was collectively responsible to parliament. Thus the prime minister had the right to select and appoint ministers to his cabinet and that the stipulation that he must consult with the state council before appointing a state minister was merely a directive and not an order. Maung Maung, *Burma's Constitution Comes to Life* (Madras: Diocesan Press [n.d.]. Reprinted from the *Indian Year Book of International Affairs*, 1958). Also in U Zan Htar Sin, *Democracy Upside Down* (Rangoon: Nantha Press, February 1990), 66–67.

55. *The Constitution*, section 162.

56. "Proposed Amendments to the Union Constitution," 21.

57. *The Constitution*, section 164 (2).

58. "Proposed Amendments to the Union Constitution," 21.

59. *The Constitution*, section 219.

60. "Proposed Amendments to the Union Constitution," 21–22.

61. *The Constitution*, section 222.
62. "Proposed Amendments to the Union Constitution," 22.
63. *The Constitution*, Schedule III, List 1, Union Legislative List.
64. "Proposed Amendments to the Union Constitution," 23.
65. Ibid., 23–24.
66. Ibid., 24–25.
67. "Proposed Amendments to the Union Constitution," 25.
68. Ibid., 25.
69. Ibid., 25–26.
70. Ibid., 26.
71. *The Constitution*, Third Schedule, List 2. State Legislative List.
72. "Proposed Amendments to the Union Constitution," 27.
73. Ibid., 27.
74. "Proposed Amendments to the Union Constitution," 28.
75. "Proposed Amendments to the Union Constitution," 29–30. Explanation given by U Chan Htoon in his address to members of the Supreme Court about whether or not the 1953 Agricultural Land Nationalization Act included the states. *The Union of Burma*, 30.
76. "Proposed Amendments to the Union Constitution," 29–30.
77. Ibid., 30.
78. Ibid.
79. Ibid., 31.
80. "Proposed Amendments to the Union Constitution," 31.
81. Minutes of the All States Conference, 41.
82. *The Nation* (Rangoon), March 1, 1961.

Chapter 18

1. See appendix 40 for the list of those attending the meeting.

The document for revising the constitution was submitted to the States Scrutiny Committee on March 8, 1961, and to the Constitution Amendment Committee led by Dr. E Maung on March 11, 1961. Minutes of the All States Conference, 45.

2. According to the present constitution, the states have limited powers, whereas all the residuary power is left with the Union. "Proposed Amendments to the Union Constitution," 30.
3. Record of seventy-ninth meeting of the States Scrutiny Committee, held on March 15, 1961. HDR: 3AP/1987.
4. See appendix 41 for the list of those attending the meeting.
5. Records of the Special Meeting of the States Scrutiny Committee, held on March 20, 1961. HDR: 3AP/1987.
6. Minutes of the seventy-ninth meeting of the States Scrutiny Committee. HDR: 3AP/1987; Minutes of the special meeting of March 20, 1961. HDR: 3AP/1987.
7. Ibid.
8. Ibid.
9. Ibid.
10. Minutes of the seventy-ninth meeting of the States Scrutiny Committee. HDR: 3AP/1987.
11. SCOUHP had been inactive after 1952, and an attempt had been made to revive it but without success. (Minutes of the Taunggyi All States Conference), 24.
12. *Botataung Daily*, March 19, 1961; Minutes of the All States Conference, 15; *The Nation* (Rangoon), March 19, 1961.

13 *Botataung Daily*, March 19, 1961; *Myanmar Alin Daily*, April 20, 1961.

14. *The Rangoon Daily*, April 21, 1961; *The Guardian*, April 20, 1961.

15. *The Rangoon Daily*, April 21, 1961; *Discussions between the Shan State leaders and the prime minister, May 21, 1961*. Directorate of Military Intelligence.

16. *Discussions between the Shan State leaders and the prime minister, May 21, 1961*. Directorate of Military Intelligence.

When U Nu held a press conference on April 20, 1961, reporters asked him about the letter from Singapore and he answered: "In the past month, before I left for the Chin Hills, a letter came into my hands. That letter was from an American from Singapore to a Bamar in Burma. The letter, posted in Bangkok and addressed to an American in Singapore, said that a revolutionary party had been set up in the Shan State and that the party was led by a very prominent person in Burma. The Shans from that party would endeavor to bring about the secession of the Shan State from the Union and to establish its independence. To be able to secede, [they would need] foreign help, which should be immediately given, lest the attempt be crushed by the Bamars." *Myanmar Alin Daily* newspaper, April 16, 1961.

Former President of the Union, Ex-Speaker of the Chamber of Nationalities, and member of the Chamber of Nationalities, Sao Shwe Thaike, and the *mahadevi* arrived in Yangon by train from Shwenyaung on May 20, 1961. On receiving the news of Sao Shwe Thaike's return to Yangon, reporters waited for his arrival at the railway station. As soon as Sao Shwe Thaike got off the train he was taken to the Railway Hotel, and questions were then asked. One reporter said: "Prime Minister U Nu had made an accusation that a person from the Shan State with a very high reputation was involved in communications with foreign countries. What is your opinion?" Sao Shwe Thaike replied that he had heard U Nu say that *saohpa* were among those establishing contact with foreign countries. Regarding the involvement of a person whose reputation shone "like the sun and the moon" Sao Shwe Thaike said he had not heard the prime minister say so. "I have not read the newspaper, so I do not know." *Hanthawaddy Daily* newspaper, May 27, 1961.

17. *Discussions between the Shan State leaders and the prime minister*, May 21, 1961, Directorate of Military Intelligence.

18. Ibid.

19. *Discussions between the Shan State leaders and the prime minister*, May 21, 1961, Directorate of Military Intelligence; *The Rangoon Daily*, April 22, 1961.

20. *The Guardian*, April 22, 1961.

21. *Discussions between the Shan State leaders and the prime minister; Myanmar Alin Daily*, April 23, 1961.

22. Col. Kyaw Soe, Col. Shwe, Col. Ba Shwe, Lt. Col. Gwan Shein, and Maj. Thein Shwe attended the discussions. The discussions between the army officers and the Shan State representatives were held on April 21, 1961, at 16:30 hours, at the Shan State Government Office, Taunggyi. Directorate of Military Intelligence.

23. Sao Man Hpa (Hsen Wi), Sao Htun Aye (Tawng Peng), U Aung Phu (Mong Nawng), Sao Hkun Aung (Baw), Sao Kyaw Khaung (Mong Nai), U Ba Thein (Mong Mit), U Lu Gyi (Keng Tung), U Hkun Sam Myat (Nam Kham), U Hme (Mong Yai), U San Mya (Loilem) attended the meeting.

24. Discussions between the army officers and the Shan State representatives, April 21, 1961.

25. Sao Shwe Thaike. Facts of personal interview 0043. History Dept. (Research), Yangon University.

26. *The Rangoon Daily*, April 26, 1961; *The Nation* (Rangoon), April 26, 1961.

At the meeting of the Shan State government, held on April 25, the following resolutions were passed:

1. The Shan State government, in suppressing the insurgency in the Shan State, until peace is secured, will cooperate with the army, the armed police force, and the public.
2. The Shan State government to issue a statement asking all the insurgents to renounce armed insurrection and return to the legal fold.
3. The Shan State government solemnly believes that success can be achieved if problems relating to the differences between the states and Burma Proper could be settled in a fraternal spirit.
4. The above resolutions passed by the Shan State government, to be approved unanimously at the meeting of the Shan State government and State ministers, where agreement will be reached not only to condemn the insurgents but also to cooperate with the government and the public in suppressing the insurgents effectively, until peace is restored in the Shan State. *The Rangoon Daily* newspaper of April 26, 1961.

27. The Taunggyi Conference was held to gain unity for the nationalities; however, not only were the Bamars excluded, but the Ya-Pa-La-Pha was also not invited. Only the vice president of the Ya-Pa-La-Pha U Htun Mya, U Khan, and U Aung Than were invited on personal grounds.

In accordance with the resolution of the Ya-Pa-La-Pha, U Htun Mya and friends boycotted the conference and sent letters of regret. The above statement was made known to the reporters by U Htun Aye (Nam Kham) at the press conference on June 8. *Pyidaungsu Daily* newspaper of June 11, 1961.

28. Minutes of the All States Conference, 17–21.
29. *Pyidaungsu Daily*, June 2, 1961.
30. Ibid., June 9, 1961.
31. (A) Regarding the Taunggyi All States Conference, Sama Duwa Sinwa Nawng expressed his opinion to the press, saying that the conference was tantamount to creating more problems. If the nation were to be transformed into a collection of autonomous states, he did not know what effect it would have on Shan State, but for Kachin State it would be like the explosion of the hydrogen bomb. *Pyidaungsu Daily* newspaper, June 8, 1961; *The Nation* (Rangoon), June 7, 1961.

(B) U Zahre Lian also told the press that it was impossible to implement a true Federal Principle as proposed by Shan State. *The Nation* (Rangoon), June 5, 1961.

32. Minutes of the All States Conference, 23–24.
33. Minutes of the All States Conference, 36; *Pyidaungsu Daily*, June 10, 1961.
34. *Myanmar Alin Daily*, June 11, 1961.
35. *Myanmar Alin Daily*, June 10, 1961; *The Nation* (Rangoon), June 11, 1961.
36. *Hanthawaddy Daily*, June 11, 1961. Sao Hkun Aung's name was not included on the list published by the *Pyidaungsu* and *The Nation*.
37. *Pyidaungsu Daily*, June 12, 1961; *Hanthawaddy Daily*, June 13, 1961.
38. *Pyidaungsu Daily*, June 12, 1961; *Hanthawaddy Daily*, June 12, 1961.
39. *Hanthawaddy Daily*, June 15, 1961; *The Nation* (Rangoon), June 14,1961.
40. *Pyidaungsu Daily*, June 13,1961; *Hanthawaddy Daily*, June 12, 1961.
41. *Pyidaungsu Daily*, June 13, 1961.
42. *Pyidaungsu Daily*, June 14, 1961; *Hanthawaddy Daily*, June 14, 1961.
43. *Pyidaungsu Daily*, June 14, 1961.
44. Minutes of the All States Conference, 38.
45. Ibid., 37.

46. Ibid.
47. Ibid.
48. Ibid., 39.
49. *Pyidaungsu Daily*, June 14, 1961.
50. *Pyidaungsu Daily*, June 17–18, 1961; *The Nation* (Rangoon), June 17, 1961.
51. Minutes of the All States Conference, 40; *Hanthawaddy Daily*, June 16, 1961.
52. Minutes of the All States Conference, 40–41.
53. Ibid., 40–42.
54. Ibid., 42–46.
55. Ibid., 46.
56. Ibid., 47–48.
57. Ibid., 48.
58. Ibid., 48–49.
59. Ibid., 50.
60. Ibid., 51.
61. Ibid., 51–52.
62. Minutes of the All States Conference, 54; "Proposed Amendments to the Union Constitution," 31.
63. Minutes of the All States Conference, 54.
64. "Proposed Amendments to the Union Constitution," 1; Minutes of the All States Conference, 54.
65. "Proposed Amendments to the Union Constitution," 1.
66. Minutes of the All States Conference, 54–55.
67. Ibid., 55.
68. Constituent Assembly is the term U Zahre Lian meant to use here.
69. Minutes of the All States Conference, 55.
70. Regions which had been included on the Part 1 List were the Federated Shan States.

Regions which were excluded in the Federated Shan States were Hsaung Sup, Singaling Hkamti, and Hkamti Long; Rakhine Hill Tracts; Chin Hill Administered Area; Myitkyina, Bhamo, and Katha Administered Areas of the Kachin Hill Regions; Triangle Area Region; Hukawng Valley regions lying north of Chindwin Administered Areas; Salween Administered Areas; and other regions of nonadministered areas.

71. Regions included on the Part 2 List were those small parts of Myitkyina and Bhamo, Mawlek Subdivision; Homalin Subdivision of the upper Chindwin Administered Areas; former rural areas of Tamu township; Myawaddy District of Kawkareik, Kya In, townships in areas east of Taungoo Administered Areas; and ranges of mountains of the Administered Areas of Hsahton.
72. Minutes of the All States Conference, 55.
73. Constituent Assembly, 1/4, 71.
74. Minutes of the All States Conference, 56–57.
75. Ibid., 57.
76. Ibid., 57–58.
77. Ibid., 58–59.
78. Ibid., 59.
79. Ibid., 59–60.
80. Ibid., 60–61.
81. Ibid., 56–57.
82. Ibid., 61.
83. Ibid.

84. Ibid., 61–62.
85. Ibid., 63–64.
86. Ibid., 64.
87. Ibid., 64–65.
88. Ibid., 65.
89. Ibid.
90. Ibid., 66–67.
91. Ibid., 67.
92. Ibid.
93. Ibid., 68.
94. Ibid.
95. Ibid., 69; Personal interview 0127, History Dept. (Research), Y.U.
92. Minutes of the All States Conference, 69.
93. Now Tharthana Yeiktha Road.
94. Minutes of the All States Conference, 69.
95. Ibid.
96. Ibid.
97. Ibid.
98. Ibid., 70.
99. Minutes of the All States Conference, 70; *Pyidaungsu Daily*, June 16, 1961.
100. *Pyidaungsu Daily*, June 18, 1961; *The Nation* (Rangoon), June 17, 1961.
101. *Pyidaungsu Daily*, June 18, 1961; *The Nation* (Rangoon), June 17, 1961.
102. *The Nation* (Rangoon), June 17, 1961; *Pyidaungsu Daily*, June 17–18, 1961.
103. Minutes of the All States Conference, 78–79.

Resolution No. 1 was proposed by the Rakhine representative U Maung Maung (Ya Ta Nya) and seconded by the Kachin representative Duwa Lawan Li (member of parliament). Resolution No. 2 was proposed by the Kayah representative U Chit Maung (Kayah National Headquarters) and seconded by the Shan State representative U Htun Myint (Taunggyi), the Mon representative Nai Ngwe Thein, and the Kayin representative Saw Thin Sein. Resolution No. 3 was proposed by the Mon representative Nai San Myaing and seconded by the Rakhine representative U Ba Pyu (Ya Pa Nya Ba). Resolution No. 4 was proposed by the Kachin representative U Zan Hta Sin and seconded by the Shan State representative U Kyaw Sein (member of parliament). Resolution No. 5 was proposed by the Shan State representative U Soe Maung and seconded by the Kayah State representative U L. Aung Sein (Kayah Youth Organization).

Chapter 19

1. *The Hanthawaddy Daily*, June 27, 1961. Two other members of the group, Minister Sao Hkun Hkio and Sao Htun E, the *saohpa* of Hsa Mong Hkam, arrived in Yangon on June 29, 1961, according to the *Myanmar Alin Daily* newspaper of June 30,1961. While the Shan representatives were in Yangon, U Kyaw Nyein, the vice president of the AFPFL, went to meet Prime Minister U Nu on June 29, to present his party's view on the federal issue. He admitted that the states did have grievances that, if their cause were removed, would negate the need to revise the constitution. If the Shan proposals were adopted, bickerings would arise between the Shans and the Bamars, between the Kachins and the Bamars, leading to mistrust and dissension. Therefore it was not the correct way to proceed, and the AFPFL could not accept the Shan proposal. *Pyidaungsu Daily*, June 30, 1961.

2. *Pyidaungsu Daily*, July 2, 1961; *The Mirror Daily*, July 2, 1961.

3. *Pyidaungsu Daily*, July 2, 1961; *The Mirror Daily*, July 2, 1961. *The Nation* of July 2, 1961, carried a report that the Kachin leaders who supported the Federal Principle adopted by the

Taunggyi All States Conference had formed their own working committee to implement the Federal Principle, and that members of that committee—Duwa Zau Lawn and U Zan Hta Sin of the Kachin National Congress, Duwa Zau Rip and Duwa Htain Baing La of the Kachin Youth Paungyaung National Party, Duwa Hkun Hpong, Duwa Ban In Ban, and Duwa Nang Zing La of the People's Economic and Cultural Development Party—had also come down to Yangon. They were planning to meet with the leaders of political parties, including Prime Minister U Nu, as well as the members of the Government Advisory Committee on the Amendment of the Constitution, headed by Dr. Ba U.

4. *The Mirror Daily*, July 2, 1961.

5. Ibid. The PVO's message to the Taunggyi All States Conference said that many difficulties had been encountered in implementing the present constitution, and that these difficulties could be resolved only by revising it and forming a Republic of all States. All nationals must repel the attempt of the expansionist colonialists to sow seeds of disunity, and must work for the preservation and strengthening of independence, and, using the strength of national unity, join in the fight for internal and international peace.

6. *The Mirror Daily*, July 2, 1961.

7. *The Mirror Daily*, July 6, 1961.

8. *The Mirror Daily*, July 7,1961.

9. *The Mirror Daily*, July 8, 1961; *The Nation* (Rangoon), July 8, 1961.

10. *The Mirror Daily*, July 9, 1961; *The Nation* (Rangoon), July 9, 1961.

11. *The Mirror Daily*, July 9, 1961.

12. *Botataung Daily*, July 12, 1961.

13. This and the following paragraphs are taken from the *Pyidaungsu Daily*, July 12, 1961.

14. *Mandaing Daily*, July 12, 1961.

15. *Mandaing Daily*, July 12, 1961; *Botataung Daily*, July 12, 1961.

16. *The Nation* (Rangoon), July 12, 1961.

17. *Botataung Daily*, July 12, 1961.

18. Ibid.

19. Ibid.

20. Ibid., July 14, 1961.

21. *Ban Mai Mong Tai, Khit Thit Shan Pyi* (The New Shan State). Printed in the Shan language at the White Tiger Press, Hsi Paw. The publisher was U Aung Ba, elder brother of U Kya Bu, former principal agricultural officer, Shan State. From the publication of the Office of the Director, Military Intelligence Service (MIS), entitled *Shan State Political Actvities and the Origins of the Federal Principle 1954–1962* (in Myanmar).

22. The *Mandaing Daily*, July 14, 1961.

23. The *Mandaing Daily*, July 14, 1961; The *Botataung Daily*, July 14, 1961.

24. The Shan State government had decided not only to condemn the Shan insurgents but also to suppress the insurgency with the help of the people of the state until peace was restored, and the decision was publicized on April 25, 1961. *The Rangoon Daily*, April 26, 1961.

25. *The Nation* (Rangoon), July 15, 1961.

26. *Report of the Government Advisory Committee on the Amendment of the Constitution*, as proposed by the Shan State government and its people. 1962 (Yangon: Printing and Stationery Department. Government of the Union of Myanmar), 5. In subsequent notes this publication will be referred to as *Report of the Advisory Committee 1962*.

27. *Report of the Advisory Committee 1962*, 12; *Botataung Daily*, July 23, 1961.

28. *Report of the Advisory Committee 1962*, 13–17.

29. Section 151: If at any time it appears to the president that a question of law has arisen, or is likely to arise, which is of such a nature and of such public importance that it is expedient

to obtain the opinion of the Supreme Court upon it, he may refer the question to that court for consideration, and the court may, after such hearing as it thinks fit, report to the president on it.

30. K. C. Wheare, *Federal Government*, 3rd ed. (London: Oxford University Press, 1953), 12.

31. *Report of the Advisory Committee 1962*, 24. All sebsequent references to this document are noted in the text by page number in parentheses.

32. William Anderson. *The Nation and the States: Rivals or Partners?* (Minneapolis: University of Minnesota Press), 1955.

33. *Report of the Advisory Committee 1962*, 29–34.

Third Schedule. List 3. Concurrent Legislative List

1. Land—
   (i) Regulation of land tenures, including the relation of the landlord and tenantand the collection of rents, transfer, alienation, and devolution of land.
2. Forests, Mines, and Oil fields—
   (i) Regulation of forests, mines, and oil-fields (including labor and safety in mines and oil fields) and mineral development.

34. *Myanmar Alin Daily*, January 20, 1962.

35. *Pyidaungsu Daily*, January 21, 1962.

36. *Pyidaungsu Daily*, January 21, 1962; *Myanmar Alin Daily*, January 21, 1962.

37. *Pyidaungsu Daily*, January 21, 1962; *Myanmar Alin Daily*, January 21, 1962. Besides Dr. Saw Hla Tun, the rest of the representatives who met with U Nu were members of the provisional Executive Committee of the States Unity Organization, formed by the All States Conference in Taunggyi. At the time of the Taunggyi conference, Dr. Saw Hla Tun was abroad on government business.

38. States Unity Organization document. All sebsequent references to this document are noted in the text by page number in parentheses.

39. (a) States Unity Organization document, 8; As the attorney general, U Chan Htoon made this statement in the Supreme Court during arguments whether the Land Nationalization Act extended to the states or not. *The Nation* (Rangoon), July 2, 1962.

40. Section 222 (1) In this constitution, unless the context otherwise requires, the following expressions have the meanings hereby respectively assigned to them, that is to say–"Unit" means (a) any state forming a constituent unit of the Union of Myanmar; (b) all the territories of the Union of Myanmar not forming part of any state.

41. Section 199. Parliament may by Act admit to the Union a new state upon such conditions including the extent of representation of the state in parliament as may be specified in the Act.

42. Chapter 11 contains provisions concerning amendments to the constitution.

43. States Unity Organization Document, 9.

44. *The Nation* (Rangoon), February 13, 1962.

45. Ibid., February 14, 1962.

46. *The Nation* (Rangoon), February 19, 1962.

47. *The Rangoon Daily*, February 19, 1962.

48. Ibid., February 20, 1962.

49. Widhura Thakin Chit Maung: *The Shan Principle and the Future of the Union* (Yangon: Kyemon Press, 1962), a–d.

50. Speech of Prime Minister U Nu at the conference on the Federal Principle held in the Main Hall of the Myanmar Broadcasting Service, on Pyay Road, Yangon, on February 24, 1962. HDR:RT/0016/Sp-62/1990. This will be referred to in subsequent notes as U Nu's broadcast speech.

51. The speech of Minister Sao Hkun Hkio, delivered at the Conference on the Federal

Principle, held in the Main Hall of Myanmar Broadcasting Service, Pyay Road, Yangon, on February 24, 1962. HDR:RT/0016/SP-62/1990.

52. Section 8. All powers, legislative, executive, and judicial, in relation to the remaining territories of the Union of Myanmar shall, subject to the provisions of section 180, be exercisable only by, or on the authority of, the organs of the Union.

53. The speech of the Kachin State representative Duwa Zau Lawn, delivered at the Conference on the Federal Principle, held in the Main Hall of the Myanmar Broadcasting Service, Pyay Road, Yangon, on February 24, 1962. HDR:RT/0016/SP-62/1990.

54. He seems to be alluding to sections 166 (2), 167, 174 (2), and 175 (3) of the constitution which contain the terms "Kachin" and "non-Kachin," and that of the twelve seats in the Chamber of Nationalities to be filled by representatives from the Kachin State, six were to be filled by Kachins and six by non-Kachins.

55. The speech of the representative of the Chin Special Division, Captain Mang Tung Nung, delivered at the Conference on the Federal Principle, held in the Main Hall of the Myanmar Broadcasting Service, Pyay Road, Yangon, on February 24, 1962. HDR:RT/0017/SP-62/1990.

56. The speech of the representative of the Shan State, U Htun Myint (Taunggyi), delivered at the Conference on the Federal Principle, held in the Main Hall of the Myanmar Broadcasting Service, Pyay Road, Yangon, on February 24, 1962. HDR:RT 0017/SP-62/1990.

57. The Shan State representatives involved in the drafting of the constitution initially wished to engage the services of Barrister Mr. Dawood as constitutional adviser, but finally selected U Myint Thein as their legal adviser.

58. The speech of Kayah U Sein, delivered at the Conference on the Federal Principle, held in the Main Hall of the Myanmar Broadcasting Service, Pyay Road, Yangon, on February 24, 1962. HDR:RT/0018/SP-61/1990.

59. U Nu's broadcast speech.

60. The speech of Thakin Chit Maung, delivered on the second day of the Conference on the Federal Principle, which was inaugurated in the Main Hall of the Myanmar Broadcasting Service, Pyay Road, Yangon, on February 24, 1962. HDR:RT/SP-62/1990. This speech was published by the Kyemon Press in book form as Widhura Thakin ChitMaung's *The Shan Proposal and the Future of the Union*. All sebsequent references are to the published speech, noted in the text by page number in parentheses.

61. *The Daily Mail* correspondents Lt. Col. J. C. Tulloch and Ian Campbell had links to Force 136, one of the British intelligence units, and were instigators of the Kayin uprising in 1948. U Thant. *Pyidawtha Khayee* 2nd vol. (Yangon: Sarpay Beikman Press 1961), 108–112.

62. The speech of U Ba Swe delivered on the second day of the Conference on the Federal Principle, held in the Main Hall of the Myanmar Broadcasting Service, Pyay Road, Yangon, on March 1, 1962. HDR:RT/0019/SP 62/1990.

63. The following information is put in, because not to do so would make U Ba Swe appear very casual with his facts. The largest state in the US is Alaska, covering an area of 586,412 sq. miles, and the smallest state is Rhode Island, covering an area of 1,214 sq. miles. The state with the biggest population is California with 29,760,021 and the state with the smallest population is Wyoming with 453,588 (1990 census).

64. *The Shan Proposal and the Union* Gagyi–Nga.

65. Speech of the chairman, Minister Dr. E Maung, delivered at the conference between Burma Proper and the states, presenting the views of the Union Party, Yangon. Union Party Headquarters. 3–4.

66. See annex (3).

Chapter 20

1. Personal interview 0126, History Dept. (Research), Yangon University.
2. *Botataung Daily*, March 3, 1962.
3. HDR: 1 AP/1990.
4. Personal interview 0126, History Dept. (Research), Yangon University.
5. Personal interviews 0125, 0125, History Dept. (Research), Y.U.
6. Personal interviews 0126, 0124, History Dept. (Research), Y.U.
7. Personal interview 0126, History Dept. (Research), Y.U.
8. Now called Shweli Road.
9. Now called Saya San Road.
10. Now called Taw-Win Road, Dagon Township.
11. *Hanthawaddy Daily*, March 5, 1962; *The Nation* (Rangoon), March 3, 1962; Personal interviews 0126, 0125, History Dept. (Research). Y.U.
12. *Botataung Daily*, March 3, 1962; Record of the coup d'état by Kayah U. Sein, hand-written script.
13. *The Nation* (Rangoon), March 3, 1962.
14. Personal interview 0126, History Dept. (Research), Y.U.
15. HDR: I AP/1990.
16. Personal interview 0126, History Dept. (Research), Y.U.; *Botataung Daily*, March 3, 1962; *The Nation* (Rangoon), March 3, 1962.
17. *Hanthawaddy Daily*, March 4, 1962.
18. *The Nation* (Rangoon), March 4, 1962.
19. *Botataung Daily*, March 4, 1962; *The Nation* (Rangoon), March 4, 1962
20. *Hanthawaddy Daily*, March 4, 1962; *The Nation* (Rangoon), March 4, 1962
21. *Hanthawaddy Daily*, March 3, 1962; *The Nation* (Rangoon), March 3, 1962.
22. Ibid.
23. Ibid.
24. Record of coup d'état; *The Nation* (Rangoon), March 3, 1962.
25. Record of coup d'état.
26. Record of coup d'état; *The Nation* (Rangoon), March 3, 1962.
27. Until 1988 this encampment was used as the Institute of Political Science. Now it serves as an extension of the Myanmar Military Hospital.
28. Personal interviews 0125, 0144, History Dept. (Research), Y.U.
29. Inge Sargent, *Twilight over Burma* (Honolulu: University of Hawaii Press, 1994), 174.
30. *The Nation* (Rangoon), March 3, 1962
31. *Hanthawaddy Daily*, March 3, 1962; *The Nation* (Rangoon), March 3, 1962
32. Ibid.
33. *Hanthawaddy Daily*, March 3, 1962.
34. Ibid.
35. Ibid.
36. Ibid., March 6, 1962.
37. Ibid., March 4, 1962.
38. Shan State Political Movements and the Origins of the Federal Principle, 1954–62. Directorate of Military Intelligence. Here in after referred to as Shan State Politics.
39. Members of the All Shan States Organization who lost in that election were U Ohn Pe (South Loi Lem), U Tin Ko Ko (North Yawnghwe), and U San Hla Baw (Mong Mit). *Record of the Third Pyithu Hluttaw*. The Union of Myanmar (parliament), vol. 2. Meeting Minutes Record No. 22 (Yangon: Government Printing and Stationery. 1961), 2362–2364.

40. Originally U Tun Aye (Nam Kham) was designated by Sao Hkun Hkio as an observer at the All Nationals Conference, but U Nu permitted him to attend the conference as a representative so that he would have the opportunity to speak and give his views. *The Nation* (Rangoon), February 25, 1962.

41. *The Nation* (Rangoon), March 4, 1962

42. U Ding Ratang, member of the Chamber of Nationalities, for Myitkyina (North constituency, supported the AFPFL federation.

43. U La Wan, member of parliament from the Bhamo Constituency in Kachin State, was added as a member of the Kachin State Supreme Council on March 12, 1962. *The Nation* (Rangoon), March 23, 1962.

44. All civilian members were members of the former state council. All of them were supporters of the AFPFL federation. Chairman Dr. Saw Hla Tun was interested in the Federal Principle. He was the only one from among the heads of state of the Pyidaungsu government who was reappointed chairman by the Revolutionary Council. Some of the persons appointed as Supreme Council members were members of the AFPFL. Therefore at the press conference held on March 9, 1962, questions were raised whether such appointments were made out of regard for the AFPFL. Brigadier Aung Gyi replied that in forming Supreme State councils, appointments were made on the basis of personal integrity, ability, and honesty, and that such appointments do not reflect any prejudice against or hatred of any political organization. *Hanthawaddy Daily*, March 10, 1962.

45. Ibid., March 4, 1962.

46. *Hanthawaddy Daily*, March 5, 1962.

47. Ibid., March 10, 1962.

48. Ibid., March 3, 1962.

49. Ibid.

50. Ibid.

51. Ibid.

52. Ibid.

53. *Hanthawaddy Daily*, March 3, 1962.

54. Ibid., March 8, 1962.

55. *The Nation* (Rangoon), March 8, 1962.

56. *Hanthawaddy Daily*, March 10, 1962.

57. Ibid.

58. Ibid.

59. *The Nation* (Rangoon), March 10, 1962; *Hanthawaddy Daily*, March 10, 1962.

60. Personal interview 0125, History Dept. (Research), Y.U.

61. *Shan State Politics.*

62. Ibid.

63. *Shan State Politics.*

64. On March 2, 1962, when the Revolutionary Council seized power, Mahadevi Sao Hern Hkam was in England. Sao Shwe Thaike died in November 1962 and the *mahadevi* returned to Myanmar. In the later part of 1963 she went across to Thailand. From Thailand she led the Shan State Liberation Army and the Shan National United Front. Chao Tsang Yawng Hwe. *The Shan of Burma* (Singapore: Institute of Southeast Asian Studies, 1987), 17–18, 173.

65. *Shan State Politics.*

66. Ibid.

67. At the All Nationals Conference, held on February 24, 1962, at the broadcasting station on Pyay Road, Yangon, U Htun Myint (Taunggyi) said: "Nationals from our state are very much united in regard to our Federal Principle. We have established firm national unity concerning our

pure Federal Principle and our demand for equality. We have already passed a strong resolution to march on until the emergence of a pure Federal Principle; we will continue our efforts with patience and in a family spirit until this pure Federal Principle is understood and accepted by all nationals of the states and Myanmar Proper. In conclusion I respectfully request that those people who cannot agree with us and accept our pure Federal Principle discuss this matter with patience and in a family spirit. Long live friendship among Shan, Bamar, Kachin, Chin, Kayin, Kayah, Rakhine, and Mon peoples! Let a true union emerge quickly." HDR:RT/0016/SP-62/1990.

68. *Shan State Politics.*

69. Personal interviews 0124, 0125, History Dept. (Research), Y.U.

70. Personal interview 0125, History Dept. (Research), Y.U.

71. Personal interview 0124, History Dept. (Research), Y.U.; HDR: 1 AP/1990.

72. Personal interviews 0124, 0125, History Dept. (Research), Y.U.; HDR: 1 AP/1990.

73. Personal interview 0125, History Dept. (Research), Y.U.; Statement made by the head of the Shan State, Sao Hkun Hkio, at the Seminar of Nationalities, held on February 24, 1962, at the broadcasting station on Pyay Road, Yangon. HDR:RT 0019/SP-62/1990.

74. Speech delivered by Prime Minister U Nu on February 24, 1962, at the Conference of the Nationalities, held at the broadcasting station on Pyay Road, Yangon. HDR:RT/0019/SP-62/1990.

75. Speeches of U Nu. HDR:RT/0019/SP-62/1990.

76. Personal interview 0043, History Dept. (Research), Y.U.

77. Personal interviews 0043, 0022, History Dept. (Research), Y.U.

78. Personal interview 0144, History Dept. (Research), Y.U.

79. Ibid.

80. Personal interview 0022, History Dept. (Research), Y.U.

81. Personal interview 0122, History Dept. (Research), Y.U.

82. Brigadier Tin Pe (retired) has said that he knew nothing about the move to pass the National Service Act at that time.

83. OC: Officer Commanding

84. CO: Commanding Officer

85. Personal interview 0131, History Dept. (Research), Y.U.

86. Personal interview 0122, History Dept. (Research), Y.U.

87. Reported in *The Nation* (Rangoon), March 4, 1962.

88. Ibid.

89. Ibid.

90. *The Nation* (Rangoon), March 3, 1962.

Glossary

Akun ahmat	revenue officer
Alelet	central division, applied to area now composing South Hsenwi
Ahmat	minister
Ahmatchoke	chief minister
Baan	village
Bohmu	title of Myanmar provincial military officer
Chao	lord
Duwa	powerful chief
Haw	palace or residence of a Shan chief
Heng or hein (Shan), Ne-baing (Myanmar)	a minor Shan official in charge of a small district; provincial officer
Hkun	lord, a title frequently applied to Shan chiefs
Hpai	dam
Htamong	a minor Shan official
Kadaw	homage, tribute
Khao	rice
Keng	state
Kon nam	water wheel
Kong	drum
Kulla	a foreigner
Kyaung	a Buddhist monastery
Kyaungtaga	one who has built a monastery
Kyemmong	heir apparent
Legun	tax on wet-paddy land
Letpet so	pickled tea
Mong	state
Myelat	area in southwestern Shan States bounded by Myanmar on the west, Lawsawk on the north, Yawnghwe on the east, and Loilong on the south
Myook	Myanmar title for a political officer of low rank
Myosa	Myanmar title for the ruler of a Shan substate or state of lower standing than that ruled by a sawbwa
Na	paddy field
Nawmong	heir presumptive
Ngwehkunmu	Myanmar title, lowest of the three ranks of Shan chief
Paokchok	ruler, governor
Parabeik	Shan folded books of paper made from hsa tree bark
Pawmong	elder state officer
Payataga	builder of a pagoda

Pem	basket
Pu kye	headman
Pwe	festival
Se	large territory
Sanad	patent or appointment order, letter of appointment
Sao	prince
Saohpa (Shan), Sawbwa (Myanmar)	title used for the more important Shan chiefs
Saohpalong	title used for a Shan head of state, higher than that of saohpa
Sawpya (Kayah)	title use for a Kayah head of state
Sheko	to make obeisance
Sitke	Myanmar provincial official
Taungya	slash-and-burn or shifting cultivation
Thathamada	house tax
Thanapet	leaf used for cheroot wrappers

Bibliography

Books

Adem, Nel. *My Vanished World: The True Story of a Shan Princess.* London: Horseshoe Publications, 2000.
Anderson, John Gottberg. *Burma.* Hong Kong: Apa Production, 1981.
Anderson, William. *The Nation and the States: Rivals or Partners?* Minneapolis: University of Minnesota Press, 1955.
Andrus, J. Russel. *Burmese Economic Life.* Stanford: Stanford University Press, 1948.
Aitchison, C. U., Comp. *A Collection of Treaties, Engagements and* Sanad *Relating to India and Neighboring Countries.* Vol. 14. Calcutta: 1876–1931.
Ba Maw. *Breakthrough in Burma, Memoir of Revolution, 1939–1946.* New Haven: Yale University Press, 1968.
Barpujan, H. K. *The Comprehensive History of Assam.* Guwahat: Publication Board Assam, 1994.
Basu, Nirmal Kumar. *Assam in the Ahom Age 1228–1826.* Calcutta: Sanskrit Pustak Bhandar, 1970.
Bennison, J. J., ed. *Burma Census.* Vol. 11 in *Census of India, 1931. (*Part 1, Report; Part 2, Tables). Rangoon: 1933.
Berval, René De. *Kingdom of Laos, the Land of the Million Elephants and of the White Parasol.* Limoges, France: A Bontemps, 1959.
Burma and the Insurrection. Rangoon: Ministry of Information, 1949.
Burma During the Japanese Occupation. Vol. 1. Rangoon: Intelligence Bureau, Government of Burma, 1943.
Chula Chakrabongse, Prince. *Lords of Life: A History of the Kings of Thailand.* London: Alvin Redman, 1960.
Chao Tzaung Yawnghwe. *The Shan of Burma.* Singapore: Institute of Southeast Asian Studies, 1987.
Chen Yi Sein. *Ancient Tai.* [Written in Chinese without place, publisher, or date.]
Chibber, H. L. *The Geology of Burma.* London: Macmillan, 1984.
Chit Maung, Widhura. *The Shan Proposal and the Future of the Union.* Yangon: Kyemon Press, 1962.
Christian, John Leroy. *Burma and the Japanese Invader.* Bombay: Thacker, 1945.
Cochrane, W. W. *The Shans.* Vol. 1. Rangoon: Superintendent, Government Printing, Burma, 1915.
Collective Defense in South East Asia. London: Royal Institute of International Affairs, 1956.
Colquhoun, Archibald Ross. *Amongst the Shans.* New York: Scribner and Welford, 1885.
The Constitution of the Union of Burma. Rangoon: Government Printing and Stationery, 1957.
Cooke, C. B. Captain. *The British Burma Manual. The Treaties Concluded with the Kingdom of Ava and Siam.* Vol. 1. Calcutta: Thacker, Spink and Government Place, 1878.
Crosthwaite, Charles. Sir. *The Pacification of Burma.* London: Frank Cass, 1968.
Dautremer, Joseph. *Burma Under British Rule.* London: Adelph; Terrace, 1913.
Davies, H. R. Major. *Yunnan: The Link Between India and the Yangtze.* London: Cambridge University Press, 1909.
Deignan, H. G. *Burma—Gateway to China.* Washington: The Smithsonian Institution, 1943.

Dodd, William Clifton. *The Tai Race, Elder Brother of the Chinese*. Cedar Rapids, Iowa: The Torch Press, 1923.

Donnison, F. S. V. *British Military Administration in the Far East, 1943–1946*. London: His Majesty's Stationery Office, 1956.

Dudley, Stamp L. *An Intermediate Commercial Geography*. London: Longmans Green, 1963.

Elias, Nay. *Introductory Sketch of the History of the Shan in Upper Burma and Western Yunnan*. Calcutta: The Foreign Department Press, 1876.

Elliott, Patricia. *The White Umbrella*. Bangkok: The Post Publishing, 1999.

Encyclopaedia Britannica: A New Survey of Universal Knowledge. Vol. 19. London: Encyclopaedia Britannica, 1786.

Enriquez, C. M. Capt. *A Burmese Loneliness: A Tale of Travel in Burma, the Southern Shan States and Keng Tung*. Calcutta: Thacker Spink, 1918.

———. *Races of Burma*. Delhi: Manager of Publications, 1933.

Farley, Miriam S. *United States Relations with South East Asia*. New York: American Institute of Pacific Relations, 1955.

Fifield, Russel H. *The Diplomacy of South East Asia*. New York: Harper and Brothers, 1958.

Fraser-Lu, Sylvia. *Burmese Lacquerware*. Bangkok: Orchid Press, 2000.

Furnival, J. S. *Introduction to the Political Economy of Burma*. Rangoon: People's Literature Committee and House, 1957.

Gear, Donald and Joan. *Earth to Heaven. The Royal Animal-Shaped Weights of the Burmese Empires)*. Chiang Mai: Silkworm Books, 1992.

George, E. C. S. *Ruby Mines District. Burma Gazetteer*. Rangoon: Superintendent, Government Printing and Stationery, Union of Burma, 1962.

Ghosh, Lipi. *Burma: Myth of French Intrigue*. Calcutta: Naya Udyog, 1994.

Gogoi, Lila. *The Tai Khamti on the North-East*. New Delhi: Omsons Publication, 1970.

Grabowsky, Volker, and Andrew Turton. *The Gold and Silver Road of Trade and Friendship: The McLeod and Richardson Diplomatic Missions to Tai States in 1837*. Chiang Mai: Silkworm Books, 2003.

Grant, J. W. *Burma Fruits and Their Cultivation*. Rangoon: Superintendent Government Printing and Stationery, 1961.

———. *The Rice Crop in Burma*. Rangoon: Superintendent, Government Printing and Stationery, 1949.

Greenwood, Nicholas. *Guide to Burma*. 2nd ed. London: Bradt Publications and Connecticut, US: Globe Pequot Press Inc., 1995.

Grierson, G. A. *Linguistic Survey of Burma*. Vol. 2. Delhi: Motilal Banarsidass, 1973.

Guide to the National Museum of Anthology. Tokyo: The National Museum of Anthology, 1991.

Hall, D. G. *A History of South-East Asia*. London: Macmillan, 1964.

Hallett, Holt S. *Thousand Miles on an Elephant in the Shan States*. Bangkok: White Lotus, 1988.

Hansard's *Parliamentary Debates*, vol. 443, no. 12. London: His Majesty's Stationery Office, 1947.

Harvey, G. E. *History of Burma*. London: Frank Cass & Co., Ltd., 1967.

Hayashi Yukio, ed. *Dynamics of Ethnic Cultures Across National Boundaries in Southwestern China and Mainland Southeast Asia: Relations, Societies, and Languages*. Chiang Mai: Ming Muang Printing House, 2000.

Hayashi Yukio, and Sayavong Khamdy, eds. *Cultural Diversity and Conservation in the Making of Mainland Southeast Asia and Southwestern China Regional Dynamics in the Past and Present*. Collected papers. Chiang Mai: Ming Muang Printing House, 2003.

Hertslet, Edward. Sir. *China Treaties*. 3rd ed. Hertslet with the assistance of Edward Parkes. 2 vols. London: Blackie, 1908.

The Hmannan Mahayazawintawgyi. Vols. 1 and 2. Yangon: Department of Information, Ministry of Information, 1972. Vol. 1, 3rd ed., 1992.

Hoontrakul, Likhit. *The Historical Researches of the Siamese-Chinese Relations*. Bangkok: Debsriharis Law Office, 1953.

Howard, Michael C. *Textiles of the Hill Tribes of Burma*. Bangkok: White Lotus Press, 1999.

The Hsen Wi Chronicle. Blue Book, Burmah, 1886.

Htun Myint, *Taunggyi, U. The Saohpas and the Shan State*. Yangon: Thamada Press, 1952.

———. *Shan State [a component] of Equal Status within the Union*. Yangon: Myanmar Byuha Press, 1960.

Innes, R. A. *Costumes of Upper Burma and the Shan States (in the collection of Bankfield Museum, Halifax)*. Halifax: Halifax Museum, 1957.

Johnstone, William, C. *A Chronology of Burma's International Relations 1945–1958*. Rangoon: Rangoon University, 1959.

Kahin, George Me Turnan, ed. *Governments and Politics of Southeast Asia.* New York: Cornell University Press, 1959.

Kuomintang Aggression Against Burma. Rangoon: Ministry of Information, Government of the Union of Burma, 1953.

Lee, C. Y. *The Sawbwa and His Secretary: My Burmese Reminiscences*. New York: American Book, Stratford Press, 1958.

Lefevre, E. *Travels in Laos: The Fate of the Sip Song Pana and Muong Sing. 1894–1896.* Translation and introduction by Walter E. J. Tips. Bangkok: White Lotus, 1995.

Levi, Werner. *Modern China Foreign Policy*. Minneapolis: University of Minnesota, 1953.

Liangwen, Zhu. *The Dai or the Tai and Their Architecture and Customs in South China*. Bangkok: D. D. Books, 1992.

Lishi, Gao. *On the Dai's Traditional Irrigation system*. Translated by He Changyi and Environmental Protection in Xishuang-bana. Kunming, Yunnan: Nationality Press, 1998.

Lowis, C. C. *The Tribes of Burma*. No. 4, Ethnographical Study of India. Rangoon: Superintendent, Government Printing and Stationery, 1949.

Mangrai, Sao Sai Mong. *The Padaeng Chronicle and the Jengtung State Chronicle Translated*. Ann Arbor, Michigan: University of Michigan, Center for South and Southeast Guides, 1981.

———. *The Shan States and the British Annexation*. New York: Cornell University, 1965.

Marshall, H. I. *The Karen People of Burma: A Study in Anthropology and Ethnology*. Columbus: University of Columbus, 1920.

Maung, Maung, Dr. *Burma's Constitution Comes to Life*. Reprinted from the Indian Year Book of International Affairs. Madras: Diocesan Press, 1958.

———. *Burma in the Family of Nations*. Amsterdam: International Educational Publishing House, 1956.

———. *Burma's Constitution*. The Hague: Martinus Nijhoff, 1959.

———. *Grim War Against KMT*. Rangoon: Nu Yin Press, 1953.

Maung Maung, U. *Burmese Nationalist Movements 1940–1948*. Edinburgh: Kiscadale Pub, 1989.

Maung Maung Tin. *Konbaungset Yazawun*. Vol. 3. Rangoon: Letimandy Press, 1967.

Metford, Beatrix. *Where China Meets Burma: Life and Travel in the Burma-China Border Lands*. London: Blackie, 1935.

Milne, Leslie. *Shans at Home*. London: John Murray, Albemarle, 1910. Repr., Bangkok: White Lotus, 2001.

Mitton, G. E., ed. *Scott of the Shan Hills: Orders and Impressions*. London: Butler and Tanner, 1936.

Mix, H. W. *English and Shan Dictionary*. Rangoon: American Baptist Mission Press, 1920.

Moreland, F. T. *The Forests of Burma*. London: Green & Co., 1944.

Nagara, Prasert N. A, and A. B Griswold. *Epigraphic and Historical Studies*. Bangkok: The Historical Society, 1992.

Ni Ni Myint. *Burma's Struggle Against British Imperialism (1885–1895)*. Yangon: University Press, 1983.

1947 Constitution and the Nationalities. Vols. 1 and 2. Yangon: Universities Historical Research Center and Inwa Publishing House, 1999.

Nisbet, John. *Burma Under British Rule and Before*. Westminster: Archibald Constable, 1904.

Nu, Thakin. *Burma Under the Japanese: Picture and Portraits*. London: Macmillan, 1954.

Ohn Kin, U. *Burma Under the Japanese*. Lucknow: Lucknow Publishing House, 1947.

Pe Kin, U. *Pinlon: An Inside Story*. Yangon: The New Light of Myanmar Press, 1994.

Peltier, Anatole-Roger. *Sujavanna*. Chiang Mai: A-R Peltier, 1993.

———. *Tai Khoeun Literature*. Chiang Mai: Social Research Institute, Chiang Mai University, 1987.

Pe Maung Tin and G. H. Luce. *The Glass Palace Chronicle of the Kings of Burma*. Rangoon: Rangoon University Press, 1960.

Phayre, Arthur P. *History of Burma*. London: Wanstead, 1967. First published 1883 by Trubner & Co., Ludgate Hill, under the title *History of Burma Including Burma Proper, Pegu, Taungu, Tenasserim, and Arakan*.

Phukan, Girin, ed. *Indian Journal of Tai Studies. Vol. 4*. Moranhat, Assam: Institute of Tai Study and Research, 2004.

Phukan. J. N., Romesh Buragohain, and Ye Hom Buragohain. *Chao-lung Siu-ka-pha Documentary History of the Ahom*. Vol. 1. Assam, India: Celebration Committee 77th Anniversary Year of Chaio-Lung Siu-Ka-Pha, 1997–98.

Rodger, Alex. *A Handbook of Forest Products of Burma*. Rangoon: Superintendent, Printing and Stationery, 1963.

Royal Institute of International Affairs: Survey of International Affairs, 1951, 1952, 1954. London: Oxford University Press, 1954, 1955, 1956.

Sainson, Camille. *Nan-Tchao Ye-che histoire partculière du Nan-Tchao traduction D'une histoire de L'ancien yunnan*. Paris: Imprimerie Nationale, 1880.

Santasombat, Yos. *Lak Chang: A Reconstruction of Tai Identity in Daikong*. Canberra: Pandanus Books, Research School of Pacific and Asian Studies, 2001.

Sargent, Inge. *Twilight over Burma: My Life as a Shan Princess*. Chiang Mai: Silkworm Books, 1994.

Scott, J. George, and Hardiman, J. P. *Gazetteer of Upper Burma and the Shan States*. 5 vols. Rangoon: Superintendent, Government Printing, Burma, 1900–1901.

———. *Burma: A Handbook of Practical Information*. 3rd ed. London: Dela More Press, 1921.

———. *Burma, from the Earliest Times to the Present Day*. London: T. Fisher Unwin, 1924.

Sein Win. *The Split Story*. Rangoon: The Guardian, 1959.

Selection of Papers Regarding the Hill Tracts Between Assam and Barmah, and on the Upper Brahmaputara. 7 vols. Calcutta: Sanskrit Pustak Bhandar, 1873.

Shan Reader. History. Chiang Mai: Shan Culture and Education Central Committee, 2004.

The Shan State Manual. Rangoon: Government Printing Office, 1933.

Shintani Tadahiko L. A. *Linguistics and Anthropological Study on the Shan Culture Area*. Tokyo: Institute for the Study of Languages and Cultures of Asia and Africa, 1999.

Silverstein, Josef. *Burma: Military Rule and the Politics of Stagnation*. Ithaca: Cornell University Press, 1977.

Slim, William, Sir. *Defeat into Victory*. 2nd ed. London: Cassell, 1956.

Smales, C. B. *A Sample Key to One Hundred Common Trees of Burma*. Rangoon: Public Relations, 1945 [Repub.].

Spencer, J. E. *Shifting Cultivation in Southeastern Asia*. Los Angeles: University of California Press, 1966.

Steinberg, David Joel, ed. *In Search of Southeast Asia: A Modern History*. Rev. ed. Sydney: Allen and Unwin, 1987.

Stuart, John. *Burma Through the Centuries*. London: Kegan Paul, Trench, Trubner, 1909.

Suriyabongs, Luang. *Buddhism in Thailand*. Bangkok: University of Thammasat Printing Press, 1955.

Tan I: *Hou-han-shui-chih: Lieh-chua*. [Written in Chinese without place, publisher, or date.]

Tanabe Shigeharu, ed. *Religious Traditions Among Tai Ethnic Groups: A Selected Bibliography*. Bangkok: Ayutthaya Historical Study Center, 1991.

Taw Sein Ko. *Hluttaw Hmattan*. Rangoon: Government Printing and Stationery, 1960.

Tern Moeng, Sao. *Shan-English Dictionary*. Kensington, Maryland: Dunwoody Press, 1995.

Terwiel, B. J. *The Tai of Assam and Ancient Tai Ritual*. Vols. 1, 2. India: The Catholic Press, 1980, 1981.

Thayer, Philip W. *Nationalism and Progress in Free Asia*. Baltimore: The Johns Hopkins Press, 1956.

Thorpm Ellen. *Quiet Skies on Salween*. Oxford: Alden Press, 1945.

T'ien Ju-K'ang. *Religious Cults of the Pai-i Along the Burma-Yunnan Border*. Southeast Asia Program. New York: Cornell University, 1986.

Tinker, Hugh. *The Union of Burma: A Study of the First Years of Independence*. 3rd ed. London: Oxford University Press, 1961; 4th ed., 1967.

———, ed. *Burma: The Struggle for Independence 1944–1948*. Vols. 1, 2. London: HMSO, 1983–84.

Trager, Frank N. *Burma: From Kingdom to Republic*. New York: Frederick A. Praeger, 1966.

———. *Burma: Japanese Military Administration, Selected Documents, 1941–1945*. Pennsylvania: University of Pennsylvania, 1971.

———. *Burma's Role in the United Nations, 1948–1955*. New York: Institute of Pacific Relations, 1956.

Treaties, Conventions, Etc., Between China and Foreign States. 2 vols. 2nd ed. Inspector General of Customs. Shanghai: [s.l.], 1917.

Wheare, K. C. *Federal Government*. 3rd. ed. London: Oxford University Press, 1963.

White, Herbert Thirkell. *Burma*. London: Cambridge University Press, 1923.

Who's Who in Burma. Rangoon: People's Literature Committee and House, 1961.

Wilhelm Klein, Gunter Pfannmuller, Hans Johannes Hoefer, John Gottberg Anderson. *Burma*. Hong Kong: Apa Productions, 1981.
Williams, Clement. *Through Burmah to Western China, Being Notes of a Journal in 1863*. London: Nilliam Blackwood, 1868.
Wood, W. A. R. *A History of Siam, from the Earliest Time to the Year A.D. 1781, with a Supplement Dealing with More Recent Events*. Bangkok: Chalermnit Bookshop, 1924. Repr. 1959.
Zan Htar Sin, U. *Democracy Upside Down*. Rangoon: Nantha Press, 1990.

British government publications

Burma and the Insurrection. Rangoon: Government of the Union of Burma Publication, 1949.
The Burma Gazette, 1922, 1947, 1948, 1949, 1952, 1958.
The Burma Gazette, Northern Arakan District, vol. A. Rangoon: Government Printing and Stationery), 1960.
Constitution of the Union of Burma. Rangoon: Government Printing and Stationery), 1957.
"Federated Shan States Law and Criminal Justice Orders (1926)." *The Burma Gazette*, no. 33 (June 28, 1926).
Frontier Areas Committee of Enquiry, 1947. Rangoon: Government Printing and Stationery), 1947.
The Future Administration of the Northern and Southern Shan States in Burma. Government of India: Home Department, Publication, no. 11, 1921.
KMT *Aggression. Translation of the Honorable Prime Minister's speech in the Chamber of Deputies*. March 2, 1953. Rangoon: Government Printing and Stationery), 1953.
Mong Kung. India Office, November 1930.
"Shan States Civil Justice Orders (1900)." *The Burma Gazette*, May 19, 1900, Political Dept., May 16, 1900, no. 3, Rule 1–3, 5–6, 372–73.
———. "(Subsidiary) Order (1906)." *The Burma Gazette*, December 1, 1906, Political Dept., November 23, 1906, no. 23, Rule 1–4, 835–36.
"Shan States, Kareni, Chin Hills and Pakoku Chin Hills." *Imperial Gazetteer of India*, Calcutta: Superintendent of Government Printing, 1908.
"Shan States Law and Criminal Justice Orders (1894)." *The Burma Gazette*, July 13, 1895, P1, Political Dept., July 13, 1895. no. 33, 262–268.

Articles

"Acceptable." *Time* 65 (January 31, 1955), 21.
Ady, P. "Economic Bases of Unrest in Burma." *Foreign Affairs* (April 1951), 475–481.
"Aggressor Condemned." *New Times* (Moscow), (May 6, 1953), 19–16.
"American Aid to Burma." *Burma Weekly Bulletin* 41 (January 13, 1954), 323–326.
Andrus, J. R. "Japan's New Gifts to Thailand." *Foreign Commerce Weekly* (September 4, 1943), 3–9, 38.
"An Annual Publication of the Institute of Tai Studies and Research." Moranhat, Assam, India: *Indian Journal of Tai Studies*, vol. 1, January 2001.
Aree, J., Mc. "Burma Faces the Communists." *Current History* 20:340–3 (June 1951).
Aung Thein, U. "Intercourse Between Burma and Siam." *Journal of Burma Research Society* 25 (1935).
———. "Intercourse Between Burma and Siam." *Journal of Burma Research Society* 28 (1938).
Bailey, F. M. C. I. E. Lt. Col. "Behind the Burmese Road." *The Field* 172 (July 1943), 84–85.
Ballis, W. B. "Power Struggle in Asia and American Far Eastern Policy." *South Atlantic Quarterly* 52 (January 1953), 20–8.
"Bangkok Negotiations." *New Times* (Moscow), 28 (July 8, 1953), 12–13.
Barrington, James. "The Concept of Neutralism: What Lies Behind Burma's Foreign Policy." *Atlantic* 201 (February 1958), 126–128.
———. "The United Nations and Burma." *Burma Weekly Bulletin* 5 (November 1, 1956), 230–231.
———. "United Nations Through Burmese Eyes." *Burma* (Rangoon) 4 (July 1954), 39–45.
Blagden, Charles O. "Shan Buddhism." *Journal of the Royal Asiatic Society* (1912), 495–496.

Bowles, Chester. "Burma and Vietnam: Contrasts and Lessons." *New York Times Magazine* (June 13, 1954), 14–15.

———. "Ten-Point Program for the United States in Asia." *Foreign Policy Bulletin* 31, (April 15, 1952), 1–2.

"Burma Accuses Chinese Nationalists." *The Economist* 167 (April 11, 1953), 71–2.

"Burma at the United Nations." *Burma* (Rangoon) 3 (April, 1953), 36.

"Burma Incident." *The New Republic* 126 (February 11, 1952), 8.

"Burma Reports to UNGA Against Foreign Aggressors." *Burma Weekly Bulletin* 25 (September 23, 1954), 194.

"Burma's Chief Delegate on KMT Aggression in Burma." *Burma* 12 (December 1, 1953), 1–11.

"Burma's Chief Delegate Speaks on Continued Presence of KMT Forces in Burma." *Burma* (Rangoon) 11 (November 16, 1953), 1–3.

"Burma's U Nu Sizes Up His Peking Neighbors; Interview Nu." *Newsweek* 45 (May 2, 1955), 34.

Cady, J. A., Jr. "The Situation in Burma." *The Far Eastern Survey* 22 (May 2, 1955), 49–54.

———. John F. "The Situation in Burma." *The Far Eastern Survey* 22 (April 22, 1953), 49–54.

Callendan, A. L. M. "Traveling Among the Lu, July 10, 1920." In *Presbyterian Church in USA Records*. Chiang Mai, Thailand: Payap University Archives, 1920.

"Can Burma Be Saved for Democracy?" *Christian Century* 73 (February 29,1956), 261.

Carey, J. A. Jr. "US Position on Evacuation of Foreign Forces from Burma." *US Department of State Bulletin* 29 (November 30, 1953), 761–4.

———. "A Trip to the Chinese Shan States." *Geographical Journal* 14 (1899), 378–94.

Chary, Chery, Sun. "Sino-Burmese Frontier Problems." *Yenching Journal of Chinese Studies*, Monograph series no. 15, Peiping, 1938.

Cheng Te-k'un and Ling Ch'ao-tao. "An Introduction to the Southwestern Peoples of China." *Journal of the West China Border Research Society*, (Chengtu, ser. A) 16 (1945), 23–38.

"China, Burma and Wa." *The Economist* 180 (August 18, 1956), 570–571.

"Chinese in North Burma." *Eastern World* (November 15, 1956), 10.

"Chinese Troops in Burma." *International Council* 499 (September 1954), 34–6.

Christian, John L. "Burma Roads of the Past and Present." *Journal of the United Service Institution of India* 74 (April 1944), 202–209.

———. "Burma: Where India and China Meet." *The National Geographic Magazine* 84 (October 1943), 489–512.

Cochrane, Archibald. Sir. "Burma in Wartime." *Asiatic Review* 37 (October 1941), 681–696.

Cochrane, Wilbur W. "An Ahom (Shan) Legend of Creation from an old MS." *Journal of the Royal Asiatic Society* (1911), 32–42.

———. "Shans and Buddhism of the Northern Canon." *Journal of the Royal Asiatic Society* (1912), 487–95.

Cohn, D. L. "Communist Approach to Burma." *The Atlantic* 198 (September 1956), 41–3.

Collis, Maurice. "Courts of the Shan Princes." *Asiatic Review* 35 (1939), 330–42.

"Complaint Before the General Assembly by Burma regarding Aggression Against It by the Republic of China." *International Organization* 7 (August 1953), 384–5; 8 (February 1954), 52–5.

Coryton, J. "Trade Routes Between British Burmah and Western China." *Journal of the Royal Geographical Society* 45 (1875), 229–249.

Cowles, J. "U.S. and Asia." *Foreign Policy Bulletin* 33 (June 15, 1954), 1–2.

Cuzen, Seerye N. "The Siamese Boundary Question." *The Nineteenth Century* 34 (1893), 34–35.

"Dangerous Game." *New Times* (Moscow) 5 (January 28, 1953), 2–4, 23–24.

"A Dashing Exploit." *St. James's Gazette*, July 3, 1888.

"A Dashing Exploit." *The Echo*, August 18, 1888.

Douglas, Robert K. "China and Burma." *Asiatic Quarterly Review* 1 (1886), 141–64.

Dunlop, R. "Straws in the Burmese Wind." *Christian Century* 69 (March 12, 1952), 310–12.

Durrenberger, Paul E. "The Shan Rocket Festival: Buddhism and non-Buddhist Aspects of Shan Religion." *Journal of Burma Research Society* 71 (1983), 673–74.

"Economic Development Program in Burma." *U.S. Department of State Bulletin* 27 (October 27, 1952), 660.

"Evacuation of Troops from Burma Awaited Before Further Discussion." *U.N. Bulletin* 15 (December 1, 1953), 519–34.

"Explanation by Burma of Evacuation of Chinese." *U.N. Bulletin* 16 (April 15, 1954), 322.

"The Federated Shan States: Their New Constitution." *Rangoon Gazette, Weekly Budget*, April 2, 1923, 5–30.
Fifield, R. H. "What Shall U.S. Do About Formosa?" *Foreign Policy Bulletin* 31 (April 15, 1952), 5–6.
Fitzgerald, Patrick. "The Yunnan-Burma Roads." *The Geographical Journal* 95 (1940), 161–74.
"Foreign Forces in Burma Condemned." *U.N. Bulletin* 14 (May 1, 1953), 323–5.
"Formation of Karen States." *Burma* (Rangoon) 5 (November 21, 1951), 1-3.
Foster, W. G. "New Hope Comes to Formosa." *Reader's Digest* 58 (May 1951), 30–2.
"Free Thai Movement." *Eastern World* 8 (January 1954), 18–19.
"Further Efforts to Evacuate Forces from Burma Urged by Assembly." *U.N. Bulletin* 16 (January 1, 1954), 40–3.
Garthew, M. "The History of the Thai in Yunnan, 2205 B.C.– A.D. 1253." *Journal of Southeast Asian Studies* 40 (1) (1952) , 1–38.
"Getting the KMT Out of Burma." *The Economist* 168: 13 (July 4, 1953).
Gerini, G. E. "Shan and Siam." *Asiatic Review* (3rd. Ser.) 5 (1898) 145–63.
Gogoi, Nomal Chandra. "Tai, Thai and Dai: Origin Evolution and Dissemination of Tai Culture in China and Southeast Asia with Special Reference to the Ahoms of Assam." Mangshi, Yunnan: The International Conference on Comparative Studies on the Dai Culture in the Four Rivers Valleys in Yunnan Province, 2003.
"Has Burma Become Asia's Most Vulnerable Spot?" *Christian Century* 68 (August 1, 1951), 885.
Hendershot, Clarence. "The Role of the Shan States in the Japanese Conquest of Burma." *Eastern Quarterly* 2 (May 1943).
Henley, David. "A Forgotten Invasion: Thailand in Shan State, 1941–45." CPA Media, the Asia Experts. http://www.cpamedia.com/history/thailand_in_shan_state/
Hillier, W. R. "Notes on the Manners, Customs, Religion, and Superstitions of the Tribes Inhabiting the Shan States." *Indian Antiquary* 21 (1892), 116–21
Holm, David. "Works on customary law among the Dai: a brief bibliography." *Tai Culture: International Review on Tai Cultural Studies*, vol. 6, no. 1 & 2, SEACOM ed. Berlin: SEACOM, 159. 2001.
Hughes, T. C. C. B. E. "The Campaign in and Evacuation of Burma." *Journal of the Royal Central Asian Society* 31 (January 1944), 80–92.
"Imperialistic Politics South of the Clouds." *The China Weekly Review*, September 30, 1933.
"Intrigues of Kuomintang Bandits in Burma." *The Current Digest of the Soviet Press* 5 (December 30, 1953), 9.
"Is U.S. Stirring Up Burma?" *U.S. News and World Report* 32 (March 14, 1952), 33–5.
J. G. S. "The Start of the War in Burma." *Journal of the United Service*. Institution of India, 72 (July 1942), 198–218.
Kozicki, Richard J. "The Sino-Burmese Frontier Problem." *Far Eastern Survey* 26 (March 1957), 33–38.
Kudryavtsev, V. "Talks in Bangkok." *The Current Digest of the Soviet Press* 5 (August 15, 1953), 17.
"Kuomintang Aggression in Burma." *Burma* (Rangoon) 1 (March 13, 1953), 1–4.
"Kuomintang Aggression in Burma." *China Monthly Review* (June 1953), 86.
"Kuomintang Aggression into Burma." *New Times* (Moscow) 35 (August 26, 1953), 19.
"Kuomintang Troops in Burmese Territory." *New Statesman* 46 (August 8, 1953), 146.
Lambert, E. T. D. "A Short Account of the Ahom People." *Journal of Southeast Asian Studies* 40 (1) (1952), 39–65
Leach, Edmund R. "The Frontiers of Burma." *Comparative Studies in Society and History* 3 (1960), 49–68.
Leach, F. B. "Burma: A New Strategical Position." *Asiatic Review* 37 (1941), 841–845.
———. "The Invasion of Burma." *Contemporary Review* (June 1942), 337–342.
Lertluamsia, Ranee. "The Worldview of the Ancient Tai: a study of the Tai Ahom documents." *Tai Culture: International Review on Tai Cultural Studies* 3 (1), 48–60. Berlin: SEACOM, 1998.
Levi, Werner. "American Foreign Policy Toward China." *Journal of International Affairs* 11 (2) (1957), 150–9.
"Liberate the Mainland." *Life* 34 (March 2, 1953), 14–23.
Lindsay, Michael. "The Policy of the Chinese People's Government in Asia." *Journal of International Affairs* 11 (2) (1957), 143–150.
Linebarger, Paul M. A. "Taipei and Peking: The Confronting Republics." *Journal of International Affairs* 11 (2) (1957), 135–143.
"Little Discourtesy." *Time* 68 (December 24, 1956), 22.

Lloyd, J. "Planning a Welfare State in Burma." *International Labor Review* 70 (August 1954), 117–47.

Luce, G. H. "The Early Syam in Burma's History." *The Journal of the Siam Society* 46, part 2. Bangkok: November 1958.

———. "The Tan (A.D. 97–132) and the Ngai-Lao." *Journal of the Burma Research Society* 14, part 2, 1960.

MacMahon, A. R. "Anglo-Chinese Convention and the Burmese Frontier." *Imperial and Asiatic Review* 9 (1895), 439–62.

Mahoney, C. H. "Foreign Forces in Burma: with Text of Agreed Resolution on Evacuation." *U.S. Department of State Bulletin* 31 (November 8, 1954), 709–711.

Maung Maung, U. "Burma Looks Ahead." *Pacific Affairs* 25 (March 1952), 40–48.

———. "Kuomintang Aggressors in Burma." *Eastern World* 7 (June 1953), 13–14.

———. "Pyidawtha Comes to Burma." *Far Eastern Survey* 22 (August 1953), 117–119.

Mende, Tibor. "Report from the Burma Border." *The Reporter* 8 (May 12, 1953), 17–21.

Morris, T. O. "Copper and Bronze Antiquities from Burma." *Journal of Burma Research Society* 15 (1924), 115–128.

———. "The Prehistoric Stone Implements of Burma." *Journal of Burma Research Society* 25 (1935), 1–39.

"Mr. U Nu Goes to Moscow." *Christian Century* 72:1323 (November 16, 1955).

Nartsupha, Chatthip and Ranoo Wichasin. "The State of Knowledge of Ahom History." *Tai Culture: International Review on Tai Cultural Studies 3 (1)*, SEACOM ed. Berlin: SEACOM, 16–47. 1998.

"Neighborly Incursion." *Time* 68 (August 13, 1956), 20.

Orestov, O. "In Thailand." *The Current Digest of the Soviet Press* 5 (July 4, 1953), 16.

———. "The Kuomintang Adventure in Burma and its Instigators." *The Current Digest of the Soviet Press* 5 (December 9, 1953), 18.

Osipov, V. "What Is Behind Kuomintang Aggression in Burma?" *The Current Digest of the Soviet Press* 5 (October 31, 1953), 17.

Parker, E. H. "The Old Tai or Shan Empire of Western Yunnan." *China Review* 20 (1893), 337–46.

———. "Shan and Siam." (A reply and discussion). *Asiatic Review* (3rd. ser.) 5 (1898), 401–5.

Parkinson, C. N. "American Policy in Southeast Asia." *Fortnightly* 18 (August 1954), 75–9.

"Peaceful Coexistence As It Looks in Asia." *U.S. News and World Report* 39 (August 5, 1955), 80–3.

Pearn, B. R. "A Burma Diary of 1810." *Journal of Burma Research Society* 27 (1937), 283–307.

———. "The Commercial Treaty of 1862." *Journal of Burma Research Society* 27 (1937), 33–52.

Phukan, Jogen. "Towards an approach to Tai Ahom Law through the study of titles regalia." *Tai Culture: International Review on Tai Cultural Studies* 6 (1, 2), 121–133. Berlin: SEACOM, 2001.

Pitchford, V. C. "The Wild Wa States and Lake Nawnghkio." *Geographical Journal* 90 (1937), 223–32.

Pleshakov, A. "The Aggression Against Burma." *New Times* (Moscow) 17 (April 22, 1953), 11–13.

Plyshevsky, I. "Kuomintangites in Burma." *The Current Digest of the Soviet Press* 5 (May 9, 1953), 9.

Pu Loi Hom & Pu Loi Tun. "The Founding of Mong Kawng." *Golden Jubilee Shan State Magazine*, Yangon, The Taunggyi Association, 1997.

Raendchen, Oliver. "Social Aspects of the Ban-Mong System of the Tai Dam, in Northern Vietnam" Proceedings of the 6th International Conference of Thai Studies, vol. 1, Chiang Mai, October 14–17, 1976.

———. "The Design for a Proposed Cultural System for the Tai People." *Tai Culture: International Review on Tai Cultural Studies* 7 (2). Berlin: SEACOM, 1998.

———. "The *hiit-khoong* codes of the Lao." *Tai Culture: International Review on Tai Cultural Studies* 6 (1, 2). Berlin: SEACOM, 159. 2001.

"Recapture of Monè from the Rebel Leader Twek-nga-lu." *St. James Gazette*. July 3, 1888.

Rau, S. Rama. "Peace, Rice, Friendship, and the Burma of U Nu." *The Reporter* 14 (April 19, 1956), 18–22.

Roth, Andrew. "The Crucial Role of Li Mi." *Eastern World* 6: 32–34 (February 1952).

Roucek, J. S. "Southeast Asia and the U.S." *Current History*, 23: 66–72 (August 1952).

Schubert, P. "Uncle Sam's Overseas Watchdogs." *Saturday Evening Post* 226 (July 4, 1953), 30–1.

Scott, J. George. "The British Shan States." *The Asiatic Quarterly Review*. July 1889.

———. "Buddhism in the Shan States." *Journal of the Royal Central Asiatic Society* 24 (1911), 717–34.

Seidenfaden, Erik. "Review Article of Burma and Beyond by Sir George Scott." *Journal of Southeast Asian Studies* 29 (1937), 141–51.

"Seventh Session of the U.N. General Assembly." *The Current Digest of the Soviet Press* 5 (May 30, 1953), 10–12.

Notes on discussion of the Eastern Shan State. F.N. 264 S.G.(A) 50.
Note of a discussion on Shan States matters on 13 December 1924 at Taunggyi, 16, NAD. Acc. No. 7714, 1/1 (B).
Notification of the Government of the Union of Burma, Ministry of Judicial Affairs, Judicial Branch. December 6, 1949.
Order issued on July 24, 1948 by the Shan State Government. F.N. 118. S.G. (A) 48.
Pa-Ah-Ma-Sa, *Pa-O National Unity Organization*. F.N. 113 Ya Pa (A) 56.
Pitchford, V. C. *Report on the Part of Yunnan Between the Bhamo Frontier and the Salween*. Indian army intelligence branch report, Rangoon, 1895. Confidential.
Political Department Notification No.16, May 5, 1923.
"Political Discussions at Pang Long" *Second Pang Long Conference*, appendixes C and D (Secret), 1946.
Private letter from Mr. Leiden to Sir Gilbert Lathhwaite. February 25, 1947.
Proceedings of the Constituent Assembly of Myanmar, vol. 1, *Meeting Minutes*, no. 4. Yangon: Myanmar Government Printing Press, 1947, 73–83.
Proceedings of the Twelfth Session of the Federal Council of the Shan Chiefs held in Taunggyi, February 24 to March 1, 1934. 9 National Archive Department. F. 96534. Accession No. 5054, 1/1(A).
Proposal for the withdrawal of Military Administration. F.N. 271 S.G.(A) 50.
Proposed Amendments to the Union Constitution submitted by the Shan State, Doh-Ta-Wun Press, Rangoon, 31–32.
Record of General Conference of the Shan State Council from 1 to 9, Yangon: Government Printing House and Stationery, 1953.
Record of the coup d'état by Kayah U Sein. Hand-written script.
Record of the First Conference of the Shan State Council from 1 to 7. F.N. 185 Ra (Aa) 57.
Record of the Fourth Session of the Shan State Council meeting, File no. 5 (from 1, 2, 3, 4, and 5), 5 (in Myanmar).
Record of the Second Historical Importance of the Shan State. F. N. 240 .Ya Pa (A) 53 (in Myanmar).
Record of the Shan State Committee for the Amendment of the Union Constitution, Universities Central Library, Typescript.
Record of the Sixth Shan State Council Meeting after Second General Election (in Myanmar). *The Constitution*, 57.
Record of the Shan State Council Meeting held from 31-7-1950 to 9-8-1980. Sixth Session. Insurrection in Northern Shan State. F.N. 28 S.G.(A) 51.
Record of the Shan State Council Meetings, from 1 to 8. Yangon: Government Printing House and Stationery, 1955, 7.
Record of the Shan State Council, Second Conference. File (2), 62.
Record of the Special Meeting of Shan State Council, Union of Burma (Myanmar), November 7 to 11, 1958 (in Myanmar).
Record of the Third Conference of the Shan State Council (Hluttaw), File no. 2, 5 (in Myanmar).
Record of the Third Pyithu Hluttaw. Vol. 2. Yangon: Government Printing and Stationery, 1961. Members of the All Shan States Organization who lost in that election were U Ohn Pe (South Loi Lem), U Tin Ko Ko (North Yawnghwe), and U San Hla Baw (Mong Mit) (Meeting Minutes Record No. 22)
The Report Given to the Shan State Council by the Head of Shan State. F.N. 53 S.G. (A) 49.
Report of Leveson sent to Chief Commissioner by the Superintendent of the Southern Shan States, May 1, 1893.
The Report of Sao Boonwat on the Occupation of Lashio. F.N. 92 S.G. (A) 49.
Report of Special Intelligence Officer, July 24, 1957 (in Myanmar).
Report of the Government Advisory Committee on the Amendment of the Constitution as proposed by the Shan State Government and its people. 1962. Printing and Stationery Department. Government of the Union of Myanmar, Yangon.
Report of the Insurgency Southern Shan State (in Myanmar). F.N. 17 Ya Pa (A) 53.
Report on general matters concerning Saohpas and their relatives (in Myanmar). F.N. 63 Ya Pa (A) 53.
Report on the Administration of Burma for the Year 1887–88.
Report on the Administration of Burma for the Year 1911–12, part 1.
Report on the Administration of Burma for the Year 1922–23.
Report on the Administration of Burma for the Year 1935–36.
Report on the Administration of the Northern Shan States for the Year 1890–91.

Report on the Administration of the Northern Shan States for the Year 1891–92. Rangoon: Government Printing, October 1892.

Report on the Administration of the Northern Shan States for the Year 1897–98 and Southern Shan States, 1897–98.

Report on the Administration of the Northern Shan States, 1897–98 and Southern Shan States 1897–98.

Report on the Administration of the Northern Shan States for the Year 1901–02.

Report on the Administration of the Shan States for the year 1887–88. Parliamentary Paper, February 20, 1896.

Report on the Administration of the Shan States for the Year 1889–90. Rangoon: Government Printing, August 1890.

Report on the Administration of the Southern Shan States for the Year 1892–93. Rangoon: Government Printing, August 1893.

Report on the Administration of the Southern Shan States for the Year 1901–02.

Report on the Northern Shan States, Rangoon to Lashio via Mandalay.

Report on the Shan Frontier of the Mandalay Division, 1901–02.

Report on Tour in Salween District 1913, F. O. 821/78.

Report on Town in Northern Shan States, 10R. W. 2281.

Report submitted the Shan State Government on Chinese incursion into Burma. F.N. 47 Ra (Aa) 57.

Resolution on the Reports on the Administration of the Shan States for the Year 1891–92.

Resolution on the Reports on the Administration of the Shan States for the Year 1901–02.

Scott, J. G. *Summary of the Eastern Shan States*. January 2, 1889, to December 8, 1889.

———. *Summary of the Northern Shan States for the Week Ending January 2, 1897, to May 8, 1897*. Confidential.

———. *Summary of the Northern Shan States for the Week Ending January 9, 1897*. Confidential.

———. *Summary of the Northern Shan States for the Week Ending January 16, 1897*. Confidential.

———. *Summary of the Northern Shan States for the Week Ending January 23, 1897*. Confidential.

———. *Summary of the Northern Shan States for the Week Ending January 30, 1897.*

———. *Summary of the Northern Shan States for the Week Ending February 6, 1897*. Confidential.

———. *Summary of the Northern Shan States for the Week Ending February 13, 1897*. Confidential.

Scott, J. G. *Summary of the Shan States, for the Week Ending September 17, 1887*. No. 125–16, with map of Shan States.

The Script Copy of Representations by Shan States Sawbwa to Secretary of State, 1930–31, and related documents: MF 1368.

Secret letter, "Behavior of Chinese Troops in Burma" *From Lt. Col. A. D. Mac Conachie*, New Delhi, to W. I. J. Wallace, Simla. December 1943.

———, "Behavior of Chinese Troops in Burma." *from Major E. J. Cowell*, New Delhi, December 14, 1943.

Secret Letter from W. I. J. Wallace to Maj. Gen C. F. B. Pearce, C B E, New Delhi, Simla, December 3, 1943.

Secret letter, "Misconduct of Chinese Troops in Burma," December 11, 1943.

Secret Report on Pang Long Conference.

Secret Telegraphic Letters in Regard to the Affairs of Upper Burma. 1885. F.O. 422/15.

"*Shan State, 1983 Population Census,*" *The Socialist Republic of the Union of Burma*, Ministry of Home and Religious Affairs. Rangoon: Immigration and Manpower Department, 1987.

Southern Shan States Report of 1889–90.

Special Order No. 6, 1949, issued by the President of the Union of Burma on November 23, 1949.

Siam Confidential, 409. From Mr. J. G. Scott to Marquess of Salisbury. (Received August 1).

"Summary of Findings", *The Socialist Republic of the Union of Burma, Ministry of Home and Religions Affairs*, Yangon: Immigration and Manpower Department, 1987.

Summary of speeches made by U Saw at the Pang Long Conference, 1946.

Telegram from Chief Commissioner, Rangoon to J. George Scott, received at Fort Stedman on May 15, 1888.

Telegram from Government of India to the Chief Commissioner, March 21, 1895.

Telegraph to J. G. Scott, Assistant Superintendent, Shan States from the Chief Secretary of Chief Commission, Rangoon, to Congratulate him and Fowlers on the Dash and Capture of Twek-nga-lu in Monè, May 15, 1888.

Thibaw Saohpa (memo), File no. 61 A / 1886.

Through the Assistant Superintendent Miang Yang to the Deputy Commissioner, Myitkyina, from the Office of the Tawng Ok, Hpimaw. September 7, 1944.

Transfer of Administrative Power and How to Solve the Saohpa Problem (in Myanmar). F.N. 177 Ya Pa (A) 53.
Upper Burma Proceedings. National Archive Department, Shan State. File no. 604, December 1880, vol. 2664 A.
Upper Burma Proceedings. Foreign Department. May 10, 1886, proceeding no. 2.
———. October 14, 1886, proceeding no. 3, enclosures 1 and 2 (3).
W. W. Warry to Chief Commissioner, May 10, 1893.

Shan State documents

Discussions between the Army Officers and the Shan State Representatives, 21/4/61.
Discussions between the Army Officers and the Shan State Representatives were held on 21/4/61 at 16:30 hours, at the Shan State Government Office, Taunggyi. "Office of the Directorate of Military Intelligence."
Discussion between the Shan State leaders and the Prime Minister, 21-5-1961. Directorate of Military Intelligence.
HDR (History Department (Research), Yangon University): 3AP/1987.
HDR: 1 AP/1990.
HDR:RT/0016/SP-62/1990.
HDR:RT/0017/SP-62/1990.
HDR:RT/0018/SP-62/1990.
HDR:RT 0019/SP-62/1990.
HDR:RT/SP-62/1990.
Shan State People's Federation League.
Shan State Political Activities and the Origins of the Federal Principle 1954–62. Office of the Director, Military Intelligence Service. [Ban Mai Mong Tai, *Khit Thit Shan Pyi*. Hsi Paw: White Tiger Press.] (in Myanmar).
The Shan Proposal and the Union.
Statement made by the Head of the Shan State Sao Hkun Hkio. At the Seminar of Nationalities held on February 24, 1962, at the Broadcasting Station on Pyay Road, Yangon.
States Unity Organization Document.

United Nations documents

A/2375, United Nations General Assembly (UNGA), 7th Session, March 26, 1953.
A/2379, 420th Meeting of the Plenary Session of the UNGA, March 31, 1953.
A/2375, A/C.1/L 42, UNGA, 7th Session, 1st Committee, 606th Meeting, April 17, 1953.
A/2375, A C.1/L, 42, UNGA, 7th Session, 1st Committee, 609th Meeting, April 20, 1953.
A/2375, A/C.1/L 42, A/C.1/L 43, UNGA, 7th Session, 1st Committee, 609th Meeting, April 21, 1953.
A/2375, A/C.1/L 42, A/C.1/L 43, A/C.1/L 44, UNGA, 7th Session, 1st Committee, 610th Meeting, April 21, 1953.
A/2375, A/C.1/L 42, A/C.1/L 43, A/C.1/L 44, Rev. 2, UNGA, 7th Session, 1st Committee, 610th Meeting, April 22, 1953.
A/2375, A/C.1/L 42, A/C.1/L 43, A/C.1/L 44, Rev. 2, A/C. 1/L 45, UNGA, 7th Session, 1st Committee, 611th Meeting, April 22, 1953.
A/2375, A/C.1/L 42, A/C.1/L 43, A/C.1/L 44, Rev. 2, A/C. 1/L 45, Rev 1, UNGA, 7th Session, 1st Committee, 611th Meeting, April 22, 1953.
A/C.1/L 46, UNGA, 7th Session, 1st Committee, 612th Meeting, April 22, 1953.
A/C.1/L 47, UNGA, 7th Session, 1st Committee, 612th Meeting, April 22, 1953.
A/C.1/L 69, UNGA, 8th Session, 1st Committee, October 28, 1953.
A/C.1/L 70, UNGA, 8th Session, 1st Committee, October 29, 1953.
A/C.1/L 71, UNGA, 8th Session, 1st Committee, October 30, 1953.
A/C.1/L 73, UNGA, 8th Session, 1st Committee, November 5, 1953.
A/C.1/L 89, UNGA, 8th Session, 1st Committee, November 26, 1953.
A/C.1/L 90, UNGA, 8th Session, 1st Committee, November 27, 1953.

A/C.1/L 90, Rev. 1, UNGA, 8th Session, 1st Committee, December 4, 1953.
A/C.1/L 91, UNGA, 8th Session, 1st Committee, November 27, 1953.
A/C.1/L 92, UNGA, 8th Session, 1st Committee, December 1, 1953.
A/C.1/L 93, UNGA, 8th Session, 1st Committee, December 2, 1953.
A/2423, UNGA, 7th Session, July 22, 1953.
A/2468, UNGA, 8th Session, September 11, 1953.
A/2607, UNGA, 8th Session, December 5, 1953.
A/2627, UNGA, 8th Session, December 11, 1953.
A/2643, UNGA, 8th Session, March 19, 1954.
A/2644, UNGA, 8th Session, April 5, 1953.
A/2704, UNGA, 9th Session, August 20, 1954.
A/2739, UNGA, 9th Session, September 28, 1954.
A/2740, UNGA, 9th Session, September 29, 1954.
A/2762, UNGA, 9th Session, October 20, 1954.

Unpublished material

Hendershot, Clarence. "The Conquest, Pacification, and Administration of the Shan States by the British, 1886–1897." Ph.D. diss., University of Chicago, 1936.

Speeches

The Document for the Revision of the Constitution submitted to the States Scrutiny Committee on March 8, 1961 and to the Constitution Amendment Committee led by Dr. E. Maung on March 11, 1961.

Explanation given by U Chan Htoon in his address to members of the Supreme Court in connection with whether the law on Land Nationalization was inclusive or not of the States.

The Speech delivered by Prime Minister U Nu on February 24, 1962 at the Conference of Nationalities held at the Broadcasting Station on Pyay Road, Yangon. HDR:RT/0019/SP-62/1990.

The Speech of Minister Sao Hkun Hkio, delivered at the Conference on the Federal Principle, held in the Main Hall of Myanmar Broadcasting Service, Pyay Road, Yangon, on February 24, 1962.

The Speech of Kachin State Representative Duwa Zau Lawn, delivered at the Conference on the Federal Principle, held in the Main Hall of the Myanmar Broadcasting Service, Pyay Road, Yangon on February 24, 1962.

The Speech of Kayah U Sein, delivered at the Conference on the Federal Principle, held in the Main Hall of the Myanmar Broadcasting Service, Pyay Road, Yangon, on February 24, 1962.

The Speech of Prime Minister U Nu at the Conference on the Federal Principle held in the Main Hall of the Myanmar Broadcasting Service, on Pyay Road, Yangon on February 24, 1962.

The Speech of Thakin Chit Maung, delivered on the second day of the Conference on the Federal Principle, which was inaugurated in the Main Hall of the Myanmar Broadcasting Service, Pyay Road, Yangon, on February 24, 1962.

The Speech of U Ba Swe delivered on the second day of the Conference on the Federal Principle, held in the Main Hall of the Myanmar Broadcasting Service, Pyay Road, Yangon on March 1, 1962.

The Speech of U Nu. HDR: RT/0019/SP-62/1990.

The Speech of the Chairman, Minister Dr. E Maung, delivered at the Conference between Burma Proper and the States, presenting the views of the Union Party, Yangon. Union Party Headquarters. Personal Interview, 0126: History Dept. (Research), Yangon University.

The Speech of the Representative of the Chin Special Division, Captain Mang Tung Nung, delivered at the Conference on the Federal Principle, held in the Main Hall of the Myanmar Broadcasting Service, Pyay Road, Yangon, on February 24, 1962.

The Speech of the Representative of the Shan State, U Htun Myint (Taunggyi), delivered at the Conference on the Federal Principle, held in the Main Hall of the Myanmar Broadcasting Service, Pyay Road, Yangon, on February 24, 1962.

Interviews

Heing, Long Loi Hkam of Namhkam, Northern Shan State, June 6, 1997
Heing, Long Ywat Hkam of Mong Nai, Northern Shan State, September 8, 1996.
Heing, Long Lai Sai of Manpong, Mong Yai, Northern Shan State, June 7, 1998.
History Department (Research) of Yangon University. Personal interviews 0022, 0043, 0122, 0124, 0125, 0126, 0127, 0131, 0137, 0144
Hkun, Sao Nwe Mao, Ban Panglong. Putao, Hkamti Long, April 5, 1996.
Hsae, Sai of Yawng Hwe, Southern Shan State, January 1, 1996.
Htee, Long Hkun of Loilem, Central Shan State, July 19, 1996.
Kaung, Ching Hsang, of Manhai, Hsi Paw, Northern Shan State, April 4, 1996.
Lai, Long Hkam of Heho, Southern Shan State, July 17, 1996.
Leng, Long Hkun Hkam, Ban Se U, Hsen Wi, June 6, 2004.
Leng, Long Sang Hkam of Muse, Northern Shan State, July 19, 1996.
Leng, Sai Hkam of Lang Hko, Southern Shan State, February 2, 1996.
Lin, Long Hkam of Yawng Hwe, Southern Shan State, May 3, 1996.
Loi, Nai Kyaung of Muse, Northern Shan State, March 3, 1996.
Men, Long Sang of Pang Long, Central Shan State, July 17, 1996.
Mu, Long Loi in (of) Mong Yai, March 3, 1996.
Ngan Long Soi Hkam of Nam Hkam, Northern Shan State, September 30, 1997.
Ont, Pa Nang of Mong Yai, Northern Shan State, September 19, 1996.
Pan, Long Sang of Mong Yai, Northern Shan State, May 3, 1996.
Pi, Sao Nwe Gam Hkamti Shan, in Putao, September 26, 1976.
Pwint, Long Hkun of Nam Hsan-Loi Long, Northern Shan State, July 7, 1996.
Pyinnya, Hein of Hsi Paw, May 18, 1997.
Su, Long Loi of Tang Yan, Northern Shan State, August 17, 1996.
Wan, Hkun Maha of Lashio, April 5, 1996

Index of Persons

Index of Places